Imperialism and the Developing World

Imperialism and the Developing World

How Britain and the United States Shaped the Global Periphery

ATUL KOHLI

OXFORD
UNIVERSITY PRESS

OXFORD
UNIVERSITY PRESS

Oxford University Press is a department of the University of Oxford. It furthers the University's objective of excellence in research, scholarship, and education by publishing worldwide. Oxford is a registered trade mark of Oxford University Press in the UK and certain other countries.

Published in the United States of America by Oxford University Press
198 Madison Avenue, New York, NY 10016, United States of America.

First issued as an Oxford University Press paperback 2021

CIP data is on file at the Library of Congress
ISBN 978-0-19-006962-9 (hardback)
ISBN 978-0-19-758249-7 (paperback)

1 3 5 7 9 8 6 4 2

Paperback printed by Marquis, Canada

For
Marie and Tara

Contents

List of Tables

List of Figures

List of Figures

Acknowledgments

BOOKS TAKE TIME to write. My first set of thanks goes to Princeton University for its generous leave policy. Two full years of sabbatical leave in 2013–2014 and 2017–2018 gave me uninterrupted periods during which much of this book was written. The university setting was also important in other ways. I co-taught a course on imperialism with my Princeton colleague John Ikenberry in 2007. Although the two of us approached the subject differently, I began to think seriously about this book during class discussions. Subsequently, the Princeton Institute for International and Regional Studies (PIIRS) funded a multiyear research community (2012–2016) on "Empires: Domination, Collaboration, and Resistance," which the Princeton historian Jeremy Adelman, John Ikenberry, and I codirected. My thanks to then-PIIRS director Mark Beissinger for encouraging the formation of the research community. I learned a lot from various visitors and speakers who came through Princeton under the auspices of this project, as well as from my Princeton colleagues who joined the research community (for details see http://piirs.princeton.edu/research-community/empires-domination-collaboration-and-resistance).

During the research phase for the book a number of scholars provided valuable help with data and sources. Stephen Broadberry at the London School of Economics helped me calculate some historical data on India; this is duly acknowledged in the manuscript. Manuel Llorca-Jaña of the University of Santiago in Chile also helped clarify some puzzles in the historical economic data concerning the southern cone of Latin America. Alexander Kentikelenis of Bocconi University in Italy shared his unpublished work on the International Monetary Fund and was generous enough to forward his photocopied materials from the Baker Paper archives at Princeton University. Quang Minh Pham of the Vietnam National University, Social Sciences Campus, Hanoi, was helpful with source materials on the Vietnam War, especially material from the Vietnamese perspective. Robert Vitalis of the University of Pennsylvania provided some important bibliographic references on Iraq. Last, the staff at the US Bureau of Economic Analysis was helpful in sorting out the availability of data on US portfolio investment in Latin America.

Feedback on presentations based on the materials from this book was helpful in revising the manuscript. Although I cannot thank everyone who attended these seminars and raised useful questions, those who organized the talks and acted as discussants deserve to be singled out. I presented the chapter on the East India Company (chapter 1) at Columbia and Harvard universities in the United States, and at King's College in London. Thanks are due to Akeel Bilgrami for organizing and to Partha Chaterjee for commenting on the chapter at the Columbia seminar, to Ashutosh Varshney of Brown University for organizing the seminar at Harvard, and to Sunil Khilnani for the same at King's. I also owe thanks to Vinay Sitapati of Ashoka University in India for organizing a small discussion group at his home in New Delhi, where a group of bright young scholars from his university were kind enough to read and share their reactions to the chapter. The chapter on Britain's informal empire (chapter 2) was presented first at the University of Toronto and then at the Jawaharlal Nehru University (JNU) in New Delhi. Again, my thanks go to Kanta Murali for organizing the Toronto seminar and to Niraja Dayal for the same at JNU; Chirashree Dasgupta generously commented on the chapter at JNU. I presented the chapter on early American imperialism (chapter 4) at Boston University. Min Ye was kind enough to invite me, and Andrew Bacevich was generous with his time, reading and commenting on that chapter at BU. Last, I presented an overview of the book at George Washington University—thanks are due to Adam Dean for the opportunity.

Colleagues who read and commented on the manuscript deserve special thanks—they definitely helped improve it. I acknowledge their help in alphabetical order. Jeremy Adelman brought the newer literature on global history to my attention and helped strengthen my analysis of Argentina. My Princeton colleague Gary Bass helped moderate some of my more strident claims and also provided references to useful materials on US foreign policy that I had missed. The insightful comments of Princeton's Robert Keohane helped clarify the theoretical framing of the book. Pratyay Nath of Ashoka University brought the more recent literature on the Mughal Empire to my attention.

The Princeton Historian Gyan Prakash read the Indian materials and gave me the green light that I was on solid empirical grounds. Amin Saikal at the Australian National University identified himself as one of the two anonymous reviewers for Oxford University Press (OUP). I appreciated his generous reading of the whole manuscript and his helpful suggestions, especially on the Middle East portions of the book. Richard Sandbrook, University of Toronto, forced me to clarify the underlying theory and to improve my analysis of African materials. Prerna Singh from Brown University was also generous in her comments and suggestions. Georg Sørensen at the University of Aarhus in Denmark read the entire manuscript with great care. I acknowledge his help particularly because it was both supportive and yet, in his own words, "straight talk, no diplomacy"; the best type of help a writer could want. My long-time Princeton colleague Ezra Suleiman provided the sage advice that materials written in anger ought to be read and reread before publication. And finally, the second anonymous reviewer for OUP provided useful suggestions for revisions, especially for Latin American materials in the book.

Others who helped to bring the book to completion also need to be acknowledged. Marie Gottschalk suggested the art for the cover. Alison Lowander copyedited the manuscript with great care. I owe her special thanks for improving my presentation. The University Committee on Research in the Humanities and the Social Sciences at Princeton University provided a small grant to support the copyediting of the manuscript. Esther Robinson is a graduate student in Princeton's Department of Politics, whose help with the final preparation of tables, figures, bibliography, and the index of the book I appreciate. David McBride was a supportive editor at Oxford University Press. With his own academic background in history (and prolonged experience at a major press), during our first conversation he understood right away the type of book I was writing. Subsequently, he read the manuscript and provided both advice and encouragement; I could not have asked for more from an editor.

Some personal acknowledgements are also essential because these connections remain whether I write one more book or not. My father – Dr. Jai Dev Kohli – died at the good age of ninety-four while I was writing this book. As a medical researcher he often wondered how I collected data without experiments. I regret that I will not be able to show him the book. My mother – Pushpa Kohli – soldiers on, often with a positive attitude toward life; since she participated in India's nationalist movement I think she will appreciate the book. My brother – Tanuj Kohli –, sister –Vandana Kohli – and their respective families remain a cherished part of my extended family connections. My cousin Subodh Anand remains a dear friend. We regularly share joys and troubles of our evolving lives. And finally, this book is dedicated to my life-long partner, Marie Gottschalk, and our daughter, Tara Kohli. Since they know why, I will not elaborate, except to note that they help complete my little world.

Introduction

WHEN THE UNITED States invaded Iraq in 2003, American decision-makers expected to depose Saddam Hussein quickly, install a friendly regime, and leave. The Iraq War did not follow that script. Instead, the United States confronted Iraqi nationalism. A prolonged occupation followed. Although most of the US troops left in 2011, American efforts to shape Iraq continue. During the occupation, American critics of US intervention in Iraq compared it to Vietnam. Senator Edward Kennedy suggested that Iraq was another "quagmire," a term often used during the American war in Vietnam. While these were serious comparisons, they ignored deeper historical parallels. Great Britain created Iraq after World War I by piecing together the outlying provinces of the former Ottoman Empire. British efforts to turn Iraq into an India-style colony then met swift resistance from Arab nationalists, nearly a century ago. London had to order the bombing of Iraq in 1920 to defeat this indigenous opposition. Instead of turning Iraq into a formal colony, Britain installed a pliable Arab monarch, who allowed British troops and advisers to stay and who pursued pro-British policies. Britain's informal empire in Iraq lasted well into the 1950s. The parallels between the US and British experiences in Iraq run even deeper: both expected to be welcomed as liberators to Iraq, but were not; both denied that they had any interest in Iraqi oil, but that was a lie; and, while promising to bring progress, both wreaked havoc on Iraq.

These and numerous other parallels that we will encounter in this book are more than just random repetitions of history. In fact, they constitute a pattern that is a product of Western imperialism in the global periphery. The book undertakes a systematic analysis of how imperialism has shaped the emergence of the developing world. Why imperialists imperialize and how imperialism impacts peripheral countries are the central concerns of this study.

How Britain and the United States Shaped the Global Periphery. Atul Kohli, Oxford University Press (2020).

DOI: 10.1093/oso/9780190069629.001.0001

The subject is of importance because the fate of the developing world has been intimately connected to the rise and expansion of Western capitalism. Ponder briefly how we have come to be where we are, viewed from the perspective of the developing world. From the sixteenth century on, prospering European states pursued their political and economic interests overseas: the methods varied anywhere from slavery to settling Europeans beyond their own borders in empty or occupied lands to conquering and colonizing well-established civilizations. In so doing, European colonialism dragged much of the nonindustrial world into the modern era. But the colonial journey of peripheral people of Asia, Africa, and South America to modernity was, and remains, incomplete. Some peripheral countries acquired well-constructed states under colonialism, but most did not. While some colonized economies were downright plundered—and a few colonies, populated mainly by people of European origin, prospered—most colonies became commodity producers for their colonial masters, surviving at low levels of income. Long-term relations of domination and subordination also bred norms of racial superiority and inferiority.

Waves of decolonization and the breakup of empires only led to uneven gains in national sovereignty for countries on the global periphery. The Spanish and Portuguese colonies of South America gained nominal independence following the Napoleonic Wars in the early nineteenth century, but soon became part of an informal empire, run first by Great Britain and then, over time, by the United States as it replaced Britain as the global hegemonic power. A similar process unfolded in the Middle East, where the breakup of the Ottoman Empire initially led to a variety of British protectorates to limit the sovereignty of these countries and, more recently, to efforts by the United States to establish *Pax Americana* in the region. While China was never fully colonized, a number of European powers and Japan carved it into spheres of influence. This was first evident in the forced economic opening of China by Britain during the Opium Wars in the nineteenth century, and then, even more so, as the Ch'ing dynasty disintegrated in the early twentieth century.

Life chances of people living under informal empires were better than those living under colonial rule, but only somewhat. Chaotic China experienced very little economic progress during the first half of the twentieth century. Peaceful semi-sovereign states, say, those in Latin America, were on occasion able to mobilize resources for pushing national progress. For example, Argentina and Brazil experienced economic growth in the nineteenth century and/or the first half of the twentieth century, whereas a colonized India did not. Such progress in semi-sovereign countries, however, remained limited by dependence on external economic circumstances; some progress was possible only when these circumstances were favorable. External dependence also reinforced elite-mass gaps within these political economies, making it difficult to create well-consolidated states that could exercise effective power and promote inclusive development.

The decolonization that followed World War II was most effective in creating sovereign states in Asia. Countries such as China and India mobilized their domestic populations politically, via a revolutionary path in the first case and reformist in the second, and prioritized state consolidation before turning to the task of economic progress. These countries and others in Asia are now reaping handsome rewards in terms of sustained state-led growth and poverty reduction. By contrast, political economies of Latin America have remained mired in a US-centered informal empire, especially during the era of military dictators and the subsequent period of Washington Consensus, when periods of highly unequal growth were followed by prolonged economic stagnation. Future generations in this lopsided pattern of development will pay for the benefits reaped by the few in the earlier period. As a democratic Latin America struggles to break out of these constraints, the past weighs heavily on it; most of these economies remain highly unequal and commodity dependent for their growth. The same is true for large parts of Africa, but with an added tragedy. Unlike Asia, decolonization in sub-Saharan Africa did not yield coherent states. Formal sovereignty, of course, has little meaning under the conditions of weak and ineffective states; only a well-organized and coherent state can represent the sovereign interests of a people and put them on a path of progress. Without such effective states, sub-Saharan Africa has experienced the least economic progress, so much so—and here, ironies of history abound—that now a rapidly industrializing China seeks to create its own version of an informal empire on that continent.

It ought to be evident in this brief historical recounting that both formal and informal empires have shaped the emergence of the developing world. How this process has unfolded is the central concern of this study. I analyze both the causes and consequences of modern imperialism. The focus is on British and US imperialism in the nineteenth and the twentieth centuries, respectively. The suggestion is that imperialism is moved mainly by the needs of hegemonic powers to enhance their national economic interests. They do so by undermining sovereignty in peripheral countries and establishing open economic access. The impact on the countries of the periphery tends to be negative. The central argument of this study is that in a world of states, national sovereignty is an economic asset. Since imperialism seeks to limit the exercise of sovereign power by subject people, there tends to be an inverse relationship between imperialism and development: the less control a state has over its own affairs, the less likely it is that the people of that state will experience steady, inclusive economic progress. Although national sovereignty may not be sufficient to put a country on a path of progress, it is often a necessary precondition. We should then expect the least economic development in fully colonized countries, somewhat better but still-limited possibilities in semi-sovereign states, and the best prospects under conditions of sovereign and effective state power. In due course numerous nuances and qualifications will need to be added to this blunt argument; there will be exceptions to the core argument and historical details will often defy parsimony. And yet, the complex story of imperialism and the developing world follows a discernable logic: imperialists pursue their own interests by undermining sovereignty and thus the prospects of prosperity in the countries at the global periphery.

Clearing the brush: Two old and interrelated questions are pursued throughout this study: Why do powerful states—especially hegemonic capitalist states—imperialize, and what impact does imperialism have on the developing world? Since these are huge, controversial, and well-studied themes, one more book on the subject requires justification. As is often the case, my interest in the past was rekindled by the present. During the decades of the Cold War, numerous efforts by the United States to influence developing-country polities—via regime change, military interventions and bases, or the use of economic levers to create open economies and acquiescent governments—were often justified in terms of deterring communism. But even after the end of the Cold War, such efforts did not diminish. President Barack Obama was led to characterize the United States as a nation on a "perpetual wartime footing" and President Donald Trump to boast "we are all over the world."[1] US interventions in Afghanistan and Iraq were obviously the most dramatic of the Vietnam-type of US interventions after the Cold War. Rhetorical justifications by US decision-makers aside, fresh questions arise: Why does the United States repeatedly intervene in the affairs of developing countries? Is there a pattern here that not only characterizes the US role in the global periphery but is also possibly consistent with earlier historical patterns, such as when Britain was the global hegemonic power and built a vast empire? Also, what is the impact of such recurring imperial actions on the life-chances of those who are imperialized? Does democracy and prosperity really follow such interventions? Recent US interventions in the Middle East are the tip that provokes us to re-explore the iceberg that is Western imperialism in the developing world.

The core focus of this study is a comparison of British imperialism in the nineteenth century, especially Britain's informal empire, and US role in the developing world, especially in the post–World War II phase, which is also characterized here as a form of informal empire. There are numerous other types of comparisons—over time and across regions—built into the study to strengthen the causal argument. The primary mode of inquiry is historical and comparative research. The study is mainly inductive; causal generalizations are derived from empirical analysis, though not without some theoretical priors. The key general insights will thus be best summarized in the concluding chapter, after readers have digested the historical materials. I depend on secondary materials where they are available; where they are not readily available, information is gathered from archives and newspaper accounts. Some new numerical data is also presented here and there. Since the ground covered here is well traversed, I do not claim originality in this volume. This is a work of synthesis and interpretation, with nuances and twists that make the account distinct.

It may also be helpful if I lay out an explicit rationale for the focus of this study on Britain and the United States at the beginning. Empires are age-old phenomena. So, if the aim is to generalize about causes and consequences of imperialism, why focus on the overseas empires of Great Britain and the United States? Britain and the United States are the two great hegemonic powers of the modern era of industrial capitalism. While all empires share some commonalities, these two modern empires are distinct enough from other traditional land-based empires, and even from the overseas empires of Spain and Portugal, that one can justify bracketing them together for comparative historical analysis.[2] First and foremost, these are empires of growth. Modern economic growth, which is characterized by growing productivity and which is self-sustained, began in Western Europe sometime around the seventeenth century. The emergence of such growth was accompanied by changes, first in technology and in the organization of agrarian production, along with changes in trade patterns, and eventually hastened sharply with the Industrial Revolution. Some scholars simply think of this shift in terms of the emergence of capitalism. Capitalism and self-sustained growth then altered how rulers think of national power.[3] Since more economic growth implies greater national power, rulers in the modern era typically get involved in growth promotion. Empire building comes to be seen as one more means to support economic growth. The decisions to extend the empire then must also take into account the views and preferences of the newly powerful actors in society, the growth producers, or the capitalists. These motives and dynamics have only few parallels in traditional land empires.

Second, sustained economic growth expands the tools available for establishing and maintaining imperial control. Power, which in part depends on wealth, is increasingly less of a zero-sum game. As the economic pie expands it can be shared, even if disproportionately. Intermediaries on the periphery can now become compradors or willing collaborators. With growth and profits in mind, even territorial control eventually loses some of its traditional attraction. Collaborators—more or less willing—can be found to facilitate friendly regimes in the imperialized periphery. It is more than a historical chance that informal empires were not an available option in traditional land empires but do become a major option for capitalist empire builders.[4] What good would an imperialism of free trade do for the Mongols or the Romans? And third, modern overseas empires of growth adjoin dynamic, industrializing cores with nearly stagnant, commodity-producing peripheries; this, too, has only limited parallels with traditional land empires, or even with Spanish and Portuguese overseas empires.

If bracketing modern capitalist empires can be analytically justified to be worthy of comparative analysis, why focus specifically on Britain and the United States? The focus on the United States may especially raise eyebrows because Americans often deny that they run a global empire. Why not focus on other colonizers of the nineteenth century instead, such as France or even Japan? Two responses are in order. First, this is not a study of comparative colonialism. Britain's colonial empire has been well studied. I draw on that literature in this study. The literature on French and Japanese colonialism, by contrast, is not as extensive, certainly not in English. The discussion here is informed by my own earlier work on Japanese colonialism.[5] French colonialism will also emerge, especially in the discussions of Egypt, Vietnam, and the Scramble for Africa. The more important point, however, is that this study seeks to broaden the scope of the study of imperialism beyond colonialism. Although colonialism ended, imperialism did not. Even in the heyday of colonialism, Britain's extensive informal empire complimented its colonial holdings in the nineteenth century; both British colonialism and Britain's informal empire are analyzed below. One hope of this study is, then, to revive the interest in a systematic study of informal empire as a form of imperialism.

A concern with informal empire naturally leads to a second response: the efforts of the United States to establish global influence in the twentieth century invite a comparison with similar British efforts in the nineteenth century. Britain and the United States dominated the nineteenth and the twentieth centuries, respectively. Britain used its power superiority to build both a formal and an informal empire. The United States, too, tried its hand at colonialism at the turn of the twentieth century but gave up rather early. The American way to empire has instead depended on friendly regimes, extensive military bases, economic penetration, military interventions, and even multilateral pressure. While short of formal colonialism, the United States—no less than Britain—has sought to pursue its interests in the global periphery by establishing an informal empire. American efforts to mold the periphery, moreover, continue into the present, often with the help of Britain. What drives these parallel efforts across centuries? Why do strategies for establishing influence vary? And what impact does this expansionism have on peripheral countries? These are the important questions that can be addressed via a systematic comparison of British and American imperialism.

A third brush-clearing exercise of use at the outset may be to define core concepts used in this study, especially the controversial concepts of imperialism and informal empire, but also of development. Imperialism is a process that leads to the creation of empires. It is a process that involves growing control of one state over another state or people. More often than not, the aim of control is to seek political and economic advantage. This understanding of imperialism is broader than views that equate imperialism with colonialism on the one hand but, on the other hand, it is more specific than views, such as Vladimir Lenin's, that equated imperialism with a stage of capitalism.[6] By suggesting that imperialism is intentional—it is aimed at seeking political and economic advantage—I am also distinguishing my approach from views, such as Joseph Schumpeter's, that imply that imperialism in modern age is foolish—is atavistic[7]—as well as from views that propose that imperialism is about doing good, be it spreading Christianity or democracy. Last, by emphasizing both political and economic advantage, I suggest that politics and economics are not as easily separated as many liberals, realists, or Marxists would have it—power and wealth are deeply interrelated, and imperialism is about both.

A second definition of *informal empire* is also needed. I borrow this term from John Gallagher and Ronald Robinson.[8] A relationship may be characterized as constituting an informal empire when three conditions hold:

- While the imperial metropole does not formally control the peripheral country, it maintains effective control—veto power—over policies in the periphery that infringe on the real or perceived interests of the metropole.
- More often than not, this relationship is sustained via clientelistic relationship between metropolitan and peripheral elites. This relationship may originally have been established under duress. Over time, however, many such relationships become "normalized"; both sides get something out of the relationship, at least at the level of elites.
- When the relationship of domination is challenged, the metropole is in a position to use coercion. This can take various forms: gun boats; regime change; and, in the contemporary era, even multilateral pressure. The use of coercion—overt, covert, or via latent threat—helps distinguish cases of informal empire from mere exercise of influence by metropolitan powers over peripheral countries.

And finally, the terms *development* and *modernization* are used throughout this study. By development I refer to the transformation of agrarian societies into industrial ones; sustained economic growth, especially industrial growth, captures some core elements of this transformation. The terms *modernity* and *modernization* are broader in intent. Legitimate states that govern effectively and dynamic industrial economies are widely regarded as the defining characteristic of a modern nation-state. Modernization is, then, the movement toward the creation of such a modern political economy.

With some preliminary issues set aside, the more central concerns of this study— namely, the causes and consequences of modern imperialism—can be introduced. While it is my hope that some general understanding of causes and consequences will emerge from this study, it is also the case that the nature of imperialism varies quite a bit, both over time and across space. This adds complexity to any full understanding of causes and consequences of imperialism; attempts to be too parsimonious are only likely to be achieved by sacrificing historical nuances beyond recognition. In addition to introducing general claims that frame the empirical analysis of causes and consequences, it is also important to introduce a focus on varieties of imperialism, especially on the mechanisms that lead to formal versus informal empire.

Why imperialists imperialize: Theories of imperialism are a legion. A variety of Marxists, realists, and liberals have their own distinctive interpretations of why imperialists imperialize.[9] In my own interpretation developed below, I take issue with some scholars while agreeing more with others; after examining the historical record, these issues are discussed further in the conclusion. For now, I only need lay out a synthetic organizing proposition that will frame the empirical materials that follow.[10] Throughout this study the argument is that the main motive behind imperialism is the pursuit of national economic interest. States pursue economic prosperity. They do so for a variety of reasons, but mainly because in a world of growing economies—a modern phenomenon itself—states cannot afford to sit still. Maintaining relative national prosperity is an essential component of relative national power in the modern world and thus of national interest and state security. As Kenneth Waltz explains, national security of any state eventually rests on a strong economic base.[11] Hence, states are always involved in managing national economies as an aspect of national security. In this important sense mercantilism never ended. For powerful capitalist states, this commitment to national prosperity inclines them to ensure economic opportunities for their capitalists at home and abroad. Overseas this means creating opportunities to sell products, invest, and manage financial relations. For hegemonic capitalist states, this inevitably leads to a strong desire to create a global system of open economies in which their competitive firms can outsell others and/or produce goods for others. When lesser powers resist, imperialism is likely to follow; sovereign and effective state power on the global periphery is, then, what imperialists seek to tame. Both British and American imperialism follow this logic. Both are best understood as processes of establishing global dominance—hegemony, as some may prefer—aimed at creating open-economy imperium.

As I examine this proposition against empirical materials in the following chapters, there will be occasions to modify the core logic, especially because there was plenty of imperialism before the emergence of free trade on the one hand and, on the other hand, because the commitment of imperialists to free and open economic interactions was often flexible. I also return to expand the argument in the conclusion. However, a few qualifications and clarifications are needed before proceeding further. First, the core intuition here is that powerful states imperialize lesser states in order to pursue national economic interests. Since nation is a political concept, imperialism is both a political and economic phenomenon. Who belongs to a nation, whose interests within a nation count more than the interests of others, and who decides what is in the economic interest of a nation are all issues that are defined by the political process within the imperialist state. Since politics shift, such beliefs are not immutable. Over time, however, the understanding of national economic interest that leaders of imperial states hold may well become stable, at least within broad parameters. For example, the belief that global economic openness enhances economic growth and national power may well take on an ideological quality. Like most ideologies, such beliefs not only facilitate ready action, but may also lead to costly misadventures when the understanding of national economic interest fails to adjust to shifts in circumstances. As this book goes to press in mid-2019, US tariffs on China may well indicate the beginning of one such shift.

A related problem with the proposition that imperialism is aimed at the pursuit of national economic interests is that the ruling elite of imperialist states may hold a very narrow understanding of a nation's economic interests; they may well equate national economic interest with the interests of their national economic elite. This creates problems for the study of imperialism: taxpayers and soldiers bear the costs of imperial actions but private elites often benefit. Imperialism thus involves a public subsidy of sorts, with states supporting private profitability of their capitalists overseas. If this is the case, one could suggest that imperialism is not really aimed at the pursuit of national economic interests but at supporting the interests of metropolitan capitalists. I avoid embracing this Marxist claim, however, not because it is not valid in many cases, but because it would reduce the important force of nationalism to class interests. Moreover, the suggestion that imperialism is moved by the urge to promote national economic prosperity subsumes—rather than excludes—instances where state elite pursued the narrow interests of capitalist classes via overseas expansion. The simple point is that imperialism served the narrow interests of capitalist classes of hegemonic countries in some historical cases, but the leaders of these states in other instances embraced a broader understanding of what is good for their respective economies. Such historical variation is no more complicated than the fact that some metropolitan governments were narrowly beholden to their capitalist classes, while the power base of others was broader. The resulting variation in what moved state-led overseas expansion in different instances can then be logically accommodated within a singular focus on the pursuit of national economic interest as the taproot of imperialism.

And finally, not every instance of imperial action will fit the claim that the actions were aimed at the pursuit of national economic interest. At times, security or balance-of-power considerations will loom large, and at other times policies may be driven mainly by the interests of metropolitan capitalists. Since leaders are fallible, moreover, some imperial actions will prove to be no more than acts of hubris and expensive foolishness. Yet, such exceptions notwithstanding, most imperial actions analyzed here originate in an effort of great powers to enhance their economic interests. Hegemonic capitalist states have global horizons: they pursue their national interests by establishing and maintaining an international system of open economies, at least as long as such openness benefits their producing classes. Specific instances of imperialism will then also need to be understood as part of broader efforts of imperial powers to establish systems of power, including maintaining boundaries of their respective imperial system.[12] Imperial powers do so with cooperation of ruling elites in the periphery in some cases, or via force in others. The core proposition about motives tells us little about the strategies and mechanisms of building an empire. Strategies of building empires vary both because of resources readily available to empire builders, and because of the conditions they confront vis-à-vis other great powers, as well as at the periphery. It is thus important at the beginning to have some sense of the variety of imperial formations in the modern era.

Types of imperialisms: The historical analysis in the body of this study will make clear that Britain and the United States used a range of strategies to establish influence over different types of peripheral countries, with varying results. The analytical challenge for comparative historical analysis is to do justice to the unique aspects of different instances of imperial interventions on the one hand, but on the other hand, to not lose sight of the common patterns across such cases. Imposing a few categories on the variety of imperialisms we encounter here may help this analytical task. This is because typologies make diversity manageable by facilitating causal analysis within and across categories. The most important distinction that helps organize diversity in this study is that between formal and informal empire. Of course, there are important distinctions within each of these categories. For example, British colonialism could be compared to French or Japanese colonialism; early British colonialism, say, in India, can be fruitfully compared to later British imperialism, say, in Nigeria. Although I undertake some of these comparisons, to repeat, this is not a study in comparative colonialism. What loom larger here are variations within informal empire, especially the variety of pathways to such an empire: regime change, hard militarism, or a multinational coalition of imperialists. And lurking behind these distinctions (both across and within the categories of formal and informal empire) are the differences between British and American imperialism over different centuries. A few further comments on three sets of variations—formal versus informal empire; alternate pathways to an informal empire; and British versus American imperialism—will introduce the reader to some of the important subthemes developed in this study, along with the major themes of causes and consequences of imperialism.

The main difference between formal and informal empire is the degree of control exercised by the metropolitan country. A colonial state is ultimately controlled by the colonizer. For example, the British government had the final say over the post-1857 state in British India. By contrast, Britain's influence over its informal empire in the nineteenth century, say, over Argentina or Egypt, was considerable but not final; formally sovereign rulers of these countries had some autonomy, which varied over time and circumstance. Similarly, the United States continued to exert enormous influence over the Philippines, even after granting it independence at the mid-twentieth century. The distinction between formal and informal empire then gives rise to two sets of explanatory issues, one about causes of imperialism and one about consequences. First, if the taproot of imperialism is indeed the pursuit of national economic interest, why do imperialists choose to colonize some countries but pursue informal control elsewhere? Second, what difference does it make for the imperialized whether they are ruled as a colony or as a nominally sovereign country that is in fact a client state? I explore these questions with reference to historical materials throughout this study and will return in the conclusion with fuller answers. At this introductory stage, a preview of my answer to the first question is provided immediately below, and to the second question in the Impact of Imperialism section of this introduction.

Seeking economic opportunity, imperialists acquire colonies when they can but settle for client states when they face resistance.[13] Weak or disintegrating states—or stateless people—are easier to colonize. By contrast, if metropolitan powers want to imperialize well-functioning states on the periphery, finding acquiescent ruling elites or regime change may be a more cost-effective strategy than territorial control. However, the more mobilized a citizenry of a developing country, the harder it is to establish either formal or informal control over that citizenry. In addition, balance of power politics also influences strategies of imperialism. For example, potential conflict with a rival power may deter a metropolitan power from seeking full territorial control and may lead instead to alternate solutions, such as informal empire with an open economy or even dividing up the spoils.

A number of more specific propositions then follow. If global conditions are permissive (in the sense that the imperial power does not face significant power competition) and the peripheral elites are weak and/or refuse to collaborate, it then becomes likely that imperialists will seek full political control, such as during the colonial era. The example of British colonialism in India discussed below followed this logic. The logic also holds true for the Scramble for Africa but with an added difference: given growing power competition among European powers, the spoils had to be divided. The more recent occupation of Iraq by the United States in the post–Cold War era also shares some parallels to these historical situations. By contrast, if global conditions are not permissive and peripheral elites in well-established states are more or less willing to acquiesce, then imperial patterns are likely to take the shape of an informal empire. The examples that demonstrate this logic at work include Britain's influence in Latin America and over the Ottoman Empire during the nineteenth century. The role of the United States in East Asia, the Middle East, and Latin America during the decades of the Cold War also follows this logic. One can readily imagine a combination of other circumstances leading to other types of outcomes. The introductory point is mainly to be suggestive: patterns of imperial political control reflect political-economy conditions at the core and the periphery on the one hand, and global balance of power on the other hand.

From the metropolitan standpoint, the goal of informal empire is to establish stable but subservient governments on the periphery, without controlling territory. Both Britain and the United States have created such client states—or semicolonies, as some would have it—the world over to pursue their economic interests. The pathways to establishing such entities, however, have varied quite a bit, anywhere from hard militarism to overt or covert regime change and multilateral domination. While details of specific cases will emerge in due course, readers may want a sense at the outset of the key propositions that may help explain the choice of one strategy over another. The British used hard militarism to pry open China, and the United States has pursued this path repeatedly, say, in the Philippines, Vietnam, and Iraq. The argument is that metropolitan leaders are attracted to this strategy when a weaker power stubbornly stands in the way of goals that are diffuse but grand: opening up the giant China market or establishing *Pax Americana* over an entire geographical region. By contrast, if goals are specific, such as ensuring that British or American corporations are not nationalized in, say, an Iran or a Chile, and the power disparity between the metropolitan and peripheral countries is huge, forced regime change in the periphery emerges as a preferred strategy for establishing a pliable state. And multilateral domination is the third path chosen when stakes are high and the imperial goals complex, such as maintaining open access to the Chinese economy in the nineteenth century, or ensuring debt payments by Latin American countries late in the twentieth century.

A comparison of British and American imperialism in this study is aimed at generalizing about the causes and consequences of imperialism. While pursuing that central task, the search for commonalities ought not to obliterate important differences across centuries. Three of these loom large in the analysis below and are worth flagging as introductory observations. First, unlike in nineteenth century Britain, the United States in the twentieth century emerged as a giant, continental-size economy. The United States thus depended less than Britain did on overseas economic interactions for its buoyancy. From the standpoint of national economic interests, Britain needed an empire; the United States merely wanted one. I elaborate on the distinction between *need* and *want* in chapter 4, but for now it is worth pointing out that this distinction between need and want has implications for understanding some important contrasts between the British and US modes of building a global empire: for the United States, building an empire (even an informal one) has always been more a matter of choice than a necessity. The element of choice, in turn, has added tentativeness to America's imperial quests and nearly always provoked disagreements at home.

Related to America's giant economy is a second contrast: the power superiority of the United States over the rest of the world in the twentieth century and beyond was a lot more decisive than Britain ever enjoyed in the nineteenth century. The Soviet Union briefly may have achieved nuclear parity with the United States during the twentieth century, but that military power rested on a rotten economy. No one, including American decision-makers , ever doubted the overwhelming power superiority of the United States over near competitors. The result has been that when it comes to imperial interventions, the United States has been able to indulge its ideological whims a lot more readily than the British. The British had to worry about the costs of imperialism, and thus tended to be efficient imperialists. By contrast, from time to time the United States has a tendency to exert great imperial efforts without obvious benefits. The United States then readily absorbs the costs of failed imperial efforts and gets ready for the next intervention.

A third contrast between British and American imperialism is the obvious fact that they have unfolded a full century apart. Public opinion thus matters more in the case of the United States than it ever did for the narrow ruling class of Britain. Even more important is how the global periphery has altered over that time period. Britain was able to pursue imperialism more readily because of two conditions on the periphery: local collaborators were readily available and these collaborators could as readily control and pacify the local population. However, the rise of nationalism and mass politics in twentieth century altered the social structures of countries on the periphery. While local collaborators are still available for those seeking to build empires, their ranks are thinner because of nationalist competitors. More important, the spread of plebiscitarian politics across the world has dissolved key building blocks of old fashioned imperialism. These were the feudal-like social arrangements whereby the maharajas, the sultans, the tribal chiefs, the latifundistas, and the pashas of the past could deliver the compliance of local populations. These vertical authority structures are vanishing fast, if they are not already gone, and are being replaced by the emergence of mass politics. Imposing imperial order from the outside is much more complicated in the twenty-first century because would-be subjects can be readily mobilized along nationalist lines.

While these and other diversities are accounted for, the main purpose of this study is to seek common patterns across British and American imperialism. As suggested, empirical materials will document that the key motive behind both British and American imperialism was the pursuit of national economic interest. The impact of British and American interventions on the global periphery is the second general theme of this study; it, too, can now be introduced.

Impact of imperialism: Just as theories of imperialism abound, so do debates about the impact of imperialism. Scholarship and ideology mix easily in these debates; the gap between rhetoric and evidence is often large. In colonialism's heyday, for example, colonizers evoked the white man's burden and the civilizing mission of Europeans as the rationale for colonialism, implying both benign intent and impact. Angry anticolonial mobilization across the developing world eventually challenged these claims, arguing instead that colonizers were self-interested and that the impact of colonialism was highly exploitative. Following World War II, the emergence of numerous sovereign states in Asia and Africa also succeeded in altering the tone of this debate in favor of Third World nationalists, at least for a period. A variety of anti-imperialist leaders and scholars further criticized neocolonial practices during the 1950s and the 1960s: on the one hand, some scholars of American foreign policy drew attention to the harmful effects of US interventions in support of anticommunist regimes in the developing world;[14] and on the other hand, a variety of dependency scholars underscored the "unequal exchange" that they suggested continued to characterize the economic relations of the "core" and the "periphery."[15]

After the first blush, anticolonial nationalism faded in the developing world. A variety of crises engulfed developing world economies late in the twentieth century, including the debt crisis. Western nations, now led by the United States, again reasserted themselves. Newer versions of the white man's burden emerged, this time with demands to promote human rights and democracy in the developing world. In the name of globalization, moreover, the Washington Consensus on development demanded that developing countries open their economies and join the US-sponsored world order.[16] Once again, Western claims implied benign intent and positive benefits for those who fell in line. Those countries in the developing world that were in a position to resist these demands resisted while others succumbed, at least till their angry citizens demanded a change in direction.

Given this ideological and scholarly context, no conclusions about the impact of imperialism are likely to be without controversy, let alone decisive. The debates are well rehearsed. There is also no need to deny some of the good that Western countries did on the global periphery. These included the introduction of modern education, the building of infrastructure, and in some instances, trade-led growth and/or the creation of a modern state structure. Some of these developments will be noted in due course. But on balance, the evidence examined here supports the claim that imperialism seriously undermined the prospect of sustained economic growth and prosperity on the global periphery. While this claim is hardly original, my hope is that the analysis clarifies the underlying causal mechanisms that produced this outcome, especially the role of sovereignty, or the lack thereof.

The negative impact of imperialism was most pronounced in formal colonies. With full political control, metropolitan powers molded policies of colonies to favor the mother country. Though the choice of specific policies varied enormously, they were aimed at ensuring two outcomes: that the colonial empire was self-financing and that the colony provided favorable economic opportunities for the metropolitan economy to expand. Metropolitan powers thus taxed colonial economies via one policy or another, but often at a high rate, such as in India. In turn, these resources were used, not so much to improve the life chances of colonial citizens, but to finance colonial rule. Forced economic integration of metropolitan and colonial economies may have facilitated some trade-led growth in the colonies. By and large, however, colonial economies were turned into commodity producers and takers of manufactured goods. Through acts of both omission and commission, then, colonial powers undermined the prospect of steady economic progress in the colonies. The book's analysis of British colonialism in India and Nigeria and that of the United States in the Philippines and Cuba provides evidence in support of these claims.

The economies of semi-sovereign countries have experienced more economic growth than those of formal colonies, at least during periods of economic buoyancy in the metropole. This is because the government of a peripheral country has more political room to maneuver under conditions of informal empire than under colonial rule. The underlying mechanisms are not hard to understand. Imperialists must give something to client rulers on the periphery to do their bidding. Though this something has varied over time and space, wealth and power are the main rewards. For example, when trade was of main interest to imperial powers during the nineteenth century, the incomes of commodity producers often grew as peripheral countries became more and more integrated with metropolitan economies as takers of manufactured goods. Over time, as the importance of multinational corporations grew, peripheral rulers willing to protect metropolitan investments were rewarded. And with the emergence of finance as a key dimension of cross-national links late in the twentieth century, the peripheral elites who are willing to embrace the Washington Consensus and open their economies to global finance have been feted in imperial capitals.

Client states, then, enjoy a little more political autonomy than do full colonies. Rulers of such states can use this space to transform nominal sovereignty into effective sovereignty in a few policy areas and during some time periods, leading to limited economic progress—mainly, commodity led growth. The cases of Argentina and Egypt under British influence in the nineteenth century and of Iran and Chile under the influence of the United States in the twentieth century will help document such trends in this study. However, it is also the case that economic growth experienced by such semi-sovereign countries is often lopsided.[17] Powerful commodity producers in peripheral countries monopolize the benefits of commodity-led growth. Sharp income and wealth inequalities often accompany this type of trade-led growth. More important, powerful commodity producers develop a strong vested interest in sustaining commodity exports. They thus support open economies. They also then partner with metropolitan powers to discourage nationalist efforts within peripheral countries to build diversified economies with strong industrial bases. Developing country nationalists become the enemies of both metropolitan powers and of the commodity-propelled peripheral elites who together constitute the coalition that perpetuates informal empire. The economic results include sporadic growth that depends on the buoyancy of the global demand for commodities. The political impact of informal empire is even more pernicious: dominant forces within the empire pursue systematic efforts to undermine the emergence of nationalist coalitions on the periphery that may champion a more autonomous path to self-sustained growth and industrialization.

Imperialists do not always win. When efforts to create client states go awry, a different pattern unfolds. In this study, US interventions in Vietnam and Iraq will help elucidate such trends. American efforts to mold these polities confronted nationalist opposition. Facing possible failure, American decision-makers doubled up their military efforts to defeat such opposition. Even when narrow cost-benefit calculations did not justify such military efforts, the argument in support of sustained intervention was that American credibility was at stake: as a hegemonic power, the United States could not be seen as losing to fourth-rate powers. However, the imperial project of shaping the politics and economics of a peripheral country—*nation building*, as some in the United States call it—is a very different project from militarily defeating a fourth-rate power. The United States is eminently capable of the latter but, with the spread of nationalism and the rise of mass politics, the former is increasingly difficult. Stubborn insistence by Americans to still pursue such military interventions—aimed at creating client states—have in turn led to enormous loss of life and destruction on the global periphery. Some three million Vietnamese died during America's war in Vietnam. Unexploded landmines that the United States left behind still take their toll in Vietnam, and the tragic results of the widespread American use of such chemicals as Agent Orange are still there for anyone to see.

That imperialists hurt the life-chances of those they imperialize is not likely to be a controversial claim, except for some die-hard champions of empires.[18] What is more important (from the point of view of scholarship on modern capitalist empires) is to focus on their varieties. This is more important because an understanding of how the impact of imperialism varies—and why—helps to delineate the underlying causal mechanisms. Some of the older but influential literature on empires proposed that informal empire was really imperialism by "other means;"[19] similarly, some early critical literature on the developing world argued that neocolonialism was really a disguised continuation of colonialism.[20] The driving force behind imperialism in such arguments was often unequal relations engineered by capitalism. These were serious arguments but the suggestion—implicit or explicit—that formal sovereignty is not meaningful was deeply misleading.[21] By incorporating some of these earlier insights, I refocus attention on the importance of sovereignty, the role of states, and of political autonomy in the study of imperialism.

One finding of this study is that the impact of colonialism was more pernicious than that of informal empire. Client states are not colonies. This is because of the limited but real political autonomy enjoyed by governments in client states. This autonomy can and has been used to engineer some development, albeit lop-sided development. A logical extension of this line of thinking is that full political autonomy—or sovereignty— is essential for self-sustained and inclusive development in the modern world. Sovereign and effective states on the global periphery that resist forced opening of their economies and instead mobilize national resources for the benefit of their own people are enemies of imperialists. Imperialism in the modern world thus involves an ongoing effort to tame nationalists so as to thwart them in their goal of fully sovereign states on the global periphery. While sovereignty may not necessarily lead to effective states, it is hard to imagine effective states without sovereignty. Without sovereign and effective states, in turn, it is difficult for those left behind to resist external pressures and to mobilize their economic resources successfully. Late development requires sovereign and effective national states.[22] Japan in the nineteenth century and China and India in the early twenty first century exemplify this proposition. It should not be surprising, then, that imperialism and development tend to be inversely related.

Organization of the study: The study is organized mainly chronologically but also analytically. The first half of the book focuses on British imperialism and the second half on American. A focus on the East India Company in chapter 1 helps to understand the origins of British imperialism. In the two subsequent chapters I analyze Britain's informal empire (chapter 2) and British colonialism (chapter 3), respectively. The arrival of the United States on the global scene is the subject of chapter 4. American interventions during the Cold War are analyzed in chapter 5. The most recent American interventions are the focus of chapter 6. Comparisons of formal and informal empire, as well as of British and American empires, are made throughout the study. Each of the chapters is organized to elucidate the three key themes of the book: the motives that drive imperialism; the mechanisms whereby formal or informal rule is established; and the impact of imperialism on both the metropolitan and peripheral countries. I return in the concluding chapter to summarize key trends and the argument in more detail.

PART I

How It Began

Britain and the Developing World

I

The East India Company

THE BRITISH CAME late to overseas expansion. By the time the English East India Company had established a foothold in India, in the early seventeenth century, the Portuguese had been trading for nearly a century, and had established far-flung bases in Asia, Africa, and in the New World. The Spanish conquest of the southern Americas had proceeded far, so much so that by the middle of the sixteenth century, nearly two-thirds of the indigenous population had already died of foreign diseases. The Dutch were also ahead in the fray; they had pioneered the idea of armed overseas trade organized by a joint stock company, the Dutch East India Company (Verenigde Oost-Indische Compagnie), which the EIC eventually emulated and surpassed. It would have been difficult to predict in the early seventeenth century that Britain—then a country of some four to five million people in which even the concept of "Britain" had only just begun to emerge—would go on to defeat competing European rivals to establish a global empire on which, according to those who lionized this empire, the sun never set.[1]

And yet that is what happened. With the advantage of hindsight, it makes sense to begin our study of imperialism and the developing world with the East India Company. Not only was Great Britain the most important imperial power of the nineteenth century, but also, following Britain's loss of the American colonies, India was among its most important overseas possessions. The road to formal colonial control over India in the middle of the nineteenth century had been paved by the East India Company during the preceding two centuries. The East India Company began as traders in the seventeenth century and became state-backed rulers of India in the eighteenth century. Within Britain the East India Company acted as a state within a state. In India—already a land of some 140 million people in 1600—the East India Company struggled to establish a systematic presence during the first half of the seventeenth century and then traded successfully with the Mughal Empire for about a century, using coastal

How Britain and the United States Shaped the Global Periphery. Atul Kohli, Oxford University Press (2020).

DOI: 10.1093/oso/9780190069629.001.0001

factories as its operational base.[2] As the Mughals disintegrated, Lord Robert Clive acquired Bengal in 1757. After that, the East India Company turned into a ruthless and exploitative ruler of India for nearly another century. The mercantilist East India Company eventually gave way to formal British colonialism in the mid-nineteenth century, when squeezing the Indian economy became untenable for a company, on the one hand, and on the other hand, manufacturing capitalism and free-trade doctrines emerged dominant within Britain. In keeping with the themes of this book, this chapter examines the changing motives of the East India Company and the British state as they established rule over India, the mechanisms by which rule was established, and the impact of the East India Company, on both Britain and India.

These are large, scholarly issues for a single chapter. I mainly synthesize existing information, adding new information as needed and accentuating some interpretations over others. The scholarship on the East India Company is considerable, but uneven. One set of accounts builds on the vast holdings of East India Company records in the United Kingdom and tends to focus on how the East India Company operated within the context of the British state and society.[3] Those who focus on the impact of the East India Company on India tend to be a distinct group of historians who work with variety of sources, including records of the East India Company.[4] Only some historians have tried to combine both the "metropolitan" and the "peripheral" perspectives.[5] Building on strands of these and related scholarship, the effort in what follows is to link motives, actions, and consequences. But this will not always be easy. Any analysis of motives runs into the problem of the significant gap that existed between what officials in London desired and what the East India Company's "men on the spot" in India—some twelve to eighteen months away in terms of communication—actually did. And in the study of the impact of the East India Company on India, not only are the data highly fragmentary, but also it is difficult to trace the links between imperial policies and socioeconomic trends within India. One focus that helps to overcome some of these difficulties—by linking the study of motives and of impact—is on the economic resources that the East India Company appropriated from India to enhance Britain's public and private interests.

The discussion is organized chronologically. After a brief overview of the pre-1640 situation, I first analyze the early phase of the rise of the East India Company as traders, starting, say, with the renewal of the original royal charter of 1600—that is, of the company's monopoly rights to trade in the East—during Oliver Cromwell's rule in 1657, up until the annexation of Bengal by Clive, following the Battle of Plassey in 1757. The core focus of the chapter is on the subsequent century—1757 to 1857—during which the East India Company came to rule India with the support of the British state. How the specific case of the

East India Company fits with the general themes of the study is discussed in the "Conclusion" section. Since my purpose is to develop a political and economic interpretation of the East India Company in India, it is useful to preview briefly the analytical argument that is developed below via historical materials.

First, the key motive behind East India Company operations in India was extraction of economic resources. How this was done varied. Methods included armed trade in the earliest stages; squeezing India's land revenues and using them to finance a large British Indian Army and transmitting the rest to Britain for much of the period; and last, forcibly opening the Indian economy to British manufactured goods. Indian resources thus benefited those who invested in the company—often Londoners of means, as well as the British state—which both contributed to private profitability in Britain and helped build Britain's global power. Second, the key mechanism of establishing rule was the use of coercion to defeat any and all resistance by the traditional Indian elite, which led to the elimination of the elite in some cases, acquiescence in other cases, and active cooperation in yet other cases, which facilitated the establishment of longer-term ruling alliances. Last, as to impact, the evidence is overwhelming that the activities of the East India Company in India, especially from the eighteenth century onward, benefited Britain at the expense of India. The British gained from the East India Company via a variety of channels, especially via transfer of Indian resources for private and public uses. Over time the East India Company—now less a company and more a corporate ruler—helped establish a colonial pattern of trade during the first half of the nineteenth century. The negative impact on India was also transmitted via a variety of channels, especially via the misuse of Indian savings—savings that may have been invested more productively within India—and via the destruction of indigenous manufacturing. Although this particular imperial relationship may not quite add up to an instance of "development of underdevelopment," the evidence that Britain gained at the expense of India via the East India Company is unequivocal.[6]

Background

The East India Company first succeeded in acquiring a royal charter that ensured its monopoly over the eastern trade in 1600. After a couple of successful decades, the company almost went under, because of both Dutch competition and growing political troubles within Britain. The expansionary phase of the East India Company in India began only in the second half of the seventeenth century, especially following the renewal of the monopoly charter by Oliver Cromwell in 1657. The first half of the seventeenth century is best thought of as the formative years of the East India Company.[7] To analyze these beginnings it is useful to situate the early development of the East India Company within the context of broader political and economic forces of the period.

For much of its existence, the East India Company was profoundly dependent on the British state, though the state also benefited handsomely from taxing East India Company's trading profits. But during the sixteenth century, English trade with the Mediterranean and beyond was facilitated by such overland trading companies as the Levant Company. The Tudors benefited from external trade, especially the wool trade, but, given their other preoccupations—the Reformation, power struggles between the Crown and the nobility, the growing wealth of merchants, creating a greater Britain, and warfare with European powers—overseas expansion was not as important to them as it was to the more centralized Portuguese and Spanish Crowns. Portuguese and Spanish monarchs had helped to finance overseas expansion and already believed that foreign economic resources in the form of bullion made them relatively powerful. With state support, Dutch overseas trade was also expanding rapidly during this period. By contrast, England's overseas expansion was pursued mainly by private groups. The entreaties of merchants and others for royal support met only limited success. These royal priorities eventually shifted, but only following some profoundly important political and economic developments in England during the sixteenth and seventeenth centuries.

Historical scholarship on these developments is rich and complex, and much of it is not of great relevance for this study.[8] Simplifying greatly, throughout the Middle Ages power in England had shifted between royal and baronial control, and intervention from Rome was a recurring event. These patterns were disrupted during the sixteenth and the seventeenth centuries. While Henry VIII had his own personal reasons for precipitating a break with Rome, the Reformation had strengthened England's "insular independence," creating a religion-based nationalism of sorts: "a refusal to submit to dictation from outside."[9] As gunpowder was introduced, the Tudors, especially Elizabeth I, also centralized power, often at the expense of the old aristocracy, though this meant a growing dependence on newer moneyed interests, both in the countryside and in London.[10] England thus came to resemble a modern nation-state toward the end of the sixteenth century, albeit one without much in terms of a centralized army or bureaucracy in this early stage.

Tudor peace further encouraged the longer-term economic buoyancy that was under way, fueled in part by the import of bullion on the Continent and the related increase in demand for English goods. These economic trends, especially the growth of the wool trade, led to important social and political changes within England: land became a commodity for sale and profit; the gentry's power grew; and the wealth and power of those associated with this trade in London also grew. These newer moneyed groups, especially the country gentlemen and some merchants, were increasingly represented in the House of Commons and shared an interest in the expansion of trade and commerce, including overseas trade. Elizabeth had encouraged these trends, and for a while (toward the end of the sixteenth century), the interests of the court and of the new money converged. The costs of constant warfare made Elizabeth dependent on merchants for loans, and both the country gentry and the merchants benefited from Tudor centralization and peace. Hoping to benefit from taxing the growing wealth of merchants, Elizabeth started to support overseas ventures during this phase, at least in a limited way.

An intellectual climate supporting overseas expansion was also building up toward the end of the sixteenth century. For example, British geographer Richard Hakluyt, with an eye on Spain, argued that "England's future survival and greatness as a nation lay in developing a colonial and trading empire overseas."[11] Sir Francis Drake and others similarly argued for royal support to confront the Spanish and expand overseas. While the cash-strapped Elizabeth was keen to benefit from such expansion, it was not obvious to her that many El Dorados actually existed; the Spaniards were way ahead in that game. Elizabeth's power to support expansion was also limited insofar as all extraordinary expenditures required the support of the Privy Council and the Parliament, political bodies in which the nobility, already wary of the growing power of new money, remained powerful. The limited support that Elizabeth did offer in response to private pleadings for overseas expansion was not so much financial or military—that would only happen after the profound political changes of 1640—but the granting of royal charters, which bestowed royal legitimacy and more important, monopoly trading rights on private companies. Armed with these royal charters, a variety of private actors led voyages as disparate as those that would bring settlers to the Chesapeake Bay; move fortune seekers to forcibly acquire "small scraps of land" from the Spaniards in the Caribbean; or send ships looking for cloves and luxury products, first to Bantam (in modern-day Indonesia) and then to Surat (in modern-day India).[12] Thus began England's overseas expansionary phase.

It was within this broader context that the East India Company came into being in 1600. As overland trade routes of the Levant Company were disrupted, some members of that company joined forces with privateering interests of the City of London and successfully petitioned for a royal charter. While both the English state and the East India Company hoped to profit from eastern trade, how exactly this would develop was far from obvious at the beginning. Peace with Spain and the decline of Portugal had created an opening for eastern voyages, but the Dutch offered fierce competition. Early voyages of English East Indiamen (as the eastbound European ships came to be known) brought back pepper from the

Indonesian islands but soon met Dutch resistance. With the decline of Portugal, the locus of East India Company ships shifted, first to the west coast of India (to Surat), and then to eastern India, especially to the Coromondel coast and Bengal. Unfortunately for the English, there was not much demand for wool, their main export of the period, in the warm climates of Asia. By contrast, there was growing demand in England for precious stones, exotic spices, indigo (used as a dye), and, of course, for calico (Indian textiles). After some trial and error, East India Company trade with India settled on bullion imports to India—there was much demand for silver and gold in India, especially among India's ruling classes, and given the plunder of gold and silver in Mexico and Peru by the Spaniards, the price of bullion in Europe tended to be about a third of what it was in India—and exports back to England of gems, spices, indigo, and especially of a variety of manufactured Indian textiles.

While what was to be traded was being worked out in the early decades of the seventeenth century, the underlying politics of trade was complicated, both in England and in India. The Mughal dynasty ruled India during this period. At its peak (say, during the reign of Akbar, 1556–1605), the Mughals—though they were despotic, like most agrarian bureaucratic empires of the period—provided effective control over large portions of the subcontinent.[13] Although the agrarian economy of the period was based on low levels of technology and productivity, yields per unit of land tended to be high, probably because only fertile lands were cultivated.[14] Household-based manufacturing flourished in small towns, especially crafts and textiles. Much of the trade was within the territory controlled by the Mughals, though textiles and other goods were also exported regularly, both to the Middle East and to Southeast Asia, mainly by private merchants. Some large-scale *karkhanas* (workshops) also existed; these produced armaments and luxury goods for royalty and the upper classes, and built ships that exported goods across the Indian and Arabian seas. Effective and exploitative administration by the Mughals enabled high-level taxation of these economic activities, which supported a substantial armed force, the building of large-scale monuments, and the opulent consumption in the court and among the upper classes. This opulence impressed and tempted the Europeans.[15] East India Company ships had every reason to want to trade with India, but as long as Mughal rule was intact, say, until the early eighteenth century, the East India Company also had every reason to shy away from any military confrontation.[16]

The East India Company sought (and the Mughals gave it permission) to establish a factory and to trade from Surat.[17] Since the Mughals did not rely much on taxing overseas trade, the company's presence was not perceived as much of a threat by Emperor Jahangir; moreover, the Mughal emperor welcomed gifts from the ambassador sent to the Mughal court by James I, as well as the exchange of views—especially on matters of religious tolerance and pluralism.[18] The East India Company established more inland factories to secure goods to be bought with imported bullion in India and exported back to London for sale in auctions. After some trial and error by the East India Company, calico emerged as the main item that could be bought in India relatively cheaply and sold in London at a fair profit for the company and its stockholders. The calico supply apparently was plentiful because calico was already an export item, from this region as well as other Indian regions. The local suppliers also readily adapted to the tastes and designs conveyed to them by company representatives—the factors—who stayed on in India to secure the cargo for the next voyage. While some suppliers and middlemen may have gained from this trade, the limited available evidence suggests that the English trade introduced to India at this early stage was too small a proportion of India's overall economic activity—even of export activity, since Indian merchants, the Portuguese, and the Dutch also participated in this trade—to have much impact beyond the immediate region.

Between 1600 and 1640 the East India Company sent some 170 ships, mostly to India, and of these, more than a hundred returned successfully, loaded mainly with Indian calicoes.[19] The sale of these and other goods made significant profits for the East India Company. Although profits obviously fluctuated—especially because ships were lost—the average rate of profit for the East India Company on its capital investments during these decades was nearly 70 percent.[20] Before the political and economic troubles caused by the English Civil War—which had a substantial negative impact on the East India Company—the company was not only generating very high rates of return for all those who had invested in it (mainly London merchants), but had also set up plants on the Thames that were building state-of-the-art ships and was emerging as the largest employer in London.[21] Although it was a result of private initiative, this success of the East India Company was deeply dependent on state support. Not only were the monopoly rights to eastern trade a function of the royal charter, but royal support also made the company appear to be a sound investment, and it could not have regularly taken large amounts of bullion out of the country without royal permission.[22] The Stuarts, in turn, not only greatly benefited by taxing company profits in one form or another—for example, "customs and imposts" on the East India Company in 1621 contributed "at least £20,000" to the royal treasury—but they also used the company as a source of royal loans.[23] Although the court and the East India Company continuously jockeyed for relatively favorable terms on which to sustain their mutual support, there is no denying that overseas expansion by the East India Company represented a clear and early mercantilist case of state and corporate cooperation.

During the 1620s and the 1630s, just as the East India Company was beginning to get established, it faced serious challenges from both Dutch competition and the growing political turmoil in England. The United Provinces (not quite Holland yet) were increasingly the leading European power, having eclipsed the Spanish in economic efficiency and naval power.[24] The Dutch East India Company not only competed with the East India Company for Asian trade, but its ships were armed and fully supported by the Dutch state. Royal military support for the East India Company was minimal in comparison. This put pressure on the East India Company to arm their own ships, an expense that in turn cut into the profitability of its overseas voyages. The growing domestic problems in England probably hurt the East India Company's profitability even more. The tensions between the court and Parliament put the mercantilist East India Company in a difficult situation. The company depended on royal support, but most investors in it were merchants who supported the parliamentary cause. Political uncertainty scared away investors, leaving the East India Company with serious problems of how to finance its eastern trade. A plague in London and a famine in and around Surat—the main trading port in India at the time—also hurt the East India Company's trading activities, exacerbating the economic problems. During the English Civil War, the East India Company nearly collapsed as a trading firm.

The Civil War of 1640–42 is clearly a complex historical event that has attracted considerable attention from historians. The debates over whether it was a religious conflict or a class conflict or neither, fueled instead by a series of contingent events, need not detain us here.[25] The main question for this study is, how did the political transition following the Civil War influence the English state's approach to overseas expansion, especially toward the East India Company? Even if the transition was not decisive, the evidence supporting the claim that the Civil War represented an important break in England's political evolution is persuasive; in the words of Christopher Hill, "no government after 1640" seriously attempted to prevent enclosures.[26] Enclosure—a process that fenced in common lands, making them private property for sheep pasture, often leaving peasants and tenants without land—was central to the promotion of the wool trade. The reluctance of governments to prevent or to even fine enclosures after 1640 underlined two important political changes in England of the time. First, it marked the growing power of Parliament at the expense of the monarchy within the state (the monarchy and the old aristocracy often opposed enclosures), and second, it confirmed the growing power of commercialized landowners (the gentry) at the expense of the more traditional aristocracy. Whether one thinks of the Civil War as England's bourgeois revolution or not, there is no denying the growing power of moneyed interests in the English state in the subsequent decades. Yes, the Restoration diluted some of the important changes brought about by

Cromwell and other "usurpers," but core legislation of interest here, such as the Navigation Act of 1651 that led to the strengthening of the English navy or the renewal of state support for the East India Company, remained mostly intact. Whatever "reversals" did occur, signifying more continuity than change between the pre- and post-1640 periods, the Glorious Revolution of 1688 certainly put an end to them, further clarifying the limits of royal power and marking the ascendance of parliamentary government.[27]

During the second half of the seventeenth century, the English state became more inclined to support overseas expansion. In the words of Cain and Hopkins, the interests of land and of merchants became "entwined both in the definition of the national interest and in matters of personal finance."[28] Oliver Cromwell helped establish the economic and moral importance of overseas empire, especially as he proceeded to conquer and colonize Ireland. The money of England's new moneyed class now helped finance colonial expansion, and this expansion, in turn, helped the members of this class acquire valuable Irish land. The immediate rationale for the Navigation Act of 1651 (and the one in 1660) was to protect English shipping interests, mainly against Dutch superiority, by stipulating that all England's overseas trade must be carried out by English ships. Customs from this trade, however, also boosted the revenues of the cash-starved English state; "dear money" had emerged as a crucial constraint on national power, especially vis-à-vis the Dutch.[29] Over time, the Navigation acts helped strengthen the shipbuilding industry and build up the English navy, a development that would prove crucial for successful overseas expansion. It was in this context, then—new moneyed interests at the helm, expansionism as a new state goal, and limited economic resources available to facilitate the expansive state—that Cromwell renewed the East India Company's charter in 1657 to carry on as a monopoly trader with India. Cromwell pushed the charter through despite opposition from some who wanted freer trade; free trade, however, was a long way away at this stage, and the financial needs of the state overcame such opposition. Following the restoration of the monarchy, Charles II was also keenly aware that overseas expansion would be important for bringing in new "customs revenue" and thus as "a vital new source of income."[30] He, too, continued state support for the East India Company, not only as a monopoly trader but also by providing the support of growing English naval power, ushering in a prolonged period of trade with the Indian subcontinent that eventually led to territorial control and imperialism.

The East India Company as Traders

The East India Company traded successfully with India during the century that followed the renewal of its charter in 1657. The political economy of this period is conveniently analyzed in two periods, each spanning some five decades. During the first period, trade in calico grew spectacularly when Indian textiles became mass consumer goods in England. After that, say, in first half of the eighteenth century, Indian cotton goods also became central to the slave trade—they were used to pay for slaves in West Africa and clothed slaves in the Americas—and the East India Company added Chinese tea to its Asian trade portfolio. Those associated with the East India Company made significant fortunes during the century, and taxes on the company continuously helped the English state with its war-strained finances. Since the infringements on the sovereignty of India were minimal during the first period—that is, as long as the Mughal Empire could push back, say, until the early eighteenth century—trade was mostly carried out on commercial terms. There is no evidence to suggest that these early English gains came at the expense of India. Although the trade was too small a portion of the Indian economy to benefit it as a whole,[31] bullion imports into India benefited local producers and merchants, on the one hand; on the other hand, the Mughals supported the trade because they, too, gained from the associated taxes.

During the first half of the eighteenth century, however, the power balance between England and Mughal India started to shift. The Mughals were disintegrating and English naval power was on the rise. English efforts to limit India's sovereignty grew, and along with that, the terms of economic exchange deteriorated for the Indian side. Important trends during this period help document this deterioration: the protectionist pressures within England to limit Indian textile imports grew; the English applied pressure to win major concessions from the weakened Mughals to trade in India without paying customs duties; and Indian merchant shipping declined under pressure from growing British naval power. The analytical message of the following historical discussion, then, is that sovereign power is important for warding off economic exploitation. The Mughals had succeeded in resisting British intrusions in the second half of the seventeenth century, but as power relations shifted in the first half of the eighteenth century, Britain turned its power superiority, which rested on a more dynamic national economy, into further economic advantage.

During the second half of the seventeenth century, the English state increasingly became a "national" state. With the ascendance of Parliament and moneyed interests, a shared view came to prevail that "the job of government was to increase the wealth of the country" and that "state control and direction could stimulate material progress."[32] Colonialism was very much a part of this mercantilist worldview: "It came to be widely accepted . . . that colonies were essential to the economic well-being" of England.[33] Competition over control of overseas trade and acquisition of new territories then added to the power conflicts among European states, a set of conflicts in which England was slowly but surely gaining an upper hand. For example: the First Anglo-Dutch War (1652–54) opened the Indian trade to the English; the Anglo-Spanish War (1654–60) led England to acquire Jamaica in 1655, which became central to English profits from both the sugar and the slave trade in the West Indies; and the Second Anglo-Dutch War (1665–67) enabled English ships to monopolize the West African slave trade. The English Crown, officials, and merchants increasingly "cast covetous eyes" on possible new colonies "either because they were economically desirable or because they were strategically important for the maintenance and development of existing colonies and trading routes across the globe."[34] Overseas expansion thus became a systematic English goal, both for the sake of private profits and to obtain the public resources needed for more wars and further expansion. There was nothing absentminded about how the English—and later the British—started acquiring their global empire.

It was within this broader context that Charles II continued the support for the East India Company that Cromwell had already reaffirmed in 1657. Numerous London merchants again invested in the company, lured by royal support and the promise of high returns. Among the investors were also growing numbers of Members of Parliament, who over time became crucial supporters of the company. East India Company trade thus created a cozy relationship—too cozy in some views[35]—between London-based political and economic elites. The growing profitability of the eastern trade was at the heart of that relationship. This trade grew rapidly: if in 1660 the East India Company imported 250,000 cotton piece goods from India, by 1680, the volume was up to one million pieces.[36] Since the price of the bullion that the East India Company used to purchase these goods in India continued to be low in Europe and the demand for Indian textiles in England was growing, the East India Company readily auctioned its Indian goods for high profits in London, even after paying substantial taxes. Elements of crony capitalism aside, by the end of the century the East India Company had emerged as a "financial institution of the first rank," which not only made steady and high profits for its investors but also contributed "huge sums of money to the state." For a nation incessantly at war in Europe and beyond, "the success of overseas trade proved crucial to nourishing the sinews of state power."[37]

The trade the East India Company conducted with India at the time was not international trade in the normal sense of the term today. First, the English were not really exchanging any goods with India; they were using treasure (bullion) to purchase Indian goods and then selling these goods back in England. The Spanish had looted much of the bullion from southern America. As the Spanish used this treasure to finance more wars and monuments—instead of investments, which led to the long-term economic decline of Spain—the bullion found its way to Antwerp, the financial capital of the time. The East India Company would then secure the bullion against bills of exchange in Antwerp (and later, in London, as London emerged as the new financial center), which would subsequently be paid off when the voyages loaded with Indian textiles returned and the goods were sold. The second and the more important distinguishing characteristic of the East India Company trade was that it was armed trade.[38] The Spanish conquistadores had led the way in using coercion to extract economic benefits. The Dutch had modified this strategy by sending armed voyages that looked for spices and other goods. Early on, the East India Company did not invest heavily in arming its voyages (only to learn that this put it at a disadvantage, especially vis-à-vis the Dutch). Following the Restoration, the Royal Navy provided more support to the East India Company, both to confront other competing European powers and to subdue local resistance within India. The East India Company's own ships also began to arm themselves heavily. More importantly, the factories the East India Company had established in India to conduct trade increasingly became militarized; these land bases were fortified, and manned by locally recruited soldiers armed with European arms to both protect goods and eliminate competition. The three early such factories, in Bombay, Madras, and Bengal, respectively, would grow into the three presidencies with the same names that eventually became the nucleus of the British Empire in India.

Rulers in Asia were of two minds about how much access to give to Europeans to trade with their territories. The Tokugawa rulers in Japan, for example, limited all such access, and the Ch'ing in China allowed trade but not land bases. The Mughal rulers of India probably calculated that allowing land bases on the periphery of their empire did not pose much of a threat, especially in view of the possible advantages to be derived from trade. These calculations were not necessarily inaccurate, but they assumed a cohesive rule that could confront growing English power, a set of assumptions that crashed during the eighteenth century. Even in the late seventeenth century, the portents were not good. For example, upon assuming the governorship of the East India Company in 1681, Josiah Child—an East India Company merchant, a Member of Parliament, and a close ally of Charles II—started advocating "absolute sovereign power in India for the Company,"[39] and again, in 1686, asserted that "it is impossible to make the English nation's station sure and firm in India" without controlling territory and collecting revenue from India.[40] These were not just the yearnings of one militant leader of the East India Company; the company leadership in London in 1687 again conveyed its ultimate goals in India to its representatives in Fort St. George (the old "White Town" in Madras):

> (To) establish such a politie of Civil and Military power, and create and secure such a large revenue to maintain both at that place, as may be

> foundation of a large, well grounded, sure English dominion in India for all time to come.[41]

And all this in the name of "peaceful commerce"! Since these very goals were what Clive eventually implemented in the eighteenth century, the claims of some scholars that "the growth of territorial empire in India was neither planned nor directed from Britain" are not tenable.[42] England was already seeking territory and profits the world over. There is no doubt that this aggressiveness ebbed and flowed, in a recession of sorts, under the leadership of Sir Robert Walpole, but it was again resurgent with the rise of William Pitt the Elder, when Clive made his big push into Bengal. The real issue is not whether the colonization of India was planned in England or not—of course it was—but when such an opportunity would become readily available. While Plassey was waiting to happen, India in the late seventeenth century was not quite ready for the plucking.

Child's belligerence precipitated a war with the Indian ruler Aurangzeb in 1688. By 1690 the English had lost this war. Child's defeat led to the lament that it was "very dangerous" to make war on the "Great Monarch the Mogul."[43] The English defeat marked an important fork in the road in India's colonial history. First, the event raises intriguing what-if questions of history that remain unanswerable: What if Aurangzeb had not accepted English indemnity—and a promise of better behavior in the future—and instead denied the East India Company the right to maintain land bases in India? Could India then, like China, have postponed the colonial onslaught for another century or more? Might English expulsion have created a window of opportunity for newer political forces within India, say, the Marathas, to create a new empire to replace the declining Mughals? We will never know, of course. The questions nevertheless underscore the need to maintain a scholarly mindset in which not all that happens was inevitable. Second, what we do know for sure is that cohesive Mughal power thwarted English ambitions, at least for a short while. This forced the East India Company to continue trading with India on terms that were more-or-less commercial rather than imposed politically. Sovereign power was then, and remains now, an antidote to economic exploitation.

Unfortunately for India, England's power was growing, but India's was about to begin to decline. Aurangzeb died in 1707, the same year that England and Scotland united to become the Kingdom of Great Britain. The succession to Aurangzeb did not go well. The Mughal Empire disintegrated into a variety of regional kingdoms, which provided some economic stability on the subcontinent but were no match politically for growing British power.[44] As to why the Mughal Empire disintegrated, a variety of new scholarship notwithstanding, the classic accounts of Moreland and Habib remain persuasive.[45] The Mughal rulers remained patrimonial, and unlike the rulers in China, they failed to move in a bureaucratic direction. Mughal peace encouraged the development of trade and commerce. However, the lands of the realm were managed by allocating portions as gifts to court favorites on the basis of tax farming. This created incentives to squeeze revenues from those who tilled the land, which discouraged improvements in agricultural productivity. Unlike in the England of the period, where agrarian commercialization had already initiated a series of modernizing economic and political changes, Indian agriculture, the mainstay of the Indian economy, remained more or less stagnant.[46] The struggle over nearly stagnant revenues was thus at the heart of a nearly permanent power struggle between the center and the regions in Mughal India. When cohesive, the Mughal rule was quite capable of imposing its will on intermediaries and defending India from external intrusion. The empire lacked economic or political dynamism, however, and exhibited considerable brittleness when the center weakened and external pressures grew. Whatever else may be said about Mughal India, the Mughals were not a modernizing force. India under the Mughals was not moving toward autonomous commercial or capitalist development. Whether such changes would have emerged during the eighteenth century, or, failing that, whether India could have carried out its own version of a Meiji transformation in the nineteenth century, we will never know. What we do know is that British colonial imposition closed off these possible historical pathways to modernity for India.

The British state during the first half of the eighteenth century was already working hard to strengthen its own economy and power. The success of the East India Company in importing Indian textiles to Britain during the second half of the seventeenth century led to growing demands for protectionism. Manufacturing interests were increasingly challenging the trading interests and winning. Much of the cloth and hosiery at this stage was manufactured by village artisans in England, who were often located on large country estates. The politically powerful gentry, then, had an interest in encouraging manufacturing in their villages.[47] The government in England passed laws in 1700 (first under pressure from wool manufacturers, and then again periodically) prohibiting certain types of Indian textiles—especially those that were fully processed and ready to use—to be imported into England.

The protectionist legislation did not lead to an immediate decline of exports from India, mainly because Indian textiles were much in demand: "Indian cotton cloth had no rival in Europe until late in the eighteenth century."[48] The underlying reasons were both low costs and "superior production techniques."[49] The East India Company now re-exported these textiles to a variety of countries on the Continent, but especially for purchasing slaves in West Africa and for use by slaves in the "new world." While this "triangular trade" of sorts put EICs profits on relatively secure ground during the first half of the eighteenth century—the annual profits of the East India Company during 1720–57 averaged £500,000, and the dividends paid on investment averaged 7 percent to 8 percent[50]—two caveats are important. First, the protectionist framework provided room for the British textile industry to emerge and mature during the eighteenth century. Once India was colonized, it did not have the same luxury as Britain to protect its own textiles. Britain then eventually forced an open economy on India, which contributed to the destruction of India's textile industry. Second, the East India Company sensed that heavy dependence on Indian calico for its income might prove excessive; it is around this time, in the early eighteenth century, that tea imports from China also became important to East India Company trade.

East India Company trade with India flourished during the first half of the eighteenth century. From London, the company looked like "success upon success," providing very high rates of return on investment; by the end of this period, some 28 percent of British MPs held East India Company stock.[51] As before, East India Company ships took bullion—and on occasion other goods, such as woolen cloth—from England and brought back Indian calico, chintz, and silks; some of the ships went on to China to exchange bullion for tea, for which the English had started acquiring a taste. The trade was increasingly concentrated in Bengal, from where nearly 60 percent of all Asian exports to Britain now originated. The growth of trade, however, created its own problems. Growing resistance within England to Indian textile imports has been noted. The other problem for the East India Company was a growing need for more and more bullion. Not only did this boost gold and silver prices in Europe, but also, given the mercantilist mindset of the era, there was criticism within England that the East India Company was draining national treasure—and thus power—for its own profits. The pressure on the East India Company to somehow improve its terms of trade with India was thus consistent. East India Company men on the spot in India sensed political weakness in India as central Mughal rule disintegrated. The regional powers in India were at odds with each other, and the East India Company was not only a party to these growing strategic intrigues, but also used the situation to pursue aggressive diplomacy to gain economic advantage.

Two examples will help underscore how peaceful commerce, which had already been fundamentally challenged by Child (only to be pushed back by Aurangzeb), was increasingly a thing of the past. Britain was now using its superior military might to alter the terms of economic exchange in its favor. First, the East India Company in 1717 pressured and bribed the weakened Mughal emperor to grant them a *firman* (a ruling of sorts) to trade free of customs duty.[52] This was a significant economic boon to the East India Company, which could now lower the costs of trade and enhance its profits, which it did. Some of the commercial success of the East India Company was, then, not just commercial success. Because the Royal Navy provided military support, it is important to note the collusion between the state and merchants, which underlay all such aggressive diplomacy, and the resulting high rates of return on investments. The *firman* was first applicable to Bengal, but then the East India Company sought to broaden its scope to the rest of its trading areas in India. When other regional rulers resisted the company's demands for custom-free trade, "there was always the warship and their guns."[53] The loss of custom duties deprived Indian rulers of resources that they could have spent within India—probably on consumption and warfare, but even those would have added to economic activity. Concrete estimates of economic resources lost to India are hard to come by; however, Siraj-ud-daulah, the last independent ruler of Bengal, suggested that the East India Company had deprived him—defrauded, in his claims—of nearly £2 million.[54] Whether these estimates are accurate or not, it is the case that the East India Company was now benefiting from customs-free trade and channeling these resources back to Britain. With the shift in relative political power, the process of transferring tribute from India to Britain had begun.

The importance of force for profits was also evident in an arena where English power was clearly superior, namely, on the seas. Among the early casualties of English armed trade in India was indigenous shipping. With the help of the Royal Navy, East India Company ships started plundering Indian ships, leading to a long-term decline of Indian traders. One scholar finds support for this outcome in Mughal documents and tersely notes that "the view that the East India Company deliberately enriched itself by an indiscriminate plunder of indigenous shipping is hardly the image which the Company itself projects in its own records."[55] This trend hastened as the century wore on and the Mughal Empire disintegrated: if eighty-seven Indian ships had traded off the Indian west coast in 1693, the average between 1716 and 1733 was only thirty-two a year, going down to seventeen in 1741.[56] The decline in Indian shipping paralleled the decline of the Mughal rule in India.

During the seventeenth century, Mughal rulers had calculated that allowing the English company to trade in India would not be much of a military threat and might contribute taxes from trade. With the passing of time, both assumptions turned out to be false. As noted, Mughal cohesion declined in the early eighteenth century. The East India Company could also by then count on enhanced military support from a modernizing and expansionist British state. The company then forcibly changed the terms of trade, further weakening the fragmenting Indian polity by depriving it of taxes from trade. Meanwhile, the East India Company's profits flourished, further benefiting those associated with the company and the British state. What had started out as a commercial venture was slowly but surely moving toward an imperial venture in which the British state and British capital were benefiting at the expense of India. Although these trends were weak—barely discernible—at this early stage, by the mid-eighteenth century the British imperial journey in India had begun.

The East India Company as Rulers, Phase 1

The East India Company established territorial control over Bengal in 1757. Using it as a base, and with the support of the British navy and that of East India Company's own armed forces in India, the company spread its territorial conquest, so much so that by the early nineteenth century much of present-day India, Pakistan, and Bangladesh were under British control. The relations between the British state and the East India Company also grew more intimate; the state was increasingly becoming the dominant partner in the ruling alliance. Territorial conquest enabled the British to squeeze resources—"revenues," in seemingly neutral British colonial discourse—out of the Indian economy. These resources were first used to build a British-controlled armed force within India with Indian soldiers, which in turn facilitated further conquests and further revenues. The British then designed an ingenious method of transferring the remaining but growing revenues from India to Britain: unlike the Spaniards, who simply loaded bullion from the Americas on to their ships, the British substituted their Indian revenues for bullion exports from England to buy Indian calico (as well as tea from China), and then sold these investments back in England, adding to private profits and public finances.

This pattern was in place for some five to six decades when the growing demands from manufacturing interests within England led to the dilution of the monopoly right of the East India Company to trade with India, in 1813. From then on, the East India Company increasingly became a state agency of sorts, whose main function was to rule India. Trade was now more and more in private hands. The British state, the East India Company, and private manufacturers, and traders now collaborated to turn India into a colony in the true economic sense: an exporter of raw materials and an importer of British textiles, thus contributing to the growth of a key industry in the development of Britain's Industrial Revolution. The British state also benefited directly, not only by continuing to tax Indians to finance the imperial rule over them, but also by transmitting Indian wealth to Britain via such ingenious mechanisms as using Indian revenues to facilitate the opium and tea trade with China and running favorable balance-of-payment accounts to pay for home charges, or British expenses charged to Indian revenues. Meanwhile, traditional political and economic patterns in India were deeply disrupted: the household-based textile manufacturing industry was destroyed; food production failed to grow; and the power of the indigenous ruling classes was fundamentally undermined. A significant revolt led by the Indian aristocracy in the mid-nineteenth century proved too much for the East India Company to handle, and led to the formal assumption of Crown rule over India in 1857. This political economy of British imperialism in India during 1757–1857—motives, mechanisms of rule, and impact—is analyzed in what follows, again in two phases: the more mercantilist phase that lasted until about 1813, and then, with the decline of the East India Company's trading monopoly, a second phase marked by the growth of private trade.

A brief reminder of the global and the national context in which the East India Company operated during its mercantilist phase may be helpful at the outset. The second half of the eighteenth century was a period of British ascendancy, bookended by two wars with France and punctuated by the loss of the American colonies. Challenges from the Spanish and from the Dutch Republic were already receding; both their domestic economies and their military might had failed to keep up with developments in Britain. The Spaniards joined the French against Britain during the mid-century Seven Years' War and lost, giving up to Britain—at least temporarily—their colonial capitals in both the West Indies and the East Indies (Havana and Manila, respectively). Dutch power also peaked around the mid-century: the Dutch economy grew slowly throughout the century, and toward the end Britain's national product was some nine times that of the Dutch Republic;[57] around the mid-century, the number of war ships in the Dutch navy was nearly half of that of the British navy. While France sought to challenge the growing British power, the increasing might of the British navy was already evident during the Seven Year's War, which the French lost. The British loss of the American colonies encouraged the French to challenge Britain again, as did the sense of mobilization and a few rapid military victories that followed the French Revolution. British power, however, had grown steadily: by 1780s or so, the Industrial Revolution had arrived in Britain; moneyed interests dominated British politics; and Britain subordinated foreign policy to economic policy, aggressively pursuing profits overseas, especially within the empire, which further fueled British power.[58] Napoleon was the last to really test Britain's growing might, at least for a while and at least beyond Europe. With the rise of conscription armies and the defeat of Austria during the early phases of the Napoleonic Wars, the balance of power between France and Britain appeared to hang in balance, but only momentarily. By 1815, when Napoleon was defeated at Waterloo, British supremacy had arrived, inaugurating the British century of global dominance.

At home, by the mid-eighteenth century the empire was already "seen as vital to Britain's economic wellbeing (and) to her standing as a great power."[59]

The British state now systematically pursued imperial expansion. Britain was not quite a "bourgeois" state yet; it was instead an oligarchy of commercialized landed aristocrats whose governments "made war and peace for profit, colonies and markets and in order to stamp on commercial competitors."[60] The "aggressive commercial expansion" of the British state then fed both private and public interests.[61] The warring British state was constantly starved of resources; the national debt helped finance these wars, and such institutions as the Bank of England and the East India Company in turn helped finance these debts. The constant search for new resources, not only for company and personal profits, but also to help buttress state power, was thus very much part of the modus operandi of the East India Company. Both Clive and the Battle of Plassey were products of this broader drive toward militant profit seeking overseas during this period.

The power of the British state, of course, rested on a growing economy, an economy that during the last third of the eighteenth century was being transformed by industry. The questions of whether the shift to industry was revolutionary or gradual, and of why England experienced this fundamental shift first, have been widely debated. Most of these debates need not detain us here.[62] It will suffice to suggest, following Hobsbawm, that among Britain's advantages in the late eighteenth century, three stand out: the domestic market, the empire, and an activist state.[63] The "great size and the steadiness" of the home market provided the "broad base for a generalized industrial economy," especially for the development of food-processing industries, coal, and, of course, the industry central to the first phase of Britain's Industrial Revolution: textiles. The development of cotton and textiles, in turn, was also deeply connected to Britain's imperial links: all cotton was imported, first from slave-owned plantations in the West Indies and then from the same in the United States; manufactured textiles were in turn exported, and the colonies were taking up nearly two-thirds of all exports toward the end of the century. During the nineteenth century, as we will see, India became a central market for British textiles. An activist state was essential to the early stages of the Industrial Revolution; a laissez-faire state was not the cause but a result of industrial success in Britain. The British state was run by commercial interests, and, in turn, it consistently intervened to support profit-making by both merchants and manufacturers: The Naval acts turned much of colonial trade into a monopoly; protectionist legislation kept Indian calico out of Britain, providing room for the textile industry to mature; support of the slave trade and colonization of the West Indies provided cotton imports; and much of foreign policy took systematic account of economic costs and benefits. The origins of Britain's Industrial Revolution are clearly complex. For our purposes, it is mainly important to keep Hobsbawm's emphasis on the imperial connection of the Industrial Revolution in mind: "Behind our Industrial Revolution there lies this concentration on the colonial and 'underdeveloped' markets overseas, the successful battle to deny them to anyone else . . . Our industrial revolution grew out of our commerce, and especially our commerce with the underdeveloped world."[64]

It was in this mid-eighteenth century context that the East India Company fundamentally shifted its profit-making strategy in India away from trading on commercial terms to conquering territory and squeezing resources via political mechanisms. There are a variety of explanations in the historical literature as to why the East India Company turned to territorial conquest of India, some of which are not persuasive. It is best that I set these aside before proposing my own interpretation. First, there is a seemingly modest indecisiveness among some scholars, suggesting that the underlying motives are "hard to explain."[65] It is difficult or even pointless to disagree with such a nonargument, except to say that such indecisiveness is part of a misplaced broader interpretation that British imperialism in India was unplanned and accidental, that it all happened in a fit of absent-mindedness. As I suggest, this was simply not the case; I further propose that Clive's conquest and plunder of Bengal—a set of efforts that initiated the process of territorial control of India— was part and parcel of the broader militant turn British foreign policy took in the mid-eighteenth century when Pitt supplanted Walpole. A second argument accepts that territorial conquest was far from accidental but proposes that the strategic shift was aimed mainly at enhancing the private fortunes of such men on the spot as Clive.[66] I do not find this overly persuasive because the search for revenues via territorial conquest was long an East India Company goal, and the British navy actively supported Clive as he moved from one military conquest to another. A third argument accepts that the territorial conquests in India were part of the broader British imperial advance in the mid-eighteenth century, but suggests that the underlying motives were less economic and more about the "agrarian patriotism" of the British ruling class.[67] This, too, is unpersuasive because the old aristocracy, which some may suggest was moved mainly by considerations of honor, duty, and patriotism, though I have doubts—was really not politically salient anymore; Britain's ruling class (the gentlemanly capitalist class) by then was instead a thoroughly profit-oriented gentry, allied with commercial interests.[68] Following the Seven Years' War, the manufacturers also started gaining political significance within the ruling class. As I have already suggested, this class made war and acquired colonies mainly for profit, though there is no need to deny that elements of patriotism and honor may also have played some role.

Robert Clive was born to a political family and his career in India began as a small-time clerk—a factor—in the East India Company outpost in Madras.[69] During his first decade in India (1744–53), he became more and more a soldier, and distinguished himself as a military strategist of sorts while participating in wars involving local South Indian rulers and the French East India Company. After a notable military victory in 1751, his reputation grew and he was lauded in London, including by Pitt, as a "heaven-born general." Upon his return to Britain, Clive briefly joined Parliament, and his aggressive oratory again made an impression on Pitt. Meanwhile, Pitt's demand for a more militant approach toward France in the post-Walpole years was increasingly gaining acceptance in British politics. When Clive left for India for the second time, in 1755, Pitt's power was on the rise. After some ups and downs, Pitt joined a coalition government and became the British prime minister in 1757, the same year Clive established territorial control over Bengal. As a military man with close ties to the merchant community associated with the East India Company, and because of his connection to the British political establishment via his family, Clive was very much in tune with the hopes and desires of Britain's ruling class.

On matters of foreign policy during the eighteenth century, the political elites in Britain were not united. A little-England policy of sorts—a policy of war avoidance—was supported by a group of politicians, including Walpole, who represented the interests of those who paid heavily for these wars, the tax-paying gentry.[70] This political tendency held sway in the first half of the century. But by mid-century a more militant foreign policy had come to the fore. It was led by another group of politicians, including Pitt, who had the support of many London merchants. This group argued that "war and colonial conquest were the way to national wealth and power."[71] Since wars and colonial conquests were expensive, and since there was reluctance at home to pay for them, the supporters of a militant foreign policy also supported aggressive expansion overseas as a strategy to boost public revenues. Many in the East India Company—and certainly Clive—supported this political tendency. When Pitt led Britain into the Seven Years' War, the struggle with France to control commerce and profits became global: the recovery of Canada opened up the fish and fur trade; the capture of Guadeloupe opened up a new supply of sugar; the conquest of Senegal further facilitated the gum and slave trade; an attack on Manila gave Britain control over tea trade with China; and, of course, the territorial control over India by Clive opened up new source of revenues.[72] None of these were accidents; they were part of the British turn toward aggressive commercial expansion in the mid-century. No doubt, Britain gave up some of these gains during the Treaty of Paris, when moneyed interests—both the gentry and in London—refused to pay for the consolidation of victories. However, the gains in India were not among those that were returned to France; the Indian gains held a promise that went way beyond the gains of trade on commercial terms.

When Clive left for India for the second time, in 1755, he was sent not only as an employee of the East India Company but also as an officer of the Royal navy. Consistent with broader foreign policy goals, his mission was to secure British interests in and around Fort St. George in Madras against both the French and local rulers. Naval ships under the command of Vice Admiral Charles Watson were also sent to India to help Clive. Trouble emerged in and around Calcutta soon after Clive's arrival in Madras: the ruler of Bengal had defeated British forces and imprisoned British residents. This was no 1688, however, when Aurangzeb had defeated the East India Company's military ships and the company had retreated; the deeper political and military balance had by now shifted decisively in favor of the British. The ruler of Bengal was a poor shadow of the Mughal ruler Aurangzeb. The British navy and military technology, including the quality of British cannons on ships and muskets on land, had improved steadily in the interregnum. Clive shifted north with his troops, along with the British naval ships, and did what anyone British in his position would have done, or at least would have attempted: defeat the local powers to secure the interests of the East India Company and the British Crown. That Clive made a personal fortune in the process was also only unusual in the size of the fortune he made.[73] Clive's conquest of Bengal is best understood at two levels: at a general level, it was one strand in the broader British turn to a more aggressive foreign policy that was aimed at securing economic advantages overseas; and, at a more specific level—ignoring numerous details of who did what to whom—it reflected India's growing political fragmentation and the simultaneous rise in British military power.

Clive's military conquest led to an immediate plunder of Bengal. The personal treasury of the ruler of Bengal was worth close to £2 million, a sizable sum at that time, considering that the entire income of the British state during this period was less than £10 million.[74] Clive appropriated this fortune, passing some on to other East India Company officials and soldiers, and keeping a substantial sum for his personal use. Over the next several years, Clive continued to collect gifts from various indigenous rulers, who in turn squeezed the local peasantry harder to please their British conquerors. Christopher Hill estimates that between 1757 and 1766 the East India Company and its employees squeezed some £6 million as gifts from Bengal and adds that "there had been nothing like it in history since the Spanish conquistadores looted the Aztec and Inca civilizations."[75] Clive, of course, eventually returned to England with this personal fortune as a nabob, bought some country estates, and joined Parliament. Clive's successor, Warren Hastings, continued to plunder Bengal, proudly distinguishing himself from Clive by suggesting that he never defrauded the East India Company. The only question he asked himself instead when pocketing Indian money was, "whether it would go into a black man's pocket or my own."[76] I return later to how this plunder impacted Bengal, including the famine of 1769–70, when several million Indians perished.

As Clive acquired the rights to the taxes of Bengal, the British state became concerned about how an individual can have rights to conquered territory—and beyond the legal principles, the state wanted a share of those resources—and started to get more and more involved in managing both Clive and the East India Company. Thereafter, the process of the state gaining the upper hand in the state-East India Company relations was fairly rapid. Following the military victory at Plassey, Clive and his successors conquered more and more territory in India over the next several decades: Arcot in 1761, Awadh at Baxar in 1774, and so on, until the final significant military victory over the Marathas in and around Bombay in 1818, after which the territorial conquest of India was very nearly over. These military conquests facilitated more Indian land taxes, but there was often a time lag before new taxes could pay for warfare, which led to deficits. Most of these deficits were financed by loans, raised either in India or in Britain by floating bonds. The British state also stepped in to subsidize the East India Company's costs of war and, in return, sought more control over the company affairs. According to a historian of the East India Company, the relations between the British state and the East India Company had become so involved by 1763 that "divorce ceased to be an option."[77] The financial contributions of the East India Company to Britain also grew, via both private profits and tax revenues. The importance of these contributions was substantial enough that British "national interest" was increasingly linked to the "security of territorial empire in India," and already, by 1773, there was a growing sense that the loss of India would produce "a national bankruptcy" in Britain.[78] Legislation in 1773 created a governor general for all of India, an appointment that was to be controlled by the Crown. Last, with Pitt's India Act of 1784 (by then, William Pitt the Younger), Parliament established a Board of Control to manage the affairs of the East India Company in London, reducing the company to an "agency of imperial government."[79]

It may be noted that while the East India Company was establishing territorial control over India during this period, company officials and British legislators continued to deny having any interest in the territorial conquest of India. Robert James, the secretary of East India Company, is known to have commented in 1767—a decade after Plassey—that "we don't want conquest and power; it is commercial interest we look for."[80] And in 1784 (the year Pitt's India Act was established), a British legislator commented in Parliament that "to pursue schemes of conquest and extension of dominion in India, are measures repugnant to the wish, the honor, and the policy of this nation."[81] These denials were so inconsistent with the ground reality that one wonders about their purpose. In all probability, the comments were aimed at mollifying the East India Company's critics within Britain. But clearly, these denials were also lies. The use of imperial lies then raises a broader point about the ideology of imperialism. Although ideological issues are not central to this study, we will encounter in these pages the fact that imperialists often lie about their intentions in order to mollify critics, at home or abroad. There is a noticeable pattern. Spokesmen for would-be hegemons deny the intent to seek hegemony. And once they become hegemons, they claim that greatness was thrust upon them and that in any case, "our hegemony is benign and needed."

To return to the main narrative, the primary goal of the state-supported East India Company in India continued to be "how to enrich the mother country."[82] The acquisition of territory and of taxes from that territory, however, changed the problem of how to enrich the mother country. There was enormous enthusiasm within the East India Company in London at the prospect of new riches that territorial control of Bengal might facilitate; the company directors gave orders to their agents in India, "to enlarge every channel for conveying to us as early as possible, the annual produce of our acquisitions."[83] When Clive and his successors squeezed excessive surplus out of poor Indian peasants, leading to famine and decline in agricultural production, the company directors further ordered those on the spot to "use robust methods and force if they deemed it necessary for the collection of taxes."[84] Ruthless and despotic rule aside, the collection of substantial revenues in India did create the problem of how to transfer a portion of these back to Britain. A conscious decision was made to not repeat what the Spaniards had done in the Americas. India, to the East India Company leaders, was "a hen which lays a golden egg a day." The lesson from the analogy was inescapable: "if you draw off in bullion the revenues of that country you kill the hen to get all her eggs at once."[85] The solution to the problem of how to enrich the mother country with Indian revenues, then, had two parts: the first part was to use these resources to alter the nature of Britain's trade with India, and the second part was to use Indian revenues to pay for the costs of the growing British Indian Army.

The total revenue the East India Company collected in India between 1782 and 1857 is recorded in Table 1.1. The first thing to note about this data is that revenues grew steadily and were even higher in the post-1857 colonial period (see chapter 3 for a fuller discussion of the colonial period). Revenues from Bengal in the post-Plassey years, say, 1766 to 1771—for which good data that are specific to Bengal are available—averaged from £2 to £3 million per year.[86] It is clear in Table 1.1 that as the empire spread over India, these revenues grew to some £16 million by 1813—that is, until the end of the mercantilist phase—and then to some £33 million by 1857. What is also clear in the table is that the main source of these revenues—nearly 60 percent of the total revenues—was land tax. Other significant sources of revenue included taxes on salt, the sale of opium, customs duties,

Table 1.1 Revenue and Expenditure of the East India Company, 1782–1857*

Years	Average Annual Revenue (in million £)	Percent of total revenue derived from land revenue	Percent of total expenditure in India on military
1782–1791	6.5	64.4	58.0
1792–1801	8.5	59.0	55.7
1802–1811	15.6	55.0	50.9
1812–1821	18.4	65.8	50.5
1822–1831	21.7	62.9	46.8
1832–1841	20.1	60.2	42.6
1842–1851	24.7	55.9	44.1
1852–1857	28.4	55.8	40.0

* The figures in the last column are percentage of East India Company expenditures within India, which after 1800 tended to be some £1–£3 million less than the East India Company's overall revenues in India; the balance was transferred back to Britain via a variety of mechanisms that are discussed in the text. *Source*: Adapted from Richards, "Finances of the East India Company," tables 6 and 9. It may be of interest to the reader that Richards, who was an economic historian at Duke University, collected this data with great care but unfortunately passed away before he could put it to full use.

and tribute paid by local rulers. As to expenditures, it is again clear in Table 1.1 that nearly half of all the money the East India Company spent in India was spent on the military (I return to a discussion of this later). Other major East India Company expenditures included the costs of running the empire—civil administration and police absorbed some 15 percent to 20 percent of the total—and a significant portion of the balance was transferred back to Britain through one mechanism or another.

Recall that Anglo-Indian trade prior to Plassey mainly involved exchange of bullion from Britain for calicoes from India. With the acquisition of Bengal revenues initially—and, eventually, all India revenues—there was no further need for the East India Company to send bullion in ships to India. Instead, the company now used the taxes it collected in India to buy Indian products, mainly textiles, either for sale in London or, given protectionism on some items, for re-export, chiefly to facilitate the slave trade. Since the high costs of running the empire in India were also borne by Indian revenues (save for the costs of shipping and the meager salaries paid to the company's employees), the East India Company was essentially securing Indian products for free and selling them for substantial profit. No wonder East India Company trade grew substantially: if by 1700 the East India Company sent some eleven ships annually to India, by 1800 it was sending nearly a hundred ships a year. During the second half of the eighteenth century, these ships would take instruments of rule to India, including cannons, and bring back Indian calico (and over time, more and more Chinese tea) for sale in London. Indian revenues paid for all of this; profits to the East India Company and to the British state, in turn, were substantial. I will return to a fuller discussion of British gains; suffice it to note for now that the British state—leaving aside private profits or profits to the company for the moment—gained some 7 percent to 10 percent of its total receipts from the custom duties on East India Company trade during this period, say, between 1767 and 1812.[87]

As the East India Company's corporate empire in India became a matter of national concern in Britain, efforts were made to systematize company rule in India. Charles Cornwallis was appointed governor general of India in 1786 by Prime Minister William Pitt the Younger, or more accurately, by Henry Dundas, Pitt's secretary of state for war. Cornwallis continued the process of military conquests and control over India that had begun with Clive and Hastings. What was new were the conscious efforts to reduce corruption within the East India Company in India, improve the legal underpinnings of rule, and systematize property rights and revenue collection, at least in the Bengal Presidency. The East India Company paid its employees meager salaries and, for the most part, allowed them to make private fortunes as compensation. These private fortunes had started cutting into company profits, leading to higher compensation and stricter rules of behavior; this was the beginning of a process of transforming company employees into civil servants of sorts in an imperial agency. Cornwallis also succeeded in creating a permanent settlement in Bengal, essentially granting de jure property rights to the tax collectors of Bengal, the zamindars (landlords), in exchange for substantial land revenues, settled in perpetuity. A similar experiment was attempted in the Madras Presidency, but it was eventually abandoned because it led to a decline in revenues. I will return to a further discussion of these issues.

These personnel and land reforms stabilized and enhanced the East India Company's revenues from India (Table 1.1). Meanwhile, there was growing resistance within Britain to Indian textiles as the British textile manufacturing was maturing. A new solution to the problem of how to enrich the mother country with the growing Indian revenues, then, was in part to resell Indian textiles elsewhere in the world, but more important, to slowly abandon Indian textiles as the main product bought and sold by the East India Company and to shift to Chinese tea. Tea was by now a popular drink in Britain and elsewhere, including the American colonies. The East India Company then started using Indian revenues to buy bullion in India and to ship this bullion to China to buy tea for sale in Britain. Over time, it became clear that there was market for opium in China.

Instead of sending bullion from India, Indian revenues were used to purchase Indian opium and exchanged for Chinese tea. By the end of the century, this mode of transmitting Indian revenues via tea bought in Canton became the most profitable part of the East India Company's Asian trade.

Besides financing trade, the other major use of Indian revenues was, of course, to cover the costs of ruling the growing empire in India, especially the building of what would eventually become the British Indian Army. Throughout this period, the size of British armed forces in India grew. These sepoy armies consisted mainly of soldiers recruited and trained along European lines in India by East India Company officers, with the help of British royal forces.[88] By 1805, the numbers of troops in these regional forces of the East India Company were significant: 64,000 each in the Bengal and Madras Presidencies, and another 26,500 in the Bombay Presidency.[89] From the British perspective, there were numerous problems associated with these forces—they were not unified and they were under- professionalized, not to mention expensive; nonetheless, they were effective war-making forces that facilitated more military conquests in India. As is clear in Table 1.1, nearly half of the Indian revenues were used to pay for these armed forces and for arms brought from Britain to rule India. Squeezing land resources out of India by imposing political control and building armed forces in India were mutually supportive goals of the East India Company.[90] These East India Company contributions to running what was essentially fast becoming a British empire led to significant debates in London over who should bear the costs. Whenever the company's finances became troubled, the British state helped out, but then resumed taxing it for further benefits. Leaving these state and company tugs of war aside, at minimum, it ought to be clear that by the end of the century, the East India Company was no longer a mere trading firm. It was, instead, a full-blown, imperial British agency that combined economic and military functions as it established an empire in India.

The East India Company's exploits in India during this period brought significant benefits to Britain, often at the expense of India. This is not to ignore that there were some important lines of criticism of the East India Company within Britain at the time. The personal aggrandizements of Clive and Hastings came in for some sharp parliamentary rebukes, but talk of disciplining the East India Company seldom made much headway, especially in the post-Plassey years. The East India Company was too important a source of national revenues to be tampered with. Over time, more consequential were the shifting state controls over the East India Company. But these, too, were aimed either at rationalizing the East India Company or ensuring the state's fair share of the Indian loot; seldom were they aimed at moderating the ongoing plunder. The criticisms that proved to be most significant were those that emerged from the growing manufacturing interests within Britain. Manufacturers wanted to dilute the East India Company monopoly on eastern trade, and they eventually succeeded (around 1813). I return to that next phase in the evolution of the East India Company.

The issue of how East India Company actions in India benefited Britain is complicated during this period by the fact that the East India Company was no longer just a trading company, as it had been in the earlier period. By now it was instead a corporate imperial agency to which the British state had essentially outsourced the conquest and squeeze of India. Observers of the East India Company during the period well understood this role: "Remitting the surplus revenue of India . . . [is] perhaps the best reason" for the East India Company's existence.[91] This surplus revenue of India, to repeat, was used to both facilitate the East India Company's trade and pay for running the Indian empire, especially the sizable British Indian Army. The commercial advantages the East India Company generated for Britain were both relatively direct, in the form of supporting British balance of payments and public revenues, and indirect, in the form of generating profits and employment in the British economy. Similarly, building up an Indian army was not only central for ruling and squeezing India; it also enabled Britain to project power in and around the Indian Ocean.

Britain's balance of payments between 1765 and 1812 are summarized in Table 1.2. It is worth underscoring that the annual net inflows to Britain from its Indian trade averaged some £2.4 million. In the context of Britain's global trade during this period, these amounts were considerable and went a long way to balance the current account deficits that Britain ran regularly during this period, mainly as a result of warfare. According to Javier Cuenca Esteban, the Indian inflows were the "least dispensable" element of Britain's foreign accounts.[92] It is important to reiterate that this trade was not trade in the normal sense; India was not importing any goods in return. The trade surpluses were coerced out of India by Britain. As imperial rule spread over India, Britain taxed India's land wealth first, and then other economic activities, and used a portion of the revenues to buy Indian calico and Chinese tea that were sold in London and elsewhere. This was highly political trade: the East India Company "remained free to benefit from coercion over Indian weavers, from barrier to entry of potential competition in India, from local judicial control, and from monopoly or taxing powers in saltpeter, rice, salt, cotton, raw silk and opium."[93] There was clearly overlap between the contributions of Indian trade to the British balance of payments and public revenues, but it is also important to recall that the customs duties on Indian trade collected by the British government amounted to some 7 percent to 10 percent of its total annual revenues from customs and excise duties. These were resources that Britain could use to fight wars without further taxing its own population, and thus contributed to both British power and wealth.

Table 1.2 British Balance of Payments, 1765–1812*

	1765–75	1776–82	1783–92	1793–1807	1808–1812
Balance of trade and services, excluding India	845	−1203	−140	2503	4001
British war expenses, excluding India	−14	−644	−96	−3513	−11657
Balance of debt service	−548	−590	−513	475	2459
Balance of above	**282**	**−2438**	**−750**	**−534**	**−5195**
Total inflows from India	**1969**	**2345**	**2612**	**3354**	**2268**
Inflows from Ireland	579	719	965	1165	1202
Current account balance	2831	626	2828	3986	−1725

* All figures are in 000 £ and are annual averages for the period. The inflows from Ireland in row six are listed separately because they were not strictly related to direct imports and exports; instead, they included inflows resulting from reselling of Irish goods to British America and remittances related to British-owned lands in Ireland. Note that the figures for Britain's trade surplus with India are higher than the figures for what the East India Company spent annually during this period on goods that it bought and exported from India. The discrepancy makes sense because exported goods were sold at considerable profit, especially those that were re-exported either to the Continent or to West Africa for slave trade, and balance of payments included transfers other than earnings on exported goods. *Source*: Adapted from Javier Cuenca Esteban, "India's Contribution to the British Balance of Payments, 1757–1812," *Explorations in Economic History* 44, no. 1 (January 2007): 154–76, table 4.

The broader impact of the East India Company's economic activities on the British economy at the time is harder to document because it tended to be diffuse and multifaceted. Still, H. V. Bowen's recent work in this direction is heroic, and his findings on the jobs that the East India Company helped create and on the company's expenditures within the British economy are well worth summarizing. After a careful sorting of relevant data, Bowen suggests that at its peak, in 1800, the East India Company created some 93,500 jobs.[94] Britain at that time was a country of roughly twenty million people, with some eight million employed adults, nearly 60 percent of whom were employed in industry or services.[95] The

East India Company was thus responsible for some 2 percent of British employment in industry and services. As to company expenditures in the British economy, Bowen estimates that these averaged some £8.5 million annually during this period, or between "one-quarter and one-fifth of the figure attributed to annual government expenditure" at the time.[96] Last, the numerous private fortunes that were made in India by all those connected to the East India Company, first by plunder, and then, more systematically, via company profits, dividends, and private trade, were spent in Britain, adding to the economic vigor.[97] Bowen's overall conclusion is thus useful: "During the late eighteenth and the early nineteenth centuries the funds that flowed out of East India House added to the commercial, financial, and industrial strength of the metropolis, and the private fortunes generated by those connected to the Company became increasingly tightly woven into the economic fabric of imperial Britain."[98]

In addition to these economic benefits to Britain, the other major use of Indian revenues discussed here was the steady buildup of an armed force in India that would become the British Indian Army. Although organized as regional regiments at this early stage, this British army in India comprised more than 150,000 troops in 1805, including some 24,000 British troops. It was one of the world's largest standing armies at the time, and it was all paid for by Indian revenues, including the imported muskets and uniforms. A giant share of the revenue the East India Company collected in India—as high as two-thirds in some years—went toward maintaining this army. The use of this armed force to spread the British Empire in India has been noted. What has to be added in the present discussion is that this armed force also provided essential support to Britain in the wars it fought to spread the empire beyond India. For example, as the French troops captured Amsterdam in 1795, Britain used Indian troops to colonize such areas of former Dutch influence as Ceylon, Malacca, and the Moluccas. Indian troops were also used in a parallel campaign against the Dutch on the Cape of Good Hope, first in 1795, and then again in 1806. During the Napoleonic Wars, British Indian troops allied with Ottoman armies to defeat the French in Egypt. Then again, in 1810, Britain used its Indian troops to capture Isle de France, the last French foothold in the Indian Ocean, renamed it Mauritius, and ruled it till 1968. Last, British Indian troops helped Britain capture Java from the Dutch in 1811. In sum, the British Indian Army provided important support to Britain's growing global dominance.

Thomas Mortimer, a British political economist, declared in 1772 that the East India Company was "one of the chief sources of the power and commercial prosperity of Great Britain."[99] Even allowing for some exaggeration, the economic and political evidence reviewed here very much moves in this direction. While the more extreme claims that the Indian revenues financed Britain's Industrial

Revolution may not be tenable today, neither are the seemingly confident claims of some that the contributions of the Indian Empire to Britain during this period were not of "major importance."[100] The evidence available at present seems to corroborate the findings of a British parliamentary committee that reviewed the affairs of the East India Company in 1793. The committee concluded that, as a result of East India Company activities in India, British

> manufactures have been supported, encouraged, and improved; its shipping has been increased; its revenues augmented; its commerce extended; its agriculture promoted; and its power and resources invigorated and upheld.[101]

Subsequent scholarly sparring aside, then, contemporaries understood—fully and rightly—the importance of the East India Company and of India to Britain. This importance, moreover, went beyond the economic and military benefits to which one can assign numbers. As some scholars have suggested, the empire also helped to craft the emerging British national identity, especially because the Scots played such a large role in the company, as did the Irish in the British Indian Army.[102]

Britain's gains were executed politically and these were often at the expense of India. Before I discuss impact of the East India Company on India, several caveats are in order. First, any assessment of impact always imagines some counterfactual condition—even if it is implicit—of what may have happened. Since this is very hard to know, it will be useful to keep in mind that Mughal India, though prosperous by premodern standards, was not a modernizing economy or polity, and that the rulers taxed the economy at a high level. Second, the influence of the East India Company on India during the second half of the eighteenth century was concentrated mainly in the Bengal Presidency, and it had a growing role in South India toward the end of the century. Muslim rulers of South India were only subdued during the 1790s; the Marathas in Western India were finally defeated in the early nineteenth century; and much of North Central India remained either independent, such as Punjab and Kashmir, or enjoyed considerable autonomy, such as Awadh and Rajputana, during this period. Third, the net impact of the East India Company rule on India is not easy to assess in any precise manner. Data for this period are fragmentary, and how trade, production, and employment might influence each other in a coercive political economy remains conceptually and empirically murky.

With these caveats in place, it should be reiterated that the main mechanisms the East India Company used during this period to take advantage of Bengal, and to an extent other parts of India, were two: first, to destroy, subdue, or to reduce the claims and powers of the indigenous ruling class; second, having acquired political power, to squeeze taxes out of the local economies—mainly land revenues at the beginning—and to use them, in part, to buy goods to sell in Britain and elsewhere, but mainly to support a growing British Indian armed force that was used to further support Britain's imperial goals in India and elsewhere. The destruction of the indigenous ruling class in India was at the heart of the imperial project. It should be added that the indigenous rulers were hardly progressive or enlightened; they, too, lived off the taxes of the poor peasantry and used the revenue for warfare and conspicuous consumption. Nevertheless, since these rulers were indigenous, the monies they spent supported the Indian economy. Both warfare and luxury consumption by indigenous rulers supported large workshops and an artisan class, and these went into decline following the ascension of the East India Company.[103] As discussed here, the way the East India Company used the resources that it extracted from India did not have a similar impact. Over the longer term, loss of sovereignty had lot more serious consequences—a theme that runs through this volume—such as an inability of more enlightened indigenous rulers to emerge and, in turn, to protect and enhance the interests of the inhabitants of the subcontinent.

Over the short to the medium term, the mode and the amount of revenues that were squeezed out of the Indian society were a major determinant of the pernicious impact of British rule during the period. As noted, the immediate economic transfers following Clive's victory at Plassey, in 1757, took the form of plunder. Once the East India Company gained the right to collect taxes in Bengal, in 1765, the process of collecting land revenues began in earnest; the revenues collected in Bengal between 1766 and 1771 averaged some £2.4 million annually, of which nearly £2.2 million were land revenues.[104] These revenues probably equaled the "highest assessments made by previous Indian regimes."[105] Nearly half of these overall revenues helped to finance the East India Company's growing military force and about one-third were used to buy textiles (and some other goods) for sale in Britain and elsewhere.[106] As to how the new processes initiated by the East India Company impacted the economy and the society of Bengal, two sets of outcomes are especially notable. First, the East India Company used its "dominant position to fix the terms of exchange" in the local textile industry, especially "pushing down the share of wages toward the subsistence level."[107] In spite of the company's growing demand for textiles, there is no evidence to suggest that the local weavers benefited; if anything, the enhanced political leverage of the East India Company may have made them worse off.

A second major and early impact of the East India Company on Bengal was the famine of 1769–70. The East India Company's own court of directors (and then, Warren Hastings) estimated that the famine killed nearly one-third of Bengal's population;[108] some ten million people—yes, ten million—perished. The famine was not caused by the East India Company; famines were and continued to be common in India. While all famines are rooted in natural causes and the related crop failures, as we have learned from Amartya Sen and others, famines also have political origins;[109] this famine was no exception. The East India Company's actions contributed to the massive human tragedy in at least three different ways. First, the company's relentless demand for revenues had led the "impoverished zamindars" to alter traditional practices; they were now "reluctant" to help out the local peasantry by writing off "the arrears of rent during periods of natural calamities."[110] Second, under the East India Company regime, there was an increase in the area under commercial crops at the expense of food production for subsistence. Third, and most directly, the East India Company—anticipating a famine—used its cash reserves to buy large amounts of rice from the market to feed the army in 1769 and then again in 1770. In addition, private employees of the East India Company and their Indian middlemen starved the market by setting up "local monopolies of grain."[111] Man-made shortages exacerbated the impact of nature's occasional havoc, which led to a severe famine. As the famine unfolded, the East India Company also did not undertake any positive steps to ameliorate the misery and death of local inhabitants. On the contrary, company officials were focused on ensuring that despite the sharp decline in production, there would be no decline in revenue collection. According to these officials, revenue did not diminish "owing to its being kept up violently to its former standards."[112]

As the East India Company consolidated its hold over Bengal and brought more and more of India under its rule during the last quarter of the eighteenth century, a central issue it faced was how best to squeeze revenues out of the Indian society so as to govern and create profits. Between 1782 and 1813, East India Company revenues grew from some £5 million to £16 million (Table 1.1). As noted, land revenues provided the lion's share of these revenues. How to collect land revenues was a major preoccupation of the British in India throughout this period and beyond. The settlement with the zamindars of Bengal in 1793 sought to systemize the collection of land revenues by offering landowners de jure rights to private property in exchange for their payment of significant-but-fixed taxes on that property. Around the same time, the East India Company in the Madras Presidency experimented with what has come to be known as the Ryotwari System. This system was based on the direct collection of taxes from ryots (peasants) by government officials, without the mediation of the zamindars (the landlords). Faced with numerous problems of direct tax collection, the East India Company abandoned the Ryotwari System in 1801, experimented again with the Zamindari System, but then reverted to the Ryotwari System in 1822, which stayed in place till the end of British colonialism in India in the mid-20th century. In the early nineteenth century, a ryotwari system of sorts was adopted in the Bombay Presidency, and a version of the Zamindari System was extended to the Awadh in north-central India.

The Zamindari Settlement in Bengal has been well studied for its impact on the local society, both at its apex and on the poor peasantry.[113] A scholarly consensus of sorts has emerged that the British probably mistook the tax collectors of the Mughal period as landowners and bestowed property rights on them. However, onerous demands for revenue from the East India Company also led to considerable turnover in this class; many lost their estates because of their inability to meet their contractual obligations. Those who bought these estates tended to be mainly the lower gentry, or those who were probably closer to being the customary landowners of Mughal India; in addition, some new money from Calcutta (and some government officials in the know), also bought these estates as investments. Over time, by the turn of the century, incomes from these estates grew, and this class of substantial landowners evolved into the real zamindari class of the Bengal Presidency. They became allies of the British rulers, collecting land taxes for them in return for growing incomes and legal and political rights. By contrast, the impact on sharecroppers and landless laborers was negative. Although the evidence is murky, especially on the issue of whether landlessness increased, it is the case that most Bengali zamindars continued to be absentee landlords. With a turn to more commercial agriculture and continued pressure to meet revenue demands, layers of tenancy grew, leading to both commercialization and an increase in sharecropping. There is no evidence to suggest that the landowners invested their incomes back into the estates or that productivity of incomes on land improved. On the contrary, the overall evidence tends to move in the direction that "the conditions under which peasants continued to cultivate the land were much worse than before."[114]

Last in this discussion of the impact of the East India Company on India during the mercantilist phase, it is important to pull together some of the broader points. Since all governments tax their populations, and since the upper classes everywhere often benefit disproportionately as a result, in what sense was East India Company rule in India at this stage exploitative? The answer is that the East India Company used its power superiority to extract significant amounts of resources from Indian society but never reinvested them back in a manner that might have benefited India. For example, during 1794–1810 (a period for which good data are available), the East India Company collected some £200 million in total revenues (or an average of £12 million annually in India);[115] very roughly, this annual amount represented some 22 percent of the GDP of the Indian land area that the East India Company systematically controlled at this stage.[116] As noted, the largest portion of these revenues—nearly half—were spent on the British Indian Army. While the salaries paid to Indian soldiers indeed became part of the Indian economic stream, the net economic contribution of this was probably no more than a redistribution of the incomes of poor peasants—who bore the ultimate burden of land revenues—to soldiers. Unlike in Mughal India, warfare during this period did not support local industries; cannons, muskets, and even uniforms were imported from Britain. As noted, the British frequently used the Indian Army to pursue their imperial ambitions in the near abroad, well beyond India. None of these uses of Indian savings added much to India's economic progress.

Moreover, the East India Company in London ordered its officials in India to set aside at least £1 million of the revenues it collected every year to buy Indian goods for sale in London. This was the main source of profit for the company. The actual data for these years show that the average annual expense on cargoes from India was some £1.4 million. An additional £380,000 per year of Indian revenues were used to run the East India Company's London offices. Some 15 percent of Indian revenues were then simply transferred from India for the benefit of the East India Company, and for the benefit of the British state and economy. By contrast, the East India Company government in India invested some 1 percent to 2 percent of the revenues collected during these years on building roads and public works and virtually nothing on education or on improving agrarian technology. These patterns of revenue extraction and expenditures were repeated year after year and decade after decade. Over time, they were bound to contribute to economic stagnation in India, and they did.

The East India Company as Rulers, Phase 2

Although the East India Company provided significant benefits to Britain, there was also growing criticism of the company within Britain toward the end of the 18th century. The East India Company divided British liberals: John Stuart Mill, a company employee, defended it in Parliament, and Adam Smith—in agreement, at least on this issue, with the not-so-liberal Edmund Burke—unleashed a scorching critique of the East India Company, including in his *Wealth of Nations.* More consequential was the pressure in Parliament from manufacturing interests to break the East India Company's monopoly on the eastern trade. Throughout the eighteenth century, British textile manufacturers had succeeded in limiting imports of finished Indian calico. As textile and other industries in Britain matured, the nature of these demands shifted: at minimum, the manufacturers now demanded cheaper cargo rates on the East India Company's eastern-bound ships, but more and more, they simply wanted the East India Company's monopoly on trade ended. From the standpoint of the British state, the East India Company was increasingly needed, not so much as a trading company, but as a political force in India. A turning point came in 1813, when the East India Company lost much of its monopoly to trade in India. The East India Company's role in India as a trader over the next decades shrank, and its role as a ruler expanded; the East India Company was very much a state agency of sorts by then. The 1813 charter had left the East India Company with a monopoly to trade Indian opium for Chinese tea. The monopoly on China trade also ended in 1833, after which the role of the East India Company in India was that of a ruler. This phase, too, was short-lived. A major revolt within the East India Company-controlled Indian Army ended the company's role in India altogether, and the British Crown assumed sovereign control over India in 1857. In the discussion that follows, I analyze the political economy of East India Company rule in India during the first half of the nineteenth century.

Before delving further into East India Company's role in India, some additional comments are in order. By the end of the Napoleonic Wars, in 1815, Britain's global power was unassailable. Traditional challengers like the French, the Spanish, and the Dutch no longer posed a fundamental obstacle to Britain's worldwide ambitions. New challengers like Germany and the United States were yet to emerge; for example, steel production in both the United States and Germany surpassed that of Britain only during 1890–95. British hegemony during the nineteenth century rested in part on a vibrant domestic economy and in part on extensive control over colonies. At home, British industry was surging, with textiles in the lead. When the growth in textiles slowed toward the middle of the century, the second phase of the Industrial Revolution—in iron, coal, and railways—began, helping Britain to maintain its economic lead till the end of the century. A growing economy helped to finance and to build a powerful, armed force, especially a navy. Control over colonies, especially India, added to British power, in part because colonial resources strengthened the British economy, and in part because the large Indian Army provided a highly subsidized instrument for Britain to project power in Asia, North Africa, and the Middle East. The navy and the Indian Army were the hammer and anvil of British global power.

Britain used its hegemonic position to further strengthen its worldwide empire, both formally and informally. As we will see, India provides the clearest case of the spread of the formal British Empire during the middle of the nineteenth century. But the first half of the nineteenth century was also a period during which Britain started using force to impose treaties on peripheral economies, seeking to buy raw materials on favorable terms and opening these economies to British goods and investment. Examples include Argentina and Brazil in the early nineteenth century; Egypt and Turkey during the 1830s; and the Opium Wars in

China in the 1840s.[117] (See chapter 2 for discussion of Britain's informal empire) The important point to note is that Britain's political and economic hegemony in the early nineteenth century led to further imperial expansion. These developments pose an intellectual challenge to a number of important views on British imperialism—namely, that the rise of free trade led to a decline in the imperial urge in the mid-Victorian era; that imperialism was really a product of late-century balance-of-power politics; or that no, imperialism was, instead, driven by the growing power of finance capitalism within Britain. I further address these theoretical issues in the conclusion of this chapter.

The gentry dominated the British Parliament in the first half of the nineteenth century. What global policies Parliament would or would not support, however, was not easy to derive from who dominated it. As noted, the gentry was a highly commercialized force that often worked in alliance with the financial interests in London. Also noted is that throughout the eighteenth century, especially after the mid-century, this coalition had supported a militant and aggressive foreign policy that included the imperialism of Clive, Hastings, and others in India.[118] Manufacturing interests became an additional political force as Britain's global hegemony coalesced in the early nineteenth century. Among the early political victories of these interests was the 1813 East India Company charter, which diluted its monopoly over trade. But the Corn Laws of 1815, which protected agricultural products, underscored that landowning forces also remained politically powerful. Policy battles over free trade went back and forth during the first half of the century and culminated in the victory of Richard Cobden's pro-textile and pro-Manchester interests and the simultaneous loss for the Conservative Party in 1846, when the Corn Laws were abolished.

A victory on tariff policy, however, was not a victory for peace. Cobden lost when he sought to promote a less imperial Britain. For much of the period under consideration, despite political tussles over policies and the shifting powers of one faction of capital against another, there remained a consensus across much of Britain's ruling class on some key issues that linked domestic and foreign policy. Cain and Hopkins delineate elements of this consensus: "Britain's" power abilities "depended critically on the pace of economic development"; the economic development of Britain would remain a function of "continuing capitalist development"; healthy capitalist development in the period required finding "new markets for industry and commerce in the underdeveloped world," including by force; and, in the words of Lord Palmerston, "it is the business of government to open and secure the roads for the merchant."[119] This marriage of the power interests of the state and the profit interests of the economic elite is really the key to understanding British imperialism, not only in the first half of the nineteenth century, but also, with some modifications, before and after this period.

The East India Company needed to adapt rapidly to these basic changes in both the British political economy and Britain's global position during the first half of the nineteenth century. As if to symbolically mark the loss of its trading monopoly in 1813, the East India Company finally disbanded its London-based committee on preventing the growth of private trade—that battle was lost. More substantively, the continuing goal of how to enrich the mother country now had to be pursued on two tracks in India: a fiscal track, in which the East India Company was the primary actor, and a trading track, as trade increasingly shifted into private hands (but on which, as rulers of India, the East India Company also continued to play an important supportive role). Both tracks can now be analyzed in turn. It is important to keep in mind in analyzing this period that the East India Company was by now highly dependent on the British state.

The East India Company already controlled much of India in 1813; the remaining bits were incorporated over the next few decades, the conquest of the Punjab in 1849 being the last significant acquisition. The revenues that the East India Company extracted from India grew steadily during this period, from some £16 million in 1813 to £33 million in 1857 (Table 1.1). India's GDP in 1813 and 1857—very roughly—was £222 million and £240 million, respectively, in nominal prices.[120] The revenues the East India Company was collecting in India then amounted to 7 percent to 8 percent of the Indian GDP in 1813, and increased steadily thereafter to some 16 percent to 17 percent of the Indian GDP in 1857 (Table 1.3). More than half of these originated in land taxes and the rest from various monopolies that the East India Company controlled, especially opium trade to China.[121] The East India Company's capacity to extract these fiscal resources rested on a "very military state" that the East India Company continued to operate in India.[122] A vast army undergirded this state. A civil service of sorts helped collect land taxes in the ryotwari areas. In large parts of India, however, a variety of traditional rulers and new landowning classes became junior allies of the British in the process of mobilizing and extracting land revenues. These classes, in turn, benefited from both de jure rights on property and from the conservative British policy to "respect traditions," and related to that, to forego any "modernizing" changes in Indian society, such as introduction of education.[123]

The key problem the East India Company faced was how to use the substantial revenues it collected in India to benefit Britain. A major use of the revenues continued to be to finance the British Indian Army. This army had some 300,000 soldiers by 1820. In addition to helping the British impose rule on India, the Indian army continued to be used, as before, to spread the British Empire in the vicinity: examples from this period include the Straits Settlements of 1824 that

Table 1.3 Indian Revenues of the East India Company, 1801–1871*

Year	Total Revenues (million rupees; 1871 prices)	Territory under control (1,000 square miles)	Revenue per square mile** (rupees)	Revenue as a percentage of Indian GDP	Revenue as a percentage of the GDP of the controlled territory
1801	104	247	423.4	4.8	17.6
1811	155	333	440.4	7.5	20.4
1821	203	506	401.7	10.3	18.4
1831	208	514	405.4	10.2	17.9
1841	269	597	450.8	12.3	18.6
1851	385	771	499.3	16.1	18.9
1861	413	837	494.0	17.3	18.7
1871	514	904	568.7	20.6	20.6

* The post-1857 data record, of course, not the revenues collected by the East India Company but by the British colonial state in India.

**For comparison, note that the revenue per square mile in 1600 under the Mughals was 479.1.

Source: Raw data is from Broadberry et al., "India and the Great Divergence," various tables.

brought Penang, Malacca, and Singapore under British control; periodic participation in the Great Game to keep Russia out of Afghanistan; interventions in Burma in 1842 and 1852; and the Opium Wars in China in 1839–42 and 1856–60. Some 40 percent to 50 percent of Indian revenues during this period went toward supporting the army; and another 7 percent to 10 percent, to support a growing police force.[124] By contrast, expenditures on public works remained below 2 percent of the total revenues. The army and the police, then, absorbed substantial resources and were at the heart of the despotic imperial state that the East India Company maintained in India during the first half of the nineteenth century.

A substantial portion of the remaining Indian revenue was remitted to Britain. This was achieved via a variety of mechanisms. The first mechanism was what the British called "home charges." These were a variety of expenses in Britain that were charged to Indian revenues; they included dividends to East India Company shareholders, interest on public debt that the East India Company had accumulated in India, and a variety of salaries and compensations for East India Company employees, both in India and in Britain. For the period under discussion, home charges averaged from £2 million to £3 million annually (or some 10 percent of total Indian revenues).[125] As we see in chapter 3, this amount went up significantly in the post-1857 period. Since the Indian revenues had to be transmitted in British pounds, the East India Company also worked hard to always maintain a balance of trade in favor of India. Leaving aside the old mercantilist debate about whether the home charges added up to a drain of wealth from India to Britain, there is no doubt that these unilateral capital transfers from India to Britain brought very little to India in return.

The second mechanism was a "well-regulated tea trade" via China that provided a ready "channel through which funds could be remitted from India."[126] The East India Company ran a production and distribution monopoly for opium in India. (See chapter 2 for more detailed discussion.) The profits from sale of opium added to the company's revenues in India. More sinister and profitable was the further exchange of this opium in China for tea: as the Chinese were becoming addicted to opium, tea was becoming a graceful drink in Britain and beyond. Tea shipped from China was auctioned in London and provided significant profits for the East India Company; in 1834, for example, an East India Company tea auction fetched it a handsome sum of over £4 million, which was more than half the expense of the British navy.[127] Since the root of these profits was a "very military state" in India, East India Company rule there during this period has been aptly described as the first "narco-military empire" in the world.[128] And last, when the East India Company was strapped for cash and all else had failed in terms of ways to transmit Indian revenues back home, the company reverted to the early strategy of the conquistadores that they had supposedly foregone, namely, to put bullion in chests and load it on ships headed home. According to Bowen, such transfers occurred on a "semi-regular" basis and the sums involved were "considerable." Referring to bullion shipments from India, William Astell, the company chairman, acknowledged in 1830: "I hardly know how we could get on without them."[129]

The other major development during this period was the rapid growth of private trade. Following the East India Company's loss of its trading monopoly in 1813, Indian trade quadrupled by 1858. The composition of the trade also altered fundamentally.[130] British textiles were globally competitive by the early nineteenth century. They no longer required protection, and they were ready to be exported the world over. Britain then increasingly argued for free trade. The demand for Indian calico fell simultaneously, as did such Indian exports as indigo, which was processed in India as industrial dye for textiles. Some related data are provided in Table 1.4. If in 1814–15 Indian textiles and indigo composed some 34 percent of Indian exports to Britain, by 1857–58, they had declined to 9 percent. Instead, India's major exports by the mid–century were raw cotton and

Table 1.4 India's Main Exports, 1814–1858 (Figures as Percentage of Total Value)

Year	Industrial dye (indigo-based)	Manufactured cotton goods	Silk	Cotton	Opium	Sugar
1814–15	20.0	14.3	13.3	8.0	NA	3.0
1828–29	27.0	11.0	10.0	15.0	17.0	4.0
1834–35	15.0	7.0	8.0	21.0	25.0	2.0
1839–40	26.0	5.0	7.0	20.0	10.0	7.0
1850–51	10.0	4.0	4.0	12.7	34.1	10.1
1857–58	6.1	2.9	2.9	15.6	32.7	4.3

Source: Figures adapted from K. N. Chaudhuri, ed., *The Economic Development of India under the East India Company* (Cambridge: Cambridge University Press, 1971), table 2, p. 26.

opium—especially opium, which alone accounted for more than one-third of all Indian exports.

Indian imports also shifted. One may recall that in the past India hardly imported anything from Britain; instead, prior to Plassey, the East India Company used bullion to buy Indian goods for sale in England and then, after Plassey, used Indian land taxes to do the same during the second half of the eighteenth century. With the British textile industry maturing and India in no position to protect its own textile industry, India's main imports during the first half of the nineteenth century became cotton yarn, finished textiles, apparel, metal goods, and plenty of wines and spirits, presumably for consumption by the Indian Army. It was during this period that India's trading pattern morphed into what we now recognize as a typically colonial pattern: India's exports became primary commodities, and there was a corresponding concentration on manufactured goods in her imports.

Although the ideologies of free trade were gaining in significance in Britain during this time period, it is important to underscore that Britain's trade with India remained highly politicized. It was not free trade. The East India Company played a decisive role in managing this trade, and was quite self-conscious of its achievements:

> This Company has in various ways, encouraged and assisted by our manufacturing ingenuity and skill, succeeded in converting India from a manufacturing country into a country exporting raw produce . . . [in addition it has succeeded in] . . . extracting from the latter three millions of money for Home charges (annually).[131]

How did the state-supported East India Company achieve this transformation? India was for all practical purposes a colony by this point. Since the East India Company controlled the government and policies in India, there was nothing Indians could do to protect their own economic interests. Ideas of protectionism were in the air. Alexander Hamilton and Friedrich List were developing national doctrines supporting protectionism, in opposition to Adam Smith. Sovereign and powerful states such as the United States and Germany even adopted these ideas in the nineteenth century so as to industrialize successfully while maintaining protections against the more advanced British economy. This option was simply not available to colonies like India. Related to this, Britain's empire helped British economic competitiveness both through its monopoly over shipping and the protection to commerce provided by the Royal Navy. Many Indian merchants (and ships) had been displaced or destroyed by the East India Company in the preceding century. It was not as if they could now take Indian calico and try to sell it cheaply in the near abroad, much of which was increasingly controlled by the British or other Europeans.

More specifically, Britain managed its imperial trade so as to maintain a balance of payment in favor of India. This was essential for transmitting Indian revenues in sterling to pay for the substantial home charges discussed here, as well as to cover private export of capital and payments to liquidate the public debt. The economic historian K. N. Chaudhuri estimates that during this time period, India's unilateral, annual capital exports to Britain averaged some £5 million to £6 million.[132] That this had to be generated politically is especially evident if one keeps in mind that following the decline of demand for Indian calico, what India could export to Britain was not obvious. The East India Company intervened systematically to encourage the production of commercial crops for export in India. When these did not generate enough foreign exchange to pay, not only for the purchase of British manufactured goods, but also for regular capital transfers, the solution was found in the triangular trade adjoining Britain, India, and China: Indian opium was sold in China and generated large balance-of-payment surpluses for India because India hardly bought anything from China; the earnings from the sale of opium were used to purchase tea in China; Chinese tea was then sold in Britain and provided handsome profits for the East India Company and, via taxation, for the British state; and Indian balance-of-payment surpluses facilitated both imports of British manufactured goods and capital transfers from India. At the heart of this system was the opium monopoly controlled by the East India Company in India: the East India Company laid out targets for the production of opium for Indian peasants, mainly in Bengal and Bihar, and then maintained exclusive rights to purchase, process, and pack this opium in chests for auction to various merchants who were ready to take them to China. The British

Indian armies, as well as the Royal Navy, were readily available around ports in southern China to ensure that the sale of opium went smoothly.

John Sullivan, a senior revenue official of the East India Company in Madras, summed up the role of the East India Company in India during this period rather succinctly: "Our system acts very much like a sponge, drawing up all good things from the banks of the Ganges, and squeezing them down on the banks of the Thames."[133] To elaborate, East India Company rule in India continued to benefit Britain at the expense of India, though the modalities and the specific nature of the impact altered in the early nineteenth century. Britain's benefits were both direct and indirect. The most important among the direct benefits continued to be access to a very large British Indian Army, for which the British did not pay, but which remained available to both impose rule on India and to spread the British Empire. Other direct benefits included substantial capital transfers from India that added to the British private and public economy—on the order of £5 million per year, or roughly 1 percent to 2 percent of the British GDP annually. The growth of private trade was a new development during this period and provided significant indirect benefits to Britain. To be fair, India could also have benefited from the growth of this trade, though several conditions mitigated such gains: the Indian economy was still nearly three times larger than the British economy in the early nineteenth century; Indian exports were increasingly low-value-added commodities, especially opium, which was replacing food production and being shipped to China; and the East India Company bought the opium with revenue it collected from other Indian peasants, recirculating resources more than contributing to the growth of the economy. By contrast, India provided a large market for British manufactured goods, especially textiles. By the middle of the nineteenth century, Britain relied heavily on its colonies as markets for textile exports—by the end of the century nearly 90 percent of British textile products were exported—and India was central among these colonial markets. While the claim that Britain owed its industrial leadership to its empire, including India, is an exaggeration—Britain's Industrial Revolution was of its own making—it is hard to believe that textiles, Britain's major first industry, could have grown as rapidly as it did without its colonial markets, especially India.

On the receiving end of the relationship, British textile exports to India in the early nineteenth century undermined India's textile industry. This old, controversial claim is supported by a variety of data. Trade data cited above (including in Table 1.4) clearly suggests that during this period Indian textile exports declined sharply and that imports of the same from Britain rose correspondingly. But given the size of the Indian economy, this may or may not have led to "de-industrialization," as some critics claim. Employment data are more telling: over the nineteenth century, India's workforce employed in industries declined from some 18 percent to 8.5 percent and, within the industrial workforce, workers in cotton spinning and weaving declined from 62.3 percent in 1809–13 to 15.1 percent in 1901.[134] Regional evidence from India further supports this macro picture. For example, there was growing unemployment of spinners and weavers in the Bombay Presidency during this period; even the "Parsis abandoned weaving altogether," contributing to the "gradual decay of the native manufacturers."[135] The evidence from the south also leads a foremost scholar to conclude, "Madras became largely an exporter of primary goods."[136] Even contemporary British observers noted the growing misery caused by textile imports: "Many industrious people in different parts of India are thence thrown out of employment and reduced to distress."[137] Last, a recent study recreates India's historical national accounts and adds the final nail in the coffin of this controversy. These data are reproduced in Table 1.5 and make India's industrial decline in the early nineteenth century clear. Broadberry and colleagues thus conclude, "The scale of the decline was so catastrophic that the net effect was an absolute decline in Indian industrial production in the first three decades of the nineteenth century, rather than just a reduction in the share of industry in economic activity."[138]

The other mechanism via which the East India Company rule hurt India's developmental prospects was, obviously, the extraction and use of Indian savings. The East India Company through this period extracted revenues worth some 11 percent to 12 percent of the Indian GDP annually, reaching as high as 16 percent to 17 percent at the end of the period under discussion (see Table 1.3). The uses to which these revenues were put, such as to support a large army and to

Table 1.5 India's Industrial Output, 1801–1871 (1871 = 100)

Year	Home Industries	Export Industries	Total Industry and Commerce	Total Real Output
1801	90.2	457.9	127.0	87.5
1811	82.3	304.7	104.6	82.9
1821	78.6	183.2	89.0	79.2
1831	84.3	65.2	82.4	81.8
1841	97.0	56.6	92.9	87.3
1851	105.2	49.5	99.6	95.9
1861	112.9	56.3	107.3	95.6
1871	100	100	100.0	100.0

Source: Stephen Broadberry, Johann Custodis, and Bishnupriya Gupta, "India and the Great Divergence: An Anglo-Indian Comparison of Per Capita GDP, 1600–1871," *Explorations in Economic History* 58 (2015): table 11, p. 69.

facilitate capital transfers to Britain, have been discussed. What is notable is that these Indian savings were not invested in India by the East India Company in a manner that would facilitate economic progress in India; on the contrary, the East India Company squeezed the revenues out of India and used them for its own purposes. And this, then, is the real tragedy from the point of view of the Indian poor: had these Indian savings been well invested, they might have added 1 to 2 percent per annum to India's economic growth in the first half of the nineteenth century. But as it was, the Indian economy continued to stagnate: best estimates suggest that per capita GDP growth in India between 1811 and 1861 barely budged.[139]

Conclusion

Britain's overseas expansion began with state-supported chartered companies. The East India Company was foremost among these British companies. In this chapter I have used historical materials to provide an interpretation of the motives, mechanisms, and impact of East India Company rule, both on Britain and on India. To recapitulate very briefly, I argue that the main motive that took the East India Company to India was profit. Over time, as the East India Company came to depend more and more on the British state, this narrow goal of company profits broadened to how to enrich the mother country. Beyond company profits, then, the East India Company became India's rulers and in the process, devised a variety of methods to use Indian resources to support British interests: these included financing a large armed force in India for British use, transferring Indian revenues to help the British state and economy, and opening the Indian economy under duress as a taker of British manufactured goods. The East India Company's main mechanism of rule was coercion. While it had its share of Indian collaborators, the East India Company's imperialism from the Battle of Plassey to the very military state of the early nineteenth century was mainly brutal; it literally exchanged force for profits. And last, I argue that Britain benefited at the expense of India. Both private wealth and British state power were enhanced by East India Company rule in India. By contrast, India's nascent industries were destroyed, and most of all, India lost significant portions of its savings to the East India Company—every year, every decade, for a century—which the company used for a variety of purposes other than the economic betterment of India.

To conclude the chapter, it may be useful to link the specific study of the East India Company to the broader themes of this book. The case of the East India Company in India is somewhat unusual insofar as it preceded formal colonialism. Squeezing a country of the size of India would have been difficult for any imperial force but was especially so for a company. It is the case that the East

India Company was highly dependent on the British state and that within Britain it acted as a state within a state. It is also the case that the East India Company succeeded quite handsomely in squeezing economic resources out of India for a while. In the end, however, the East India Company was not a state; it did not have the benefit of national economic and political resources to support its imperial ventures. When sections of the Indian aristocracy and some army battalions revolted against East India Company rule in 1857, the political and economic situation became untenable for the company. It was very nearly bankrupt when the British Crown formally took political control of India in 1857. But despite a somewhat unique instance of early corporate imperialism, which well preceded the emergence of full-blown industrial capitalism in England and elsewhere in Europe, certain notable general tendencies marked the early experience of the East India Company—tendencies that recurred in numerous future instances of imperialism.

First, what motivated and sustained the East India Company's expansion into India was a search for economic resources, including both profits for private, moneyed interests and revenues for the state. A similar alliance of state and capital in the search for overseas economic benefits, we will see, has been at the heart of a variety of subsequent cases of imperial expansion. Second, what also emerged very early—and continues—is the need of imperialists to deny any malign, self-serving intent. Imperial actions instead sought to be justified in terms of legitimacy norms suitable for the period. In the case of the East India Company, for example, there was a constant tendency to claim that the company was merely a trader that did not seek territory, even as it was acquiring more and more territory via coercive means. This was because trade was a perfectly legitimate activity for a company like the East India Company during this period, whereas controlling territory was something only states did. In subsequent cases, we will notice that justification for state-led imperialism similarly came to be sought in terms of prevailing norms of legitimacy: the white man's burden; civilizing mission; and, in more modern times, when the norms of sovereignty emerged, the effort to deter communism and promote democracy and human rights and, most recently, to seek security from terrorists or unsavory regimes.

Third, the East India Company case reveals the central role of political power in imposing economic exploitation: the relationship of the East India Company to India was a lot less exploitative in the seventeenth century when Mughal rule was intact, but then turned a lot more exploitative after the Mughal Empire disintegrated in the eighteenth century and the company used political means to extract economic benefits. This pattern will recur in a variety of other cases analyzed here. Although the rise of industrial capitalism and free trade eventually altered this nearly naked, feudal-like exploitation, even free trade and other open-economy interactions are seldom all that free. They are facilitated instead by deeply asymmetrical power realities across political units in the global economy.

Last, the interpretation of the East India Company in India developed here sheds light on broader debates concerning an understanding of British imperialism. One realist view, of sorts, which developed especially to explain the subsequent Scramble for Africa, stresses that imperialism was mainly a byproduct of power conflicts among core powers.[140] If so, Britain's tightening grip over India during the first half of the nineteenth century (when Britain's power was largely uncontested) is a major anomaly. The Hobson-Lenin thesis on the importance of finance capitalism as the taproot of imperialism also runs up against the case of the East India Company in India. While economic forces were important drivers of British imperialism in India, a glut in finance hardly characterized the British economy during the period of British expansion in India in the late eighteenth and early nineteenth centuries. India's territorial revenue was, instead, crucial during the eighteenth century. In the nineteenth century it was British manufacturing interests, especially textile exports, that were central to British interests in India. The failure of these theories to explain British imperialism in India is especially significant because India was lot more important to Britain than were its African colonies; any explanation of British imperial behavior that fits Africa but not India will simply not do. Another, more liberal view holds that the British imperial urge went into decline in the mid-Victorian era—once it had achieved economic leadership, especially leadership in manufactured goods. The underlying logic of this argument is that with its competitive economic edge, Britain did not need to use force to open markets. This is, of course, the view that Gallagher and Robinson challenged successfully, but it keeps creeping back.[141] The Indian case offers a basic challenge to this view, too, as do the numerous cases of Britain's informal empire during the Victorian era that we will visit in the next chapter; the victory of free trade and imperial expansion went hand in hand in mid-nineteenth-century Britain.

In sum, a strict power view of British imperialism falls short because no one has yet satisfactorily demonstrated that there exists some upper limit on the amount of power to which a hegemonic power might aspire and because the decision-makers of hegemonic powers can always imagine future challengers. Lenin's view on imperialism both overestimates the power of finance and, ironically, underestimates the power of the state in reconciling and redefining the factional interests of capitalism with some understanding of the national economic interest. And the free trade view on imperialism turns out to be inadequate because free trade is often not all that free, as we have seen. We will further see not only that Britain's trade was helped by a variety of monopolies, but also that those who resisted were forced to open their economies under duress. Instead of these interpretations,

I argue for a more synthetic interpretation that imperialism is best understood as an overseas strategy that powerful capitalist states pursue to enhance national economic interests. The underlying logic is that powerful states conceive of relative prosperity as a national security issue. For these states, this commitment to national prosperity inclines them to ensure economic opportunities for their capitalists at home and abroad. When political actors in peripheral economies resist such encroachments, imperialism becomes likely. The imperial urge is, then, moved by a convenient marriage of the power interests of the state and the profit interests of the economic elite.

2

Britain's Informal Empire

ARGENTINA, EGYPT, CHINA

THROUGHOUT THE NINETEENTH century Britain used its political and economic superiority to open markets abroad. This expansion took a variety of forms. Toward the middle of the century, and then again at the end of it, British expansion in India and in large parts of Africa was structured as formal colonial control. (I analyze British colonialism in chapter 3.) Relations with white dominions also evolved during this period. Since the primary concern of this study is imperialism in the developing world, such instances of British influence abroad are not discussed in detail here. The focus of the discussion in this chapter is the third major form of British expansionism in the nineteenth century: the building of an informal empire in parts of Latin America, the Middle East, and East Asia. The countries within the scope of Britain's informal empire were neither fully sovereign nor formal colonies.[1] They were something in-between, countries in which Britain exercised significant political influence without controlling territory. A number of important questions can be raised about Britain's informal empire: Why did Britain seek influence without control in some parts of the world, but pursue formal territorial control in others? What were the mechanisms it used to establish an informal empire? And, of course, what was the impact of political and economic subordination on the countries that came to be integrated with the British political economy? In this chapter, I develop answers to these questions while analyzing three countries that were part of this informal empire.

Britain's informal empire grew in fits and starts. Its heyday was bookended by the end of the Napoleonic Wars in 1815, which marked the beginning of British hegemony, and the First World War, which was the culmination of the growing power challenges to that hegemony. As we have seen, Britain's global power peaked toward the middle of the century. By then, Spain was no longer a threat; France remained a major power but had mostly accepted a global position second

How Britain and the United States Shaped the Global Periphery. Atul Kohli, Oxford University Press (2020).

DOI: 10.1093/oso/9780190069629.001.0001

to Britain; Russia could be meddlesome but only in territories bordering on its vast expanse; and effective challenge from Germany and the United States was still a few decades away. At home, although this was the age of Karl Marx, capitalism was increasingly triumphant, and the abolition of the Corn Laws marked a victory of industry over agriculture. Britain's foreign policy was dominated by Lord Palmerston (Henry Temple), who was first the foreign secretary and then prime minister. Well before the presidency of Woodrow Wilson and the emergence of the American version of liberal messianism, Palmerston expressed Britain's growing self-confidence, if not arrogance:

> I may say without any vainglorious boast, or without great offence to anyone, that we stand at the head of moral, social and political civilisation. Our task is to lead the way and direct the march of other nations.[2]

Although Palmerston cloaked his imperial pursuits in the ideology of "world betterment via opening of markets," his actual policies were informed by a core view (noted in chapter 1), namely, that "it is the business of government to open and secure the roads for the merchant." The underlying motivation was explicit: "[T]he rivalship of European manufacturers is fast excluding our products from the markets of Europe and we must unremittingly endeavor to find in other parts of the world new vents for the product of our industry."[3] Caudillos, khedives, and recalcitrant emperors would have to be dealt with—with force, if needed.

The scope of Britain's informal empire became vast over the nineteenth century. It came to include significant portions of what used to be Spanish and Portuguese America, the Ottoman Empire, and Ch'ing China. Given the breadth of the subject matter, I use empirical materials selectively in this chapter to develop some general themes. I focus on Argentina to exemplify Britain's political and economic relations with Latin America. Of course, no single country can capture the diversity of British–Latin American relations.[4] Argentina is, nevertheless, a significant case. This is not only because of its economic importance but also because the study of Argentina as an example of Britain's informal empire poses significant analytical challenges: Argentine elites often cooperated with the British, especially later in the century, and per capita incomes of Argentinians grew steadily throughout the nineteenth century. What sort of informal imperialism, then, did Britain exercise in Argentina? By contrast, it can be argued that Brazil provides a more obvious example of Britain's informal empire in Latin America: Britain clearly used its superior political power to structure economic exchange with Brazil on highly favorable terms; and Brazilian per capita incomes mostly stagnated throughout the century while businessmen in both Brazil and

Britain made handsome profits. I have analyzed the political economy of Brazil in the nineteenth century in some detail elsewhere.[5] Instead of repeating that material, I focus here on the analytically more difficult case of Argentina—using Brazil as a comparative point of reference—suggesting that in spite of their differences, both Argentina and Brazil evolved under British influence as producers of commodities and takers of manufactured goods and capital.

As the Ottoman Empire weakened during the nineteenth century, rival centers of power emerged within the empire; Anatolia and Egypt were the two main regions. No one doubts that Britain came to exercise significant influence over the Ottoman Empire during this period. Among the reasons I chose to focus on Anglo-Egyptian relations are the following. First, in the first half of the century, Egypt was only nominally under Ottoman control; for all practical purposes it was a sovereign country, which Britain came to control more and more as the century wore on. Second, Britain deliberately undermined efforts by the Egypt's rulers at mid-century to industrialize the Egyptian economy. From then on, Egypt became far more integrated with the British economy than Anatolia,[6] providing cotton for British textile production, acquiring substantial foreign debt, and eventually succumbing to British occupation toward the end of the century. Egypt, then, is a prototypical example of the forces that moved Britain to build an informal empire and of the impact of such coerced political and economic integration on peripheral societies.

Third, the rationale for focusing on Britain's role in China during the nineteenth century is fairly obvious. As discussed in chapter 1, the East India Company had already established a triangular trade, of sorts, in Asia, in which India was the primary taker of manufactured goods from Britain; Indian opium was the main good sold to China; and large amounts of Chinese tea exports were either absorbed by Britain or sold by British merchants elsewhere. When this highly profitable trade was threatened by Chinese rulers, the infamous Opium Wars resulted, leading to the forced opening of China and the growing influence of Britain over it. While Britain never came close to influencing all of China—it was shared with other imperial powers and the interior was often beyond control—it did establish treaty ports, acquired Hong Kong, and controlled customs revenues during the second half of the century and beyond. The already weakened Ch'ing rulers were thus further weakened by imperial incursions, which led to the emergence of an unstable republic in the early twentieth century. While the Chinese case thus follows some of the main patterns of Britain's informal empire on the global periphery (especially the coerced economic opening for the sake of profits, with damaging consequences for those on the receiving end), the imperial experience in China also pointed toward the future. Two of these emerging trends are worth underscoring at the outset. First, the experience of sharing imperial spoils with other imperialists clearly took shape in China—as it had in Egypt, though there it was only between France, and Britain was clearly the senior partner—and pointed toward the shape of imperialism to come during the Scramble for Africa. Second, competition over the Chinese market brought an emerging hegemon, the United States, into the fray. The Open Door policy of the United States was put forward by the American statesman John Hay in the context of seeking access to China. As we will see, the content of these policies could have been lifted straight out of the policies enunciated by British statesmen Lord Castlereagh (Robert Stewart) and George Canning a century earlier, when Britain, then the emerging hegemon, sought to establish influence over Latin America. The Open Door policies proved crucial to framing the US approach not only to Asia but also elsewhere and during subsequent periods.

It may be helpful to preview the main themes developed here with reference to specific historical materials. First, there is the issue of motives, or of the forces that moved Britain to expand overseas during the nineteenth century. As one might expect, the scholarly terrain here is well rehearsed and often controversial. John Gallagher and Ronald Robinson set the terms of the debates in the 1950s by suggesting that despite popular claims that free trade encouraged anti-imperialism, Britain built a vast informal empire during the Victorian period. What moved Britain were the needs of economic expansion, which, led to bringing more and more territories under influence and to turning them into producers of raw materials and takers of manufactured goods.[7] Others demurred, especially D. C. M. Platt, who denied the utility of the concept of an informal empire because in his view, Britain's economic gains, especially in early nineteenth-century Latin America, were minimal, and gunboats were used only rarely to establish influence. He argued instead that Britain turned imperialist mostly toward the end of the century, but by then strategic considerations were at the forefront.[8] More recently, P. J. Cain and Anthony Hopkins have returned to the Gallagher and Robinson argument but with a twist: they suggest that what moved Britain to build an informal empire was less the pressure to seek markets for manufactured goods and more financial interests pursued by "gentlemanly capitalists," especially during the second half of the nineteenth century.[9] These are serious arguments. As I examine the empirical materials, it will become clear that Platt's objections are often untenable and that Cain and Hopkins, though persuasive for some periods, underestimate the importance of industrialization, on the one hand, and of the power motives driving British expansionism, on the other hand. Gallagher and Robinson remain the most persuasive, although more recent evidence leads to qualifications and modifications.

I argue that Britain's growing military superiority in the early nineteenth century rested on a vibrant domestic capitalism, especially through the lead it had in industrialization. As noted, there was a growing consensus within Britain during the first half of the century that sustaining economic dynamism required overseas markets, especially beyond Europe, and that it was the role of the British state to open such markets. British leaders then used the nation's military superiority to secure markets for British entrepreneurs; these leaders were responding in part to the demands of manufacturing and other business interests at home, but they were also cognizant that the resulting economic buoyancy fed British state power. To repeat the general point made in chapter 1, a marriage of the power interests of the state and the profit interests of the economic elite is the key to understanding modern imperialism, both formal and informal. For example, textiles were the key to British manufacturing success in the first half of the nineteenth century. The British state systematically supported the expansion of the British textile industry abroad during this period through trade treaties, political manipulation, and the occasional drubbing by gunboats of Argentina and Brazil; the undermining of Muhammad Ali in Egypt and turning the land of the pyramids into a producer of raw cotton for British textile manufacturers; and keeping China open for opium to sustain the exports of textiles to Asia via the triangular trade. A buoyant industrial economy, with textiles as its core, was in turn central for supporting Britain's global power ambitions.

As British competitiveness in textiles was challenged during the latter half of the century, railways and other heavier industries became the cutting edge of the second industrial evolution. The British state again supported railway construction abroad, especially by ensuring that dependent governments, such as in Argentina, guaranteed the profits of private investors. Novel forms of foreign investment emerged to support the spread of railways, which facilitated the growth of foreign trade with interior regions of the underdeveloped world. The construction of railways in these economies also stimulated interest—mainly on the part of rulers of these countries, such as the khedives of Egypt—in a variety of such infrastructure projects as the building of ports and public utilities. With British finance houses such as Barings and Rothschild becoming global players, public loans abroad grew, both to build such projects and, on occasion, to support the unrealistic ambitions of the peripheral elite. Over time, countries as diverse as Argentina, Egypt, and China became heavily indebted. The reactions of the British state provide early examples of too big to fail and structural adjustment, of sorts: the British state systematically intervened in these countries, consolidating its hold on the respective state finances and thus on the state structures, with the hope—at times, a fading hope—of ensuring that British bondholders and financiers were protected, along with the British economy and power status.

Economic motives were thus at the forefront as Britain built an informal empire in parts of Latin America, the Middle East, and East Asia. There will be occasions here to qualify the economic thrust of this argument by noting the role of strategic considerations as well, such as the need to prop up the Ottoman Empire as part of the Great Game with Russia. For now, it is more important to introduce the second main theme that runs through the empirical analysis, namely, the mechanisms Britain used to establish and sustain its informal empire. While these varied, the role of superior power was central. Britain used power overtly when British ambitions were resisted; but more often, given its enormous power superiority, ruling elites in underdeveloped regions turned themselves into obsequious allies: Muhammad Ali thus repeatedly promised to secure for the British their route to India via Egypt; Latin elites swore by Adam Smith; and even Chinese emperors accepted—if reluctantly and quietly—British demands. It is not surprising that Platt and others searching official British records do not find explicit orders, say, from a Palmerston, to the British navy to go secure the Barings loan in Argentina.[10] That is not how power operates. As we will see, when pressure was needed, the sight of naval vessels and whispers from proconsuls were often enough to bend the will of rulers on the periphery (although the overt use of force, as in the Opium Wars, was hardly rare).

More important were the deeper political forces that came to the fore. The forced opening of underdeveloped countries typically led to the penetration of their economies by British products, investments, and a variety of official and private British actors—often exempt from local laws—with well-adorned clubs and cricket grounds. The indigenous elites who came to the forefront in these settings were those best suited to profit in a dependent political economy; they included the ranchers in Argentina, the coffee barons in Brazil, the cotton growers and merchants in Egypt, and the compradors in the treaty ports of a disintegrating China. These indigenous elites benefited from British dominance and often sought cooperation with it; if they learned English, played cricket, and knew how to use forks and knives properly, it helped the relationship. Such comprador elite became British agents—self-interested but agents nevertheless—in underdeveloped regions. When alliances were in place and effective, which was often, they minimized the need for Britain to use overt force to accomplish its goals. Stable subservience is what the British hoped for in client regimes. The overt use of force tended to be most pronounced in the early stages, when a *Pax Britannica* had to be imposed, and then again when such oppositional elites as nationalists, populists, or communists emerged.

Last, the third major theme developed here concerns the impact of Britain's informal expansion on Britain, but more importantly, on the underdeveloped regions. This, too, is controversial terrain. First, a caveat: since the beneficiaries of informal empire included both the metropolitan and the peripheral elite, it is important in any analysis of impact to not create too strong a sense of the metropole versus the periphery. In Britain, for example, the costs of imperial expansion were often borne either by British taxpayers or by those who were imperialized; the benefits accrued to private parties. As long as few business groups benefited from the forced opening of one peripheral economy or another, the British state—not a very democratic state in the nineteenth century—had enough incentive to continue its imperial expansion. Similarly, the incomes of some commodity exporters on the periphery often grew sharply within the frame of informal empire, but the skewed nature of the benefits defies the suggestion that the whole nation benefited.

Within the context of this caveat, I suggest that Britain gained handsomely from its informal empire. The gains were mainly economic, though on occasion, strategic gains were also significant. For much of the century foreign trade played a central role in sustaining the buoyancy of Britain's export-led economy.[11] While a fair amount of this trade depended on the competitiveness of British products, those with the political power to protect their own national economies, say, Germany, the United States, France, and even some of the white dominions, used tariffs and other measures to regulate their trade. These policy options were closed off to countries within the orbit of Britain's empire, most readily in its formal colonies, but also in those it controlled informally. The result was that these countries evolved into providers of raw materials for the expansion of British manufacturing and, in turn, absorbed British manufactured products. As the century wore on, those with excess capital in Britain also sought opportunities for direct investment and loans abroad. In the uncertain conditions of peripheral economies, the British state often intervened to ensure satisfactory rates of returns on such investments. Along with Britain's economic interactions with formal colonies like India, then, and with such white dominions as Canada and Australia, informal colonies in Latin America, the Middle East, and in East Asia helped sustain Britain's economic dynamism and global leadership position during the nineteenth century.

The literature on informal empire was not concerned with the impact of such arrangements on peripheral political economies. These issues were left to trade or dependency theorists. By emphasizing the similarity between formal and informal colonialism, Gallagher, Robinson, and other scholars have probably done a disservice—inadvertently, I suspect—insofar as their stand legitimizes the view that the impact of colonialism and neocolonialism were similar and equally negative. My findings move in a different direction. The impact of informal imperialism was quite complex, and both positive and negative, but on balance, it tended to be less pernicious than that of formal colonial control. On the positive side, I document that, unlike formal British colonies, say, India, Egypt and

Argentina experienced steady growth during the nineteenth century. Although not all countries within the orbit of informal empire experienced steady growth, for example China, many did. Part of the explanation for such growth is of course the nature of complementarities between the metropolitan and peripheral economies. That the benefits of growth were quite skewed is undeniable. Still, decades of steady economic growth is nothing to scoff at; champions of free trade can use such historical instances to support their beliefs. Sustained growth within the scope of informal empire, however, had political roots: since these countries were not quite colonies, they enjoyed a semblance of sovereignty. As a result, trade with these economies was carried out mostly on commercial terms, facilitating the growth of the incomes of commodity producers and of the economy. A commodity-exporting economy also gave rise to agrarian oligarchies, which became politically influential, and supported limited sovereignty in exchange for economic benefits as a class.

Over time, the limits on sovereignty also took an economic toll. The countries of Britain's informal empire may have experienced economic growth, but they failed to evolve into complex economies with an industrial base. Many scholars, some in the dependency school, others not, have thus concluded that forced integration of peripheral economies with Britain in the nineteenth century led to "lop-sided development."[12] These insights remain relevant. What remains to be done is to integrate them systematically with a study of imperialism. In the discussion here I proceed cautiously, avoiding any suggestion that Britain's informal imperialism was solely responsible for the failure of industrial capitalism to take root in countries within its imperial orbit. That claim would be grossly misleading; numerous internal constraints within these countries also inhibited a move toward more complex economic development. Where British influence was significant and pernicious, however, was in encouraging the development of a commodity-producing economy, in turn strengthening the political position of the commodity producers and exporters—the agrarian oligarchs—in respective state structures. Britain also actively discouraged the emergence of competitive manufactured goods in peripheral economies, on the one hand, and of nationalists in their respective political spheres, on the other hand. The net impact was to preclude the emergence of nationalist developmental coalitions that might have put these countries on a different path to modernization. There were to be no Meiji Restorations in Britain's informal empire.

I take turn analyzing Britain's informal empire in Argentina, Egypt, and China, respectively. In the conclusion, I will not only make some comparative comments across the case studies but will also link its themes to the broader themes of the study.

Argentina

Well before the nineteenth century, Britain had coveted South America. It mainly sought bullion (chapter 1), which played a vital role in facilitating Britain's profitable eastern trade. With the Industrial Revolution, however, Britain increasingly started viewing South America as a potential market for its manufactured goods, especially textiles. Since Spain—still a formidable power in the late eighteenth century—would not allow Britain to trade freely with its American colonies, the British goods that reached South America were shipped either legally from Cadiz, after being taxed by Spanish authorities, or as contraband from Britain's Caribbean outposts. Both the British and indigenous merchants in South America resented the profits made by the middlemen, especially the Spaniards, which provided the basis for a longer term, anti-Spanish and free-trading alliance. The Napoleonic Wars, however, had significantly undermined Spanish and Portuguese power in South America, and Britain was eventually able to reorder its economic relations with South America on its own terms, including with Argentina.

The informal empire that Britain established in Argentina during the nineteenth century can be roughly divided into two main phases, which correspond to Britain's first and second industrial revolutions, textile exports dominating the first half of the century and a variety of foreign investments, especially the building of railways, leading the way toward the end of the century. The political framework for these economic interactions was established via trial and error during the early part of the nineteenth century and deserves to be discussed at the outset. There is no doubt that Lord Castlereagh (Britain's secretary of state for war and colonies, 1807–12, and secretary of state for foreign affairs, 1812–22) was the architect of Britain's informal empire in South America.[13] The key ingredients needed to establish British economic dominance in South America, however, had been recognized even earlier. For example, after conquering Trinidad in 1797, British commander Sir Ralph Abercrombie proposed further military expeditions to "liberate" Spanish America, not with an eye to "conquest" but to lay open "the whole trade of that extensive continent." Mere opening, he argued, would be sufficient because "from her enterprise, from her capital, and from her industry," Great Britain "would in reality possess nine parts in ten" of the great economic prize of southern America.[14] It was left to Castlereagh and his successors in office to turn these notions into what can best be described as the British doctrine of informal empire.

During the Napoleonic Wars, Castlereagh rightly anticipated a weakened Spain and Portugal in the future. Thinking ahead, in 1807 he asked how Britain might secure "the opening to our manufactures of the markets of that great continent" of South America.[15] Colonial annexation was ruled out because the continent was "vast" and because of the "temper" of the population;[16] in other words, the costs of conquest were likely to be high. Conquest was also not needed. The main goal instead was to open the continent for commerce and profit. Britain was already economically competitive. Britain merely needed to be the paramount, rather than the exclusive, power on the continent. Establishing paramount power, in turn, implied the need to keep other major powers out of liberated Spanish colonies, on the one hand, and to encourage cooperative but subordinate elite to emerge into positions of power in these sovereign territories, on the other hand. If these were the goals, the path to achieving them was far from smooth; it took a fair amount of trial and error before satisfactory arrangements emerged.

Keeping other powers out of Spanish America proved easier, mainly because of Britain's growing naval superiority. The British navy blockaded the southern Atlantic in 1808, which not only kept the French out of South America, but also protected independence movements in Spanish America from Spanish interventions and encouraged British merchants to open new markets. In case the Spanish did not get the message, the British navy forced Spain to lift a blockade of Buenos Aires in 1810, which again encouraged British trade. Ferdinand VII may have reasserted Spanish authority over its American colonies during 1815–20, but the British navy made this impossible. The power of the United States loomed on the horizon, and Canning (who succeeded Castlereagh after he committed suicide in 1823) was fully aware of the implications, but the Monroe Doctrine of 1823 did appear at the time to be mainly "windy rhetoric," because the words were not backed by a commensurate naval force.[17]

If naval superiority gave Britain a clear advantage vis-à-vis other powers in South America, finding stable governments in the region that would facilitate British commercial interests was not always easy, and certainly not in the early part of the century. A variety of independence movements failed to cohere in a manner that would fill the vacuum created by the dissolution of Spanish colonial power. From Great Britain's view, Brazil was an early success, a model of sorts, to be replicated elsewhere in South America. Brazil, however, was a Portuguese (not a Spanish) colony. The relative political stability of Brazil was replicated in Chile, but not elsewhere in Spanish America; the underlying political processes were distinct. British ships escorted the militarily weakened Portuguese emperor to the Portuguese colony of Brazil in 1810, where he was safe from Napoleon's armies. He was accepted as the legitimate ruler of Brazil—at least for a time—and the thankful emperor in turn signed a commercial treaty giving Britain enormous advantages; for example, tariffs of 15 percent to 25 percent were now to be imposed on imports from countries other than Britain.[18] The result was that

British goods flooded Brazil early in the century, and Brazil became an "emporium for British Manufacturers."[19] Moreover, British policy in Brazil amounted to "dictation," because it "circumscribed the powers of the Brazilian government to raise revenue or to impose protectionist measures," at least till the mid-century.[20] Brazil, then, readily became part of Britain's informal empire; though nominally a sovereign country, it was "in fact," and to a significant degree, "a British colony."[21]

The creation of a similar client regime—orderly, subordinate, and willing to open the economy—proved more difficult in Argentina during the early stages, mainly because of political instability. If one considers Admiral Home Popham's "unauthorized" invasion of Argentina in 1806 as the starting point of Britain's official contact with Argentina, then the 1825 Anglo-Argentine Treaty of Friendship, Commerce, and Navigation is best thought of as the culmination of the early phase in which Britain installed the framework of an informal empire in Argentina.[22] Although political order was in short supply in Argentina during this period, British trade grew rapidly. How did this happen? Argentina was a sparsely populated country of the size of India with a population of less than 500,000 people, many concentrated in the city and the province of Buenos Aires.[23] Unlike Brazil, where a labor-intensive sugar-and-mining economy encouraged slave imports in the eighteenth and nineteenth centuries, the labor needs of Argentina's cattle-ranching economy were minimal: in the early nineteenth century, one foreman and ten peons could look after ten thousand head of cattle on the pampas.[24] As a result, Argentina imported relatively fewer slaves. Most of the population in the early nineteenth century was either of European origin or mixed race and, of course, the indigenous Indians—those who had survived the early Spanish onslaught, but who, too, would be brutally killed off for the sake of land during the British-dominated century.

Within the Spanish Viceroyalty of River Plate (dissolved in 1810), Buenos Aires had already emerged as the center of both power and economic dynamism in the region that would eventually become Argentina. The interior provinces tended either to be economically self-sufficient—besides agriculture, they had developed household-based manufacturing behind protectionist walls, such as woolen clothing and tools—or were linked to the colonial silver economy centered in Lima. Both patterns were about to be disrupted, with significant political ramifications. Buenos Aires, by contrast, was growing as a trading center, exporting hides and other animal products, and importing a variety of consumer products, mainly from or via Spain, especially for the elite. As Spanish power declined, so did Spanish protectionism and trade, and the British navy ensured that British merchants filled the vacuum. Lest there be doubt that such a marriage of force and profit was planned in London, notice the instructions from Castlereagh to his naval commander John Whitelocke in Buenos Aires in 1807: "As the speculations of the British merchants seem to deserve every Encouragement, I am to desire you will attend to their interests as far as in your Power."[25] The local elites in Buenos Aires were no fools; they understood well that power was shifting rapidly from Spain to Britain and that the British sought access to commerce. When British ships brought the news that Napoleon had deposed the Spanish monarchy, a ruling junta composed of Creoles took power in Buenos Aires. A ruling triumvirate, which included the once anti-British but increasingly a pro-British future leader of Argentina, Bernardino Rivadavia, accepted the British merchants' demands to reduce tariffs on trade and proclaimed a commitment to a variety of liberal values.

The liberal order being proclaimed in Buenos Aires was, of course, not readily accepted by many Argentinians. As British goods flooded in, the provinces in the interior sensed a growing threat, both from free trade and from British domination of Buenos Aires. A variety of caudillos and gaucho armies from the interior challenged the edicts of Buenos Aires. Buenos Aires was also by now armed and mobilized. Political order thus remained in short supply. While there were numerous cleavages around which conflict precipitated in these early decades in Argentina, one enduring cleavage was that between the unitarios and the federales—that is, between those who preferred a strong central government (often, merchants in the city of Buenos Aires) and those who preferred a more decentralized federation (often, those who resisted economic opening of the interior provinces). Although the British were not directly responsible for the growing political strife in Argentina—it was actually harmful to their commercial pursuits—the forced opening of the Argentine economy to British trade did become "a major source of political strife and failure after 1810."[26] What growing trade with Britain also facilitated during this early phase, however, was the emergence of an export-oriented agrarian oligarchy, especially in the province of Buenos Aires.[27] These ranching interests, in alliance with merchants—led by Rosas—eventually provided some semblance of political stability to Argentina, although that order was never institutionalized; stable constitutional rule emerged only in the mid-century, and even then, rulers continued to be authoritarian and personalistic.[28]

Establishing *Pax Britannica* with such a mobilized and unstable polity required considerable finesse, a task that Castlereagh facilitated brilliantly. The failure of British invasions in 1806–7 had already clarified to the British leadership that military occupation of Argentina—or, for that matter, of other parts of South America—would be very costly and best not pursued. It should be underlined that along with the military failure, Britain also failed in its effort to impose a Brazilian type of unequal trade treaty that would have given Britain highly favorable access to the Argentine market; for the British, the 1825 free-trade treaty was thus a second-best alternative. Castlereagh also chose not to support the anti-Spanish independence movements, in part because Spain became a British ally in the war against Napoleon in 1809, but also because antigovernment rebellions might leave these territories "without any government." British strategy was instead to let Napoleon destroy Spanish power. Then, according to Castlereagh, "We shall present ourselves as auxiliaries and protectors" to the emerging governments. This would facilitate what was needed in a country like Argentina, namely, "silent and imperceptible" economic penetration.[29] As it turned out, the economic penetration was neither silent nor imperceptible. As noted, with British gunboats sitting offshore, the Creole junta in Buenos Aires offered British traders significant concessions in 1810. Although these were challenged temporarily by others in Argentina, in 1811 Rivadavia again sought more open support of the British. The British were then allowed to take silver out of Argentina as payment for British exports in 1814. As British trade grew, taxes on related profits became a major source of public revenues, making the rulers in Buenos Aires more dependent on British commerce.

Following independence, the British entered Buenos Aires in a big way: some 240 business houses were established; consular agents were appointed; intelligence was gathered; goods were insured in London; and, of course, bilateral treaties were signed.[30] British merchants were, moreover, a coherent lot, who met in exclusive "British Commercial Rooms" in Buenos Aires and became politically influential, both locally and in Britain.[31] British textile manufacturers in Lancashire and Manchester were already petitioning politicians in London to recognize South American republics—a simple act that in the context of the period would have amounted to an open announcement that British hegemony had supplanted Spanish power—to facilitate textile exports. The British rulers hesitated; they were moved to recognize these republics only in 1823, following the proclamation of the Monroe Doctrine by the United States, underlining the fact that both the interests of manufacturers and the reasons of state molded policy. Meanwhile, Rivadavia offered "lavish concessions" to the British in 1821;[32] the British navy started providing safe passage for the bullion owed to textile merchants on armed ships to London; and the British came to monopolize government contracts in Buenos Aires. The Friendship Treaty of 1825 that Canning negotiated was thus a culmination of these growing interactions—which had begun after Popham's invasion in 1806—and that came to provide the framework for economic interactions in the subsequent decades. While the treaty was indeed a real free-trade treaty insofar as it allowed all nations to trade freely with Argentina, decision-makers in Britain well understood that given Britain's competitive economy, and given how costly it would have been to eke out a more exclusive arrangement, such a treaty would suffice to secure disproportionate access to trade. It is not surprising that it was in this context that Canning famously claimed, "Spanish America is free and if we do not mismanage our affairs sadly, she is English."[33]

British trade with Argentina, or for that matter with much of South America, boomed during the independence era and proved to be "crucial" for sustaining Britain's textile exports: if British textile exports in 1804–6 amounted to £1.1 million, or 2 percent of total British textile exports, by 1824–26 they had grown to £5 million, or some 13 percent of total British exports.[34] Brazil was clearly important in this trade expansion, but the Southern Cone countries, including Argentina, were not far behind. For example, if twelve ships left Britain in 1807–8 for the South American west coast, encouragement from British government ensured that in 1808–9 thirty British ships arrived in Buenos Aires.[35] Thereafter, British exports to the Southern Cone grew steadily; by late 1820s some 200 British ships were calling at Buenos Aires annually; and, as one wit added, these were no cruise ships. During this period, British exports to the Southern Cone grew at some 4 percent to 5 percent per annum in value terms and, because textile prices were declining, at a steeper rate in terms of volume (see Table 2.1).[36] By 1822, half of all imports—and nearly all the imports of manufactured goods—coming into Buenos Aires were British in origin.[37] Mule and ox-cart trains from Buenos Aires carried these products to the interior, where they played havoc with the local economies. Argentina paid for these imports by exporting hides and bullion: exports of hides and of other animal products from Argentina grew at some 4 percent to 5 percent in the post-1810 period, and bullion—received via Chile and Peru—played a "sizable" role in financing British exports in this early period.[38]

The Barings loan also originated during the end of this period, casting a long shadow on British-Argentine relations. Since the government in Buenos Aires

Table 2.1 British Textile Exports to the Southern Cone, 1815–79

Growth in Value (annual average in percent)		Growth in Volume (Cotton Goods) (annual average in percent)	
1817–37	5.4	1819–29	28.4
1837–57	3.6	1829–39	13.1
1857–77	2.4	1839–49	4.3
1857–74	5.3	1849–59	5.2
		1859–69	2.7
		1869–79	2.9

Source: Adapted from Llorca-Jaña, *The British Textile Trade in South America*, tables 2.1 (p. 25) and 2.4 (p. 33).

taxed the profits on the growing trade—and thus had access to higher revenues, in sterling, to boot—there was increasing confidence in the British merchant community that loans could safely be extended to Argentina. Local liberal factions were also keen to encourage British investments in Argentina. Rivadavia worked with the Baring brothers to secure a loan of £1 million, mainly to establish the Banco Nacional. The terms of the loan were downright usurious.[39] After commissions and fees, Buenos Aires received only about half the loaned amount. The Banco Nacional itself was dominated by British merchants, who used it to finance more British imports, and to support the political ascension of Rivadavia, a move that was fiercely opposed by caudillos from the provinces. Political and economic problems contributed to Argentina defaulting on this loan, leading, in turn, to a long dry spell in British loans to Argentina; this situation was only resolved in the 1860s. I will return to discuss the post-1860 developments, but for now it should be clear that by the end of the first quarter of the nineteenth century, the British navy and clever diplomacy had first pried open Argentina for profitable commerce, and then established a broad framework—a framework of informal empire—within which, as we will see, political and economic relations continued to evolve for the rest of the century.

Those who argue that British relations with Argentina did not constitute an informal empire focus on the few decades following 1825, especially the disappointment resulting from the default on the Barings loan in 1825. Platt, for example, rests his case on this period and makes two related arguments. First, British trade with Latin America, including with Argentina, prior to, say, 1860, was not all that significant: "Latin America could sell nothing to Europe, so that it could buy nothing in return."[40] And related to this, since the region was not important economically, "British government intervention" in the region was "extraordinarily limited."[41] As indicated at the beginning of the chapter, I argue that both these arguments are wrong. On Britain's relations with Latin America in this period, I build on Alan Knight's argument that British policy was "belligerent, interventionist and meddlesome," and on trade, I will use a variety of data, especially Llorca-Jaña's recent data, to document why Platt seriously underestimated Argentina's economic importance to Britain.[42] Use of superior force by one polity on another for the sake of profit is indeed the essence of informal empire.

Rivadavia's ascension to power in 1826 as the first president of Argentina (or the United Provinces of South America, as Argentina was then called) was facilitated by British merchants around the Banco Nacional, as was his decline the next year when the British withdrew their support.[43] Of course, Rivadavia's writ barely reached beyond Buenos Aires. While the British were keen to support the liberal factions, of whom Rivadavia was a prominent member, the context of a war with Brazil had shifted the balance of power in Argentina toward those caudillos capable of mobilizing armed force. Britain intervened decisively in the Brazil-Argentina war—both the Brazilian and Argentine navies were at this time commanded by former British naval officers—and helped to create the sovereign state of Uruguay.[44] This resulted in recriminations and a civil war, from which General Rosas, in 1829, emerged as the new ruler of Argentina. As is well known, Rosas dominated Argentine politics until 1852, when he was overthrown and moved to England where, with his blue eyes, he blended in and led the life of a country gentleman until his death in 1877.

Whereas politics in many parts of Latin America during this period is best characterized as "anarchy of *caudillos,*" Rosas provided a semblance of political stability in Argentina.[45] Rosas was a "classic *caudillo*": personalistic, charismatic, dictatorial, and ruthless.[46] He also sought to enhance a measure of freedom for Argentina within the core constraints of British lordship. In Argentine politics he represented first and foremost the interests of cattle ranchers of the province of Buenos Aires. As a third force of sorts in the conflict between the unitarios and the federales, Rosas over time forged a working alliance between agro-exporters and the merchant traders. A key strategy was to forcibly bring more and more land into the orbit of the export economy. Armed campaigns led to the extermination of some 6,000 Indians as Rosas acquired large tracts of land. He in turn transferred these lands, in the form of mega-estates, to cronies, as well as sold them at basement prices to other investors;[47] Ferns characterized this exchange as "*estanciero* socialism" (socialism for the ranchers).[48] Both cattle-based exporters from large estates and free traders in Buenos Aires, including the British merchants, very much benefited from these new developments. The historical record seems to indicate very few protests by or remorse from the British about this profitable extermination of Indians in the pampas. The British ultimately even found Rosas's ruthless dictatorial rule acceptable: "I dislike and condemn the System of Rosas, as all Liberal men must do, but I conceive it would be a great evil should he be vanquished, as this system gives protection to life and property, more particularly that of Foreigners, and it is based on Order."[49]

Britain's policy toward Rosas was moved by the goals of expanding trade and ensuring that debts were honored. Following Palmerston's dictum that the role of government was to promote the interests of manufacturers and merchants, Britain intervened in Argentinian affairs as needed to ensure that these goals were met. It is important to note that even though Argentina was mostly a white country by now, Britain did not treat it as it did its white dominions. Palmerston lumped Argentina with China and other "half civilized governments," which periodically required "dressing down":

> Their minds are too shallow to receive any impression that will last longer than some such period and warning is of little use. They care little for words and they must not only see the stick but actually feel it on their shoulders.[50]

Both sticks and words backed by sticks were used to ensure favorable outcomes. For example, no sooner had Rosas come to power than, in 1829, British proconsuls in Buenos Aires made "verbal representations" on behalf of British bondholders, urging the new government to honor a variety of debts, especially the Barings loan.[51] When Rosas did not readily oblige, the issue festered, which led to repeated representations and, eventually, to an armed Anglo-French intervention, aimed at pressuring the Rosas government to pay the bondholders. When Rosas successfully resisted this intervention, he also pleaded to the resident British diplomats, in 1842: "I am grieved that circumstances forbid me in this instance to yield to the desires of Her Majesty's government."[52] Although the British temporarily accepted this setback, they also sided with forces that eventually overthrew Rosas in 1852.

British interventions on behalf of trade promotion were even more belligerent. Throughout this period the British negotiated navigation treaties that allowed the British navy and private ventures to open the internal waterways of the River Plate and Paraná system for navigation and the expansion of trade in the interior. Flooded with British goods, Rosas sought to impose some mild tariffs in 1835–37. Whether this was a conscious effort at import substitution or not, related ideas were in the air; Alexander Hamilton's protectionist ideas had been practiced in the United States for a few decades by then. Rosas was, of course, fully sanguine about British interests in this domain and about British power over Argentina; he excluded textiles from the new tariff regime, since they were the main British export. Still, the British strongly objected to the move lest the policies became attractive to others in the region; Palmerston wanted British representatives in Buenos Aires to lecture Rosas on the virtues of free trade. Since words had to be followed by sticks for these "half civilized governments," the "Murray Memorandum" on trade with Latin America argued, in 1841, for active intervention by the British government to promote the interests of both the manufacturers and of Great Britain; this was needed because "the merchant thinks but of time present. . . . The Government of a country, on the other hand, looks not only to the present but to the future: how national interest can best be promoted permanently."[53] A more succinct statement of the "relative autonomy" of the state from capital is not likely to be found in government records! Aimed at securing such interests, the Memorandum continued, "Secret instructions might be given to offer succor"—diplomatic speak for the possible use of coercion—in order to secure favorable trade and investment treaties.[54] Rosas quietly withdrew his tariffs shortly thereafter, without enough time having passed to influence any significant investor response.

Rosas was hardly an early Argentine nationalist, and even less a radical. He was a ruthless dictator whose policies mainly benefited the big ranchers and trade merchants. He accommodated British interests as much as possible; as a lighthearted example, when the civil war against Rosas was in its last stages, and a siege was laid on Buenos Aires, the only people allowed to move freely in and out of Buenos Aires were the British, mainly because their cricket field was outside the city boundary.[55] And yet, Rosas's unwillingness to totally toe the British line (on loans and free trade) put him at odds with those who really mattered. Eventually—in an early example of regime change—the British put pressure on Rosas. Although the civil war that toppled Rosas involved anti-Rosas Argentine forces from the interior that had allied with forces from both Uruguay and Brazil, the Brazilian forces acted as a proxy for the British. When Rosas was overthrown, Palmerston congratulated the Brazilians for their "liberal" sensibilities in ousting a ruthless caudillo from power.[56] Ever gracious, if also duplicitous, in their imperial relations, however, the British also enabled Rosas to travel on a British navy ship to England, along with his daughter and enormous personal wealth.

After Rosas, Argentina was a divided country. A transition phase of sorts ensued for the next decade or more, during which a more national polity emerged.[57] Customs on growing trade enabled the creation of a bureaucracy. The same trade also provided an incentive for political compromise. Provincial politicians increasingly represented the interests of the large landholders in the interior, who were rapidly joining the agrarian export-oriented economy. The political forces in the interior thus found common cause with merchants of Buenos Aires, who facilitated this trade economy. A trade-oriented alliance of the landed oligarchy and merchants emerged, facilitating a federal polity in which provincial interests became dominant. The city of Buenos Aires was separated from the province of Buenos Aires and became a national city, somewhat subservient to the emerging rule of provincial politicians. There were voices that argued for a stronger center with a more national economic program, including tariffs, import substitution, and the diversification of an agrarian export economy toward more industry. These were imported ideas in the case of Argentina, however; indigenous economic interests, especially the ranchers, wanted nothing to do with tariffs, and the ideas for a more national project got lost. The ranchers and merchants were happy with the liberal option of relying on open trade for their prosperity and letting foreign investment to do the rest of the job of developing the country.[58] A coalition to invite dependent development thus came to the fore in Argentina, as had happened in other parts of Latin America.

The role of the British during this transitional political phase was both indirect and direct. In terms of indirect influence, the key actors of the new liberal ruling coalition of provincial agro-exporters and merchant traders had of course gained prominence because of the integration of the Argentine economy with the British economy over the past half-century. In such situations, it becomes difficult to identify where external influences stop and where internal developments can be viewed as autonomous ones; this was a key insight of the dependency literature that remains relevant. Beyond such indirect influence, however, the British also intervened more directly during this phase to facilitate political outcomes they deemed preferable. They viewed the political change through the prism of which Argentine forces would encourage continued open trade and, most of all, help to settle the old, outstanding Barings loan; those forces were to be supported. According to Ferns, Britain influenced Argentina to move in the direction of a federal polity in which "rural and provincial interests had a prominent place."[59] The British preferred this kind of confederation because it successfully subordinated Buenos Aires, putting the city's resources at the disposal of the whole republic, available to pay off the Barings loan.[60] The British then went further, threatening military intervention in Argentina if the new political rulers did not agree to a favorable settlement of the Barings loan. The Foreign Office thus instructed Frank Parish, the British proconsul in Argentina, who had prior experience in India to boot, that they "would be perfectly justified in proceeding at once to the adoption of other and stronger measures" to ensure the settlement of the loan; in a private note to Parish, "coercion" was suggested as a possibility.[61] Parish apparently worked on the finance minister of Argentina—an Argentinian gentleman who was a partner in a Liverpool financial firm—and, shortly thereafter a favorable settlement was reached for the repayment of the 1824 loan, heralding the beginning of a new phase in British-Argentine relations.

During the first six decades of those relations, the British periodically intervened to form and deform the emerging country of Argentina. To recapitulate, important instances of overt imperial interventions in support of trade and investment promotion included the 1806–7 invasion; naval blockade of the South Atlantic in 1808; trade concessions from rulers of Buenos Aires under duress in 1810; the role of the British navy in transferring bullion throughout the era of independence; the 1825 free-trade treaty; verbal representations, from 1829 on, to demand the repayment of the Barings loan; anti-tariff moves against Rosas during the 1830s; the Murray Memorandum of 1841 threatening force to establish free trade; armed pressure on Rosas during the 1840s and then again to support his overthrow in 1852; the support for a more federal polity in the post-Rosas period; and the threat of armed intervention in 1856–57, leading to favorable terms for the settlement of the Barings loan. Some of these interventions failed;

the issue of success or failure, however, does not speak to the issue of intent and motives. This list of the more obvious instances of British intervention neither includes the various indirect influences that have been discussed nor the "whispers" and the more subtle but continuous interventions in Argentine politics by resident British diplomats.[62] In face of such evidence, the claims of some scholars that Britain did not intervene in Argentine politics are simply not tenable. British interventions are also more comprehensible if they are seen as facilitating economic gains for British manufacturers and merchants, a set of issues to which I now turn.

During this first phase, Britain's economic relations with Argentina centered on trade, with textiles as the main export and cattle products the main import; by contrast, export of metal goods, railway construction, and related foreign investments came to be dominant during the second phase, say, in the post-1870 period. The older view that British trade with Argentina (or, more broadly, with Latin America) during the first phase was not significant has been substantially revised by economic historians.[63] British political interventions were aimed at enhancing trade, and enhance trade they did. According to François Crouzet, the volume of British trade with Latin America between 1814 and 1873 grew at an annual rate of 3.4 percent, which compares favorably with trade growth with the United States during the same period at less than 3 percent per annum.[64] Nearly 60 percent of all the British exports were textiles; Latin America in 1840 took nearly a third of Britain's cotton exports; Brazil and Argentina together absorbed about half of these regional exports.[65] The new estimates of Llorca-Jaña (see Table 2.1) suggest that the rate of growth of British trade with the Southern Cone—mainly Argentina and Chile—between 1817 and 1874 was an impressive 4.2 percent per annum in terms of value; however, the volume of cotton exports between 1817 and 1879 grew at a staggering 9.4 percent per annum.

The question that arises is how Argentina paid for the growing volume of British goods, especially textiles. The earlier claim that countries like Argentina had nothing to sell to the British has now been discredited. Not surprisingly, Argentina's main exports continued to be cattle products: hides, salted meat, and tallow. Wool exports also grew rapidly, though it is unlikely that they went to Britain; after all, Britain was itself a successful wool producer and manufacturer. Ferns calculated that over the twenty-two years leading up to 1851, hide exports grew by 300 percent, salted meat by 250 percent, tallow by 275 percent, and wool exports (starting from a low base) by 2,100 percent. He further suggested that this growth in trade was reflected in increase in shipping: if 200 ships were calling at the port of Buenos Aires annually in the late 1820s, over 500 ships were visiting the port annually during the 1840s.[66] Newer aggregate estimates of Argentine exports are consistent with this finer-grained analysis. By one estimate, if Argentina's exports in 1830 were 12 percent of the GDP, by 1870 they had risen to 20 percent; the annual rate of growth of per capita exports during the same period averaged some 2 percent per annum.[67] Two other estimates are considerably higher: one suggests that per capita growth of exports between 1810 and 1870 was 3.5 percent, and of total exports, 5.5 percent (4 to 5 percent between 1810 and 1850 and 7 to 8 percent between 1850 and 1870);[68] the estimates of Llorca-Jaña for 1810 to 1850 are identical: according to him, also, Argentine exports during this period grew at 4 percent to 5 percent per annum.[69] While Britain was by far Argentina's dominant trade partner, Argentina also exported to other countries. There is evidence to suggest that Britain exported more to Argentina than it imported back. The balance was made up by bullion payments, which were "sizable" throughout the period; since Argentina had few mines, silver and gold came into Argentina via Peru and Chile and, in turn, was carried back to London on British navy ships, to avoid loss to pirates.[70]

These data put to rest any doubts raised in earlier scholarship about the economic importance of Latin America to Britain more broadly and of Argentina specifically. The data also underscores that the actions of Castlereagh, Canning, and Palmerston were quite successful in prying open the markets of new world countries such as Argentina, leading to growing imports of raw materials and the export of manufactured goods. That Argentina became very much a part of Britain's informal empire is, then, hardly in doubt. What complicates the argument is the economic impact of these imperial relations. Argentina, or at least the elites, benefited from these new political and economic patterns, though these developments were lopsided, with long-term consequences. As we have seen, the trade pattern that the British established facilitated the growth in the incomes of agro-exporters (ranchers and merchants) in Argentina and also discouraged indigenous manufacturing. Both trends are borne out by data. Propelled by the growing incomes of ranchers and merchants, the Argentine economy grew steadily during this period: per capita economic growth between 1820 and 1870 averaged some 0.8 percent. This rate is not that far behind the 1.0 percent per capita growth in Western Europe at the same time, and the 1.3 percent growth in the United States.[71] By contrast, Brazil's economy was nearly stagnant.[72] The contrasting growth performance of Argentina and Brazil is not readily explained. And though this is not the place for an extensive analysis of the subject, looking at the contrast does shed light on the Argentine situation.

Argentina and Brazil were both part of Britain's informal empire. Both traded extensively (though Argentina's trade-to-GDP ratio was somewhat higher), and both sold commodities to and bought manufactured goods from Britain. If anything, Brazil was politically more stable and should have benefited economically from this stability. The best explanation for its relative sluggishness during the nineteenth century is probably its slave economy, which did not readily generate demand for mass goods, and thus for much local production.[73] This explanation is even more persuasive if one keeps in mind that economic growth in Brazil, including in manufacturing, picked up later in the century, after slavery was abolished. In addition, though data on terms of trade are notoriously difficult to come by, we do know that Brazil's exports exhibited more boom-and-bust cycles than did the products of Argentina's ranching economy. Last, the leaders of the monarchial government of Brazil were even more subservient to the British than were Argentina's various rulers, especially Rosas. As I have argued elsewhere, the Brazilian state, especially the regional state of São Paulo, became more interventionist in the postmonarchial period (say, after 1890), and contributed to manufacturing and economic growth.[74] Whatever the correct explanation for Brazil's economic stagnation during much of the nineteenth century, the case does underline that a proposition about trade-led growth—that the Argentine case on its own might support—does not follow readily.

The steady growth in the imports of cheap British manufactured goods to Argentina, on the one hand, led to the decline of indigenous, household manufacturing in the interior and, on the other hand, reinforced the existing political and economic obstacles to developing modern manufacturing.[75] Economic inequalities also grew sharply. Land ownership came to be highly concentrated, with the expected political and economic ramifications: in the province of Buenos Aires, for example, 825 estates controlled 33 million acres in 1840.[76] As another example of growing regional inequalities, land prices in Buenos Aires toward the end of this period were some forty times higher than prices in the interior, and the revenues of Buenos Aires were fourteen times more than those, say, of Cordoba.[77] One estimate suggests that the Gini coefficient of wealth in Argentina during 1855–56 might have been as high as 0.73.[78] So, toward the end of this period Argentina was already becoming a political economy that was, on the one hand, "dynamic and opulent" but, on the other hand, was acquiring "structural imbalances and distortions that were to afflict its later development"[79]

To the extent that new phases in historical development can ever be marked, the rise of General Bartolomé Mitre to power in Argentina (1862–68) marked a transition to a new phase of British-Argentine relations, one that would last until about World War I, when British hegemony over Latin America was undermined. It was characterized by a more consolidated domestic polity in Argentina, routinization of the asymmetrical relations between Britain and Argentina, and a transition away from the textile-centered British trade to the construction of railways in Argentina and to significant inflows of new British investments. This new phase was, of course, a product of deeper forces at work, both in Britain and in Argentina. Within Britain, the thrust of the Industrial Revolution was shifting the economic focus away from textiles and toward heavier industries, including metal industries, especially the construction of railways. The Companies Act of 1862 encouraged the pooling of risks; this in turn facilitated overseas investments from Britain, especially in companies that would go on to build railways in diverse parts of the world. Among other notable developments within Argentina, the agreement to settle the Barings loan, in 1856–57, raised the confidence of British investors in Argentina and loans and investments resumed. The more liberal elements now in power in post-Rosas Argentina were, moreover, committed to attracting foreign resources to develop the country without altering the commodity-exporting nature of the economy in any fundamental way. These local ambitions helped create a convergence of interests between British investors and Argentine elite well into the new century. The results included significant growth of profitable British trade and investment with Argentina. On the receiving end, there is no doubt that the Argentine economy grew handsomely during much of this period, but a number of other developments were pointing toward a less rosy future: the economy's continuing reliance on exports from mega-ranches; the related power within the state of the agrarian oligarchs; sharp inequalities; limited industrialization; and deep dependence on British finance and investments to sustain the agro-export economy and on British goods to sustain the lavish lifestyles of the local elite.

During the second half of the nineteenth century, a central government consolidated territorial control over Argentina and a ruling class committed to dependent development came to firmly control the state. The political compromise that had led to a federal polity with a weak center has been discussed. In the next phase, the center imposed order on the outlying territories. As often happens, a war (with Paraguay during 1865–70) provided the first significant occasion of state control, when Mitre used the armed forces to subdue recalcitrant regional elites and tame gauchos and Indians in the interior. General Roca pursued these goals in subsequent decades with even greater intensity, and proclaimed the conquest of the wilderness as a priority. This led to more massacres of Indians and the acquisition of enormous amounts of land that was in turn virtually given to ranchers, further strengthening the ruling alliance. Argentina was increasingly a white country. Immigration from Italy and Spain hastened. Despite the continuing massacre of Indians, the overall population jumped from approximately one million in 1857 to 3.3 million in 1890.[80]

Ranchers, merchants, and those who represented these groups controlled the politics of the state. Arguments were occasionally put forward about the need to impose tariffs and undertake indigenous manufacturing. Rosa's ambassador to the United States had already reported back about the use of infant-industry protection by the great northern neighbor, and he urged Argentina to do the same. These arguments fell on deaf ears, however, because neither the indigenous economic elites nor their British overlords had any interest in Argentina pursuing this alternate pathway to the modern world. Similar arguments arose again a few times during the 1870s and the 1880s; they, too, were drowned out. Very few in the political class had any real concern for the "long-term interests" of their country.[81] The influential among the generation that came to the fore during the second half of the century had matured and benefited within the frame of the British-dominated political economy; they were not about to challenge or abandon that frame readily. The main approach to development this ruling group pursued instead was to promote agro-exports and, in turn, use British investments and goods to provide a semblance of modernity, albeit superficial modernity.[82] The trade-led-growth model may even have made eminent sense during the period: an immense amount of land was available; the labor requirements of a ranching economy were minimal; immigration provided this labor; the terms of trade for Argentine products were favorable; the British were willing to invest in other needed fields and to provide manufactured goods; and governments that basically understood this pathway to be desirable were in control of the state apparatus. Why could such prosperity not go on forever? As we know, it did not. We will see that even at the time, problems were evident but that the costs of recognizing them were too high. Blindness paid! Argentina thus pursued an easy-growth model, easy because it was achieved without much capital accumulation, without significant technical or organizational know-how, with low levels of education, and because the points at which any value was added to output were controlled by foreigners, mainly the British—as long as they could, until they could not.

One conventional understanding of British-Argentine relations in the post-1870 period is that they were mostly noninterventionist.[83] This is mostly correct, but the implications of this view need to be properly understood, even qualified. First, some real interventions by the British did take place. Take the crisis in Santa Fe in 1876. The provincial elite of Santa Fe wanted the British-owned London and River Plate Bank to ease restrictions on bank discounts. When it refused, the local authorities arrested the bank manager, and the bank was closed. The British sent a gunboat to Rosario, but the local authorities successfully resisted the armed pressure. The British then turned to the authorities in Buenos Aires and threatened to demand immediate payments on the guaranteed railway profits. The national government then negotiated with Santa Fe, and the British bank was reopened. In the words of one scholar, the incident underlined, "the influence the British had come to command in Argentina. . . . They had secured great power in their guise as the government's creditor."[84] Such interventions, moreover, sparked resentments. After the Santa Fe incident, politician Vincente López argued in a congressional debate for reducing the "country's heavy reliance" on Britain and for following the examples of Germany and the United States in protecting and building industry, calling free trade "a conspiracy of the strong nations to dominate the weak."[85] As noted, these arguments were lost on all those who stood to benefit from free trade, at least for the time being.

Second, the new Barings crisis of 1890 highlighted the growing power of British finance over countries like Argentina. The repatriation of guaranteed profits on huge railway investments and payments on loans to the government had created a situation in which financial outflows from Argentina to Britain were often greater than the inflows.[86] When one such debt crisis emerged in 1889, subscribers to the giant London-based financial firm Baring Brothers held back payments, threatening a financial crisis, not only for Barings, but possibly also for Britain. In an early example of too big to fail, the laissez-faire British government quietly agreed with the governor of the Bank of England to bear half of any loss that the Barings crisis might create, renewing confidence in the financial community.[87] Meanwhile, the Argentinians tried to raise a loan from the United States to pay back their British debts. The Americans wanted a naval base in return and did not want to open their meat market—the shape of "big stick imperialism" was beginning to emerge.[88] Eventually, the desperate Argentinians turned to the other giant British global financial firm, Rothschild, which restructured the loan on terms that led to "the imposition of unpopular austerity measures, a striking reduction in real wages, and the sale of state enterprises to foreign bankers."[89] The settlement, according to Carlos Marichal, represented a "capitulation to the dictates of the international banking community in almost every sphere of the economy."[90] It is not surprising that the credibility of the government was undermined and that a motley opposition comprising students; Catholic groups; and opportunistic leaders, such as the former dictator Mitre, now arguing for democratic reforms, emerged, pointing toward the political future of Argentina.[91]

What needs to be underscored in all this is that the nature of British intervention in Argentina was changing, not the fact of domination and the use of superior power for economic ends. A leading scholar of the subject suggests that by the turn of the century Anglo-Argentine "diplomatic intercourse" had acquired a "humdrum character."[92] The use of British gunboats or even of diplomatic pressure to further British economic interests was indeed becoming less common. This was in part because Argentine elites were by now quite cooperative, and in part because the United States increasingly would have objected to the use of such strong-arm British tactics in its backyard. Nevertheless, a sharp "asymmetry of power and influence" continued to define Anglo-Argentine relations during this period.[93] This was increasingly rooted in deep economic dependency, which as noted, the Argentine elites were not about to challenge: Britain by now was "the bank, stockbroker, railway builder, and supplier of Argentine Republic."[94] The results included "a close alliance of merchant bankers, companies and government officials defending and promoting British interests" in Latin America, including in Argentina.[95] What, then, was the need for overt intervention? A US consul in Buenos Aires in 1890 aptly summed up the situation in Argentina: "[T]he English have the preference in everything pertaining to business and business interests in the country—as ultimately as though it were a British colony."[96]

British trade and investment with Argentina expanded rapidly during this second phase, especially investments and especially in the post-1890 period (Table 2.2). It may be helpful to express these absolute figures as proportions of overall trade and investment before discussing the process that led to these outcomes. By 1913, Latin America was taking 10 percent of all British exports and 20 percent of total British foreign investments.[97] Argentina was a leading destination, absorbing 40 percent of British exports and nearly a third of British foreign investment in Latin America.[98] During World War I, British investments in Argentina constituted nearly 10 percent of its total global investments, at par with what Britain at that time invested in Australia or South Africa.[99] No one should doubt the economic importance of Argentina for Britain. As for Argentine dependence on Britain, by 1913 nearly a quarter of its exports were absorbed by Britain, mainly agricultural products: beef, maize, and wheat.[100] Although reliable aggregate figures on British investments in Latin America are hard to come by, best estimates suggest that in 1913 they were in the range of £1 billion and that Argentina took nearly 40 percent of this total.[101] Much of the then-modern sector of the Argentinian economy, including railways, ports, meat-freezing plants, utilities in

Table 2.2 Anglo-Argentine Trade and Investment, 1860–1913 (in million pounds)

	British Imports from Argentina	British Exports to Argentina		British Foreign Investment (Direct and Portfolio) in Argentina
1860	1.1	1.8	1865	2.7
1880	0.9	2.5	1875	22.6
1900	13.1	7.1	1885	46.0
1913	42.5	22.6	1895	190.9
			1905	253.6
			1913	479.8

Source: Adapted from Miller, *Britain and Latin America*, tables 5.3 (p. 108), 5.5 (p. 111), and 6.2 (p. 122).

the cities, and banks, was foreign owned, mainly by the British. The Argentine economy grew handsomely during this period, especially after 1890, until the Great Depression hit in 1928, when Argentina's foreign commerce and growth collapsed, never to return to its glory days again.

Anglo-Argentine economic relations changed dramatically in the post-1870 period, due at least in part to changing technology. The introduction of the telegraph enabled rapid communication; freezing plants and steamships enabled the export of beef, and the introduction of railways facilitated the movement of goods from and to the interior. Textiles continued to be an important British export to Latin America, including to Argentina, but their importance declined in this second phase: if in 1860 nearly 70 percent of all British exports to Latin America were textiles, by 1913 they were down to 30 percent.[102] Some of this decline was due to tariffs and deliberate import substitution, such as in Mexico and Brazil. But those policies were not as pronounced in Argentina. As noted, the ruling groups in Argentina did not prioritize national industrialization during this period. The textile exports to Argentina peaked as late as 1912, when German and US goods became more competitive.[103] The new British exports to Argentina were connected to the second industrial revolution, especially the growth of railways. These included iron and steel products, machinery, paints, chemicals, and coal. The intensification of Anglo-Argentine trade during this period highlights two points that are worth underscoring: first, although Britain faced growing competition or protection against its goods (or both) in various parts of the world, this was not the case either in its colonies or in countries like Argentina within the scope of its informal empire; second, the basic trade pattern whereby Britain exported manufactured goods in exchange for commodities rooted in a very limited sector of the Argentinian economy—the ranch economy—continued and deepened.

If trade patterns exhibited some continuity, the investment boom during this second phase was a new phenomenon. Prior to 1870 Argentina took very little of British foreign investment; most British financial interests in Latin America were in Mexico and Brazil, and they were mainly in the form of loans to the governments of these countries. In the post-1870 period, British foreign investment in Argentina grew rapidly, especially in the post-1890 period, following the settlement of the Barings crisis. Between 1885 and 1895, for example, British investment in Argentina quadrupled, and then doubled again between 1905 and 1913.[104] Much of this new investment financed the construction of railways and public utilities. While there is no doubt that financial glut in Britain toward the end of the century generated pressure to look for profitable opportunities abroad, one should not overemphasize the disconnect of finance from the developments in the "real" economy, especially in manufacturing.[105] What drove British railway investments in Argentina was emphatically not the work of "financiers and speculators" but the promise of "a new market for British manufacturers."[106] The development of joint stock companies enabled investment overseas, but this investment moved to countries, such as Argentina, where there was confidence, and confidence, in turn, was boosted by opportunities for selling British products that yield even more profits, such as the railways. It is not surprising that nearly 60 percent of British gross capital flows into Argentina between 1865 and 1914 went into railways. This was not primarily gentlemanly capitalism pushing an imperial agenda; these were folks with coal stains on their fingers, creating opportunities for profit.

The ranching interests in Argentina had their own stake in encouraging railway building. Very simply, railways enhanced the value of their lands and their products. What is surprising is not that these interests wanted railways but why none of them (or the government they supported) undertook railway building on their own, even if with borrowed technology and finance.[107] (We will see that around the same time, the Egyptian government undertook railway construction.) Be that as it may, the liberal Argentinian government heavily subsidized railway construction: not only by providing land and liberal tax exemptions but by guaranteeing British railway investors a rate of profit of 7 percent.[108] The state subsidies proved very attractive to British investors. In 1857 there were only six miles of rail tracks in Argentina. By the end of the century there were 6,000 miles of tracks, and nearly 21,000 miles of tracks by 1913. Much of this—70 percent—was British owned by four major companies. That railway revenues did not always keep pace with their growth was not a major deterrent because of the government's profit guarantees. The pressure to continuously remit these profits, in turn, put enormous pressure on Argentina's balance of payments and eventually contributed to the financial crisis of 1889–90, scaring away investors. Even though British investments resumed following a structural-adjustment agreement devised by the Rothschilds, the pressure to pay the guaranteed profits did not readily ease in Argentina.

A few comments on the contrasting developments in Brazil may again put the Argentine case in sharper relief. While developments in Argentina and Brazil exhibit strong parallels during the nineteenth century, especially the fact that both became producers of commodities and takers of manufactured goods within the frame of the British informal empire, as noted, the Brazilian state's increased interventionism toward the end of the century helped to promote some industry in the post-1890 period. These developments were of long-run significance, a set of issues to which I return toward the end of the book in chapter 6. Following the end of Brazil's monarchy, which the British had propped up, a ruling elite emerged in the Old Republican State (1889–1930), especially in powerful states like São Paulo, which was not totally subservient to external actors.[109] These new rulers intervened to support coffee incomes and also imposed tariffs on a variety of consumer goods. Brazilian industry grew at 4 percent to 5 percent per annum during 1890–1930; by 1930, Brazil was pretty much self-sufficient in textiles, shoes, processed food, and a number of other light consumer industries. When it was faced with financial and balance-of-payment pressures similar to those of Argentina, Brazil's solution was also more interventionist: it borrowed abroad and used the money to nationalize the British-owned railways toward the end of the 19th century.

As World War I approached, the era of Britain's great influence over Argentina also approached an end. The main determinant of this shift was, of course, the growing political and economic significance of Germany and the United States. Goods and investment from these countries were increasingly competitive in Latin America. From the 1890s on—even before the Spanish-American War of 1898—the US Navy grew substantially, adding muscle to what had up to then been considered the windy rhetoric of the Monroe Doctrine. Within Argentina, too, mass politics with nationalist and populist themes began to emerge. After the war, these mobilized groups effectively challenged the power monopoly of pro-British liberals. Over this period, to recapitulate, the Argentine market absorbed large quantities of British goods and provided an outlet to numerous British companies for profitable investment. While there is no doubt that the nineteenth century dynamism of the British economy was at the root of its expansion abroad, it was also the case that Britain used its superior power to create and consolidate such opportunities. As documented here, Britain used overt force during the first half of the century and then, as relations of asymmetrical power took on a routine quality, relied more and more on patron-client types of relations that a self-interested set of elites in Argentina perpetuated.

The Argentine economy also grew handsomely during this period, especially toward the end of it. But it had not diversified within the constraints of an informal empire, pointing toward a troubled future. On the eve of the Great War, the Argentine economy was still largely a pastoral one that exported agricultural goods and imported manufactured ones. This is not to deny some growth of manufacturing in consumer industries, especially as the war cut off economic relations with Europe and encouraged some de facto import substitution. However, much of this growth was handicrafts and small-scale industry; the number of employees in firms, for example, averaged somewhere between eight and twelve, suggesting that large industrial factories were rare in Argentina.[110] In addition, to repeat, the economy and society were characterized by sharp inequalities, low savings levels, and the absence of skilled, well-educated manpower. Wise statesmen in Argentina might have used the wealth of agro-exports to mitigate such lopsided development. However, the political and economic context did not bring such statesmen to the fore. As we have noted, Argentina's ruling coalition was extremely self-serving—well satisfied with a profitable dependence on Britain—without much concern for either the long term or for the public good. As a matter of fact, it could be argued that such a ruling coalition was integral to the functioning of an informal empire in which Britain exercised great influence in Argentina without formal political control, certainly in the post-1870 period. As opposition to this narrow ruling coalition grew, the economic elite could not hold on to state power, populism came to the fore, and a dysfunctional state further contributed to the poor functioning of a lopsided economy in the twentieth century. This part of the story, however, does not belong in this chapter on the nineteenth century.

Egypt

If the ongoing threat from Russia was not enough, both the French and the industrial revolutions at the end of the eighteenth century put pressure on the Ottomans to reform the state and the economy of the empire. As a semiautonomous region of the Ottoman Empire, Egypt also experienced these pressures. The Egyptian response to the rise of the West was nearly heroic during the first half of the nineteenth century, when Muhammad Ali undertook vigorous state-led efforts to modernize Egypt. Toward the middle of the century, however, the British undermined these efforts. From 1850 to 1882, the descendants of Muhammad Ali sought to negotiate a difficult way forward, seeking room to maneuver within the British-imposed constraints, using British and French resources to build infrastructure (including the Suez Canal), and hoping to export their way to prosperity. These efforts failed when an indebted Egypt was occupied by Britain in 1882. From then on until at least 1922 (although many might suggest until the rise of Nasser in 1952), Egypt pretty much became a British colony. As for Argentina, then, I analyze the motives, mechanisms and the impact of Britain's informal—and at times nearly formal—empire in Egypt over the long nineteenth century.

At the turn of the nineteenth century Egypt was a country of some four million people, whose per capita income had stagnated for several centuries.[111] Over these centuries Egypt had been ruled by the Mamluks, a military oligarchy of initially sovereign rulers and then, following the annexation of Egypt by the Ottomans in the early sixteenth century, vassals of the Porte. As long as the rulers in Egypt paid tribute regularly, the Ottomans left them alone to manage their own affairs. When the Mamluk rulers were threatened by growing European power in the eighteenth century, they initiated some reforms late to collect additional land taxes and use the revenue to build a better armed force. These reforms made very little progress, however, especially because Napoleon conquered Egypt in 1798. His motives were mixed: conquest of Egypt was part of the post-Revolutionary French expansionism that brought the long-established Franco-Turkish alliance to an end; the British land route to India passed through Egypt; and Egyptian grain could feed southern France. The French occupation thus drew Egypt into the vortex of European conflicts and ended its relative isolation as a mere province of the Ottoman Empire.

The British reaction to French occupation of Egypt was swift. Henry Dundas, the war minister, declared to the British cabinet in 1799 that "the possession of Egypt by any independent Power would be a fatal circumstance to the interests of this country."[112] What exactly were British interests in Egypt at this early stage, however, was unclear; even the often-repeated claim that Egypt provided an overland route to India was probably not all that pressing, because the route was in disrepair during this period, and only became viable again with the introduction of steamships a couple of decades later. Instead, following the principle that any French gain was a British loss—and viewing the weakening Ottoman Empire as an arena of potential political and economic advantage—the British pushed Napoleon out of Egypt within three years. Brief though it was, the French occupation left its mark on Egypt. The French sought to impose a Napoleonic model of state and economic reform that Muhammad Ali admired, and the French left behind technocrats, many of whom were followers of Henri Saint Simon, with a belief in state-led, top-down model of socioeconomic change, which Muhammad Ali eventually employed.[113] The British occupation of Egypt was also short-lived because by now the Porte had become a British ally. The British sought to restore the authority of the Ottomans, but in a classic divide-and-rule tactic they also maintained a treaty-based right to protect the weakened Mamluk rulers from Ottoman authority.[114] Muhammad Ali, at the time an Albanian military adventurer in one of the Ottoman armies, took advantage of the resulting authority vacuum, rode his way to power in Cairo in 1805, and established a ruling dynasty in Egypt that would last—albeit with only nominal powers during the twentieth century—until Nasser's coup in 1952.

Muhammad Ali ruled Egypt for more than four decades. During this period he centralized rule, used state power to expand Egyptian agricultural production and exports of Egyptian long cotton, mobilized resources to initiate import substitution type of industrialization in textiles and armaments, expanded state revenues and Egyptian armed forces, and then used these forces to expand Egyptian power in the near abroad, threatening the Ottoman Empire from within. It is not surprising that historians of Egypt disagree in their assessment of Muhammad Ali and his policies.[115] From my standpoint, the key controversial issue can be phrased as such: Was Muhammad Ali a modernizer-from-above, say, an earlier version of the nationalist Meiji oligarchs, whose experiment in national transformation was deliberately undermined by the British? My answer tends toward yes, with two important qualifications. First, although Muhammad Ali may indeed have been an early nationalist of sorts, he was no Egyptian nation-builder. He was Albanian, probably of Kurdish stock, with blond hair and hazel eyes. He fancied himself a Turkish gentleman, a pasha, and mainly spoke Turkish, ruled with the help of his kin, and "despised the Egyptians" as an "inferior race of dirty peasants."[116] Second, his rule tended to be quite personalistic. While Muhammad Ali consolidated state power, the state during this reign never acquired a bureaucratic character. His efforts at state-led development were also hampered by personal interventions, enormous centralization, and the use of brute force.[117]

Despite these limitations, Muhammad Ali's policies and their results added up to an important early experiment in what we today might call deliberate development. The historical evidence also supports the claim that the British interpreted Muhammad Ali's success as a move against their regional economic and political interests and so, in turn, they set out to deliberately undermine his experiment—and succeeded. Both points can now be elaborated on. The facts of Muhammad Ali's actions in Egypt are not in doubt.[118] After military victory in 1805, he successfully consolidated power by eliminating possible challengers, including the Mamluks, whom he invited to a party (some two dozen leading members), trapped them in a Cairo alley, and systematically killed them all. Following Napoleon, he moved to the model of a conscription army. This required significant new resources, the acquisition of which provided one important incentive for the economic policy changes discussed here. A viable army, in turn, enabled Muhammad Ali to enhance his autonomy from the Porte (while he paid lip service to the authority of Mahmud II in Constantinople), and to conquer neighboring territories.[119] The British were wary of Muhammad Ali, first, because he posed a challenge to the authority of the Ottomans and, second, because of his later statist economic policies. They were not considering formal annexation of Egypt as a colony, however, in the early part of the century. With wars with Napoleon on, any such action might have driven the Ottomans back into the embrace of the French. Reminiscent of the Creole resistance to Popham in Argentina, moreover, Muhammad Ali had already repulsed a small British military attack in 1807, underscoring that conquest would not have been easy. Muhammad Ali in any case understood full well that he could not achieve much without the "goodwill of England;" he thus promised the British safe passage to India via Egypt and grain for their armies.[120] He and the British thus had an uneasy but working relationship in the early nineteenth century, at least for a while.

Muhammad Ali was a mercantilist.[121] Needing revenues to build state power, he sought state control and transformation of the Egyptian economy. He employed French advisers and first completed the cadastral survey begun by Napoleon. This enabled him to not only enhance agricultural taxes, but also to undertake significant changes in the land-tenure patterns. For example, he abolished communal ownership of land and established de facto, though not de jure, rights of land ownership. Since squeezing existing resources had its limits—and Muhammad Ali was far too ambitious to settle for a second serfdom—he invested in irrigation, the main bottleneck to expansion of agricultural production in Egypt. Increase in grain production enabled Egypt to export grain to fighting European armies. The chance discovery of long-staple cotton in a Cairo garden led to slow but steady expansion of commercial cotton cultivation in the post-1821 period. Cotton production quadrupled between 1821 and 1835.[122] A significant portion of this increase was exported, though, as discussed here, Muhammad Ali also used cotton to facilitate indigenous textile manufacturing. Textile production was in full swing in Britain during this period. Egyptian cotton was thus in high demand in Lancashire, not only because of its high quality, but also because it only needed to travel across the Mediterranean. While the Egyptians were importing finished cloth—both British textiles and Indian muslin that East India Company merchants were prohibited from selling in England—exports of Egyptian cotton doubled between the 1820s and the 1840s.[123] The need to sustain exports and to maximize revenues led to other changes. The port of Alexandria was improved and linked by canal to the Nile. Muhammad Ali also established state monopolies for exports, buying products from peasants at low prices and selling them at considerable margin of profit.

These early economic developments in Egypt (or for that matter in other parts of the Ottoman Empire) paralleled the developments noted in Latin America during the same period: slow but steady integration with the British economy as a producer of commodities and taker of manufactured goods. However, the similarities end there, at least until the middle of the century. Muhammad Ali was no free trader. His hope instead was that "this country [Egypt] would have the least possible need for foreign products and that it would become capable of supplying such products to its neighbors."[124] With these ambitions, he used state revenues collected from agricultural taxes and commodity exports to facilitate state-led industrialization. His rate of domestic savings and investments may have been as high as 10 percent of Egypt's GDP during the period.[125] He used these monies to import machinery and technicians to establish new factories, whose products were protected by tariffs on imports. By 1830, state-owned factories were producing "cotton, woolen, silk, and linen textiles, sugar, paper, glass, leather, sulfuric acid and other chemicals."[126] In addition, ships were being built with the help of Greeks and a variety of arms and simple machinery were produced in government-run factories. Some 200,000 workers (or nearly 4 percent of the working age population) were employed in industrial establishments, excluding the substantial handicraft industry.[127] Muhammad Ali also sent some 300 young Egyptians to Europe to learn modern techniques, and many more studied in newly established "schools of medicine, engineering, chemistry, accountancy and languages and in the military and naval colleges."[128]

The British were irritated by these developments in Egypt. In spite of Palmerston's claims to support "world betterment," "the British had no desire to see the success of this attempt to diversify the Egyptian economy."[129] The irritation was at times expressed as disbelief that Egyptians or Turks were capable of such economic advances; in the words of the ever culturally sensitive Palmerston, "what energy can be expected of a people who have no heels on their shoes."[130] Richard Cobden, the ardent British free trader, was also deeply critical of Egyptian efforts at modernization: Egyptians were going against the norms of free trade, wasting good Egyptian cotton that could be put to much better use in British textile factories.[131] Such displeasures expressed in free-trade ideologies aside, what really irked the British manufacturers and government officials were Egyptian tariffs on textiles, Britain's main industry at the time. These tariffs had to be tolerated from politically powerful states like Germany, the United States, and France, but not from weaker political entities like Egypt. Prior to the 1820s, cheap British textiles had "flooded" the Egyptian market.[132] With the tariffs imposed by Muhammad Ali, these imports were replaced by Egyptian cotton goods that were now used to make much of the army's clothing and the djellaba (cotton smock) worn by numerous Egyptian peasants. Worse, from the British standpoint, Egypt was also exporting cotton goods during the 1820s and the 1830s to other parts of the Ottoman Empire, especially Hijaz (now a region in Saudi Arabia, containing the holy cities of Mecca and Medina) and Sudan, which Egypt had conquered militarily. By the 1830s British consuls in Egypt were expressing "misgivings about Egyptian competition" and conveying them back to London.[133]

The Ottoman rulers were also concerned about Muhammad Ali's growing economic and military power. The British, by now clearly the hegemonic power, not only in the region, but also worldwide, offered to help the Ottomans limit Muhammad Ali's expansionism. In return—and the British always demanded a return on their help—they imposed the Treaty of Balta Liman, in 1838, on the entire empire, including Egypt. According to this treaty, all state monopolies operating within the Ottoman Empire had to be dissolved and their tariffs on imports removed. Although the policy was justified in terms of the virtues of free trade and laissez faire, it fundamentally undermined Egypt's modernization strategy. The Treaty of London in 1840 ensured that Egypt remained part of the

Ottoman Empire but within the frame of British guardianship. Further European military intervention in 1841 led to severe limits on the size of Muhammad Ali's military. This move was not only consequential in the obvious sense of limiting his power, but also because the military was an important market for Egyptian manufactured products. Following these developments, much of Egyptian industry went into decline, not to recover until well into the twentieth century. Egypt increasingly became a producer and exporter of raw cotton (Table 2.3). By contrast, British exports of manufactured cotton goods grew spectacularly: if in the early 1830s British exports of cotton goods to Egypt were valued at £82,000, by the mid-century they had grown fourfold, to more than £350,000 (Table 2.3).

Some scholars suggest that Muhammad Ali's industrial experiment was doomed to failure, with or without the forced opening of the Egyptian economy by the British, mainly because his state-owned industries were inefficient and all state-led experiments in import substituting industrialization end up poorly.[134] These arguments are not persuasive. Yes, Muhammad Ali's industries suffered from inefficiencies, but all newcomers to industrialization face such difficulties; that is why nearly every country, including England, started its industrialization while protecting its nascent industries. What is more, Muhammad Ali was quite aware of such issues when he suggested to a British consular, "You (England) had your beginnings as I have, and they were as expensive to you as they are to me: I do not expect to begin with much success, but I shall succeed by and by."[135] What the evidence suggests instead is that within two decades of a state-led experiment in deliberate industrialization, Muhammad Ali was beginning to succeed, enough to worry the British. The British in turn used their superior military power to

Table 2.3 Anglo-Egyptian Trade, 1820–1850

Cotton Exports from Egypt (volume in cantars, annual averages)		British Textile Exports to Egypt (declared value in pounds, annual averages)	
1821–25	124,252	1827–29	27,939
1825–29	186,641	1830–34	81,968
1830–34	180,610	1835	131,672
1835–39	222,939	1836–39	198,120
1840–44	195,653	1840–44	179,328
1845–49	236,392	1845–49	307,114
		1850	354,427

Source: Owen, *The Middle East in the World Economy*, tables 4 (p. 67) and 7 (p. 85). While most cotton exports from Egypt went to Britain, the figures on the left include exports to other countries as well, especially France. One cantar equals 94 pounds.

forcibly open the Egyptian economy in a way that benefited British trade and undermined Egypt's industrial beginning. Charles Issawi's early conclusion thus still rings true: "The collapse of Muhammad Ali's schemes points out one of the major obstacles to economic development in Egypt, an obstacle that was not removed until the 1930s: the lack of political autonomy."[136]

With the imposition of the Treaty of Balta Liman and the placement of limits on the size of the Egyptian army, the British had narrowed Egypt's future political and economic options. This was a key turning point. A framework of informal empire was now in place. The next phase of Anglo-Egyptian relations was bookended by the demise of Muhammad Ali in 1849 and British occupation in 1882. During this phase, a number of Muhammad Ali's kin emerged as rulers. They continued the efforts to modernize Egypt but in highly constrained circumstances. The results were, at best, mixed. The Egyptian economy grew throughout the period but was propelled mainly by growth in cotton production and exports. Infrastructure facilities needed to support the cotton economy, such as railways, ports and canals, were also built. Egypt imported manufactured goods (for example, textiles) from Europe, especially from Britain, to both facilitate consumption and to build infrastructure (for example, railways). If the parallels with Latin America are striking, they go even further. Egyptian rulers borrowed heavily to undertake these modernizing projects. Only some of these loans led to genuine investments. For the rest, Egypt became a "Klondike on the Nile," where foreigners hoodwinked the locals and made a killing, and culpable rulers made poor decisions.[137] Growing debt led Egypt to take on further debt to pay back the original debt and, as usually happens, when a global financial crisis of sorts struck, in 1873, new loans stopped. As the British and the French demanded that their bondholders be paid back and as Egyptians started protesting, the British bombarded Alexandria, killed or imprisoned the protestors, and initiated a new phase to which I will return after a fuller discussion of developments during this period.

Following the death of Muhammad Ali in 1849, dynastic rule continued in Egypt. His kin, especially Abbas, Said, and Ismail, dominated the polity until the British takeover in 1882. Unlike Muhammad Ali, however, these subsequent rulers were considerably more constrained by European (mainly British, but also French) needs and demands. The British approach to the Ottoman Empire, including Egypt, was dominated during this period by such Liberal politicians as Palmerston and William Gladstone on the one hand, and the Conservative leader Benjamin Disraeli on the other hand. The British foreign policy of propping up the Ottoman Empire to minimize the gains of other European powers was consistent with the growing British control over Egypt during this period: Egypt, as a result, was no longer a military threat to the Ottomans and the growing economic penetration of Egypt benefited British manufacturers and bankers. Of course, the Ottoman Empire faced restiveness within and a series of military challenges from without during this period; the Tanzimat reforms failed to revive the empire against these challenges, and the British, in 1876, abandoned the policy of propping up the empire when Robert Gascoyne-Cecil—Lord Salisbury, then the secretary of state for India—concluded that "some territorial rearrangement" of the Empire would be necessary.[138] This shift paved the way for the British annexation of Cyprus in 1878 and the occupation of Egypt in 1882.

Meanwhile, on the economic front, flush from the victory against the Corn Laws in 1846 and suffering growing protectionism against British textiles in Europe and the United States, Palmerston and others vigorously sought raw materials and markets for British manufacturers. While India and other colonies were already secure markets, the establishment of an informal empire over areas as diverse as Latin America and the declining Ottoman and Ch'ing empires, were part of the new British effort in the nineteenth century. The economic importance of Egypt for Britain grew throughout this period of global economic expansion, first and foremost because of the cotton exports from Egypt, but also because of the construction of the Suez Canal, through which British commerce passed, and finally because of Egypt's growing indebtedness.

The options open to the Egyptian state were increasingly narrow. As noted, those who inherited power from Muhammad Ali could not establish any more monopolies or impose tariffs; treaties imposed by the British prohibited such policies. As Muhammad Ali's nascent industries died, exporting cotton to Britain and importing manufactured goods from Britain—especially textiles and luxury goods—emerged as the only available pathway to both modernizing Egypt and improving the incomes of Egyptian elites. Thus began Egypt's integration with the global economy. Soon after coming to power, Abbas (1848–54) needed the help of the British to deal with the Porte. In exchange, the British first pressured Abbas to open up grain sales to British merchants; this undermined one important source of revenue of the Egyptian state. The British state also pressed Abbas to facilitate British private investments in railways.[139] While the development of railways was in mutual interest (insofar as it helped the development of the cotton economy), unlike Argentina, Abbas, following Muhammad Ali, decided to involve the Egyptian state in the construction and operation of railways. Nevertheless, the similarities with Muhammad Ali were superficial: loans, equipment, contractors, and, eventually, even the personnel in the ministry of railways of the Egyptian state came from Britain.[140] The first railway was opened as early as 1853, and by 1858 Cairo was linked to both Alexandria and Suez. Thereafter, railway construction continued at a rapid pace; by World War I Egypt had some 4,000 miles of railway tracks in operation.

The development of cotton exports—free of state control—also led to other changes.[141] The remaining restrictions on the private ownership of land were removed, leading to the creation of a class system in the countryside. Because foreign ownership of land was also allowed, this led to significant foreign financial interest in the buying and selling of land; foreign capital entered mortgage and other types of loan markets in a big way. During Ismail's rule (1863–79), the area under irrigation expanded vastly, facilitating an increase in cotton production and exports. Canals that would facilitate transportation were also built, some of which were navigable year around. Telegraph lines came to cover the country. All these developments required significant public expenditures. Some of the resources were mobilized internally by taxing agriculture. During the American Civil War, Egyptian cotton exports boomed; this, too, eased the resource constraint. But in the end, much of the infrastructure development was financed by foreign loans. The public debt was growing throughout this period and was seriously exacerbated by the construction of the Suez Canal.

If British economic interests in Egypt were focused on selling textiles, building railways, and buying cotton, the building of the Suez Canal was really a French project. As the *Economist* quipped in 1869 (the year the canal was opened), the Suez was built "by French energy and Egyptian money for British advantage."[142] How the Suez was built is a sordid tale of French intrigue and fraud, of Egyptian dependence and gullibility, and of the British capacity in the nineteenth century to always come out on the top. The details need not detain us here.[143] The idea of the canal had been around since the days of Napoleon's occupation of Egypt but was opposed by Muhammad Ali because, prescient as he was, he understood that such a canal would undermine Egypt's independence. Not even Palmerston at the outset thought that Suez was a commercially viable project, especially because it would compete with the British-built railways in Egypt. The project was pushed instead by Ferdinand de Lesseps, a French Cecil Rhodes of sorts, who had befriended the "corpulent" and "insecure" Said when he was a boy, apparently feeding him spaghetti in secret while Muhammad Ali lectured him on the need to lose weight.[144] When Said became the ruler of Egypt in 1854, Lesseps rushed back to Cairo to finally pursue his long-held dream of building the Suez Canal. Said trusted Lesseps as a mentor of sorts, but Lesseps talked Said into agreeing to terms for the project that turned out to be "usurious."[145]

According to the terms on which the Suez was constructed, Said was obliged to buy a significant portion of the canal's shares, thus financing its construction, and to provide free Egyptian land and corvée labor. Some 100,000 Egyptian laborers died digging the canal with their bare hands.[146] By one calculation, Egypt paid 70 percent of the cost of building the canal for a 15 percent share of the profit.[147] Said, meanwhile, commissioned an opera for the canal's ostentatious opening ceremony in 1869. Short of cash, when Said was unable to buy the shares he had signed on to buy, he borrowed heavily. As much as one-third of promised loans went into paying commissions and other dubious charges made by bankers. And when the debts on the loans became pressing, Said and subsequent rulers borrowed still more. When Egypt was in dire straits, Prime Minister Disraeli borrowed £4 million from the Rothschilds on behalf of the British government, bought 40 percent of the shares of the Suez Canal, and then boastfully told Queen Victoria, "[I]t is yours, ma'am."[148] It was an exaggeration at that point; however, the French defeat in the Franco-Prussian War had weakened France, which was now in no position to further its claims on the canal. A few decades hence, much of the traffic passing through the Suez was British, and "the British treasury was receiving dividends to the tune of about £1,500,000 a year in return for the original investment of £4,000,000."[149]

Besides the payments on loans for building Egypt's infrastructure, including the Suez, the capitulations were an added strain on Egyptian finances. To repeat, these capitulations originated much earlier, aimed at protecting Christians within the Ottoman Empire. During the nineteenth century, these protective clauses were increasingly modified to protect the Europeans in Egypt from taxation and other edicts of the state. Such Mediterranean cities of the Levant as Alexandria had long attracted other Europeans. As the Egyptian state lost sovereignty during the second half of the nineteenth century, foreigners felt more protected against state incursions than ever, and their numbers grew rapidly; if in 1850 there were some 6,000 Europeans in Egypt, by 1880 some 100,000 foreigners had migrated to Egypt, a majority to Alexandria but also to Cairo and other places. These foreigners came to control significant portions of the dynamic sectors of the economy while paying minimum taxes, weakening the state. Foreign counselors, especially British and French, further ensured that their respective citizens enjoyed autonomy from local laws; in the words of one historian, "threatening and cajoling, blustering and bullying, resorting even to gunboat diplomacy, the consuls demonstrated beyond any doubt their emergence as the new politicians of Egypt."[150]

Following the death of Muhammad Ali and prior to the second British occupation in 1882, Egypt's foreign trade and indebtedness grew. As to foreign trade, it is clear in Table 2.4 that cotton exports grew throughout this period—nearly 80 percent of them going to Britain—and even more spectacularly during the next phase of British occupation, as we will see. While this growth in exports facilitated rising incomes, Egypt was now rapidly becoming a specialized economy, with one commodity as its main export; the limits of this pathway to growth would emerge sharply in the early twentieth century. Moreover, much of the profitable cotton economy was increasingly attracting foreign investment

Table 2.4 Egyptian Trade, 1850–1882

Annual Cotton Exports (in million pounds)		Annual Total Trade (imports and exports, in million £E)		Annual imports of main manufactured goods, 1870–74 (in million £E)	
1850–54	0.92	1850	3.7	'Manufacturers'	1.9
1855–59	1.3			Marble	0.16
1860–64	6.1	1860	5.1	Hardware	0.11
1865–69	10.2			Hats	0.11
1875–79	8.4	1880	21.8	Shoes	0.09

Sources: Columns 1 and 3 are from Owen, *Middle East in the World Economy*, table 22 (p. 136) and table 24 (p. 150) respectively. £E stands for Egyptian pound; the value of Egyptian pound was nearly identical to the British pound during this period. The data in middle column is from Issawi, "Egypt since 1800," p. 8.

in sales, transportation, loans, irrigation, and even some land ownership. As the total trade figures in Table 2.4 suggest, Egypt's imports also grew during this period. Not surprisingly, these imports were dominated by manufactured goods, especially textiles and materials for building railways and other infrastructure projects; the imports of luxury items (for the use of Egyptian and the sizable foreign elite) are also notable. As in the case of Argentina, then, Egypt during this period also began its journey toward becoming a commodity exporter and taker of manufactured goods.

The other major development throughout this second phase was Egypt's growing public debt and, related to it, the growing control of the Egyptian state by foreigners. Muhammad Ali's death was followed by a "spectacular growth of banking activity" in Egypt: by 1877, eight banks had provided telegraphic exchange with London and Paris.[151] These and other European financial institutions helped finance a variety of projects pursued by Egyptian rulers; these have been discussed and include investments in activities deemed essential to facilitating the development of cotton exports—building of railways, ports, and irrigation, as well as such megaprojects pushed by the Europeans as the Suez Canal. Although some of the borrowed money was well invested, a fair amount of it was not. Not only were the terms of the loans often onerous, there was downright fraud: for example, by 1880 Egypt owed nearly £100 million, of which only £65 million had gone into its coffers; the balance went toward a variety of commissions and fees, creating enormous "fraudulence."[152] The ambitious but gullible Said had incurred much of this debt, which Ismail inherited. Ismail, in turn, borrowed further, in part to pay off Suez-related debts, but also to build railways. By

1873, Egypt's annual interest on this debt—some £5 million—was already more than its revenues.

Ismail made a serious proposal for debt restructuring that the British rejected. The Cave Mission of 1876, created to study the debt situation in Egypt, instead suggested that there had been financial incompetence on part of Ismail and led to a dual control over Egyptian finances by the British and the French. From here on the decisions of the Egyptian government on revenues and expenditures were to be controlled by the French and the English, mainly the English. At the center of this growing drama of debt and further loss of Egyptian sovereignty was the British representative, Sir Evelyn Baring, of the Baring family, whose firm had lent large sums of money to Egypt. After the British occupation of Egypt in 1882, Baring returned from India, in 1883, to be "crowned" the "king" of Egypt; he popularly came to be known as Lord Cromer.[153] Meanwhile, he played a central role in persuading the British government to not accept Ismail's proposal for financial restructuring and, in 1879, became the British representative in control of Egyptian finances. Evelyn Baring was also part of the group that in 1880 promulgated the "law of liquidation," which effectively put "a stranglehold on Egypt," committing it to firm payments on its debts to its creditors, including to his family firm, the Baring Brothers, which we encountered in the context of the Barings loan to Argentina.[154]

Although the Egyptian state was increasingly coming under French and British control, it is important to underscore that by 1880, British interests "clearly predominated." The "British were taking 80 percent of Egypt's exports, supplying 44 percent of its imports, and owned much of the public debt . . . [moreover] 80 percent of its [Suez] traffic was British and Disraeli had snatched 44 percent of the Canal Company's share from Ismail in 1875."[155] So, when a nationalist reaction of sorts set in against the growing foreign control over Egypt, it was the British who were most concerned. The so-called Urabi revolt, with its rallying cry of "Egypt for Egyptians," was aimed, first, at the khedives for accommodating the demands of foreigners and then, eventually, at the foreigners, especially the British. As a variety of factions among the religious and commercial elite joined forces with the military leader Urabi Pasha, the revolt took on the proportions of a possible national revolution.[156] The British ruthlessly suppressed this revolt, first by bombarding Alexandria from its offshore navy ships, killing and arresting many of Urabi's supporters, and then proceeding inland, arresting Urabi and occupying Egypt.

Gladstone's occupation of Egypt has been much debated by historians.[157] Not only did the systematic dismemberment of the Ottoman Empire begin with this occupation, but arguably, it was also the beginning of the European "scramble for Africa."[158] One line of thinking that proposes that such "men on the spot" as

Cromer persuaded the Liberal Gladstone to occupy Egypt will simply not do.[159] Disraeli's claims notwithstanding, the Liberals were as imperialist as the Tories during this period; in the words of George Trevelyan, both were inclined "to extend the boundaries of the Empire."[160] Moreover, during a period when Britain was extending its empire left, right, and center, the most men on the spot did was influence the timing and the modality of imperial control; the brain behind the systematic imperial expansion was located in London. The simple fact is that by 1882 Britain already exercised enormous influence on Egypt, and the economic and strategic importance of Egypt had grown steadily since the end of Muhammad Ali. Links between trade, foreign investment, and debt have been noted, as has been the growing importance of Suez. When these interests were threatened by indigenous forces, Gladstone and Lord Granville took account of the power situation in the region—especially the growing weakness of the Ottomans and the renewed aggressiveness of the French, as was manifest in the grab of Tunis in 1881—and intervened militarily to consolidate British control over Egypt.

The perennial issue of whether the importance of Egypt to Britain was more strategic or more economic also ought to be addressed. As I have argued all along, economic versus strategic interests are not as easy to separate in the study of imperial motives as some simplistic arguments involving realists versus Marxists would have us believe; states promote the interests of their capitalists, in part because capitalists are politically influential and because they create wealth, and wealth is the basis of national power. One ready candidate for what really moved Britain to intervene in Egypt could have been the need to ensure that British banks and bondholders were paid back the money owed to them by the Egyptian authorities. In Cromer's own words, "[T]he origin of the Egyptian question in its present phase was financial."[161] The importance of finance in the study of British imperialism, in turn, has a long pedigree, anywhere from the classic works of Hobson and Lenin to the more recent scholarship of Cain and Hopkins.[162] While Egypt's public debt was clearly an important concern of some in Britain, so was the importance of Egypt as a source of high-quality raw cotton for others; for yet others, it was the need to protect the numerous British investments there, especially in railways. Control over the Suez Canal was also of great importance by then. Nearly 80 percent of British trade with India had passed through the Suez by 1880; this shorter route not only reduced the cost of private trade, but revenues from the Suez also added handsomely to the British treasury. Egypt was thus clearly of considerable economic importance to the British by 1882. As Urabi demanded "Egypt for Egyptians," and power competition in Europe over the fate of the Ottoman Empire was heating up, Gladstone and others decided to risk alienating other European powers, took preemptive action, and gobbled up Egypt.

Following British occupation, Egypt pretty much became a British colony.[163] Unlike post-1857 India, Egypt was never a formal colony of Britain. However, also unlike with Argentina, no one is likely to debate that post-1882 Egypt was about as close to being a British colony as you can be without being a colony. At the start of World War I, Egypt became a formal protectorate of Britain. Arguments for self-determination notwithstanding, Woodrow Wilson accepted this status for Egypt. And then, in 1922, Egypt formally gained sovereignty, which in effect was severely restricted until the early 1950s. Consistent with the focus of this chapter on Britain's nineteenth-century informal empire, my discussion here will mainly analyze the trends in Anglo-Egyptian relations up to World War I, including only a few comments on the subsequent developments.

For much of this period, Egypt was ruled by Evelyn Baring (Lord Cromer, 1883–1907), followed by the proconsuls Eldon Gorst and Herbert Kitchener. As noted, Lord Cromer was a member of the Baring family, and had been a central figure in Egypt during Britain's financial negotiations with Ismail. After that, and before taking up his position as a proconsul in occupied Egypt, Cromer did a stint in India, and he brought that experience to Egypt. Cromer has been described as among the "cleverest" of British proconsuls, who represented the "best and the worst" of the men who occupied such roles in Britain's imperial history: "The patrician pose and pompous oratory were accompanied by commercial obsession and counting-house meanness, the professed magnanimity by practiced pettiness, the Olympian project by trivial errors, the attention to detail by neglect of basic trends, a sense of the broad sweep of world history by adherence to the narrow Victorian code of an officer and a gentleman."[164]

After Britain began occupying Egypt, the British dissolved the Egyptian army and reorganized it under the control of British officers. With Cromer in charge, much of the government also came to be controlled by British civil servants: if in 1885 there were about a hundred senior British civil officials within the Egyptian state, by 1906 the number had grown to more than 1,000.[165] Following the Indian model of colonial rule, Cromer also established a ruling alliance with large landowners that helped "safeguard imperial interests in the countryside."[166] British colonial administration in Egypt attached the "highest priority" to maintaining "regular payments on the external debt."[167] With that as the primary goal, Cromer did in Egypt what foreign debtors, then and now, have always demanded: cut government expenditure, improve revenue collection, and develop the export economy to collect ample foreign exchange to pay back foreign debt. There is evidence to suggest that Cromer imposed an efficient government on Egypt that was considerably less corrupt and wasteful than the preceding governments.[168] His economic policies, however, mainly benefited the bondholders and other British investors.

Cromer successfully encouraged increases in cotton production and exports. The main vehicle for this was an increase in investment in irrigation. As newer lands came under cultivation, or the same land began supporting more crops per year, cotton production and exports grew.[169] The growth of cotton production, however, as well as the rate of growth of overall agricultural production, decelerated in comparison to what had come before. Between 1820 and 1878, for example, cotton production had grown some fifty times—albeit from a low base—and per capita farm output, more than five times.[170] Driving this growth, as we have seen, were the early public investments in irrigation by Muhammad Ali and then the continuing efforts in the same direction by his highly constrained—but still partly sovereign—progeny. Once Cromer took over, and his early efforts at "structural adjustment" went into effect, public expenditures were cut back, and investments into irrigation decelerated.[171] Good land for cultivation was also becoming scarce. Although cotton production did increase, this was often at the expense of other food crops such as beans and barley, and commercial crops such as sugarcane. The rate of growth in agricultural production decelerated; between 1878 and 1899, per capita agricultural production grew at some 0.5 percent per annum. This was still good in comparison to what followed: from 1899 onward, per capita agricultural output in Egypt declined steadily until World War I, and then did not climb back to its late nineteenth century levels until the 1960s.

Other actions and inactions of British colonial authorities in Egypt also had a pernicious impact. For example, consider the fate of Egypt's industrial development. Muhammad Ali's early import-substitution efforts were by now nearly forgotten, and Ismail's limited moves toward this end could not succeed without the policy autonomy he needed to provide some protections. With their enormous advantage in cotton production, however, the Egyptians again made efforts to establish textile factories. These might have succeeded. However, the British authorities, concerned about Lancashire producers, insisted that the factories "pay a countervailing duty of 8 percent on all their products."[172] So much for a commitment to laissez-faire! With the colonial state actively discouraging industrialization, it is not surprising that Egypt's industrialization did not commence again until the 1930s, when the global depression and nationalist demands created some policy autonomy within Egypt to impose tariffs. Cromer and his colleagues also had no interest in encouraging education in Egypt. This reflected both a concern for limiting public expenditures and for political considerations. Cromer had no use for Egyptian nationalists; using words that were nearly identical to those his counterparts were using in India, he argued that there was no Egyptian nation and that Egyptian nationalists were only a self-serving elite, "worse than Irishmen."[173] Since the link between education, the rise of an indigenous middle class, and the emergence of nationalism was clear to Cromer from his Indian experience, he—and others in Africa, too, in subsequent decades—shied away from investing in education. The Egyptian economy throughout the period under discussion thus remained an agricultural economy of some eight to ten million people, with low levels of literacy and a foreign middle class. The per capita incomes of Egyptians reflected trends in agricultural production: by one good estimate, if per capita GDP had been growing in Egypt during the late nineteenth century, these incomes declined in the early twentieth century, and then stagnated thereafter until World War I.[174]

As importantly, Egypt now became extremely dependent on the export of one commodity—cotton—for any possible source of dynamism. Meanwhile, Cromer was achieving what he had set out to achieve. Egypt's foreign trade grew rapidly. Between 1880 and 1912, Egyptian exports more than doubled, and "both the level and rate of growth of per capita exports from Egypt far exceeded the average for medium sized" peripheral economies of the period.[175] By the turn of the century, nearly 90 percent of these exports were cotton exports. Imports also grew rapidly, textiles from Britain being the single most important item.[176] Under Cromer, Egypt also ran a favorable balance of payments; it had to, to pay back the interest on its public debt and dividends on private foreign investment, which also grew during this period.[177] Foreign investors felt more secure after the occupation and foreign investment grew rapidly. Between 1888 and 1914, direct foreign investment increased from some £23 million to £111 million, or nearly fivefold.[178] The sectoral distribution of this investment is telling. Nearly half if it was in mortgage companies, which were helping to finance land and other investments related to the profitable cotton production for exports.[179] Much of the remaining investment—excluding the investment in the Suez Canal, of course—was also oriented toward cotton production, going to irrigation and transport. By one account, "close to three-fourths of all foreign direct investment in Egypt between 1880 and World War I was related to the boom in agricultural land, primarily cotton land."[180] By the beginning of the war, Egypt had become a classic colonial economy: a large, foreign-controlled cotton plantation of sorts (with the pyramids and the Nile), which attracted investment to support cotton production, sold its cotton to Britain, and bought British manufactured cotton goods in return. This "lop-sided development," to use Charles Issawi's felicitous phrase again, would not serve Egypt well in the future.[181]

To conclude this discussion on Britain's informal empire in Egypt: It is clear that British motives in Egypt during the nineteenth century were somewhat more mixed than they were, say, in Argentina. As we have seen, British interest in Argentina, or for that matter in Brazil or other parts of Latin America, was mainly economic. Since British interests reflected developments in Britain's domestic economy, it is not surprising that we see a similar pattern in the case of

Egypt: opening the economy for trade in the early part of the century, including destroying indigenous efforts at industrialization, and then focusing on cotton-related investments during the second half. In addition to economic interests, however, Britain's policy toward Egypt had to keep additional considerations in mind: Egypt was nominally part of a weakening Ottoman Empire, whose fate concerned many other powers; initially, Egypt was located on Britain's overland route to India, and then, with the opening of the Suez Canal, much of British trade to India passed through Suez; and despite their relative military weakness, the French were an important power in the region. These factors complicated Anglo-Egyptian relations during this period but did not alter the core focus on trade and investment. In Palmerston's own words, while the Ottoman Empire was clearly of political importance, Britain's commercial interests in the region, including in Egypt, were "of no less importance."[182]

As to mechanisms of rule, over time, British influence on Egypt became more and more direct. This pattern contrasted with that in Argentina, where, as the nineteenth century progressed, a collaborating indigenous ruling class reduced the need for the overt use of force. British influence over Egypt started out indirectly, when it imposed economic openness on the Ottoman Empire as a whole, which then led to economic penetration of Egypt. Muhammad Ali and his kin, however, were dynastic rulers, not totally beholden to an export-oriented agrarian oligarchy; they were also reluctant free traders. As these rulers succumbed to British pressures, more nationalist indigenous political forces rebelled, leading to Britain's overt use of force and imposition of near colonial control over Egypt. Although the mechanisms of British influence over Egypt and Argentina thus differed—mainly because politics in these respective polities were organized differently—the impact was similar. Egypt, like Argentina, benefited from the development of an export economy, especially insofar as the per capita incomes of the producing classes grew. However, as in many other cases of commodity-focused economies, this did not lead to the development of a more complex economy. Egypt became heavily dependent on cotton production and exports; when these reached their limits in the early twentieth century, the British did not encourage diversification of the economy. Egypt only regained some policy autonomy during the 1930s, to begin afresh its journey toward an industrial economy; this was nearly a century after the British had destroyed Muhammad Ali's efforts in this direction in the nineteenth century. A whole wasted century!

China

In the early nineteenth century, China was a giant, insular country that was moderately well governed, at least by the standards of traditional agrarian monarchies.

Throughout the eighteenth century, China's population had grown rapidly, from under 200 million to nearly 400 million people, straining resources and encouraging restiveness. Because it was a relatively self-satisfied civilization that had grown wary of foreigners due to repeated invasions by barbarians, Chinese rulers sought to minimize contacts with the outside world. Although China was not quite as insular as Japan was in the period, it limited trade with Westerners to the southern port city of Canton. British contacts with China at Canton in the early nineteenth century were mediated mainly by the East India Company, whose ships regularly brought opium, cotton, and silver to Canton (mostly from India), and took tea and silk back to London. As the century progressed and British expansion became worldwide, the British opened up China, too, often using gunboats. The century-long operation of Britain's informal empire in China is analyzed here in three rough phases. During the first phase, say, from the turn of the century to the Opium Wars in 1839–42 and 1859–60, opium trade grew steadily until the Chinese authorities threatened to shut it down. Britain's forced opening of China that followed in the second phase then led to trade growth, the imposition of indemnities, and slow but steady control over China's public finances. Other major powers joined Britain in sharing the fruits of the open door. Japan's invasion of China in 1895 marked the beginning of the third phase, which lasted until World War I. Britain's investments in China grew during this phase, as did loans, both for economic projects and to bolster a failing state. The scramble for China also speeded up, involving several major powers, which carved up China, especially coastal China and the Yangtze region, into their respective spheres of influence. The 1911 revolution within China and the coming of World War I marked the end of Britain's informal empire in China. From then on, Japan's influence over China grew substantially. Meanwhile, central authority in China disintegrated, leading to a half-century of internal warfare, as foreigners picked off what they could and the communists gained power.

Early British interest in China was mainly commercial. As discussed in chapter 1, the East India Company had a monopoly on trade in Asia in the eighteenth century. This monopoly on trade with India lasted until 1813; and on trade with China, until 1833. It is thus not surprising that early British patterns of trade with China reflected the interests of the East India Company. As the East India Company conquered more and more of India during the second half of the century, the company rulers gained access to substantial land revenues. Much of this revenue was used to build the British Indian Army and to rule India; a portion was also used to buy Indian calico, which sold handsomely in London and made a neat profit for East India Company stockholders, who included numerous members of the British Parliament. This wonderful system of transferring the resources of poor Indian peasants to the London elite ran into problems when the emerging manufacturing classes in Britain succeeded in their demand that Indian calico be kept out of the British market. The company then channeled some Indian calico to feed the Atlantic slave trade, and also turned its attention to Chinese tea as a commodity to be bought at Canton, paid for with Indian revenues (often in the form of silver), and sold back in London, where the taste for tea was growing. Such were the beginnings of Britain's commercial relations with China.

Certain important developments in the late eighteenth century put this nascent Anglo-Chinese trade on a forward footing. First, Britain now wanted to encourage the export of manufactured cotton goods to conquered India. And, since the demand for Indian commodities in Britain was not always reliable, finding a steady outlet for some Indian commodity was also a priority for the East India Company. The discovery that Indian opium could be sold in China was, then, the second development of great significance for Britain's eventual relations with China. Why the Chinese developed a taste for smoking opium, but not the Indians, will probably never be known. Be that as it may, the demand for opium in China led the Calcutta-based East India Company to establish a monopoly on the growth and production of opium in eastern India in 1773. From then on, the East India Company was quite deliberate in cultivating the Chinese demand for opium; in the words of one of the company's British opium examiners, "[T]he great object of the Bengal opium agencies is to furnish an article suitable to the peculiar tastes of the population of China."[183] Unused Indian revenues could now be used to produce opium in India, which was then packed neatly in chests that were shipped out of Calcutta and then exchanged for tea in Canton for sale in London. Meanwhile, the demand for tea in Britain was growing: if Chinese tea worth £1.5 million was sold in London in 1785, by 1815 the amount had doubled, to £3 million.[184] A triangular trade of sorts—created and nurtured by British interests—thus began to take shape: manufactured British cotton goods to India, British Indian opium to China, and Chinese tea to Britain.

Britain's trade with China grew but not briskly in the early nineteenth century. One significant obstacle early on was the reluctance of the Chinese authorities to open China to Western trade. An early British trade mission to the Chinese emperor, led by Lord Macartney in 1792–93, was a total failure; instead of entertaining British requests to ease trade restrictions, Emperor Qianlong famously told the British ambassador, "[W]e have no use for your country's manufacturers."[185] If the British blamed this failure on Chinese "imbecility" and "obstinacy," the Chinese returned the compliment, arguing that the British were "greedy adventurers, who were devoid of any cultural graces."[186] Beneath the apparent cultural divide, the Chinese had good political and economic reasons to remain insular. Chinese rulers had always worried about barbarian attacks from the north. The Manchus had come from there; they knew the dangers of foreign intrusions. Now they also worried about the barbarians from the south. The threat of peasant restiveness and disaffected elites—especially of regional elite at the periphery of the empire—was ever-present. For Chinese authorities, maintaining the delicate power equilibrium required minimum external intrusion. Moreover, the Chinese already produced high-quality goods. For example, the correspondence in the early nineteenth century of Jardine, Matheson, and Co., a prominent British trading firm in Canton, talks of the "superiority of the Chinese native nankeen cotton cloth over Manchester cotton goods in point of quality and cost."[187] Whereas the British were able to force their textiles into India during this period, the Chinese authorities resisted as long as they could, until the gunboats arrived.

Under restrictive conditions, British trade at Canton in the early nineteenth century grew but did not flourish. The East India Company and a few private traders were allowed to establish "factories" outside the Canton city walls, where they lived and from where they carried on their trade.[188] Some of these private traders were from countries other than Britain, but others were British on Austrian or other national passports, avoiding the British monopoly laws that protected the East India Company. Members of the East India Company were very much in charge of representing the interests of these foreign traders to the Chinese. On the Chinese side, a loosely organized group of private traders, the cohong, were authorized by the emperor to undertake the trade. The cohong, in turn, were under the supervision of a public official, the superintendent of maritime customs (the hoppo), who reported back to the emperor in Peking via intermediaries. The cohong licensed the Chinese compradors who worked for British traders and carried out the actual buying and selling. The compradors procured tea and silk from various parts of China for the East India Company to purchase. Since the Chinese were not keen to buy British manufactured goods, trade at this early stage was not balanced: between 1792 and 1807, for example, company's shipments from Canton were worth £27 million, but shipments of English goods into Canton amounted to only £16.6 million.[189] The East India Company paid the balance with silver and, of course, opium.

The opium trade was contraband and was organized differently. After some initial forays into smuggling opium directly into China, the East India Company outsourced the illegal part of the trade to private British agency houses, such as Jardine, Matheson, and Co. and Dent and Co. The company auctioned the Indian opium to these private traders in Calcutta. Large, armed, private ships loaded with opium from India would then dock some distance from Canton, or at the nearby island of Lintin. Chinese traders would put in their opium orders with the comprador and often pay in cash. After the British private traders approved

Table 2.5 Old Trade at Canton, 1817–33 (Annual Averages in Million pounds)

Year	China's Exports via Canton (mainly tea)	Imports into China, via Canton (including opium)	Opium Imports
1817–22	2.5	2.8	1.7
1823–28	2.7	4.0	1.8
1829–33	2.7	4.6	2.6

Source: Greenberg, *British Trade and the Opening of China*, app. 1, Tables A (p. 217) and D (pp. 220–221). Dollar figures in the original have been converted into pound sterling at the prevailing rate of £1.00 = $4.85.

the sale, they often exchanged this cash with the East India Company for notes that would be exchanged for sterling in London. The East India Company would use this cash to buy tea to sell in London, and then the proceeds were used to pay the private merchants who held promissory notes from Canton and the custom duties to the British state, and, of course, profit for the company. Meanwhile, in China, fast-moving boats rowed by Chinese boatmen would take the opium from the docked British freighters and scurry them up the mouth of the Pearl River for sale and distribution throughout the country. Since the trade was both lucrative and illegal, it encouraged massive corruption; according to a missionary posted in China at the time, "[I]n China every man is a smuggler in opium, from the Emperor downwards."[190]

By the time the East India Company lost its Chinese trade monopoly in 1833, the triangular trade—involving, to repeat, British textile exports to India, Indian opium to China, and Chinese tea to London—had matured. (see chapter 1 on British textile trade with India. I return to this topic in chapter 3.) The scale of the trade involving China is evident in Table 2.5. Chinese tea continued to be the main item of interest to the East India Company, but it is also clear from the table that it would have been difficult for the East India Company to sustain these exports without the opium imports from India to China. Figures 2.1 and 2.2 further help to put this early Anglo-Chinese trade into perspective. It is clear in Figure 2.1 that British trade with China was fairly stable at a low level until the forced opening of China in the 1840s. The consistent gap between exports and imports until late in the century is also notable. Even after China's forced opening, the British could not sell enough goods to the Chinese. This gap was consistently made up by the opium from India, which is not included in Figure 2.1 (because opium exports to China from British India were officially Indian,

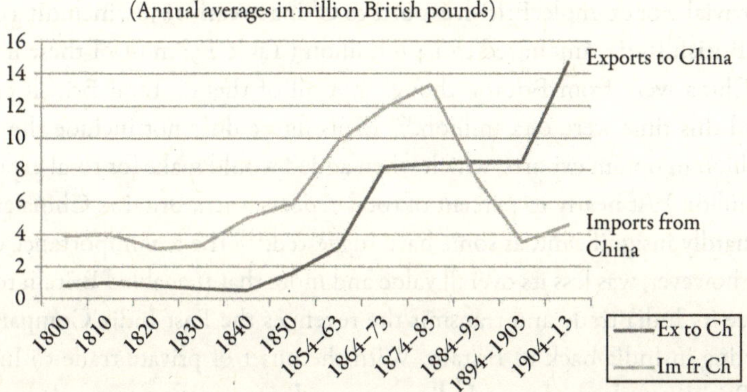

FIGURE 2.1 British Trade with China, 1800–1913.

Source: The 1854–1913 data are from E. M. Gull, *British Economic Interests in the Far East* (London: Oxford University Press, 1943), pp. 51–52; the earlier data are from Britten Dean, "British Informal Empire: The Case of China," *Journal of Commonwealth and Comparative Politics* 14, no. 11 (1976): p. 72.

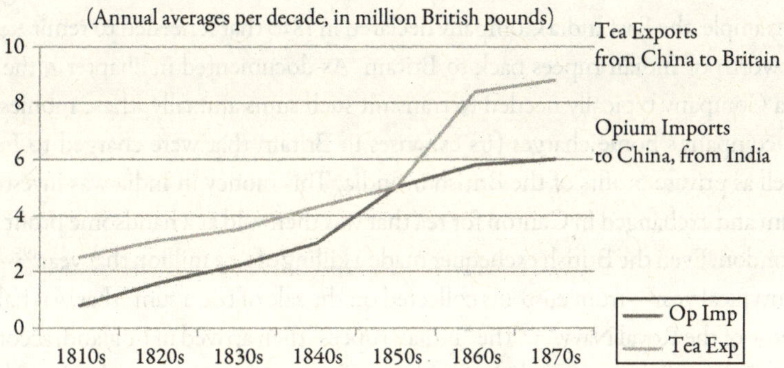

FIGURE 2.2 China, opium imports, and tea exports, nineteenth century.

Source: The data on opium imports are from Yen-P'ing Hao, *The Commercial Revolution in Nineteenth Century China* (Berkeley: University of California Press, 1986), 69. Mexican (or Spanish) silver dollars were converted at the rate of £1 = 6 M$, following the conversion rates given in Greenberg, *British Trade and the Opening of China*, viii. The tea data are estimated from Dean, "British Informal Empire," p. 73.

not British, exports). The pattern of opium exports to China from India and tea imports from China to Britain are depicted in Figure 2.2. It ought to be clear from this data that the growth of tea imports to Britain depended on the growth of opium imports to China.

The old Canton trade was important for Britain, but the nature of its importance needs to be spelled out. Although the overall amount was small, it was far from trivial. For example, British exports to China in early 1830s, including opium from British India, amounted to £4.6 million (Table 2.5; most of these imports into China were from Britain, though not all of them). Total British exports around this time were £42 million.[191] (This figure does not include the nearly £3 million in opium exports, which when added would make for total exports of £45 million.) At nearly 10 percent of total exports, then, Britain's China exports were hardly insignificant, as some have suggested.[192] The real importance of this trade, however, was less its overall value and more that it enabled Britain to both balance its India trade and transmit the revenues the East India Company was collecting in India back to Britain. With the onset of private trade to India in 1813, British textile exports to India grew rapidly, amounting to nearly a quarter of the total volume of its textile exports by the mid-century.[193] Since Indian goods were not selling readily back in Britain—but Chinese tea was—Indian opium to China helped balance this trade: "For the Lancashire exporter, the most profitable mode of remittance from India was via China. Calcutta led to Canton."[194]

Even more important from the British point of view was the fact that Canton trade enabled the East India Company to transmit Indian land revenues to England. For example, the East India Company declared in 1830 that it needed to remit £4 million worth of Indian rupees back to Britain. As documented in chapter 1, the East India Company typically needed to transmit such sums annually; these monies covered company's home charges (its expenses in Britain that were charged to India), as well as private profits of the British in India. This money in India was invested in opium and exchanged in Canton for tea that was then sold at a handsome profit back in London. Even the British exchequer made a killing of £3.3 million that year[195]—not an untypical year—from customs collected on the sale of tea, a sum "that was half the expense of the Royal Navy."[196] The "Indian rupees" then arrived in England, according to Fay, "concealed, so to speak, inside chests of congou, souchong and pekoe."[197] Fay goes on to summarize the whole British-run Asian trading system nicely:

> What a marvelous interlocking system it was—and at the bottom of it, opium! Its sale in Calcutta contributed significantly to the revenue of the Government of India. Its sale at Lintin financed the purchase of England's teas, while at the same time making it easier for returning English nabobs and the government of India to get Indian rupees home. In England, Whitehall depended upon the tea duty for a considerable part of its revenue. How convenient the drug was, how indispensable even—but at the same time how dangerous to the future."[198]

The danger lay, of course, in the fact that opium was no ordinary commodity; it was an addictive drug, the trading of which was banned in China.

By 1816, opium smoking was already common "in all parts of the (Chinese) Empire."[199] Over the next decade or two, the price of opium fell sharply as opium from western India (the Malwa opium) supplemented the supply of the Bengal opium (the so-called Patna and Benares opium); if a chest of opium sold for some £400 in 1822, by 1832 it cost less than £150.[200] The East India Company's opium revenues continued to increase because the volume of opium imported into China grew rapidly. If China imported some 4,000 to 5,000 chests of opium annually before 1820, by 1839 it was importing 40,000 chests (this number would again double after the Opium Wars, as we will see).[201] The scale of opium imports now required exports of silver out of China to cover the costs of the opium.[202] By 1836 opium trade was substantial, so substantial that in retrospect, it has been characterized as "the world's most valuable single commodity trade of the nineteenth century."[203] There is evidence that by the 1830s opium addiction in China had spread to the literati, the mercantile classes, senior government officials, eunuchs, and members of the imperial clan.[204] Addiction even afflicted the armed forces, so much so "that the troops were incapable of combat."[205] Not surprisingly, arguments for strict prohibition on opium imports began to grow in China.

If the British had any moral qualms about pushing opium into China, they seem to have been overcome by the desire to make money. For example, William Jardine, who had helped establish Jardine, Matheson, and Co., was a leading smuggler of opium in Canton. He was a Scottish doctor who obviously did not pay much heed to his Hippocratic Oath to do no harm. He even advised his friends to invest in opium, because it was both a highly profitable and a safe investment: this was "because you got your money before you gave your order. Whatever the difficulty was in landing it afterward, you had nothing to do with it."[206] After the First Opium War, Jardine returned to Britain with a fortune, and was elected a Member of Parliament; as is often the case, a fortune washed away all sins. Even those who peddled in the market of sin—the missionaries—were intimately involved with the opium trade. They arrived on the same ships that brought opium to China, and they often acted as translators for the opium traders. God's mission in China was thus subsidized by opium profits: "Christ and opium! . . . [What] an irresistible combination."[207]

As noted, the East India Company's Chinese trade monopoly was abolished in 1833. After that China trade became private trade. The British government also sent a representative, Lord William Napier (who was the first superintendent of British trade in China, soon to be followed by others), to Canton to take over the political functions formerly performed by representatives of the East India Company. Over the next few years, however, Britain's relations with China deteriorated rapidly, leading to the first Opium War in 1839. The basic underlying dynamic was fueled by Britain's desire to forcibly open China for trade. This desire was evident from the moment Napier was appointed. He shared the concern of British private traders that trading opportunities in China were far too restricted and needed to be opened. He was a close friend of Jardine, a fellow Scotsman, and lived in his house while posted in Canton.[208] State-capital links do not get any closer! Napier fancied himself another Robert Clive, and was ready to expand British influence in China. He argued with Palmerston for "housebreaking" and suggested, as early as 1833, that "three or four frigates and brigs with a few steady British troops, not sepoys (Indian soldiers from British Indian army), would settle the thing."[209] While Napier grossly underestimated what it would take to open China up—his early effort to open China militarily with two armed ships was a total failure, and he died shortly thereafter in China—his failed gunboat diplomacy marked the beginning of Britain's militant foreign policy toward China.

As noted, Palmerston became Britain's foreign secretary in 1835. He favored a "forward policy" in China that would further not only "Britain's national interest" but also the views of the "middle-class."[210] Business groups in Britain sensed opportunity and started mobilizing to open China. Jardine and Matheson, both formerly with the East India Company, and now partners in the leading opium-smuggling firm in China, which bore both their names, became leaders of sorts in this effort. At their urging, the Manchester Chamber of Commerce sent a memorial to Palmerston, in early 1836, that drew attention to the "great importance of the China trade," because it not only provided an outlet for British manufacturers but also helped to stabilize British textile exports to India, and then argued that the British government needed to "protect' and "extend" this trade, especially in light of the failure of "Napier's Mission."[211] Similar documents from Liverpool and Glasgow followed. Opium traders based in Canton and British manufacturing interests thus made common cause as they urged the British government to break down Chinese walls against free commerce.

Meanwhile, opposition to opium imports was growing in China. By 1836 nearly 35,000 chests of opium were being imported into China. The large quantities of silver that left the country to facilitate these purchases were creating deflationary pressure in the economy. Some 10 percent to 15 percent of China's large population had become opium addicts.[212] Despite the enormous corruption and Chinese collaboration in facilitating this trade, any ruler worth his name needed to put a check on these developments. The Chinese emperor decided, in November 1836, to prohibit opium imports into China and appointed Lin Tse-Hsu as his commissioner in Canton to implement the policy. Lin justified the prohibitions by arguing that if opium imports continued, "in a few decades we shall be deprived not only of soldiers to defend the country, but of silver to pay for provisions."[213] He ordered the confiscation of all the opium on ships and in storage. Charles Elliot, who had replaced Napier, made a shrewd move that later angered Palmerston: he suggested to British traders that they surrender their opium, assuring them that their costs would be reimbursed. Lin burned much of this opium, estimated to be worth some £2.4 million. These developments in Canton raised a hue and cry in London. Many now argued for waging a war against China to protect private property and, of course, the freedom of trade.

The prohibition on opium imports in China provided the occasion for a war that the free traders in Britain were already demanding. The real motive force behind the Opium War in China was the same as that which moved Britain elsewhere during this time period: capitalizing on its global naval superiority to open markets for British manufacturers. Palmerston was a champion of this strategy. Although the China market proved not to be the largest, it certainly had that potential; from the British standpoint, the importance of an open China lay "in its taking the surplus output necessary to keep the new machines running when the home market sagged. Hence the constant pressure of the British manufacturers to open the gates of China."[214] The burning of the opium chests by Lin sent Jardine running back to London to lead a war lobby. British chambers of commerce in Calcutta and Bombay (as well as the China associations in London, Liverpool, and Manchester) also argued for war.[215] Jardine financed a campaign in Britain to "convince public opinion of peculiar horrors faced by British nationals on the China coast."; He also made a personal representation to Palmerston, "urging a tough policy at Canton including a blockade of Chinese ports to secure reparations, a commercial treaty, the opening of four new ports, and the occupation of several islands like Hong Kong."[216] It is a testament to the influence of the business community and to Jardine personally that this is exactly what followed. You do not have to be a Marxist to notice the important role of capital in driving modern imperialism.

Palmerston agreed to a war in China. The cabinet debate was a discussion not about the merits of war but about who would pay British merchants the £2 million in lost opium. Since neither Parliament nor British India was likely to do it, it was decided to make the Chinese pay, both for the war and for the lost opium.[217] The substantial indemnity imposed on China following the war was a product of this decision. The effort to open China was thus to be costless: the Chinese would pay for their obstinacy. The war force this time was to be much larger to avoid the type of embarrassment that had resulted from the Napier fizzle. Naval forces were ordered to move from the Cape of Good Hope and from India and to meet up in Singapore before proceeding to China: the total force was composed of "sixteen war ships, four armed steamers, twenty-seven transports, and about 4000 soldiers."[218] It was the first time that the South China Sea had seen such a flotilla. British traders in Canton and Macau provided additional support: "[O]pium vessels (were) leased to the fleet, captains (were) lent as pilots and other staff as translators, hospitality (was) always available as well as advice and the latest intelligence and silver from opium sales (was) exchanged for bills in London to meet the army and navy expenditures."[219]

The Chinese forces proved to be no match against this organized effort of the British armed forces and merchants: "Against those who came equipped with steam-power and Adam Smith the discipline of Confucius was of little avail."[220] Once the war had been won, Palmerston thanked Jardine "for contributing materially to England's success"[221] and expected that the victory would lead to "most important advantages to the commercial interest of England."[222] Though British victory was clear, we will see that the opening of China remained a work in progress. The Nanking Treaty that followed in 1842 and the Bogue Treaty in 1843—the first of many "unequal treaties" that foreigners imposed on China—stipulated an indemnity of more than £4 million (about half for the opium lost and the other half to cover the costs of war); opening of five "treaty ports" for trade, including Shanghai; colonization of Hong Kong; and the lowering of customs and transit duties on British goods.[223] The British era of informal imperialism in China had begun.

One British scholar has aptly described Anglo-Chinese relations during 1842–1914 as "our cock-of-the-walk period in China."[224] This was indeed the period of Britain's informal empire in China. At its peak, British merchants conducted trade from some ninety-two ports that were forcibly opened by British armed forces. British citizens also dominated much of the interior trade in and around the Yangtze Valley, controlled the collection and expenditure of custom duties, and enjoyed extraterritorial protections while residing in China. British power influenced the working of China's foreign office and British military intervened when the protection of British interests so required. Palmerston had fully supported this "forward policy," believing that China will "provide market for the thousand rills of upland industry."[225] While China never quite met the high economic hopes of foreigners (it never does), British textile exports to China grew throughout this period, as did opium imports from British India (Figures 2.1 and 2.2). As we will see, British foreign investments in China grew later in the century, especially following the Japanese invasion of China in 1895, which enabled foreigners to establish factories and other firms in China's main urban centers. British investors made numerous private fortunes and the taxes on tea imports from China continually provided a handsome source of revenues for the British exchequer. As noted, China trade also enabled the British to balance their highly profitable Indian trade. Conversely, the costs of establishing influence in China were minimal: Britain repeatedly imposed indemnities on the Chinese that made China pay for the privilege of being attacked and controlled by the British.

It took the repeated use of gunboats and a second war during the late 1850s to finally open China further for trade.[226] The defeat in the First Opium War was not treated as a calamity in Peking. The emperor and his advisers instead thought of British intervention as akin to the problems that China repeatedly encountered from barbarians at the fringes of the empire. Instead, China's ruling authorities were focused on growing domestic turmoil, especially the rebellion of the Taipings. From the British perspective, the period following the Nanking Treaty of 1842 was auspicious, but not good enough. British trade doubled between 1844 and 1845, going up from less than £1 million to more than £2.25 million.[227] Opium imports into China also rose sharply, from an annual average of some £2 million in the 1830s to £5 million in the 1850s (Figure 2.2). The Manchester Chamber of Commerce, however, led a lobby arguing that a lot more could be sold in China, a view that Palmerston shared.[228] British gunboats were already dismantling Chinese defenses along the Yangtze, but British authorities wanted to open up the Chinese interior systematically. John Bowring, the new superintendent of trade and governor of Hong Kong, was keen to spread Britain's informal empire. The Chinese government felt pressured by the growing Taiping Rebellion, and Bowring saw an opportunity: "[I]nstability invites us to avail ourselves of the changes which are inevitable."[229] Palmerston did not want to wait for what might or might not be inevitable: "I clearly see that the Time is fast coming when we should be obliged to strike another Blow in China."[230]

The Second Opium War approached against the background of Taiping Rebellion, a massive mid-century civil war in southern China in which millions of people died; it has been well studied, and much of it does not concern us here.[231] What is important for us to note instead is that Taiping Rebellion marked the beginning of the end of the old Chinese order. The state and gentry alliance—institutionalized via the examination system and the control of the bureaucracy by landed classes—that had imposed order on China in the past was increasingly under attack, both from excluded groups within China and from Western powers seeking advantage in China. Although dynastic decline was a recurring theme in Chinese history (and some of that was clearly afoot in late Ch'ing China, too, especially the decline in administration), new themes loomed larger. The rapid growth of population and the related internal migration, scarcity of resources, and restiveness have been noted. In addition, imperial incursions contributed to the emergence of the Taiping Rebellion. The opium trade encouraged the growth of an underworld in Kwangsi Province, where the Taiping Rebellion originated.[232] The First Opium War caused considerable social dislocation in the region, especially as trade moved away from Canton to Shanghai. New ideas from the missionaries were also localized to interpret the causes of growing misery and millenarian solutions. As is often the case, when those with grievances joined hands with those promising justice, an opposition movement emerged. The Taiping Rebellion then grew readily because the monarchial state was incapable of imposing order at the farther reaches of the empire. At the peak of the civil war, in the 1850s, then, Hung Hsiu-ch'üan, the leader of the rebellion, came to control much of southern China, establishing a regional capital in Nanking. By the time the Taipings were crushed, in 1864, other regional armies supported by the gentry had also emerged, especially in Hunan, and Peking was only able to establish a semblance of order with their help and the help of the British.

With the Chinese central authorities preoccupied with internal rebellions during the late 1850s, the British were looking for any and all excuses for another round of efforts at forced economic opening. An almost trivial event—the *Arrow* incident, in which the Chinese authorities seized a pirate boat with an expired British registration—provided the occasion for the Second Opium War. Between the two Opium Wars, the British were preoccupied with a massive revolt in India, in 1857, which led to the British Crown (instead of the East India Company) assuming direct power over India. Once that transition was behind them, the British again, in 1859, with the help of the French, floated some 170 warships from Hong Kong up the China coast and up the Yangtze to finally open up China.[233] Ground troops reached Peking and burned down the summer palace of the emperor. With the victory complete, a series of new treaties led to the opening of more ports for trade; the Yangtze valley was opened; a hefty new indemnity was imposed on Peking; tariffs were lowered, and the opium trade was finally legalized. By 1860, then, large parts of China were turned into "an un-colonized extension of the (British) Empire."[234]

One may usefully pause in the historical narrative at this point and raise a question of broader relevance: Why did Britain not go further and colonize China? After all, Britain was busy during this time period formalizing Crown control over India. Why not China? Throughout the nineteenth century, the idea of colonizing China was entertained in Britain but rejected. As early as 1794, the British ambassador to China, Lord Macartney, concluded that "the project of a territory on the continent of China . . . is too wild to be seriously mentioned, and especially if all can be quietly got without it that was expected to be got with it."[235] This remained the consensus view of much of the British political class through the nineteenth century, just as the consensus view of the same class was that India as a colony was indispensable to Britain's fortune and global standing. The reason that the idea of colonizing China was too wild could not have been size, given that both India and China were giant countries. Since India was already colonized—the bloody work of numerous conquests over a disintegrating empire had been done in an earlier century, and by a private company, to boot—the fear of an overextended state probably played some role,[236] although that fear did not inhibit Britain from colonizing large portions of Africa a few decades later.

The most likely obstacle to full the colonization of China was probably the same as it was in the case of the Ottoman Empire: both had moderately well-functioning governments for much of the nineteenth century. It would have taken an enormous military effort to conquer these lands. And this was deemed unnecessary because "all can be quietly got" without conquest. This was the central logic of informal imperialism: the use of limited force to open the economy so British producers could sell their surplus goods and investors could invest what they could not invest profitably in Britain. A delicate political balance had to be maintained in the imperial periphery: governments within the sway of informal empire should neither be strong enough to pursue autonomous economic policies, nor so weak that orderly government vanishes. Britain thus simultaneously supported the integrity of both the Ottomans and of the late Ch'ing, but also chipped away at their economic sovereignty for the sake of British economic interests.

Stable subservience was thus the key quality needed in client regimes for informal imperial relations to operate smoothly. The British perfected this mechanism of rule via trial and error. When other powers challenged Britain's imperial monopoly later in the century, British decision-makers decided to share economic access with them, establishing an open door, without calling it that. Britain during the late nineteenth and early twentieth centuries was thus already operating a type of multilateral informal empire that would later serve as a model for the United States to emulate. Key elements of British policy combined in the forced opening of China, preserving the integrity of an increasingly dependent Ch'ing regime and sharing some of the spoils with other major powers. As an emerging power, the United States was learning from Britain; American decision-makers eventually labeled such a policy an open-door policy and perfected it in the twentieth century for their own purposes, as they, too, sought to promote stable but subservient regimes on the global periphery.

To return to the historical narrative, China's sovereignty from 1860 onward came to be seriously constrained by the numerous treaties imposed on China, mainly by Britain. Military defeats increasingly made the Manchus realize that not all was well, that reform would be needed—even in the Celestial Empire. The emperor established a foreign office—the Zongli Yamen—headed by his uncle, which over time became sympathetic to the British. The British now dealt directly with this office to ensure that treaty obligations were met, including the payment of indemnities. Control over the collection of custom duties had already passed into British hands—in the name of the Ch'ing emperor, of course—as they came to staff and to operate the office of the Imperial Maritime

Customs Service (IMCS). Revenues collected by this agency simultaneously assured regular indemnity payments to the British, on the one hand, and added to the coffers of the emperor, on the other hand. Toward the end of the period, say, the early 1890s, the IMCS was collecting nearly a quarter of all of China's governmental revenues, approaching the amount yielded by China's main source of revenue, namely, land taxes.[237] Beyond treaties, Britain's informal empire in China, then, came to include control over a portion of China's public finances and, more important, the growing dependence of the emperor on the British.

One Robert Hart became the inspector-general of the IMCS in 1863, and he ruled it with an iron hand for a few decades. During his long tenure, customs were collected efficiently and honestly, qualities that were in short supply within China's state structure at the time. At its peak the IMCS employed some 700 foreigners, many of whom were British and were paid lavishly in the manner of the colonial Indian Civil Service. The IMCS also helped create a postal service in China, modernized ports, and built lighthouses, facilities that helped British commerce in China. But the real utility of the IMCS for Britain continued to be that it was a reliable source of indemnity payments. Robert Hart was also a colorful colonial character. Fluent in Chinese, he befriended the higher-ups in the Chinese court. He kept a Chinese concubine and sired three children with her. Before going too native, however, he returned to the fold: he married one Julie Bredon, stashed away some £80,000 in London, and was knighted upon his return to his native Northern Ireland.[238]

Empress Dowager Tzu-hsi came to power in 1861. An ambitious, crafty ruler, she made alliances with regional warlords to crush the Taipings in the south. The British attitude toward the Taiping Rebellion had shifted over time. Early sympathy had given way to hostility when it became clear that the Taipings were threatening, not only British trade in the Yangtze valley, but also other British economic interests in Shanghai. In the post-1860 period, British policy in China increasingly sought to strengthen a pliable monarchy in Peking. The British thus threw their weight behind the Ch'ings against the Taipings, who eventually were crushed, in 1864. The success of the Ever Victorious Army, a modern, Western-style army led by Charles George "Chinese" Gordon that fought with the forces supporting the Empress Dowager, initiated an era of British involvement in the reform of the Chinese armed forces. Consular jurisdiction grew during this period, putting many urban centers of China beyond Chinese law and transforming concessions into numerous "urban micro-colonies," some of which boasted "the finest Race and Recreation Clubs in the world."[239] These micro-colonies became the centers for the spread of Western goods, commerce, and eventually, investments. Over time, foreign influences from these ports became a "flood" and "contributed heavily to the disruption and the transformation of China's traditional state and society."[240]

Britain's main interest in China following the Opium Wars remained economic, especially trade. But opening China for trade had required not only two major military interventions, but also periodic use of gunboats thereafter. To ensure that military interventions did not become a burden on the exchequer, Britain regularly imposed indemnities on China to pay for the use of the navy, troops, and ammunition. As noted, the Treaty of Nanking led to an indemnity of more than £4 million, nearly half of which was to cover the costs of war (the other half, to pay private merchants for the loss of opium revenue). Following the Second Opium War, Britain, as part of the Convention of Peking in 1860, imposed another indemnity of £2.6 million (or 8 million Chinese taels; the French were promised the same amount) on China. Between 1861 and 1886, foreign powers (mainly Britain) forced some £11 million out of the Chinese state, mainly in the form of indemnities. Considering that the annual budget of the British navy during this period averaged some £5 to £8 million, these sums were far from trivial. With these indemnities, then, began the Chinese government's period of financial dependence on Britain and other external powers, especially Britain, which continued into the future. As we have seen, British control over Chinese customs and duties, in turn, helped to ensure that the Chinese met their obligations. Thus Britain's informal empire in China was, to an important extent, self-financed; the Chinese paid for the British rule over China.

Britain's trade with China grew in the post–Opium Wars period. A glance back at Figures 2.1 and 2.2 underscores several trends. Britain's direct exports to China grew but continued to lag behind imports from China. This trend as depicted in Figure 2.1 is incomplete, for the same reason as for the earlier period discussed here, say, 1800 to 1840—because it does not include opium imports to China from British India. Following the Opium wars, Opium imports into China resumed and grew steadily (Figure 2.2), at least until the 1880s, when China's domestic opium production begun undercutting Indian imports. And in the post–Opium Wars period Britain was finally able to sell its textiles to China. Nearly two-thirds of direct British exports to China (Figure 2.1) during this period were cotton goods.[241] If, in 1850, Britain exported some 5 percent of the volume of its textile exports to China, by 1896, China's share was up to more than 10 percent.[242] There is no denying that this amount is dwarfed by the share that India took in 1896: nearly 40 percent of all British textile exports! However, two observations will help put the importance of China trade for Britain in perspective. First, at 10 percent, the share of British textile exports to China in 1896 was greater than what Europe and the United States combined were willing to buy from Britain.[243] As other advanced countries raised tariffs and developed their own textile industries, colonies and near colonies helped to stave off the decline of British textile industry. Second, China trade continued to help balance Britain's India trade via the opium imports.

Opium imports into China grew steadily in the post-1840 period. They actually doubled between the 1840s and the 1870s, both in terms of value (Figure 2.2) and in terms of volume: in 1839, China imported 39,000 chests of opium; by 1884, it was importing 81,000 chests.[244] Opium imports into China also exceeded the value of textile imports for much of this period. Since this is what the two wars were fought for, the British authorities and merchants must have found the outcome satisfactory, even as millions of Chinese were becoming addicts. In retrospect, pushing narcotics under the threat of guns and in the name of free trade casts a long shadow on Palmerston's claim—with which this chapter began—that during the nineteenth century Britain stood at the "head of moral, social and political civilisation." The indictment of the opium trade by John K. Fairbank came much closer to the mark: "[T]he most long-continued and systematic international crime of modern times."[245] Since winners influence the writing of their own histories—and certainly do not get punished for international crimes—many continue to take seriously Palmerston's claim that the forced opening of markets in the far corners of the globe was aimed at world betterment.

China's main exports to Britain during this period continued to be tea and raw silk. As is evident in Figure 2.1, British imports also rose steadily following the Opium Wars and maintained the upward trajectory until the early 1880s. Thereafter, China's exports to Britain declined, in part because European rivalries began to affect China trade, but mainly because tea from India and Ceylon was undercutting Chinese tea exports. For example, in 1879, 70 percent of tea imported into Britain came from China; by 1900, this share was down to 10 percent. Darjeeling had replaced Lapsang Souchong. Meanwhile, however, it is clear in Figure 2.2 that tea exports from China continued to grow for much of the period under discussion, say, between 1810 and 1880. Given Britain's continuing trade imbalance with China (well into the 1880s), opium exports from British India remained essential to facilitate tea exports. Within China, the tea trade was organized largely by the compradors employed by large British trading firms. Over time, many of these compradors started investing in British firms, giving rise to a variety of commercial networks linking the Chinese and the British in such treaty ports as Shanghai. Chinese nationalists and communists would eventually target these micro-colonies as creations of imperialism. In the interim, tea exports to Britain not only brought profits to private traders but the custom duties levied on this trade also contributed significant resources to the British exchequer. For example, during the 1850s and the 1860s, customs revenues on tea contributed nearly 10 percent of Britain's total government revenues annually.[246]

Trade remained Britain's main economic interest in China until the 1890s. After that, investments and loans also became quite important. A turning point of sorts was the Japanese invasion of China in 1894–95 that led to Japanese control over Korea, Taiwan, and parts of Manchuria. The huge indemnity that the Japanese imposed on China led to major new loans, including from Britain, and the new set of treaties that the Japanese imposed on China opened it to foreign investors, including British investors.

To understand the next and last phase of Britain's informal empire in China, say, following the Japanese invasion of China during 1894–1895 up to World War I, it may be useful to look briefly at internal political developments in China. A major development in China during the second half of the nineteenth century was the growing inability of the Chinese state to deal with the pressing challenges it faced. These included the peasant restiveness that has been mentioned and the foreign encroachments on its sovereignty. The Meiji Restoration in neighboring Japan during this period, which had propelled Japan to the rank of major emerging power, highlighted how state reform could put a nation on a path to economic modernization. Such political reforms continued to elude China for much of the next century.

Given China's size and Britain's limited political control over the country, it would be a stretch to hold British imperialism primarily responsible for the growing state failures in late nineteenth-century China.[247] More likely, the relationship was mutual: state weakness in China allowed the British to make inroads, and the limits the British put on the Chinese state, in turn, made it that much more difficult for China to undertake state reform. But the deeper roots of the failure of the Chinese state to reform itself and to initiate modernizing reforms were internal. Specialists on nineteenth-century China have debated the related issues;[248] these debates need not detain us here. Suffice it to note that the most persuasive of these accounts suggest that the Chinese state was unable to generate a modernizing impulse because it was deeply penetrated by those who had the most to lose from such reforms, namely, the traditional landowning classes.[249] The Empress Dowager, for example, sensing China's relative weakness, initiated a self-strengthening movement aimed at both industrialization and military modernization. However, as in the case of Russia at around the same time, the resources needed to pursue a grand modernizing scheme from above were simply not available. The lion's share of such resources would have had to come from China's landowning classes, who controlled much of the state bureaucracy via the examination system. Reforms thus continued to flounder, until the Manchu dynasty, as well as the Chinese state, disintegrated in the early twentieth century.

While the major causes of growing state failure in China during the second half of the nineteenth century were indeed internal, British influence unquestionably further contributed to state weakening and eventual disintegration. To recapitulate, the two Opium Wars—and the unequal treaties that resulted from them—undermined China's sovereignty, established pockets of territorial control, put British subjects beyond Chinese law, and forced open a narcotics trade that increased addiction among the upper strata of China's working male population. The First Opium War also undermined the legitimacy of the Chinese rulers in southern China, and created social dislocation that fed into a major civil war (the Taiping Rebellion). The repeated imposition of war indemnities put pressure on state finances, as did the limits the British imposed on tariffs. With custom duties fixed at 5 percent, the Chinese state had difficulty mobilizing resources other than the taxation of land wealth. And even the collection of these resources came to be controlled by the British-run IMCS, which ensured that the state's financial obligations to foreigners were met first, before resources were transferred to Chinese authorities. The role of the IMCS became even more pronounced during the next phase, when the significance of foreign loans grew. Most important, the more dependent the Ch'ing rulers became on foreigners, the less legitimate they appeared to Chinese citizens, which gave rise to various forms of nationalist opposition.

Britain's economic interactions with China in the post-1895 period developed against the background of a weakening Chinese state, on the one hand, and growing rivalries with other powers seeking access to China, on the other hand. The Japanese military victory over China created a frenzied sense among rival powers that a scramble for China might lead beyond spheres of influence to a formal partition of China. The British wanted to deny, and succeeded in denying, the Japanese any share of the rich trade of the Yangtze valley, which they considered their district. By contrast, Britain did not consider Korea or Manchuria to be part of its sphere of influence in China, and it accepted Japanese advances into these areas. Not so Russia, however, which shared borders with both regions. The Russians were willing to fight the Japanese for influence, which they eventually did in 1904–5, with disastrous results. While the French were busy consolidating their position to the south in Indo-China, they kept a close watch on developments in China, so as to not lose their established positions. The Germans, too, were relatively new to China; they now sought access to railway concessions, for which a scramble was beginning. And last, sensing a threat to its own commercial interests, the United States also joined the fray of nations seeking influence over China.

Following its victory in the Spanish-American War in 1898, the United States acquired the Philippines (along with Cuba) as a colony (see chapter 4). It now wanted to use the Philippines—America's Hong Kong—as a base to access the potentially much larger Chinese market. If the Europeans and the Japanese were to carve up China formally, however, this would exclude the United States. With its power growing, the United States wanted to avoid such an outcome. It was in this context that the United States developed the Open Door notes (about which I will have a lot more to say in chapter 4). For now, suffice it to note that the United States took the lead in moderating imperial competition in China by suggesting an "Open Door" (equal access for all to carry-on trade and investment in China). The United States also took it upon itself to support the territorial integrity of China. American success on both policy fronts was extremely limited: neither the British nor the Japanese allowed other powers to compete economically in their respective districts within China; and of course, the Chinese state disintegrated in 1911. The significance of the American Open Door Policy in China lay elsewhere. As I will argue in the Part II, it was the beginning of one American pathway to building a global informal empire, mainly in the post–World War II period: advocating multilateral collaboration among the major powers to maintain openness in peripheral economies, with the United States in the lead.

But that runs way ahead in the story of imperialism and the developing world. Faced with this changing context, Britain nonetheless managed to maintain its cock-of-the-walk position in China up to World War I. It did this by strengthening its hold on key areas. Britain still enjoyed military superiority, even though others were catching up. Britain's established positions in China could not be readily challenged. Britain denied everyone access to the Yangtze trade, arguably the most profitable foreign trade in China. Britain strengthened its hold over the IMCS, even using loan contracts to formalize British control over that key financial agency within the Chinese state. Major trading ports like Shanghai remained Western outposts within China, with a very strong British presence. Hong Kong, of course, continued to be a British colony. Much of China's trade continued to go through Shanghai and Hong Kong. And as we will see, the British government also forged close partnerships with British financial firms that became quite important in funding loans to and investment in China.

British economic interests in China grew during this last phase of Britain's informal empire; trade continued, but direct foreign investment and loans to the Chinese government also became part of the new, profitable business. British exports to China grew steadily through this period, though imports from China declined (Figure 2.1); overall trade grew from some £12 million at the turn of the century to more than £19 million at the eve of World War I.[250] The basic underlying dynamics have been noted: Chinese exports declined mainly because they faced competition from British Indian tea and Japanese silk, although the Boxer Rebellion and other political instabilities also hurt trade. Trade imbalance could be sustained over the short term because China was increasingly selling goods to other markets, especially Japan, but also because capital inflows into China were growing. Over time, capital outflows surpassed inflows (more on this to follow), and the trade imbalance with Britain added to China's foreign-exchange woes. Meanwhile, British exports to China continued to grow. Cotton goods continued to be nearly 60 percent of total British exports to China through the end of this period.[251] New British exports now included iron, steel, and electrical goods. Demand for these was generated in part from new railway construction, but also from some industries that the Chinese were beginning to establish as a result of the self-strengthening movement initiated by the Empress Dowager.

New British foreign investments also started moving into China. Prior to the Japanese invasion in 1895 there was some British foreign investment in China, but not much; most of it was in real estate in Shanghai and in other trade-related activities in treaty ports. The military indemnities imposed on China following the Opium Wars, as well as some small loans, have been mentioned; one presumes that these were mostly paid off by 1895. The treaty impositions by Japan on China following the 1895 invasion—the Shimonoseki Treaty—opened up China's treaty ports to direct foreign investment. British direct investment started moving in, slowly at first and then fairly rapidly in the new century. New British loans to the Chinese government also grew in the new century. Summary estimates of Britain's investment interests in China are provided in Table 2.6. It is notable that direct investments more than doubled and that loans nearly doubled between 1902 and 1914. Several related issues deserve further comment.

Table 2.6 British Foreign Investment in China, 1897–1914 (in millions of pounds)

Year	Total Investment	Direct Investment	Loans to Chinese Government
1897	36.3	24(66)	12.3(34)
1902	54.2	31.4(58)	22.8(42)
1914	127	84(66)	43(34)

Note: The figures in parentheses are percentage of total investment.

Source: C. F. Remer, *Foreign Investments in China* (New York: Howard Fertig, 1968). Data for 1902 and 1914 are from tables 2 (p. 352) and 4 (p. 361). I estimated the direct investment figure for 1897 on the basis of a business investment figure for 1897 of £14.3 (p. 348) and scaled it up by two-thirds to take into account real estate in Shanghai and other investments. This is the same procedure that Remer used to generate his estimates for 1902. The loan figures for 1897 are from table 1 (p. 34), excluding the loan of 1898. Boxer indemnity is not included here. The original figures in dollars have been changed to pound sterling at the exchange rate of 4.8.

Historical data on British loans to the Chinese government are a lot more reliable than on British direct investments.[252] Still, we have some sense of where British direct investments were concentrated; this, in turn, gives us an inkling of the impact of this investment on China, a discussion to which I will return. In 1902, British foreign investment was concentrated in areas related to foreign trade and in real estate, especially in Shanghai. As foreign investment grew rapidly over the next decade, the pattern changed, but not dramatically. In 1914, for example, the three main areas of concentration included two older areas, activities related to import-export trade (about £20 million), and real estate (another £18 million); the new area that was added was manufacturing, involving some £20 million. A fair amount of this investment in manufacturing catered to the market created by foreigners living in treaty ports. Only some of the investment was aimed at the internal market of China. Two of the main investments were cigarette production and sugar refining. To keep the importance of this investment for China in perspective, it should be noted that between 1902 and 1914, the outflow of profits and other remittances was some 25 percent greater than the total inflows.[253]

Most of the loans prior to 1902 were "general purpose" loans to the Chinese government, aimed mainly at paying back military indemnities. Only a few loans—around 10 percent—during this early phase were for railway construction.[254] Over the next decade, however, a scramble for railway concessions was well under way and, given a preponderance of power, the British got their fair share. Both Jardine, Matheson, and Co. and the Hong Kong and Shanghai Banking Corporation (HSBC) were involved in making loans to China, and official support was "a regular feature" in the post-1900 period.[255] By 1914, nearly 40 percent of the total loans went toward railway construction; that is, if the British share of the Boxer indemnity of some £7 million is not included in the loans (or 33 percent, if the Boxer indemnity is included). Most of these loans were made to fund specific railway projects; the principal and interest were often guaranteed by the Chinese government, which in practice meant the IMCS, that in turn was controlled by the British.[256] Other government loans were also secured against funds under the control of the IMCS. Loan business in China was thus not only profitable but also deeply political; as had happened with Egypt and Argentina, at the turn of the twentieth century in China, financial imperialism was added to the imperialism of free trade.

A brief comment on the Boxer Rebellion is in order at this point because it both added substantially to the financial difficulties and underscored the growing failure of the Chinese state.[257] Antiforeigner sentiment in China increased after the Japanese victory in 1895. Since the Ch'ing state was reaching a variety of accommodations with foreigners, including an agreement to pay Japan's substantial war indemnity, the Manchus were also implicated. While it was not quite nationalist, the Boxer Rebellion was a proto-nationalist, antiforeigner movement, and especially anti-missionary, which took on threatening proportions for the foreign powers that had carved up China in the late nineteenth century. Rival powers now came together to repress the Boxers. The Empress Dowager played an ambiguous role, shifting between repression and support of the movement in its early stages, but then joining the Boxers in a disastrous antiforeigner war. Eight foreign powers—including Britain, Japan, Russia, and, eventually, Germany—collaborated against the Ch'ing and the Boxers, and inflicted a decisive military defeat. While the Empress Dowager was allowed to return to the throne in 1901, Chinese sovereignty and the power of the Ch'ing dynasty over China had been seriously undermined; the end of monarchial rule in China was now near, only a decade away. These victorious powers slapped a huge indemnity on the Chinese state—£67.5 million over thirty-nine years—to cover the costs of the anti-Boxer war; the British portion of the indemnity alone, at 11.25 percent, was nearly £8 million. It was increasingly clear that the Chinese state was not only coming apart but was also getting deeper and deeper into debt. For the moment, however, the payment on the debt appeared to be assured because the British continued to control China's custom revenues. From the point of view of financial firms that were still willing to lend money to the Chinese state, then, foreign interventions and indemnities were good business.

Still, the role of financial imperialism in China at the turn of the century, though real, should be kept in perspective. British trade with China continued to grow during this period. While British foreign investment also grew significantly, it is clear (see Table 2.6) that nearly 60 percent of this was direct investment and that the balance was pure loans. In 1914, for example, the Chinese owed the British some £50 million, including Britain's share of the Boxer indemnity. Of this, about one-third consisted of railway loans that were directly connected to the real economy insofar as they facilitated enhanced imports of steel, iron, and electrical goods. Some £34 million was, then, involved in what may be termed "pure finance," or money that the British financial houses lent to the Chinese state at a guaranteed profit so that it could pay back its debts, including to the British. This sum is not trivial but it is hardly enough to sustain a scholarly case, à la Cain and Hopkins, that Britain's main interests in China by now were financial.[258] British interests in China around 1914 were, instead, quite diverse: the sum of £34 million in pure finance must be compared to £84 million in direct investments, £16 million in railway loans, an ongoing annual total trade of £19 million, and some opium that was still coming in from British India.

As we move toward a conclusion of the China discussion, the historical materials can now be used to delineate the key analytical themes of the present study, namely, motives, mechanisms, and the impact of Britain's informal empire in China. There can hardly be much disagreement on the definitional point that Britain's mode of influence over China during the nineteenth century qualifies as a type of informal imperialism. We have seen that Britain repeatedly used its superior power to gain economic advantage in China during this period, including in the two opium wars that opened China for trade; the forced establishment of treaty ports that put British citizens beyond Chinese jurisdiction and became beachheads for the spread of Western commerce; the military intervention to help maintain order in China (such as against the Taiping Rebellion); the repeated imposition of indemnities following military encounters; the control over a significant portion of China's public finance; the use of a first-among-imperialists position to seek advantages for British firms; and the leading of a multilateral imperial alliance against the Boxers and the Empress Dowager that marked the beginning of the final decline of China's monarchial state. All this certainly adds up to a situation of informal empire.

Britain's main interest in China during the nineteenth century was economic, or if political, only as far as was necessary for "the protection of commerce."[259] Britain had very few strategic interests in China, at least until the new century, when the rise of Japan led to an Anglo-Japanese alliance. If this much is clear, what is still difficult to disentangle is the extent to which the British state was moved to imperialize China at the behest of private British capital versus some broader conception of a national economic interest. We have seen that before the Opium Wars, British manufacturers had lobbied for a forced opening of China, and opium smugglers such as Jardine had made personal appeals to Palmerston for a war. At the same time, stuck with a bill of £2 million for the confiscated opium, Palmerston had every reason to shift the burden of these payments away from the national exchequer and on to the Chinese. The customs on the tea imports facilitated by the opium trade generated annual revenue equivalent to half the cost of the British navy. So, though there is no doubt that the opium wars were motivated economically, it is less clear whether the primary economic interests at stake were those of private capitalists or of the national state. Chances are that it was the coincidence of the two that provided the motive for war. The same was the case in financial imperialism: military indemnities covered the costs of war, but the HSBC was the loan agent that benefited while servicing these indemnities. Railway concessions helped specific British firms, but simultaneously created a market for new exports, generating support for Britain's export-dependent economy. In sum, when we unpack the economic interests that led the British to establish an informal empire in China, it leads to a general point that I made in the introduction: in a capitalist economy in which the state and capital work closely, private economic interests and national economic interests overlap extensively; it is not surprising, then, that the imperialism of hegemonic capitalist powers is moved by a hope to strengthen both domestic capitalists and the national economy.

As to mechanisms that helped the operation of an informal empire, the case of China is especially instructive. While the British clearly used force to open China, over time, they also made an effort to institutionalize the exercise of influence. Without formal control, the British hoped that a stable but subservient regime in Peking would help routinize their domination in China. Achieving stable subservience, in turn, was a process of trial and error, fraught with problems. The British bludgeoned the Ch'ing monarch during the two opium wars (and even burned his summer palace). When the Ch'ing capitulated under British pressure, the problem from the British point of view became the opposite—namely, the danger of too weak a monarchy. The British then sought to support the monarchy—not too much but just enough to maintain order while China met its treaty obligations. Examples of this support included helping the monarch crush the Taiping Rebellion and providing regular financial support from customs revenues. A stable but subservient regime was thus established in Peking, facilitating informal dominance, say, between 1860 and 1900. But when others in Chinese society came to understand the game, they challenged the arrangement. The Boxer Rebellion was one such challenge. Sensing the state's growing weakness, even the Empress Dowager threw her weight behind the Boxers. Both stability and subservience were now challenged. After a decisive military defeat, the Ch'ing may have again settled for subservience. However, by now stability was vanishing. The breakdown of order, along with growing power challenges to Britain's cock-of-the-walk status, spelled the end of the British informal empire in China.

Britain's economic gains from its informal empire in China are evident in trade, loans, and direct investment. Trade dominated Anglo-Chinese economic interactions until late in the century. There is no doubt that many in Britain were disappointed with the opening of China; trade gains did not match their expectations. But then China has always been a tough nut to crack. Also, this disappointment reflected unrealistic expectations. As we have seen, British trade to China grew steadily following the Opium Wars. Direct British exports to China in the early 1880s were about one-third of what Britain exported to India. Although this may support the disappointment perspective, what should be kept in mind is that the forced opening of China was essentially free for Britain, whose war expenses were paid by the Chinese in the form of indemnities. Direct Anglo-Chinese trade data also do not fully capture the importance of the China trade for Britain. As I emphasize, Britain's China trade was really a triangular trade that also involved opium trade from British India, which helped both to balance textile exports to

India and to facilitate tea exports from China. Viewed this way, the China trade was of great benefit to the British: numerous private fortunes were made; opium exports became a mechanism for transferring Indian land revenues to London; customs from tea helped the British exchequer; textile exports to both India and China could be sustained, even when global competition became formidable; and last, a forcibly opened China provided an outlet late in the century for the products of Britain's Second industrial revolution, such as the steel and machinery that fed the building of railways.

Later in the century both loans and direct investment also became important components of British interests in China. As discussed, HSBC and the British government built a close relationship to take advantage of the Chinese situation. When the British government (as well as other powers) imposed indemnities on the Chinese state, the British encouraged HSBC to provide loans to the Chinese state. This was profitable insider business because the British also controlled the IMCS, which collected customs revenues in China against which the loans were secured. In addition to indemnities, general-purpose loans and railway loans added up to considerable business for Britain's financial industry. Direct investments also grew rapidly. A fair amount of this growth was related to imports and exports. However, as treaty ports were further opened up—this time by the Japanese as imperialism in China became more multilateral—numerous new British firms sprang up to supply the needs of the foreigners living in the treaty ports and in Hong Kong. Major new investments aimed at upriver trade included cigarettes and sugar refining. By 1914, British investments in China were estimated at some £127 million, of which two-thirds was direct investments and the balance was loans (Table 2.6). Although this was less than half the British investment in the much smaller country of Argentina, "China received more British capital than any other Asian country except India."[260] In sum, if one takes into account the full range of British interests in China, including trade, loans, and direct investments, it is hard not to agree with the conclusion of E. M. Gull, the secretary of the London-based China Association, that Britain's policies in China during the nineteenth century (viewed strictly from the British perspective) were a "howling" success.[261]

The impact of Britain's informal empire on China is harder to assess, both because China was a giant political economy and because British impact on China was seldom decisive. British impact in some areas was in fact benign, although on balance it was quite negative. Scholarly assessments have varied, ranging from seeing the good that the "foreigners" did in China to finding the imperial roots of China's underdevelopment.[262] This is also no place to intervene decisively in such important debates. Based on the limited evidence analyzed here, I am led to the conclusion that the main roots of China's political and economic problems in the nineteenth century were internal. The British impact, however, made matters worse. Although the impact of trade and investment was ambiguous—even marginal—that of encouraging opium addiction and of the systematic undermining of the Chinese state was deeply pernicious. Each of these issues can now be discussed in brief before I conclude this case study.

First, it will be useful to set aside the classic issue of economic dependency. Unlike in the cases of Argentina and Egypt, Britain's economic penetration of China was quite limited. China never became a dependent economy in the sense of becoming a producer of a few commodities linked to the growth of international trade. The steady growth of tea exports still did not come close to displacing land that was under food-crop production. Much of Chinese agriculture continued to cater to China's huge agrarian population. The reason is fairly obvious: China's exports remained very small in relation to its GDP, on the order of 2 percent to 5 percent during the second half of the nineteenth century. Moreover, outside the treaty ports, the British hardly made any incursions into Chinese agriculture. They did not own agricultural land in China. China's landowning classes never became champions of free trade, allied with the British. Imperial incursions in China were thus mainly urban, and the British allies there were the Chinese compradors. Compradors may have eventually matured into full-fledged Chinese capitalists—some did, but mainly in Hong Kong or in the Chinese diaspora—but the communist victory in China cut that process short.

None of this should be taken to minimize the negative impact of the forced opening of China. Besides the opium trade, which is in a class by itself, there is evidence that growing imports of machine-made yarns ruined the spinning of yarn—China's major handicraft industry in the post-1860 period.[263] But there is also evidence that these imports led to the dispersion of a handicraft industry instead of an overall decline.[264] Some who focus on foreign investment inflows into China during this period underscore the modernizing impact of such investment, especially in the areas of technology and organization.[265] There is no reason to deny such gains, but the overall impact must be kept in perspective. Chinese GDP in current prices in late 1880s has been estimated to be roughly in the range of £1.1 billion.[266] It is clear in Table 2.6 that foreign-investment inflows into China between 1897 and 1914 averaged £5 million per year. In a billion-dollar economy, this was not enough to make a serious dent. Moreover, outflows of the profits on foreign investment and remittances outpaced inflows during this period. This must have at least neutralized any possible positive impact, and possibly hurt China's economic growth during the period.

But again, if the impact of British trade and investment on China was not dramatic, that of opium imports and of the undermining the Chinese state was significant. Toward the end of the century, some 10 percent to 15 percent of Chinese citizens had become opium addicts. While a taste for opium in China predated the British, what the British consciously encouraged was the availability of large amounts of cheap, high-quality opium, and that at gunpoint. As noted, it is difficult to be precise about how China's opium addiction may have impacted its capacity for governance and economic development. However, we can be sure that the results were negative, maybe even sharply negative. In the modern day and age, when the health of between 10 percent and 15 percent of a country's population is seriously impaired, say, by HIV, it is considered a crisis that demands global attention. As mentioned previously, opium addiction was concentrated among working-age males in China across social strata, including at the top layers of society and among soldiers in the armed forces, who were sometimes paid in opium. How could this not have had a deleterious impact on the society? The British forced opium into China for the sake of profit while preaching free trade. Nothing, then, underscores the hypocrisy of nineteenth-century British liberalism more sharply than the opium trade.

The issue of why per capita incomes in China during the nineteenth century were stagnant, or may even have declined, is clearly complex. A glance at what neighboring Japan achieved during this time period reminds us of the failure of the Chinese state to reform itself and to put China on a modernizing path. There is no doubt that the Chinese state was deeply influenced by the Chinese landowning classes, who had much to lose if a determined, Japanese-style effort to undertake modernization from above was repeated in China. The ultimate responsibility for China's failure to modernize in the nineteenth century has to rest on the alliance of a monarchial state with traditional landowning gentry. Nevertheless, this is another area in which the role of British imperialism was also significant and negative. As we have seen, Britain's informal empire rested on undermining the efficacy of the Chinese state; its economic autonomy had to be undermined for the British to pursue their economic interests. This they did systematically and brutally. Wars led to treaties that reduced tariffs and duties, sources that may have augmented the resource base of the Chinese state. The British came to control the use of custom duties, significant portions of which went to pay indemnities. And tariffs as a policy option were not available to Chinese rulers, making it difficult to encourage domestic industry later in the century when the Empress Dowager initiated the self-strengthening movement.

Resource constraints made it difficult to build armed forces and to impose order on rebellious groups. The more dependent the Chinese state became on warlords below and the British above, the more the state lost its legitimacy. Economic exploitation in a nearly stagnant, resource-constrained political economy alone would probably have been enough to generate disaffection in China.

The loss of the heavenly mandate to rule further fed challenges to state authority. The Empress Dowager tried to save her power and the monarchial state by joining forces with the Boxers. A decisive defeat at the hands of foreign power then put the last nails in the coffin of the Chinese state. Unlike Meiji restoration in neighboring Japan, the Chinese state in the nineteenth century proved incapable of initiating modernization. Britain's informal empire over nineteenth century China reinforced domestic trends within China to ensure that there would be no Meiji-like restoration in China.

Conclusion

Benjamin Disraeli famously declared that "colonies do not cease to be colonies because they are independent."[267] In this chapter, I have explored some important instances of how this worked in practice in three countries within Britain's informal empire, and examined imperial motives, mechanisms, and impact in each.

In light of the historical evidence presented here, what generalizations can be made about Britain's motivation to expand into these far corners of the world? The evidence is overwhelming that Britain's primary concern was economic gain, without force if possible, but with force if necessary. By the late eighteenth century, Britain had a head start in the development of industry. Industrialists sought markets for their goods. British naval superiority also had been established by the end of the Napoleonic Wars. British economic and political elites then came to share the view that Britain's global dominance would depend on a buoyant capitalist economy and economic buoyancy, in turn, would require expansion into peripheral regions of the world. By the mid-century, Palmerston explicitly supported such a position and went on to argue that a key function of the British government ought to be to open overseas markets for the merchant and the producer. Dynamic capitalism in this shared worldview would serve both the interests of capitalists and of the state. A marriage of force and profits is what drove Britain to seek gains across the world. When indigenous rulers did not readily succumb to British ambitions, force was used to subjugate them until open economies could be established. In all the cases discussed here, this was the main pattern leading to the creation of Britain's informal empire.

In Argentina and in Brazil, the British first sought an outlet for their growing textile industry in the first half of the nineteenth century, then sought to build railways, and last, lent them large sums of money as a profitable business. Force was used periodically to establish and maintain these economic interactions, so much so that British foreign policy during the period has been characterized as belligerent, interventionist, and meddlesome. Still, within a comparative context, British use of overt force in Argentina was less pronounced than in Egypt and

China. A ruling class of European origin, instead, came to the fore in Argentina, made fortunes in a dependent economy, and was often happy to facilitate stable subservience. By contrast, the ancient civilizations of Egypt and China did not as readily capitulate to Britain. Muhammad Ali in Egypt sought to emulate European industrial gains via an early Egyptian version of a Meiji-type restoration. This was brutally undermined by the British, who then turned Egypt into a supplier of high-quality cotton for its textile industry. Egypt, along with Turkey, absorbed its share of British manufactured goods and substantial foreign loans, including for the Suez Canal. Given its location, strategic concerns were also more important in British imperialism in Egypt than in Argentina or China. It was domestic opposition to imperialism, however, that eventually precipitated a colonial-type of takeover of Egypt. Last, economic motives were paramount in China, first to push opium so as to facilitate revenue transfers from India, then to sell manufactured goods, and finally to absorb foreign investments and loans. Force was used overtly to open the Chinese economy, and then military superiority was used to construct a variety of mechanisms to ensure subservience, including control over public finances.

Without full political control, informal empire was often a work in progress. In addition to the periodic use of overt force, the ideal arrangement was to have in-place client regimes that were pliable and capable of maintaining order. Such stable subservience was achieved more readily in some places and during some periods than in others. The British had considerable success in this regard in Argentina, though political stability could prove challenging. Most rulers of Argentina during the nineteenth century represented the interests of the ranching economy, which proved complementary to the British economy and flourished; convergence of interests between Argentinian and British upper classes, in turn, facilitated a degree of routinization of a stable and subservient relationship. After being bludgeoned, rulers in Egypt and China also came to see their own interests in terms of enhancing British opportunities in their respective countries. However, unlike Argentina, rulers of Egypt and China never quite became representatives of a dependent class that saw its interests in terms of continuing dependency. Rulers in Egypt, for example, were quite personalistic; some were more willing to work with the British and the French than others. As important, urban opposition to imperial rule emerged early and had to be put down by force. In China, the informal empire remained mainly an urban phenomenon; foreigners seldom penetrated the agrarian economy, arguably the core of China's economy in the nineteenth century. Both the monarchy and the agrarian classes in China remained opposed to modernization, failed to embrace commerce, and thus never established a type of cross-national class alliance of the type we observe in Argentina. In other words, a class base for building the institutions of stable subservience were absent in China.

Chinese emperors also learned to accept British demands. What else could they do? But these arrangements were not deeply enduring. The Empress Dowager even supported the Boxers with the hope of expunging the foreigners, inviting a massive retaliation and her eventual demise.

How well did the British succeed in their goal of expanding into the global periphery with the hope of economic gain? The evidence reviewed here suggests that they succeeded very well indeed, especially if one keeps in mind the costs of creating relations of informal empire were either borne by British tax payers—not always the same groups as those who benefited from the empire—or by the imperialized, as is sharply evident in the case of military indemnities imposed on China. In addition to the evidence reviewed in each of the cases above, Tables 2.7 and 2.8 provide some sense of the economic importance of peripheral economies to Britain's continued economic expansion in two important areas: textile exports and capital investments. By mid-century it is clear (see Table 2.7) that peripheral economies were absorbing nearly three-quarters of Britain's leading product, textiles. By the end of the century this share was more than 90 percent. Colonized India took most of these cotton goods, with Latin America a close second; the shares of both the Levant, including Egypt, and of China were also far from insignificant. Turning to capital exports, other industrializing economies, including colonized neo-Europes, absorbed about half of the total late in the century. Countries on the global periphery absorbed the other half. Of these, it is clear in Table 2.8 that Argentina was the leader, with India a close second, and again the Levant and China absorbing their share. It thus seems fair to conclude that British economic expansion in the nineteenth century depended to a significant degree on its access to markets on the global periphery. When countries were not colonized, informal empire ensured ready access to these markets.

Table 2.7 British Textile Exports, 1820–1896 (Volume as Percentage of Total)

To	1820	1850	1896
Europe and USA	67.8	27.4	8.2
Latin America	21.3	23.9	15.7
Levant	3.2	11.5	8.1
India		23.2	39.1
China		5.4	10.4
Africa	0.7	2.2	5.0

Note: The combined British textile exports to India and China in 1820 were 5.7 percent of the total. Breakdown by individual countries is not readily available.

Source: Adapted from Farnie, *English Cotton Industry*, table 5 (p. 91).

Table 2.8 Gross British Capital Flows to the Global Periphery, 1865–1914

Region/Country	In Million pounds	Percent of Total
Latin America	760	48
(Argentina)	(349)	(22)
India	317	20
Ottoman Empire	108	7
(Egypt)	(66)	(4)
China	74	5
Others	312	20
Total	**1571**	**100**

Source: Adapted from Alan P. Taylor, "Foreign Capital Flows," in Victor Bulmer-Thomas, John Coatsworth, and Roberto Cartes-Conde, eds., *Cambridge Economic History of Latin America,* vol. 2, *The Long Twentieth Century* (Cambridge: Cambridge University Press,), 2006, table 2.3 (p. 73). I have followed Taylor's definition of which regions and countries are included in the periphery and which are not. Note that total British capital flows during this period were £3,366 million; capital flows to the periphery thus constituted 48 percent of Britain's total capital outflows, the balance going to Europe, neo-Europes, and the United States.

Last, some will object to the tenor of this discussion by arguing that surely, British global economic expansion brought economic and other benefits of modernization to the global periphery. I have argued against such a position in each of the cases here, though there is also no need to deny the benefits that peripheral societies did gain from their contacts with Britain and other European powers. Argentina is the clearest case in which prolonged and deep economic integration with Britain facilitated significant economic growth during the nineteenth century. The economic penetration of Egypt, too, was quite deep but periods of economic growth were intermittent at best. The Chinese economy was never penetrated as deeply. The roots of nineteenth-century economic stagnation in China were also mainly internal to China. Such evidence can be used to support a case that the impact of Britain's informal empire varied, was not always pernicious, and was—perhaps—even benign in some cases. Such a position would not be inconsistent with the thrust of my argument that privileges sovereignty as an economic asset. Countries within the scope of informal empire often had more autonomy to direct their economies than colonies on the periphery. This limited sovereignty could be used in some places and during some periods to the economic advantage of the peripheral society. Such claims, however, should not be exaggerated. The British impact on countries within the scope of its informal empire was often pernicious.

Even in the case of Argentina, where the economy indeed grew, growth was lopsided insofar as it rested mainly on the development of a ranching economy.

Some industry did develop but much of it was small scale manufacturing that depended on external factors for its limited success. Britain discouraged the emergence of nationalist rulers to the fore and made it difficult to use tariff and other policy instruments to create a more complex economy with a deeper industrial base. In the case of Egypt, even the growth was not as continuous. It is telling that the Egyptian economy grew in periods when local khedives maintained some degree of sovereign control over their economies; as British control became decisive later in the century, economic growth also vanished. Meanwhile, Egypt became one large cotton farm feeding the British textile industry, incapable of diversifying beyond simple commodity production. While China's economic penetration remained limited to treaty ports, the Chinese state was repeatedly drained of resources and delegitimized by imperial incursions, contributing to its demise. Eventually, China broke out of these constraints in the twentieth century but not before significant political discontinuity and serious costs associated with revolutionary consolidation. A common theme that runs through the cases here—one that is central to this study—is that, irrespective of economic growth in some cases, Britain, via its informal empire, undermined the possibility of a more nationalist building of more complex economies on the global periphery. Many countries continued to struggle with this nineteenth-century legacy in the twentieth century, and beyond.

3

Varieties of Colonialism

INDIA AND NIGERIA

INDIA BECAME A formal British colony in 1858 and remained one until 1947. Nigeria was colonized as part of the broader Scramble for Africa at the end of the nineteenth century, and remained a British colony until 1960. In this chapter I analyze British colonialism in India and Nigeria to both examine varieties of colonialism and to shed light on the broader issue of causes and consequences of imperialism in the developing world. For some scholars, imperialism is synonymous with colonialism, or with a formal empire. I have adopted, instead, a broader approach to imperialism in this study, an approach that naturally follows from Disraeli's dictum, cited in chapter 2: "[C]olonies do not cease to be colonies because they are independent." Still, no study of imperialism can be complete without an understanding of Britain's formal empire. India was central to British colonialism—the jewel in the crown—and Nigeria was arguably the most important British colony in tropical Africa (excluding Egypt and South Africa). I undertook a comparative analysis of these two cases in an earlier book, as well, although the focus of that study was mainly on the impact of British colonialism on state building and economic changes in India and Nigeria.[1] I draw on that earlier study in this chapter but the focus here is as much on the motives as it is on the impact of colonial rule. The discussion in this chapter is also organized to facilitate a comparison with instances of informal empire.

By the time India became a Crown colony in 1858, the task of conquering India—which had been going on for nearly a century—was nearly complete. As we saw in chapter 1, the East India Company was moved primarily by economic motives, depended on coercion to impose rule, and over time, helped to enrich Britain and itself at the expense of India. While British rule evolved over the next century—a century is a long time and circumstances change—the underlying theme that remained a near constant was how India could help enrich the mother

How Britain and the United States Shaped the Global Periphery. Atul Kohli, Oxford University Press (2020).

DOI: 10.1093/oso/9780190069629.001.0001

country, Britain. Crown rule in India over the next century can be divided conveniently into two phases, before World War I and after World War I. During the first phase—the true phase of *Pax Britannica*—India lay prostrate at the feet of the British. Britain sought to consolidate its rule over India by rationalizing the state structure (especially the army), modifying the ruling alliances with indigenous elite, and broadening the sources of revenues to finance this rule. Of primary concern was the trading relationship with India. Many colonial policies—everything from the building of Indian railways to how the exchange rate was managed—were influenced by the focus on trade. India continued to absorb significant portion of British exports, especially textiles. By contrast, Indian commodity exports to Britain often lagged behind. The trade imbalance helped Britain to deal with its balance-of-payment problems elsewhere. But it was also the case that Indian products sold briskly in other parts of Europe and Asia. The favorable balance of payment enjoyed by India in real trade helped Britain manage a variety of imperial expenses in India, turning India into a creditor nation.

After World War I, Britain faced global competition—both economic and political—from other emerging powers. The British century was over. Britain faced growing opposition to its rule by Indian nationalists. Its colonial policies in India during this second phase became more reactive, as the British sought to deal with global competition, on the one hand, and with the need to co-opt or repress Indian nationalists, on the other hand. After World War II, a profoundly weakened Britain finally granted the mobilized Indians independence in 1947. The legacy colonialism left behind was a despotic state and a colonial economy that imported manufactured goods in exchange for commodities. Within this frame, productivity of Indian economy barely changed, population grew, per capita incomes were nearly stagnant, and most Indians remained illiterate and poor, with a life expectancy of thirty two years.

Britain's earlier interest in coastal West Africa was intimately tied to the slave trade. After it officially abolished slavery in the early nineteenth century, Britain established coastal bases, such as in Oil Rivers and Lagos, to promote legitimate trade with the interior. During the nineteenth century, palm oil emerged as a product of interest to British merchants. The growth of trade, however, depended on sustained access to the interior, which was threatened, initially by political instability and later by the encroaching French (and Germans), who, as late industrializers preferred protected rather than open economies. During the Scramble for Africa that followed, Britain established colonial rule over the area that eventually become Nigeria. Britain sought to rule Nigeria on the cheap; the minimal goals were to maintain order, keep the French out, and facilitate trade. The level of political and economic development in Nigeria was relatively low to begin with, and the British did little to improve on what they found. Making a virtue out of indirect rule, the British failed to create a centralized state structure in Nigeria (unlike in India) that might have been manned by a professional army and civil service. There was some direct taxation. But for the most part the British collected indirect taxes, especially on trade, to make colonial rule self-financing. Although the missionaries provided education, this was limited to the southern half of the country—education threatened the power of Islamic emirs of the north, who had joined the colonial ruling structure as junior partners—and therefore aggravated regional inequalities. The British invested little in technological or economic developments in areas beyond the trading economy. When the British left Nigeria in 1960, they left behind a poorly functioning state and a profoundly undeveloped economy.

The historical analysis of British rule in India and Nigeria helps shed light on the motives, mechanisms, and the impact of colonialism. The main argument with reference to each of these themes that emerges here may be usefully summarized at the outset. British expansion overseas was driven mainly by economic needs. This was as true for Britain's informal empire as it was for British colonialism. Of course, economic needs varied and at times, noneconomic factors were also important in overseas expansion. The real world is always complex. However, the most important case of British colonialism in India clearly demonstrates the centrality of economic considerations. As documented in chapter 1, naked plunder, squeezing and appropriating land revenues, and forced trade were all part of how the East India Company exploited India. It will become clear here that a major vehicle via which Britain continued to derive economic benefits from India during Crown rule was still trade. Under pressure from other late industrializers, it was the captive Indian market that helped the British textile industry sustain growth in the second half of the nineteenth century and beyond. Over time, other products entered the picture, especially during the second industrial revolution. The importance of India for managing Britain's balance of payments also continued during the post-1858 phase. In addition, British investments in India became sizable, often supported by rates of return that were guaranteed by the colonial state, for example, in the railways. India provided jobs for the British in substantial numbers, and indentured Indians replaced African slaves as a source of labor on British plantations in the West Indies. The British Indian Army also continued to support Britain's global rule, without costing a penny to the British taxpayer. But following World War I, some of India's economic importance to Britain declined. The how and why of this will be discussed in due course, but this shift eventually eased the pain of decolonization for Britain at the mid-century.

In contrast to India, Nigeria's economic importance for Britain turned out to be not all that great. Except for Egypt and South Africa, this was probably true of most of the other British colonies in tropical Africa, as well. Nevertheless, the level of economic benefits eventually yielded by Nigeria does not tell us much about the early motives to colonize Nigeria. When Britain colonized Nigeria, economic motives were at the forefront. The colonial efforts were initially spearheaded by Sir George Goldie (a Cecil Rhodes–like figure in search of a fortune) and his company, the Royal Niger Company, which, as we will see, resembled the East India Company. Of the various theories that have been developed to explain the Scramble for Africa, economic theories remain the most relevant, though not of the Hobson-Lenin variety. Arguments that prioritize strategic considerations make no sense, considering the limited strategic significance of many African countries like Nigeria. And if the argument is that what drove Britain's urge to acquire a new empire in Africa was the need to save the old empire in India,[2] then, given India's economic importance to Britain, this is quite consistent with economic arguments. I argue, instead, that what moved the British to take a lead in the scramble, especially in West Africa, was the urge to seek "access" to possible markets in the African interior. The hope was that open access would provide important raw materials in exchange for British manufactured goods, which toward the end of the century faced increasing competition elsewhere in the world.[3] Some of this hope was borne out, even in Nigeria, though not as much as in Egypt or South Africa, not to mention India.

Since colonialism involves formal political control of one polity by another, the mechanisms of rule are less of a mystery than they are in cases of informal empire. Britain used superior military strength to conquer both India and Nigeria, and then established governments in these countries that for the most part were run from London. Interesting issues for analysis instead are variations within this formal framework: more or less direct rule, more or less repressive rule, and the role of the indigenous elite. Following the Sepoy Mutiny of 1857, the British established a despotic and conservative rule in India that championed order over change. For reasons of economy, however, the British also sought to educate Indians so as to create a pool of cheaper officials for the colonial state. Out of the ranks of these educated Indians emerged Indian nationalists, the likes of Mohandas Gandhi and Jawaharlal Nehru. After World War I, colonial statecraft in India oscillated between co-opting and repressing these new indigenous elites, and eventually yielded power to them. The British used the lessons it had learned in India to establish rule in Nigeria. The most important of these was a near fetish with indirect rule that was supposed to facilitate a cheap and effective ruling strategy. Although the Muslim emirs eventually collaborated with the British to establish such rule in Northern Nigeria, the absence of similar authority structures in the South led to more direct colonial rule. The nationalist reaction to colonial rule in Nigeria was also relatively weak, both because of late introduction of higher education and because of a decentralized colonial state that fragmented nationalist mobilization along ethnic lines. When the British yielded power in Nigeria, the political legacy they left behind did not augur well for a well-functioning state.

As to impact, my argument suggests that Britain gained at the expense of its colonies. In due course this argument will be qualified and the nuances will be elaborated. But at a blunt level, British gains from its Indian colony were substantial and sustained for nearly two centuries. As noted, during the period of direct Crown control, the British gains were especially significant before World War I, after which both global competition and opposition within India (not to mention the two world wars and the depression of the 1930s), cut into the British capacity to squeeze a colony of the size of India. To repeat, at the peak, British gains from India came via a variety of pathways: trade, investment, and help with balance of payments; employment opportunities for the British and the use of indentured Indian labor in other colonies; and nearly a free use of the Indian Army to pursue a global role. British gains in Nigeria were more modest, though they have to be assessed against the minimal costs the British incurred running its empire in parts of Africa. It was the genius of the British Empire that the natives paid for the privilege of being ruled by Britain.

The impact of the colonial experience on India and Nigeria, in turn, was far from benign. I do not subscribe to the thesis that colonialism created underdevelopment. Nevertheless, it is hard to ignore the fact that the main role of the colonial state was "squeeze and neglect": the British squeezed economic resources out of these economies, and then used the resources for purposes other than betterment of the indigenous societies. Moreover, the colonial state forcibly kept these economies open to metropolitan producers, investors, and financiers, hampering their long-term development. Per capita income in India over two centuries of colonial rule barely budged, though India was more fortunate than Nigeria. India at least ended up with a functioning state and infrastructure, such as the railways. Nigeria, by contrast, inherited an economy with very low levels of technological development and a poorly constructed state.

The discussion here is organized by country cases. I first discuss British colonialism in India and then in Nigeria. Comparative analysis of the two cases, comparisons with cases of informal empire, and a discussion of some relevant theoretical issues is woven throughout the narrative. I return in the conclusion of the chapter to link this chapter to others of this study, and to sharpen some more general conclusions.

India

India's revolt against British rule in 1857 took the British by surprise. Prior to the revolt the British had mistakenly interpreted the acquiescence of Indians as willing collaboration. When a section of traditional Indian elite and Indian soldiers took up arms against colonial rule, they were disabused of this comfortable interpretation. The British called the revolt a "mutiny"—Indians called it "the first war of independence"—and then crushed it with their superior military force. The reaction of the British statesman Richard Cobden captured the sentiments of the British political class at the time: "One stands aghast and dumbfounded at the reflection that after a century of intercourse with us, the natives of India suddenly exhibit themselves greater savages than any of the North American Indians who have been brought into contact with the white race."[4] The real savagery, however, was what the British unleashed on the revolting Indians over the next two years, with their guns and cannons, including the recently introduced 80-pounder smoothbore muzzle-loading cannon that could readily blow buildings and humans to smithereens. We know that 2,392 British died in India between 1857 and 1859—the British kept good records of their own dead—but reliable estimates of the number of Indians who were killed during the mutiny are not available. Most scholars agree, however, that many, many more Indians died than Britons; the number of Indians who died directly in warfare—soldiers and civilians alike—probably ran into the hundreds of thousands (the number that is most often cited is 800,000), and if one includes the deaths caused by the famine and disease that followed, the number might be in the millions.[5] Be that as it may, reliable scholars have concluded that Britain's "retributive savagery" in India between 1857 and 1859 constituted "one of the most shameful episodes" in Britain's imperial history;[6] the origins of *Pax Britannica* in India were anything but peaceful.

Following the revolt, India became a direct Crown colony. The East India Company's commercial monopoly in India had already declined steadily during the first half of the century (see chapter 1), and then the revolt of 1857 exhausted the company politically and militarily. As the British state took direct control of India, the shift in power from East India Company rule to Crown rule within Britain was relatively smooth. A fair amount of continuity was also maintained because the British government chose to work with the infrastructure of colonial rule the East India Company had crafted in India. For example, most East India Company employees in India were kept on and became public servants. Some important changes followed, but first it is important to focus on why hardly anyone in Britain questioned the need to hold on to India as a colony. The question is not totally ridiculous. During this very period, the Opium Wars had generated a significant discussion in Britain about the merits of colonizing China (see chapter 2). Just as there was near unanimity in Britain that the project of turning China into a formal colony was foolhardy, there was near unanimity that holding on to India was essential. Why the difference? One obvious difference of course was that the East India Company had already done the expensive work of conquest in India. By contrast, the monarchy in China was still intact and efforts to conquer China in the mid-nineteenth century would have been very expensive—maybe even impossible. As important, the key goal of seeking economic advantage in China via trade could be accomplished within the frame of an informal empire. However, additional factors were also at work for the British in India. India by the mid-nineteenth century was central to Britain's global role, both because of its economic and military importance to Britain and because any lack of will in India might have weakened Britain as a committed imperial power elsewhere. Both issues are worth further elaboration because they help us understand Britain's continuing colonial motives in India.

By the mid-nineteenth century hardly anyone in Britain doubted India's economic and political importance. In the words of Robinson and Gallagher, "[To] all Victorian statesman, India and the British isles were the twin centres of their wealth and strength in the world as a whole."[7] We have seen how India was used to enrich the mother country during the century prior to the revolt of 1857 (chapter 1). The only issue worth reiterating is that during the first half of the nineteenth century, trade with India had supplemented Indian land revenues as a major source of economic advantage for Britain. We have seen that India was a key market for the British textile industry at the mid-century—nearly one-quarter of Britain's textile exports went to India[8]—and the textile industry, in turn, gave Britain its global edge, especially in the first half of the century. Investments in India were also growing. Around the time of the revolt, for example, plans to invest heavily in building railways across India were maturing. The role India would play in Britain's second industrial revolution was then about to begin. Indian revenues also supported a giant army that was critical to Britain's pursuit of a variety imperial ambitions, especially in the Middle East and the Far East. Again, for example, around the time of the revolt the British had used the Indian Army to pry open China during the Opium Wars (1839 and 1856) and had sent Indian troops to Persia, in 1856, to deal with one threat or another. The costs of these interventions were borne not by the British but by Indian taxpayers. The British political class fully understood that control of India—and its economic and political resources—was essential for maintaining Britain's global hegemony. From the British standpoint, a revolt by some foolish Indian princes and backward Hindoo soldiers, who objected to the use of cowhide in the making of ammunition, could not get in the way of an objective as grand as maintaining the British Empire. The revolt had to be crushed, and crushed it was.

In addition to the concrete economic and political importance of India for Britain, imperial psychology drove the British to act decisively—and brutally—in India. In the words of a senior colonial official during the period, "[T]he

British Empire is so vast and so unwieldy that it is all important that the whole world see that it has not overgrown its strength, but that it possesses quite as much energy, vitality and power of action at the extremities as at its centre."[9] The revolt in India thus had to be crushed so the rest of the world would be impressed with Britain's imperial commitments and capacities, even at the extremities, halfway across the world. This is an important point because it underscores imperial thinking. More than a century later, Henry Kissinger would similarly argue that the United States needed to prevail in Vietnam so as to demonstrate America's credibility (see chapter 5.) What these vastly disparate examples reveal is how those who run an empire think of empires as systems of power. Just as any modern state cannot tolerate armed rebellions within its borders, imperial powers are often moved to crush any and all challenges to their authority within the imperial system, lest disturbances in one part travel to other parts, creating a domino effect. Unlike Vietnam and the United States in the second half of the twentieth century, however, India was of great economic importance to Britain in the nineteenth century. It thus moved with full force in India, crushed the revolt, and initiated another century—or, nearly a century—of rule over India.

The British colonial project in India was always a work in progress. To the extent that colonial rule was ever routinized, it was during the four or five decades following the establishment of Crown rule. This phase ended in the early twentieth century with a number of important developments: the partition of Bengal in 1905, World War I, and the emergence of Mahatma Gandhi and Indian nationalism. During this first phase, which lasted from about 1860 to the turn of the century, the "British had India at their feet."[10] The British government used its power superiority to introduce political and economic changes in India. The modifications of the state structure that the British undertook in post-1857 India reflected colonial interests and beliefs. First, following the revolt, there were to be no more mutinies. British rule thus had to be centralized and, if necessary, despotic. Power was increasingly concentrated in a single office in London, that of the secretary of state for India, and pressed upon India via a viceroy who implemented a number of centralizing reforms, including reform of the armed forces. Second, the mutiny also clarified for the British the limits of exercising despotic power from afar. As a result, they sought to strengthen their alliances with local powers, especially the gentry and the aristocracy: the maharajas, zamindars, and the taluqadars. And third, all such changes had to be consistent with the British understanding of good government. The colonial state would thus have to be efficient and economical; in other words, it would have to be run by resources mobilized within India, with Indian revenues—that is, without any cost to the British taxpayer.

An urgent task after the revolt was to reorganize the Indian armed forces. The British went about this with great care and, judged from the point of view of colonial goals, rather successfully.[11] The reform of the armed forces followed two principles. First, the European presence in the armed forces increased. This was an expensive undertaking, but it was deemed essential if future mutinies by natives were to be avoided. The proportion of British regiments relative to sepoy regiments thus grew. As importantly, officers were recruited in Britain and trained at Sandhurst; well into the twentieth century the officers of the Indian Army were nearly all British. The second principle that guided the reorganization of the army was "divide and rule." This informed the policy of recruiting soldiers from regions and social strata deemed more loyal to the British. Ethnic cohesion within regiments was also considered important: a more loyal regiment could be used to suppress a disaffected regiment. While the three separate armies of Madras, Bombay, and Bengal were maintained—again, with divide and rule in mind—a central command was also established in Calcutta; the latter followed the parallel but competing need to centralize colonial rule. The army was then professionalized. Officers lived in plush, gated communities—the cantonment—and the soldiers were also isolated from civilian life, helping create esprit de corps.

A giant professional army—with 150,000 Indian soldiers, 74,000 British troops, and some 2,700 British officers—was at the heart of British colonial state. India thus became the military barracks of the British Empire. The British Indian Army served a dual purpose. On the one hand, it was an essential tool of the British for maintaining order in India. While day-to-day government was run by civilians, the army set the boundaries on any possible dissent against colonial rule; eventually, even the nationalists felt compelled to keep their protests nonviolent, so as to not provoke the heavy hand of the colonial state. On the other hand, the substantial Indian Army continued to be essential to the British projection of global power, especially in regions close to India. During the period under consideration, for example, the British used the Indian Army in numerous imperial projects: in China, 1859; Persia, 1859; Ethiopia and Singapore, 1867; Hong Kong, 1868; Afghanistan, 1878; Egypt, 1882; Burma, 1885; Nyasaland, 1893; and Sudan and Uganda, 1896.[12] Since Britain did not pay for any of these imperial interventions, the financing of the Indian Army molded colonial policies in India. I will return to this issue. Suffice it to note for now that nearly half of the budget of the British colonial government in India helped support the operation of the Indian Army.

The other key focus of state reform was, of course, the civil service. The British had introduced an exam-based civil-service system in India as early as 1853, at around the same time as such a system was created in Britain itself. During the period under consideration, this civil service became deeply routinized, formally becoming the Indian Civil Service (ICS) in 1892. The ICS performed the core tasks of the colonial state; it collected revenues, maintained order (with the help of the police and the army, as needed), and implemented government policies in far-flung regions of India, especially in regions that were under direct rule[13] The service was relatively tiny: some 1,000 officers—mostly British during this time period—ruled an Indian population of some 250 to 300 million. The young British officers who came to India were often products of the British public school system and the elite British universities, Oxford or Cambridge. They entered the service after passing a competitive exam. Following brief period of formal training, they learned the job while working under more senior officers in isolated districts of India. The highly professional—and conservative—service then developed its own internal norms that served the colonial purposes of maintaining order and revenue collection rather well. Over time, Indians started joining the ICS, especially during and after the First World War, when the supply of British officers dwindled. Those who valorized colonial rule described the ICS as the steel frame that held India together. Even Indian nationalists swallowed their pride and quietly maintained this civil service—just changing its name to Indian Administrative Services, or IAS—as a key agent of rule in sovereign India.

The British left behind a professional army and civil service in India. Many would argue that this was a positive legacy of British colonialism in India. The distinctiveness of this colonial heritage can be underscored by juxtaposing British rule in India to other types of British imperialism. One point of comparison is with cases of informal rule (chapter 2). Obviously, informal empire did not involve direct British rule; the British thus played a much more limited role in molding the state structures of countries like Argentina, China, or even Egypt, than they did in India. When nationalists across the developing world eventually challenged the power of comprador groups, Indian nationalists inherited a better functioning state structure than did the countries under informal British sway. While this is hardly surprising, the fact is that the Indian case is distinctive even when compared to other cases of British formal rule, such as Nigeria. The Indian Army and the civil service worked to attain essential British goals in India: extracting revenue, maintaining order, and projecting power in the near abroad.

A second key aim of colonial statecraft in the post-1857 period was to modify relations with indigenous ruling classes. Prior to 1857, the British had already forged a variety of working arrangements with Indian princes, de facto landlords, and other local notables, who were turned into de jure landlords. The revolt had made it clear to the British that they could push the Indian traditional elites only so far and still hope to work with them as allies. This realpolitik conclusion was now often justified in terms of respect for local customs and traditions. The result was a deeply conservative alliance that joined the autocratic colonial state with the despotic traditional elite of India. This alliance, in turn, influenced colonial policies. Most obviously, it limited the capacity of the colonial state to tax the income of Indian elites. Sources of public revenues thus had to be diversified away from taxing land incomes. Policies that might offend traditional interests and sensibilities also had to be avoided. The ramifications were deep and widespread; essentially, this meant that modernizing changes that might threaten the power of traditional Indian elites were not to be pursued. This is not to imply that the modernization of a backward India was ever part of the British colonial project. But even rudimentary progressive impulses were sacrificed to stabilize the conservative ruling alliance. If traditional Indian social structure was built around caste domination, the exploitation of tenants and poor farm hands, and low levels of health and literacy, the colonial state left these patterns more or less intact. Modernizing economic changes that might undercut the power of agrarian elites were also sacrificed. The urban Indian elites who eventually emerged, then, soon formed an opposition to the colonial ruling alliance, in the name of nationalism.

Prior to 1857, the East India Company's twin goals of territorial acquisition and revenue enhancement had been mutually supportive. As we saw in chapter 1, the process of acquiring territory very nearly came to an end in the early nineteenth century. When the revenue imperative became pressing after the 1857 revolt, not only were new territories not available for conquest, but the tacit arrangements with the landowning classes had also limited land as a source of new revenues. And yet, the colonial authorities in India continued to collect revenues at a high rate. We saw in Table 1.5 that in 1871, the revenues collected by the colonial state in India might have been as high as 20 percent of the Indian GDP. Nearly half of all revenues collected in India were still drawn from land in the second half of the century; but thereafter the land share declined, especially in the early twentieth century.[14] Other sources of revenue during the period under consideration are evident in Table 3.1. After land, the most important source of revenue was the pernicious opium trade with China. As discussed in chapter 1, the procurement and sale of opium was a state monopoly, especially in Bengal. Profits from this trade provided substantial revenues, followed by a number of other state monopolies, such as in salt. The share of customs and excise duties as sources of revenue also began to grow. However, the taxing of foreign trade was especially controversial, both in Britain and in India, a subject to which I will return. The direct taxing of incomes hardly played a major role as a source of government revenues during this period.

The expenditure side of the ledger is what truly reveals the nature of the colonial design. From half to two-thirds of the public revenues were spent on maintaining the army and on civil administration. In other words, the colonial state extracted significant revenues from India and then spent most of them on financing its own existence. Thus the Indians paid for their own colonial domination.

Table 3.1 India, Sources of Revenues, 1858–1901 (Percentage of Total Revenues)

Revenue Source	1858–59	1870–71	1900–01
Land revenue	50	40	53
Opium	17	16	Not available
Salt	7	12	16
Customs and Excise	12	11	19
Income tax	0.3	4	3
Others	13	18	9

Source: Adapted from Kumar, "The Fiscal System," table 12.4, (p. 916) and table 12.7, (p. 929).

The colonial state invested very little in agriculture, such as in improving irrigation, which remained during this time the main source of livelihood for most Indians. Health and literacy were also neglected; at the turn of the century public expenditures on education and on medical services during 1900–1901, for example, averaged about 2 percent per annum each.[15] The promotion of industry in India was nowhere on the minds of India's colonial rulers.[16] The contrast with Japan during this period is stark. As we have seen, after the Meiji Restoration, in 1868, the Japanese state undertook a variety of modernizing changes that put Japan on a path to becoming an industrial nation. The British in India, by contrast, ensured that the economic backwardness of the subcontinent would be perpetuated well into the twentieth century. The main task of the British colonial state in India in the nineteenth century was to collect revenues, maintain order, and open the Indian economy for the benefit of British economic interests, a set of developments to which I now turn my attention.

The consolidation of Crown rule over India facilitated a deeper economic integration of India with Britain. The changes that followed were evident in trade, investment, and in the financial relationship of Britain to India. Political stability and forced economic openness led to a sharp increase in trade. The opening of the Suez Canal in 1869 and the construction of railways in India also facilitated movement of goods. On the demand side, industrialization in a number of Western countries created new needs for raw materials. As we have seen, during the period under consideration, Indian exports grew at some 3 percent to 4 percent per annum; the value of exports jumped nearly tenfold, from 253 million rupees in 1856 to 2,490 million rupees in 1913.[17] In the second half of the nineteenth century, about half these exports went to Britain, and nearly one-third went to China. India's major export items to Britain included raw cotton, jute, indigo, wheat, and, as the century wore on, tea. As we have seen, opium was the main export to China. While small farmers produced most of these commodities (except for tea), British-controlled state enterprises in India mobilized the supply for exports and British traders—along with British ships—controlled the trade. The colonial state and numerous British private interests were the beneficiaries.

A few additional characteristics of this trade are worth noting. First, the rapid growth notwithstanding, India's exports in the second half of the nineteenth century were still too small a portion of the national income (in the 7 percent to 8 percent range) to make a substantial impact on national income. Nevertheless, trade expansion probably enhanced the incomes of those most closely associated with the trade, as well as to some economic growth. Although hard data are not available, the upward trend in both national and per capita income during this period is consistent with these observations (see Table 3.3). Second, though some value was added to exported goods, for the most part India was by now a classic colony, producing primary commodities for the metropolitan economy or, as in the case of opium to China, for another semicolony. Third, leaving opium aside, India's most important export to Britain during this period was raw cotton, which was a "vital source" for Lancashire.[18] And fourth, India imported more from Britain throughout this period than it exported to Britain. It was only the opium exports to China—along with some other exports to the Near East and other European countries—that gave India a surplus of foreign earnings in trade.[19] I will return to a discussion of the importance of this balance-of-payment surplus in merchandise trade in India for Britain.

Britain's exports to India also grew rapidly in the post-1857 period. As a matter of fact, exports to India jumped nearly 75 percent between 1855 and 1859.[20] Thereafter, they grew steadily: if in 1870 India absorbed some 8 percent of Britain's exports, by 1913 this share had grown to 16 percent. At the eve of World War I, then, India was Britain's single most important export market.[21] Britain's exports to India were nearly all manufactured goods: some 40 percent to 50 percent of the total exports during this time period were cotton textiles, and another 15 percent to 20 percent were metals, machinery, and railway materials.[22] The growth of Britain's textile exports to India in the post-1857 period needs to be emphasized. As noted, British textiles were facing growing competition and tariffs in much of the world. The United States and countries in Europe and Latin America took a decreasing share of Britain's global textile exports. But as a colony, India had no policy choice; Britain manipulated tariff policy in India to the advantage of British textile producers (more on this to come). The result was that India's share of British textile exports grew from some 23 percent in 1850 to 39 percent in 1896 (see chapter 2, Table 2.7). It is hard to imagine that Britain's pioneering industry—textiles—could have continued to grow during the second half of the nineteenth century without captive markets, such as in India. This was no free trade! The conclusion of Cain and Hopkins is thus persuasive: "Britain's export industries gained greatly from the extension of British sovereignty over India and in particular from the transfer from Company to Crown rule in 1858."[23]

The back and forth on tariff policy in the post-1857 period gives us a good sense of the tug of war between the national economic interests and class demands that molded British economic policy in India.[24] After the mutiny, the costs of the war had to be paid, and the British colonial state in India faced pressing revenue needs. It was a bedrock principle of British imperialism that colonies ought never to become a drain on the British exchequer; the revenues thus had to be raised in India. As noted, British officials deemed it unwise to press the Indian landed interests any further to meet these revenue needs. A ready alternative was taxing foreign trade. A duty of 10 percent on cotton textile imports was then imposed in 1859. British textile manufacturers reacted sharply and argued that the tariffs might hurt their profits, encourage textile producers in India, and violate the cherished principle of free trade. The tariff duties were then reduced. Lord Salisbury, the secretary of state, declared that thenceforth, any tariff policies in India had to take Lancashire's interests into account. Tariffs were virtually abolished in 1882. But the government in India, again facing pressing financial needs, re-imposed tariffs in 1894. Anticipating sharp protests from Lancashire, the colonial government in India imposed an equivalent tax on Indian manufacturers to neutralize any possible incentive toward import substitution. This satisfied both the governmental needs for revenue and demands of British textile manufacturers; however, the costs were born by Indian producers and consumers. Not only that, but these policies had serious legitimacy costs for the British colonial government in India.[25] Over time, the tariff issue became part of the case that Indian nationalists made against the pecuniary nature of British policy in India, loud professions of the principles of free trade notwithstanding.

As noted, British investments in India also grew rapidly in the second half of the nineteenth century. Following the assumption of Crown rule and before World War I, "some £286m was raised for India on the London stock market, 18 percent of the total for the Empire."[26] India thus became one of the largest recipients of British investment overseas.[27] Much of the investment in India was in infrastructure that facilitated trade, especially railway building. From the mid-century on, Lancashire merchants and other interests in Britain lobbied for the development of Indian railways.[28] The underlying reasons are not hard to fathom: railways would open India's interior for both raw materials and as a market for British manufactured products. The Indian government also favored railway construction as a means to project the power of the Raj to distant corners of the subcontinent. What followed over the subsequent decades was the construction of one of the world's largest railway systems.

As in the case of trade, railway investments in India were politically managed. The consolidation of Crown rule in India ensured that cheap land and labor would be available. The prospects of enhanced trade made investment in railways an attractive proposition. But what finally attracted British investors was a government guarantee on the investment at the rate of 5 percent per annum. These returns would, of course, be financed by the home charges imposed on Indian revenues. Railways thus provided "the British a sound opportunity on which a steady return was guaranteed at the cost of Indian revenues"; railway investments in turn provided opportunity for the products of Britain's second industrial revolution to be sold to India: "[A]ll the equipment, machinery, materials and technology were imported from Britain."[29] Whether the railway investment was profitable or not mattered little. What did matter was that the railways facilitated trade and helped the Raj consolidate its hold on India, and that the rate of return on the investment was guaranteed by Indian revenues. Over time, Indian nationalists came to understand that the terms of British railway investments in India were onerous for Indians. But there was little policy autonomy on such questions under colonial rule to modify the terms of the contract. A contrast with cases of informal empire, such as Brazil, is instructive on this point. British investment into railway construction in Brazil in the nineteenth century also followed a pattern of government guarantee on rate of return. But British influence over Brazil was informal; the Brazilian government had some policy autonomy. By the turn of the century, Brazilian rulers came to understand the "one sided" nature of British profit guarantees, bought the British off by turning guaranteed investments into government bonds, and brought the railways under national control.[30] India had to wait five more decades—until independence, that is, to modify the exploitative economic arrangements of the past.

Last, in this discussion of colonial economic links in the second half of the nineteenth century, a few comments are in order on how Britain managed India's balance of payments to its own advantage. Table 3.2 provides an overview of the relevant data. Several issues revealed by these data are worth elaborating. First, the figures in column 1 document that India exported more than it imported throughout this period. These figures hide the important point that Britain exported more to India than it imported from India. This enabled Britain to sell its manufactured goods to India and also to use the surplus foreign exchange to pay for a variety of its other global obligations. But British state enterprises in India also mobilized Indian resources to export opium to China. Substantial earnings from this, and over time, from other primary exports to other parts of the world, gave India the trade surplus evident in column 1. Britain then used

Table 3.2 India, Balance of Payments on Current Accounts, 1869–98 (Five-Year Averages, in Millions of pounds)

Time Period	Balance of Trade	Invisible Charges (home charges, remittances)	Balance of Payments on Current Account
1869–73	14.2	−24.4	−10.6
1874–78	14.6	−17.3	−12.7
1879–83	16.7	−28.4	−11.7
1884–88	14.6	−30.3	−15.7
1889–93	15.5	−32.9	−17.4
1894–98	15.1	−32.8	−17.7

Source: Adapted from B. R. Tomlinson, *The Economy of Modern India, from 1860 to the Twenty-First Century*, 2nd ed. (Cambridge: Cambridge University Press, 2013), table 1.3 (p. 13).

these surplus earnings to pay for a variety of invisible charges (column 2). This was the naked return, so to speak, on the political investment of colonialism. The two most important components of the invisible charges were home charges and profit remittances. The home charges made by the East India Company (see chapter 1) continued during Crown rule and included the payment of pensions to British citizens who served in India, bills for military equipment and stores, and interest on the public debt. Remittances included profits on private investments, interest on the railway investment, and payments for a variety of private services. These payments were large enough to turn India into a debtor nation throughout this period (column 3). The debt was managed by loans from British banks or by government bonds, payments on which again were in turn made from Indian revenues as part of home charges.

What is evident is that British colonial authorities put surplus Indian export earnings to such uses as paying the pensions of British colonial servants and defraying the costs of the guaranteed returns on railway investments by British citizens. This was subtler than naked plunder, but these drains of Indian resources did constitute new methods for extracting colonial tribute. Early Indian nationalists—for example, Dadabhai Naoroji and Romesh Chunder Dutt—recognized these arrangements for what they were and protested vigorously.[31] The British either ignored their protests or denied any wrongdoing. But a next generation of Indian nationalists was listening. Naoroji, for example, was among the early founders of the Indian National Congress (INC) and influenced Gandhi. In retrospect, it is clear that Naoroji and Dutt exaggerated—or misunderstood—the pernicious impact of the drain of wealth on poverty in India. While the British indeed engineered regular transfers of wealth from India to benefit both private British citizens and the British state, the size of these transfers was only a small share of the large Indian economy. British benefits were thus substantial but the impact on India was not enormous. The real roots of India's poverty and destitution lay elsewhere. There was plenty of poverty and destitution in India before British colonialism. The real evil of British rule in India was not so much that it created poverty in India, but that it maintained and perpetuated it. (For discussion of the main mechanism of this impact, see chapter 1; I will return to the issue after discussing the developments during the interwar period.) Suffice it to note for now that the British extracted a large portion of savings out of the Indian economy—in the range of 10 percent to 20 percent per annum, for two centuries—and regularly used these resources for purposes other than the betterment of India and Indians.

Many of the post-1857 patterns of British rule in India that we have discussed so far underwent important changes in the first half of the twentieth century. Again, the rise of other industrial powers—Germany, Japan, and the United States—challenged Britain's global dominance. British exports and investors even faced competition in the colonies. British exports to India thus declined during the first half of the new century. Within India, too, a new class of educated, urban Indians began to protest British colonial rule. If Britain set the agenda for colonial rule in India in the second half of the nineteenth century, British polices in the new century became more reactive. The partition of Bengal in 1905, for example, sparked serious political opposition to British colonial rule. The British backtracked. India was no longer at Britain's feet. Moreover, some 1.2 million Indian soldiers fought on the British side during World War I, and India paid nearly £150 million toward the cost of the war.[32] As an implicit "quid pro quo," E. S. Montagu—the British secretary state for India—declared, in 1917, that "the goal of the Raj was responsible government for India within the Empire."[33] The need to make such concessions further underlined both the changing nature of the world—US president Woodrow Wilson had put self-determination of subject people on the global agenda—and the shifting balance of power between Britain and India. Over the next three decades, Indian nationalism grew stronger. By contrast, the economic depression of the 1930s and then World War II further weakened Britain, leading to the end of British colonial rule in India in 1947. The political and economic changes that marked British colonial rule in India in the first half of the twentieth century can now be discussed in brief.

The colonial state did not undergo any major transformation in the new century. Central authority was still exercised from London and agents of rule in India continued to be a large army, a small but professional civil service, a judiciary, and a police service. But within this framework, important changes that would have long-term consequences had begun. Following World War I, the size of the Indian Army shrank, and cost considerations also led to a reduction in the presence of British soldiers. A sizable armed force of some 150,000 Indian soldiers remained in place, but Indian officers began to play a more significant role. The same was true of the ICS: by 1929, for example, the ICS had 367 Indian and 894 British officers.[34] Similar trends were evident in the judiciary and the police service. The tasks of government officers were changing, especially with the rise of the nationalist movement. I will return to this issue. For now, the theme of continuity is worth underscoring; the role of high-ranking Indians in the colonial state structure grew in the interwar period, and they would eventually go on to form the backbone of the sovereign Indian state, as well, leading to the caustic—and unfair—observation of a critic that the Congress-led independence of India was little more than "substituting the brown for the white."[35]

If the colonial state structure exhibited a fair amount of continuity in the new century, the politics with which this state had to cope changed dramatically. Instead of presiding over the nearly docile Indian society of the second half of the nineteenth century, the state now had to cope with the rise of anticolonial nationalism . Under the leadership of Gandhi and Nehru, Indian nationalists mobilized successfully against British colonial rule. The British tried to ignore, co-opt, or repress these nationalists, until it was clear they could not, and then they gave up. The motives of those who led and those who joined India's nationalist movement were, of course, mixed: patriotism, dislike of the British, self-interest. Leaving aside communist revolutions, such as China's, India's nationalist movement was one of the most significant mass movements in the developing world. The details of the movement do not concern us here.[36] What concerns us instead are some key themes that help to shed light on the major focus of this study, namely, how imperialism has shaped the developing world.

The nationalist movement in India emerged as a reaction to British colonialism, and once the nationalists were in power, leaders such as Nehru shaped the evolution of sovereign India. Three key characteristics of the Indian nationalist movement will help us further understand the impact of British colonialism on India, as it was mediated in the twentieth century by the rise of nationalism: the creation of unity in diversity; defeat of the ruling alliance that adjoined colonial interests and the traditional Indian ruling classes; and a commitment to gradual change with a multiclass alliance at the helm.

The nationalists succeeded in uniting India's diverse ethnic, class, and caste groups in a relatively cohesive nationalist movement, which found its institutional expression in the INC. The INC eventually evolved into India's premiere ruling party, the Congress. We know that both the inclusive and the cohesive characteristics of the INC were far from perfect: a variety of groups in India, especially Muslims, but also those on the political left and right, did not readily embrace the INC, and even among the middle-of-the-road Congress elite, there was frequent, even bitter, discord. Nevertheless, led by an urban intelligentsia, the INC succeeded wildly in mobilizing a mass following that included a variety of India's linguistic and religious communities, businessmen, workers, students, and peasants, and even some landowning groups, especially the lower gentry. The core aim of the INC was to oust the British. During the process of mobilization the INC helped to create a national consciousness in India that, in turn, was of great significance for the political future of sovereign India. Mobilized nationalism both gave legitimacy to the goals of the leaders in post-independence India and limited the fissiparous impact of private and sectional interests.[37]

A question of some significance for a comparative analysis of colonialism may be raised at this point: Why did India succeed in mobilizing a relatively cohesive, mass-nationalist movement? The import of this question will become clear when I discuss the case of Nigeria, where the nationalist impulse against British colonial rule remained relatively weak and fragmented. While a full explanation will require reference to a number of underlying differences, one important difference that is worth highlighting is the significance of a centralized colonial state in India, something that was missing in Nigeria. As Anil Seal argued—persuasively, to my mind—Indian nationalism ought to be understood as a reaction to a centralized colonial state.[38] If Indians were to succeed in mobilizing against the great power of the British colonial state, they had to come together. As early as 1916, the prominent Congress leader Bal Gangadhar Tilak was urging the bickering Congress elites to come together on the following terms: "When we have to fight against a third party—it is very important that we stand on this platform united, united on race, united in religion, united as regards all different shades of political creed."[39] Over the subsequent decades, Gandhi and other Congress leaders repeated similar messages over and over again. We have seen that divide and rule was a recurring British tactic to undermine Indian nationalists. If opposition was to be mobilized against a despotic and centralized colonial state, unity in diversity was a political necessity. A centralized colonial state thus encouraged a cohesive nationalist movement.

Colonial rule in India rested on an alliance of the colonial state with traditional Indian elites, many of whom were large landlords. When at mid-century, the INC replaced the British as India's new rulers, the days of the maharajas, zamindars, and taluqadars were also numbered. Unlike the communist revolution in China, the process of political change in India was gradual. In both cases, however, the traditional elites lost out to new, modernizing leaders: Mao Zedong and Nehru. One prominent scholar of large-scale historical transformations called the victory of Indian nationalists India's "bourgeois revolution."[40] Although

I do not subscribe to that interpretation—mainly because the Indian nationalists were more a political class than representatives of a nascent bourgeoisie—the grain of truth in the suggestion underscores the decisive nature of a political break in India at mid-century. India's nationalist leaders committed India to a self-sufficient, industrial future. State-directed development sought to minimize India's economic dependence on the West and prioritized heavy industry over consumer industry or agriculture. The nationalists then consolidated a hard-won sovereignty, at times, even sacrificing short-term economic well-being. The details of India's successes and failures on this journey need not detain us here.[41] What needs to be emphasized instead is that decolonization in India marked the victory of those who spoke in the name of the new Indian nation over an alliance of colonizers and the traditional Indian landed elites. A comparison is again in order. While nationalists came to the fore in much of the developing world following World War II, the victory of nationalists in many Asian countries, including India, was a lot more decisive than, say, it was in the countries of Latin America, where nationalists remained constrained by the continuing power of agrarian oligarchs and foreign capital. I return to this contrast in subsequent chapters, especially in chapter 6.

A third important characteristic of India's nationalist movement was its multiclass, reformist orientation. The INC was never tightly organized; it was more like an umbrella organization. Although the diversity of interests and identities of the national movement helped to create its oppositional power, pulls and pushes inside the INC also diluted its capacity to develop clear-cut programs. Nevertheless, on balance, the pluralist character of the INC proved to be a positive attribute; it was simultaneously well suited to undermining the legitimacy of British colonial rule, and to accommodating a variety of Indians within its fold, paving the way toward a democratic polity. That India's emerging political class participated in limited elections, especially in the post-1935 period, further strengthened the tendency to embrace democracy as a route to power and legitimacy. Comparisons are again in order. First, the British more or less allowed this form of middle-of-the-road nationalism to emerge in India, insofar as the colonial state repressed oppositional movements on the right or the left—the *extremists,* in colonial terminology—much more fiercely. The contrast with the French in Vietnam is notable on this point because the French intolerance of all forms of nationalism drove Vietnamese nationalism underground and into the hands of communists (see chapter 5). And second, while the multiclass, reformist character of Indian nationalism may have facilitated some valued ends, it also contributed to the creation of an ineffective state in sovereign India. As is widely recognized, India's "soft state" promised far more than it ever delivered.[42] This low level of state performance in India contrasted with the much more efficacious sovereign state of China, which proved capable of doing both good and evil on a much more heroic scale.

Turning our attention from politics to economics, India's economic value to Britain declined in the first half of the twentieth century. This decline was more evident in trade than in capital movements. As noted, after World War I, Britain exported less and less to India: if Britain exported 13 percent of all its exports to India in 1913, by 1940 this share had declined to some 8 percent.[43] India's exports also declined. India's overall trade during this period declined at some 2.5 percent per annum.[44] The two world wars and the economic depression disrupted trade worldwide, and India was no exception. Additional factors at work in India were poor agricultural performance in this period and, again, British tariff policy. Needing revenue and to stave off competition, the British colonial government in India again imposed tariffs on imports. The protests of Lancashire merchants were no longer heeded because textiles were less and less central to Britain's global interests. The tariffs, however, including imperial preferences, failed to keep the exports of other industrializing countries out of India. Protection also contributed to the emergence of import substitutes within India. Both of these developments contributed to the decline in British exports to India. Indian exports fluctuated—gaining during the war years mainly due to increased demand for jute products—but on the whole, also declined due to war-related disruptions and especially due to the decline in demand associated with the Great Depression.

British investments into India during this period continued, though growth was sluggish. The big-growth era of railway investments was already over. Without government support, British private investors preferred the white dominions to colonies like India, and the nationalist fervor in India made private investors wary. Nevertheless, British investments in India in 1936 were 13.5 percent of total British investments overseas, nearly double the 7 percent share in 1914.[45] The fact that these investments were relatively secure—Britain did, after all, rule India—was arguably "the greatest benefit that Britain received" from its colonies during this period.[46] The debt on loans was serviced regularly and profits were remitted regularly. Since Britain "depended heavily on income from overseas investments," the significance of these steady earnings from India was considerable.[47] It is also important to recall that the servicing of foreign debts and profit remittances in sterling was deeply tied to how Britain managed its trade in India. The home charges and charges on other invisibles continued, helping Britain's balance of payments. India even developed a surplus in its visible trade with Britain during the 1930s.[48] Because gold was also exported, Indian earnings financed Britain's dire balance-of-payment situation during the Depression years. The argument that India's economic importance to Britain declined during the interwar years has to be kept in perspective.

What about the economic impact on India? For this concluding discussion it is best to take the entire period of British Crown rule as a whole. The data for India's economic growth in the modern period are recorded in Table 3.3. It is evident from these data that per capita income in India between 1870 and 1950 grew at an annual rate of some 0.2 percent or nearly stagnated. The contrast with economic growth in the post-independence period is striking: the per capita incomes of Indians in the post-independence period (say, from 1950 to 2016) have grown at an average rate of 3 percent per annum. While long-term stagnation versus growth are complex issues, anyone who doubts the pernicious impact of colonialism ought to reflect on these data and be prepared to come up with an alternate explanation for the striking contrast between colonial and post-colonial economic performance—one that does not depend on the role of colonialism. In addition to the growth record, only some 17 percent of Indians were literate at the time of independence, and life expectancy at birth was 32 years.[49] The India that Britain then left behind after nearly two centuries of rule was a seriously underdeveloped economy and society.

The impact of British colonialism on the Indian economy operated via both direct and indirect mechanisms. The patterns of foreign trade and capital movements during Crown rule have been discussed. To reiterate, patterns of trade reinforced India's position as a producer of commodities and a taker of manufactured goods. Capital was invested mainly in infrastructure—especially railways—that served strategic and trading interests, and in public loans. Capital was also regularly extracted from India to pay for home charges and to remit British profits. There is no need to deny that some Indian exporters benefited from commodity exports and that the railways and other infrastructure helped create a national market in India. There is also no reason to exaggerate the pernicious impact of

Table 3.3 Economic Growth in India, 1870–2016

Time Period	GDP (%)	GDP Per Capita (%)
1870–1913	0.97	0.54
1913–50	0.23	−0.22
1950–73	3.54	1.40
1973–2003	5.2	3.14
2003–16	7.7	6.2

Source: The data from 1870 to 2003 is from Angus Maddison, *Contours of the World Economy, 1–2030 AD: Essays in Macro-Economic History* (Oxford: Oxford University Press, 2007), tables A.5 (p. 380) and A.8 (p. 383). The more recent data is from World Development Indicators of the World Bank.

the drain of wealth on the performance of Indian economy. Continuous extraction was real but not significant enough to explain the sustained economic stagnation in India. The real roots of stagnation become evident when we focus on why Indian agriculture stagnated during this period and why industrial growth was minimal. How British colonial policy influenced the performance of Indian agriculture and industry can now be discussed.

India was largely an agrarian economy during much of the period under consideration. The livelihood of the largest majority of Indians depended on agriculture. And yet, the best data available suggest that "agricultural yields were largely static in colonial India, especially for subsistence crops that provided the basic needs of the rural population."[50] Although the roots of this stagnation were complex, the underlying determinants included the disincentives created by property relations, on the one hand, and, on the other hand, by the continuing heavy dependence on rainwater and the low level of agrarian technology. The impact of British colonial policy is evident in all these areas, in sins of both commission and omission. For example, British revenue needs led to the transformation of land relations in India. Much of this was implemented during the period of East India Company rule (see chapter 1). Scholars have documented how zamindari and taluqadari land systems may have helped the British collect revenue but also created serious disincentives for private investment in agriculture. Such settlement of land often created absentee landlords, and then layers of intermediaries underneath them, none of whom felt the need to improve agricultural production (mainly because the profits would be shared). Even in ryotwari areas (see chapter 1), over time, various types of landlords emerged, encouraging the growth of tenancy, which became a disincentive to the investment of resources or labor on land.[51] In Daniel Thorner's felicitous phrase, India's agrarian structure thus developed "built in depressors," that helped to explain both agrarian stagnation during the colonial period and the difficulty India's independent rulers faced as they sought to create a more dynamic agriculture.[52]

In addition to limited private investment, the other major factor that contributed to nearly stagnant productivity in agriculture was the lack of public investment in the agrarian sector. Tables 3.4 and 3.5 tell the story of how the British spent the substantial revenues they regularly squeezed out of the Indian economy during this period. The issue of the share and the sources of governmental revenues in national income have been discussed. It is clear in Table 3.4 that civil administration and defense took up more than half of these revenues and, if home charges are included, then nearly two-thirds of the revenue expenditure simply went toward the costs of running the Empire. Expenditures on education and health averaged some 4 percent and 2 percent of the total governmental

Table 3.4 India, Patterns of Public Expenditure, 1871–1947 (Percentage of Total)

Year	Civil Administration (including debt servicing)	Defense	Education	Medical and Public Health	Capital Outlay	Other Expenditures (including home charges)
1871–72	29	32	N.A.	N.A.	N.A.	N.A.
1900–1	28	22	2	2	17	30
1913–14	29	25	4	2	18	23
1917–18	35	33	4	2	5	21
1921–22	32	33	4	2	12	18
1931–32	40	28	7	3	5	20
1946–47	21	26	3	2	26	22

Source: Adapted from Kumar, "The Fiscal System," table 12.8 (p. 931).

Table 3.5 India, Public Investments in Economic Overheads, 1898–1938 (As a Percentage of Total Investments in Economic Overheads)

Year	Railways	Irrigation	Roads and Buildings	Others
1898–99	45	12	34	9
1901–2	45	12	34	9
1919–20	50	1	39	10
1927–28	53	12	30	5
1931–32	31	19	40	10
1937–38	24	14	52	10

Source: Adapted from Kumar, "Fiscal System," table 12.9 (p. 936). These figures on public investments in economic overheads do not correspond to any single category of expenditures in table 3.4. Investment in economic overheads averaged some 20 percent per annum of the total public expenditures during these years.

expenditures per annum during the first half of the twentieth century, and were even lower than that during the nineteenth century. Education expenditures, moreover, focused on higher education (mostly urban based) to train cheaper manpower to staff the colonial state. The possibility of a healthier and literate—and thus more productive—peasantry was thus continuously sacrificed by the colonial state.[53]

More-direct public investment in agriculture was also minimal. Of the total public expenditures in the twentieth century, the colonial state spent an average of nearly 20 percent per annum on what we would today call infrastructure, but in colonial terminology was categorized as "expenditure on economic overheads." The breakdown of these expenditures is recorded in Table 3.5. It is clear that the government was focused on railways and a variety of construction projects, most of them urban. Again, while there is no need to deny the contribution of roads and railways in creating a national market—thus helping agrarian producers, at least by stabilizing prices across time and space—the contribution of such investments to raising agricultural productivity was probably minimal. Much more significant would have been more investment in irrigation and in agrarian technology that might facilitate higher yields per unit of land. The colonial state's focus when it came to agricultural research was on export crops, especially cotton, and when it came to irrigation, on the Punjab, where retired soldiers of the Indian Army had to be settled. The British did build canals across India but the amount expended on this was fairly small, especially considering the revenues they extracted from the agrarian sector, first, directly from land, and then from taxing products of land. Investment in irrigation averaged 12 percent per annum of the total investment in economic overheads during the first half of the twentieth century (Table 3.5), or some 2.4 percent of the total annual public expenditures. And this despite widespread understanding during the period that irrigation was an important input that might raise agricultural yields, and thus, incomes. Considering that at the turn of the century, nearly 90 percent of Indians lived in the countryside and that the largest majority by far depended on agricultural incomes for their livelihood, it would be fair to surmise that the well-being of poor Indians was not of great concern to the British rulers of India.

Beyond agriculture, minimal industrial development further contributed to nearly stagnant per capita incomes in colonial India (see Table 3.3).[54] At the time of independence the share of factory production in the Indian national product was some 7 percent to 8 percent. This suggests that India experienced some industrialization during the period under consideration but not enough to sustain steady growth in per capita incomes. For a poor economy with low levels of investible savings and limited technical know-how, both the supply and the demand constraints on industrialization in India were formidable. Such constraints, however, characterize underdevelopment more broadly and are not helpful in understanding why industrialization takes off in some places—and during some time periods—but not in others. To understand such variation one needs to focus on institutional factors instead. Understanding limited industrial development in India thus requires a focus on the actions and inactions of the British colonial state.

We know that prior to World War I Britain had imposed an open-economy framework on India, and that unlike such other late industrializers as Japan (or for that matter, Germany or the United States), India simply did not have the policy autonomy to promote national industrialization in the nineteenth century, either by protecting domestic industries or by pursuing more positive policies that we today might recognize as industrial policies. The impact of such forced openness is discussed both in chapter 1 and earlier in this chapter: India became a taker of British manufactured goods in exchange for low value-added commodity exports. That the industrial impulse in such a setting was weak is, then, hardly surprising. What is surprising and revealing is that, forced openness notwithstanding, some industry did develop in India prior to World War I. British businessmen concentrated around Calcutta invested in such export-oriented industries as jute and the processing of tea. Given British demand for these products, British businessmen in India, who had a better knowledge of the British market, as well as the know-how and capital, started these industries. More puzzling is why Indian entrepreneurs did not follow suit. Economic historians have persuasively documented that once British businessmen became established, they used less-than-free-market techniques to create barriers to entry—for example, tightly knit ethnic communities of Scots excluded Indians from managing agencies that often controlled business opportunities in and around Calcutta.[55]

The Indian-owned industry that did emerge prior to World War I was of two types. First, some textile manufacturing focused on the domestic market grew up around Bombay. On the face of it, this is a bit of a puzzle because textiles were Britain's main export to India for much of the nineteenth century. Several factors help us understand this puzzle. First, the Indian producers produced low-end cloth for the poor that the British did not produce. The low cost of labor and transportation also gave Indian producers some advantage. The fact that British manufacturers lobbied so very hard to abolish even a 5 percent to 10 percent tax on textile exports in the second half of the nineteenth century suggests that they felt threatened by the potential competition from Indian producers. The battle over tariffs also underscores that had the Indian state enjoyed some policy autonomy (of the kind the white British dominions and those within the scope of Britain's informal empire often enjoyed), Indian manufacturing might have emerged successfully behind protections several decades before it actually did. The second type of industry that developed early in India was steel. The Tatas, an Indian industrialist family, initiated a steel industry in 1907. They mobilized capital by appealing to nationalist sentiments and then used borrowed know-how to begin production. World War I helped Indian industry, for some obvious and some not so obvious reasons. Because imports were disrupted, both the textile and the steel industries prospered under a de facto import-substitution regime. But export industries like jute more than made up for war-related disruptions due to the sharp increase in demand for gunny bags. Imports resumed after the war, and the Indian textile and steel producers lobbied hard for protection, to no avail. Both industries fell upon hard times at the same time Indian nationalist politics was on the rise. Indian nationalists and emerging Indian industrialists then made common cause around the issue of protection; it was an alliance of convenience that continued well into the future.

When Britain's global hegemony and the era of free trade more or less ended after World War I, Japanese imports started entering India in a big way, during the 1920s. As discussed, the revenue needs of the colonial state in India were pressing, and they led the British to tax imports into India. The average rate of tariffs had increased from some 5 percent to 25 percent by 1930. In addition to textiles and steel, Indian industrialists also entered the sugar and paper industries. Although the Depression took a toll, from 1934 on, Indian industry surged behind protections. Starting from a low base, industrial production in India doubled between 1934 and 1946. To repeat, industry was still a very small part of Indian national product, and this growth upsurge was not sufficient to boost India's overall economic growth significantly, but focusing on this limited industrial growth does underscore the factors that impeded and facilitated that growth. The role of protection was clear because the industries that did best were precisely the ones that were protected from imports: textiles, iron and steel, cement, paper, and sugar.[56] India's major business houses, including Birla, Dalmia, Walchand, Shri Ram, Thapar, and Singhanias, all came into their own during this period. It is hardly surprising that both Indian industrialists and nationalist politicians like Nehru interpreted free trade as an imperial project and, instead, converged around the need to promote import substitution to nurture both Indian industry and nation building.

To recapitulate the discussion on India, it was indeed Britain's most important colony during the period under discussion. Following India's mid-nineteenth-century revolt, no one in Britain doubted the need to hold on to India. British forces ruthlessly repressed the rebelling Indians and imposed direct Crown rule on India. Britain then rationalized the state structures within India, especially the armed and the civil services, reordered relations with the traditional Indian elite, and ensured that enough revenue would be extracted from India to meet imperial needs. As the British settled down to rule in India, their main preoccupation was with matters economic, including trade, investment, and financial relations. As documented here, British economic gains in India were significant, especially before World War I. The impact on India, by contrast, was deeply negative. There is no need to deny some positive legacies of British colonialism in India, including an effective state structure and a railway system. Nevertheless, the evidence is overwhelming that Indian economy stagnated under British rule. Tribute-like extraction was part of the story, but the economic stagnation is really a story of how British colonial policies inhibited the growth of agrarian productivity, on the one hand, and minimal industrial development on the other hand. Nearly two-thirds of the substantial revenues that the British extracted in India annually financed nothing more than the costs of running the empire. Very little was invested into what we today might consider development: low levels of investments into education or health are documented here; and most important from the standpoint of economic growth in the countryside, where nearly 90 percent of the Indians lived, was the minimal investment in irrigation. Other economic policies—especially tariff policies, but also the management of exchange rates and the availability of finance—made it difficult to initiate industrial development. When the British left India after two centuries of rule, only 7 percent to 8 percent of the national product originated in factory production; more than 80 percent of the population was illiterate, life expectancy was thirty-two years, and incomes had stagnated for the first five decades of the twentieth century.

Nigeria

Well before Britain created the protectorate of Nigeria at the turn of the twentieth century, British trading interests were already established on the west coast of Africa. Prior to analyzing the causes and consequences of British colonialism in Nigeria, then, especially in comparison to India, it may be useful to begin the discussion with some historical background, both of British trading activities on the one hand, and of the local societies that eventually became Nigeria on the other hand. Of course, British economic activities on the west coast of Africa originated during the three centuries of slave trade. After slavery was abolished in the early nineteenth century, British merchants sought to pursue "legitimate trade" during much of the nineteenth century.[57] Palm oil emerged as a product of West Africa, the demand for which grew in Britain because of its use in the making of soap, candles, lubricant in locomotives, and eventually as an ingredient in margarine. If in 1810 Britain imported 1,000 tons of West African palm oil, by 1860 the import levels were up to nearly 50,000 tons per year, and then stayed at that high level well toward the end of the century.[58] Britain's exports to the region, in turn, included wines and spirits, cotton goods, and some consumption items. While it was promising, this legitimate trade never really supplanted the highly profitable slave trade. Constraints on the further growth of trade included: Limited buying power in the region; political uncertainty along trade routes to the interior, including along the rivers that flowed into the Niger Delta; continuing slavery; and, as the century wore on, competition from other European powers, especially France.

Constraints notwithstanding, British trading activities in and around the Niger Delta grew throughout the century, albeit at a slow pace. British merchants periodically sought the support of the British state to ensure profitable trade. Palmerston and others in London eyed West Africa with interest but were reluctant to extend territorial control. One may ask, why? Palmerston and other mid-Victorians were hardly anti-imperialists. Recall the aggressive Opium Wars in China and the transfer to Crown rule in India during this period. Tropical Africa—again, excluding South Africa and Egypt—was considered promising but not of great economic importance. There was always hope for more economic gain but the importance of tropical Africa only increased toward the end of the century, with a decline in shipping costs, the prospect of railways linking the interior to the coast, and growing competition among European powers. At mid-century, Palmerston still preferred an informal empire in tropical Africa: his requirement for African states was that they should be "well kept" and "always accessible."[59] Such stable subservience could not always be ensured, however. Seeking commercial expansion in Nigeria, Britain established a coastal colony in Lagos in 1861. Lagos was to be to West Africa what Hong Kong was to China, an entrepôt. An informal empire of sorts was also established in the region of Oil Rivers—the Niger Delta that served as the highway for exports of palm oil—where the British consul "would now and then send a gunship upriver," with the hope of instilling some healthy respect for the British traders among the locals.[60]

The British traders in West Africa included Sir George Goldie, one of the two British founders of Nigeria; the other was Lord Frederick Lugard. Goldie took over an ailing family business that traded in the Niger Delta. After moving to the coast in 1877, Goldie aggressively rebuilt the business, forced mergers on other companies, bought out French companies, and established the United African Company in 1879 (renamed the National African Company in 1881), which then eventually became the Royal Niger Company, with a charter from the British government in 1886.[61] The details of Goldie's entrepreneurial adventures do not concern us here.[62] Worth noting instead are the commercial origins of growing British interest in Nigeria in the late nineteenth century. Before the Berlin Conference ratified the division of Africa among European powers in 1885—more on the Scramble for Africa to follow—Goldie was focused on turning the Niger River region into another British colony. By 1884, Goldie's company was "acting as a kind of government in the hinterland"; his gunboats patrolled the Niger and he signed treaties with African chiefs that ceded territory to his company "in perpetuity" and gave it trading monopoly.[63] Although the British government demurred, it also turned a blind eye to an individual-dominated company acquiring territory, a set of actions quite reminiscent of the East India Company and Clive in India, a whole century earlier. The Royal Niger Company charter was short-lived. The British government bought out Sir Goldie's company at a handsome price and established a protectorate in southern Nigeria. The company could not effectively deal with a variety of political and military problems that followed the partition of Africa. Not only did the Germans and the French pose challenges in the interior, but warring tribes in the Yoruba lands had to be pacified, and local emirs had to be subdued in the northern Sokoto Caliphate. Before continuing the discussion on how the Scramble unfolded in this region, then, a brief introduction to the nature of the local political economies that came to make up Nigeria will be of some use at this point.

The diverse regions that became Nigeria shared two traits: low levels of stateness and fairly rudimentary economies.[64] Unlike Asia, where the British confronted the likes of the Ch'ing emperors, the local polities on the west coast of Africa were smaller in scale and lacked centralized state structures. These ground realities influenced colonial strategies. The variety of situations that the British confronted can be reviewed in turn but in brief. The slave trade had left behind small city-states on the coast—as well as through the Delta—that were run by local strongmen who had benefited from the trade. When the British transitioned to legitimate trade, they often needed to work with these local strongmen as middlemen. Treaties were signed and few of the strongmen were incorporated under a protectorate. When some still got in the way—as in, for example, the well-known case of King Jaja of Opobo—the British government supported the demands of British traders and simply got rid of the "minor obstacles" to free trade.[65] Up from the coast and southwest of the Niger River the British had to deal with the warring Yoruba Kingdoms.[66] A number of tribes that would eventually come to be labeled the Ibos inhabited the region to the southeast of the river. Ibo tribes were easy to conquer;[67] pacifying the Yoruba chiefs required more work.

During the second half of the nineteenth century the twenty to twenty-five Yoruba kingdoms were often at war with each other. Scholars disagree about the causes of the warfare, but one important argument is that the shift from the slave trade to the palm-oil trade encouraged new men of power that undermined the stability of the old system.[68] Not all scholars agree with this view.[69] Be that as it may, what is important from the standpoint of this study is that the warring Yoruba chiefs presented the British with both obstacles and opportunities. Growth of trade required peace in the region. There was also hope that the establishment of *Pax Britannica* in the interior might open up opportunities to cultivate and export cotton, at cheaper rates than from India. And who knows, maybe there are new mines to be discovered, including diamond mines. A unified response to British encroachments by the Yorubas, say, led by the Old Oyo, could have created real obstacles. As it was, the British used their base at the colony of Lagos, worked with the missionaries, and then picked off one Yoruba kingdom and then another, cajoling, threatening, and making treaties, until the region was ready to be incorporated into a larger British colony by the end of the century.

As to the economy, slave trading had created "a barren three centuries" during which the forcible removal of "hundreds of thousands of most virile members" of the society created an "effective barrier against the development of agriculture and industry."[70] The turn to exports of palm oil and groundnuts in the nineteenth century had some positive impact on incomes but not on technological development. The bulk of economic production was aimed at domestic market, especially food production. Land was plenty and shifting cultivation was common. Land was owned communally but could be held in perpetuity by families; family farming was thus the main mode of production, though the use of slave labor was also common. Agricultural practices were striking for their "small" and "primitive" quality: "ploughing was completely unknown."[71] The hand-hoe was the primary agricultural tool, since draft animals were not used. Even the potter's wheel was still not part of the agrarian economy at the turn of the twentieth century.[72]

In the nineteenth century, situated above the *V* carved by the Niger and Benue Rivers in Nigeria were fifteen to twenty emirates, loosely confederated under the umbrella of the Sokoto Caliphate.[73] It had come into being early in the century via Islamic jihad carried out across the Sahara by North African fighters. The local Fulani elite often embraced jihad and imposed a new Islamic order on the indigenous Hausa kings; this order remained more or less intact until the British arrived. They had had limited contact with this area prior to acquiring it at the Berlin Conference in 1885.[74] By the standards of political units in precolonial, sub-Saharan Africa, the Sokoto Caliphate ranked among the most centralized, stable, and sizable.[75] By the standards of other polities that the British colonized, however, the political structure of Sokoto was fairly rudimentary. There was, as I argue elsewhere, "no central army; centralized civil administration was weak, if not nonexistent; the quality of rule varied across emirates, as well as over time; and jihads, mutual warfare, and slave raids remained common throughout the century."[76] A weak central state notwithstanding, in the second half of the twentieth century the Caliphate was more stable than, say, the Yoruba kingdoms. Some of the emirates, moreover, could mobilize effective military power. When the British then sought to transform their paper acquisition of Sokoto at Berlin into actual occupation, they met resistance. Lord Lugard and others persuaded some emirs to sign capitulation treaties, but in other cases the West African Frontier Force (WAFF)—a multi-battalion military force created by the British at the turn of the century to deal with conflicts in West Africa—had to be used to defeat and incorporate the remaining emirates.

The relative stability within the Sokoto Caliphate facilitated some economic gains over the nineteenth century, though these were built on a fairly crude agrarian economy. Unlike the south of Nigeria, which is thick with forests and mangroves, Sokoto lay in a dry savannah that trailed into the Sahara. Besides cereals, groundnuts, and cotton, indigo also grew in the region. Limited evidence suggests that the establishment of the Caliphate led to further enslavement and to the expansion of land under cultivation with the help of gang labor.[77] Increased production of cotton and indigo fed the demand for Kano textiles north of the Sahara. The handcrafted luxury cloth of Kano was carried on donkeys across the Sahara with the help of slave labor. The fact that this trade survived until late in the nineteenth century suggests that British or other European textiles had not entered the region. The minimal contact with European, or even Egyptian or Ottoman, economies also underscores the absence of any technological change for much of the century.

With this brief introduction to the regions that eventually became Nigeria, we are now in a position to return to the discussion of why and how Britain colonized Nigeria. British traders clearly took the lead in southern Nigeria. The British government supported their trading efforts, first with an informal empire of sorts, and then, after the Berlin Conference, with a move toward establishing a more formal empire. By contrast, much of the north of Nigeria became British as part of the European agreement at Berlin in 1885 to divide up Africa; formal colonization followed. The colonization of Nigeria thus has to be understood both in its own terms and also very much as a result of the broader European Scramble for Africa at the end of the century. Far too much has already been written about the Scramble for Africa. For this study, it is only necessary to take sides in existing debates; it is not necessary to reinvent the wheel. What should be added is that it is a bit surprising how many theories of imperialism rest their cases on the late-century European expansion into Africa. Africa was not even that important for Europeans.[78] The surprise diminishes, however, if one keeps in mind that many of the theories of imperialism sought to explain not only the division of Africa (though that was central), but also a variety of other expansionist moves toward the end of the century. Examples include France in Indochina, Japan in Korea and Taiwan, the United States in the Philippines and Cuba, and the carving up of China. In the words of Hobsbawm, the late nineteenth century was indeed the "age of empire."[79]

Two explanations of why Britain—and other European powers—rapidly divided Africa among themselves need to be set aside. One of these is the well-known Hobson-Lenin argument.[80] According to this line, imperialism at the end of the century was moved by the search for profits in the periphery by under-utilized capital in the metropolitan countries. As is by now readily apparent to readers, I am partial to economic arguments. But evidence does not support the suggestion that the Scramble for Africa was driven mainly by investors and financiers looking for higher rates of return. As we have seen, British investors preferred to invest in the white dominions, and then within the periphery, first in Latin America (especially Argentina), and then in India (see chapter 2, table 2.8). There is no evidence to suggest that the moneymen of London eyed Africa with any great interest, before or after the Scramble.[81] Instead, the limited interest in West Africa that is evident in the discussion here was trading interest (although there is no need to deny that this was facilitated by the lowering of shipping costs, manifest, for example, in the role of the Royal Niger Company).

The second argument that is also untenable is the suggestion that the British rush to Africa was politically motivated or, more specifically, aimed at preserving the empire in India.[82] The main evidence adduced in support of this claim was the growing political turbulence in Egypt in the early 1880s that then supposedly forced the British to occupy Egypt to preserve their routes to India, a set of actions that in turn threatened the French (and even the Germans), initiating the Scramble. Two objections to this argument ought to be noted. First, as we have seen, the importance of India to the British was deeply economic. Even if the British had been trying to preserve their routes to India—though that strikes me as far-fetched, especially for West Africa—this would hardly be a non-economic argument. And second, as discussed in chapter 2, political instability in Egypt originated in earlier British actions that were deeply motivated by economic considerations. Similarly, the instability in West Africa, such as in Yoruba kingdoms, was hardly unrelated to the British commercial penetration of the region.[83] While political factors indeed have to be taken into account, the strong critique of Robinson and Gallagher put forward by Cain and Hopkins, namely, that they confuse "symptoms" with "causes," remains persuasive.[84]

The argument that best explains late-century expansionism is that it was moved by the search for markets in the context of growing power competition among industrializing powers. Max Weber—who was definitely not a Marxist—captured the developments of his own era rather well:

> Only complete confusion and naïve optimism can prevent the recognition that the unavoidable effects of trade expansion by all civilized bourgeois-controlled nations, after a transitional period of seemingly peaceful competition, are clearly approaching the point where *power alone* will decide each nation's share in the economic control of the earth.[85]

Increased share of trade was thus the main goal, and power was the currency with which to achieve it; this was the essence of late-century expansionism, more broadly, and of the dynamics leading to the Scramble for Africa, more specifically. Following Hobsbawm and others, the key building blocks of such an argument can now be summarized. First, the economic importance of peripheral economies grew toward the end of the century. For example, European exports grew fourfold between 1848 and 1875, and then doubled again before the start of World War I. Toward the end of the century, shipping doubled between 1870 and 1910, and railway construction also grew sharply. These trends drew the "previously marginal into the world economy."[86] The spread of industrialization to Germany, Japan, and the United States added to the already significant demand from Britain for raw materials from peripheral economies: for example, oil, rubber, tin, and copper.[87] Growing consumer demand also increased the value of such colonial goods as sugar, tea, coffee, and cocoa. With the South African example in mind, feeder railways made the prospect of mining in the interior of peripheral economies a potentially profitable possibility. And if the interiors were accessible, the prospect that more manufactured goods, such as textiles, could be sold in marginal economies also became attractive, especially during the economic depression of the early 1880s.

The growing economic value of the periphery certainly does not, on its own, explain the imperial Scramble for Africa. For that one needs to add a second set of factors: political developments at the end of the century, both within the core and in peripheral countries. The industrialization of Germany had upset the balance of power in Europe, and the rise of the United States and Japan had added to Britain's anxieties about its declining global hegemony. This tightening power competition had an important economic dimension that further helps us understand the European move into Africa. European powers sought access to new markets, including in Africa, but their preferred methods of doing this varied. As noted, at mid-century Palmerston was quite satisfied with an informal empire in Africa that would ensure it was "well kept" and always "accessible." These preferences altered later in the century when access became problematic because the competing European powers also now sought it. The French mode of access was especially problematic for the British because of the French penchant for protectionism during this period. As late industrializers, the French used protection at home. To have monopolistic access to the markets of peripheral economies, they also used protections to keep the more competitive British goods out of parts of Africa. The British found this seriously objectionable. As Disraeli complained to the French ambassador in 1879, "If you were not such persistent protectionists . . . you would not find us keen to annex territories."[88] The French were not willing to back off, of course, and territorial annexation is what followed; the strategic interest of competing European powers in tropical Africa—and, as we will see, especially in West Africa—was then mainly commercial.

Political developments within Africa also created pressures for the British to occupy parts of it. The suggestion by Robinson and Gallagher that political turbulence on the periphery invited late-century imperialism is a tad too much like blaming the victim, but the grain of truth in that analysis can be reformulated. Britain's informal encroachments had created resistance—or diffuse turbulence—that the British felt moved to control if commercial relations were to flourish. This was clear in the case of Egypt (see chapter 2), when the anti-British revolt by Urabi led to the British occupation of Egypt. Nothing similar was afoot in West Africa but the political instability above the coast was also a product of prolonged British commercial penetration of the region. This, too, had to be tamed to facilitate commercial expansion. In the words of Goldie, "in uncivilized countries there can be no permanence of commerce without political power."[89] This is what the Scramble was really all about: political control to ensure sound and profitable commercial relations. Even if tropical Africa turned out to be not all that profitable, it does not take anything away from the fact that "among the original motives of the partitioners was the thought or hope of possession leading to economic benefits"; Lugard—a key architect of Nigerian colonialism—thus wrote, in 1895, that "foreign competition in manufactures and the hostile tariffs imposed by other nations, together with the depression of trade," led us to "seek new markets and new fields for our surplus energy."[90] Hyam—also no Marxist—thus concluded that the suggestion that "the British interest in West Africa was basically a trading interest is unlikely to be contested."[91]

British colonialism in Nigeria lasted some six decades. The commercial motives that fed the colonial drive having been discussed, the analysis here will focus on the causes and consequences of changing British colonial policies in Nigeria. Three key themes are developed via historical analysis. First, the British sought to run Nigeria on the cheap. This led to a fetish for indirect rule. Much of the work of colonial governance was done in collaboration with traditional African authorities. The British expended little effort to create a centralized rule, a coherent armed force, or a professional civil service. The quality of the state that the British constructed and left behind in Nigeria was fairly poor. Second, the economy that evolved over the six decades was a classic colonial economy that exported commodities—palm oil, groundnuts, cocoa, cotton, and tin—and imported such manufactured goods as alcohol, textiles, and metal products. The British depended on import taxes as the main source of revenue for running the colonial state. Little of these minimal revenues was spent on improving agriculture (except for the exportable cash crops), and even less on the promotion of technological or industrial development. When the British left Nigeria, the hand-hoe was still the main tool used for cultivation in the fields. Third, Nigeria's regions evolved along different paths. Missionary education and deeper commercial penetration created a literate, urban elite in the south, especially among the Yorubas. By contrast, the British ruled the north in collaboration with the Muslim emirs; the north was thus shielded from missionaries (and from the English-language education that they imparted). A traditional Hausa-Fulani elite continued to dominate society in the north. Over time, these differences fed distinct identities and undermined the prospect of cohesive nationalism. In sum, a poorly constructed state; a backward, commodity-dependent economy; and a fragmented political class that took power following independence in 1960 did not augur well for the future of a sovereign Nigeria.

The process of how British rule over southern Nigeria extended during the last part of the nineteenth century has been discussed. The colonization of the north was also complete, say, by 1903, when the Sokoto Caliphate fell to British armed units. Central to the colonization of the north was the figure of Lugard, subsequently Lord Lugard.[92] Lugard was born in India to a missionary family. He was educated in England, served in East Africa, and then was as an army officer in the service of the Royal Niger Company, which as we recall was headed by Goldie. While Goldie very nearly retired into private life after selling the company to the British government, the younger Lugard stepped forward and took the lead in colonizing the north. The British government first asked him to head the colonial government in the north, and then later recalled him to try to amalgamate the southern and the northern protectorates of Nigeria into a single colony before World War I, a task that was never really accomplished. Lugard is often held to be a key architect of indirect rule in Nigeria.

British colonial needs, as well as the ground realities of Nigeria, helped mold its colonial ruling strategies. The local polities and economies that Britain colonized in Nigeria were so rudimentary that it would have taken a heroic effort to craft a well-functioning colonial state and to put Nigeria on a path of a moderately productive economy. Instead of any serious effort at social engineering, however, the British did nearly the opposite in Nigeria: they established control and mostly neglected the rest. Behind the relative neglect lay limited colonial aims. After they had established territorial control, the British had two goals: first, that colonial rule would not cost London anything and second, that the local economy would be integrated with the British economy to facilitate trade and other economic benefits.[93] There was near consensus within the British government, as well as among local colonial rulers like Lugard, that Nigeria would operate with little funding from London.[94] Climate and disease also argued against a large British presence in Nigeria. Prior experience in India loomed large in the minds of most British colonial officials. India offered two rival models of how to run a colony: the core model was that of a centralized, direct rule, but a secondary model was the arrangement the British reached with a variety of Indian princely states. Since the potential to collect taxes from the very backward economies of Nigeria was doubtful, Lugard and others in Nigeria gave up on the idea of creating a centralized colonial state in the mold of India. The second-best option that might offer a cheap and effective strategy of colonial rule was, then, collaborating with indigenous authorities. The emirs of Nigeria were reminiscent of the Indian maharajas. Lugard made a virtue of indirect rule—couching it, as had colonial officials in India, in terms of respect for native customs and traditions—and settled on it as a key element of statecraft for colonial Nigeria.[95]

In the north of Nigeria, Lugard vested the power of taxation and of maintaining order in the hands of existing emirs. Such power was, of course, constrained because the emirs were supervised by British officials, especially in the key area of revenue collection and in ensuring a fair share for British colonial governance. Nevertheless, the emirs wielded considerable traditional authority—now reinforced by modern colonial power—in their local domains.[96] It is important to emphasize that this authority was personalistic; the emirs treated the areas they ruled as personal fiefdoms. Unlike in India, then, the coming of colonialism to Nigeria failed to redefine this blurring of private and public power (even at its apex), with long-term consequences. I will return to this issue. Indirect rule based on an alliance of a colonial state with traditional rulers became the main system of rule north of the Niger and Benue Rivers. This system of rule essentially stayed in place until Nigeria gained independence and, in modified forms, even beyond.

Meanwhile, the ruling strategies in the south of Nigeria had to be crafted to deal with local realities. As noted, the British moved north from their base at Lagos to colonize the Yoruba areas. Since Lagos was run directly by British officials—in partnership with well-trained Nigerian civil servants—it is not preposterous to wonder why a model of more direct rule was not extended to Yorubaland or to the Southern Protectorate, just to the east.[97] Because treaties were made with Yoruba chiefs, it was probably expedient to continue working with these traditional elite, especially because it fit the rising ideal of indirect rule. An effort was also made to find traditional chiefs in the Ibo areas, but given the cellular structure of local authority, indirect rule in this southern region remained a work in progress.[98] The difference from the north of both of the southern regions was that in the south, indigenous men of education and commerce were also emerging. In time, this new elite would challenge the power of the traditional chiefs. Why not help create more new elites and work with them? Doing so would have implied siding with the forces of modernization instead of reinforcing the power of traditional authority, a decision the British were not prepared to make. By the early twentieth century—with the examples of Egypt and India in mind—there was already a growing sense that modernized natives spelled trouble for colonial rulers. New racist ideologies had also led the British to exclude educated Africans from government. Working with chiefs and extending indirect rule, of sorts, was then a result in part of expedience, but also of changing mindsets and the lessons learned on how best to rule colonies.

The British periodically debated amalgamating the varying regions of Nigeria into a coherent system of rule, with a centralized state and a unified legal system, but they never really pursued this with any diligence. The British were always thinking in terms of costs and benefits, and there was not much of a return to be had by crafting a better state in Nigeria. The comparison with India on this dimension is telling, and I will return to that discussion. The first effort at centralization under Lugard, in 1914, was a superficial one, whose main aim was to centralize revenues. Its net effect was to take the sizable resources collected in the south—by taxing the region's growing trade with Britain—and use them to subsidize Lugard's favored emirs of the north.[99] Whether the divide-and-rule strategy was deliberate or not—probably not at this early stage—the impact was the same. The resources of the south were to be used to support the north, a set of developments that over time, southerners came to resent. The next major effort did not occur until the late 1930s, when, instead of moving toward a centralized state, the British formally divided Nigeria into three regions, the west and the east below the rivers and the north. This administrative grid, in turn, intensified regional struggles, creating a growing sense that the Yorubas, Ibos, and the Hausa-Fulani had distinct interests and identities. A third and final effort at constitutional engineering before independence was made just following World War II. A modicum of centralization facilitated by the Richards Constitution in 1947 was reversed in 1954, when power was formally devolved to the three regions. The ethnic leaders of Nigeria wanted this, as did a weakened Britain, which wanted to avoid cohesive nationalist demands for sovereignty. As a preemptive measure—this time with a healthy and deliberate dose of *divide et impera*—power devolution had significant political consequences. The politics of Nigeria from then on became less about confronting British colonialism and more about the real or imagined threats of "Fulani domination," or the "rising power of the Ibos," or the plans of the "more educated and commercially advanced Yorubas to run post-independence Nigeria."[100]

The failure of state construction in colonial Nigeria was further manifest in how the army, civil, and police services were created. Following conquest, Britain maintained a fairly small armed force in Nigeria, numbering some 3,000 soldiers. The fact that the British could always call upon the WAFF was a factor. In addition, the limited effort to construct an effective army reflected both the limited need for such forces—given indirect rule in much of the country—and the limited tax base. Nor was this an armed force designed to support centralized rule. The contrast with India was stark. The civil service the British created in Nigeria was also not all that professional; it also incorporated very few Nigerians.[101] Around 1930, for example, there were some 430 British officers in Nigeria, or one officer for every 20,000 Nigerians. Although these numbers compared favorably with those in India, the quality of officers did not. Instead of an exam-based, meritocratic civil service, the recruitment to Nigerian civil service was fairly personalistic. One individual in Britain—Ralph Furse—interviewed candidates for positions and looked for force of character rather than brainpower among graduates of Oxford and Cambridge. A lot of young British duds, with few prospects at home, ended up running countries like Nigeria; in the estimate of one scholar, out of 110 district magistrates in Nigeria in 1940, only thirteen were professionally qualified.[102] With the exception of Lagos, up until World War II very few Nigerians were also incorporated in the civil service. The ethos of an exam-based, well-trained civil service—the steel frame of colonial India—was thus never transmitted to Nigeria.

The police forces in Nigeria were of two types: the colonial police and the native police.[103] In the north of the country daily policing was the job of the native police, an ill-trained force numbering some 3,000 in 1939. Without a unified legal system, crimes were defined according to local customs and Islamic precepts. Local emirs were responsible for raising and managing the native police forces. The personalistic ethos of rule that pervaded the northern emirates also permeated these police forces. The task of maintaining political order, by contrast, was the responsibility of the colonial police, which was originally based in Lagos, but over time came to be divided into a small northern and a larger southern component. The numbers in this force ranged between 3,000 and 4,000, including some 80 British officers. As in other colonies, the British sought out ethnic outsiders for policing duties. To police parts of southern Nigeria, for example, the British recruited northern Hausas, whom they dubbed a "martial race," reminiscent of Sikhs or Gurkhas in India. While this may have been an expedient divide-and-rule colonial strategy, over time a Hausa police force in Yoruba or Ibo homelands would not augur well for ethnic peace and nation building.

Colonial government in Nigeria thus developed without centralized rule and without such core components of an effective state as a well-organized army, civil service, and police force. While this inheritance posed serious problems for sovereign Nigeria, the limited colonial state was adequate to meet the minimal British expectations in Nigeria. Take, for example, the critical area of revenue collection. The British made do with a fairly low rate of taxation: during the interwar period tax revenues were only 2 percent to 3 percent of the GDP.[104] As important was that nearly 60 percent of these revenues came from taxing foreign trade, a bureaucratic task that was much easier than collecting direct taxes. Collection of direct taxes in the north was left in the hands of the local emirs who, especially during the early years, "plundered" their respective territories to meet their obligations to the British.[105] Over time, these taxes were regularized. Direct taxation proved to be a real problem for the British in the south also, not so much in Lagos, but especially in the southeast. This is because most of those being taxed were self-employed, earnings were often not monetized, accounting practices were non-existent, and the ranks of civil servants were too thin to establish any form of systematic taxation.[106]

The meager revenue base did not pose a problem in interwar Nigeria because the British had a "very restricted conception" of the economic role of the state in colonies during this period.[107] In the words of Ajayi and Crowder, the "basic objective" of colonial policy was "to stimulate the production and export of cash crops . . . to encourage the importation of European manufactured goods, and above all, to ensure that this trade was conducted with the metropolitan country."[108] Both patterns of public expenditure and specific policies followed from these limited goals. Nearly a third of the public expenditure was for running the colonial state itself, the civil service, and the police service.[109] With trade as a priority, the colonial government introduced a new currency (pegged to the British pound), established banking, and put custom regulations in place. Public investments in infrastructure then took up another 10 percent of public expenditures annually: railways, roads, and other communication systems were put in place. To be even-handed, the British also invested in improving health and education. As a matter of fact, at some 15 percent per annum, expenditures in these areas were substantial, more so than in India. Scholars have suggested that these trends reflected the important role that missionaries played in the making of Nigerian colonial policy. I return below to a discussion of the impact of the uneven spread of education in different regions of Nigeria.

What was the economic and social impact of these colonial policies on Nigeria? Between 1900 and 1930, Nigeria's average per capita income grew at about half a percent per annum and then essentially stagnated until the end of the war.[110] (I will return to post–World War II trends.) Economic growth in the first three decades resulted mainly from growth in trade, for example, trade between 1901 and 1927 jumped from £4.2 million to £32 million, or nearly eightfold.[111] Nigeria took from Britain gin and rum, cotton goods, building materials, railway items, autos and bicycles, and other consumer items. These imports were facilitated by substantial growth in Nigerian exports of palm oil, groundnuts, cotton, and cocoa. Some of the expansion in supply was probably a market response to growing demand—the "vent for surplus"—but it is also the case that supply growth required state-sponsored institutional changes in how land and labor were organized.[112] There is also evidence that the British government offered financial aid to firms that would extract and export palm oil.[113] The demand for Nigerian exports collapsed with the onset of economic depression in 1930 and did not recover until the end of World War II. Import and export trade was controlled by a handful of British companies. For example, the Association of West Africa Merchants, made up of the United Africa Company and other European firms, controlled as much as two-thirds of this trade. The British government and British merchants, then, managed what was a fairly classic colonial exchange of commodities for manufactured goods in Nigeria.

The impact on the core economy of either the pre-1930 growth or the post-1930 stagnation in the foreign sector was probably marginal. Data are hard to come by, but we do know that nearly 85 percent of the total production during this period was in the subsistence sector.[114] Since land was abundant, agricultural production probably kept up with population changes via extensive growth. There is no evidence that agricultural productivity improved during this period. The underlying reasons are not hard to understand. First, growth in export crops was also mainly extensive, with little technological improvements or productivity growth; there was thus no spillover from one sector to another.[115] The colonial state, of course, did little or nothing to promote improvements in subsistence agriculture during this phase. One source of technological improvement that had made a difference in some other African colonies but that was also missing in Nigeria were large-scale plantations owned by foreigners. Colonial land laws made it almost impossible for foreigners to own land in Nigeria. This was in part a product of the need to preserve the ruling alliance with traditional emirs and chiefs, who often controlled land use, and in part to ensure that scarce labor remained available to grow cash crops. Whether Nigeria would have attracted settlers is hard to know, but keeping Nigerian land for Nigerians must be counted as a positive colonial legacy. However, the colonial state remained the legal owner of land—land could not be bought and sold readily—and an indigenous landlord class that may have practiced large-scale agriculture did not develop. Most agricultural production was thus dominated by small, taxpaying family farmers who avoided risk and produced mainly for subsistence. This, too, contributed to continued stagnation in agricultural productivity. Cumulatively, then, in the words of an African economist, "the system and techniques of (agricultural) production remained largely primitive" during this phase.[116]

There was very little industrial development in colonial Nigeria, a lot less than in India. By World War II there were a few soap factories in the southeast owned by Unilever, a few cotton gins and sawmills in the west, and one cigarette manufacturing plant started by the British American Tobacco Company. For the most part, British manufacturers during this period were more interested in selling their products to Nigeria than in setting up local industry. The underlying obstacles included the conditions one associates with "underdevelopment:" low demand; poor infrastructure; scarcity of skilled labor; and, more so in Nigeria than in some other colonies, difficult living conditions.[117] Indigenous entrepreneurs with experience in risk-taking and organizing large-scale production were also missing. None of this is surprising. What needs to be underscored instead is the role of colonial policies, which were far from helpful. As indicated, the colonial state did not undertake even minimal governmental activities to promote industry prior to World War II. Such activities might have included investment in technical or business education, provision of loans, technology transfer or development, public investment that might feed private endeavors or protect infant industries. On the contrary, the colonial state on occasion violated its own commitment to laissez faire and "actively discouraged" local "manufacturing activities."[118] The main aim of the policy was to protect the interests of British manufacturers. Thus, the colonial state discouraged local textile manufacturing by imposing tolls on caravans carrying local goods but not on those carrying British goods;[119] levied freight charges that discriminated against African and smaller companies;[120] and "enforced . . . stringent regulations" and "exacted . . . heavy trade licenses" on the marketing of African produce.[121]

An important socioeconomic trend during this period that is also worth emphasizing was the uneven development of the regions of Nigeria, which had long-term political consequences. This trend had its origins both in how foreign trade impacted different regions and in how education spread in Nigeria. The southwestern region traded four times more than the northern region, with the southeast somewhere in between. Since trade and commerce were the main sources of new income, it is no surprise that per capita income in the southwest was twice that of the north around World War II. Missionaries were the main agents of the spread of education (and, of course, of saving souls). As noted, part of the colonial ruling arrangement with northern Islamic emirs was that Christian missionaries would generally be kept out of the north. Missionary activities were thus concentrated in the south, first and foremost in the Yoruba areas, and then in the Ibo areas. Growing incomes from commerce and access to English education facilitated the rise of an English-speaking middle-class elite in the south. Many of them had embraced Christianity. There was no counterpart to this development in the north;[122] northern society continued to be dominated by the traditional Islamic emirs. These divergent trends spelled long-term problems for the making of modern Nigeria.

Commercial and educated elites started to challenge the authority of traditional chiefs in southern regions. Thanks to the support of the colonial state, traditional chiefs maintained some of their power and status, including land policy, which gave the chiefs power over how communal lands were to be used. Nevertheless, the new men of the south wanted more, and what stood in their way were both traditional chiefs and the colonial state. With anticolonial nationalism growing the world over in the interwar period—especially with India and Gandhi—it is not surprising that some among the educated in southern Nigeria also started imagining, if not demanding, national sovereignty. The historic surprise is, instead, why this nationalist impulse was relatively weak in Nigeria, even as late as World War II. According to Coleman, "[T]he interwar period was largely one of nationalist gestation, when new influences were being felt, new associations were being formed, and a new generation was coming of age."[123]

Two factors help us understand the feeble character of Nigerian nationalism prior to World War II. First, it was not clear to would-be-nationalists just who would become part of the new Nigerian nation. The southern elites were a product of modernizing changes and wanted more, including access to state power, but the power of the traditional northern elite rested on minimizing changes, including preserving colonialism. The southern Yoruba elites were readier to make nationalist demands than their Hausa-Fulani counterparts in the north. This fracture would continue to haunt Nigeria, and I will return to the issue of growing regional and ethnic fragmentation. The second factor prior to World War II was simply one of timing. Britain colonized Nigeria relatively late on the timeline of British colonialism. Education was also introduced late, and the ranks of those with a university education prior to World War II were still thin. For example, there were fewer than a thousand university graduates in Nigeria around World War II, and most of them were Yoruba. The pool from which a nationalist political class was likely to emerge was thus still relatively small. Anticolonial passions would grow after World War II, but not always in a cohesive fashion. It is to the political and economic developments after the war that I now turn my attention.

While many colonies gained independence after World War II, colonialism lingered in Africa for another decade or two. Britain and France were weakened, but for the most part, African nationalists were not organized enough to convincingly demand sovereignty, and even less to seize control of state power. This was certainly the case in Nigeria. To understand the postwar evolution of British colonial policy in Nigeria, then, it is important to remember the global context.[124] Britain faced serious economic problems after the war. It came to depend heavily on the United States, first to sustain its balance-of-payment shortages, and then, of course—with the Marshall Plan—economic reconstruction at home (see chapter 5). Britain lost India in 1947 in part because of its own weakness, but also because any effort to hold on to a mobilized polity at that stage would have been expensive and probably a failure. Unlike the French in Vietnam and Algeria, the pragmatic British knew when to get out. Nevertheless, the British were also keen to disguise their growing weakness. For example, during a cabinet discussion about liquidating the Raj in India, a government minister noted that the "withdrawal from India need not appear to be forced upon us by our weakness nor to be the first step in the dissolution of the Empire."[125]

In the aftermath of Indian independence, a similar set of attitudes guided Britain's decolonization policies elsewhere: be ready to let go when pressed, but always seem to be in control of policy.[126] Winston Churchill's bluster notwithstanding, both political parties in Britain shared these beliefs. This is not to suggest that Britain was in any hurry to relinquish its African colonies. Rather, the concern was how to minimize the losses. A defensive attitude had important policy implications. First, no major new initiatives were to be taken in the colonies at this late stage, especially if they cost money. This also translated into a reluctance to use force, although that depended on the perceived stakes, as evident, first, in suppressing communists in Malaya, and then, disastrously, during the Suez crisis. The stakes in much of tropical Africa were not as high. This led to a second important policy inclination: to make concessions to African nationalists in the hopes that they would somehow remain within the fold. Harold Macmillan's winds of change Africa tour of 1960 captured, on the one hand, this spirit of reluctant acceptance of the inevitability of decolonization but, on the other hand, an ardent desire that the new leaders of Africa would not all turn into more radical nationalists like Ghana's Kwame Nkrumah. Once the African colonies were made formally independent (with recognition from the United Nations), what the British wanted was that the new African leaders would accept such second-best (that is, from the British standpoint) alternatives as a dominion status or, at least, a membership in the Commonwealth. It was hoped that such a shift from a formal to an informal empire would still allow Britain the status of a major power and continuity of its economic relationships.

Nigeria gained independence in 1960, three years after Ghana did, but several years earlier than other African countries. Many of the pre–World War II political and economic trends in Nigeria discussed here continued following the war. However, some important changes also followed. Their legacy has to be part of any broader understanding of how colonialism shaped Nigeria. Specific political changes—some resulting from British colonial policy, others not—further contributed to the emergence of a fragmented polity: a weak nationalist movement, divided along ethnic lines; the evolution of the civil service; and the collection and distribution of public revenues. As to the economy, during this period a commodity boom helped economic growth, but the resulting resources were not used productively. The British made ready concessions to regional nationalists, a set of policies that both assuaged the nationalists but also kept them divided. The struggle to distribute new resources along ethnic and patronage lines was thus already beginning to take shape, even before independence.

As noted, up until World War II Nigeria was administered as three different regions. In the words of James Coleman, "prior to 1947, there really was no central government in Nigeria."[127] For a brief moment, the British tried to create a central government in 1947 (the Richards Constitution) but this effort did not last. It was too late for major policy innovations in the colonies. Nigerians protested because they had not been consulted, and the British backtracked. The revised constitution of 1954 again devolved substantial power to the three regions, the Hausa-Fulani north, the Yoruba southwest, and the Ibo southeast. In reaction, a major Nigerian newspaper at the time editorialized that henceforth, "economically as well as politically there will be three Nigerias."[128] Any move toward a proper centralized government that may have thus begun in 1947 was certainly reversed by 1954, continuing instead the longer-term trend toward a fragmented, ill-formed colonial state.

The continuing weakness of Nigeria's anticolonial movement has to be understood, at least in part, against this background of a fragmented colonial state. The prewar trends have been discussed. During the war, several developments in Nigeria contributed to growing anticolonialism but not to the emergence of a coherent nationalism. The British mobilized Nigerian resources to support the war effort. These included establishing wage controls, paying producers lower prices for exports, and further limiting credit. Nationalist politicians such as Nnamdi Azikiwe mobilized workers and others who were dissatisfied with making sacrifices for a war that was not their own. Nigerian soldiers who participated in the war came back less intimidated by white superiority and with feeling a greater sense of efficacy. This "raw material" could have fed a more effective and coherent nationalist movement, but it did not. A divided elite sapped the opposition's energy.[129] The fragmented colonial state contributed to intra-elite divisiveness via two different pathways. First, as noted, colonial policies created different types of societies characterized by the different elite interests in the north and in the south. The elite in the north had every reason to be wary of what they perceived to be southern aggressiveness. The southern elites, especially the more-educated Yorubas, wanted change, including a sovereign state. The Hausa-Fulani elite of the north, by contrast, were allies of British colonialism, and rightly concerned about their future prospects without the British. In the end, these divergent interests were hard to overcome.

A more centralized state might have forced the bickering elites to come together to fight a unified enemy, but this second factor was also missing in Nigeria. It is evident in the Indian case that India's ethnic heterogeneity was crafted into a cohesive nationalist force by Indian leaders, who repeatedly urged a divided second tier to come together to fight a tough, coherent colonial state. If the Indians could come together, why couldn't the Nigerians? To be fair, Indian maharajas had remained deeply ambivalent about the Congress in colonial India; the ambivalence of the Hausa-Fulani elite toward Obafemi Awolowo—a potential Nigerian Nehru—had similar origins in conflicting interests. Nevertheless, the INC did succeed in overcoming a variety of centrifugal forces. The problem in Nigeria was not some antecedent, primordial tribal affinities per se. A key contextual difference was that there was no centralized colonial state in Nigeria to inspire the development of a unified nationalist movement.

The underlying logic of this argument is that a powerful enemy can inspire a fragmented elite to overcome its parochial identities to forge a united front. The existence of a powerful colonial state may also have generated a sensibility that unified struggle is worth the effort because in the end, decolonization would yield significant rewards of power and privilege. But the postwar colonial state in Nigeria was neither coherent nor powerful. As nationalism finally emerged in

Nigeria after World War II, the regions were already relatively strong in terms of both resource control and regional loyalties. After the 1954 constitution, moreover, revenues derived from the regions came to be owned by those regions; marketing boards that collected taxes on trade were brought under regional control; elections in different regions were conducted according to different rules; and state officials were also regionalized. Nigeria's regional elites thus came to be more interested in preserving their regional privileges (and less in burying their differences) than in sharing the limited benefits offered by a relatively weak center. The British were also more interested in concessions and accommodation than in confrontation. Over the short run, then, both Nigeria's divided elites and British colonialists were willing to live with a fragmented polity. The longer-term tragedy would, of course, be a dysfunctional state, incapable of steering Nigeria on to a progressive path.

It is not impossible to imagine a loosely organized federation providing a solution to the problem of governing a multiethnic polity. But for that to work in Nigeria, two prior conditions—both of which, unfortunately, were missing—would have helped. First, the center would have to hold. Without a minimal agreement on how to "live and let live," the different Nigerian regions were either constantly anxious about who would control the center or perpetually busy trying to dominate the center. This was a recipe for ongoing conflict, which eventually took the form of an overt civil war—the Biafran War—only seven years after independence.[130] Second, each region would have to be well governed. The quality of government across regions, however, was quite uneven. For example, as the British prepared to leave, there was an effort to rapidly recruit Nigerians to official posts. Educated Africans were readily available in the southwest, where, with Lagos as a base, there was also a tradition of better civil service. Nigerianization there proceeded fairly smoothly, at least in early years. The giant north, by contrast, had very few qualified indigenous personnel. Fearful of southern domination, northerners preferred expatriates to southern Nigerians. The attempt of the northerners to create their own civil service was hurried and superficial. Quick training courses focused on how to wear uniforms, etiquette, and ceremonial roles rather than on how to comprehend and solve problems.[131] Political interference was also rampant in the rapid expansion of official services that followed independence. The core of the state that Nigerians inherited from their colonial past, either at the national or at the regional level, was not up to the task of providing good government.

Finally, we can take note of the economic trends that emerged during the late colonial phase, focusing on the changing economic role of the colonial state. Nigerian economy performed moderately well in terms of growth: national production grew at some 4 percent per annum during the 1950s.[132] Per capita incomes grew between 2 percent and 2.5 percent per annum, which was a considerable improvement over the interwar period. This growth was mainly driven by high commodity prices related to World War II and then to the Korean War. The growth in commodity production, in turn, was mainly extensive; it made use of the growing population and available land. Traditional agriculture that was produced for domestic food consumption still constituted nearly half of the GDP, and grew at some 2 percent per annum (meaning that it barely kept up with the growing population). Manufacturing did grow rapidly but from a low base. At the end of the period under discussion, the share of manufacturing in the national product was still only 3 percent, so what we are discussing is, essentially, a preindustrial economy. Nevertheless, there was rapid growth in manufacturing toward the end of this period, which requires an explanation.

The rapid growth in manufacturing was led by foreign investments in such products as textiles, cement, rubber products, beer and soft drinks, and oil products.[133] Manufacturing was first encouraged during the war years, when some Nigerian incomes grew, but a scarcity of shipping discouraged imports and some de facto import substitution took place. Following the war, the colonial state needed revenues and thus taxed imports at a higher rate, again facilitating import substitution. Though this was not planned, the growth in manufacturing was, essentially, of the import-substitution type. Nigerian nationalists drew the same policy lesson from this temporary delinking from the global economy as did nationalists elsewhere in the developing world—namely, that protectionism, and not laissez faire, supports national industry. But in contrast to some other parts of the developing world, such as the case of India just discussed, two differences also stand out. These differences, too, are worth underscoring because they help us understand Nigeria's limited success with import-substitution industrialization in the post-independence period. First, indigenous entrepreneurs failed to respond to the same incentives. This is because indigenous entrepreneurs with enough experience and resources to undertake large projects were simply missing at this stage of Nigeria's development.[134] Second, the economy was a house of cards, supported by high commodity prices. Short of those prices, there would be little demand in the economy to encourage foreign investors to produce consumer goods. Of course, the intensity of booms and busts in commodity prices became more dramatic after Nigeria became a major exporter of petroleum in the post-1970 period. But even during this early period, dependence on commodity prices was there for anyone to see.

The economic role of the colonial state underwent some important changes in the post-World War II period. In a word, the colonial state became more interventionist but not always in the most productive manner. During the war years, Britain had already imposed greater controls on the Nigerian economy.

Following the war, statism was in the air, supported by a variety of unlikely bedfellows: Keynesian economics and, related to that, the spread of the welfare state in the advanced industrial countries; Third World nationalism; and the influence of the Soviet Union. British colonial officials also started thinking in terms of deliberate development in the colonies. For example, a Department of Commerce and Industry was finally established in Nigeria, in 1947. But this new thinking also coincided with a period of deep economic problems in a war-weary Britain. The Colonial Office in London was not about to invest in industrial promotion in its remaining African colonies. Taxes on booming trade did facilitate some new resources within Nigeria, which the colonial state used to support new industry by giving tax concessions to potential investors and by the establishment of subsidized industrial estates. Foreign enterprises—instead of indigenous producers—again took advantage of these new policies.

Revenue collection was a second area of changing patterns of state intervention. The dependence on taxing foreign trade to generate public revenues was already in place before World War II. During and after the war, nearly 70 percent of the revenues of the colonial state still came from such taxes. While taxation of imports continued as before—although at higher levels that the commodity boom facilitated—new institutions developed to facilitate taxes on exports. These were of long-run consequence. During the war years, the British created marketing boards that bought commodities from Nigerian producers at fixed prices. The overt rationale for such price control was the need to stabilize prices during wartime. From there it was only a short step to "the introduction after the war of permanent marketing boards to control prices paid to peasant producers."[135] Since public authorities exported commodities at prices higher than paid to producers, marketing boards became vehicles for both taxing producers and as a major source of revenue for both regional and national governments. Over time, these institutional arrangements both hurt exports and acted as disincentives on peasant production.[136]

Last, state intervention in social spending increased in Nigeria during this period. From a standpoint of what would be good for common Nigerians, this shift ought to be deemed a desirable change. However, the impact was not always benign. For example, public expenditure in primary education increased considerably in the post-1955 period. Both the federal and the regional governments, especially the governments in the southern regions, financed this increase. The underlying motivation was to use education as a route to upward mobility, especially within the public sector. But the results often fell short: public contracts to construct school buildings often resulted in shoddy or incomplete construction; qualified teachers, books, and supplies were not readily available; and overall follow-through from the new political leadership was missing. As a result, by the late 1950s, "two million primary students . . . were receiving substandard education from ill-trained teachers in overcrowded and inadequate facilities."[137] New patterns of state intervention that emerged following World War II then—whether in the areas of taxation or the promotion of production or welfare—already pointed toward a troubled future.

To sum up the discussion on Nigeria, the British came to Nigeria both to look for profits and to deny them to other Europeans. The various polities and economies that the British incorporated into Nigeria were profoundly backward to begin with. Britain sought to rule Nigeria on the cheap, and expended little effort on crafting a working state or on modernizing the economy. The result included a poorly constructed state without a central authority, without a national civil service, and with a dependence on indirect taxation. The British used this minimal state to promote trade. The local economy thus evolved into a classic colonial economy that exported commodities and imported British manufactured goods. Britain's economic gains from Nigeria were modest, but the benefits have to be assessed against the costs of running the colony, which to Britain were negligible. Following World War II, new nationalist forces challenged British colonialism but they, too, failed to cohere. A fragmented colonial state encouraged the regionalization of the nationalist movement and new regional forces further tore apart the weak centralist impulse of the colonial state. State intervention in the economy also gave rise to such perverse trends as heavy dependence on taxing foreign trade, low producer prices for the peasantry, wasteful social expenditure, and ineffective efforts to diversify a commodity-centered economy. These were long-term trends in the making, with sharply negative consequences for the future of Nigeria.

British Imperialism: Some Conclusions

It may be useful to end this chapter by stepping away from historical details and drawing two types of general conclusions. First, the conclusions worth emphasizing are those that emerge from the chapter's immediate focus on varieties of British colonialism. Second, a few concluding observations are also suggested by juxtaposing the discussions of the Britain's formal empire in this chapter and Britain's informal empire in chapter 2. I will return to the issue of comparisons between British and American imperial experiences in subsequent chapters.

British colonialism in India was prolonged and deep. By contrast, British rule in Africa, including in Nigeria, was relatively short and superficial. What can we learn about the motives, mechanisms, and impact of British colonialism by reflecting on these two experiences together? Let us begin with Robert Clive (see chapter 1) and Sir George Goldie, two important figures in British expansion into India and Nigeria, respectively. Although they lived more than a century apart, what is striking is that both men went looking for fame and fortune in faraway lands. They both helped to establish British colonial rule. Both worked for private companies—East India Company and Royal Niger Company, which each had charters from the British government—whose explicit aim was to make profits. When these companies encountered local resistance, both men used force to eliminate that resistance. Both men made great personal fortunes and helped their respective companies to do the same. Of course, Clive made his fortune the old-fashioned way, through plunder and tribute; systematic revenue extraction and trade followed much later. For Goldie, the palm-oil trade was the main source of profit. The British state worked closely with the two companies these men represented, supporting their respective efforts, especially military efforts, and then shared the profits that were made. Although the process in Nigeria was a lot more compressed, it is notable that the efforts of both the East India Company and the Royal Niger Company ended when the task of establishing colonial rule became too cumbersome and expensive for them to manage as private companies. At that point, the British government bought them out and established Crown colonies in India and Nigeria. Given these historical origins, how can anyone doubt that the search for economic benefits was a significant force driving British colonialism?

Of course, these were only early motives. Over time, the colonial project became more complex and additional motives came into play, although economic motives never lost their centrality. The discussion of India in this chapter begins a whole century later after Clive, with the establishment of Crown colony in 1857. Despite a major anti-British military revolt by Indians, which the British crushed successfully, it is notable that at mid-century hardly anyone in Britain questioned the need to hold on to India. A central motive, I argue, was that the economic importance of India for both state and private capital in Britain was already well established, and sustained benefits were expected. There was also the concern in Britain that indecisiveness about India could be contagious, and indicate to others that the British capacity—or willingness— to run a global empire might be in decline. India was thus already central to British prosperity and power in the middle of the nineteenth century. It can come as no surprise that Britain used ruthless force to hold on to India for another century.

A full understanding of British motives in Nigeria must take into account the fact that the British had had little contact with much of northern Nigeria before establishing rule. Britain acquired the Sokoto Caliphate as part of the broader Scramble for Africa among European powers. Serious scholars have suggested that the British role in the scramble must be understood as a defensive political move, made to either protect existing British interests, such as routes to India, say, via Egypt, or to discourage growing French or German encroachments. As I have said, I side with an alternate line of argument, that, instead, the competition with other European powers was mainly about trade—especially, French use of protectionism—and disturbances en route to India were often caused by earlier British economic incursions. The Scramble for Africa may not have only been motivated by profits, but any discussion of the motives that led to it must situate the late nineteenth-century political expansion within the broader economic context of the period.

The colonies of India and Nigeria were both ruled from London but the mechanisms of rule differed quite a bit across the two colonies. Over time, India came to be ruled by a centralized colonial state with relatively well-established institutions. By contrast, colonial rule in Nigeria was neither centralized nor did institutions of rule put down deep roots. These varying outcomes reflected different timeframes of colonial rule in India versus Africa, changing British needs, and, of course, varying local facts on the ground. The differences were also of long-term significance for the future of India and Nigeria. The basic shape of the colonial state in India was already in place by the mid-nineteenth century, acquired via trial and error as the East India Company established rule over India. The East India Company crafted its ruling structure atop the remnants of Mughal institutions. While the mercantilist East India Company established a variety of arrangements with traditional Indian elites to facilitate rule, on balance, its rule followed military conquest and was more direct than indirect. The persistent need to collect revenue led to the creation of a professional civil service. A well-organized armed force was also needed, both to rule India, and to extend British power in the near abroad. During the post-1857 period in the discussion here, these core state institutions were modified, but not fundamentally. Key changes included a reworking of some relations with indigenous elites to encourage cooperation with the colonial state, further reorganization of the armed forces to avoid future mutinies, and civil service reforms that facilitated more efficient revenue collection. Responding to the needs of the economy—as well as to the growing demand of the nationalists—more and more Indians were also incorporated into these key services. When the British left India, the new nationalist rulers inherited a set of well-organized state institutions.

Britain came to Africa much later in its imperial quest, toward the turn of the twentieth century. Not only had capitalism fully triumphed by then, it had been embraced also by other comers, posing a serious challenge to Britain's global hegemony. British colonial needs in a place like Nigeria were minimum: keep other Europeans out; maintain order; and establish an open economy. The political space of Nigeria also lacked both tradition of centralized rule and, related to that, systematic institutions for extracting land revenues. The British in Nigeria thus did not need a well-organized colonial state, nor would it have been easy for them to create one—at least not without considerable effort. The British took the easy way out, and settled for indirect rule. They established working relations with traditional emirs and tribal chiefs, who helped maintain order and collected some revenues. The main source of revenue was also indirect, that is, taxation of foreign trade. British needs were satisfied by a decentralized ruling structure that did not reach down very far in the local society; neither a coherent civil service nor a professional army was thus developed. For the most part, Nigerians were kept out of these minimal ruling structures. In contrast to India, a sovereign Nigeria did not inherit well-functioning state institutions.

A few concluding observations about the costs and benefits of British colonialism are also in order. As with rival theories about why imperialists imperialize, discussions of the gains and losses of colonialism are also well rehearsed. The evidence examined presented here leads to a conclusion that Britain gained at the expense of its colonies. This argument is at odds with the views of those who continue to focus on the benefits that the British left behind in their colonies.[138] But the suggestion that Britain gained at the expense of its colonies is hardly an original argument; many nationalists, Marxists, and other critics of imperialism have reached a similar conclusion. The originality in the materials presented here is their nuance, especially in specifying the causal pathways. Instead of focusing on the workings of global capitalism, which is the concern of one type of dependency theory, say, that associated with the work of Wallerstein,[139] I have focused more sharply on the role of states and power. Ultimately, imperialism involves one state undermining the capacity of another state or people to determine their own political and economic path. While economic motives are often central in imperial pursuits, it is the state elites who are in the lead. State elites, in turn, often respond to the interests of one faction of capital or another and also take into account broader economic considerations, such as what is good for the country as a whole, which I have labeled "national economic interests." The argument that the British state facilitated gains for Britain at the expense of its colonies can thus be briefly recapitulated.

The argument that Britain gained at the expense of its colonies is stronger for the case of India than for Nigeria. British gains—and India's losses—prior to 1857 are discussed in chapter 1 and do not need to be restated. During the post-1857 period, British colonialism in India helped to create benefits for both private British citizens and for the British state. British capital benefited via trade, investment, and financial flows. These are documented here. Other private benefits included the creation of jobs for British citizens in India and the use of Indian labor in British colonies in the West Indies. The British state, in turn, benefited most directly from the use of a vast Indian army for which it did not pay a penny.

Other indirect national benefits included help with balance of payments, the transfer of revenues from India via home charges, and the Indian colony's overall contribution to Britain's economic buoyancy (and thus to its power). By contrast, the economic importance of Nigeria or, for that matter, of tropical African colonies more generally (again, excluding Egypt and South Africa), to Britain turned out to be more modest. Still, British trade with and investment in Nigeria were far from negligible. Trade also followed classic colonial lines: Britain bought needed raw materials from Nigeria and Nigeria, in turn, absorbed British manufactured goods that increasingly faced competition in the rest of the world. Britain's trade surplus and returns on investment contributed to Britain's balance of payments.[140] And during the two world wars Britain mobilized Nigerian resources to support its war efforts. There is no denying that these benefits are dwarfed by the British gains from its Asian colonies or white dominions, but any full assessment of British gains in tropical Africa must keep two other considerations in mind: first, everything Britain gained it successfully denied to other competitive European powers; second, the costs of running the empire in Africa were miniscule. According to Wesseling, Britain colonized 70 million Africans during the Scramble at the average cost of "fifteen pence per person."[141] And subsequently, as discussed, countries like Nigeria paid for their own colonization.

This is not to say that the British left nothing good behind in India and Nigeria. The political legacy of British colonialism in India has been noted, though Nigeria was not so fortunate. Britain also laid down an extensive railway system in India, helped to create a national market, and introduced English as a language that eventually facilitated national integration. One can note some similar gains in Nigeria, as well. Missionary education in Nigeria must also be noted on the positive side of the ledger, as should some commodity-led economic growth following World War II. Beyond these positive contributions, however, the negative legacies loom much larger.

The economic impact of East India Company rule in India is discussed in chapter 1. During the post-1857 period I examine in this chapter, the stunning fact is that while India was a formal British colony, the per capita earnings of Indians barely budged over an entire century, and continued to stagnate during the first half of the twentieth century. The steady post-independence growth of the Indian economy only makes the prior century of near stagnation that much more poignant and tragic. Among the British acts of commission and omission that contributed to this outcome, I underscore a policy pattern that I characterize as "squeeze and neglect." During the period under discussion, the British squeezed substantial amount of savings out of the Indian economy on a regular basis, and spent nearly two-thirds of them on nothing more than on running the Raj. Land policies facilitated revenue extraction but created disincentives for private investment in agriculture. Public investments in support of the rural economy, especially in irrigation, were minimal. Since nearly 90 percent of Indians at that time lived in the countryside, a large part of the explanation of stagnant incomes in India lies with the limited gains in agricultural productivity. And although I do not examine the perennial problem of famine in India here, it can certainly be added on the negative side of the ledger.[142] In addition, industrial growth was minimal. Forced economic openness made it difficult for Indians to initiate new industries. When the British left India after nearly two centuries of rule, then, they left behind a country that was largely agricultural, poor, and illiterate. At the end of the colonial period, a life expectancy of thirty-two years well captures the quality of life an average Indian could expect to have.

British colonialism in Nigeria was of a much shorter duration than in India and was relatively superficial (in the limited sense that the rule did not reach deep down in the society). Nevertheless, the impact of British rule was often deleterious. The tension between these two claims is mitigated if one keeps in mind the rudimentary quality of polities and societies that became Nigeria. Britain essentially dragged Nigerians into the modern world but did not leave them with the tools to cope with that modernity. The focus of British rule was promotion of trade, but also the taxing of that trade to finance colonial rule. A colonial pattern of exchange of commodities for manufactured goods evolved. Production growth in cash crops was mainly extensive. The British did not invest in promotion of technologies that might improve agricultural productivity. Subsistence agriculture dominated the economy and hardly underwent any significant improvement. The industrial impulse was weak, and what there was of it the British actively discouraged. Their state-building failure especially looms large as a blot on the British record. The specifics of this are documented above: failure to create a central government that was run by a professional civil service, with the capacity to tax incomes; and the accentuation of local identities and identity struggles around regions. The state failure also came to be mirrored in a fractured nationalist movement. Following independence, then, the Nigerian state was relatively dysfunctional. This was a tragedy of first order because a well-functioning state—one that gives meaning to national sovereignty—remains a key institution to facilitate development and upward mobility in the modern world.

Last, two sets of comments about formal versus informal empire are in order. First, if Britain sought economic advantage in both its formal and informal empire, why did it seek territorial control in some places, but not in others? Let us set India aside momentarily, because territorial control over India was already well advanced in the 18th century. (see chapter 1.) By contrast, an industrializing, capitalist Britain of the nineteenth century seemed to prefer informal control in places as diverse as Latin America, and the Ottoman and the Ch'ing empires (see chapter 2). If one were to juxtapose these nineteenth century cases to the case of India, one might be tempted to conclude that true colonialism was a product of a mercantilist age that came to an end with the emergence of thriving capitalism.[143] But historical developments again complicate the argument. Britain, toward the end of the nineteenth century, joined (if not initiated) the scramble and colonized large parts of Africa.

What logic, if any, can help us sort out these diverse British efforts aimed at seeking economic advantage in the global periphery? Gallagher and Robinson argued that Britain preferred an informal empire but resorted to territorial control when informal collaboration failed to secure ready access to the peripheral economies.[144] Based on the evidence presented here, this argument still rings true but also requires qualifications. The major exception to Gallagher and Robinson's argument is, of course, Britain's most important colony: India. Britain sought territory in India from the outset. It was land revenue from India that made the Raj profitable, at least in the early phase. There was never a question of running India informally. Even if one concedes the Indian exception as an exception, which I do not, with its pre-capitalist beginnings, a second qualification for the nineteenth century is that informal empire often bred the conditions for formal empire. In parts of the empire, then, informal versus formal rule were really not alternate choices as much as they were stages. Both the cases of Egypt and Nigeria exhibit the evolution along such a continuum.

Recall Palmerston's assertion that the political condition that the British needed to seek economic advantage in formal or informal colonies was that they should be well kept and always accessible. I have described this as a condition of "stable subservience": stability enabled predictability in economic interactions; subservience, in turn, assured that these interactions occurred on British terms. Why the British chose formal versus informal empire often depended on how they could secure stable subservience in one part of the global periphery or another; since conditions varied, so did strategy. The conditions that most favored an informal empire were when a peripheral country was moderately well governed and the rulers were willing to collaborate. This was the case in Argentina, especially after the violence that followed independence from Spain had settled down. The fact that the British and Argentine economies proved to be highly complementary helped because Argentinian upper classes also benefited from such an arrangement; on balance, the Argentinian rulers were then ready collaborators. Another condition that helped the emergence of an informal empire in Latin America was the power and the interest of the United States in the region. While the Monroe Doctrine was not sufficient to dissuade the British from recolonization—the British navy was far superior to that of the United States at the time—it was a factor. Britain's informal empire in Argentina thus ensured that the lion's share of benefits would accrue to British business interests, but it left open the prospects of gain for both the Argentinian elite, and over time, for the Americans to make inroads.

At the other end of the continuum of informal to formal rule, the main condition that seems to be associated with formal colonial rule is the absence of centralized rule in the periphery. In the words of Goldie, there can be no permanence of commerce without political power in unruly countries. While India and Nigeria were colonized under very different circumstances, they did share a critical condition: the absence of a central authority. Without such an authority, the question of who to collaborate with was moot. Establishing territorial control and central authority had to precede a search for collaborators at lower levels. Formal colonialism, in other words, was a prerequisite for taking sustained economic advantage of peripheral countries in which central authority was either weak or missing. Recall, for example, the case of the East India Company in India under Aurangzeb (see chapter 1). When the East India Company lost a military engagement to the Mughal ruler in 1690, trade with India had to be sustained on commercial terms for nearly half a century. The disintegration of the Mughal Empire in the eighteenth century then created opportunities for the likes of a Clive, both to initiate the long-term process of territorial control and to alter the terms of economic interactions in favor of Britain. More than a century later, the colonial advance in Nigeria followed some similar patterns. After Britain established a colony on Lagos in 1861, for a few decades it carried on trade without feeling the need to colonize West Africa. The need to expand trade, however, required access to the interior. This was difficult. Local strongmen got in the way. More important, there was no central authority to be pressured into facilitating the building of railways, searching and establishing rights over mines, expanding the production of exportable crops, and opening interior markets for British manufactured goods. The fact that the French and the Germans also wanted similar access only strengthened the need to establish territorial control, which the British eventually did.

In between the cases of easy informal empire and hard colonialism are other cases of British imperialism discussed above. Egypt and China, for example, were moderately well governed in the early nineteenth century. Unlike Argentina, however, rulers of these ancient civilizations were not willing to provide ready economic access to Britain. Both Muhammad Ali and the Ch'ing emperors resisted British encroachments, but were ultimately not strong enough to continue to do so. Britain used military power to destroy Muhammad Ali's nascent efforts to modernize Egypt and to pry open China for the opium trade. Subsequent rulers in the two countries were then forced to collaborate willy-nilly. The comparison of British attitudes toward China and India at the middle of the nineteenth century is instructive and worth reiterating: while there was near consensus in Britain that the next step for India was to become a Crown colony, there was just as strong a consensus that such a formal empire in China would be foolishness. Underlying the different attitudes was a key distinction: the Ch'ing Empire was still very much intact and a conquest of China would have been very expensive. Moreover, to repeat the words of Lord Macartney, a formal empire in China was not needed because, "all can be quietly got without it that was expected to be got with it." This was indeed the spirit that moved the British to seek informal empire: if you can get economic advantage without a formal empire, then why not. This attitude kept the British from colonizing Egypt for a while but circumstances changed. A patriotic revolt—the Urabi revolt—threatened the smooth operation of an informal empire in Egypt. The British crushed the revolt and moved toward full colonialism to recreate stable subservience in Egypt, and in so doing also initiated the Scramble for Africa.

The last observation that emerges from a comparison of Britain's formal and informal empire concerns the varying impact of these differing forms of imperialism. While the evidence that I examine is limited, and the results are mixed; on balance, countries that were colonized ended up worse off—certainly on the economic dimension—than other parts of the global periphery that came under informal sway. One obvious indicator is, of course, economic growth. The prolonged economic stagnation in colonial India is documented here. I also outline both the British acts of omission and commission that propelled this outcome: the British extracted significant savings from the Indian economy and invested very little of it to promote growth; the needs of revenue collection created a land system that discouraged private investment in agriculture; public investment to support agriculture was minimal; and deliberate policies sought to discourage the growth of industry in India. The situation in Nigeria was more or less the same, but the share of trade was larger in relation to the indigenous economy, and hence, fluctuation in demand for commodities influenced the growth process more obviously. But there was little change in the underlying productivity of the Nigerian economy during the colonial period. Colonial policies responsible for these patterns are also discussed above, including a limited focus on promoting the extensive growth of commodity exports, but the neglect of most other productive activities.

The sustained economic growth experienced by Argentina under British hegemony stands as a contrast to these cases of colonialism. The complementarities of the industrializing British and land-abundant Argentine economies were largely responsible for this outcome. Nevertheless, rulers of Argentina enjoyed a limited degree of policy autonomy that enabled them to ensure the steady expansion of commodity-based trade. Such policies included the expansion of available land (including the extermination of Indians); a shift from export of hides to meat; and choosing buyers and sellers beyond Britain to include other European countries and the United States. Such policy autonomy reached its limit when the policy issue was to move away from commodity-dependence toward a deeper diversification of the economy toward industrialization. As demonstrated in chapter 2, Britain deliberately stifled such initiatives. A segment of Argentinian elite was also always available to cooperate with the British to sustain the informal empire, with long-term, harmful consequences.

As to the other two cases of informal empire discussed in this chapter, the case of China does not really speak to the issue at hand. The British penetration of the Chinese economy was limited to urban areas. The core economy of China during the period was agrarian. The dynamics of growth in China during the period under discussion were mostly internal to China, although the growing political neglect of the economy was a function of a strained state. The case of Egypt is more telling. Egypt, like Argentina, sustained some economic growth as long as it was able to expand cotton production to meet growing British demand. Public investments by Egyptian rulers helped the expansion of production and the supply of cotton. Over time, the British grip on Egypt tightened, especially as Egyptian debt became a leading issue. Structural adjustment–type policies that ensured debt repayment then led to a decline in public investments in cotton production; this was evident first in a deceleration of economic growth and, eventually, in stagnation. A shift from informal to a more formal empire in Egypt was clearly associated with poor economic performance. While juxtaposing a colonized India or Nigeria to an Argentina under informal sway may only be suggestive, the decline of economic performance within Egypt as Britain's political grip tightened is quite revealing of the economic impact of differing varieties of imperialism.

PART II

How It Continues

United States and the Developing World

4

Seeking Influence Abroad

CARIBBEAN AND PACIFIC ASIA

BORN AN ANTICOLONIAL nation, the United States burst upon the global scene as an imperial power at the end of the nineteenth century. Following the Spanish-American War of 1898, the United States acquired control over Cuba, Puerto Rico, Guam, and the Philippines; Hawaii was also annexed during the conflict. Shortly thereafter, American secretary of state John Hay issued the Open Door notes, hoping to secure economic access to China. While debates within the United States pitched "imperialists" against "anti-imperialists," there was also near consensus among American elites on the need for overseas economic expansion; the debate was mainly over the means, especially over territorial control of peripheral economies. Over time, the United States came to prefer informal over formal imperialism. However, the use of state power to facilitate economic expansion continued unabated after the Spanish-American War. Presidents Theodore Roosevelt and William Howard Taft focused their energies south of the border, acquiring Panama in order to build a canal, forcing regime change in Nicaragua and Honduras, and establishing financial control over the Dominican Republic. By the time Woodrow Wilson had decided to join the Allies in the First World War, the United States had established a small—by British standards, that is—but far-flung empire in the Caribbean, Central America, and Pacific Asia.

Consistent with the themes of this study, in the present chapter I analyze the motives, the mechanisms, and the impact of the first phase of America's overseas expansion. I also draw parallels—or the lack thereof—with British imperialism. The scholarly literature that addresses such issues is sizable, and many of the related debates are well-rehearsed. For example, explanations of early American imperialism include the suggestion that, as in the case of Britain, it happened in a fit of absentmindedness, or that "greatness was thrust upon us," or that it resulted from a "psychic crisis." Some have even argued that American expansion

How Britain and the United States Shaped the Global Periphery. Atul Kohli, Oxford University Press (2020).

DOI: 10.1093/oso/9780190069629.001.0001

was aimed at bringing progress to the less fortunate, whether this progress took the form of promoting Christianity, economic development, or democracy. And last, serious scholars have proposed the political-economy explanation that such outward moves were inevitable as the United States emerged as a global power or that it was pushed by internal economic needs.[1] It will become clear that the historical record best supports the economic and political arguments, although how these motives combined requires elaboration. By contrast, the literature on the impact of American imperialism is more fragmented, often along regional lines. For example, those who analyze either US-China relations during the period or the American impact on the Philippines are often not the same set of scholars who study the legacy of American influence in the Caribbean or Central America.[2] Building on these and related materials, I will also develop some additional generalizations about the impact of American expansion on peripheral economies.

It may be useful at the outset to preview the general argument that is developed below with reference to historical analysis. The question, first, is what motives drove the United States to expand overseas at the end of the nineteenth century? The pressures to expand overseas had been building in the decades following the Civil War. During this period, the United States developed a powerful industrial economy. The example of Britain was very much on the minds of influential Americans, and arguments emerged that great powers must seek commercial opportunities beyond their borders, and that they needed to build military power to support those ambitions. Along with an industrial economy, then, the United States developed a powerful navy. The boom-and-bust character of a buoyant capitalist economy added to the argument that ready access to overseas markets could smooth market fluctuations and facilitate steady economic growth and national power. With much of the global periphery already colonized, however, the United States sought access to the few remaining open economic spaces. The largest of these was China, and the lure of the Chinese market loomed large in America's early overseas imagination. The Philippines was initially deemed a desirable acquisition as a stepping-stone to China; it would be America's Hong Kong. Closer to home, Britain was still a major presence in the large economies of Argentina, Brazil, and even Mexico. However, the American economy was becoming more competitive and American naval power was growing. New opportunities were opening up, especially in the Caribbean and Central America. Britain was still a formidable presence, but weaker European powers such as Spain were ready to be expelled from their few remaining colonial outposts.

Nationalist revolts against Spanish colonialism in Cuba and the Philippines provided the United States with opportunities to intervene, avowedly in support of those country's indigenous nationalists. However, quick naval victories over Spain did not lead to independence for Cuba or the Philippines, but to suppression of the indigenous nationalists and the creation of new American colonies. With naval bases in the Philippines, the United States became a Pacific power. This enabled it to claim a right—in a condominium with other major imperial powers—to full and open access to the Chinese market, the big prize all along. Stronger presence in the Caribbean led the United States to appropriate Panama from Colombia and to build the Panama Canal. The canal, in turn, was of great value, not only to the US Navy but also to manufacturing interests on the American East Coast; the canal made access to the Pacific much easier and trade routes more profitable. The rulers of weaker southern neighbors were tamed, to favor either American investors or to ensure payment of debt owed to Americans, or even to Europeans. McKinley, Roosevelt, and Taft encouraged these developments, not only because of their close ties to America's economic elite, but also because they viewed overseas expansion as essential for America's prosperity and global might.

Next, what were the main mechanisms used by the United States to establish imperial influence overseas? Unlike Britain, the United States was never comfortable acquiring full-fledged colonies. The country's anticolonial history played a role, as did important facts on the ground: at the end of the nineteenth century much of the world was already occupied by Europeans, and by then the United States had already acquired an enormous amount of continental territory of its own. What the United States now wanted instead was access to overseas markets and, on occasion, control over strategically significant pieces of land. After some trial and error—a process that included the full colonization of the Philippines and nearly full colonization of Cuba for more than half a century—the United States settled on a strategy of building an informal empire. Of course, the United States hardly invented this form of imperialism; as we have seen, informal imperialism was part of Britain's extensive imperial repertoire. And as with Britain, the essential mechanism that the United States used for building an informal empire was to create stable-but-subservient regimes on the periphery: stability was necessary for protecting property and profits, and subservient regimes were needed to do America's bidding, including maintaining favorable economic policies.

Establishing stable-but-subservient regimes in other countries is never easy. A variety of obstacles that Britain faced in the nineteenth century in Argentina, Egypt, and China have been discussed (chapter 2). By the time the United States arrived on the global scene as a late imperialist, emerging mass politics and nationalism in peripheral countries had added new and additional challenges. These had to be confronted. Even at this early stage, the United States used a range of strategies that eventually came to define America's way to empire: hard militarism, in the Philippines (and to an extent in Cuba); multilateral domination, in China; and forced regime change in neighboring countries, such as Nicaragua. We will see that these early strategies represented long-term patterns in the making. The imperial strategy of hard militarism used to establish a stable-but-subservient regime in the Philippines would be employed by the United States again in Vietnam and Iraq. Similarly, the multilateral domination of China via the Open Door policy cast the die for future American efforts to establish an open global economy regime in the post–World War II period and, more recently and more relevant to the themes of this volume, to impose the Washington Consensus on developing countries. And last, overt or covert regime change—anywhere from Iran to Chile—has become a permanent part of the repertoire that the United States uses to establish its informal empire.

As to the question of why the United States is inclined toward one strategy of domination in one place and another in a different place, early historical evidence points in a number of directions. Regime change may seem the best option when narrow economic interests are at stake (especially those of American-based overseas corporations) or when the United States enjoys overwhelming power superiority over a potential client state. For example, US efforts to change rulers in the mini-states south of the border were often aimed at ensuring the profitability of such American companies as the United Fruit Company. But when the stakes are higher and the tasks more complex, as they were in the case of maintaining open access to the Chinese economy, the implementation of an imperial agenda requires moving beyond bilateral interventions to create a system of domination. Smaller players who get in the way of the pursuit of high-stakes goals are likely to be thrashed. This was the fate of the Filipino nationalists at the turn of the century. The Open Door notes, in turn, were aimed at creating a coalition of imperialists to prevent the further carving up of China, maintain the subservient regime in power, and keep the Chinese economy open for all to exploit; the fact that the American economy could increasingly outcompete the economies of other imperial powers only helped to cement American preference for this pathway to informal empire.

Last, it is important to take stock of the impact of the costs to and benefits for both the United States and its client states. Unlike Britain, the United States was a giant continental-size economy; it depended less than Britain did on overseas economic interactions for its buoyancy. It would be hard to make the case—and I will not make it—that the United States needed colonies and client states to sustain its economic dynamism. Need and want are related but point to different degrees of desirability. A formal and informal empire was probably essential for Britain to sustain its industrial revolution in the nineteenth century; in this sense, Britain needed an empire. By contrast—there being no limit to human or national wants—the United States wanted overseas acquisitions to augment its growing wealth and power. As will become clear, this distinction between need and want has implications for understanding some important contrasts between the British and US modes of building a global empire: building an empire for the United States—even an informal empire—has always been more a matter of choice than of necessity. The element of choice, in turn, has added tentativeness to America's imperial quests and nearly always has provoked disagreements at home.

Although the economic benefits of imperialism for the United States may not appear to have been large, their value has to be assessed in relation to the cost of acquiring and maintaining them. In light of the huge power resources that the United States had begun to build by the end of the nineteenth century, the cost of most of its forays into peripheral states were marginal. When costs were significant, as, for example, during the first two years in the Philippines, they were borne by US taxpayers and soldiers; the eventual gains were mainly private. From this standpoint, overseas acquisitions led to significant gains, at least for select Americans. I document below that the growing empire provided markets for American manufacturers, cheap raw materials for an industrializing economy, and opportunities for investment in mines and commodities. At times, the benefits of empire transcended private gains, especially when such gains were political; foreign naval bases and fueling stations thus added to the American capacity to project power and so to its status as a new global power.

The following assessment of the American impact on its client states discusses both economic and political developments. Forced integration with the American economy often provided client states with opportunities for economic growth, mainly via growth in commodity exports. But such a pattern of growth also created important economic and political distortions. South of the border, for example, American corporations came to own large slices of commodity-exporting economies, and the US government often supported friendly dictators to keep protests in those countries at bay. The results included poorly governed societies with sharp inequalities, sustained low levels of living, and long-term political instability, including revolutions, as in Cuba. The case of the Philippines under American tutelage offers further parallels. The Philippines, too, experienced commodity-led growth in the early twentieth century, but longer-term developments were far from benign: there were limits to commodity-led growth; the dependent pattern of growth gave rise to enormous inequalities; political power came to be concentrated in the hands of large landlords and middle-class politicians willing to do America's bidding; and a nationalist coalition to lead industrialization failed to emerge, pushing the Philippines down a pathway that resembled the political economies of Latin America more than those of its Asian neighborhood.

The impact of US intervention on China was far more diffuse, though again, hardly benign. China was a giant political economy in which the state was already teetering on the brink of collapse at the turn of the century. As discussed in chapter 2, Britain and Japan were the major imperial powers in China; the importance of the United States was secondary. But once the United States became a Pacific power, it sided with other imperial powers to keep the Chinese economy open and to preserve the power of an ineffective monarchy. A variety of modernizing forces were beginning to emerge in China during this period, some aimed at expelling foreigners, others at reforming or abolishing the monarchy, and some at both. More often than not, the United States opposed these forces. For example, the United States joined other imperial powers in defeating the Boxer rebellion, and then supported but undermined the power of the Ch'ing monarchy by imposing huge indemnity—thus contributing to the monarchy's disintegration—paving the way to a half-century of political instability that only ended with the victory of communists.

In what follows, I first provide some background, focusing on post–Civil War developments in the United States, as well as some beyond its borders, that toward the end of the century generated pressures for overseas expansion. I then take turns analyzing US expansionism in main areas: the Caribbean and Central America; and East Asia, especially the Philippines and China. In the conclusion I return to some general themes, especially concerning the early origins of longer-term patterns of American imperialism.

Background

During the decades following the Civil War (1861–65), American political economy underwent important transformations. These transformations, in turn, greatly influenced the United States' approach to the world.[3] Notable changes in the domestic political economy included rapid industrialization and the emergence of mega-corporations as facilitators of this advance. The American state also consolidated territorial control, on the one hand, and on the other hand, power within that state became more centralized. The modernizing political economy then sought to flex its muscles overseas. A navy was developed, often supported by arguments for the need of foreign markets. While an industrializing economy provided the core strength for such expansion, economic fluctuations (the boom-and-bust quality of the late nineteenth-century American economy) added to the pressure to open global markets, especially in economies that would take America's manufactured goods. The underdeveloped but potentially huge economy of China—which was still not fully colonized—fed the imagination of the more visionary among American economic and political elite, who hoped to acquire a set of stepping-stones to China and turn the Pacific into an American lake. More pragmatic businessmen stayed closer to home, looking for opportunities south of the border. The last little parts of Spain's nearly dead empire, especially, provided ripe opportunities for the expansion that American elites were demanding. When these expansionist efforts, far or near, inevitably ran into resistance from indigenous forces, the United States used coercion to establish control over a number of countries.

The American economy grew steadily during much of the nineteenth century, at some 3.5 percent per annum in the first half of the century and at nearly 4 percent per annum during the second half.[4] The economy was mainly agricultural in the earlier periods, and cotton and tobacco were the primary exports to Europe. Under protectionist laws, industry started to grow in the first half of the nineteenth century, and then "took off" during the second half.[5] The Civil War was a turning point, of sorts. Although the war was enormously destructive of lives, its economic and political importance lay elsewhere. The needs of warring armies encouraged the rise of giant American corporations, including Swift (meat processing), Borden (dairy and groceries), and Carnegie (railways and, subsequently, steel).[6] The war Congresses—free of planter interests and dominated by northern and eastern interests—passed a series of important measures to benefit the cause of industry and corporations. These included a stronger central bank, high tariffs for emerging industries, the Homestead Act (which facilitated the growth of an internal market), the giving of land for the further building of railroads (to integrate Western markets), and contract labor laws that encouraged immigration and cheaper labor.[7]

The defeat of the South ended the power of planters in national politics and opened the way for the growing hegemony within the United States of industrial and financial interests. Corporate investors followed the armies to the South and helped create an integrated national political economy. I will return to the changes in the nature of the American national state. Suffice it to note for now that, far from being a laissez-faire state, the national state increasingly became a "promotional state," boosting the interests of capitalism and national economic prosperity.[8] Large corporations established by the likes of the Rockefellers, Andrew Carnegie, and J. P. Morgan became dominant players in the political economy. The cooperation between the state and capital facilitated rapid industrial growth. This, in turn, attracted more immigrants—also supported by favorable policies—and propelled the growth of the national economy. Between 1870 and 1913, for example, American population and the GDP grew at some 2 percent and 4 percent per annum respectively; these rates were nearly double that of Great Britain during the period. The result was that by 1913, the GDP of the United States was larger than that of Britain and France combined, with all the attendant consequences for shifts in global power.[9]

American products were also increasingly competitive in the world economy. By the end of the century, Europeans feared the invasion of American goods and multinational corporations. Though foreign trade was not a large component of America's growing economy—exports were around 7 percent of the GDP from 1870 to 1900 (compared to nearly 15 percent for Britain toward the middle of the century, when it became an "export economy")[10]—its contribution to the growth of specific industries was crucial. For example, 50 percent of iron and steel, 70 percent of the cotton crop, and 50 percent of copper were exported.[11] The Carnegies were leaders in steel, exporting to the world over, including to Czarist Russia. The Rockefellers led the kerosene trade, with a special focus on Asia. Textile manufacturers were also focused on the Chinese market. Other American companies like Singer Sewing Machine, Kodak, and McCormick Harvesters became global economic players. US exports tripled between 1860 and 1897, and by the end of the century, the United States had replaced Great Britain as the "workshop of the world."[12]

It is important to underscore that American economic progress in the late nineteenth century was far from smooth and continuous. A variety of social conflicts and periodic depressions accompanied the economic transformation. This was the Gilded Age, a period of growing wealth inequality in the United States. For example, the census of 1890 documented that the top 1 percent of the population controlled more resources than the remaining 99 percent combined.[13] More recent data collected by Piketty also documents that wealth inequality rose steadily in the second half of the nineteenth century, peaking around 1910.[14] These inequalities fed industrial and agrarian unrest, as did the periodic economic depressions, say, during 1873–78, 1882–85, and 1893–97. Examples of this unrest include the railroad strikes and urban riots of 1877, the Haymarket Affair of 1886, and then, following the economic downturn of 1893, the "rising force of Populism among western and southern farmers, the growing strength of socialism inside the labor movement, the traumatic Pullman boycott, strikes by textile workers and coal miners, and the bonus armies of Coxey," and others.[15] Periodic depressions were accompanied by bank closings, business bankruptcies, receiverships, failures to sell goods, and declining rates of profit. I will return to the issue of how such domestic problems brought forth calls for economic expansion abroad as a possible solution. For now, it is important to note that the period following the Civil War and preceding the onset of the Spanish-American War is best thought of as a period of economic boom punctuated by busts.

After the Civil War, the American state also underwent important changes. Early efforts were focused on reconstruction and the slow but steady political incorporation of the defeated South. The large armies that had fought the Civil War were dismantled, though enough military force was maintained to eliminate remaining pockets of Native American resistance as their lands were confiscated. Westward expansion continued until late in the century, when Turner proclaimed the "frontier" closed.[16] That argument supported the emerging calls for overseas expansion, an issue to which I will return shortly. Meanwhile, as already noted, power in national politics increasingly came to reside with industrial and financial corporations and free farmers. Political parties and the courts supported these interests, and the power of the executive branch grew, albeit in fits and starts. The needs of industrialization also stimulated efforts to build a centralized and professional state structure, efforts that had gained momentum by the turn of the century.[17] With its territory consolidated, rapid industrialization, and the centralization of state power, the United States was ready to project its power abroad.

The Spanish-American War of 1898 is widely regarded as the decisive event after which the United States emerged as a global power. While I, too, accept this historical periodization for my analysis here, it is important to recollect that arguments for the need to build an American empire—as well as some actual expansion[18]— predated the war. William Henry Seward—a New York senator and the secretary of state in administration of Abraham Lincoln—was already dreaming of an American empire in the 1860s: "[T]he empire would begin with a strong, consolidated base of power on the American continent and move into the way stations of the Pacific as it approached the final goal of Asia. . . . [Asia being] the prize of commerce. . . . Each area would have its own function to perform and become an integrated part of the whole empire."[19] Moreover, the American empire would be different: "conquest was not needed: Americans value dollars more and dominion less"; and "political supremacy" will follow "commercial ascendancy."[20] This early thinking is important, not because it influenced policy immediately—it did not—but because it underscored early inclinations of American policymakers: an empire was needed (mainly for commercial reasons). But unlike the British, who proceeded step by step, acquiring colonies via trial and error, the American empire would not require territorial control, on the one hand, but, on the other hand, it would be planned and constitute a well-integrated system of overseas rule.

The argument that the United States needed to expand overseas became more prominent during the late 1880s and intensified during the second half of the 1890s. The rise of industry and the growth of corporate power provided the context for the rise of these expansionist demands. As long as the economy remained mainly agricultural, land was the main factor of production (along with labor: slaves and immigrants). Absorption of more and more land on the continent had provided relief to such economic constraints as limited land in the past. With frontier closing and industry rising, the need for markets to absorb industrial production was emerging as the new constraint, focusing the attention of businessmen and policymakers on the need for such overseas markets. If US exports in the 1880s were mainly agricultural—more than 80 percent—by the turn of the century, industrial exports were nearly 40 percent of the whole. In specific industries such as iron and steel, the need to export became a near necessity; by 1886, for example, the domestic railroad construction that had hitherto absorbed much of this production came to a halt, generating surpluses that demanded an outlet. It is not surprising, then, that during these years a glut theory emerged. According to this prominent view, "America had become too productive and had created a glut of goods that could only be disposed of in foreign markets."[21]

President Benjamin Harrison appointed James G. Blaine as the secretary of state in 1889. Well before William McKinley, Blaine was a sharp critic of Great Britain, advocated protective tariff for American industry, and saw a clear connection between trade expansion and national prosperity and power.[22] Economic expansion abroad, however, was not going to be easy; many European countries had tariffs in place and much of Asia, Africa, and Latin America was either colonized or informally dominated by the British and the French. Economic expansion would require military power. Out of this logic emerged the early efforts to rebuild an American navy. Blaine worked closely with the naval secretary Benjamin Tracy, to initiate the beginnings of a big navy. It was during these years that old wooden ships were replaced by modern steel armored ships such as the *Maine*, the *New York*, the *Oregon*, and the *Olympia* (Commodore George Dewey's flagship at Manila Bay, as we will see). While a world-class US navy would only be built after the Spanish-American War—all the ships that constituted Roosevelt's Great White Fleet were commissioned after the war—these early steel ships were sufficient to defeat the Spaniards at the end of the century and to initiate the era of American imperialism. Tracy was quite clear in his understanding of the connections: "The Sea will be the future seat of empire. . . . And we shall rule it as certainly as the sun doth rise! . . . To a pre-eminent rank among nations, colonies are of greatest help."[23]

Around the same period, the writings of Alfred T. Mahan, a naval officer and the director of the Naval War College (established in 1884), gained currency, and especially influenced Theodore Roosevelt. Mahan argued that Britain's commercial and military hegemony rested on a powerful navy; if the United States wished to supplant Britain, it, too, needed a strong navy.[24] He made the logic of his argument quite clear: "[A] country's wealth and strength required overseas markets and sources of raw materials." Seaborne commerce, in turn, needed the support of a strong navy and the mobility of such a navy required overseas bases and coaling stations. Declaring, "I am frankly an imperialist," he went on to argue that the United States "must have colonies."[25] He then urged Americans to shift their perspective: "Whether they will or no, Americans must begin to look outward. The growing production of the country demands it."[26] Influential politicians including Roosevelt and Henry Cabot Lodge were especially receptive to these ideas. For example, Roosevelt and Mahan communicated directly and, before the Spanish-American War, came to agree on the need to accelerate the navy buildup, annex Hawaii, drive the Spanish out of Cuba and Puerto Rico, and to turn the Caribbean into a "highway of commerce."[27] In due course, Roosevelt sought to convince President McKinley of the virtues of these policies.

The economic depression of 1893 added urgency to what had until then been general arguments for overseas expansion. As noted, the late-century economic boom was accompanied by a number of social problems: growing class conflict; a sense that the frontier was closing; the need to integrate the large inflow of immigrants; restiveness in the black underclass; and farmers' demands for higher prices.[28] Even before 1893, many businessmen and politicians argued that access to overseas markets could help relieve these pressures. The economic crisis of 1893 then led to a balance of payment crisis and a run on gold reserves that precipitated "a collapse of much of the banking system, a shakeout of the corporate sector, a paralyzing contraction of credit, a plummeting in demand and a rapid spread in unemployment."[29] Businessmen and politicians now increasingly converged on a possible solution: enhanced exports. For example, on the private-sector side an important bankers' magazine of the period proposed that "(if) our surplus manufacturing capacity turned to the production of goods we may be able to export hereafter, at reduced cost and thus keep all our industries permanently employed, as England does, having the world's markets in which to unload any accumulation."[30] And the National Association of Manufacturers (NAM) argued for a stronger and more professional foreign service that would help promote commerce.[31]

On the policymaker side, too, John Carlisle, the Treasury Secretary in the Cleveland Administration, forcefully argued in his annual report of 1894 that America's prosperity depended "largely upon (its) ability to sell surplus products in foreign markets at remunerative prices."[32] The state department joined the chorus, arguing that "every year we shall be confronted with an increasing surplus of manufactured goods for sale in foreign markets if American operatives and artisans are to be kept employed the year around."[33] Given such widespread evidence, a scholar of the period—who is not committed to an economic interpretation of US foreign policy at the end of the century—concluded that, toward the end of the century, "almost everyone (in the United States) seemed convinced that America would prosper if it could find and control overseas markets for its surplus production."[34]

Where could the United States unload its "surplus production"? Given the growing importance of manufactured products in American economy, the underdeveloped areas of the world were the most likely markets. Since much of Asia and Africa was already colonized, Latin American markets provided one natural outlet. Businessmen then argued for building a canal to reach the Pacific coast of Latin America, for reciprocal treaties, for trade fairs, and for government help to open Latin American markets. Latin America "ought to belong to us in a commercial sense," argued a leader of a manufacturer's association.[35] While the interest in Latin America came "naturally" to American businessmen, less obviously the Depression also focused sharp attention on the potential China market.[36] Both missionaries and exports to China—especially textile exports but also kerosene—had already grown, and with growth came a larger sense of the possibilities of this giant market. According to a scholar of these themes, newspapers and businessmen around the country were lured by the China market: the economics editor of the *New Orleans Times-Picayune* characterized the American interest in China market as "immense"; the *Chicago Inter-Ocean* hoped for a "tenfold" increase in US-China trade; and NAM was excited about "the great trade" that may arise in the Orient.[37] Even the State Department, in its review of business prospects for Americans, argued that China offered "one of the most promising fields for American enterprise, industry, and capital."[38]

For America's political leaders, these growing demands for overseas economic expansion pointed to a number of specific policy directions. With respect to some countries—especially south of the border—US policymakers sought bilateral and reciprocal treaties that would ensure access to both raw materials and markets for manufactured products. For other markets, say, where British trade dominated, demands grew to displace British trading hegemony, strengthening calls for free trade. In yet other places, such as China, economic needs led to arguments for maintaining the integrity of China as a single market, with equal access among competing imperial interests. Demands for shifts in political and military policies were also not far behind economic policies. The slow but steady growth of the US Navy during this period has been discussed. The need to link the Caribbean to the Pacific via a canal gained currency in political debates. And the problem of attaining American supremacy in world markets increasingly became a central issue in presidential elections.

The internal economic pressures within the United States to expand overseas were developing in the global context of the shifting power balances that added intensity to these pressures. Several international developments in 1895 underscored these longer-term shifts in the making. First, the United States intervened successfully in Venezuela's favor in a boundary dispute between it and Britain over territory controlled by the British in neighboring British Guiana. Backed by growing economic and military power, this strong invocation of the Monroe Doctrine led Richard Olney (the secretary of state for President Grover Cleveland) to proclaim: "Today the United States is practically sovereign on this continent and its fiat is law upon the subjects of southern America."[39] The fact that the United States prevailed over Lord Salisbury—Robert Gascoyne-Cecil, Britain's prime minister—marked an important turning point in the growing power of the United States vis-à-vis Britain.[40] Second, Japan's military successes in China in 1895 both announced the arrival of Japan as a major power in the Pacific and enhanced concern within the United States about the possible partition of China among competing imperial powers, especially Japan, Britain, and Russia. American policymakers perceived such a carving of China a serious economic threat.[41] Third, José Martí initiated the Cuban revolt against Spanish colonialism in 1895, underscoring the growing problems of the Spanish empire. Before the Spanish-American War, then, American leaders understood clearly that the global power of the United States was growing, but so were concerns and opportunities, inclining them toward an expansionist path.

The proximate events that actually precipitated the War in 1898 are well known and require only the briefest reiteration here.[42] I will also return to discuss more specifically how the war led to American control over Cuba and the Philippines, respectively. The presidential election in the United States in 1896 reflected well some of these deeper trends. The election pitched William Jennings Bryan, the candidate of the Democratic Party, which was increasingly controlled by the agricultural interests of the South and the West, against the Republican McKinley. A key element in the Democratic platform was gaining freer access to overseas markets for American farm products. McKinley accepted the need to promote agricultural exports but added the more complex demands of industrial and corporate interests of the Northeast to the Republican platform.[43] Corporate demands in the period also included access to overseas markets but without always embracing free trade. McKinley formulated these more complex policies as such: "I believe in practical reciprocity," one that will open the "world's markets for our surplus products [but] shall not destroy wages or surrender American markets for products which can be made at home."[44] Although the electoral rhetoric used by Bryan and McKinley was "embittered," they "agreed on the necessity and desirability of expanding the American marketplace, and of extending American power and influence around the globe."[45] When McKinley entered the White House, in 1896, then, he was "committed to a program of vigorous overseas economic expansion," though not to a war with Spain over Cuba; that decision would come two years later.[46]

A political commitment to pursue economic interests seldom comes with a manual of instructions on how to do so. The Spanish-American War was no different. When McKinley became president, the Cubans were rebelling against their Spanish overlords; so were the Filipinos, though hardly anyone in the United States was aware of this, save Roosevelt and a few other Asia hands. Major American newspapers—owned by the likes of William Randolph Hearst and Joseph Pulitzer—argued for American intervention in support of Cuban independence; to them, instability in Cuba threatened American interests. The destruction of the USS *Maine* off the coast of Cuba brought forth jingoism—"belligerent nationalism" in the words of one historian[47]—and pushed the demands for a war with Spain to a fever pitch. President McKinley was reluctant at the outset but not so Roosevelt, his forceful assistant secretary of the navy. Roosevelt—who "valued war for its own sake"[48]—and others argued for American intervention and eventually succeeded. The US Congress authorized the use of force against Spain in April 1898, and war followed on April 25. It lasted for only three months—"a splendid little war," according to Secretary Hay—and led to the rapid destruction of Spain's decrepit navy. Victory, in turn, led the United States to acquire control over Cuba and Puerto Rico in the Caribbean and Guam and the Philippines in the Pacific; formal annexation of Hawaii followed shortly thereafter.

While accidents, national mood shifts, and forceful individuals are what precipitated the war—such factors always play a role—they were not the deeper causes. Against the view that the Spanish-American War was an accident or that an empire was "thrust" upon the United States,[49] one should note that before the war, war planning, of sorts, was already on the way. Roosevelt thus pushed for Dewey to command US forces in the Pacific in 1897, knowing full well that Dewey shared his views about the need to act against Spain in the Philippines.[50] And then again, Roosevelt cabled Dewey in February 1898—before the war began in April—to "keep full of coal" and, if needed, undertake "offensive operations in the Philippines."[51] As in the case of Britain then, there was nothing absentminded about the United States acquiring an empire. To repeat, numerous historians have documented that the pressures for the United States to expand overseas had been building for some time, along with the rise of industrial capitalism in the post–Civil War period. The fear that such growth might be hampered by economic downturns only intensified these pressures. Thinkers like Mahan provided explicit connections between economic needs and military buildup. Political figures like Roosevelt, in turn, embraced these ideas and pushed them toward action.

Caribbean

The United States often champions self-determination for other nations but then frequently turns around to limit moves toward such autonomy when American interests are threatened. Nowhere was this contradiction as clear during this first phase of American expansion as in its own backyard, the Caribbean[52] and Central America. The economic reach of Americans in the region had grown during the 1880s and the 1890s. After the Spanish-American War in 1898, the United States acquired Cuba and Puerto Rico from Spain. Over the next decade or so, American influence in the region continued to grow: for example, it forcibly acquired Panama from Colombia, and the construction of the Panama Canal was begun in 1903; the Roosevelt Corollary was proclaimed with reference to the Dominican Republic, and US control over its finances was established in 1904–5; a nationalist leader of Nicaragua was overthrown by an American-supported coup in 1909; and in 1910 the US Navy intervened in Honduras to provide support to pro-US factions and to ensure debt repayments. A review of these well-known instances of early American expansion, especially into Cuba, serves several analytical functions in the discussion that follows: besides shedding light on the issue of American motives and impact, looking at the patterns of US intervention in the region are helpful for understanding America's emerging approach to building influence abroad.

US interest in the Caribbean region grew during the 1880s and the 1890s. A canal that might link the Caribbean Sea and Pacific Ocean had been on the minds of US businessmen and policymakers even earlier, especially since the 1860s, when the building of the Suez Canal confirmed that such a project was technologically feasible. The Americans started buying sugar cane and tobacco plantations on the Caribbean Islands after the abolition of slavery and reconstruction at home. Investments in banana farms in Central America followed. Production of commodities for exports also encouraged investments in processing industries and transportation. Cuba was the largest and most advanced island in the Caribbean region, with some 1.6 million inhabitants, nearly half of slave origin. While still a Spanish colony in the 1890s, Cuba already took a lot of American investments and goods: before the Spanish-American war, US investments in Cuba (mainly in sugar and mining) totaled some $30 to $50 million and such American goods as hardware, shoes, canned goods, and sewing machines sold "briskly" on the island.[53] Havana was also a cosmopolitan city in the region, an economic hub and a playground of sorts, with some two hundred brothels servicing Spaniards and Americans.

During the second half of the nineteenth century, antislavery and pro-independence movements became frequent in Cuba.[54] This often scared the local elites, who openly hoped that the United States might annex them. For the most part, however, the Spaniards were able to control these movements, say, during the Ten Years' War in the 1860s and the 1870s. US leaders had also periodically expressed the desire to annex Cuba for strategic reasons; well before the Spanish-American War, for example, the American secretary of state Blaine had recommended such a course of action. But not much came of such desires until the 1890s, when, as discussed, the needs of an industrializing economy pushed the United States toward its expansionist phase. Cuba's independence movement in 1895, led by Martí, thus raised concerns to a new level. By then, US economic interests in Cuba had grown, as had American naval power. Also important was the fact that the Cuban rebels were combining nationalist demands with demands for social justice; their promises of land redistribution were of special concern to Americans since much of their investment in Cuba was in agriculture. When the struggle between the Cuban nationalists and Spaniards morphed into guerilla warfare, life and property were threatened. The anti-imperialist US president, Grover Cleveland, suggested that American concern over Cuba was by no means "wholly sentimental or philanthropic . . . our actual pecuniary interest in it is second only to that of . . . Spain."[55] Despite the considerable sympathy for Cuban nationalists within the United States, then, Cleveland chose not to recognize the legitimacy of insurgents. Proclaiming neutrality, the United States nonetheless leaned toward Spain in the early phase of the conflict, hoping that Spain would repress the nationalists, establish stability, and protect American interests.

McKinley took office in 1897, committed to restoring the confidence of American business groups, including via overseas economic expansion in the Caribbean and Pacific Asia. Both indigenous nationalists and Spanish colonialism stood in the way of this goal; eventually the United States defeated both militarily. The decision to go to war with Spain over Cuba emerged only serially. Though the avowed goal of the war was to liberate Cuba from Spanish colonialism, it was clear even before the war that like his predecessor, McKinley had little sympathy for Cuban independence. For example, McKinley's then secretary of state, John Sherman, had argued before the Spanish-American War that US policy toward the Cuban nationalists "must be controlled by commercial interests rather than by sympathy with a people struggling for liberty";[56] and then, while making a case for the war to the US Congress, McKinley argued explicitly that it would not be "wise or prudent" for the United States to recognize "the independence of the so-called Cuban Republic," because such recognition would put an "embarrassing" constraint on US "intervention," that of "approval or disapproval of such government."[57] Clearly, Cuban sovereignty was not high on McKinley's policy agenda.

What, then, was the real purpose of the War? I have discussed the broader, contextual forces, emphasizing the economic origins of American expansionism. Among the more proximate triggers historians have established, too, prior to the war, Cuban nationalists were on the verge of defeating Spain, exposing its weakness and threatening American commercial interests.[58] American businessmen—especially sugar and banking interests with Cuban connections—sent a memorandum to McKinley in February 1898, pointing out that some $100 million had been lost in commerce during the Cuban War of Independence, and requesting American intervention to establish peace in the interests of commerce.[59] McKinley, in the address to the Congress arguing for war with Spain, noted, "[O]ur trade has suffered, [and] the capital invested by our citizens in Cuba has been largely lost." When McKinley sent the *Maine* to Cuba, among the considerations must have been the threat that Cuban conflict posed to American commercial interests. A variety of other pressures then helped precipitate the war. It is well-known, for example, that when the *Maine* was blown up, war hysteria grew; the role of Hearst newspapers in whipping up these sentiments has been described as "one of the most shameful episodes in the history of American press."[60] The US Congress signed on only after an amendment to the war resolution—the Teller Amendment—seemed to provide an assurance that the United States did not seek to colonize Cuba. Their conscience thus relieved, US congressmen fully participated in the growing jingoism: they sang "The Battle Hymn of the Republic" as they authorized a war against Spain. Roosevelt meanwhile ordered a uniform from Brooks Brothers so he could form the Rough Riders and join the war effort.[61]

The Teller Amendment also assured some Cuban rebels, such as General Calixto Garcia, the leader of Cuban revolutionary force, that US intervention was aimed more at Spanish colonialism than at them. The Cuban rebels and the American forces then cooperated, albeit briefly, in defeating Spain. However, it became immediately evident that the United States had no intention of allowing the Cuban nationalists to form a government. As noted, it was never in the cards. Ignoring the Teller Amendment, the United States occupied Cuba, promising it some sort of control, eventually, over its own affairs—that is, "when the conditions were right." While the Cuban nationalists were unhappy, unlike in the Philippines, they chose not to fight the United States militarily. The asymmetry of power was overwhelming and the geography only intensified this imbalance. Moreover, instead of withdrawing American forces, in 1899, McKinley sent in more US forces to pacify Cuba. Garcia and his compatriots then accepted a financial settlement from the United States to disband the revolutionary army. Between 1899 and 1903, the United States experimented with a variety of political arrangements for Cuba, eventually settling on a set of conditions, codified under the Platt Amendment, that turned Cuba into an American protectorate. This legal arrangement lasted until 1934, although Cuba's political and economic dependency continued well beyond, until Fidel Castro's revolution.

Following Spanish defeat, some among the Cuban elite—mainly the creole, planter class—feared the indigenous nationalists, who were often in the military and of darker skin color—and hoped for closer links with the US. US annexation of Cuba, however, was nixed rather early by US policymakers as a long-term option. Why? The question is of some relevance because the United States did annex neighboring Puerto Rico. Why not Cuba? The Teller Amendment might have played some role. So did racism; in the words of an American general who explained to Cuban creoles the American reluctance to annex Cuba: "Uncle Samuel has too many niggers already."[62] Probably more important, however, was the fact that within the frame of America's turn to expansionism, Puerto Rico was of strategic value, whereas Cuba's importance was mainly economic. Puerto Rico had a third of Cuba's population at the time. Its location made it of great value to the United States as a coaling and naval station; Mahan and others had singled it out as one of the stepping-stones needed for the United States to establish a global presence. Though Cuba also had strategic importance, much of this was satisfied by annexing the southeastern tip of Cuba at Guantánamo Bay (where the United States to this day has a naval base along with a detention center). For the rest, the importance of Cuba during that period was mainly economic. Moreover, US policymakers believed that Americans did not need to annex Cuba to pursue these economic interests; instead, after some trial and error, they came to the conclusion that their economic interests could be pursued within a framework that offered "the best of all worlds by more indirect control and the illusion of Cuban self-government."[63]

After McKinley's assassination, Roosevelt became president. His rhetoric on Cuba followed that of the Republican leadership and was already a match for Woodrow Wilson's subsequent "idealism": "[O]ur aim is high. . . . We hope to do for them [the Cubans] what has never been done for any peoples of the tropics—to make them fit for self-government after the fashion of the really free nations."[64] Nothing of the sort followed, of course. The immediate task in Cuba following war victory was how to withdraw most of the American troops—needed to satisfy the Teller Amendment—while also limiting the options of the Cubans. McKinley delegated this task to Elihu Root, the secretary of war at that time. He, in turn, worked closely with General James G. Wilson, who was serving in Cuba in 1899. Wilson developed the ideas that Root then turned into proposals and passed them on to Orville Platt, a senator from Connecticut, for approval in the Senate.[65] Once approved, these proposals came to be known as the Platt Amendment.

According to this amendment, the United States would withdraw troops from Cuba in exchange for some severe limits on Cuban sovereignty. These limits included: No independent foreign policy; a US right to intervene in Cuba to ensure a government that would protect "life, property, and individual property"; and a right to lease military bases.[66] When the Cubans resisted the incorporation of these demands into their constitution, the United States refused to withdraw troops until they did so, and they eventually did. American policymakers fully understood the implications of their actions. General Leonard Wood, McKinley's commander in Cuba, wrote in a private correspondence to Roosevelt: "There is, of course, little or no independence left Cuba under the Platt amendment."[67] United States then withdrew its forces in 1902, while the Platt Amendment ensured American control over Cuba. Even the anti-imperialists within the United States cheered the withdrawal of American forces; to them this underlined that the United States was unlike the real imperialists of Europe.[68] Slowly but surely, then, Americans had begun to discover the type of informal empire that might serve their needs and with which they could live. *Plattismo* would, in turn, became a model of sorts that the United States applied elsewhere in the region; even beyond the region, the United States eventually put into practice the idea of forcibly molding the constitutions of other states to advance American interests.

From then on, until Castro's revolution, Cuba's evolution was deeply conditioned by its northern neighbor. For much of this period Cuba was an American "colony in all but name."[69] While Cuba was, supposedly, pacified by 1902, neither Cuban nationalism nor the Cuban forces demanding social justice were—or could be—readily eliminated. Periodic US military interventions followed, for example, in 1906, 1912, and then again in 1917, to ensure political stability and investor profits. Within this framework, set by the Platt Amendment and buttressed by periodic military interventions, Cuba's foreign trade, investment, and finances became deeply dependent on the United States. A full discussion of these developments is not needed for the present purposes; fine studies of the subject are available elsewhere.[70] All that is needed here is a quick review of some developments that will enable an assessment of the American impact on Cuba during this early phase, say, prior to the emergence of Fulgencio Batista as Cuba's ruler in 1933.

A reciprocity treaty in 1902–3 opened Cuba to American goods—more or less forcing out European goods—and enabled Cuban exports, mainly sugar, to be sold in the American market without tariffs. The Cuban economy also started using dollars as the medium of exchange. Sugar exports from Cuba to the United States had already been significant prior to war with Spain, but they then grew rapidly in the early twentieth century: sugar production in Cuba doubled between 1900 and 1910, and doubled again between 1910 and 1920, but then crashed around 1930 with the onset of economic depression in the United States[71] Much of this sugar was exported to the United States. Tobacco exports from Cuba also grew during this period. In exchange, the United States sold a variety of manufactured goods and, paradoxically, food to Cuba, needed because sugar production had displaced more traditional agriculture on the island. By the First World War, then, nearly three-quarters of Cuban trade—imports and exports—was with the United States.

Profitable commodity exports also attracted American investments in Cuba, especially in land. Americans—individual citizens and companies—bought enormous amounts of land in Cuba, mainly for producing sugar cane. Indigenous planters sold land in part because war years had impoverished them, and in part because they did not understand the growing American appetite for sugar as well as American investors did. American investors also understood that the United States was in Cuba to stay and that the US government would protect their property and investments. Specific US policies in Cuba also helped American investors insofar as Cubans—especially the smaller landowners—could not always come up with clear land titles. The US military government regularized land titles, which advantaged American buyers and "swept away thousands of Cuban squatters and small holders."[72] The United Fruit Company, for example, bought up nearly 400,000 acres of Cuban land—first with the hope of planting bananas but then shifting to sugar, given its relative profitability—and R. B. Hawley, a congressman from Texas, led the effort to form the Cuban-American Sugar Company, which, by 1910, had grown into the world's largest sugar plantation.[73] Over time, American corporations came to own 75 percent of plantation land in Cuba; the Rockefeller group alone owned some 1.25 million hectares of land.[74]

The Cuban economy thus became a classic colonial economy: exporter of one major commodity (sugar) to one major buyer (the United States), and taker of manufactured goods from that buyer. More so, the majority of the productive sugar-cane plantations came to be owned by American companies. The process of acquiring this land and turning Cuba into a large American-owned sugar plantation was, of course, far from smooth.[75] The weakening of the Creole planter class made it a less effective comprador class; over time, the United States came to need indigenous military rulers to protect American interests instead. Those displaced and marginalized by the massive land grab also revolted frequently. For example, poor Cuban blacks revolted in 1912 (the Negro Revolt) and threatened property; Americans intervened militarily to repress the revolt. Then, displaced peasants became social bandits, threatening property and property owners, again inviting American military intervention in 1917. Clearly, the Platt Amendment only provided the broad framework for establishing informal empire. The profit-making process was often brutal and therefore required tools tougher than constitutional engineering to sustain it. Direct military interventions faded only in the 1920s, when local strongmen who were willing and capable of doing America's bidding came to control the Cuban government.

It is difficult to document the growth and distributional trends in Cuba in the first half of the twentieth century. Hard data is not available; systematic growth data is only readily available for the post-1929 period, though earlier population data is available. Fragments of data support the conclusion that US economic influence facilitated economic growth in Cuba during the first two decades of the twentieth century but the same influence then also "undermined its long-term prospects."[76] US investments in Cuba grew rapidly prior to World War I. Most were directly related to sugar: plantations, refineries, and transport. By World War I these totaled some $215 million (about the same as British investments), and then grew very rapidly to $1.36 billion by 1924–25.[77] During the war, sugar prices went up sharply, attracting more economic activity. The rapid growth in sugar production and exports during these years has been noted. Since sugar constituted nearly a third of Cuba's overall production during this time period, this must have contributed to overall growth. American exports to Cuba also grew sharply. Some of these were displacing European exports, but the growing demand in Cuba must have also contributed. And finally, immigration into Cuba also grew during this period, suggesting that a growing economy probably provided the attraction. All in all, the scattered evidence suggests that the Cuban economy probably grew—and may even have grown rapidly—during the two decades following the imposition of Platt Amendment.[78]

It is doubtful that this growth either led to significant per capita gains or was shared. Along with growth, the Cuban population also increased rapidly, from 1.7 million in 1900 to 3.8 million in 1930.[79] This population was absorbed in and contributed to a pattern of growth that was mainly extensive: more and more land was brought under sugar-cane production. Without a significant increase in productivity, it is unlikely that this would have led to major gains in per capita income. Good estimates of per capita income of Cuba are available from 1929 onward. In 1929, for example, just before the US stock-market crash, Cuba's per capita income was about the same—actually, a little lower—than that of its poor neighbors Nicaragua and Guatemala.[80] On distributional issues, too, scattered evidence suggests that those at the bottom—generally the black Cubans—did not gain much from this pattern of growth. The periodic revolts by those who were displaced when Americans bought up Cuban land have been noted. Low farm incomes were maintained by the practice of importing labor from neighboring islands during peak seasons. The main beneficiaries of the sugar boom were American corporate interests and the Spanish middle class that controlled trade and commerce. Some Cubans eventually gained via access to the state, where corruption was rife and real power absent.

Cuba's sugar boom came to an end during the 1920s. Partially, this was a result of natural saturation of the market within the constraints of available land and technology. For the rest, global conditions were important. After the First World War, global sugar prices leveled off; as a result there was very little new investment in Cuban sugar mills after 1926.[81] The Great Depression of the 1930s followed. Lower demand and the imposition of tariffs in the United States had a traumatic impact on Cuba's highly dependent economy: Cuba's GDP declined by one-third between 1929 and 1932.[82] Unlike other Latin American countries, such as Brazil, where coffee-support and import-substitution policies provided opportunities for growth during the 1930s,[83] the Cuban state simply did not have the policy autonomy to experiment with imaginative solutions. Instead, the economy continued its slide, and Americans withdrew capital from Cuba during these years. Cuba's GDP in 1940 was lower than it had been in 1929. The resulting social unrest brought new types of politics to the forefront. Instead of military intervention, the United States now encouraged a military man—Batista—to the forefront of Cuban politics during 1933–34. Batista would not only do America's bidding over the next few decades but would also maintain a highly corrupt and dictatorial rule that fed Castro's revolution.

The history of Cuba under Batista and then on to the Castro revolution is not part of the main story that I tell here.[84] My main purpose has instead been to delineate the motives and mechanisms of American expansion into Cuba at the turn of the century, and then to give some sense of the impact of American rule. It should be clear that specific American companies benefited greatly from the US control over Cuba. Cuba was acquired for economic reasons and, despite its small size, for the economic benefits it delivered. By the mid-1920s, Cuba was the sixth-largest overseas market for US goods.[85] As noted, US foreign investment in Cuba during the mid-1920s also totaled some $1.4 billion; this constituted nearly a quarter of total US direct foreign investments at the time.[86] These trade and investment trends continued during the Batista years, when the sugar trade recovered and corporate investments again grew.

In considering the impact on Cuba, I have also noted that the economy grew during the early phase (say, 1902–25), but not necessarily the standards of living of the population. The growth was also maldistributed. In subsequent periods, Cuban economy grew in fits and starts, but per capita GDP in 1960 was only 25 percent higher than it was in 1929, implying less than 1 percent growth per annum over three decades. Growth and distributional issues aside, the real tragedy of Cuba is that it was transformed into a one-commodity economy, highly dependent on the United States. This left little room for economic diversification.

Despite some flourishes by Batista, who was trying to become another Getulio Vargas or Juan Perón, the Cuban state was not sovereign enough to pursue a nationalist-developmental project. Moreover, since both the state and economy were heavily controlled by the Americans, the government's corrupt and dictatorial politics fueled anti-Yankee sentiments in Cuba. The combination of failed domestic capitalism, repressed nationalism, socioeconomic inequality, and illegitimate rulers was volatile; it invited a revolution. Following Batista's overthrow by Castro, President John F. Kennedy described the US-Cuba relationship up to that point as follows: "I believe that there is no country in the world including any and all countries under colonial domination, where economic colonization, humiliation and exploitation were worse than in Cuba, in part owing to my country's policies during the Batista regime."[87]

Besides Cuba (and Puerto Rico), the other Caribbean island that posed a challenge for American foreign policy during this early phase was the Dominican Republic ([DR], then called Santo Domingo). Even before the Spanish-American War, Americans had debated annexing Santo Domingo off and on but always decided against it. During the early 1900s, however, the island's internal instability and economic debt raised the possibility of a German intervention. After the Venezuelan boundary dispute of 1903, the United States wanted no more European interventions in the American hemisphere. Some in the United States again argued for simply annexing Santo Domingo, following the model of Puerto Rico, or even the Philippines. President Roosevelt's reaction, however, was telling: "I have as much desire to annex it (Santo Domingo) as a gorged anaconda wants to swallow a porcupine wrong-end-to."[88] Only five years into its colonialist phase, the United States was already tiring of territorial annexation; the cost of imposing imperial authority on the Philippines must have been on Roosevelt's mind. An alternate policy was needed that would leave the formal sovereignty of Caribbean countries intact but also keep the Europeans out of the region.

It was in this context that Roosevelt added what has come to be known as the Roosevelt Corollary to the Monroe Doctrine: in case of "wrong-doing" in the "Western Hemisphere," it was the United States that would exercise "international police power."[89] With this policy the United States committed itself to maintaining order in the region. Roosevelt exercised this big-stick policy in the DR in 1905. With American warships patrolling the coast, Roosevelt secured control over the DR's customhouses. The arrangement was modeled very much along the lines of control that Britain and France had imposed on Egypt's finances around 1880 (see chapter 2). The avowed goal was to use the financial resources to satisfy debtors—German and British, as well as American—on the one hand, and to help facilitate political stability within the DR on the other hand. While the debtors might have been satisfied, the political situation hardly became stable.

Within a decade, US marines landed again in the DR. Because they sided with sugar interests, peasant resistance grew, leading to a nearly decade-long American occupation, followed by the dictatorial "era of Trujillo," which lasted until 1961.[90]

Leaving aside the Caribbean, the Spanish-American War also led to growing American influence over the smaller countries of Central America. Like much of Latin America, this region had been part of the Spanish empire. It gained its independence in 1823. Regional territories then organized and reorganized over the next few decades to become what we now recognize as the Central American countries. For much of the nineteenth century, a relatively few Spaniards continued to dominate the Indian populations of these countries. Meanwhile, as in other parts of Latin America, Great Britain wielded significant political and economic clout in the region. American influence in the region grew in the second half of the nineteenth century, especially economic influence but also political—as underscored by the Venezuela boundary crisis of 1895–96, discussed above—and then increased sharply after the war. For example, the United States forced the secession of Panama from Colombia in 1903 and then built the canal and established a protectorate in Panama over the next decade; American interventions turned Honduras into a typical banana republic; and the United States forced a regime change on Nicaragua in 1909. The brief review of these developments that follows will help clarify the variety of methods used by the United States to establish an informal empire in the region.

Ever since the completion of Suez Canal in 1869, Europeans and Americans entertained the idea of building a similar canal across the isthmus in Central America.[91] US policy to keep the Europeans out of such a project was set rather early: President Rutherford B. Hayes informed Congress in 1880 that "the policy of this country is a canal under American control."[92] The early attraction of a canal was mainly commercial: a shorter route to the Pacific, including to the fabled China market. As the United States built a modern navy, strategic considerations also favored such a canal. Even before the Spanish-American War, then, Roosevelt suggested to Senator Lodge: "I do wish our Republicans would go in avowedly to annex Hawaii and build an oceanic canal."[93] Presidential candidate McKinley had argued for such a canal during the 1896 election campaign, and cited the need to reach markets in the Pacific as the primary reason. The canal project then became imminent in the aftermath of the war.

For reasons of feasibility and expense, the first choice to build the canal was across Nicaragua. But a group of lobbyists with interests in Panama used "political pressure and bribes to win congressional support of the Panamanian site then ruled by Colombia."[94] When Roosevelt's negotiations with Colombia to secure rights to a strip of land across the isthmus broke down, he encouraged a secessionist rebellion by Panamanians against Colombia. The pro-Panama lobbyists in the United States helped fund this rebellion, and Roosevelt sent a warship to ensure that Colombian government could not crush the rebellion. Panama thus became a "sovereign" country in 1903, via "as brazen—and successful—an act of gunboat diplomacy as the world has ever seen."[95] Thereafter, Panama became an American protectorate in which the United States had a right to intervene as it saw fit. The construction of the canal took nearly a decade. While it was clearly a significant technical achievement, much of the labor was provided by black West Indian workers; nearly 5,000 canal workers died of disease while working on the canal.[96] By the time the canal was completed in 1914, Panama was "pretty well an American colony . . . along the lines of Cuba."[97]

Honduras came to typify a banana republic. By the end of the nineteenth century, the banana industry had grown rapidly. Over the next decade, nearly 80 percent of the banana plantations in Honduras came to be owned by American companies, especially United Fruit. These companies collaborated and conspired with indigenous politicians to ensure profitability, so much so that the country became "indistinguishable" from the fruit companies. The US government was actively involved; the US consul pretty much appointed the country's rulers.[98] The US government in Honduras was, of course, supportive of the banana companies, but its interests were also broader. In 1908, for example, Honduras faced a debt crisis; it owed nearly $120 million, mostly to British lenders. The United States stepped in, took control of the customs houses, and cut a debt-restructuring deal designed by the financier J. P. Morgan, who, in turn, came to control the railroads of Honduras. When some indigenous political elites opposed the deal, they were forced to accept a settlement, on board an American warship off the coast. American-supported "Sam the Banana Man" Zemurray then took effective power in Honduras and collaborated with the United Fruit Company to turn the country into a "prototype of a banana republic."[99] The United States Marines Corp then periodically intervened in Honduras—seven times between 1903 and 1925—to ensure a succession of stable governments that would protect the interests of American investors.

Last, the United States has had a long history of intervening in Nicaragua, which began during this first expansionist phase. From 1893 to 1909 Nicaragua was ruled by Manuel Zelaya, a dictatorial and a nationalistic modernizer, of sorts. The United States favored him when the plan was to build the isthmus canal across Nicaragua. But once Panama was chosen, Zelaya's nationalistic policies, especially his effort to secure better terms from Nicaragua's American-owned mining companies, raised alarm in Washington. President Taft, who replaced Roosevelt in 1909, promised dollar diplomacy in lieu of the big-stick policy of his predecessor. He also appointed Philander Knox to be his secretary of state. Knox was close to the Fletcher family, owners of the gold-mining concession in

Nicaragua (one Fletcher brother managed the company and the other worked at the State Department; this would not be the last time that such personal connections influenced US policy at the highest levels. I discuss the Dulles brothers in chapter 5.)[100] The State Department then orchestrated a campaign to remove Zelaya from power.

To ensure that pro-American rulers consolidated power in Nicaragua, the USS *Venus* was anchored off the coast. Adolfo Diaz had been handpicked by Americans to replace Zelaya. When Diaz failed to impose rule on nationalistic dissenters, Taft, in 1912, sent 2,600 US marines to protect American interests in Nicaragua. They stayed until 1933.[101] During these years, the marines confronted a powerful anti-American revolt led by Augusto César Sandino. This movement combined elements of nationalism and social justice, and Sandino became a symbol of anti-American resistance in much of Latin America. Sandino's defeat led to the ascension of Anastasio Somoza to power, who, in turn, established an American-supported dictatorial dynasty that lasted forty years. Thus the Somozas and the Sandinistas of Nicaragua were both very much products of US efforts to shape the country to enhance American interests.

To sum up the discussion so far, US influence in the Caribbean and Central America expanded sharply in period following the Spanish-American War. American interests in the region were mainly economic but, on occasion, also strategic. The United States decided rather early to eschew colonialism, but its control over Cuba came close to it and provided a framework in which American trade and investments flourished. The preferred form for establishing influence in the region was to keep stable-but-subservient regimes in power. Stability, however, was often elusive, and nationalists just as often challenged this subservience. The United States then periodically used force to put stable-but-subservient regimes in power and to protect them; between 1898 and 1920, for example, US marines entered the region twenty times.[102] More often than not, these dictatorial regimes were controlled by militaries that ruled in alliance with local oligarchs and American investors. The longer-term impact on the region included poorly governed countries with commodity-dependent economies, poverty, and sharp inequalities.

Pacific Asia

Prior to the 1890s, American contacts with Pacific Asia were limited. Commodore Matthew Perry had forcibly opened Japan at mid-century, and American commercial interests grew in Hawaii during the latter part of the century. The United States had cooperated with the British—as a junior partner—in expanding trade with China. As discussed in chapter 2, American ships had participated in supplying opium to China. During the 1850s, American trade with China was significant—about a third of China's entire trade with the West.[103] American missionaries going to China and Chinese coolie labor coming to the United States was the other early people-to-people contact. Although Seward and others had argued as early as the 1860s for the need to expand into Pacific Asia—with the China market as the ultimate goal—direct involvement by the US government in the region emerged only later in the century, following the rapid industrialization and state consolidation in the aftermath of the Civil War and Reconstruction.

As noted, during the 1890s, the idea that the United States needed to expand overseas to maintain its national prosperity gained currency among influential Americans. In addition to its own neighborhood of the Americas just discussed—regions that were traditionally delineated as being within the American sphere of influence by the Monroe Doctrine—the China market offered great possibilities in the Far East. Even if self-serving returning missionaries had originally propagated this idea, many businessmen came to share the view that the giant economy of China—one of the largest preindustrial countries that was still not colonized—might offer an outlet for America's rapidly growing industrial production and investment needs.[104] American businessmen, however, could not go it alone in China. Other country governments were already providing systematic support to their own businessmen, including the governments of Great Britain, Japan, Germany, and Russia. Many policymakers in the United States were then persuaded not only of the importance of the China market, but also of the need of governmental involvement. Once the lure of the China market became great, the US made a "conscious, purposeful and integrated effort to open door to China"; from then on, the United States used traditional realpolitik to seek open economic spaces in distant China.[105]

Gaining open economic access to China was not going to be easy, however. Not only was China becoming turbulent at the end of the century, but other major powers also were already on the ground there. Access to China would thus require governmental support, and in practical terms, that meant the support of a growing navy. The navy, in turn, would require bases and coaling stations on the way to China. Influential thinkers such as Alfred Mahan and Brooke Adams understood these requirements; they argued not only for building a stronger navy to support America's overseas commercial ambitions, but also for acquiring colonies—or near colonies—as way stations to China. The economic depression in the United States in 1893 intensified these demands for access to the China market. The Japanese victory over China in 1895 reinforced the concern that China might be partitioned among rival imperial powers. This, it was argued, would be a huge loss for American interests.[106] The need of the China market and the fear that the United States might lose out contributed to the decision to acquire islands on the way to China. Viewed from this standpoint, the acquisitions of Hawaii, Wake, Guam, and the Philippines in the Far East were neither accidental nor a product of a policy of large imperialism; that is, they were not acquired because of their own economic worth. They were acquired in an "eclectic effort to construct a system of coaling, cable, and naval stations for integrated trade route which could help realize America's overriding ambition in the Pacific—the penetration and ultimate domination of the fabled China market."[107]

The Philippines turned out to be America's most important colonial acquisition after the Spanish-American War. A country of several thousand islands, the Philippines in 1900 was inhabited by some eight million people, a population larger than that of Persia and two-thirds that of Korea at the time. The plan to acquire the Philippines had begun several months before the start of the war. Senator Orville Platt (of Platt Amendment fame), suggested to President McKinley that "Manila had become one of the most important ports of the Orient and that the importance of that station demanded most careful attention." Shortly thereafter, the assistant secretary of the Navy, Theodore Roosevelt, wrote a Navy Department memorandum, which President McKinley had examined, arguing that in case of a war with Spain, the Asiatic Squadron "should blockade, and if possible take Manila."[108] As noted, Roosevelt subsequently, in 1897 (well before the war) ensured that a sympathetic naval officer—Dewey—took command of the Asian fleet and instructed him that when "needed," he should undertake "offensive" actions against the Philippines.[109] And then, even before the news of Dewey's rapid victory over Spain in the Manila Bay had reached Washington, the McKinley Administration had decided to send "an army of occupation" to the Philippines.[110] In light of such historical evidence it is hard to understand the claims of some contemporary scholars that the Philippines was "an accidental conquest."[111]

While the premeditated approach to acquire the Philippines was meant to provide access to the China market, developments within China intensified the pressures to move in that direction. After their military victory over China, the Japanese in the post-1895 period had started consolidating their gains. This threatened British policy in China to prop up the Ch'ing monarchs. As discussed in chapter 2, the British could have been satisfied either by joining the land grab or creating an open door, enabling all the imperial powers to compete within China; eventually they settled for protecting their own share of the China trade. Before that, however, Britain invited the United States, in early 1898, to join in an "open door condominium" to ensure that China was not partitioned.[112] The United States did not respond, in part because it was preoccupied with the coming of the Spanish-American War, but also because it had no real power in the Pacific at that point. To join Britain in its major policy proposal over the future of China would have made it a junior partner to that agreement; however, the United States was increasingly unwilling to accept such a secondary status. This claim is supported by the fact that, after acquiring the Philippines, the United States pursued an identical open door policy in China, but now it was in the lead. What is important to note is that the growing informal partition of China by Japan, Britain and others underscored a further need for the United States to become a Pacific power that, in turn, would be facilitated by the United States acquiring its own Hong Kong in the Pacific.

By the time American ships challenged the decrepit Spanish fleet in the Manila Bay, Spanish colonial control over the Philippines was already under considerable pressure from Filipino nationalists. While this is not the place to recount that history, a few comments will help clarify what the Americans found on the ground after they came to occupy the islands.[113] As elsewhere in its empire, Spain had colonized the Philippines nearly three centuries earlier by granting large pieces of land to colonizers. Over time, these estates passed on to a mestizo stratum that became the indigenous ruling class in the islands. Spain ruled in alliance with this class and a set of local officials, the cacique. When Spain ended its mercantilist policies in the nineteenth century, such Philippine products as sugar, copra, and hemp found markets in industrializing Europe, enriching the landowning oligarchy. Children of landowning classes, in turn, often received education in Europe and returned; they came to constitute an urban middle class, an intelligentsia, of sorts.

Early Filipino nationalists emerged from the ranks of this rich intelligentsia, or *illustrados,* as they were called locally.[114] While most of the members of this political class were conservative—demanding no more than a share of Spanish privileges—a few undertook popular mobilization, combining demands for independence and social justice. Andres Bonifacio and the Katipunan (KKK), a nationalist and revolutionary organization that he helped create in 1892, represented this trend. By 1896, for example, KKK boasted a membership of 400,000 and a significant armed wing. Although the group was internally factionalized, the KKK posed a serious threat to Spanish hold over the Philippines. After an internal power struggle within the KKK, Bonifacio was executed, and Emilio Aguinaldo emerged as the new leader. Aguinaldo was more conservative politically than Bonifacio but was also an impressive military leader. He defeated the Spanish forces and even formed a provisional government. The Spanish, however, pushed back, and offered Aguinaldo a large sum of money to leave the country, and he accepted exile to Hong Kong.

This was more or less the situation in the Philippines when Dewey arrived in Manila Bay aboard the USS *Olympia,* the lead cruiser of the Asiatic Squadron. As is well known, the Spaniards in the Philippines, as in Cuba, proved to be no match for the Americans and the US victory was both rapid and decisive. But the real battle to establish control over the Philippines lay ahead; if the Spanish were readily defeated, the Filipino nationalists were not easy to pacify. Dewey contacted Aguinaldo in Hong Kong quite early. Though the historical record is murky, Dewey apparently sought Aguinaldo's help in the fight against Spain, and in return offered some sort of autonomy to the Philippines under Aguinaldo's leadership.[115] Aguinaldo helped the United States but, following the military victory over Spain, Dewey did not allow Aguinaldo to enter Manila. Instead, he would be allowed only a lesser government, in Malalos, some thirty miles north of Manila. Dewey and others had no intention of giving the Filipinos independence; as discussed, this was never the real American policy, despite whatever private commitments Dewey may have made to Aguinaldo. Aguinaldo, in turn, felt deeply betrayed and remobilized the nationalist forces, this time against the Americans. Thus began the mostly forgotten but brutal Philippine-American War, which lasted for some three years; at its peak, it involved 70,000 American soldiers, and led to the deaths of some 20,000 Filipino soldiers and 200,000 Filipino civilians.

The Philippine-American War has been described by a respected observer as "an unalloyed American conquest of territory and among the cruelest conflicts in the annals of Western imperialism."[116] In addition to superior force, the United States used torture—especially water cure—concentration camps, and scorched-earth tactics to crush the Filipino nationalists and establish American rule.[117] As in the case of Cuba, the United States demonstrated no sympathy for Filipino nationalism; instead, it deliberately sought conquest, and conquer the Philippines it did. The historical evidence provides no support to the claims of American statesmen of the period that the aim of the Spanish-American War was to help Cuba and the Philippines gain sovereignty from Spain. The Spaniards were defeated, and American order was forcibly established over these countries instead. The Anti-Imperialist League in the United States, which included such significant members as Andrew Carnegie, objected to these overtly colonial policies.[118] In the end, however, the league did not prevail. We noticed in the case of Cuba that the Platt Amendment had satisfied many of the anti-imperialists. As to the Philippines, the arguments of the likes of the Indiana senator Albert Beveridge prevailed: "Our largest trade henceforth must be with Asia . . . The Pacific is our ocean . . . . China is our natural customer. . . . The Philippines gives us a base at the door of all the East."[119] When the Senate voted to hold on to the Philippines, most of the anti-imperialists withdrew their objections. Even William Jennings Bryan voted for the resolution.

Although the Filipino resistance to American occupation of the Philippines continued, in 1900 McKinley appointed future president Taft to head the

American colonial government in the Philippines. The United States from then on pursued a two-prong colonial strategy: ruthless suppression of any real demands for Philippine independence and co-optation of those elements within the Philippine elite who were willing to collaborate. The landed oligarchs had been allies of the Spanish colonial rule, and they readily switched allegiance to Americans. The urban middle classes, however, the *illustrados*, could have posed a serious challenge to American rule by perpetuating nationalist demands. But Taft and other future American viceroys of the Philippines skillfully co-opted these elements into a governing structure that offered them limited power, on the one hand, but plenty of opportunity for graft and self-aggrandizement on, the other hand. A working colonial arrangement was thus constructed: for the next few decades the Americans talked about democracy while running a colonial state, and Filipino elites talked about independence while cooperating with the Americans. Most Filipinos were, of course, excluded.

Americans introduced democratic institutions to the Philippines: elections, legislatures, the rule of law, and a free press were brought into being. Although the colonial authorities controlled key powers and American claims that they were bringing democracy to their little brown brothers were at best hypocritical, it is also important to emphasize that American colonialism in the Philippines was less brutal than, say, Japanese colonialism was in neighboring Korea during the same period. The limited practice of democracy provided some constraints on the exercise of arbitrary power. At the same time, however, and judged from the standpoint of the long-term development of the Philippines, the colonial state evolved to become a fairly ineffective one. Two emerging features especially contributed to this ineffectiveness.

First, whatever real power Filipinos could exercise within the colonial state came to be exercised by narrow elite groups, especially the agrarian oligarchs.[120] American rule in the Philippines was based on an alliance with these oligarchs and American policies further strengthened their power in the state and society. Over the long term the oligarchic families turned the Filipino state into an instrument, not of national development, but of personal aggrandizement. Second, following their own model, the Americans in the Philippines hardly put any effort into creating a Weberian bureaucracy. With the focus on elections and parties, the state qua state also became patrimonial, serving more the interests of office holders than of Filipino society. A corrupt state controlled by landed oligarchs was then a highly ineffective state in the making. The contrast with neighboring Korea under Japan is again striking. The Japanese in Korea severed the connection between the landowning classes and the state on the one hand, and on the other hand, built a rational-legal bureaucracy in the image of their own Prussia-inspired state structure; though brutal and certainly not democratic, this colonial state of Korea evolved into a developmental state.[121] Not so in the Philippines. In the words of one scholar, the combination of oligarchic rule and a patronage-based state eventually helped give rise instead to "booty capitalism."[122]

The United States did not acquire the Philippines for its own economic worth. But once it was acquired and naval bases were established, the issue of what to do with the islands was at the forefront. The economic framework for governing the Philippines was not obvious at the outset. A variety of interest groups in the United States lobbied for favorable policies. For example, those who produced sugar and tobacco within the United States were threatened by the prospect of free trade with the Philippines; whereas the manufacturing interests welcomed the opportunity to enhance their exports, especially at the expense of the British and other Europeans. The legal status of the Philippines, and of other insular acquisitions, was also ambiguous; while they were certainly not sovereign countries, they were also not part of the United States. This made the choice of tariff and other policies difficult. Given the anti-imperial streak in American political discourse, those in charge of the Philippines, such as Taft, the investment banker William Cameron Forbes, and others, also did not want to be seen as exploitative imperialists; they identified themselves as progressives and sought to follow some of those values. US economic policies in the Philippines thus evolved via trial and error, though not without some core underlying considerations.

The United States had decided at the outset that rule over the Philippines was to be financially self-sufficient. This meant that the resources of the colonial state would have to be mobilized within the Philippines. Initially, the United States followed the Spanish practice of depending heavily on custom duties. But once the US Supreme Court ruled, in 1901, that the government could not impose tariffs on trade with its insular acquisitions, Taft shifted to a highly regressive flat tax—one that America's key Filipino allies could support—as a source of governmental revenues.[123] Without an effective bureaucracy, even this was difficult to collect. The revenues of the American colonial government averaged some 7 percent of the GDP, not much higher than that of the decrepit Spanish colonial government that preceded it.[124] Since most of these resources covered the expense of running the colonial state, capital expenditures in the Philippines throughout the colonial period remained less than 2.5 percent of the GDP, below what the Japanese colonial state spent in neighboring Korea and Taiwan.[125] All public investments over the nearly five decades of colonial rule were financed within the limits of these meager resources.

American authorities made good use of these limited resources. Two areas of public investment are especially noteworthy. First, the United States invested in education and public health. Literacy rates in the Philippines improved, as did life expectancy.[126] The impact of the educational policies, however, needs to be qualified: textbooks were used for propaganda purposes, especially to denigrate nationalist aspirations;[127] economic productivity during the period did not improve;[128] and "in the end the American attempts at social engineering brought about little fundamental change."[129] Second, the colonial state invested in irrigation, mainly during the first fifteen years of colonial rule. This was aimed both at improving sugarcane production—sugar exports were the main source of the growing incomes of the state's key supporters, the landowning oligarchs—and rice production, so as to feed the colony. Unfortunately, the fiscal situation became strained following the passage of a free trade act, Payne-Aldrich Tariff Act of 1909—taxing trade became difficult in the aftermath—and investments in irrigation declined. But as long as public investments in irrigation lasted, they helped growth of agriculture. Agricultural growth, in turn, was a key component of the positive growth in per capita incomes during the first two decades of colonial rule.[130]

The 1901 ruling of the US Supreme Court on insular cases enabled the Philippines to export to the United States without paying tariffs. The 1909 Payne-Aldrich Act put a cap on tariff-free sugar exports to the United States but no limit on what the United States could sell tariff-free in the Philippines. Its passage reflected the power of the sugar lobby in the United States to restrict imports, on the one hand, and the prowess of industrial groups that wanted to sell their products to the Philippines, on the other hand.[131] Another important ruling that reflected the power of the US sugar lobby prevented American citizens or corporations from buying large tracts of lands in the Philippines.[132] The avowed goal was to protect the Filipinos; in fact, the sugar interests in the United States worried that, as in the case of Hawaii, Cuba, and elsewhere, Americans would buy up sugar plantations on the Philippine islands and thus threaten domestic sugar production on a giant scale. These considerations within the United States then set the basic framework for US-Philippine trade relations during the colonial period.

Sugar exports from the Philippines to the United States grew rapidly, from 29,000 metric tons in 1903 to 463,000 metric tons in 1925.[133] Since Americans could only own limited pieces of land, these exports helped raise the wealth and income of the indigenous landowning oligarchy. Along with growth in rice production, growth in sugar production and exports contributed to the growth of the GDP, at least during the 1900 to 1920 period. The distributional consequences of this pattern of growth were quite uneven, however. Not only did the incomes of landed oligarchy grow, but US tariff policies also subsidized this growth in the following sense: since sugar exports to the United States from other countries could not enter the United States without tariffs, Philippine exporters received a large subsidy.[134] As noted, the inability to collect customs duties, in turn, had led the colonial state to mobilize revenues via a flat tax. The negative impact of US colonial policies on distribution should thus be clear: the United States subsidized the incomes—and thus the power—of the landed oligarchs of the Philippines, while the rest of the Philippine society bore the burden of financing the colonial state. No wonder the oligarchs had no use for indigenous nationalists and warmly embraced the American colonial project.

American exports and investments into the Philippines also grew during the colonial period. Most of the exports came to be manufactured goods, and the foreign investments included a sizable share in mining. So, even though the Philippines were not acquired for economic reasons, US-Philippine economic relations became colonial: Philippines exported commodities, absorbed American investments in the production of exportable commodities, and took American manufactured goods. While this was a long-term pattern in the making, two short-term implications of these economic relations are also worth noting. First, during the first two decades of colonial rule, Philippine incomes had grown. This, in turn, stimulated some import-substitution type of growth in the manufacturing of simple products of everyday consumption. The trend came to a near halt, however, as the growth of production in manufacturing decelerated after manufactured imports from the United States accelerated.[135] This contributed to a slower growth of per capita incomes in the post-1920 period, as did the abovementioned crucial decline in public investments in irrigation, which led to lower rice yields per unit of the new lands that were being added to sustain a growing population. Second, the trade framework that the United States created with the Philippines increasingly privileged American producers and investors at the expense of those from Europe or Japan. So, while the United States was professing an open door in China, its practice in the neighboring Philippines was quite exclusionary. The contradiction could not have escaped the attention of other powers, which, over time, chose to ignore American entreaties for equal access to the Chinese market.

Colonial economic relations influenced US-Philippine political relations, which during the colonial phase were characterized by a back and forth on the issue of Filipino independence. Within the United States, the Democrats tended to support some sort of independence for the Philippines more than the Republicans. When the rhetoric was set aside, however, the differences were not dramatic. Woodrow Wilson, for example, favored independence but never pushed the issue too far. The Republican president Warren G. Harding then rescinded even these limited gestures, suggesting that the stability and economic development of the Philippines must precede political autonomy. Interest groups within the United States were also pulling in different directions. As we have seen, tariff-free imports of sugar from the Philippines raised the ire of domestic producers, especially during the Depression years; these demands then even contributed to the eventual decolonization of the Philippines.[136]

Within the Philippines, the United States crushed any nationalists who tried to mobilize popular opposition to American rule. And since the majority of Filipino elites, both agrarian and urban, made peace with American rule (as noted, the landowning oligarchs gained wealth and the urban elites gained access to the colonial state), nationalist demands from among these groups were, at best, moderate. No wonder the Forbes-Wood Mission, in 1921, recommended, and President Harding accepted, that the Filipinos were not ready for independence in following terms: "Like most Orientals they [the Filipinos] seem to be more interested in the form than in the substance [of independence]. . . . [Independence] could be hedged around with so many conditions lodged in the hands of representatives of the United States that their actual powers would be limited. . . . In essence beneath the velvet glove must be the strong hand."[137] Despite intermittent nationalist outbursts in the Philippines, then, a "strong hand" in a "velvet glove" provided the formula for US colonial rule in the Philippines.

To conclude the discussion on the Philippines, American colonial rule in the Philippines was not all bleak. After its ruthless conquest of the islands, the United States introduced a limited democracy. There were modest gains in per capita incomes during the colonial period and literacy and health conditions improved. The longer-term impact of US rule, however, must be judged negative, even sharply negative. Spanish colonialism had left behind an indigenous society ruled by a narrow landowning oligarchy. Thus US rule cannot be faulted for creating this oligarchy; the United States inherited it. Where the US rule can be faulted is that, instead of reforming what it had inherited, American policies accentuated these political and economic inequalities. Within the frame of a superficial democracy, the Philippines evolved into a dependent political economy. Agrarian oligarchs and a political class benefited at the expense of most Filipinos. Over time, these elites preferred to collaborate with the United States rather than to put the Philippines on a nationalist path of modernization that might benefit the whole society. The Philippines have thus remained an exception in a booming Asia. The roots of this exception lie in the colonial period that helped generate an ineffective state run by personalistic politicians and supported by a narrow group of landowning oligarchs.

Moving away from the Philippines, beyond the Philippines lay China. As we have seen, the promise of the China market and the threat of losing it to competitive imperialism of other powers had contributed to the Americans' decision to acquire and to hold on to the Philippines. The colony of the Philippines now provided a base from which to project power and to influence developments in China. American goals in China were mainly commercial, but for commerce to flourish, the goals quickly had to become political: from the American standpoint, it was important that other imperial powers did not carve up China as "pieces of melon," and that the Ch'ing monarchs maintained some semblance of regime stability. In the end, American policy in China achieved mixed results. US trade to China did improve following the Spanish-American War, even dramatically in some products. The gains for American investors and bankers were more modest. While the China market was not quite a myth, gains often did not match expectations. Regime stability in China also proved to be elusive, as Britain, Japan, and others carved up their respective spheres of influence and the rule by the Ch'ing dynasty disintegrated. Many of these developments are discussed in chapter 2; there is no need to repeat that analysis. The only point that is worth reiterating is that, in my judgment, the causes of China's disintegration in the early part of the twentieth century were mainly internal to China. To the extent that imperialism played a role, Britain and Japan were the key external actors. The United States was a relatively minor actor in China. Its role did grow in the post–Spanish American War period, but it was never decisive. The main reason to discuss the American role in China during this phase, then, is in part to complete the story of where the lure of the China market led, but more importantly, it helps us understand the emerging US approach to building influence in distant political economies. Both the promulgation of the Open Door policy and the US intervention against the Boxers in China thus require discussion as examples of the United States' road to an informal empire.

As noted in chapter 2, the first set of Open Door notes were promulgated by John Hay, then the US secretary of state, in 1899. They were addressed to all the foreign powers in China, and argued that China should be kept open for all foreign citizens to do business, without prejudice or special favors bestowed by political or military influence. Although China was not consulted about the wisdom of these policies, the other powers —Russia being a significant exception— more or less agreed with the principle of maintaining open economic access to China. These and the second set of Open Door notes, in 1900, which argued for maintaining the territorial integrity of China, have been widely studied and interpreted quite differently. Some scholars have suggested that the Open Door policy was of great importance because it set the framework for a long-term American approach to building an informal empire, one that combined anticolonialism with economic imperialism: maintaining territorial integrity of peripheral states but ensuring that they remained open to American goods and investors.[138] Others have minimized the importance of these policy statements because it is argued that they were mostly ineffective and were in the "windy rhetoric" tradition of the Monroe Doctrine, in which the United States makes grand "unilateral assertions" that do not amount to much.[139] The historical evidence seems to suggest that the

Open Door notes were, and remain, important because they help us understand one emerging approach of the United States to building global influence.

We have seen that the Japanese military victory over China in 1894–95 raised concerns within American business and policy circles that Britain and Japan might carve up the Chinese market. We have also seen that the United States was not in a position to influence developments in distant China until the Spanish-American War, in 1898, however, and that United States became a Pacific power only after winning a military victory in the Philippines. It was in 1898 that major American business groups with interests in China joined the newly formed American Asiatic Association, with the aim of influencing US policy with respect to "safeguarding" the Chinese market.[140] This was also the year that Hay—already a convert to the concept of an open door policy in China—was appointed secretary of state by McKinley. Hay was sympathetic to the demands of America's China-oriented businessmen. As noted, Hay, who had just returned to the United States after having served as US ambassador to Britain, was also fully aware of the British interest in an open-door type of policy in China. The coming together of these trends, then, paved the way for the American promulgation of the Open Door policy.

Since Hay was not a Far East specialist, he appointed William Rockhill, a worldly Asia hand who spoke Tibetan and had been learning Chinese, to come up with a policy statement. Rockhill, in turn, was close to one Alfred Hippisley, a British national and an employee of the Chinese Imperial Maritime Customs Service (CIMCS) in China (see chapter 2), who was visiting the United States at that time. Rockhill and Hippisley were both concerned that an imperial partition of China would lead to a decline in CIMCS revenues, which would mean fewer resources available for the Ch'ing monarch and, in turn, would further weaken the already troubled Chinese state.[141] Hippisley then drafted some notes that, without much change, eventually became the American Open Door policy toward China. The Open Door notes were, then, very much British in origin, both in the sense that Ambassador Hay was sympathetic to them when the British first proposed them, and in the sense that they were drafted by a British national who hoped to perpetuate the British imperial project in China. Despite the lofty American claims then that the United States was the only anticolonial power in China, the fact is that the substance of its Open Door policy in China was British in conception, the central aim of which all along was to maintain imperial relations with China, unilaterally if possible, multilaterally if not.

The first set of Open Door notes provided a brief reprieve in the intra-imperial frenzy to carve up China. The Boxer Rebellion broke out in 1900. As we saw in chapter 2, the Boxers were proto-nationalists, mostly driven by anti-missionary sentiment, but also committed to purging China of growing imperial incursions: in the words of a prominent American who was an eyewitness, the "uprising was one of the most splendid exhibitions of patriotism witnessed in modern times."[142] The Boxers pressured the Empress Dowager to expel foreigners from China, who wavered, but eventually threw her weight behind the Boxers. As discussed, all the foreigners in China then came together to both crush the Boxer Rebellion and to maintain the symbol of monarchial rule over China. Within a decade, however, the Ch'ing dynasty was overthrown by Chinese nationalists, including Sun Yet Sen. The United States had joined the imperial alliance to crush the Boxers. President McKinley ordered 5,000 American troops to China, most of which were based in the Philippines. More would have been sent but for logistical problems in both Hawaii and the Philippines. After crushing the Boxers, the American troops remained in Peking. This, in turn, gave Americans influence over future developments, including the shape of the substantial indemnity that was imposed on the Chinese state. Contrary to American claims, then, historical evidence strongly suggests that the United States was very much part of the Western and Japanese imperial coalition bent on shaping China.

Following the Boxer Rebellion, key economic policy decisions in China came to be controlled by the victorious alliance of imperial powers. Some of the policy discussions were especially revealing of American intentions. Members of the imperial alliance in China, especially Japan and Britain, were concerned as to how China would pay the sizable indemnity imposed on it. This concern pointed to the continuing need for efficient collection of revenues within China, especially customs revenues controlled by the British-run CIMCS, and possibly toward raising tariffs to enhance these revenue sources. American interest, by contrast, was in maintaining a demand for American goods in China. This pointed to allowing some economic growth in China, but also to a tariff policy that would favor American goods.[143] By now, Theodore Roosevelt was president and Hay had appointed Rockhill as the American ambassador to China. The key American concern was how "China might become a better market without becoming an eventual industrial competitor." Rockhill communicated to Hay that "the encouragement of the manufacturing industries of China . . . [may] have far-reaching and highly prejudicial results" for the United States. Hay agreed. He instructed Rockhill to negotiate tariff policies in China that would encourage "agricultural implements and simpler forms of manufacturing machinery," but that would discourage consumer or heavy industries. Irrespective of the intellectual merits or the success of American policies in China, then, American intentions were quite clear: China's economic modernization was to be limited so as to provide a market for American manufactured goods.

While the post-1900 economic recovery within the United States reduced some of the lure of the China market, Roosevelt did not want to lose the focus: "[I]t is necessary for us to keep the road of trade to the East open. . . . We must see that they [the Asian markets] are managed primarily in the interest of the country, that is, of the commerce of the country."[144] However, the rising power of Japan complicated this quest.[145] Japan defeated Russia in the well-known Russo-Japanese War of 1904–5 and proceeded to ignore America's Open Door policies. The American companies Standard Oil, Swift Meatpacking, and British-American Tobacco Company were thrown out of Manchuria. These economic losses notwithstanding, Roosevelt pursued classic realpolitik, maintaining close relations with both Britain and with Japan in the Far East. The Taft-Katsura Agreement in 1905 helped alleviate American concerns about maintaining control over the Philippines by giving Japan green light to gobble up Korea. Wary of Japan's growing power, Roosevelt then sent the Great White Fleet around the world, aiming especially to impress Japan with American naval might; this ignited a naval buildup in both Japan and Germany, pointing toward the coming of WW I.[146]

President Taft shifted the focus of American policy in the Far East back to commercial concerns. Despite his experience in the Far East (as the governor-general of the Philippines), his Far East policies were mostly a failure. While trade continued, Taft wanted to encourage investors and bankers in China. But the political situation in China was increasingly turbulent. Taft also miscalculated. He proceeded to make a large loan to China, believing that the Ch'ing would continue in power. The loan actually triggered protests within China, precipitating the overthrow of the baby Manchu emperor—who had replaced the Empress Dowager after her death—and the final end of the Ch'ing dynastic rule in 1911.

If the motives (mainly economic) and mechanisms (mainly collaboration with other imperial powers and a weak Chinese monarchy) of American informal empire in China are relatively clear, a few comments on the impact will help bring this discussion to a conclusion. Any discussion of impact, however, must begin with a reiteration of some obvious historical facts; they will help keep the analysis in perspective. Both the United States and China were giant economies during the time period under consideration; for example, their GDPs around 1900 constituted some 15 percent and 10 percent of the world GDP, respectively. The United States exported only 7 percent to 8 percent of its total production, and of that, the share of American exports to China was only 1 percent to 2 percent of total American exports. China, too, was coming apart because of its inability to respond effectively to Western and Japanese incursions. Britain was the main imperial power in China in the nineteenth century, and Japan's role grew steadily during the first half of the twentieth century. The US role grew in the aftermath of the Spanish-American War, but the United States remained a distant third. In light of such obvious facts, it would be absurd to claim that the United States had gained handsomely from its incursions into China or that China had been hurt precipitously by American interventions. I make no such claims. What needs to be briefly discussed instead is the direction of change as American influence in China grew.

We have seen that American policy in China was aimed mainly at trade expansion. As it turned out, trade indeed did expand following the adoption of Open Door policies. If in 1900 American businessmen had exported $15 million worth of products, by 1905 exports had jumped sharply, to $53 million (Table 4.1). Most of these exports were sold in northern China, especially Manchuria. Nearly half of all American exports to China in 1905 were textiles; more telling is that the Chinese share of total US textile exports had increased from some 12 percent in 1895 to 55 percent in 1905.[147] While the share of all US exports that went to China remained miniscule, it did double between 1902 and 1906; for some industries, such as textiles, the gains were decisive. Textile exports declined sharply after Japan gained control of Manchuria. Kerosene and cigarette exports grew instead in the subsequent periods, and they remained America's main exports well into the 1920s. As noted, the United States' investments and loans in China were not of great significance; for example, on the eve of World War I, the share of American foreign investment in China was only 3 percent of the total foreign investment in China, while that of Japan was nearly 35 percent. The

Table 4.1 US exports to Cuba, China and the Philippines, 1890–1920 (in Millions of US dollars, Except Where Stated)

Year	Total	Cuba	China	"Other" Asia[1]	Philippines[2]
1890	858	13	3	12	
1895	808	13	4	9	
1900	1394	26	15	24	67[3]
1905	1519	38	53	30	
1910	1745	53	16	40	99
1915	2769	76	16	82	
1920	8228	273[4]	106[4]	348	299

1. The "other" Asia data in the Census excludes trade with China and Japan; during 1900 and 1915 much of this American trade with "other" Asia was with the Philippines.

2. This data is in million pesos.

3. The data is for 1902.

4. The data is for 1919.

Source: Taken from US Bureau of the Census, *Historical Statistics of the United States*, pp. 903–4. The Philippines-specific data in the last column is from Hooley, "American Economic Policy in the Philippines," table 4, p. 476.

Open Door policy was aimed at expanding trade, not investments, and trade did expand. Though the overall gains were not dramatic, the gains of some specific industries were substantial. Lobbyists from such industries as textiles, kerosene, and cigarette, in turn, continued to press US policymakers to maintain access to the China market.

The real impact of the growing American influence in China was political and, judged from the standpoint of a sovereign and effective state within China, the impact was largely negative. Like the British in the nineteenth century, American policymakers desired stability and economic openness in China; they decided that these goals would be best met by supporting a pliable monarchy. A rule of sorts seems to be in operation here: whenever imperial powers chose not to colonize a peripheral country, a stable-but-subservient government in that country often emerged as a preferred pathway to establishing influence. Be that as it may, the United States' decision to join other imperial powers in China to prop up the disintegrating rule of the Ch'ing was a mistake, even from the standpoint of America's own longer-term goal of political stability in China. The United States was an anticolonial and antimonarchical power. American decision-makers should have known better. Instead, they were in a hurry to join the club of big imperialist powers. They therefore ignored the powerful emerging forces within China that were demanding modernization. The Taiping and Boxer Rebellions were early manifestations of this churning; a variety of nationalists and communists would soon join the clamor. The Empress Dowager's decision to throw the weight of the Chinese state with the anti-foreigner Boxers, further delegitimized the monarchy. When it was overthrown, there was no ready force in China to establish central authority. It would take few decades of internal Chinese initiatives to re-establish such authority and to expunge imperial powers from China.

Conclusion

In a comparative study of British and American imperialism published in 1981, Tony Smith argued that prior to World War II the United States was, on balance, a friend of nationalism in the underdeveloped regions of the world. He went on to suggest that the United States only became an "anti-nationalist" or a "counter-revolutionary" power in the post–World War II period, when Third World nationalism joined forces with communism, as exemplified, say, in the Chinese Communist Revolution and the related war in Korea.[148] I am afraid that the historical evidence examined above does not support this conclusion. The evidence suggests instead that well before the advent of communism, the United States consistently fought nationalist forces to establish influence over peripheral political economies. This is evident in the cases we have examined thus far. In Cuba,

Americans were wary of the supporters of José Martí and suppressed the nationalists to establish control; in Nicaragua, the United States orchestrated the overthrow of the nationalist ruler Zelaya in favor of pro-American governments; in the Philippines, the United States ruthlessly defeated the forces of the nationalist Aguinaldo and then systematically discouraged the emergence of any nationalist challenge to American colonial rule; and in the case of China, the United States sided with other imperial powers against the proto-nationalist Boxers and even took a position against the Ch'ing monarch when she decided to ally with anti-foreigner forces within China.

These American interventions followed a logic. The American economy had industrialized rapidly toward the end of the nineteenth century. Many in the United States were arguing for economic expansion abroad, especially into regions that could absorb US manufactured products. It built a powerful navy, in part to support these ambitions. Since much of the underdeveloped world was already colonized, American expansionist efforts focused either on regions that were close to home or on distant islands in the Pacific that would ensure that the United States reached the great China market. As the United States sought to expand, it often ran into resistance from nationalist forces whose goals were at odds with those of the Americans. The United States systematically eliminated this nationalist resistance. Rightly or wrongly, policymakers in the United States concluded that American interests in the Caribbean, Central America, and the Far East—mostly economic, but on occasion, strategic—would instead be best served by pliable governments that could ensure order and openness. As in the case of Britain's informal empire, then, the creation of stable-but-subservient regimes in the peripheral countries emerged as the means to expand commerce and establish American influence overseas.

The historical evidence we have examined suggests that the United States pursued a variety of approaches to establishing stable-but-subservient regimes abroad. Three of these approaches are worth underlining in this conclusion because they proved to be of long-run significance. The first was hard militarism, most clearly evident in how the United States established control over the Philippines. Thousands of American soldiers were employed in a three-year war that led to the death of some 200,000 Filipino civilians. Thus was the American peace established! It will become clear in subsequent chapters that this early instance of hard militarism in the Philippines has more than a passing resemblance to strategy the United States used in subsequent periods as well, in, say, Vietnam and Iraq. Overt or covert regime change was the second strategy that the United States used during this early phase to establish pro-American rulers. This was clearest in the case of Zelaya in Nicaragua. Beyond Nicaragua, the practice of periodic military interventions aimed at either taming governmental behavior or changing rulers outright was also evident in the cases of Cuba and Honduras. Over time, we will notice—especially in cases of Mossadegh in Iran and Allende in Chile—that forced regime change also become a key strategy in the American repertoire for establishing pro-American governments abroad. The third approach, most clearly evident in the case of China, was the collaboration with other imperial powers to ensure a stable-but-open government. Multilateral collaboration is, then, a strategy that the United States has continued to pursue in recent times, the clearest example being the use of structural adjustment programs via the World Bank and the International Monetary Fund (IMF) to ensure that developing countries paid their debts to first world bankers.

Why did the United States pursue different strategies to establish influence in different parts of the developing world? A full answer will emerge only in due course, after I have reviewed additional historical evidence. For now, the limited evidence points to some tentative generalizations. The Philippines was acquired mainly as a stepping-stone to reach a critical goal, namely, access to the China market. American aims in the Philippines itself were thus vague, but resistance to American domination was rather strong. This combination of vague goals on the way to something great, but also strong resistance, then, seems to attract hard militarism as an imperial strategy. We will have an opportunity to examine this proposition further in the case of American interventions in Vietnam and Iraq. By contrast, when American goals are specific—say, creating economic opportunities for corporations—and the relative power advantage of the United States is considerable, then regime change seems to emerge as the appropriate strategy to create pliable rulers. This logic was clearly at work in the case of Nicaragua, and we will examine it further in the cases of Iran and Chile. Finally, the case of American expansion into China suggests that multilateral collaboration is needed to establish dominance when the power resources of the United States are not sufficient to accomplish the task at hand. Again, there will be an opportunity to examine this proposition further against more contemporary evidence, especially the effort to impose the Washington Consensus on development on Latin America.

Whether one judges American economic gains from its expansionist efforts as modest or significant depends on the standards one brings to bear on the subject. The American economy was already a giant economy and depended mostly on internal resources and markets. The United States exported less than 10 percent of its products overseas, and most of these went to Europe or Canada. Prior to the Spanish-American War, US direct investments overseas were also trivial. From this standpoint, one could legitimately conclude that the United States hardly needed to expand into underdeveloped regions to maintain its prosperity or build its national strength. That is why I began this chapter by making a distinction between need and want—whereas Britain needed an empire, the United States merely wanted one. Many in the United States, though not everyone, thought that economic expansion abroad would both help smooth out the boom-and-bust quality of rapid capitalist expansion and also provide long-term outlets to solve the problem of glut in the American economy. The results of the American efforts suggest that such thinking was not wrong, that American gains from its expansionist efforts were far from insignificant.

It is clear in Table 4.1 that US trade expanded rapidly in the countries in which it established political sway following the Spanish-American War. The gains in Cuba and the Philippines, especially, were steady and even dramatic. Trade also jumped sharply in China following the Open Door policy, but then declined rapidly when Japan closed off Manchuria to the United States and as a result of the growing political turmoil in China. Over time, however, the United States recovered from these setbacks and re-established a strong trading position. American direct investments overseas also grew sharply after the that war: if before the war total US foreign investments were under USD 1 billion, by 1914 they had grown to USD 5 billion, and then to nearly \$8 to \$10 billion in the 1920s.[149] More telling, nearly half of this investment in 1929 was in Latin America, mostly in the Caribbean; little Cuba alone took \$1.4 billion of American foreign investment that year. The evidence, then, supports the contention that perceived economic needs within the United States led to imperial expansion, and both trade and investment followed the flag.

The impact of American expansion on its protectorates was pernicious. There is no need to deny that commodity exports in places like Cuba and the Philippines helped generate some economic growth, but mainly over the short run. Over the longer term, however, American protectorates became classic colonies that produced commodities and took manufactured goods. Commodity producers, in turn, became both wealthy and powerful. While such groups—and their political representatives—were happy to cooperate with the United States, they seldom had enough legitimacy to establish orderly polities. Economic inequalities and illegitimate rulers gave rise to poorly governed societies. Creating sovereign and legitimate states might have put these countries on a progressive path. Unfortunately, the weight of American influence was often in the opposite direction; US influence tended to undermine nationalist leaders who may have commanded the majority support needed to create effective, developmental states.

5

Fighting Third World Nationalism

IRAN, VIETNAM, AND CHILE

FOLLOWING WORLD WAR II, the United States enjoyed enormous power superiority over the other great powers, including the Soviet Union. American leaders sought to use this power to create a global order that would enhance their country's interests and values. At the heart of this new order was to be an open global economy—populated by capitalist democracies—with the United States in the lead. Americans believed that open doors were not only good for their own economic growth and power but would also help others prosper. Great Britain and France eventually accepted this hegemonic design. Others, like Germany and Japan, which had lost the war, had no choice but to accept the American-led order. But a significant portion of the world was not persuaded and did not bend readily to American desires. The Soviet Union sought to maintain a state-controlled economy and a land empire in its near abroad. The United States was unable to stop Mao's revolutionary forces from winning and consolidating power in China. A variety of postcolonial nationalists, such as Nehru in India and Nasser in Egypt, also hoped to create state-directed economies. Americans were puzzled and angered by such insubordination; they believed that the spread of such autarkic or semi-autarkic economies would frustrate a key element of their global design, namely, an open global economy. Over time, those who sought to get in the way of American postwar ambitions—especially communists, but also nationalists—bore the brunt of American power. In this chapter I examine American interventions in the developing world—or the Third World, as it came to be called during the Cold War years—that were aimed at taming nationalists, some revolutionary and others reformist.[1]

More than Britain in the nineteenth century, the United States in the mid-twentieth century conceived of its global interests as deeply interconnected. As I analyze American interventions in the developing world, it is important to

How Britain and the United States Shaped the Global Periphery. Atul Kohli, Oxford University Press (2020).

DOI: 10.1093/oso/9780190069629.001.0001

keep in mind this interconnected nature of America's understanding of its own interests. With global ambitions, American leaders believed that challenges to its domination over any one part of the world could be contagious, leading to losses elsewhere; credibility was the currency with which the United States hoped to maintain its informal empire. Although the American approach to establishing influence was more coercive in some parts of the world than in others, what also connected these efforts was the belief that the hegemonic project was indivisible. In the early postwar years, America's top priorities were mainly in Europe. The economic recovery of declining powers like Britain and France was not only deemed to be central for continuing American prosperity, but also necessary to forestall the emergence of nationalist and redistributive politics in Western Europe; latter trends were deemed to favor the Soviet Union. To help avoid the mistakes made at Versailles, Americans also decided to reindustrialize West Germany and Japan while ensuring that they will never again pose a military threat. Americans then used a proverbial stick and carrot—anything from the well-known Marshall Plan to lesser-known efforts to help these declining European powers maintain their colonial economic links—to incorporate Western Europe (and Japan) within the American orbit.[2]

When Stalin refused to accept a subordinate position in the American-led order, the Cold War erupted.[3] A brutal dictator in a war-devastated country, Stalin had a very Russian understanding of what was good for the motherland: control over neighboring territories so to avoid future wars. When Western powers refused to let Stalin have regional influence, Stalin imposed harsh control over Eastern Europe, lowering what Winston Churchill famously described as the Iron Curtain. These closed economies of Europe posed a serious challenge to the American postwar hopes for an open global economy. From then on the United States fought the Cold War from a position of considerable strength, aiming first to contain communism and then to roll it back. Because communism offered an alternative to capitalism, the Cold War also went well beyond a classic realpolitik struggle; it became a struggle over how best to organize national states and markets, on the one hand, and, on the other hand, it took on the proportion of a crusade in which might was needed to protect what was right. Mao Zedong's victory in China, war in Korea, and growing nationalist demands in European colonies quickly exacerbated American anxieties, giving the struggle against communism a global dimension. Communism then had to be fought everywhere, because it threatened what Americans perceived as their core interests and values.

During the Cold War era, the United States intervened in numerous developing countries, especially ones in East Asia, the Middle East, and Latin America.[4] American efforts to revive war-devastated capitalist powers and to confront communist ones provided the context for these developing-country interventions. An incomplete list of major American interventions—either to support or to oppose emerging political trends—might include the following: China, Philippines, Korea, Taiwan, Vietnam, Laos, Cambodia, and Indonesia in East Asia; Israel, Saudi Arabia, Iran, and Egypt in the Middle East; Congo in Africa; Guatemala, Cuba, Nicaragua and other small countries in Central America; and Brazil and Chile in Latin America. The United States sought indirect influence over yet other developing countries via regional treaties or through such grand schemes as the Alliance for Progress. I have chosen three cases of direct American interventions in the developing world for detailed analysis: Iran, Vietnam, and Chile. These three cases capture a range of America's regional and global interests and the covert and overt methods that American leaders used to achieve their goals. American efforts were also more or less successful across these cases. Although the discussion that follows is surely less than comprehensive, it does shed light on the issue at hand, namely, America's efforts to build an informal empire in the developing world.[5]

In Iran, Americans helped Britain to covertly overthrow the elected Iranian nationalist leader, Muhammad Mossadegh, in 1953.[6] Mossadegh had earlier nationalized the Anglo-Iranian Oil Company. When the negotiations over the compensation for nationalization bogged down, the CIA helped to orchestrate a coup that led to Mossadegh's overthrow. In the aftermath, the power of a pro-Western and pliable Shah was restored and the rights to Iranian oil came to be shared equally between British and American corporations. Beyond the historical details (some well-known, others less so), the discussion of the Iranian case will help highlight several relevant themes: the importance of oil (and thus, of the Middle East in the American postwar global calculations); the growing significance of multinational corporations in global affairs; the willingness of the United States to support declining colonial powers (but at a price); how a short-term American victory turned pyrrhic over a longer time frame; and, of course, America's early inclination to thwart developing-country nationalists who sought to use state power to benefit their own country.

A similar but much more violent and prolonged confrontation between imperial ambitions and nationalism unfolded in Vietnam, the second case I discuss. The details of the American War in Vietnam—what the Vietnamese call the Vietnam War—are relatively well known, although new research keeps deepening our understanding of the conflict. When the Vietnamese sought to get rid of the French, in the early postwar period the United States helped France to restore colonial rule. Following the French military defeat in 1954, the United States took on the imperial mantle to limit the gains of revolutionary nationalists like Ho Chi Minh, both because of America's global campaign to contain communism but also because open economic access to Southeast Asia—a central part of the old co-prosperity sphere—was deemed important for Japanese economic recovery. Over time, the reasons for the United States to be in Vietnam became more and more muddled; even American leaders admitted that they could not win the war, but that they also could not withdraw. Maintaining American credibility became a reason to stay in the war because credibility was deemed to be central to the exercise of influence elsewhere in the world. In the name of credibility, the United States dropped more bombs on a sliver of a country than were dropped during all of World War II. To resist, hardline communists in Vietnam won out; they were willing to make enormous sacrifices of their own people in the name of the nation, such as during the Tet Offensive in 1968. The United States eventually lost the battle of wills. Some three million Vietnamese died during the conflict, that is, half the number of Jews killed during the Holocaust. Nearly 58,000 Americans also died. The tragic costs of American imperial ambitions in Vietnam were enormous.

While the United States was losing the war in Vietnam, it also, in 1973, undertook a much more successful intervention in Chile to overthrow a democratically elected president; it was as if a victory was needed in the backyard to compensate for the defeat in distant jungles. The overthrow and murder of Salvador Allende is the third case of US intervention I discuss here. Allende was a leader of the left who sought wealth redistribution and the nationalization of the American corporations that dominated Chile's commodity-dependent economy. American antipathy to nationalist and socialist leaders south of the border was hardly new; Jacobo Arbenz, Fidel Castro, and others had already experienced American wrath. American intervention in Chile fits the recurring pattern of American efforts to undermine nationalists and socialists who seek to limit external dependency. But the Chilean case is also distinctive because it is in a region that has long been dominated by the United States. Compared to the other cases discussed here, US economic influence in Chile was more significant, as were American contacts with Chilean military leaders. Richard Nixon and Henry Kissinger could realistically ask the CIA to make the "Chilean economy scream" and undercover operatives to encourage Chilean military leaders to depose a democratically elected president. The results included prolonged repressive and authoritarian rule, on the one hand, and a failure to diversify a commodity-dependent economy, on the other hand.

Here, as in the other chapters of the volume, historical materials help to build an analytical argument about the motives, mechanisms, and consequences of imperialism. A brief preview of these themes at the outset may be helpful to the reader. It would be easy to conclude from these three cases that US interventions were aimed mainly at fighting communism; after all, this was the era of the Cold War. While not wrong, such a conclusion would be both superficial, and ultimately, misleading. The evidence below will make clear that fighting communism was but an excuse for American interventions in Iran and Chile. By contrast, the United States indeed confronted a revolutionary communist force in Vietnam but what the United States was fighting was national, and not global, communism. More important, as we notice in chapter 4, US interventions in the developing world began well before the emergence of the Cold War and as will become clear in the next chapter, have continued well after the end of the Cold War. Clearly, a fight against communism cannot be held as the main factor that drove interventions during the Cold War era. In such cases as the US involvement in the Korean War and then in South Korea, as well as in protecting Taiwan, Cold War politics was clearly of primary significance. In most other cases of US intervention during this period, however, a fight against communism was one factor, but not the dominant consideration. So, either we believe that American interventions in different eras (or places) had different motives—an epistemological position I do not share—or we search for deeper patterns that help make sense of a variety of American interventions in poor countries of the world.

One such deeper pattern is revealed if we focus on the American effort to establish a global hegemony—more accurately, an informal empire—during this period, with an open global economy as a centerpiece. This urge to open the economies of other nations, by force if necessary, runs through the long American twentieth century. Of course, American economic needs evolved over this time. While early efforts were aimed at free trade, as the century wore on, securing overseas corporate investments and ensuring that foreign debt was paid back also became important. America's century-long efforts are thus bookended by demanding an open door in turn-of-the-century China and by implementing the Washington Consensus on development toward the end of the century. This is not to deny that some American interventions did not fit this pattern. Since history is seldom neat, the evidence reveals that ideology and security concerns complicated the pursuit of national economic interests overseas; the case of Vietnam is especially salient from this standpoint. Nevertheless, seeking open doors was a central motive in many of the more important cases of US interventions in the developing world. During the Cold War period, then, American efforts to establish a global hegemony led it to confront communists and nationalists alike, because both sought to create closed or semiclosed economies. What we notice in all three cases is a pattern of confrontation between the imperial ambitions of the United States, on the one hand, and, on the other hand, Third World nationalists, who sought to chart independent paths for their respective countries.

It is not the case that American leaders were not sympathetic to nationalism in the developing world. Over and over again, the historical record reveals that policymakers in the Truman and Eisenhower administrations noticed the emerging trends and sought to accommodate them. American leaders thus rightly concluded that the era of colonialism was over; they also did not shy away from conveying this message to their British and French counterparts. However, American leaders also wanted to limit the autonomy of the emerging developing countries, especially if their leaders were perceived to be opposed to American designs. Such limits were essential if the United States hoped to establish a global order in its own image. The puzzle for American foreign policymakers was how to do this without asserting formal control over the emerging sovereign countries.

The Americans believed that they were perfecting a model of informal control in the Philippines, Cuba and elsewhere, that combined nominal independence and substantial control over key policies. The hope was that this model of informal empire would enable American leaders to incorporate other developing countries within the orbit of the free world. The key mechanism of extending American influence was thus to encourage and support pro-American governments within the developing world. Covert or overt interventions were often aimed at putting friendly regimes in power. A variety of carrots, for example, foreign aid, and sticks, for example, military bases, were then used to keep these regimes pliable. Since the overt use of force to bend the will of nationalist rulers was both costly and too Old World for the new era, it was also important that the American word—of support or threat—was taken seriously. That is why credibility of American commitments took on such enormous significance within the scope of the American order. In the best of worlds, America's informal empire was to operate via friendly regimes that complied with American desires because they took American wishes seriously, backed as they were by enormous economic and military resources.

The last general theme that runs through the historical discussion is the consequences of American interventions, for both the United States and for these three developing countries. Whether the United States benefited from its interventions will not always be easy to assess, in part because what they were trying to achieve was far from explicit, and in part because the short- and longer-term consequences varied. In the cases of Iran and Chile, for example, the United States certainly succeeded in overthrowing elected nationalist leaders and in replacing them with pro-American authoritarian rulers, who in turn facilitated benefits for American corporations. However, the longer-term consequences in the two cases varied. The short-term success in Iran also bred enormous anti-Americanism that eventually contributed to a theocratic revolution in 1979, the difficult consequences of which are still unfolding. By contrast, US foreign policymakers may well have considered the Chilean intervention more of a success because, over a longer term, Chile not only became democratic, but also sustained an open economy that produced needed commodities and absorbed foreign investment. In contrast to these mixed cases, and still judged from the standpoint of American imperial ambitions, the prolonged intervention in Vietnam was an unmitigated disaster. Not only was the effort to stop Ho Chi Minh extremely expensive for Americans in human and material terms, it also failed. Hegemony rests not only on domination but also on some legitimacy; the United States lost a lot of high moral ground as a result of the Vietnam War. Ironically, the United States also lost credibility in the aftermath, something that American leaders thought was worth fighting for.

Assessing the impact of American interventions on Iran, Vietnam, and Chile will also not be easy, in part because of time frame and in part because American interventions were only one of many sources of change in these countries, but also because standards for judging good or bad outcomes can be deeply subjective. Still, it is clear that in both Iran and Chile, democracy—more nascent in Iran than in Chile—was deeply damaged by the American interventions. As importantly, American interventions empowered ruling coalitions in these countries that favored open and dependent economies. Nationalist coalitions that might diversify economies via deliberate industrialization thus failed to emerge, at least over the short- to medium term. By contrast, American loss in Vietnam paved the road to a nationalist consolidation of power. The war, of course, devastated Vietnam. The communist government that emerged victorious has also been highly repressive. Nevertheless, Vietnam is now charting its own development journey. Notable achievements already include near eradication of poverty and high rates of economic growth, including in manufacturing.

The rest of the chapter is organized in a fairly straightforward manner. I first discuss some background, especially the making of the early Cold War and how the developing countries fit into the interests and anxieties of the US. Within this context I then move to the discussion of the three interventions: Iran, Vietnam, and Chile. I return in the conclusion to integrate the main findings of this chapter with the central themes of the volume, including some comparisons with Britain's informal empire in the nineteenth century.

Background

As discussed in chapter 4, following the Spanish-American War, the United States acquired a small but far-flung empire. But by nineteenth-century British standards, before World War I, the United States was still a regional power, with a strong presence only in South America and in parts of the Pacific. Even before Woodrow Wilson became president, however, its global ambitions were already evident. In the words of Theodore Roosevelt, "[P]eace cannot be had until the civilized nations have expanded in some shape over the barbarous nations."[7] This expansionist urge to achieve valued goals was given full expression by President Wilson. As is well known, Wilson provided the ideological clothing for America's global ambitions. He justified American entry into World War I in terms of making world "safe for democracy," and argued that the United States was destined to be "the justest, the most progressive, the most honorable, the most enlightened Nation in the world."[8] At the end of the war, he clearly saw the growing ascendance of the United States and urged Americans to "accept what is offered to us, the leadership of the world."[9]

Wilson's famous "Fourteen Points" statement, made in response to Lenin and the Bolshevik's revolution in Russia, sought to outline the nature of American leadership of the world. The statement was wide-ranging, but most relevant to this study is Wilson's emphasis on the self-determination of nations. Many nationalists in European colonies were encouraged by what they interpreted as America's anticolonialism. As it turned out, however, Wilson's emphasis on self-determination applied primarily to the subjugated people of the Austro-Hungarian Empire, secondarily to the Ottoman Empire, and hardly at all to the European colonies. European colonizers, especially Great Britain, were to be part of a global condominium of civilized powers instead, and thus could not to be alienated. Wilson's idealism did not extend to America's global economic interests. He made this clear as early as 1907: "[S]ince trade ignores national boundaries and the manufacturer insists on having the world as a market, the flag of his nation must follow him, and the doors of the nations which are closed must be battered down." Very much reminiscent of the British case for the forced opening of China to sell opium, this is about as clear a rationale as one is likely to find for the early use of American state power to open the global economy and to build an informal empire. That these were not just empty words—or quoted here out of context—is then underscored by the fact that Wilson's secretary of state, William Jennings Bryan—yes, the great anti-imperialist—eventually praised Wilson as a president who had "opened the doors of all the weaker countries to an invasion of American capital and American enterprise."[10]

Ever since Wilson, Americans have often clothed the hardheaded pursuit of their narrow interests in the garb of spreading democracy.[11] Wilson's rhetoric fell well short of his accomplishments, however, so it is not surprising that his failures set back America's global project, at least for a few decades. His successors—Warren Harding, Calvin Coolidge, and Herbert Hoover, all Republicans—were not so much isolationists, as they were hemmed in by circumstances. On the political and military front, for example, during the 1920s the United States was not quite ready to put its hegemonic ambitions into practice; there was far too much turbulence in the world for anyone to be hegemonic: Britain's global power was declining but still formidable; Japan was getting more aggressive, especially in China; Germany was smarting under the terms of the Treaty of Versailles; and, of course, the Bolsheviks were consolidating power in Russia. An international naval conference of major powers held in Washington in 1921, which gave the Japanese a naval edge in East Asia, essentially confirmed that during the interwar period the United States was willing to live in a world of regional powers, in which American power would be supreme only in the Western hemisphere. These agreements, in turn, provided a framework for American diplomacy between 1921 and 1941.[12]

But if the Republicans Harding and Coolidge were willing to accept some political limitations, their approach to the economy was much more aggressive. The American manufacturing economy, especially textiles, was still not competitive enough to favor open trade. Pro-business administrations thus helped raise the average tariff rate to 33 percent in 1922, well before the Great Depression. With organized labor under strict control and a variety of other pro-business policies in place, the American economy boomed during the 1920s; industrial production doubled between 1921 and 1929.[13] This could have become a model for capitalism in one country. However, income inequality at home limited the domestic market, so both businessmen and public officials sought markets abroad. The traditional European markets remained a key focus. American banks lent money to the Germans so they could buy American products. The Germans used some of this money to pay back their war-related debts to France and England, which, in turn, absorbed more American goods. This was a tight chain waiting to snap. US tariffs made it difficult for other countries to sell products to the United States. America thus ran favorable balance of payments during the decade. However, when other countries also raised tariffs, American money started staying home, moving more and more into speculative investments, with crushing, and crashing, results that initiated the Depression in 1929.

In addition to the traditional European markets, the poor countries of the world—not yet recognized as the Third World—also offered economic opportunities to the United States during the 1920s. America's trade and investment with South America was already considerable but also grew during this period. Americans, as we have seen, were not shy about using coercion in the region to put malleable regimes in power. And when the United States conceded a naval edge to Japan in East Asia, Americans sought in return—and got, at least for a period—open access to the Chinese market. Beyond Latin America and the Pacific, the new area of economic interest was the Middle East. Following the First World War, oil emerged as a commodity of key strategic significance. European and American corporations then struggled during the interwar period for a share of access to Middle East oil. Without effective governments, Middle East was ripe to be carved up, which it was by rival Western corporations that drew a map with a red pencil and decided to share the region's wealth among themselves.[14]

The United States was thus hardly isolationist during the interwar period. Instead, the American approach to the world during the period is probably best characterized as a "half-way house between isolationism and full-blown, consistent internationalism."[15] The United States continued to seek influence in the poor parts of the world, mainly as sources of raw materials, such as oil, and as additional markets in which to sell American goods, both agricultural and industrial. Of course, with the onset of the Depression the world was carved into regional economic blocks, some more inward-looking, and others expansionist: along with a racist ideology, the Nazis promulgated the idea of *lebensraum*; the Japanese intensified their imperial efforts to build an East Asian co-prosperity sphere; the Soviet Union continued to build socialism in one country, which in effect was a land empire; Britain and France focused on their colonies; and the United States intensified its economic and political links with South America. These arrangements produced neither prosperity nor peace. Following World War II, then, the United States sought to establish a more open global economy. And the Americans' planning for such a postwar world began well before it formally entered the Second World War.[16]

After a variety of efforts to pull the American economy out of the Depression failed, President Franklin Roosevelt had concluded by 1938 that a solution might lie in exports. His secretary of state—the ardent free-trader Cordell Hull—then announced during the same year that "an endeavor by any country in any part of the world to establish itself in favor of a preferred (economic) position in another country is incompatible with the maintenance of our own and the establishment of world prosperity." And two years later, Hull further explained that "the primary object (of American foreign policy) is both to reopen the old and seek new outlets for our surplus production."[17] These were the early, foundational statements of what was to follow after World War II, namely, a well-integrated plan to extend open-door principles to a global scale. The thinking along these lines matured during the war years, especially as American leaders assumed that victory would be theirs and started planning for the postwar world. They understood well that war-related public spending had finally helped pull the American economy out of the Depression; the issue was how economic buoyancy would be maintained following the war. Assistant secretary of state Dean Acheson bluntly told a congressional committee, in 1944, that the key problem facing the American economy after the war would not be production, but markets: "[W]e cannot have full employment and prosperity in the United States without the foreign markets."[18] The committee members raised some questions, but pretty much agreed with this diagnosis and suggested solution—namely, the need for open markets.[19] Many postwar developments, then, including the American antagonism toward countries that did not want to open their markets readily, have to be understood in light of this emerging but overarching American commitment to an open global economy.[20]

How were the poor, agrarian countries to fit into this new global design? While the focus of postwar planning during the war years was naturally on the great powers—and that meant Europe and Japan—systematic thinking quickly revealed the part that poor countries would need to play in the new, integrated global order: they would continue to provide raw materials and markets for the recovery of the core industrial powers and for the prosperity of the United States. American policymakers were also well aware of these connections. One "powerful" career official in the State Department predicted that Britain's global power would decline after the war and "the United States would emerge with an imperial power greater than the world has ever seen"; and in the words of another senior career official, "[W]e shall in effect be the heirs of Empire, and it is up to us to preserve its vital parts."[21] More concretely, efforts to "preserve" the "vital parts" led to a policy view that "the periphery in the Pacific rim, the Mediterranean basin, and Latin America would be integrated, under American aegis, into a global market economy, its resources equally open to all core powers."[22] American policymakers were also fully sanguine that their economic and technological prowess would give them the leading position in any open economic order. Even before the end of World War II, then, the anticolonialism of the United States notwithstanding, American planning about the postwar world included the goal of integrating core and periphery economies, but this time with the United States in the lead.

After the war was over, the United States emerged as the most powerful country in the world. The European economies were in tatters. Some 20 to 30 million Russians (and non-Russians) had perished in the Soviet Union during the war. By contrast, the American economy, business profits, and employment had boomed during the war. The United States then clearly held "preponderant power," and the power of the next major competitor, the Soviet Union, "paled next to that of the United States."[23] While Harry Truman might have entertained some ambiguity about the atomic bomb, he also boasted that the bomb was "the greatest thing in history." His secretary of state, James Byrnes, announced that postwar American prosperity and power were not compatible with a world made up of "exclusive blocs"; he went on to warn all those who were in "conflict" with the American "creed" that the United States would use its surplus power to establish an open global economy.[24] It followed that all those with national ambitions to establish either closed or semiclosed economies would have to be tamed. From here on, an American commitment to "economic internationalism" came to be pitched against "political nationalism" in other parts of the world.[25] This persistent tension between internationalism and nationalism, in turn, helps make sense of some important interconnected developments in America's postwar relations with Western Europe, the Soviet Union, and, of course, most important from the point of view of this study, the Third World.

The history of American efforts to rebuild Western Europe (and Japan) and of the emergence of the Cold War has been told many times, and from varying perspectives.[26] In what follows, I will review just enough of this history to provide a sense of the context in which US interventions in the developing world unfolded.

After the war, rebuilding war-torn Western Europe was an American priority. In addition to civilizational links, the region was of both economic and security importance. Before the war, the region was one of the world's most advanced economically; during the 1920s, the United States conducted nearly half of its trade with the region. Revived Western European economies would, then, clearly offer significant economic opportunities for trade and investment in the postwar period. While there was a clear security concern that Soviet armies could march over the area, subsequent analyses underlined that this concern was probably exaggerated; moreover, as early as 1945, American intelligence had already concluded that the Soviet Union would not pose a serious military threat for some fifteen years after the war.[27] As pressing a concern was that left-leaning political parties would make electoral gains in these war-devastated countries. If this came to pass, leftist governments would prioritize redistribution, nationalize industries, and pursue an economic model that would probably be at odds with the American project of market-oriented, open economies.[28] Such governments might also make peace with the Soviet Union and pursue a neutral path in foreign affairs. That, too, would endanger America's hegemonic ambitions: Rebuilding Western Europe in a manner that would maintain "friendly control"[29] over the region was then a major postwar American preoccupation.

By most counts, American efforts in this direction were successful.[30] Evolving relations with Britain shed further light on the twists and turns along the way.[31] Following the war, Britain faced serious economic problems, both at home and abroad. Rebuilding the domestic economy was going to require imports, but Britain faced serious balance-of-payment constraints. It lost India shortly after the war, and other colonies were likely to follow, threatening the loss of cheap raw materials and assured markets. To pay for the war, the British had sold quite a few of their investments in Latin America to Americans during the war years, further reducing sources of foreign exchange via repatriation of profits. The United States had already made it clear in the Atlantic Charter (1941) that following the war, Britain would have to abandon its "imperial preferences," that is, the trading and currency arrangements within the empire that benefited Britain but kept out other core industrial powers, such as the United States. British policymakers, including John Maynard Keynes, were well aware that the free-trading arrangements codified at Bretton Woods left British firms quite vulnerable to their more-competitive American counterparts. The United States, in turn, was keen to establish open-economy arrangements, both to generate an export surplus and to tame the left-leaning Labour government in Britain. Over the short run, a large American loan to Britain helped achieve these ends; the US Congress only sanctioned the loan when the Truman Administration sold it as a means of coping with the growing Soviet threat. Well before the proclamation of the Truman Doctrine and the Marshall Plan, then, the outline of things to come was already clear.

It was in this context that a weakened Britain withdrew its commitment to support pro-Western forces in Greece and Turkey. The Americans quickly stepped in to fill the power vacuum. The ongoing process of the changing of the imperial guard now became official. The Truman Doctrine followed, and the United States joined the Cold War that Stalin and Churchill had already proclaimed about a year earlier. Although a crisis in Greece may have provided the occasion for the deeply anti-Soviet Truman Doctrine, historical research has established that the Soviet Union was not a significant player in what was essentially an internal civil war within Greece; not only that, Truman was aware of this.[32] What, then, had been the deeper forces at work? Truman had already embraced the need for "economic and financial policies to support a world economy rather than separate nationalist economies."[33] It was this commitment that was driving American foreign policy. The real motive behind the Truman Doctrine was the fear of a rising democratic left, not only in Greece but also in Italy and France.[34] To reiterate, such governments in power were likely to pursue more redistributive and nationalist economic models at home, and neutrality between the United States and the Soviet Union in their foreign policies. These developments would seriously jeopardize the American hegemonic project and had to be thwarted.

While the Truman Doctrine spelled out the broad anticommunist principles of the new American foreign policy, the actual economic, political, and military plans followed over the next three years, first with the Marshall Plan, and then with NATO and the National Security Council paper NSC-68, which sharply militarized the Cold War. The motives behind the Marshall Plan were largely economic, although in such matters politics is rarely far behind.[35] The large aid package was justified in terms of both anticommunist and humanitarian goals. But a key issue facing Western European countries was the "dollar gap."[36] A shortage of dollars in these war-torn economies made it difficult for them to absorb American exports. While there is no need to deny, or to even minimize, the benefits of US foreign aid to Europeans, it is the case that American largesse—mainly in the form of public monies—also subsidized the exports and profits of private

American firms. Moreover, financial aid to these countries was conditional on policy changes, an early version of what would come to be called "structural adjustment" during the Washington Consensus years at the end of the century (more on this in chapter 6). American aid forced left-of-center governments in Britain, France, and Italy to "reduce foreign debts, balance budgets and keep a lid on wages," and thus sought to move these countries "irrevocably away from nationalism and autarky toward internationalism and free convertibility."[37] The dollar-gap issue faced by Britain and France helps us see the importance of colonies to these countries for raw materials and markets. This posed a dilemma for the Americans because they wanted to dismantle the old imperial system and also wanted colonies to remain integrated with Western economies. I will return to this central issue.

Animosity between the United States and the Soviet Union predated the Cold War, and even Russia's Bolshevik revolution.[38] For example, the United States and Russia confronted each other in the late nineteenth century over Manchuria, the United States wanting an open door and the Russians seeking political and territorial control. Contrasting strategies for seeking influence beyond their respective borders—informal versus formal empire—were thus evident even before the advent of communism. These animosities deepened with the coming of communism in Russia. Wilson sent 10,000 US troops between 1918 and 1920 to destroy the Bolsheviks, an effort that obviously failed but underscored American hostility to Lenin and communism. Again, Stalin wanted American help to limit the Japanese influence over Manchuria but, after coming to power in 1933, President Roosevelt did not respond. Whereas Adolf Hitler forced the Allied powers to work together, even during the war, Roosevelt and Churchill delayed Stalin's plea to open a second front in France, leaving the Soviet troops to engage 80 percent of the German army.[39] A paranoid man under the best of circumstances, Stalin, then, had his own reasons to distrust the deeper motives of his wartime allies.

Despite this suspicious past, there was a brief moment of hope following the famous meeting at Yalta that the Big Three would be able to work together because the United States and Britain might be willing to concede a sphere of influence in Eastern Europe to Stalin. As we know, this was not to be. With Roosevelt's death and the atomic bomb, the American position hardened. Truman recognized clearly that US power was now preponderant and argued that the United States "had to have its way 85 percent of the time."[40] Stalin was not willing to accept such constraints, especially in his "backyard." For both security and economic reasons, he imposed brutal Soviet-style regimes on Eastern European countries. Eastern Europe was not of great economic importance to the United States. The reasons Stalin's control of the region added deeply to American anxieties lay elsewhere. First, it signaled to American policymakers that Stalin was not willing to "accept a subordinate role in *Pax Americana*."[41] Second, Stalin's refusal to allow elections in these countries violated deeply cherished preference in the United States for democratic rule. And finally, prior to World War II, Eastern European countries had been important source of raw materials and markets for Western Europe.[42] Soviet control over these economies was now a serious blow to the US design to control the Eurasian landmass, rebuild Western Europe, and keep the economies of the region open as part of an open global economic order. In sum, Soviet efforts to establish a more traditional land empire over its neighboring countries collided with American ambition to establish a global informal empire of open economies, precipitating the Cold War.

Following the Truman Doctrine and the Marshall Plan, the United States took the lead in creating the North Atlantic Treaty Organization, or NATO, a military alliance of Western powers. In retrospect, some scholars have wondered why NATO was needed if US power was already preponderant. Besides containing any possible future expansionism on the part of the Soviet Union and controlling Germany, one important suggestion has been that a key purpose of NATO was to ensure that Western European countries did not drift toward neutralism. Senior American policymakers, such as Acheson, considered neutralism "a shortcut to suicide."[43] During the Senate debate over the formation of NATO, one US senator bluntly stated the core American motive: "[T]he Atlantic Pact is but the logical extension of the principle of the Monroe Doctrine."[44] Over time, containing communism and establishing friendly control over Western Europe was, of course, not enough. After the Soviets announced that they, too, had an atomic bomb, and after China fell to Mao's forces, American anxieties about the communist threat deepened. At home, the debate on who lost China fed the anticommunist hysteria in the form of McCarthyism. Feeling on the defensive, American foreign policymakers turned more aggressive, which led to the policy changes laid out in NSC-68. As is well known, these policy changes led Americans to sharply increase military expenditures; pursue the hydrogen bomb; and, if possible, to undermine "totalitarianism" and to roll back communism.[45] With the communist revolution in China, the focus of the Cold War shifted to Asia, a set of developments to which I will return after a brief discussion of how the developing world fit into America's global design during this early phase of the Cold War.

Rebuilding the industrial core and containing communism provided the essential context for the emerging American approach to the developing world. Scholars have debated whether the importance of the developing world to the United States during the Cold War was more economic or political.[46] This is a false debate. As Truman declared rather early, "[O]ur foreign relations, political and economic, are indivisible."[47] More specifically, in the postwar period, American foreign policymakers understood national power in terms of economic strength, and to them, economic strength included reliable access to raw materials and markets abroad.[48] This is where the developing world fit into America's global ambitions; it, too, had to be integrated into an open global economy. The importance of different regions of the developing world naturally varied. American decision-makers never doubted that Central America and South America would need to remain within the American orbit.[49] Not only was the region important for trade, it also attracted the attention of foreign investors. Both communist and other capitalist European powers would thus have to be kept out of the region. Given America's global power superiority, this would not be difficult in its own backyard. The policy problem instead would be how to maintain regional influence in an era of assertive nationalism within Latin American countries.

Large parts of Asia, the Middle East, and Africa, by contrast, had been colonies of Britain, France, Netherlands, and Japan. The United States wanted direct access to these markets, especially to oil in the Middle East, which Truman characterized as "one of the greatest material prizes in world history."[50] American influence over Saudi Arabia had already been growing since the 1930s, first via ARAMCO and then more directly by the actions of the US government.[51] As we will see, Iran was similarly soon brought under American tutelage via covert regime change. Large parts of sub-Saharan Africa were still full European colonies; they would not enter American political and economic calculations for another decade or more. Instead, it was in the European colonies of Asia—many of which had been occupied by Japan during the war—that the United States eventually faced its most serious challenges, especially after Mao's victory in China. The United States prioritized economic recovery of Western Europe and Japan. American policymakers believed that recovery in the industrial core would require sustained access to the periphery.[52] The emerging clamor for national sovereignty notwithstanding, "dreams of industrialization" in Asia will have to be thwarted and colonial-type of economic ties maintained.[53]

Toward the end of World War II, US foreign policymakers were clearly aware of the political difficulties that lay ahead in facilitating neocolonial links in Asia, or, for that matter, elsewhere in the periphery. According to the US Department of the State, Asian and Pacific countries contained "a substantial part of the world's supply of many critically important primary commodities."[54] The access to these resources in the last couple of centuries had been controlled, first by Western powers, and more recently by Japan. But toward the end of the war, "rising nationalism in Asia has led to a demand for freedom from this political and economic subjection." The challenge faced by US policymakers at the end of the war was to "harmonize" the goal of bringing an "increased measure of self-government" to colonized people, but without alienating key industrial allies. How might this be done? US officials thought that American control over the

Philippines and Cuba offered a model for how to reconcile nominal sovereignty with substantial control in Asia. They hoped to persuade their European allies to follow in the American footsteps of forsaking formal colonial control, but settling for something more suited to the new era, informal control.

What would this informal control look like in practice? Again, with reference to the Philippines, a few years later, US foreign policymakers clarified the stakes and how the United States was putting the model of informal control into practice. Dean Rusk, the future secretary of state, argued, "[I]t is vital we hold the Philippines whatever the cost—unless we are prepared to write off Asia."[55] Since the Philippines was now an independent country, how did the United States plan to hold on to it? The thinking of American foreign policy officials is worth quoting in full:

> It is recognized that the United States must continue for an indefinite period to assume responsibility for the external defense of the islands, to provide military and economic assistance, to take appropriate measures to assure the institution of necessary political, financial, economic and agricultural reforms, and in general to participate in the defense and administration of the country. Such continued participation in the affairs of an independent country has its undesirable aspects but in the context of the present world situation there is no acceptable alternative.[56]

Maintaining substantial control over key policy areas in formally sovereign countries was the key to maintaining influence in the new postcolonial era. There was nothing new in such imperial strategies; as I discuss in earlier chapters, Britain during the nineteenth century had built a far-flung informal empire, such as in Argentina and Egypt, where it achieved substantial policy influence without full colonization. With rising nationalism in the post-World War II period, the United States now offered its Philippine model of decolonization to its European allies, especially to the French in Indochina, as a way of maintaining the vital links between the industrial core and the agrarian periphery.

As the United States would soon learn, the Philippine model of establishing informal control worked mainly when the ruling elite of a client state—often dependent on commodity exports—could be readily coopted. This, in turn, was more likely in situations where the elite-mass gap in the targeted country was substantial and the ruling elite could control the masses via some combination of clientelism and repression. Both Latin America and the Middle East were populated by such political economies. It is not surprising that American efforts at establishing stable-but-subservient regimes in the post–World War II period were concentrated in these regions. The American interventions in Iran and Chile also exemplify this trend. By contrast, the nationalist elite in many Asian countries mobilized their respective masses against both colonialism and other forms of external interventions. Mass nationalism would prove much more difficult for the United States to accommodate within its global hegemonic project. The British learned this lesson in India and bowed out. Americans, too, decided not to confront Mao—certainly not with a sustained military effort. However, the Dutch in Indonesia and the French in Indochina learned this lesson the hard way. The French actually faced military defeat at the hands of the Vietnamese in 1954; the United States then entered this fray at considerable expense and eventual failure.

That, however, is getting way ahead in the story. The adoption of NSC-68 did not alter American global goals in any fundamental way in the post-1950 period: the overarching goal was still to "co-opt the industrial core of Eurasia, integrate it with the Third World periphery, and maintain America's preponderant position."[57] Following the Chinese Communist Revolution, however, US attention shifted more and more toward Asia. Rebuilding Japan—the Germany of the east—now became a policy priority, both because of geopolitical concerns and because Japanese economic recovery might help further ease the shortage of dollars in Asia that limited exports of American producers.[58] Prior to 1945, the Japanese economy had rested heavily on regional markets, several of which were Japanese colonies, including Manchuria in China. With China lost in 1949, the economic recovery of Japan was now going to require re-establishing some elements of the old co-prosperity sphere, or in the words of George Kennan, "some sort of empire toward the south."[59] In addition to the security importance of Southeast Asia, the region was deemed to be of considerable economic importance, both as source of raw materials and as a region that already had substantial European investments and could continue to absorb Japanese products.[60] Communists or nationalists could not be allowed to get in the way of ready economic access to the region, or at least to the portion of the region that remained open after Mao's victory in China. It was in this context—and before the Korean War—that the United States decided to support the efforts of industrial powers to maintain (or re-establish) colonial-type economic relations in the region; these included the Dutch in Indonesia, Britain in Malaya, Japan in Burma and Thailand and, of course, the French in Vietnam.[61] During and following the Korean War, then, NSC-68 was put into practice. Prior to the war there had been reluctance within the United States to fund defense spending at the high levels suggested by NSC-68. In Acheson's words, then "Korea came along and saved us."[62] Defense spending rose sharply during the war. After the war spending came down but remained high by pre-NSC-68 standards. Not only did military-Keynesianism help boost domestic economic growth within the United States but Japanese economy also benefited from the Korean War effort. Overseas the United States now increased its commitments to Formosa (Taiwan), Indo-China, Indonesia and the Philippines in Asia and to Western Europe, including rearming of West Germany. As importantly, the weak urge American officials felt to accommodate Third World nationalism was now also set aside. American ambition to establish clear preponderance in a global system of domination required that the United States maintain: "a) strength at the center; b) strength at the periphery; (and) c) retraction of Soviet power."[63] The United States increasingly thought of its global interests as constituting a system of power in which disturbances anywhere could become contagious and had to be dealt with. It is this system of domination that I have chosen to characterize as America's informal empire. One could call it "hegemony," as many scholars do, but hegemony implies a degree of legitimacy that was often missing in the cases of US interventions in the developing world.[64]

Dwight Eisenhower and John Foster Dulles replaced Truman and Acheson in the United States; then Stalin died, and Nikita Khrushchev took over in Russia. Though Khrushchev was very much an aggressive communist with global ambitions, he made some peaceful overtures toward the United States. Eisenhower, however, wanted all or nothing; even Churchill demurred at American reluctance to entertain the possibility of incremental progress. Dulles wanted to roll back communism.[65] This hardening of the Cold War did not bode well for the developing world. Although Eisenhower and Dulles's priorities were still in Europe, the Third World was beginning to intrude. Though the developing world would only become a priority for the US during the Kennedy years, many anticolonial, nationalist leaders were already beginning to entertain the idea of nonalignment and a third camp. For the strongly anticommunist Dulles, however, even neutrality between the blocs was immoral. His underlying reasoning was that Third World neutrals might be taken in by Khrushchev's overtures and that the results would be intolerable "given the industrialized nature of the Atlantic community and its dependence upon broad markets and access to raw materials."[66] Any drift away from the block of free world nations thus had to be stopped. It was in this context that the United States intervened in Iran (and Guatemala), and deepened its involvement in Vietnam. I now turn to more detailed analysis of these cases. The US intervention in Chile came later, toward of the end of American involvement in Vietnam during the Nixon-Kissinger years. I will provide further background on the subsequent phases of the Cold War in due course.

Iran

In 1953, the American government used covert means to depose Iran's elected leader, Muhammad Mossadegh, and replaced him with a more pliable monarch, the Shah of Iran. The American role in the intervention is not in doubt; the CIA, in declassified documents, confirmed in 2011 that the coup in Iran was "conceived and approved at the highest levels of the (U.S.) government," and was "carried out under CIA direction."[67] The real issues for debate, instead, are why the United States intervened and with what impact. As one might expect, some scholars view US intervention primarily in the context of the Cold War, while others suggest that economic motives—especially access to Iranian oil—were key.[68] I argue that the United States intervened to depose Mossadegh because he was a nationalist committed to Iranian control of Iranian oil. The United States hoped to achieve a number of goals by forcing a regime change in Iran: shoring up Britain's troubled economic position; opening access to American corporations in Iran; and, most of all, establishing the norm that national control of raw materials, especially oil, was not an acceptable policy option in the developing world. The United States achieved these goals, but mainly over the short term. Over the medium term, oil resources in Iran, or for that matter, nearly the world over, were nationalized. The client regime of the Shah was then violently overthrown in 1979 by sharply anti-American, theocratic rulers. After providing some background information about pre-1950 Iran, I focus below on the period of oil nationalization and US intervention.

Well before the advent of Christ, Persian empires ruled large territories that spread from modern-day Egypt to India. Arab invasions in the seventh century brought Islam to Iran, supplanting Zoroastrianism. Over the subsequent centuries, indigenous empires waxed and waned. With the rise of the Safavid dynasty in the sixteenth century, Iran also emerged as the center of Shia Islam. The Safavid rulers of Iran were contemporaries of the Ottomans in the west and the Mughals in the east. These great Muslim empires of Asia shared not only a level of opulence that attracted Europeans but also an inability to modernize, paving the way for growing European encroachments.[69] When the Safavids disintegrated toward the end of the eighteenth century, Iran escaped full colonization only because Russia and Britain vied for regional influence. Even as the Qajar dynasty unified Persia in the nineteenth century, both Russia and Britain played their "great game" in the region and came to exercise enormous influence over the country, sharing "zones of influence" in the north and the south respectively.[70]

A British company struck oil in southern Iran in 1908. This company soon metamorphosed into Anglo-Persian Oil Company (the Anglo-Iranian Oil Company after 1935; APOC and AIOC, respectively). Once Churchill had completed the British navy's shift from coal to oil (see chapter 3), Iran's importance to Britain grew sharply. Iranian oil became vital to sustaining both the British navy and power, especially in Asia. Having more than 50 percent voting rights in the APOC, the British government chose to control the company directly, and it occupied Iran during World War I (and again during World War II) to protect its investments and access to oil.[71] The Qajar dynasty in Iran during this period was disintegrating. A variety of new political demands were being made, including the demand to limit the power of the monarchy via constitutional means and nationalist calls to limit the influence of both Russia and Britain. Following World War I, the Bolsheviks withdrew from Iran—at least for a moment—and the British tried to turn Iran into a protectorate. The anti-British nationalist reaction within Iran was swift. The British move even drew the ire of President Wilson.

It was within this context that Mossadegh's political reputation as a "patriotic and honest" leader began to grow.[72] Mossadegh was born to an aristocratic family. Like many developing-country nationalists of his generation, he studied in Europe (France and Switzerland). He received a doctorate in law, and returned to Iran in 1914, well placed to play an important political role. From early on, he championed constitutionalism (limiting the power of the monarchy) and nationalism (Iranian control over Iranian affairs, especially oil). When Reza Shah established the Pahlavi dynasty in 1925, Mossadegh's political position became difficult. Reza Shah sought to modernize Iran, including by centralizing state power, building railways, and renegotiating the terms on which APOC extracted oil from Iran. Mossadegh supported the reformist instincts of the shah, but he and others in Iran's political class knew that the British had financed and facilitated Reza Shah's rise to power. Reza Shah started concentrating power in his person and declared himself a monarch, the head of a new dynasty. Following his nationalist and constitutionalist principles, Mossadegh started opposing Reza Shah, which, in turn, forced Mossadegh out of active politics, at least for a time. Although he was formally out of office during much of the Reza Shah period, Mossadegh's reputation as a selfless leader grew; he came to be seen in Iran as a leader who was ready to stand up to both autocracy and British influence.

As World War II began, Britain and Russia occupied Iran, promising to leave at the end of the war. Americans also established a presence. Reza Shah—who was under suspicion for sympathy with the Nazis—abdicated in favor of his young and insecure son, Mohamed Reza Shah, who in time would mature into the Shah of Iran. With much of high politics under the control of occupying powers, and a weak monarch at the helm, a variety of Iranian political forces started to emerge, which would intensify at the end of the war. On the left was the Russian supported Tudeh Party, and on the right were various popular clerics and some Nazi-inspired goons and gangs. A variety of nationalists occupied the broad central political space; while these groups were factionalized around personalities, they shared the political goals of limiting the power of foreigners as well as of the monarch, viewed by many as an agent of foreign powers. Mossadegh re-entered active politics during this period. As he started arguing for a neutral

Iran, he was increasingly viewed as a leader of the nationalist-constitutionalist factions at the center of Iranian politics.

Within this fragmented political situation, the Allied powers began to struggle over Iranian oil. While the AIOC controlled the oil fields—and often the politics—in the south of the country, the north of the country was supposed to be under Russian influence. British and American companies, however, supported by their respective governments, now sought oil concessions in northern Iran. The Russians pushed back; they asked Iranian authorities for their own concessions instead. Even though they were war allies, the British resented the Americans' encroachment in Iran; the Russians resented both the American and British efforts to move into the Russian zone; and the British and Americans were suspicious of Russian motives in the north of Iran. According to one scholar, British and American bids for oil in the north "triggered the first Cold War crisis in Iran."[73] Be that as it may, Mossadegh and others used the nominal power they enjoyed within the Majles (the Iranian Parliament) to deny Russians any new oil concessions in the north. Although the British and the Americans appreciated this Iranian move, Mossadegh's argument that Iranian oil ought to be controlled by Iranians soon focused attention on the role of AOIC itself. The terms on which the AIOC operated within Iran then emerged as a matter of key importance in Iranian politics.

Following World War II, who controlled the AIOC—the Iranians or the British—became a highly contentious issue, the struggle over which eventually led Americans to intervene in Iranian politics on the British side. The AIOC was of great economic and political importance to the British. Iran was the world's largest oil producer at the time, and the AIOC was Britain's largest overseas investment. Britain depended heavily on Iranian oil, and oil exports provided much-needed foreign exchange. As noted, the dollar gap was a critical issue for Britain and other European countries in the post–World War II period, a gap that Americans sought to fill with the Marshall Plan; Americans had a vested interest in Britain maintaining its sources of foreign exchange, even if it required maintaining colonial-type links. A war-weary Britain was also about to lose India, and it desperately wanted to preserve its other imperial connections, especially those like the AIOC, which were lucrative. For Iran, the AIOC represented a form of British colonialism. The terms on which the company operated within Iran came to be viewed as highly exploitative: the AIOC paid more in taxes to the British state than it paid in royalties to Iran; the AIOC operated as a classic foreign-owned enclave, in which the Iranian workers were treated poorly, colonial-type racism flourished, and more profits were invested elsewhere than within Iran; and AIOC officials and British consular officials cooperated regularly to manipulate Iranian politics. The financial terms the AIOC had negotiated with Iran also irked Iranian nationalists, but the real issue for them was "national sovereignty": concessions that gave "large foreign corporations . . . complete control of resource exploration and exploitation . . . galled [Iranian] nationalists."[74]

Anticolonial nationalism was on the rise in much of Asia after World War II. Iran was no exception. Although Iran was not a formal colony, Iranian nationalists harbored strong anticolonial sentiments against the British. By the late 1940s, they were demanding that the AIOC renegotiate its deal with Iran, emboldened by developments around the world: the American oil giant ARAMCO was in the process of finalizing a fifty-fifty agreement with Saudi Arabia (whereby Saudi Arabia and ARAMCO would share profits evenly), which was a lot more favorable to the host country than the terms of the AIOC deal with Iran; the same thing in Venezuela; and toward the end of the war, while the powers were preoccupied, Mexico had nationalized its oil industry. The AIOC, however, refused to negotiate with Iranian nationalists in good faith. The British belittled the Iranians, hoping to make minimal concessions while strengthening the hand of the more pliable Shah. The British refusal to accept a revised fifty-fifty contract—and the Iranian refusal to accept the less generous terms that the AIOC offered—hardened the political divide. Mossadegh re-entered politics in early 1950. While running for a seat in the Majles, he argued, not for further negotiations with the British, but for nationalizing the AIOC. This stand made him deeply popular in Iran—the local press dubbed him Iran's Gandhi.[75] After Mossadegh's electoral victory from a constituency in Teheran, then, the issue of oil nationalization had reached the top of Iran's political agenda.

Mossadegh, first and foremost an Iranian nationalist and a champion of constitutional government, was, in the words of his biographer, "the first liberal leader of modern Middle East," who "went on to lead the most enlightened government his country has ever known."[76] After winning his seat in Parliament in 1950, he became the leader of the National Front, an umbrella political organization. At the heart of this organization were "middle class" and "nationalist" elites who enjoyed broad support in Iranian society.[77] Although the clerics on the right and the communists on the left were suspicious of Mossadegh (the Soviet-supported Tudeh Party criticized him and his supporters as "comprador bourgeoisie"[78]), they, too, backed his call for nationalizing the AIOC. Mossadegh then, with broad political support, introduced a bill to nationalize the oil industry. A major strike in the oil industry contributed to a national mood in support of national control over oil. After Mossadegh became Iran's prime minister, in 1951, the bill to nationalize the AIOC passed with overwhelming support; even the Shah signed it—on May 1, International Labor Day, to boot—turning it into law. For Iranians, the nationalization of oil was a deeply emotional and gratifying moment. The AIOC logo came down in Abadan, and the Iranian flag was hoisted instead. In the words of a foremost student of the subject: "For many in Iran, the raising of the national flag showed the world that the country had finally gained true independence. Oil nationalization was for Iran what national independence was for many former colonies in Africa, Asia, Latin America, and the Caribbean."[79]

Western reaction to the nationalization of the AIOC was swift and sharply negative. The British government was ready to do whatever it took to reverse the decision, the oil majors—the "seven sisters"[80]—cooperated to impose an economic embargo on Iran, and the Americans entered the fray, first as brokers, then as leaders of the coup that ousted Mossadegh from power. Even though the Iranians had offered financial compensation to the AIOC, British foreign secretary Herbert Morrison announced that "Persian oil is of vital importance for our economy" and said that Britain must do "everything possible to prevent the Persians from getting away" with nationalization.[81] Britain moved an invasion force off Abadan; Americans, however, discouraged a naval attack—and the highly dependent British complied—lest the Russians also react militarily. The British government then imposed sanctions so that no one could buy oil from Iran. When that did not prove sufficient to reverse Iran's decision, British policymakers continued to negotiate with the Iranians, on the one hand, but also secretly sought to oust Mossadegh, on the other hand. When Mossadegh discovered the plans for a coup, he shut down the British embassy in Iran, in 1952. From then on, the British had to depend on the United States to take the lead in organizing a coup to get rid of Mossadegh.

Imposing sanctions on Iran would not have worked without the full cooperation from the major oil corporations, as well as from the governments of Britain and the United States. The British government froze Iran's sterling balances in London and halted exports of such scarce commodities as sugar and steel.[82] The AIOC, in turn, controlled technicians and tankers, without which Iran could not continue to extract and export its oil. The purpose of this economic warfare was to "bring Iran to its knees and thus force Mossadegh into an oil settlement that suited British purposes."[83] Other oil companies might have taken advantage of the situation and decided to buy and sell Iran's nationalized oil. However, supported by the US government, the other six sisters cooperated with their threatened seventh sister and refused to help Iran. The underlying thinking was that if Iran benefited from nationalization, it could threaten foreign investments worldwide. The US State Department's position was virtually identical: "The U.S. Government should not make the nationalization of Iranian oil a success for others to emulate."[84] Meanwhile, the economic warfare worked. Iran's oil exports dropped dramatically, from some $400 million in 1950 to some $2 million after the nationalization.[85] The sharp decline in revenues seriously hurt the

Iranian economy, created shortages, and contributed to growing domestic political turmoil.

To understand the American role in Iran in the early 1950s some background will be helpful. American involvement in Iran prior to World War II had been modest. Missionaries had been active in Iran since the nineteenth century, and American oil companies had sought access to Iranian oil in the interwar period, which the British had successfully opposed, but otherwise, there was little official contact between the United States and Iran until the 1940s.[86] Americans came to Iran in significant numbers only when the Allied forces occupied Iran at the beginning of the war. American interest in Iran grew during the war years, however. The unsuccessful efforts of American companies to secure an oil concession in Iran around this time created tension, serious enough that Churchill and Roosevelt exchanged notes, assuring each other that they would not encroach on the other's oil interests in Iran and Saudi Arabia, respectively. Meanwhile, ARAMCO was developing rapidly in Saudi Arabia. This led Secretary Hull to argue in 1943 that "it is to our interest that no great power be established on the Persian Gulf opposite the important American petroleum development in Saudi Arabia."[87] Now with British support, the United States sent several missions to Iran, including military missions. The Shah and others in the royalist circle welcomed the American presence. Mossadegh and other nationalists, however, sensed—rightly, as it turned out—that the American presence was likely to strengthen the hand of the British and the monarchy, and they started opposing America's role in Iran.

At the end of the war, wary of the enormous British influence and of the Americans' increasing involvement, the Russians delayed withdrawing their forces from Iran. Russia's motives were probably the same as those in Eastern Europe, namely, to maintain an empire in the near abroad to strengthen Russian postwar security—if more oil could be had in the bargain, so much the better. The British were too weak to do much about this violation of an earlier agreement. Americans, in cooperation with the Iranian government, then pressured the Russians to leave Iran, in 1946. America's key interest in the region was and remained oil, but the Russian intransigence in Iran contributed to growing American anxieties about Soviet intentions. Thus, in an important sense, economic and political issues were hard to untangle in the region. The United States worried about the Russian presence precisely because the region was so oil rich. Meanwhile, as noted, the political situation in Iran was rather chaotic. The growing American presence in Iran took several forms. The American ambassador established close and personal relations with the Shah; they played tennis regularly and discussed politics afterward, often over a whiskey. An increase in US military aid and cooperation was aimed at strengthening the Shah's hand against internal disorder. The Americans were clearly lining up on the side of a dependent autocrat and against the emerging democratic and nationalist forces within Iran. As British power declined—a trend sharply underscored by the crisis in Greece, which brought forth the Truman Doctrine in 1947—Americans began, slowly but surely, to replace Britain as the major Western power in Iran. Mossadegh and other nationalists can be excused for believing that a new imperial force was pushing its way forward in Iran, either to support or supplant the old one.

As the oil issue heated up in Iran, Americans started meddling in Iranian politics, following the precedent set by the British. For example, the new US ambassador to Iran, John Wiley (appointed in 1948) is known to have pressured the Shah to appoint General Ali Razmara, considered to be pro-American, as Iran's prime minister.[88] Razmara was deeply unpopular with the nationalists and with the Islamists. He was in power only a few months before being assassinated by a fedayeen, in early 1951. Because the whole incident was widely covered by the local media, Iranians started taking note, and the nationalists started disapproving, of the growing American involvement in their politics. As antiregime and anti-imperial political forces came to the fore, the British quietly advised the Shah to impose martial law; the United States, in turn, let it be known that it would view such a move with "understanding" and "sympathy."[89] Clearly, a friendly autocrat was to be preferred to an emerging popular movement. The Shah resisted, probably because he had misgivings about his own political capacity to crush nationalist and democratic politics in Iran. Razmara's assassination then led directly to the popular push for Mossadegh to become Iran's prime minister and for oil nationalization. US policy from then on was to work with the Shah and gently pressure Britain and the AIOC to give the Iranians better terms, but also to put enormous pressure on Iran to accept something less than oil nationalization. US and British authorities were also constantly in touch, consulting each other on the next appropriate move in Iran.[90]

One George McGhee, a Texas oilman and a Rhodes Scholar, was Acheson's point man on Iran. McGhee had worked hard to persuade the oil majors, as well as independent oil companies, to support the British economic embargo that followed the nationalization of AIOC.[91] But economic pressures failed to break Mossadegh's will; control of their oil was for the Iranians not only a matter of dollars and cents, but also of sovereignty. For the Americans and the British—government officials, as well as oil interests—nationalization was to be resisted. The United States by now had established global institutions that would facilitate open trade. Protecting and facilitating Western foreign investment in the raw materials of the developing world was the next frontier in the American ambition to establish an open global economy. As noted, American policymakers at the time believed that access to such raw materials, especially to cheap oil, was essential for the economic recovery in Europe in the short run, but also for sustained economic prosperity of the West over the long term. Open access and control over developing-country commodities was deemed to be of great significance. If Iran's nationalization succeeded, who knows what might follow? Other oil nationalizations? The nationalization of mines and minerals beyond oil? And for the British, even Suez might be vulnerable! If Mossadegh continued to stand firm, initiating what might soon have become a dangerous trend—falling economic dominoes—then he would have to be removed. British and American thinking on how to deal with the nationalization of the AIOC then started converging around removing Mossadegh from power via a coup.

There is no need to deny that fear of a communist takeover may also have contributed to American anxieties over Iran. Certainly, much of the American public discourse on Iran was couched in such fears. This is also not surprising. Following the Chinese Communist Revolution, the Soviet possession of an atomic bomb, the Korean War, and McCarthyism at home, Americans came to view many political developments in the developing world through the prism of the Cold War. Moreover, Russia, and then the Soviet Union, had long exercised influence over parts of Iran. The Tudeh Party was a well-organized communist party, supported by the Soviet Union, and it had support among the working class, especially workers in oil refineries. Given Iran's political instability, a plausible case could be made, and many in the United States and Britain made it, that Iran was on the verge of a communist takeover, thus justifying covert intervention to save Iran for the free world. A security-oriented analysis of US intervention in Iran, however, does not survive close scrutiny. As noted, by the early 1950s the United States was well on its way to containing the USSR in Europe. Although there were new anxieties in Asia, the NSC-68 and the Korean War had allowed the United States to increase defense spending sharply. After Eisenhower became president, American decision-makers felt emboldened enough to want to go beyond containing communism to rolling it back.

Within Iran, as noted, the United States' successfully pushed back the Russians in 1946. Then again, Iranian decision-makers, including Mossadegh, had successfully denied the Russians oil concessions in the Iranian north, in 1947. Much was made of the potential role of the Tudeh Party in the early 1950s, but scholars have since concluded that, at the time, the Tudeh had neither the capacity nor any intention to seize power.[92] More importantly, British intelligence had also reached this conclusion at that time, and the CIA, which depended on British intelligence during this early period of American involvement, accepted its analysis: "Although the UK believes that lack of oil revenues will result in progressive economic and political deterioration in Iran, it does not appear to regard a communist takeover in Iran as imminent."[93] Acheson saw the problem clearly: "Britain stands on the verge of bankruptcy . . . . The cardinal purpose of British policy is not to prevent Iran from going Commie; the cardinal point is to preserve what they believe to be the last remaining bulwark of British solvency; that is, their overseas investment and property position."[94] At the time, Churchill's private secretary noted that "there were no signs that Persia was nearer communism."[95] When US and British authorities met to discuss oil nationalization in Iran, they agreed, "[T]he present situation contained no element of Russian incitation and ought not to be seen primarily as part of the immediate short-term 'cold war' problem."[96]

Mossadegh was no communist. He was a member of the Iranian upper class. What he wanted for Iran was national control over Iranian oil. And nationalization was hardly a radical policy during this period. In fact, the ruling Labour Party under Clement Attlee had just nationalized several important industries in the UK. Mossadegh, then, was a real problem for both Britain and the United States because he was a genuine Iranian nationalist and a constitutionalist who had been elected to power; he was furthermore hard to discredit because he had "no weakness for girls, boys, money, wine, the pipe or Karl Marx."[97] The issue that the United States and Britain faced with Mossadegh was not communism but nationalism and "neutralism," or what in the very near future would come to be called *nonalignment*. Before the coup in 1953, the US government had already concluded that "Iran's reversion to an attitude of neutrality" was not acceptable.[98] If Mossadegh insisted on maintaining democracy at home, including giving the Tudeh the freedom to operate, nationalizing the oil industry, and possibly pursuing a foreign policy that put Iran equidistant between the West and the Soviet Union, then Mossadegh had to go. The pliable Shah was a far more reliable ally of the free world.

The plans to remove Mossadegh from power via a coup were already under consideration in mid-1952, after he was elected prime minister. American officials continued to broker a deal between Iran and Britain while planning his overthrow. As prime minister, Mossadegh's popularity soared. He passed a series of reform-oriented pieces of legislation that promised to enhance the income of the peasantry and to extend suffrage to women. Since these moves were likely to help Mossadegh consolidate his popularity, the US and British ambassadors in Iran concluded in mid-1952 that the only way to get rid of him was via a military "coup d'état."[99] The CIA and MI6 (the British intelligence service) met during late 1952 to plan the coup; Allen Dulles, brother of the better-known John Foster Dulles and soon to be appointed director of the CIA, attended these meetings. The plans were ready when Eisenhower took office in 1953. He and Secretary Dulles hardly needed to be persuaded. They, along with Churchill, who was now back in power in the United Kingdom, were closer to business interests. Eisenhower and Dulles were also ready to roll back communism and limit the spread of neutralism. Iran, then, provided an early opportunity to try covert intervention as a strategy to depose a developing-country ruler who was proving to be too independent and popular.

The coup was a two-step plan: create a broader economic and political crisis in Iran first and then work with the Shah and pro-American elements within the Iranian military to depose Mossadegh. The coup planning also involved influencing elite public opinion within the United States that the threat of communism in Iran was imminent. The effort to create a sense of crisis in Iran proceeded on several fronts. The economic crisis created by the successful Anglo-American oil embargo was discussed above. The results included sharp reductions in Iran's oil income and thus, in foreign exchange, government revenues, and the buying power of all of those who depended on the oil economy. A growing economic crisis, in turn, started breeding political discontent. While Mossadegh was deeply popular, opposition to him also started growing, and rival elites sensed an opportunity. The CIA then went fishing in the troubled waters.

MI6 had a well-established espionage network across Iran, especially in Tehran. The CIA established some of its own contacts but worked mainly with British recruits in Iran. Since the British embassy was closed, the Americans directed the coup-related activities. Kermit Roosevelt, a Harvard man and Teddy Roosevelt's grandson, was the CIA's main man in Teheran, and Donald Wilber, a Princeton scholar, was in charge of psychological warfare. The CIA had access to an enormous amount of funds, which it started channeling to those who might oppose Mossadegh, including newspapers, opinion leaders in the bazaar, clerics with the capacity to mobilize crowds and gangs, members of the Iranian Parliament, and key members of the military. Operating in a fragile democracy with a long tradition of court intrigue and external dependency, the Americans were quickly able to create a substantial network of Iranians willing to help undermine Mossadegh. Key supporters of Mossadegh, who had first pushed him as the leader of the National Front, betrayed him, and some were eventually found to be on CIA's payroll. Well-known clerics like Ayatollah Kashani, who had joined Mossadegh at one point, also defected and mobilized street crowds in opposition; Kashani, too, was subsequently discovered to be cooperating with the Americans, if not on their payroll.

In addition to mobilizing opposition against Mossadegh in Iran, MI6 and the CIA undertook a deliberate campaign to exaggerate the threat of communism within Iran. Montague "Monty" Woodhouse of MI6 recalled that in his dealings with the Americans over Iran, he deliberately downplayed the British "need to recover control of the oil industry" and to "emphasize" instead the "communist threat."[100] The CIA's Wilber boasted that his task was to "fan to fever pitch public opinion against Mossadegh."[101] The CIA then planted stories aimed at undermining Mossadegh's credibility, especially in the American media. It is a shameful fact that during the summer of 1953, just prior to the coup, major American publications bought into the CIA propaganda and ran anti-Mossadegh stories. The *New York Times* dubbed him a "dictator"; *Newsweek* suggested that he was facilitating a "communist takeover"; and *Time* went all out to claim that Mossadegh and Iran were "one of the worst calamities to the anti-communist world since the Red conquest of China."[102] The American and British intelligence agencies were, then, rather successful in harnessing anti-Mossadegh political forces within Iran and in generating anti-Mossadegh public opinion in the West, especially in the United States. One reliable observer summed up the cumulative impact as follows: "[I]t is clear that Mossadegh's government was by now the object of pitiless acts of war by two hostile powers. The crippling embargo; the bombardment of disinformation; the conspiracies to riot, murder and abduct; it is not necessary to send armies in order to wage a war, and there is no glossing the ruthlessness of the Anglo-American campaign" against Mossadegh and Iran.[103]

It was in this context that CIA operatives in Iran orchestrated the coup against Mossadegh in August 1953. The details of the cloak-and-dagger operations are not that important for my brief account.[104] The first coup effort failed, and the Shah had to escape from Iran because he feared retribution at the hands of the nationalists. But a second coup followed and succeeded. Mossadegh was deposed and put under house arrest; many of his supporters faced harsher retributions, including death. The Shah returned to Iran and regained his throne, with the blessings of Loy W. Henderson, the US ambassador to Iran at the time, who recommended an "undemocratic" Iran to the Shah; the Shah hardly needed to be persuaded.[105] American support for the Iranian military and for internal law-and-order forces began immediately. With American support, the Shah was now in a position to bypass popular political forces in Iran and to appoint key political officials, including a new prime minister to replace Mossadegh. The CIA-led coup then rapidly transformed Iran into an autocracy, supported by the United States.

The real prize was, of course, Iranian oil. Mossadegh's efforts to nationalize the AIOC were reversed. Although the Shah tried to maintain a fig leaf of national control over Iranian oil, for all practical purposes Iranian oil had been denationalized by 1955. The AIOC recovered some lost ground but nothing close to its old glory; its share of the new consortium responsible for extraction and export of Iranian oil was 40 percent. After decades of failed efforts, several American oil majors finally gained access to Iranian oil; they also came to control another

40 percent of the new consortium. Even the smaller independent companies that had cooperated in the oil embargo were now rewarded with their own smaller shares. The Dulles brothers' old law firm negotiated these new oil contracts. Politics and oil were deeply intertwined in the case of US intervention in Iran; the post-coup developments only further underscored these links.

What was the legacy of the coup, both for Iran and the United States? Some causal connections are easier to suggest than others, but even those only for a short- to medium time frame. US intervention certainly derailed the possibility of Iran's evolution toward a democratic and secular polity. Whether Iran, left to its own resources, would have moved in that direction is hard to know. What we do know is what actually happened: a democratically elected leader was deposed by a coup and replaced by a US-supported monarch. Over the next quarter century, the dependent Shah concentrated power in his person and suppressed nationalist and secular politics. The only opposition forces that survived in the tyrannical polity were those suited to form another type of tyranny—religious fundamentalists, who burst forth in 1979 and who continue to rule Iran. As to Iranian economy during the Shah, per capita incomes certainly grew handsomely. However, much of this growth was driven by oil incomes; the correlation between oil income and per capita income growth in Iran (during the Shah period, as well as beyond) was nearly perfect.[106] National control over oil was postponed for nearly a quarter of a century. The Shah was no nationalist. Even with the resources available, he undertook few serious efforts to put the Iranian economy on a dynamic path. His priorities, instead, were to live off oil wealth and to keep the United States happy, which included using Iran's oil resources to buy American goods, especially armaments. As a result, agriculture was neglected, which turned Iran into a food importer, and the share of manufacturing in the economy hovered around 10 percent of the GDP, a low level for an economy with ample resources. For the most part, Iran under the Shah remained a commodity-dependent economy.

Although the United States did not acknowledge the coup, it considered the regime change in Iran a huge American success. Allen Dulles personally congratulated Kermit Roosevelt on his leadership. The Iranian coup became a model for the CIA of how to engineer covert regime change in developing countries: "[S]tart with a propaganda campaign, proceed through a wave of destabilizing violence, and culminate in an attack staged to look like a domestic uprising."[107] Shortly after the overthrow of Mossadegh, the same process was repeated in Guatemala.[108] Jacobo Arbenz was elected president of Guatemala in 1951. A nationalist and a social democrat of sorts, he sought to nationalize the United Fruit Company and other American foreign investments in Guatemala. Eisenhower and the Dulles brothers—who owned stock in United

Fruit—painted Arbenz as furthering the Soviet Union's agenda in America's backyard, although little evidence was ever found to support this charge. Since this was unacceptable, the CIA engineered a coup against Arbenz, initiating rule by a series of brutal military dictators. The point that any efforts to nationalize American investments in Guatemala—or elsewhere—would be deeply costly was made loud and clear.

The immediate benefit of the coup in Iran to Americans was, of course, economic. American corporations had for decades sought access to Iranian oil but had been blocked by the British. As noted, when British power was in decline after World War II, the United States was willing to help with its economic recovery but in a manner that also enhanced its own interests. This was as true of the Marshall Plan as it was when the United States stepped into Britain's imperial shoes, first in Greece and Turkey, and then in Iran. After the coup, the British regained some of their access to Iranian oil (their 40 percent), but Americans had led the coup; they ensured that American corporations also got a substantial share—their own 40 percent. Besides the specific benefits to American corporations, a more profound benefit came in the form of a steady and cheap supply of oil for the global market, especially for Western economies. As we have seen, by the mid-1970s, Iran was also using oil revenues and foreign exchange to buy nearly half of all the arms the United States was selling overseas, thus contributing to American economic growth.

If a case can be made that in the short and medium term the United States benefited from the coup in 1953 at the expense of Iran, a longer-term perspective muddies this clarity. Even after an internal revolution that overthrew the Shah in 1979, the rule by clergy in Iran has brought neither greater prosperity nor better governance to the people of that country. Although Iran's continuing internal difficulties cannot be fully blamed on external machinations, even Madeline Albright, the secretary of state for President Clinton, eventually recognized that US intervention in Iran in 1953 had been "a setback for Iran's political development." Short-term American gains also need to be balanced against longer-term costs. Following World War II, Iranians had a very positive view of Americans. Over time, especially after the coup and the prolonged tyrannical rule by US-supported Shah, anti-Americanism has become a strong force in Iranian politics. The ayatollahs have mobilized this force into a ruling strategy. Iran is now a sizable country of nearly a hundred million people, with enormous oil wealth and the capacity to create nuclear weapons in a region of great importance to the United States. The short-term economic gains for the United States that followed from the coup indeed appear pyrrhic when set beside the reality that this important Middle Eastern country is now deeply anti-American, at least in part due to earlier American actions.

Vietnam

Prior to World War II, the French had colonized Indochina, and the United States took little interest in the region.[109] Following the war, however, American leaders supported French efforts, parallel to their support for Britain in Iran and elsewhere, to re-establish a colonial-type of influence over Vietnam. When Ho Chi Minh's forces defeated the French militarily in 1954, the United States committed itself to saving southern Vietnam from communism. The Vietnamese revolutionaries were just as fiercely committed to national unity. The prolonged conflict that followed lasted some two decades. Only after enormous destruction did the United States withdraw its military forces from Vietnam, in 1973; Vietnam was then unified in 1975. I now examine this second case of US intervention in the developing world during the Cold War. After laying out the central argument in brief and providing some historical background, the analysis follows the chronology of the War, focusing on developments in both the United States and Vietnam.

The literature on the American intervention in Vietnam is extensive; the quality of this literature is often quite good, even though it tends to focus more on developments in the United States and less on those in Vietnam.[110] A central theme in this literature is that US intervention in Vietnam was a giant mistake. While realist scholars in this genre argue that the United States had no real interests in Vietnam, many liberals suggest that US policymakers underestimated the nationalist commitment of Ho Chi Minh, mistaking him for a stooge of global communism.[111] I build on this literature, especially on the claim that Vietnamese communists were also nationalists. However, I will depart from the core suggestion that the United States had no real interests in Vietnam. Instead, I argue that the United States pursued real interests in Vietnam—or, at least, what American policymakers thought were real American interests—but lost.[112] In the early stages of the US intervention, American leaders hoped to support France's and Japan's economic recoveries by keeping Southeast Asian markets open to them. But over time, as the French and Japanese economies recovered, the war in Vietnam dragged on and got mired in the Cold War in Asia, and maintaining American credibility itself became the reason to continue American intervention in Vietnam. Given hegemonic ambitions, credibility was a key currency for the United States to maintain an informal empire on a global scale. That the United States eventually lost the war—and with it some credibility—should not be a reason for scholars to judge the pursuit of credibility during the period as irrational.

Like Iran, Vietnam is an ancient civilization. Historical records document a settled agrarian society around the Red River Delta—just east of modern-day Hanoi—as far back as 2500 BCE. For the first ten centuries of the modern era, the northern parts of modern-day Vietnam were annexed by China. Although the Vietnamese periodically fought the Chinese for independence, they also embraced Confucian culture and modes of organizing the state and economy. North Vietnam has thus been a lot more Sinicized than the southern half, where a variety of Hindu, Moslem, and other influences via Southeast Asia helped mold the state and society. After throwing off the Chinese yolk in the tenth century, though never once and for all, rulers from North Vietnam eventually sought to incorporate what is now the southern part of Vietnam into a unified Vietnam, in the fifteenth century. The geography of the country—slim, mountainous, and with a nearly 1,000-mile coastline—was a major obstacle to sustained unity in premodern times. Nevertheless, more or less centralized rulers came and went; over time, a strong sense of Vietnam, defined especially in terms of opposition to China, also emerged. By the time France made its presence felt in Vietnam, first with missionaries in the seventeenth and the eighteenth centuries and then as colonizers in the nineteenth, Vietnam was mainly a rice-producing economy, divided between a mandarin-like land-controlling class and the peasantry, with a weak center and strong regions.[113]

France colonized Indochina during the second half of the nineteenth century. Missionaries and commercial interests within France had already been pressuring the French government to establish influence over Indochina. The immediate catalyst in the middle of the century was British success in the Opium Wars and the subsequent forced opening of the China market (see chapter 2). As we have seen, the British Crown took over the responsibility of ruling India in 1857. British hegemony was thus on the move at mid-century, and France was afraid of falling farther behind; French authorities thus recommitted to more overseas acquisitions. It was during this period that the French government supported private efforts to build the Suez Canal in Egypt (chapter 2). In East Asia, though, the French had secured some trading rights in China following the First Opium War, and their anxieties about losing out to Britain were enhanced during the Second Opium War. France sent a naval expedition to Vietnam in 1857; more followed. Vietnam was to become France's Hong Kong, an entrepôt to the Chinese market. Saigon was colonized first. Slowly but surely thereafter, other parts of Indochina were conquered, a process that was very nearly complete by the mid-1880s. Considering that the French joined the British in the Scramble for Africa (see chapter 3) from the early 1880s onward, this period in the second half of the nineteenth century was a high point of French imperialism.

French rule over Vietnam was highly repressive and exploitative.[114] According to a leading analyst, the French commitment to the *mission civilisatrice* (civilizing mission) notwithstanding, there is no doubt that "the primary objectives of French colonial policy in Indochina were economic."[115] France turned Vietnam's subsistence economy into a classic commercialized colony that produced commodities for exports and took French manufactured goods as imports. Rice cultivation increased sharply under French direction, as did rice exports. This might have contributed to an improved standard of living for the Vietnamese, but for the fact that the local population also increased sharply in the early twentieth century, and the French imposed onerous levels of taxation on the Vietnamese countryside. Rubber and coffee plantations in the south and the mining of coal and minerals in the north were other major economic activities that facilitated commodity exports. Some infrastructure was developed to facilitate colonial rule, as well as exports; urban centers also came into being. Colonial tariff policy, however, deliberately encouraged the import of French manufactured goods and discouraged "the development of local industries that might compete with French goods."[116] As one might expect in a colonial economy then, commerce and manufacturing seriously lagged behind, and what did come into being was owned either by the French or by members of the Chinese and Indian migrant communities.

French rule was more direct in the south than in the north, but for all practical purposes, the indigenous landowning classes—in cooperation with an officialdom directed by the colonial state—exercised local control. As landowners cooperated with the French to facilitate rule and extraction in the countryside, old patron-client ties that linked landlords and peasants were disrupted, only to be replaced with growing class-conflict-like tensions and hostilities.[117] This shift in the social relations in the countryside eventually provided the raw material for peasant mobilization in Vietnam, both against landlords and, more importantly, against foreign rulers. Meanwhile, the emerging intelligentsia started to question the legitimacy of French rule.[118] As in many other colonies, the early questioning took the form of holding the French responsible for not meeting their avowed commitments to *mission civilisatrice*, and then slowly but surely moved to issues of national emancipation. Both Sun Yat-Sen's revolution in China and the earlier Meiji transformation in Japan provided inspiration for what Vietnam might become. These early nationalists were often elitist, without much mass support. The French also repressed any and all nationalist agitations, imprisoning potential leaders or sending them into exile or both. The repression of moderate nationalists then provided an opening for more radical nationalists to come forward.

Among these radical nationalists was Ho Chi Minh, who founded the Vietnamese Revolutionary Youth League in 1925. By the time Ho Chi Minh had formed the league, he had already been well exposed to global political currents. While working in Paris, he had petitioned Woodrow Wilson, the champion of self-determination, and the French Socialist Party to consider the cause of Vietnamese independence at Versailles. Both ignored him. Ho Chi Minh then turned to the writings of Lenin and became a founding member of the French Communist Party. He subsequently trained in Moscow to be an agent of the Comintern and was then sent to China to work with the emerging communist movement. It was in southern China that Ho Chi Minh formed the league, in association with other Vietnamese nationalists who had also been exiled by the French. The league gained popularity in Vietnam under Ho's charismatic leadership. Other student members came to include Pham Van Dong and Truong Chinh, who would eventually go on to lead sovereign Vietnam. The league was transformed into the Indochinese Communist Party (ICP) in 1930. The ICP had a brief moment of success at the onset of the Depression, when economic difficulties increased support among Vietnamese workers and peasants. But heavy French repression sent the leadership either to prison or exile. Ho Chi Minh's political fortunes went into decline for much of the 1930s, but recovered when growing Japanese power in the Pacific reduced the Vichy French government to the status of junior colonial collaborators in Vietnam. In 1941, Ho Chi Minh and others then formed the Viet Minh, a united front, of sorts, aimed at liberating Vietnam from both the French and the Japanese.

Whether Ho Chi Minh was more a communist or a nationalist has been long debated. I accept his biographer's wise conclusion that "in his own way, he was both."[119] More important: "[T]here seems little doubt that for Ho Chi Minh the survival of his country was first and always his primary concern."[120] Communism and revolution were thus means to an end for Ho Chi Minh. The valued end was an independent Vietnam. Ho Chi Minh was thus part Lenin and part Gandhi. For him, Leninism would pave the way to what the man-of-the-people Gandhi most valued in India—nationhood. He made this means-ends relationship clear even when he founded the ICP. "[T]he French imperialists' barbarous oppression and ruthless exploitation have awakened our compatriots, who have all realized that revolution is the only road to survival and that without it they will die a slow death."[121] Over the years, as the "national question" became more pressing, "social questions" concerning property redistribution took a back seat. By the time a pragmatic Ho Chi Minh formed the Viet Minh, the mobilizing platform had thus become quite inclusive: "National salvation is the common cause of our entire people. Every Vietnamese must take part in it. He who has money will contribute his money, he who has strength will contribute his strength, [and] he who has talent will contribute his talent."[122]

Ho Chi Minh and the Viet Minh built up considerable popular support within Vietnam during the Japanese occupation, especially in the northern and central regions. Japanese occupation neutralized some of the fear of the white man's omnipotence that French rule had created. A reformist program enabled the Viet Minh to mobilize the support of the peasantry without fully alienating the landowning interests. Members of the Viet Minh could then move in and out of villages without the fear that all the landowning interests were collaborating with the occupying powers. Relief activities conducted by the Viet Minh during a famine further boosted its popularity, at the expense of the colonial officialdom and its local collaborators. One local study in central Vietnam—where the Viet Minh was not as powerful as it was farther north—thus estimated that "during the World War II years 70 to 80 percent of My Thuy Phuong's [a village just south of Hue] people supported the Viet Minh."[123] In addition to popular support and organization in the countryside, the Viet Minh also started—quietly, of course—building up armed units. When the Japanese deposed the Vichy government in Vietnam in early 1945—and appointed Bao Dai as a puppet leader—the colonial state apparatus more or less vanished. Before the Japanese could rebuild this coercive structure, however, the United States dropped atomic bombs on Japan, and Japan surrendered.

Ho Chi Minh had rightly anticipated the Japanese loss. He and the Viet Minh quickly moved in to fill the power vacuum, and declared Vietnamese independence in 1945. The Viet Minh's political presence was stronger in the north and in the center of Vietnam than it was in the south of the country. Nevertheless, Ho was already a popular national leader. He established a sovereign national government in Hanoi and asked for international recognition. Neither Stalin nor Truman recognized Vietnam as a sovereign country. In retrospect, one wonders if the tragedy of the Vietnam War could have been avoided had both Stalin and Truman supported Ho Chi Minh at this critical historical juncture. However, we know that this was not to be. Stalin was a Europhile who barely trusted such an oriental revolutionary as Mao to run a successful revolution in China; Ho Chi Minh in Vietnam was even farther down on Stalin's list of those deserving support. At the end of World War II, moreover, the Soviet Union was so preoccupied with its postwar problems elsewhere that it only opened an embassy in Hanoi in 1950, following the Chinese Revolution and China's support for North Vietnam. Meanwhile, following the decisions at Potsdam, Allied forces entered Vietnam to take over from Japan; British forces took control in the south, and Chinese nationalist forces in the north. The British, in turn, enabled the French to restore colonial rule in the southern half of the country.

Why did the United States not recognize Vietnamese independence in 1945? This is an important question because America's failure to recognize Vietnam marked the beginning of American support for French colonialism in Indochina. For a moment during World War II, it appeared that the United States might support the indigenous nationalist forces instead. Roosevelt, in a conversation with Stalin in 1943, remarked, "[A]fter 100 years of French rule in Indochina, the inhabitants were worse off than they had been before." Roosevelt and Stalin agreed that after the war, "the old French colonial rule" in Indochina ought not to be restored and that Indochina ought to be governed instead as some sort of a "trusteeship" that would prepare the region for eventual "independence."[124] American intelligence agents also cooperated directly with Ho Chi Minh during World War II. They sought his help in recovering US pilots downed by the Japanese, gave him some arms, and the OSS (Office of Strategic Services, a precursor to the CIA) dubbed him Agent 19. Ho Chi Minh, then, had some real reasons to believe that the Viet Minh and the United States were both fighting Japanese fascism and that, following Japan's defeat, an anticolonial United States might support the Vietnamese quest for independence. But US policy had changed by the end of the war. Acheson, in 1945, let it be known that "the US had no thought of opposing the reestablishment of French control in Indochina."[125] What happened? How do we explain the US support for French colonialism well before the communist revolution in China?

Roosevelt's support for trusteeship types of arrangements in postwar Southeast Asia was opposed by European colonial powers. Indochina, Malaya, and Indonesia were of great economic importance to France, Britain, and the Netherlands, respectively.[126] None of these Western powers was about to give up its colonies readily. Both Churchill and Charles de Gaulle conveyed their reservations to Roosevelt. American policymakers, who had begun to think about the shape of the postwar world, imagined Britain and France as junior partners in the new order. As noted, toward the end of the war, rebuilding both the war-destroyed British and French economies was emerging as a key priority for the United States. It was then reasoned that the European powers would need to hold on to their colonies to facilitate rapid economic recovery. The European desk at the US State Department thus opposed the idea of trusteeship for Southeast Asian countries, as did a variety of Europe-oriented American policymakers. Once again, America's ideology of anticolonialism was sacrificed for the more pressing needs of its European allies. By the time Roosevelt met with Churchill and Stalin at Yalta, the US position on the fate of Japanese-held European colonies in Asia had already changed, even if quietly. By now Roosevelt had accepted the idea that France would probably return to Indochina after the war, and that any "trusteeship" arrangement would emerge only if France agreed to it "voluntarily."

France was not about to give up Indochina, however, and certainly not voluntarily. At stake were issues of national pride, a possible contagion effect on such other valued colonies as Algeria, and most importantly, the direct economic importance of Indochina, especially Vietnam. The colony was important for both trade and investment. As an exporter of rice and rubber, Vietnam had access to ample foreign exchange. This enabled Vietnam to not only absorb light manufactured goods from France, but also to help ease France's postwar foreign exchange shortage. French foreign investment in Indochina was sizable, nearly $2 billion during this period. France owned "all the rubber plantations . . . two-thirds of the rice, all the mines, all the shipping, virtually all the industry, and nearly all the banks."[127] French colonialism in Vietnam was thus rather lucrative. France had every reason to want to re-impose control over its distant colonies in Indochina.

With tacit approval of the United States, British forces helped France return to Indochina, especially in the south. Ho Chi Minh was aghast at the cooperation among Western powers to reimpose colonial control over Indochina. Although the French quickly established control over select southern cities like Saigon, the Viet Minh had already put down roots in the southern countryside. Even in the south, French control was uneven. By contrast, the Viet Minh ran a government in Hanoi and the Chinese nationalists did not press them very hard, except to demand a more plural government here and there. France did re-establish some presence in the north as well, mainly in urban centers, but the Viet Minh was clearly dominant in that part of the country. The battle lines between the French and the Viet Minh were, then, increasingly drawn. Ho recognized his global isolation and often sought compromise with the French and made numerous appeals to the United States. The French, however, had decided to recolonize Vietnam, and the Americans, some misgivings notwithstanding, decided to stand by their key Western ally. US secretary of state George Marshall clarified this policy position in 1947. The "key our position," he wired to US representatives in Paris, Saigon, and Hanoi, is that we are "essentially in the same boat as French, also as British and Dutch. We can-not conceive setbacks to long-range interests France which would also be setbacks our own . . . . In particular we recognize Vietnamese will for indefinite period require French material and technical assistance and enlightened political guidance."[128] Whether Marshall really believed that French imperialism added up to assistance and enlightened guidance, or whether these were just diplomatic niceties, is not all that relevant. What is important instead is the clear American assurance to France that they were on the same side in the growing conflict between nationalism and imperialism.

Although the United States did not provide direct military aid to France in Vietnam before the Chinese Communist Revolution, post–World War II, US assistance to France was channeled to the conflict in Indochina and the United States did not object. After the revolution, in 1949, however, US support for France became more direct. As I noted previously, following the revolution in China, the onset of the Korean War, and NSC-68, the Cold War became more intense and the focus shifted to Asia. Vietnam bordered on China. And although Ho was a Vietnamese nationalist, he was also a communist. Even though there was little evidence at the time of any direct Soviet support for the Viet Minh, the Americans now argued that all communists were under the direction of Kremlin, and they had to be stopped.[129] Moreover, once the United States decided that the Japanese economy had to be rebuilt, the economic importance of Southeast Asia increased markedly in American thinking. Dean Rusk argued that "control over the economic resources of Southeast Asia would be a key prize in a world conflict. Japan regarded such control as a *sine qua non* in the last war."[130] If Japan had to be reindustrialized, it would now need the old co-prosperity sphere—minus China, of course—as a source of raw materials and markets for its recovering industries. While France may not readily open Vietnamese economy to the Japanese, the importance of Vietnam lay elsewhere; Vietnam became the new frontier for US policymakers, where communism had to be stopped, so as to save all of Southeast Asia. The domino theory was applied to Vietnam ad nauseam. Truman then made the fateful decision of supplying military aid to France in 1950. By 1952, the United States was bearing one-third of the French costs to run the war in Vietnam.

Meanwhile, Ho Chi Minh's failure to secure any concessions from the French or the Americans empowered harder-line communists within the Viet Minh. Some land redistribution followed. The popularity of the communists grew in the countryside. In addition to Ho Chi Minh, Pham Van Dong, and Truong Chinh—the old troika among the founding members of the Indochinese Communist Party—the leadership in Vietnam now included Vo Nguyen Giap, the cosmopolitan professor turned army general, who eventually led the Vietnamese against the French in Dien Bien Phu, and Le Duan in the south, who in time became the hard-line leader of Vietnam against American intervention.[131] While there were differences among the top leadership, especially on the issue of the appropriate strategy to oust the French, they were also united in the goal of achieving independence for Vietnam.[132] The North built up both guerilla and regular armed units, and started attacking French positions. As US support for the French in Vietnam grew, Mao's China now started supporting Vietnam. Ho made secret visits to China and the Soviet Union to try to secure arms and aid, successfully in China but not in the Soviet Union. With Chinese support for Vietnam growing, however, the Soviet Union eventually established a relationship with Hanoi, in 1950. What was a classic struggle between nationalism and colonialism was now increasingly characterized by Americans as a struggle between global communism and the "free world." Following the armistice in Korea, for example, Eisenhower declared that the costs of losing Indochina would be "incalculable to the free world."[133]

Given the value the United States had placed on Vietnam, it is somewhat surprising that it chose to not support France in 1954 during the battle of Dien Bien Phu. American policymakers discussed providing support, including the option of using a nuclear weapon to get rid of communism once and for all in the region.

But in the end, Eisenhower chose not to support the French effort. Underlying reasons included a belief among US elites that the French were incompetent, the British argument that the French were fighting a losing war, and, with Korea in mind, hesitation on part of Eisenhower of yet another Chinese intervention, this time in support of Ho Chi Minh.[134] Following the French military defeat, the subsequent negotiations in Geneva led to the division of Vietnam, with an agreement to hold a national election by 1956. Many observers believe that the Geneva Accords were a major turning point in the evolution of the Vietnam conflict, especially because they led to the creation of the separate, noncommunist state of South Vietnam, which the United States decided to preserve, even at a high cost.[135] Much of what followed militarily followed from this political decision.

As is well known, the United States put Diem in charge of South Vietnam in 1955, and then chose to not support national elections in Vietnam in 1956, which had been promised in the Geneva Accords.[136] A key reason was that Ho would have won any such election with a wide margin. This outcome was not acceptable to US decision-makers. The American foreign-policy elite had concluded, rightly, that Ho was a communist but, wrongly, that he was a stooge of the Soviet Union or China. Western coordination to re-impose colonial control on Vietnam had pushed Ho Chi Minh to seek support of the communist giants. Whether, under different circumstances, he would have become a Tito of the east, was not entertained as a serious possibility by the Americans. If the failure to recognize Vietnamese sovereignty in 1945 was the first opportunity that the United States missed on its road to the Vietnam War, failure to support elections in 1956—just because the likely results were not acceptable—was clearly another important miscalculation. Although historical counterfactuals are hard to demonstrate, a democratically elected Ho might have united Vietnam a full two decades earlier, without the loss and destruction that the subsequent war unleashed; such elections may also have tamed some of the more extreme communist tendencies among the Vietnamese leadership. Last, support for such an election would also have put the United States firmly on the side of democracy, which it repeatedly argued it was fighting for.

Meanwhile, Ho and General Giap emerged as Vietnamese heroes following victory at Dien Bien Phu. With wind behind his sails, why did Ho accept half a loaf at Geneva? Both China and the Soviet Union—especially China—pressured the Vietnamese to accept a temporary division of the country. The United States was already supporting anticommunist governments in South Korea and Taiwan. Mao was concerned about the United States entering Vietnam in a big way.[137] In retrospect, it is also possible that Ho misread US intentions, and held on to a view that national elections would be held in Vietnam in 1956. Irrespective of Ho's beliefs, Le Duan and other hardliners in the Vietnamese communist party already questioned the wisdom of the compromises that Ho had offered to the French and the United States at Geneva.[138] For the next few years, the leaders of North Vietnam chose to pursue a North-first policy that implied consolidation in the North and political struggle—instead of military or guerilla action—in the South. These moderate priorities were also opposed by Le Duan and his compatriot Le Duc Tho, who had a political base in the South and who preferred a focus on liberating the South militantly and on national unification. When land reforms initiated in 1953 did not go well[139]—the leadership admitted as much in 1956—it weakened Ho and his associates' position in the communist party. And last, when it became clear that the United States did not support national elections in Vietnam in 1956, this, too, strengthened the hands of the Vietnamese communist party hardliners. By late 1950s, Le Duan's political fortunes were rising. His ascendance was especially manifest in the fact that in 1958, Ho put him—in lieu of General Giap—in charge of policies toward the South.[140]

The US government installed Diem in power in South Vietnam in 1955 and then was complicit in his assassination in 1963, the same year President Kennedy was assassinated in the United States. During the years in between, the United States tried to create a stable, noncommunist South Vietnam but failed. Why? This is an important historical question because the political failure led directly to military intervention and a prolonged war. It also addresses the deeper issue of nation building by an external power, an imperial project par excellence. The failure to create a stable South Vietnamese state was rooted in part in American policies and in part in the sociopolitical situation within South Vietnam.[141] Diem was a Catholic in a land where most people were Buddhists. As a strong anticommunist who had spent time in New Jersey, Diem may have been a suitable American choice to lead South Vietnam, but his legitimacy in his own country was limited, especially because he was widely viewed as a puppet of the United States. The political society within South Vietnam was also rather fragmented. In addition to the important ethnic divide between majority Buddhists and minority Catholics, important religious sects and mafia-like gangs could mobilize support when their interests were threatened. Class divisions were also politicized, especially in the Mekong Delta countryside, where the Viet Minh enjoyed a fair amount of support. Diem discriminated against the Buddhists, sought to undermine the support of the Viet Minh, and, when challenged, tended to pursue repressive politics. With Diem in charge, the American claim that they were trying to keep communism out to promote democracy in South Vietnam often rang hollow.

The Eisenhower Administration channeled some $1.5 billion in aid to South Vietnam during 1955–60, much of it toward building a South Vietnamese army. The army turned out to be of poor quality. The contrast with a parallel situation in South Korea is instructive. In South Korea, the Americans had worked with a core of Japanese-trained Korean soldiers to build an effective armed force. But the French had left behind an ineffective state in Vietnam.[142] The new armed force that the Americans then created in a hurry was more mercenary and corrupt than professional and patriotic. It was also trained to fight a regular war, not a guerilla war. US-sponsored nonmilitary projects were also less than successful. Once again, the inheritance from the French did not help; whereas Korea under Japan had industrialized rapidly, industrial output of Vietnam in the early 1950s was under 2 percent of the national product. American aid to South Korea had gone mainly into rebuilding the war-destroyed industries. By contrast, nonmilitary foreign aid to South Vietnam financed imports of light manufactured goods, especially from Japan. Compared to South Korea, land reforms in South Vietnam were also poorly implemented. Whereas American troops had overcome the internal resistance to land reforms in an occupied South Korea, Diem and the landowning interests blocked any such efforts in South Vietnam. This failure, in turn, probably cost the leadership much support among the poor peasants in the countryside.

By 1960, Diem's regime in South Vietnam was in trouble: he faced protests in the cities from Buddhists and students; guerilla activities in the countryside were significant; the armed forces were both ineffective and not reliable; and his own popularity was sinking. Around the same time, leaders in the North also decided to make a concerted effort to support the revolution in the South, overthrow Diem, and reunite the country. The National Liberation Front (NLF) was formed during this period to facilitate such goals of northern leaders. To support the pro-communist forces in the South, routes for transferring arms and personnel via Laos and Cambodia were opened. Over time, these routes will be dubbed the Ho Chi Minh trail. American policymakers were alarmed but stood by Diem for a while, hoping that some combination of more aid, repression of communists, and accommodation of Buddhists might strengthen his hold on power.

Diem's diagnosis of his own political problems, however, was not one that Americans shared or could share; he came to believe, instead, that his dependence on the Americans, though essential for his survival in power, also tainted him as a puppet, and was thus a key source of his weakness. He sought to distance himself from the Americans. He proposed compromises with Ho Chi Minh, with the aim of creating a neutral South Vietnam, a Yugoslavia of sorts. Charles De Gaulle supported this approach and offered to mediate. However, the United States was strongly opposed to any move toward neutralism. This was first the view of Eisenhower and Dulles, but then also of President Kennedy and his secretary of state, Dean Rusk. The Cold War was pretty much near its peak by then—the Cuban Missile Crisis happened in 1962—and no one in the United

States wanted to be seen as soft on communism, which is how any move toward a neutral Vietnam was likely to be viewed within the context of American politics at the time. Kennedy and his aides distanced themselves from Diem, conspired to have him overthrown, and watched as he was assassinated by pro-US military men in Vietnam.[143]

During the brief Kennedy presidency the motives and mechanisms of the US intervention in Vietnam changed in important ways, and with them the impact of the war on both the United States and Vietnam. During the Truman and Eisenhower administrations, American intervention in Vietnam was motivated by what were perceived to be concrete economic and political interests: they wanted to preserve colonial markets in Indochina to help the economic recovery of France and then ensure that the critical domino of Vietnam did not fall, to both stop the global spread of communism and to enable economic recovery of Japan via continued access to the rich Southeast Asian markets. By the time Kennedy came to power, the issue of French and Japanese economic recovery had fallen into the background. While a struggle against global communism was very much at the forefront, Kennedy's advisers had concluded that "the insurgency in South (Vietnam) was indigenous" and that "there was no evidence of Chinese or Soviet involvement."[144] What, then, was the need to increase American involvement in Vietnam?

The issue for Americans now was the credibility of their own commitments. The United States had created South Vietnam as a state, and now it had to be preserved as a noncommunist outpost where the line against communism would be held. American policymakers believed that a loss of South Vietnam would have "damaging consequences for the credibility of US policy and the security of the world."[145] Following a trip to Saigon, Vice President Lyndon Johnson thus argued that "a stand must be taken over Vietnam," and the national security adviser, McGeorge Bundy, proposed that sending combat troops to Vietnam had by now "become a sort of touchstone of our will."[146] As I discussed earlier in the chapter, credibility was a key currency for maintaining America's global informal empire. Maintaining that credibility became an interest in its own right in Vietnam, starting in the Kennedy years, but continuing with a vengeance during the Johnson and Nixon years.

When Kennedy took office, there were 800 American military personnel in Vietnam, mostly assigned to train the South Vietnamese army. By the time of his death in 1963, some 16,000 US soldiers were in Vietnam, now fighting directly to "save," in Kennedy's own words, "our off-spring," that is, South Vietnam. Kennedy's advisers—the Robert McNamaras and the McGeorge Bundys, the best and the brightest, and all that—turned what was essentially a political problem in America's imperial project—how to create a stable, legitimate government in South Vietnam—into a military problem that could now be solved by technology and management techniques.[147] Counterinsurgency programs were added to the offensive repertoire, with the help of British experts.[148] President Kennedy also authorized a "crop destruction program"—with the help of airdropped chemicals—in Vietnam, which supposedly would get rid of communist peasants from the countryside.[149] The best and the brightest do not seem to have raised any serious concern as to what such chemical warfare might do to the apolitical peasant who was merely struggling to make ends meet. By the time Diem and Kennedy were assassinated in 1963, then, the indirect American approach to stabilizing South Vietnam—by creating a functioning South Vietnamese state—had more or less been abandoned. The Americans now owned the war. From here on, it would have to be won or lost directly by American armed forces.

President Johnson escalated the Vietnam War in 1965. The ghastly details of the bloody, decade-long conflict that followed are available elsewhere.[150] The three years between 1965 and 1968 were the peak years of the war. Johnson first escalated the war and then, after the Tet Offensive in 1968, de-escalated it. For this study, the analytical questions that are worth pursuing for this phase of the war are: Why did Johnson escalate and then de-escalate, and why did the North Vietnamese leaders go on the offensive in 1968, when the odds of a military victory were virtually zero? Nixon won the presidency as a peace candidate, but he hardly brought the war to an immediate end. He and Kissinger pursued "peace with honor" instead, and got neither. The United States eventually withdrew from Vietnam in 1973. The North then attacked and captured South Vietnam in 1975, uniting the country and bringing an end to the war. The analytical issues for this phase are the following: Why did the U.S. continue along a path that was clearly not yielding results; and understanding the North's road to a victory that has much to teach would-be-imperialists about the force of mass nationalism.

Johnson escalated American intervention because from the American perspective, the news from South Vietnam in the mid-1960s was continually bad. The leaders who took over from Diem enjoyed even less legitimacy and were often brutal and corrupt. Buddhists and students continued to challenge US-supported rulers, staging periodic protests in Saigon and Hue. Most worrisome for the Americans was the growing insurgency in the countryside, led by the NLF. Johnson's advisers—most of whom he inherited from Kennedy and kept—concluded that stabilizing a noncommunist South would require military escalation, including the bombing of North Vietnam. Johnson, in a crucial address at Johns Hopkins University, explained the need for Operation Rolling Thunder, the campaign to bomb North Vietnam. At the top of his list of "why we are in Vietnam," was the fact that "we have a promise to keep." Such a promise of "support to the people of South Vietnam," he added, had been kept by "every

American President" since 1954.[151] Johnson was not about to be the first to betray "our off-spring." And then again, during an important discussion at the White House with his advisers, including McNamara, Rusk, and others, he made the case for military escalation, going against State Department adviser George Ball's proposed caution in terms of American "credibility."[152] And in yet another meeting the next day, McNamara spelled out the domino effect of loss of credibility: if South Vietnam was lost, the next to fall to "communist domination would be Laos, Cambodia, Thailand, Burma," and "Malaysia" would "surely" be affected; ripple effects would then travel to "Japan and India"; "we would have to give up some military bases"; Pakistan "would move closer to China"; "Greece (and) Turkey would move to a neutralist position"; and "communist agitation would increase in Africa."[153] As serious political analysis these claims would be laughable except for the fact that they were made by deeply influential policymakers. Be that as it may, what these claims underscore is that to American policymakers, Vietnam was not important in its own right. It had instead become the frontier in the far greater American project of maintaining pro-American regimes in power—stable but subservient—in a large part of the world.

Following the logic of these deeper goals, American policymakers concluded that saving South Vietnam would require a twofold strategy: destroy the insurgency in the South and discourage the North from supporting the southern insurgents. The first goal required putting more American troops in South Vietnam, and the second required bombing the North and the supply routes from the North to South. This is precisely what followed. Johnson sent 100,000 US troops to Vietnam in July 1965. And as the southern insurgency continued, the United States sent more and more troops. Johnson explained his "gradual" escalation in Vietnam in his own colorful language: "I'm going up her leg an inch at a time . . . I'll get to the snatch before they know what's happening, you see."[154] To grab the "snatch," one supposes, by 1967–68 Johnson had placed nearly a half million American troops in southern Vietnam. In addition, Johnson ordered bombing of the North. American B-52s bombed the industrial and other centers of military and political significance in the North. This did not break the North's will, and so the Ho Chi Minh trail was bombed repeatedly—American media called it "carpet" or "saturated" bombing—including in Laos and Cambodia. Americans dropped eight million tons of bombs during the Vietnam War;[155] that compares to 3.4 million tons of bombs that the Allies dropped over Asia and Europe during all of World War II. The bombing effort was supported by chemical warfare: 388,000 tons of napalm and 100 million pounds of Agent Orange were also dropped over Vietnam, the damaging consequences of which are still noticeable in Vietnam. The CIA estimated that some 2,800 Vietnamese, many of whom were civilians, were dying each month during these peak years of the War.

In spite of the enormous damage and suffering the United States inflicted on Vietnam, the Vietnamese kept fighting. From the American perspective, victory—whatever that may have looked like—was nowhere in sight. American military generals kept insisting that there was light at the end of the tunnel. General Westmoreland, for example, argued that if the United States killed enough Vietnamese, sooner rather than later the communist leadership would be unable to find enough manpower to replace all those killed. The United States would then prevail. The morality of the destroy-a-country-to-save-it logic was so dubious that protests against the war started to grow in the United States. As is well known, significant American antiwar protests began in the mid-1960s, grew rapidly thereafter, and then spread worldwide. The details again do not need to be repeated here.[156] What is important to keep in mind is that the war in Vietnam became deeply controversial within the United States. Protests against the war began with students on university campuses, then became intertwined with other such issues as civil rights and the draft, and eventually entered national politics, especially during the 1968 elections. The sharp disagreements over the war within the United States do underscore a deeper issue, namely, the tentativeness of popular support for American imperial projects, especially if the benefits of the project are not clear but domestic costs in terms of personal sacrifice, lives lost, expense, and the violation of cherished values are palpable.

How did the Vietnamese cope with the devastation unleashed on their land by the world's greatest power? The first thing to note is that many did not cope at all. Millions perished; they are no longer around to tell their tales. Survival strategies for the rest varied: the North dug some 30,000 miles of tunnels and moved much of its war-related production underground; a half million noncombatants—many of them women—worked continuously to repair damage caused by bombs, especially on the Ho Chi Minh trail; they made inflatable bridges that could sink underwater during the day; during 1965–67, nearly 65 percent of Vietnam's budget was financed with the help of such external powers as China and the Soviet Union; leadership and the armed forces were deeply committed to the national cause; and guerilla warfare was hard to defeat with regular soldiers and B-52 bombers.[157] None of this should suggest—as communist propaganda often did—that the Vietnamese were happy warriors. For example, a "true" account of the Vietnam War in the brilliant novel by Bao Ninh, *The Sorrow of War*, captures well the suffering, malnutrition, and morale problems that afflicted soldiers and civilians alike in North Vietnam.

The North Vietnamese took to military offense in early 1968. The Tet Offensive was a well-coordinated, massive attack by the North and the NLF on urban centers in South Vietnam that followed Tet, the lunar New Year, when most Vietnamese families get together and stay home to celebrate. The attack took the

Americans by surprise. But after initial defeats, the American and southern forces recovered quickly, pushed back successfully, and recovered lost ground, including the city of Hue. Northern forces and the NLF suffered enormous losses of manpower and equipment. As a military battle, the North suffered a humiliating defeat. However, the Tet Offensive also turned out to be a major political victory for the North. Most scholars of the Vietnam War consider the Tet Offensive of 1968 a major turning point because the US troop strength in Vietnam peaked at about a half million around this time. The policy of gradual escalation came to an end in 1968. The response of American leaders to the growing opposition to the war so far had been to say that there was light at the end of the tunnel. What the Tet Offensive underscored instead was that anti-American forces, both regular and guerilla, remained very strong in Vietnam. Americans could have prevailed militarily, of course, but the question then became, at what cost? The light at the end of the tunnel, as one wit noted, might be an approaching train! The claims of the war's supporters that victory was in sight were no longer persuasive. Antiwar demonstrations grew and American public opinion turned sharply against the war. Even McNamara, the former hawk, quit the war coalition and moved to the World Bank. What the Tet Offensive accomplished for North Vietnam, then, was that, the military defeat notwithstanding, it helped turn the tide against the war within the United States

The Tet Offensive also raises the issue of what the communist leadership in the North hoped to accomplish with such a massive attack against a superior military force. Communist Party archives are not open to scholars and the information that can address this issue is limited. The answers are bound to change in the future as more information becomes known. Based on the limited information now available, it seems that the planning for the Tet Offensive began in 1967. Though the party elite shared the goal of throwing the Americans out and uniting Vietnam, they were divided among themselves about the virtue of an all-out attack.[158] Le Duan and Le Duc Tho favored such an attack while others, including Ho Chi Minh and General Giap, preferred a more protracted struggle. By then, Le Duan's faction was ascendant within the party. The hardliners prevailed, and they purged and even executed dissenters—even Ho Chi Minh left the country, ostensibly for medical reasons—especially to maintain the secrecy of the attack. Be that as it may, it also seems clear that even Le Duan never thought they would achieve a military victory against the Americans.[159] The hope, instead, was that an all-out military attack would unleash a popular revolt in the South, possibly toppling the US-supported government and eventually forcing an American withdrawal. As we know, no popular uprising followed the military attack; Le Duan and others were heroically mistaken, and their mistakes cost the Vietnamese dearly in terms of life and expense. At the same time, however, the Tet Offensive also demonstrated the power of well-organized revolutionaries. Following Tet, more and more Americans concluded that the United States could either not prevail in Vietnam or, if it did prevail, the costs could not be justified.

A war-weary Lyndon Johnson decided not to run for a second term in 1968. Growing opposition to the war was a factor in his decision, as was the likelihood that he could lose to other antiwar candidates, such as Robert Kennedy. Johnson also denied Westmoreland's request for more troops, announced limits on the bombing of North Vietnam, and initiated peace talks to try to bring the war to an end. While there was no fundamental change in the US policy of securing a noncommunist South Vietnam—it would take another five bloody years of savage bombing and warfare before that policy change was accepted—Johnson's declarations did bring to an end the era of gradual escalation of the Vietnam War, especially in terms of the commitment of American ground troops. How does one best understand this important turning point? Since mass public opinion is seldom decisive in major policy decisions in the United States,[160] one needs to look at the changing elite opinion during this period.

Following Tet, the political and economic elite started questioning the wisdom of continuing American involvement in Vietnam.[161] McNamara's growing disillusionment has already been noted. Acheson and Averell Harriman, the old Cold Warriors, let it be known that the war was increasingly counterproductive, and was detracting attention from "real interests" in Europe. While hawks like Rusk and the national security assistant Walt W. Rostow still pressured Johnson to not make any concessions to antiwar groups within the United States or to communists abroad, and important military leaders insisted that the war in Vietnam could still be won—just give us more resources—many close to Johnson started disagreeing. John Fowler, Johnson's treasury secretary, started worrying about the costs of the war. McNamara's replacement, Clark Clifford, the new defense secretary, communicated to Johnson that support for war in key business and legal circles had declined. The support in Congress for a tax hike, which Johnson would need to press on with the war, was weak. A group of Wise Men—a senior advisory group that Johnson had gathered that included the likes of Cyrus Vance, Henry Cabot Lodge Jr., Ball, and Bundy, with Acheson in the chair—recommended "disengagement" in Vietnam because the goal of a noncommunist Vietnam was probably "unattainable;" a frustrated Johnson then supposedly remarked that "the establishment bastards have bailed out."[162]

The establishment bastards, with their deep connections to the world of business and commerce, understood better than most that the costs of the Vietnam War were contributing significantly to the economic crisis that engulfed the United States in 1968.[163] At the root of the "gold crisis"—as the economic crisis in 1968 came to be called—were Johnson's simultaneous pursuit of the Great

Society program and the Vietnam War without increasing taxes. The resulting pressure on the budget and on the balance of payment weakened the confidence in the dollar, which at the time was pegged to gold. In March 1968, rapid selling of the dollars in other major economies and a drain on gold reserves created a sharp sense of crisis in Washington. Though the crisis was patched over—like the war, it would take another five years before Nixon took the United States off the gold standard and the post-OPEC era of stagflation would begin—scholars have concluded that the economic crisis of 1968 marked the beginning of the end of the "postwar boom" and therefore contributed to the "passing of postwar U.S. economic hegemony."[164]

Be that as it may, for our purposes what is important is that Johnson's key decision to change course in Vietnam—to stop sending more American troops there—was made against the backdrop of this major economic crisis at home. While Johnson also faced numerous political pressures to move in this direction, the economic need to de-escalate was clear to important decision-makers: Senate Majority Leader Mike Mansfield advised Johnson that expanding the war in Vietnam would lead to "more inflation, more balance of payments complications, and possibly financial panic and collapse"; Acheson, the leader of the Wise Men, concluded that the dollar crisis required that we "disengage (from Vietnam) in a limited time" and that the "gold crisis . . . has dampened expansionist ideas." And Johnson later explained his own decisions on Vietnam by noting that the "monetary and budgetary problems were constantly before us as we considered whether we should or could do more in Vietnam."[165]

American intervention in Vietnam had come full circle. It may be helpful at this point to step back and to rethink how each major step led to another. The initial logic of the US intervention in support of French colonialism in Vietnam following World War II was twofold: France was a key ally in the American project to create an open global economy, and the perception was that France's economic recovery and political stability depended on maintaining its colonial links. The Chinese Revolution brought the Cold War to Asia and contributed to the American decision to reindustrialize Japan. The Japanese need for markets, in turn, enhanced the strategic value of all of Southeast Asia. Following the French defeat at Dien Bien Phu in 1954, American policymakers stepped in to create and preserve a noncommunist South Vietnam; South Vietnam came to be viewed as a key domino in the struggle to keep Southeast Asian economies open and communism at bay. The more resources American presidents committed to Vietnam, the more the credibility of American commitments itself became a reason to commit yet more resources: how could the United States maintain a far-flung empire if it did not follow through on its commitments?

With American credibility at stake, Johnson sharply escalated the war in Vietnam in 1965. Numerous war-related corporations benefited from this escalation and, for the most part, the establishment elite supported the war effort, at least initially. The Vietnamese, however, put up a fierce resistance. The goal of creating a stable political order in South Vietnam remained elusive. Within three years, the human and material costs of stabilizing a noncommunist South Vietnam became enormous. An economic crisis in 1968 especially underscored these costs. The interests of a few war-related industries aside, the corporate elite let it be known that they increasingly did not support the war. The political elite concluded that the war was now beginning to undermine national economic interests. What had started out as a project to maintain American power and prosperity had become increasingly detrimental to both. A retreat of sorts was in order. To reiterate, Johnson's retreat was both real and limited. The United States had not altered its main goal of preserving a noncommunist South Vietnam. How this was to be done without committing more American troops, however, was the challenge that Johnson bequeathed to Nixon and Kissinger.

The last phase of the American intervention in Vietnam during the Nixon-Kissinger era was deeply brutal and tragic—even more so than in earlier phases because it was clear by 1968 that the United States could not prevail in Vietnam. The peace candidate Nixon as president could have ended the war in 1969; the final outcome in Vietnam would have been no different than it was in 1975. Seeking an honorable exit, the United States bombed Indochina for another four years instead. Nearly a million more Vietnamese died between 1969 and 1973, and large parts of Indochina, including Cambodia and Laos, were destroyed. Prime Minister Olaf Palme of Sweden compared the Nixon-Kissinger bombing of Indochina to Nazi war crimes. Resisting the urge for further moral condemnation,[166] I will now discuss a few analytical issues from this last phase of the war to help bring the discussion of the Vietnam case to an end.

Nixon was a deeply anticommunist leader. His early career highlights included membership in the House Un-American Activities Committee (while a freshman congressman from California), the vice presidency in the Eisenhower Administration, and a hawkish Cold War presidential candidacy against Kennedy in 1960. The 1968 election was highly charged: it followed the assassinations of Martin Luther King Jr. and Robert Kennedy, race riots, growing protests against the Vietnam War on campuses, and a riotous Democratic Party convention. Nixon had promised to end the war, but following his victory over Hubert Humphrey, he returned to his hawkish self, championed law and order, and prolonged the war in Vietnam for another four to five years. Kissinger, his comrade-in-arms in this bloody venture was a fellow Machiavellian, who was initially Nixon's national security adviser and subsequently his secretary of state.

Kissinger was a Harvard professor of international relations of German-Jewish background. His proximity to the apex of administration gave Nixon's decisions an air of respectability, as if the decisions being made emanated from centuries-old cunning—realpolitik—learned from Europe's bloody history. They were nothing of the sort. As I have already noted, many realists, both scholars and policymakers, had already declared their opposition to the Vietnam War, mainly on the grounds that American interests in Vietnam were meager. Why, then, did Nixon and Kissinger continue a war that was clearly not yielding results?

Kissinger laid out his thinking in an article in *Foreign Affairs* in 1969.[167] He agreed with his fellow realists that Vietnam was not all that important to the United States, at least not at the outset. He implicitly criticized Kennedy and his best and the brightest for overestimating the geopolitical importance of Vietnam in the early 1960s. That was then, however. By early 1969, when he was increasingly in a position to influence policy, Kissinger argued that it had become hugely important for the United States to prevail in Vietnam. Why? To his way of thinking, "the commitment of 500,000 Americans had settled the issue of the importance of Viet Nam. For what is involved now is confidence in American promises." It is American "credibility" that for Kissinger helps sustain "stability" in faraway places in "the Middle East, Europe, Latin America, even Japan." A failure to prevail in Vietnam would then only encourage "erosion of restraints."[168]

These are important claims by a senior American foreign policymaker. Two observations are warranted. First, in line with the judgment of many of his predecessors, for Kissinger credibility remained a key resource in the American arsenal of managing global influence without the burden of a formal empire. Pro-American regimes, some democratic but many not so (especially in Latin America, the Middle East, and Asia during that period), needed assurance that the United States would stand by them to help restrain popular and nationalist opposition. Second, it is hard to assess whether Kissinger was right. If the United States failed to prevail in Vietnam, would it really make the rule of a king in Saudi Arabia or of a military junta in Brazil less stable? I have my doubts: for example, Saudi monarchs are still in power and the end of military rule in Brazil in the 1980s had little to do with the American loss in Vietnam in the 1970s—but that is not relevant. As long as American policymakers believed that such nebulous cause-and-effect relations were real, any and all effort in Vietnam or elsewhere could be justified.

The United States had made a commitment to create and preserve a noncommunist South Vietnam; it had to be kept. However, the resources available to Nixon and Kissinger to pursue this commitment were limited. Johnson had initiated the withdrawal of troops from Vietnam. Any effort to reverse this decision would have met fierce political resistance at the time; even Nixon's secretary of defense (Melvin Laird) and secretary of state (William Rogers) were opposed to sending more American troops to Vietnam. The main policies available, then, were the same as those initiated by Johnson, namely, to strengthen the government and the military in South Vietnam—Vietnamization of the war, that is—on the one hand, and, on the other hand, to drop bombs, lots of them, on North Vietnam and on the supply routes from the North to the South, including those in Cambodia and Laos. In addition, Nixon and Kissinger, being the realists that they were, counted on the changing global situation, especially the growing Sino-Soviet rift, to be a new power resource. American policymakers thus hoped that Soviet Union and China, following rapprochement and recognition, respectively, might put pressure on Vietnam to accept a separate, noncommunist state of South Vietnam during negotiations in Paris. Nixon and Kissinger vigorously pursued these various policies, but failed.

The Tet Offensive took a toll on North Vietnam. However, there is no evidence to suggest that this led to any basic rethinking on the part of the communist leaders. For the North, the goal of the war remained the reunification of Vietnam under a communist leadership. Since Americans were also not willing to change their primary objective of a noncommunist South Vietnam, the prospect of reaching a negotiated peace in Paris was not promising, at least not unless one side changed its mind. The conflict in Vietnam between 1969 and 1973 was thus shaped on one side by strenuous American efforts to force the North to a "breaking point," and on the other side by the North's fierce and costly resistance in the name of a unified nation.[169] Following Tet, however, the North did have to adapt its strategies. The military defeat had forced the North to step back, regroup, and prepare for another battle another day, which came in the form of the Easter Offensive in 1972. Meanwhile, Le Duan sent his main deputy, Le Duc Tho, to Paris to participate in peace negotiations. The available evidence suggests that Le Duan was very much in charge of crucial decisions in the North at this stage.[170] The decisions to participate in talks with the United States but to not make any major concessions were probably made at the apex of the Communist Party, without much dissent. The United States and Vietnam were, then, both participating in Paris talks while remaining fully committed to resort to war as needed to achieve their respective goals.

As the number of American troops in South Vietnam declined from 1969 onward, the Nixon-Kissinger team expanded air campaigns to Cambodia and Laos, with the hope of destroying communist sanctuaries and supply routes from the North to the South. This is no place to discuss the impact of such bombings on broader Indochina; suffice it to note that many analysts trace the roots of the Pol Pot–led genocide in Cambodia back to the massive destruction of that country unleashed by Nixon.[171] Nixon also repeatedly ordered more bombing of

North Vietnam, inflicting further economic and military damage. Since North Vietnam was not about to capitulate—living with B-52 bombs had become a tragic way of life in North Vietnam—the second strand of American strategy focused on strengthening the southern military, as well as reforming social conditions in the South. There is evidence to suggest that the efforts at Vietnamization were making headway in the early 1970s, although they were too little, too late.[172] Southern troops deserted in large numbers during and following the Easter Offensive, underscoring the southern army's less-than-ready state.

Nixon and Kissinger's calculation that Soviet Union and China could pressure North Vietnam to accept something less than a united communist Vietnam also proved incorrect. They underestimated the commitment of the northern leadership to a united Vietnam and, like their predecessors, misunderstood the nature of Vietnam's dependence on the big communist powers. There is no doubt that the North was receiving substantial economic and military aid from China and the Soviet Union. Le Duan and his compatriots effectively played China against the Soviet Union and received aid from both. It did appear in the early 1970s that both of the communist giants may have been willing to sacrifice the interests of North Vietnam for the sake of better relations with the United States. Afraid of being sold out, the North attacked the South again in 1972, with the hope of a rapid end to the war. As we know, the North again suffered heavy military casualties, but it succeeded in making a broader point: neither China nor the Soviet Union could pressure Vietnam into accepting a pro-American compromise in Paris.

The three-pronged strategy pursued by Nixon and Kissinger in Vietnam—massive bombing, Vietnamization, and rewarding the Soviet Union and China for pressuring Vietnam—did not yield the expected results. North Vietnam and the revolutionary forces in the South dug in, knowing full well that a steady decline in the presence of American troops would lead to eventual victory. The die for this outcome had been cast by Johnson's decision to de-escalate the war. A few efforts by Nixon and Kissinger to prolong the war beyond the Christmas bombings notwithstanding, war-weariness had set in. Domestic constraints on continuing the war were significant: huge antiwar protests; racial and drug problems within the US armed forces; congressional refusal to fund the war further; continuing pressure on the balance of payments; and Nixon's growing political problems captured by the Watergate scandal. Globally, Vietnam was now less important to American decision-makers: better relations with China and the Soviet Union had reduced the intensity of the Cold War in Asia, and other priorities around the world demanded attention. General Nguyen Van Thieu, the president of South Vietnam at the time, understood that the steady decline of US troops was the beginning of the end of South Vietnam. Not surprisingly, Thieu repeatedly objected to the shape of the agreements in Paris, which the United States eventually forced Thieu to accept. The North Vietnamese also understood that the Paris agreement of early 1973 would lead directly to their military victory, as it did, in 1975. In Hanoi, in 2016, I asked Ambassador Nguyen Khac Huynh, a senior member of Le Duc Tho's team in Paris that negotiated with the American team led by Kissinger, if the Vietnamese side was ever concerned during the talks that the 1973 peace agreement might be a repeat of the Geneva Accords of 1954. His answer was a flat no: "[W]e understood clearly that the ground realities in 1973 were very different than in 1954." After regrouping, then, North Vietnam attacked the south again in 1975. Without American support this time, the South crumbled. The Vietnam War was finally over.

Chile

US intervention in Chile led to the overthrow and the death of the democratically elected socialist leader Salvador Allende in 1973. The military coup that deposed Allende also led to the establishment of a harsh military dictatorship under Augusto Pinochet that the United States supported. The basic facts of what happened are, again, well known.[173] Well before Allende's election in 1970, American leaders had decided that having a socialist leader in Chile was not acceptable. In spite of secretive efforts, however, the United States was unable to prevent Allende's electoral victory. Nixon and Kissinger then ordered the CIA to derail Allende's ascendance to power. Again, they failed. Once Allende assumed power, Nixon and Kissinger unleashed American fury—again, covert—to topple him, and succeeded. The main questions for the analysis of this third case of US intervention in the developing world during the Cold War era, then, are: Why did the United States choose to depose Allende? How the Americans achieved this goal and with what impact will also be discussed, although briefly. After summarizing my argument and providing some background on Chile, I focus on US involvement in Chile in the decade leading up to the military coup in 1973 (on 9/11 of that year, as a matter of fact).

As we might expect, scholars have put forward a variety of arguments to interpret the end of Chile's prolonged democracy in 1973. One set of arguments focuses on internal political and economic problems in Chile; this line of thinking often "blames the victim," suggesting that Allende "invited" a coup because he was "incompetent" or "too radical" or made "bad policy choices."[174] Related to this view, we could also interpret (as some have) that the 1973 coup in Chile was part of a decade-long regional trend in Latin America toward "bureaucratic authoritarianism." The regional political pattern in this argument resulted from such shared economic "bottlenecks" as the "exhaustion of easy import substitution."[175]

For a full understanding of the Chilean coup, we would very much need to take these internal political and economic considerations into account.[176] In the face of overwhelming evidence, however, most scholars now tend to treat the US intervention in Chile as a major, if not the decisive, factor—in fomenting the 1973 coup. Whether the United States was moved more by a fear of the Soviet Union's growing influence in Latin America or by a perceived need to protect its economic interests is debated.[177] As I interpret the evidence, economic arguments are the most persuasive, though nuances and qualifications matter, too.

My argument begins with the observation that Allende was a democratic socialist. American officials understood clearly that Allende was not a stooge of the Soviet Union and was not likely to become one. What Kissinger and other key policymakers feared most was that Allende's democratic socialism would succeed and that the Allende model would then spread to the rest of Latin America. What was so threating about the Allende model of development? It was certainly not such internal redistribution programs as land reforms; even the US-sponsored Alliance for Progress had stressed the need for land redistribution in Latin America. What worried American decision-makers more was Allende's plan to nationalize American investments in Chile, especially in copper. Nationalization would clearly hurt specific American corporations but more important, if allowed to succeed, it could encourage a broader trend in the region. Such nationalist assertion—national control over national resources—could not be allowed, not in a region that the United States so clearly dominated. The plan to thwart Allende, then, has to be understood as a "boundary setting" exercise in which the United States sought to clarify how far a country in Latin America could go in exercising economic sovereignty. Rulers who crossed these boundaries—or violated the implicit norms of America's informal empire—had to go. In Kissinger's own words, "[W]e set the limits of diversity."[178] Other considerations also entered American calculations—they always do, and I discuss some of these, too—a key consideration that moved Nixon and Kissinger to plan a coup against Allende was limiting the spread of economic nationalism in Latin America.

As part of the Southern Cone of the New World, Chile shared many of the early political and economic patterns with Argentina (see chapter 2). Chile was not an important colony for Spain, mainly because, unlike Peru or Mexico, but like Argentina, it was not a ready source of precious metals. Chile's main exports were agricultural products, especially wheat and flour, but it also exported hides and some minerals, including copper and silver. At the time of its independence from Spain, unlike Argentina or much of Spanish America, Chile escaped having a period of political instability.[179] Britain quickly supplanted Spain to become Chile's main trading partner, with an important difference: Britain now exported manufactured goods directly to Chile, especially textiles, and took agricultural products in return.[180] The domestic political economy was organized around *latifundios*, with a working population mainly of European origin—indigenous Indians were slowly killed off and, unlike in Brazil, few African slaves were imported—and a political system that followed constitutional norms, but in which power was concentrated in the hands of a narrow oligarchy.[181]

During the second half of the nineteenth century, the importance of mineral exports grew. A copper boom (and bust) was followed by a nitrate boom. Chile annexed nitrate-producing regions of Bolivia and Peru—such are the ironies of imperialism; over time, victims and victimizers can trade roles—and Britain soon came to own much of Chile's nitrate production and exports. Toward the end of the century, demand for copper again grew, but this time the small and declining copper mines, which had once been owned by Chileans, were in the hands of American companies. By the end of World War I, American capital was more important than British capital in Chile: if US investment in Chile in 1912 was some $15 million, by 1928 it had grown dramatically to $451 million.[182] Most of this investment was done by two copper-exporting companies, Anaconda and Kennecott. American-owned copper mines in Chile were geographically concentrated, isolated from the main population centers, and constituted classic examples of an enclave economy. Copper exports also dominated Chilean exports and thus its foreign exchange earnings, public finance, and prospects of deliberate industrialization.

These patterns of dependency were not challenged during the first half of the twentieth century, both because Chilean oligarchs benefited from them—the taxation of foreign companies, for example, allowed very low taxes on large agricultural holdings—and because political power was again concentrated in the hands of the oligarchy; for example, only 5 percent of the population voted in the elections in 1915. Over time, however, Chilean politics was becoming twentieth-century politics—that is, mass politics—and the older patterns of dependency were bound to be challenged (and they were, especially following World War II). During the first half of the century, Chile experienced some industrialization.[183] Much of this was a result of de facto import substitution, facilitated by such global circumstances as World War I and the Great Depression in the 1930s. A middle class of sorts emerged; urban centers grew; labor, especially in the mines, was unionized; and left-leaning parties came into being. Yet despite the growing middle class, Chilean society was characterized by sharp inequalities. When suffrage eventually expanded in Chile, after World War II, it was in the context of an economy that depended heavily on copper exports owned by American companies, and a society in which a vast gulf separated the few rich from the many poor. It would have been a miracle if democratic politics in such a setting had not led to demands for redistribution and to a politics of economic nationalism.

As happened in much of the developing world after World War II, the issue of what model of economic development to pursue became a topic of political debates within Chile. The economic problems of Chile included low growth, commodity dependence, foreign ownership in key sectors, and poverty and inequality. Recurring problems in the balance of payments, budgetary deficits, and inflation reflected these deeper problems. Within the frame of a functioning democracy, scholars and politicians offered different remedies with differing implications for who got what, when, and how. During the 1950s, these debates started to congeal around three sets of political-party platforms that can loosely be characterized as right, centrist, and left. Jorge Alessandri was the leader of the more conservative forces, whereas the Christian Democrat Eduardo Frei represented a middle of sorts, and Allende was the leader of the left. As one might expect, these leaders differed on how best to control inflation (monetarism versus structuralism), how best to facilitate growth (state-led versus foreign-investor led), and redistribution (modest versus radical.)[184] Alessandri won the election in 1958, but Allende finished a strong second. Frei then won the 1964 election. It is worth underscoring that by the time Allende won the election in 1970, the right and the middle candidates had each had a six-year term in which to attack Chile's main problems, and Chilean electorate found the results wanting both times. It was in this economic and political context that the United States became deeply involved in Chilean affairs.

Salvador Allende was a doctor who, in his student days during the 1930s, was a founding member of Chile's Socialist Party. He regularly contested elections, served in the Chilean Congress, and became the health minister in a coalition government in 1940. Though very much a leader of the left, he was "deeply committed to parliamentary government" and his "bourgeois" tastes in "dress, drink, and the enjoyment of the good life" also made him very much a part of the Chilean political class.[185] Allende was a classic social democrat and a nationalist. His political program was "not couched in terms of class struggle," and he made a "special effort to reassure the small businessman" that under an Allende administration their interests would be "protected."[186] Allende also insisted that the changes he called for, such as land redistribution and the nationalization of large foreign corporations, could and would be carried out within the frame of "existing institutions." The road to "socialism" for Allende was thus going to be "peaceful." The nationalist in Allende, however, insisted, "[W]e Chileans demand the right to seek our own solutions and to follow the roads that best suit our habits and traditions."[187] This nationalist assertiveness, manifest in the policy commitment to nationalize American-owned companies in Chile, piqued American officials, who started labeling him a "communist," a "dupe," and a "commie-liner."[188]

That the United States has exercised considerable influence over Latin America in the twentieth century is nearly a truism.[189] Chile came in for special attention during the second half of the century, especially after Allende finished a strong second in the 1958 election and when, after the Cuban Revolution in 1959, the United States became concerned about a possible leftward turn in Latin America. While the Cold War provided the immediate context for growing American anxieties, the economic importance of Latin America also loomed large. For example, the total exports of the United States in 1960 were goods worth some $20 billion.[190] Of this, Latin America took nearly $4 billion, or 20 percent, more than what the United States exported to the United Kingdom, France, and Germany combined, and more than what it sold to the rest of the developing world in Asia (excluding Japan) and Africa. American direct foreign investment in Latin America in 1960 was also quite significant: of a total of some $32 billion that Americans had invested overseas in 1960, $7.5 billion was in Latin America (nearly 25 percent of the total), which was more than what Americans had invested in all of Western Europe or in all of Asia and Africa combined. With such high economic stakes, American officials found the emergence of anti-imperialist and pro-redistribution politics in much of Latin America threatening. A victory of such political forces could disrupt profitable economic relations. It was to forestall this leftward political drift that President Kennedy created the well-funded Alliance for Progress in 1961, a set of programs that was designed to bring about a "middle class revolution" in Latin America instead.[191]

Chile came to occupy a central place in the Alliance for Progress. The economic problems of Chile were widely shared in the region, especially commodity dependence, sharp inequalities, and high levels of American investment. Moreover, Chile had a lively democracy that offered seemingly clear political alternatives. Kennedy was especially keen to discourage the nationalist and leftward trend Allende represented. American officials decided to turn Chile into a "showcase" for the Alliance for Progress.[192] The aim was to facilitate private-sector-led growth, implement land reforms, and ensure that Allende did not win the presidency in 1964, when the next set of elections were due. The United States then started pouring both overt and covert funds into Chile. Over the next decade, US foreign aid totaling some $1.2 billion—a huge amount for the period—went to Chile.[193] To appease growing economic nationalism in Chile, US government officials "pressured" Anaconda and Kennecott to modernize their plants and increase their copper investments in Chile; the governmental "pressure" included a highly subsidized, "sweetheart" deal in the form of "political risk insurance" for these corporations.[194] Although Chile faced no internal or external security threats, the United States increased its military assistance; the aim was "a clear effort to establish closer ties to Chilean Generals."[195] Some 4,000 Chilean military officers were trained at the American military base—the US Army School of the Americas—during the 1950s and the 1960s, where the training went well beyond military training to also emphasize the importance of armies as anticommunist modernizers.[196]

Beyond the above-board intensification of relations, covert American efforts to shape the fate of Chilean politics also increased sharply in the early 1960s, well before the Nixon-Kissinger onslaught on Allende in the early 1970s. Kennedy wanted to ensure that Allende would not win in the three-way race for the Chilean presidency in 1964 (among Alessandri, Frei, and Allende)—this when the electoral platforms of Allende and Frei "were not very different from each other."[197] After meetings with both Alessandri and Frei, Kennedy decided that the reformist Frei was best suited to move Chile toward the centrist goals set by Alliance for Progress. With the CIA in the lead, then, covert operations to support Frei's election bid began in earnest in 1961. Over the next three years the CIA's massive secret funding in support of Frei included some $3 million to underwrite Frei's campaign directly and another $3 million to support an anti-Allende propaganda campaign.[198] These monies were channeled to a variety of pro-American groups within Chile: student groups, trade unions, political parties, and, especially, the media.[199] CIA-inspired editorials appeared "almost daily" in *El Mercurio*, a conservative daily whose rich editor—Agustín Edwards—eventually played an influential role in coup planning. President Johnson continued these policies, and eventually, the CIA took credit for Frei's electoral victory. An election postmortem by a US intelligence official concluded that US intervention in favor of Frei in 1964 was massive, "blatant," and "obscene."[200]

Despite this enormous American support, as noted, the results of Frei's six-year term in power were lackluster. The economy grew at a lower rate than during Alessandri's regime, around 3 percent per annum.[201] Frei had run on a platform that privileged the private sectors, both domestic and foreign, but was also committed to the Chileanization of the copper industry, land reforms, and a better deal for the working class. As one might expect, this centrist program was full of internal tensions and proved hard to implement; in the early years, it tilted to the left but then moved right, satisfying no one. Some efforts to enhance national control over the copper industry were made, but Anaconda and Kennecott were offered very generous compensation. Some land reforms were implemented, but numerous problems plagued the program. Workers made some gains, but both the government and the corporations turned against them, which led to strikes and even violence. The important point to note is this: under Frei, Chilean politics became more polarized. The centrist Frei had legitimized the goals of achieving greater Chilean control over Chile's natural resources, land redistribution, and better income distribution, but had failed to meet them. This set the stage for Allende's victory in 1970; Allende's platform established goals similar to those proclaimed by Frei, but he also promised to vigorously implement them.

When Allende won the election in September, Nixon had been in power for nearly two years. Neither Chile nor Latin America was a priority for Nixon. He and Kissinger were focused on other big powers, especially on secretly improving relations with China, détente with the Soviet Union, and, most of all, the Vietnam War. Still, Latin America was too important to be ignored. Nixon had no use for the Alliance for Progress and let it be known. He was happy, instead, to work with military rulers of the major Latin American countries, who had come to power (for example, in Brazil and Argentina in 1964 and 1966, respectively). Chile also required attention because of enormous prior American efforts in shaping the country's political path. For the most part, the Americans had assumed that with Frei out of the running, Alessandri would win the 1970 election. Since he was quite acceptable, American intervention against Allende prior to the election was not as significant as it had been in 1964. But not wanting to take any chances, Kissinger approved a sum of $300,000 in mid-1970 for an anti-Allende propaganda campaign, adding as a rationale, "I do not see why we need to stand by and watch a country go Communist due to the irresponsibility of its own people."[202] Moreover, before the elections Kissinger had ordered a study of the implications for the United States of an Allende victory in Chile, and the CIA and others had worked on contingency plans in case Allende won.

The conclusions of this secret "review of U.S. policy and strategy in the event of an Allende victory" (called NSSM 97) carried out by the intelligence community are worth quoting in detail because they laid the foundation for subsequent US policy in Chile.[203] On the one hand, the review concluded, "[T]he U.S. had no vital national interests within Chile," and an Allende victory neither threatened "peace of the region" nor would alter "the world military balance of power." On the other hand, this did not mean that an Allende victory would not have any costs for the United States The review added that an Allende victory would produce "tangible economic losses" for the United States. As importantly, an Allende victory would have "considerable political and psychological costs." What might these be? First, "hemispheric cohesion would be threatened," and second, "an Allende victory would represent a definite psychological setback to the United States and a definite psychological advance for the Marxist idea." In sum, according to the US intelligence community, an Allende victory would not pose a security threat to the United States but would directly threaten economic interests; moreover, it did pose the indirect threat that an Allende-model might encourage others to move in the same direction. The review then discussed the pros and cons of a staging a coup against Allende, underscoring the fact that well before Allende's victory, the possibility of a coup in Chile was already on the minds of American decision-makers.

Following Allende's narrow electoral victory, American government officials started discussing various policy alternatives to block Allende from coming to power or, if he assumed power, to overthrow him. As one might expect, a range of views was in circulation at that time, with a significant subset suggesting that fostering a coup would be a "nearly impossible, diplomatically dangerous, and (an) undesirable operation."[204] But it was Nixon who directly and personally tilted the balance toward ousting Allende. We know this because of declassified secret documents. Nixon issued explicit instructions, which Richard Helms, the CIA director at the time, recorded by hand, directing that Chile had to be "saved."[205] To do so, Nixon ordered the CIA to make the Chilean economy "scream," and to come up with concrete plans within "48 hours." Moreover, Nixon added that "risks" in pursuing such an operation could be ignored, that the US embassy in Chile was not to be involved, and that plenty of funds would be made available. The next day, Helms informed an operational group within the agency that President Nixon "had decided that an Allende regime in Chile was not acceptable to the United States. The President asked the Agency to prevent Allende from coming to power or to unseat him."[206] The CIA then proceeded to put the project, which had the codename FUBELT, into action.

Why did Nixon decide that Allende could not be allowed to rule Chile? While we will never know the answer for sure—even Nixon would probably lay out a number of considerations that weighed on him—we do know more about this case than other similar cases of secret interventions. The immediate trigger for Nixon's decision was probably a meeting with Agustín Edwards—one of the richest men in Chile, publisher of the conservative *El Mercurio* and the distributor of Pepsi-Cola in Chile—on the morning of September 15, 1970. Edwards was deeply connected to the American corporate elite with economic interests in Chile; for example, his meeting with Nixon that morning was arranged by one Donald Kendall, then the CEO of Pepsi-Cola, who was both a former business partner of Edwards and a close friend and a financial supporter of Nixon. Edwards impressed upon Nixon that "if Allende was allowed to take office, he would nationalize the Chilean economy, force American businesses out, and steer Chile into the Soviet-Cuban orbit."[207] Kissinger later recounted, in his book *White House Years*, that this meeting had "triggered" Nixon into action; after all, it was later that afternoon that Nixon issued his instructions to make the Chilean economy "scream" and to undermine Allende. More sober analyses, however, rightly caution us to situate any such immediate "triggers" within the broader context, especially because a variety of contingency plans to deal with Allende were already in the pipeline, before the crucial meetings of September 15, 1970.[208] (I return to a discussion of this broader context below.)

Even if corporate lobbying was not decisive in fomenting a coup, Edwards's role in triggering Nixon into action does draw attention to the important role corporate interests played in blocking a move toward democratic socialism in Chile. Two observations are pertinent. First, major American corporations like Anaconda, Kennecott, and ITT (International Telephone and Telegraph) were heavily invested in Chile. Between 1958 and 1973—a fifteen-year period of vigorous democratic politics in Chile—each of these corporations played a direct or an indirect role toward derailing Allende. For example, Anaconda and Kennecott contributed funds to support Frei against Allende during the 1964 elections; ITT officials worked with the CIA in Santiago—John McCone, a former CIA director, was on the board of ITT and provided a key link[209]—to promote Alessandri over Allende during the 1970 election; and, once Allende was inaugurated, Anaconda, Kennecott, ITT, and other American corporations with investments in Chile, such as Firestone, Bethlehem Steel, and Dow Chemical, formed an ad hoc group that worked alongside the CIA to create a "coup climate" by generating economic chaos in Allende's Chile.[210] Second, the anti-Allende power bloc consisted of a nearly seamless alliance adjoining Chilean economic elite and conservative political forces, on the one hand, and American corporations with interests in Chile and American officials, including Nixon and Kissinger, on the other hand. Edwards's lobbying of Nixon to intervene in Chile captures well the nature of this underlying anti-Allende alliance.

Based on such evidence, one could almost sustain a vulgar-Marxist hypothesis that the coup against Allende was an instance of the American state protecting the interests of transnational capital. While such a suggestion would not be wrong, certainly not in the case of Chile, it is too narrow and, ultimately, misleading. American leaders do prioritize the pursuit of economic interests in the developing world. However, the interests they prioritize are national economic interests; that is, they think more broadly in terms of what is good for sustaining American economic health and thus power. The pursuit of the national economic interest may sometimes coincide with the interests of few specific corporations, but not always, and maybe not even in most cases. Thus, in the case of Iran, US intervention indeed supported specific corporate interests, but the broader motive was to establish the norm that nationalization of oil in the developing world was not acceptable, certainly not on terms deemed adverse. Economic motives played only an indirect role in the case of America's prolonged war in Vietnam, but they were important; the United States became involved with the hope of helping France to maintain its colonial economic links so that it could become part of the new American-led, open-economy order. Over time, the United States justified its war in Vietnam in terms of maintaining credibility, which of course was a key resource in sustaining an informal empire (with an open economy as its centerpiece) on a global scale. Narrow corporate interests played a much more direct role in the overthrow of Allende in Chile. Even in this case, however, the evidence discussed here indicates that Nixon and Kissinger thought in regional terms: they wanted to ensure that the success of Allende did not encourage an expropriation movement to spread through Latin America.

Before I discuss Nixon and Kissinger's motives, it is also important to set aside the view that the coup in Chile was instigated by American security concerns (especially the fear that Allende might turn into another Castro, and thus provide a beachhead for the Soviet Union in the Southern Cone). While such concerns often appear in the written records of the period, the evidence available to Nixon and Kissinger from their own officials moved sharply in the opposite direction. Before Allende's election, for example, the Joint Chiefs of Staff had concluded that "the spectre of the monolithic, continental communist threat" in Latin America was a "bogeyman."[211] More directly, with reference to Chile, in 1970 CIA officials conveyed to Kissinger that Allende "will be hard for the (Chilean) Communist Party and for Moscow to control."[212] US intelligence in Santiago had also conveyed to Washington that Soviet diplomats in Santiago had let it be known—six months before Allende's election—that because of the Cuban albatross that was already around their neck, they would not be in a position to "support an Allende government."[213] Kissinger's top aide on Latin America, Viron Vaky, cautioned that it would be "hard to argue" that Allende posed a "mortal threat" to the United States.[214] Scholars who have reviewed White House tapes on the subject further note that they reveal "no preoccupation with Cold War concerns."[215] Last, following Chile's return to democracy in 1990, a US Senate Select Committee on Intelligence conducted a thorough investigation of the evidence that was available to Nixon and Kissinger on Chile prior to the coup, and concluded that Chile "was charting an independent, nationalist course. There never was a significant threat of a Soviet military presence."[216]

So what did move the Americans to encourage a coup in Chile? We know that contingency plans for how to deal with an Allende victory in Chile were already in the pipeline in September 1970, when Nixon ordered the CIA to overthrow Allende and "save" Chile. Declassified secret documents from around this period help us piece together the underlying American motives. A detailed memo (the "Kissinger memo," from here on) that Kissinger sent to Nixon in preparation for an important National Security Council meeting about Chile in November is revealing.[217] As I analyze this and other documents, it is worth keeping in mind that Kissinger was no specialist on Chile or on Latin America; as he nearly boasted to the Chilean ambassador in 1969, "I am not interested in, nor do I know anything about, the southern portion of the world from the Pyrenees on down."[218] Nevertheless, imperial hubris allowed Kissinger to lay out for Nixon what was really going on in Chile and how Nixon should think about it. Given Kissinger's lack of expertise, it is also not surprising that his memo to the president reflected some of the main conclusions on Chile reached earlier by the US intelligence community in NSSM 97.

Kissinger impressed upon Nixon that Allende's election posed "*for us one of the most serious challenges ever faced in this hemisphere*."[219] While situating the challenge in the context of the Cold War, Kissinger also implicitly set aside the Soviet "bogeyman" by arguing that an Allende government was more likely to be "Titoist," an independent socialist country in Latin America. What was the threat posed by a socialist government that was elected democratically? First, Kissinger points to direct economic threats in Chile: loss of American investments totaling some $1 billion and possible default on debts owed to American institutions, totaling some $1.5 billion. Second, Allende's success would be dangerous for American interests in the hemisphere because the "Allende model" could readily spread: "the 'model' effect can be insidious." Third, if the United States failed to block Allende, "our failure" will be judged as "impotence" in a "region long considered our sphere of influence." Although overthrowing a democratically elected government carried risks, "*in my judgment*," Kissinger argued, "*the dangers of doing nothing are greater*." Playing Machiavelli to the Prince, Kissinger thus recommended to Nixon that he should "make a decision that we [the United States] will oppose Allende as strongly as we can and do all we can to keep him from consolidating power, taking care to package those efforts in a style that gives us appearance of reacting to his moves."

Since Nixon had already ordered secret preparations to overthrow Allende, he hardly needed to be persuaded. What Nixon needed instead was the well thought-out rationale that Kissinger laid out. It is clear from the declassified records of the NSC meeting held the next day, the day after Kissinger had penned his memo, that Nixon more or less embraced Kissinger's underlying reasoning as his own.[220] At the meeting, secretary of state William Rogers and defense secretary Melvin Laird agreed with the Nixon-Kissinger-Helms line of thinking that Allende needed to be "brought down," while retaining an "outward posture that is correct." Nixon then spelled out the reasons this policy was needed. "Our main concern in Chile," Nixon told all those assembled "is the prospect that he (Allende) can consolidate himself and the picture projected to the world will be his success." This cannot be allowed because if other "potential leaders in South America think they can move like Chile," the United States "will be in trouble." Echoing the Kissinger memo, Nixon added that Allende was not the same as Tito, because in Europe "we have to get along and no change is possible."

However—and this is the key—"Latin America is not gone, and we want to keep it." About a year later, Nixon repeated these sentiments to Haldeman and Kissinger in an Oval Office conversation about Chile, underscoring that the fear of the Allende model was truly the driving force behind the move to overthrow him: "I know the argument, of course, that if we get out, we lose our (stroke?) there. The Russians will be happy to come in, and so forth and so on. But the fact is that he (Allende) is just gonna (wheel or reel?) us in, frankly, and also treating him well is going to encourage others to go do likewise. That's what I'm more concerned about."[221]

If we situate these specific conversations within the broader context of the period, we are in a position to get a good sense of what moved the United States to encourage a coup against Allende. Nixon and Kissinger were hoping to improve relations with China and to move toward détente with the Soviet Union. In terms of problems in the developing world, Nixon and Kissinger hoped that such a great-power realignment might enable the United States to facilitate an honorable peace in Vietnam. Whether it came to pass or not, there was a growing sense that Vietnam was probably lost. The likelihood of defeat created both a defensiveness among American decision-makers but also a tendency to "draw lines" when it came to core interests; both of these sentiments are evident in Nixon's suggestion that "Latin America is not gone, and we want to keep it." How did Allende's election threaten the American "hold" over Latin America? Again, it is clear that the growing Soviet influence in the region might have been a factor, but it was far from a pressing concern; even Nixon discounted it. What really concerned Nixon and Kissinger was Allende's democratic socialist commitment to nationalizing the American-owned copper companies, redistributing wealth, and pursuing a nationalist path of development. This was the real threat. Apart from hurting American economic interests in Chile, Allende's success could be contagious, encouraging more nationalist and social-democratic dominoes to tumble across Latin America. In Kissinger's world, what was really threatening about Chile in 1970 was the potential "insidious" effect of the Allende model. Nationalist assertiveness in Latin America would be truly threatening because of the substantial economic interests in the region. The United States needed subservient rulers in South America who were committed to development pathways favorable to American economic interests. Allende challenged these imperial ambitions of the United States and thus, had to go.

Once the decision to overthrow Allende was made at the highest level of the US government, the CIA went to work. The cloak-and-dagger details of how the United States encouraged the coup against Allende are readily available elsewhere.[222] Repeating them here would not serve the main analytical concerns of this study. The point that is worth repeating is that the United States first tried to block Allende from coming to power and, failing that, put in motion forces that led to Allende's overthrow. In the language of the CIA, they pursued two tracks—Track I and Track II—to derail Allende. Since Allende had only won a plurality of the presidential votes, his appointment to the presidency needed to be confirmed by the Chilean Congress. American Track I operations at this stage focused on a variety of "constitutional" methods, including bribing Chilean legislators to vote against Allende's confirmation. Given Chile's strong democratic tradition, however, there was little support for derailing Allende that way. He had won the election. The country was at peace. And that was that. Even Frei did not cooperate when the Americans sought his support to block Allende.

The focus of American efforts then turned to Track II, which was focused on creating a "coup climate" that would make a coup more likely. These efforts involved the ruthless manipulation of the Chilean economy and society, on the one hand, and, on the other hand, the encouragement of pro-American military officials to overthrow Allende. (This approach followed closely the one that had led to the successful overthrow of Iran's Mossadegh.) American officials, corporations, and international institutions—those the Americans could readily influence—then collaborated to make the Chilean economy "scream." As the country's economic problems worsened, a vigorous anti-Allende propaganda campaign sought to exaggerate the communist threat that Allende posed. A variety of CIA-supported political groups, including right-wing militias, took to streets. The head of the armed forces—one General Schneider—did not support the idea that the growing political instability necessitated a coup. He was murdered. The CIA then let it be known to senior military figures, who would likely lead the coup, that the United States would strongly support any such move. Once the coup happened, it was far from bloodless. Allende killed himself. Pinochet became Chile's US-supported dictator.

It is difficult to assess the full impact of the coup in Chile. Some outcomes can be linked more clearly to the overthrow of Allende than others. The clearest impact was the destruction of Chilean democracy, at least for the next seventeen years. Pinochet's ruthlessness has been well documented.[223] Again, the gory details need not be repeated here, except to note that the new regime killed some 3,000 Chilean citizens in the process of consolidating power, and that "thousands more were subjected to savage abuses such as torture, arbitrary incarceration, forced exile, and other forms of state-sponsored terror."[224] The best evidence suggests that the United States was aware of these developments, turned a blind eye to them, and having instigated the coup, offered both overt and covert support to Pinochet. A second clear outcome was that Pinochet moved quickly to pay off the American corporations that Allende had nationalized. Within a year Anaconda Copper company received "253 million [dollars] in cash and promissory notes for its expropriated assets"; Kennecott Copper received $66.9 million; and the conflict with ITT was settled for $125.2 million.[225] Without exaggeration, one can conclude that US intervention in Chile benefited American corporations at the expense of Chile: Chilean democracy was destroyed, thousands of Chilean citizens were either killed or brutally repressed, and Chilean taxpayers paid American companies handsomely to placate the United States.

What about the broader, more indirect impact of US intervention in Chile? Is Chile better off today because of the brutal Pinochet interregnum? Did the United States succeed in its boundary-setting goal of discouraging nationalist and social democratic experiments in Latin America? Here, we are on more slippery ground. The answers are likely to be heavily colored by ideological predispositions. Moreover, even if we could set those aside—nearly impossible in such matters—American influence is only one factor among many that molded patterns of change in Chile or in other countries of Latin America. (See chapter 6, for a fuller discussion of economic performance in Latin America in the era of Washington Consensus.) For now, and to conclude this discussion of Chile, only two comments are necessary, one about the longer-term impact on Chile and the other concerning regional implications.

First, the United States clearly had some success in achieving its longer-terms goals by sponsoring a coup in Chile. Following the coup, the free-market experiment of Pinochet allowed American companies to invest again in Chile and for the United States to maintain a trading pattern in which Chile exported commodities in exchange for American manufactured goods. American economists also worked closely with the Pinochet regime to stabilize the Chilean economy. They had some success insofar as some of the worst macroeconomic distortions were removed and the economy grew at a respectable rate. What we do not know is how well an Allende government that had support rather than adverse pressures might have managed the economy. It also needs to be underscored, however, that Pinochet's market-Leninism notwithstanding, two basic characteristics of the Chilean economy did not change: Chile remains highly dependent on commodity exports, and income distribution within the country is highly skewed. I argue in chapter 6 that commodity dependence and sharp inequalities also characterize much of Latin America, hampering the development of the region (especially in comparison to many Asian countries, which are pursuing more nationalist paths to modernization).

The second and last comment concerns the implications of the coup for the region and beyond. The United States clearly achieved some of its regional goals insofar as military dictators over the next decade pursued policies that on the whole were not antithetical to American interests. There were to be no more Allende-type experiments. Even when the left returned to power in

Latin America in the twenty-first century, it shied away from expropriating the investments of American companies. The United States had clearly defined the limits—in retrospect, Kissinger's imperial view that "we set the limits on diversity" had prevailed—and helped change the development paradigm in Latin America. Although this shift might have served American interests, the impact on the region was far from benign. (Chapter 6 discusses Latin America's lack luster economic performance under continuing American tutelage.) The coup was also not without costs, especially political costs, for the United States. These can be hard to assess concretely, but no one can doubt that public revelation of American support for a coup against Allende hurt American legitimacy in Latin America and beyond. Claims that America respected national sovereignty and was a champion of democracy were especially challenged by the intervention against Allende. If in early 1973, the Paris Accords signaled the limits of American power to prevail in Vietnam, the Chilean coup in late 1973 underscored the hypocrisy of liberal American claims. With the limits of both power and legitimacy exposed, 1973 may well have been a low point in American hegemonic ambitions.

Conclusion

After World War II, the United States emerged as the world's most powerful state. The United States then used its power superiority to mold a world order that fit its values and interests. The centerpiece of this world order was to be an open global economy. While capitalist Europe and Japan joined this global order, many others did not. In addition to the Soviet Union and the states within its land empire, a variety of communist and nationalist regimes in the poor countries—in the so-called Third World—also sought to pursue state-led development, with closed or semiclosed economies. The United States tolerated some of these, either because they did not challenge significant American interests (e.g., some postcolonial countries in Africa) or because, as, for example, in the case of India—the costs of imposing a *Pax Americana* on them would have been very high, especially in relation to the perceived potential gains. In much of the developing world, however, the United States did confront communists and nationalists who stood in the way of America's desire to establish an open global economic order. To repeat, a list of clear US interventions in the developing world during the Cold War era, in support or in opposition to emerging trends, might include China, Philippines, Korea, Taiwan, Vietnam, Laos, Cambodia, and Indonesia in East Asia; Israel, Saudi Arabia, Iran and Egypt in the Middle East; Congo in Africa; Guatemala, Cuba, Nicaragua and other small countries in Central America; and Brazil and Chile in Latin America. Of these, I have in this chapter analyzed three specific interventions—Iran, Vietnam, and Chile—with the aim of understanding the causes and consequences of America's imperial actions.

The motives behind, mechanisms, and impact of American interventions during the Cold War have been traced throughout this chapter via historical materials. My understanding of these key themes was also summarized above in the introduction to this chapter. Only a brief restatement is thus necessary at this point. What really moved the Americans to intervene in the developing world was not so much the threat of communism but the danger assertive nationalists posed to America's hegemonic ambitions: Iran's Mossadegh not only threatened key economic interests of an already weakened ally, Britain, but also posed a broader danger of creating an unacceptable norm for who controls the production, supply, and profits of an important commodity, oil; the revolutionary nationalism of Ho Chi Minh similarly threatened important interests of another weakened ally, France, but then the more the United States got involved, the more America's global credibility became an issue, prolonging a costly and tragic war; and Chile's Allende posed a direct threat to American corporations, as well as the broader danger of encouraging a nationalist and a democratic socialist pathway to development in America's backyard.

Since overt colonialism was not on the United States' Cold War agenda, the main mechanism of control was the creation of stable but subservient governments in power. The covert support for coups against Mossadegh and Allende had led to the installation of the Shah and Pinochet, respectively, who both did America's bidding. Similar cases that are not discussed in this chapter might include the US-supported overthrow of Arbenz in Guatemala and the assassination of Patrice Lumumba in the Congo. The case of Vietnam was more overt but the American hope there, too, was to create a stable-but-subservient regime in South Vietnam; the covert overthrow and death of Diem also followed a pattern similar to those in Iran and Chile. Once client regimes were installed, the United States sought to maintain them using a variety of carrots and sticks. The most common tools were foreign aid (especially military aid) but also establishing American military bases, which limited national autonomy. The hope was that given America's enormous power and economic resources, most client states would simply take America's preferences seriously; after all, it is an old axiom of politics that the truly powerful need not use their power to secure preferred outcomes. That is why maintaining credibility became so important for the United States. The failure in Vietnam was thus a turning point in American efforts to create and sustain an informal empire.

The consequences of American interventions are not easy to assess. Did the United States benefit from the intervention cases I have discussed here? I have suggested that the US intervention in Vietnam cost the United States dearly, not only in terms of the tragic loss of life, but also materially and in terms of both credibility and legitimacy. By contrast, the more covert efforts to overthrow rulers in Iran and Chile served short-term American interests, both economic and political, insofar as the efforts led to the installation of pro-American governments in power. Longer-term impact, however, varied in the two cases: whereas Chile eventually became a democracy, a strongly anti-American theocratic regime is still in power in Iran.

What about the impact of US interventions on developing countries during the Cold War? As a qualification to the thrust of the argument developed in this chapter, it should be added that US intervention in other cases such as South Korea or Taiwan during this period do not readily fit this pattern. In these cases, American intervention was driven much more by realpolitik considerations. As I have argued elsewhere, the benign impact of US intervention in South Korea included enacting land reforms, rebuilding war-damaged industries with US foreign aid, and then, of course, providing a security umbrella that enabled South Korea to flourish economically.[226] It is thus important to acknowledge the mixed nature of the evidence. History seldom follows a neat pattern. It is, however, important to decipher the dominant tendencies. From this standpoint, the impact of US interventions is better captured by the cases of Iran, Chile, and Vietnam; South Korea and Taiwan are the exceptions that highlight the modal pattern.

So what about the impact of US intervention on Iran, Chile, and Vietnam? The US intervention in Iran and Chile overthrew elected leaders and installed pro-American dictators who, in turn, ruled with ruthless force. Both Iran and Chile experienced some economic growth during the rule by the Shah and by Pinochet. However, narrow authoritarian rule also precluded the possibility of more broad-based power coalitions that might have supported the diversification of commodity-dependent economies and better economic redistribution. Vietnam suffered enormously at the hands of the United States: some three million deaths; widespread economic destruction; and substantial human and ecological damage caused by chemical warfare, the effects of which still linger. After the Vietnamese communists consolidated power, however—ruthless though they, too, are—they put Vietnam on an autonomous development trajectory, prioritizing growth, industrialization, and the eradication of poverty.

Juxtaposing these post–World War II interventions against the US interventions that followed the Spanish-American War (chapter 4) helps to shed light on a key theme of this study. The important point to note is the strong parallels between the interventions in the first half and in the second half of the twentieth century. Although American interventions in the Philippines and in Vietnam were certainly not identical, it is hard not to notice the use of prolonged American militarism against indigenous nationalists in both cases, as the United States kept its broader regional interests in mind. Similarly, the ouster of the nationalist Jose Santos Zelaya in Nicaragua was a harbinger of a trend that would follow in the post–World War II period, when the covert overthrow of such leaders as Mossadegh, Arbenz, Lumumba, and Allende became a regular part of America's imperial agenda. There is no doubt that the United States intervened more intensely and in more places after World War II than it did during the expansionist period that followed the Spanish-American War. This was a function of the scope of America's relative power in the second half of the twentieth century. Nevertheless, what these parallels underscore is that fighting communism could not have been the most important driving force behind the American interventions discussed in this chapter. The deeper threat represented by communism in the developing world during the Cold War era was the same threat that had led to interventions well before the Cold War—namely, the threat of assertive nationalists who could mobilize mass support to enhance national autonomy. Such autonomy imperiled American interests, especially economic ones (although also, at times, political and ideological interests). America's interventions, overt and covert and involving warfare or the forced overthrow of rulers, were aimed at taming nationalists who challenged American ambitions to establish an informal empire on a global scale.

Last, a comparison with Britain's informal empire in the nineteenth century (see chapter 2) helps to underscore some important analytical issues, too. I return to this comparison to highlight the central arguments of this study in the concluding chapter. For now, the main point of the comparison is to sharpen the argument here. It was clear in the case of Britain that an informal empire in Argentina, Egypt, and China complemented Britain's formal colonies in Asia and Africa. For the United States, by contrast, an informal empire emerged as the main instrument of pursuing its overseas interests; the United States did not want colonies and, in any case, following World War II, with the emergence of anticolonial nationalism and mass politics in much of the developing world and the norms of self-determination globally, any effort to establish formal colonies would have proved very costly. Nevertheless, the force that drove both Britain and the United States to establish an informal empire was the search for profits, supported by force. These causal connections were clearer in the case of Britain than in the American case, mainly because the United States defined its economic interests in global terms: the need to establish an open global economy. Those who got in the way were thrashed. Taming nationalists is then a key trend that runs through both British and American efforts to establish control over poor parts of the world. When successful, these efforts discouraged the emergence of developmental coalitions in power, and perpetuated poorly governed societies with commodity-dependent economies.

6

Global Assertion, Soft and Hard

THE WASHINGTON CONSENSUS (LATIN AMERICA) AND THE MIDDLE EAST (IRAQ)

FOLLOWING THE END of the war in Vietnam, there was a lull in American assertiveness abroad. It did not last very long, however. Within a decade, President Ronald Reagan proclaimed, "It's morning in America," and promised to renew America's global assertiveness. This assertiveness included sharply increasing defense expenditures, taking a hard-line approach vis-à-vis the Soviet Union, laying to rest any lingering self-restraint born of the Vietnam Syndrome, and spreading of the forces of free enterprise the world over. With the decline of the Soviet Union, any hesitations about the limits of American power, which the loss in Vietnam had generated, also vanished. American triumphalism and hubris now knew no limits, at least until reality hit back. Following Reagan, subsequent American presidents have also sought to further incorporate still unincorporated parts of the world into a *Pax Americana*, with mixed results.

American interventions in the developing world in the post-Cold War period proceeded along both economic and military paths. Financial globalization and the related debt crisis in the 1980s provided the occasion to impose the Washington Consensus on development, first in Latin America and Africa, and then, following the Asian financial crisis of 1997, in parts of Asia. These pressures were aimed at both rescuing major American banks and opening up state-directed economies in the developing world to foreign capital and goods. Military efforts were focused instead on "rogue states," especially in the oil-rich Middle East, but also others. These were states perceived to be standing in the way of America's grand design in a unipolar world, whatever that design may be. Very much part of a pattern that had begun well before the Cold War and that has continued beyond the Cold War, the United States in the most recent period has

How Britain and the United States Shaped the Global Periphery. Atul Kohli, Oxford University Press (2020).

DOI: 10.1093/oso/9780190069629.001.0001

again sought to tame both economic nationalism and insubordinate states in the developing world. I analyze two significant instances of contemporary American interventions, which I characterize as modern forms of old-fashioned imperialism in the global periphery: using debt as leverage to open up peripheral economies, mainly in Latin America, and using military interventions in the Middle East, especially in Iraq.

Financial globalization accelerated following the two significant increases in oil prices orchestrated by the Organization of Petroleum Countries (OPEC) in the mid- and late 1970s. Massive amounts of Eurodollars became available in the global economy for loans at low interest rates. Many middle-income countries, especially in Eastern Europe and Latin America, borrowed heavily, hoping to invest in industries and to export to advanced industrial countries, thus speeding up the growth of their respective economies. Believing that countries do not go bankrupt, commercial banks were keen to lend to these countries. But economic problems in the United States jeopardized the hopes and plans of many developing countries. In the face of shifts in American policies, especially the high interest rates that resulted from the Volcker Shock of 1981, payments on the variable interest rates of many Latin American countries skyrocketed. Following Mexico's inability to make its interest payment in 1982, international liquidity dried up and a full-blown financial crisis arrived. Major American banks were now exposed, especially to a handful of large Latin American countries such as Brazil, Argentina, and Mexico. How the U.S. sought to resolve this crisis is the first of the two cases of recent American interventions in the developing world that I analyze in this chapter.

The United States worked through such multilateral organizations as the International Monetary Fund (IMF) and the World Bank to deal with the Latin American debt crisis of the 1980s. American government's early priority was to ensure the solvency of major American banks. Multilateral institutions offered loans to Latin American countries so they could continue to make payments on their loans to commercial banks. In exchange, these Latin American countries were asked to undertake policy changes—so-called structural reforms—that would ensure that they would have enough resources to continue to service their debts. These policy changes included minimizing state intervention in their respective economies, balancing budgets, privatization, opening their economies, and focusing on exports. Very soon, these policy packages were dubbed "the Washington Consensus" on development. Under pressure from the United States and US-controlled multilateral institutions, numerous countries in Latin America embraced these policies during the 1990s. Even if it were understood that policies associated with the Washington Consensus would jeopardize economic growth, the US and multilateral institutions maintained a discourse that policy reform was pro-growth. Poor countries in Latin America were forced to accept these policies to benefit American economic interests. The impact on Latin America included poor economic performance during the last decades of the century, especially in contrast to many Asian countries, such as China and India, which charted a more autonomous path to industrialization and prosperity.

As for the Middle East, the United States has long considered it a region of considerable strategic and economic interest; both oil and Israel have focused the minds of American foreign policymakers on the region. During the early years of the Cold War, dependent monarchs in Iran and Saudi Arabia—two of the largest oil producers of the region—ensured American influence over the critical Persian Gulf. However, a number of developments in the late 1970s upset these arrangements: a revolution in Iran that toppled the pro-American Shah from power; a second increase in oil price (again orchestrated by OPEC); and the Soviet intervention in Afghanistan. President Jimmy Carter then explicitly underlined the importance of oil for the United States and declared the oil-rich Middle East to be vital to American interests. US military presence and expenditures in the region increased. During the Reagan years, the United States—working with Saudi Arabia and Pakistan—supported the anti-Soviet Mujahedeen in Afghanistan. These religious militants later morphed into the Taliban. Wanting to neutralize Iran's regional ambitions, during the 1980s the United States also supported Saddam Hussein's forces in the prolonged Iran-Iraq War. Saddam misunderstood the nature of American support. When Iraq annexed Kuwait in 1990, the United States intervened with a massive show of force to restore the status quo. Although Saddam was easily defeated, the United States for its own reasons let him stay in power. Following 9/11, the United States again intervened heavily in the region, first in Afghanistan, and then in Iraq. American war in Iraq in the new millennium is the second case of recent American interventions in the developing world that I analyze here.

Why the United States went to war in Iraq a second time remains murky. The overt suggestion of the US government that Saddam Hussein had to be removed from power because he possessed weapons of mass destruction turned out to be the least persuasive of possible motives. No such weapons were ever found. More likely, the Iraq War was a product of an imperial hubris that post–Cold War triumphalism engendered. In this mindset, Saddam was perceived as a significant obstacle to the broader American design to remake the Middle East in its own image. This design included putting in place friendly and obsequious rulers—who could be made to look like democrats—who would facilitate control over the key resource of the region, oil, as well as enhance the security of such allies as Israel and Saudi Arabia. While it would be an oversimplification to suggest that the United States invaded Iraq to control its oil, it is also the case that the

United States would have had very little interest in Iraq had it not had oil. Oil wealth and a ruthless, ambitious ruler at its helm made Iraq an attractive target to American decision-makers, who were keen to expand American influence in a unipolar world.

Invading Iraq and toppling Saddam from power turned out to be the easy part of the war in Iraq. Given America's enormous military superiority, this result was hardly a surprise. By contrast, the efforts to rebuild a functioning Iraq turned out to be another American nightmare. Installing pro-American rulers seldom resolves the legitimacy crisis in a client state because the ruled readily see the rulers for what they are—namely, puppets of a foreign power; this was as true of Rhee in Korea, Diem in Vietnam, and the Shah in Iran as it was in more recent Iraq. In addition, the United States grossly miscalculated how welcome it would be in Iraq. Dissolving the existing state structure was also a huge political mistake, if the goal of US occupation included restoring order and prosperity to Iraq. But it may well be that the United States did not care what happened to Iraq. Under US occupation, Iraq has moved from one weak government to another, with enormous violence. It may well be that this outcome fit American needs, as long as the oil kept flowing. Resistance to both the United States and to US-supported Iraqi rulers also grew. Over time, this resistance became armed. With or without the US troops, Iraq at the time of this writing remains a deeply troubled state. The violence resulting from the American war may have led to as many as half a million deaths in Iraq between 2003 and 2011.[1] The costs of war to the United States have also been enormous; in addition to the death of soldiers, the war has been dubbed a "trillion dollar war."

A preview of the argument may be helpful. Following defeat in Vietnam, the United States could have become a more inward-looking power that was satisfied with being a gentler giant. That was not to be, however, not then, and then not again, even after the decline of the Soviet Union. Why the hegemonic urge runs relatively deep in the United States is for specialists in the study of American politics to untangle. From the standpoint of this study, what is striking instead is that assertive nationalists can readily mobilize this urge, as was evident in the popularity of Reagan—and of other subsequent presidents—who promised to maintain America as number one. US leaders use this nationalist political base to undermine national autonomy elsewhere, with the hope of furthering American interests. Be that as it may, the motives and modalities of US intervention in Latin America during the 1980s are easier to comprehend than those that have led the United States to be so heavily involved in the Middle East in the new millennium.

The debt crisis in Latin America threatened the solvency of major American banks. The United States intervened, both directly and via multilateral organizations in which the United States was a dominant force, to ensure that Latin American countries paid back their debts to US banks. The crisis also provided an occasion to further open up Latin American economies to US goods and capital. While the avowed goal of structural reform in Latin America was to promote development, it is more likely that US decision-makers understood, or at least had an inkling, that policies associated with the Washington Consensus would hurt economic growth in Latin America but still pushed them because they served American economic interests. As we have seen, the US intervention in Latin America during the 1980s was part of a long pattern of soft economic imperialism (discussed in earlier chapters under the rubric of informal empire) to forcibly open doors the world over to sustain and enhance American prosperity.

Economic motives were also behind the US military intervention in Iraq, but in less obvious ways than in Latin America. Among the factors that make the Middle East of great strategic importance to the United States is the concentration of world's oil resources in the region. Whether friends or foes control the production, distribution, and pricing of oil is, then, a matter of considerable US concern. As noted in chapter 5, the US was party to the overthrow of Muhammed Mossadegh in the 1950s in order to deny Iran national control over its own oil. The client status of the Saudi monarchy serves American regional interests well. Ever since the overthrow of the pro-American Shah, the US has sought to deny Iran a significant regional role. It even supported Saddam Hussein against Iran during the prolonged Iran-Iraq War of the 1980s. No one doubts that the US intervened to liberate Kuwait from Iraq in 1991 because Kuwait swims in oil. The motives behind the Second Iraq War—the focus of the present chapter—need to be understood within this historical and regional context. I argue that the United States went to war in Iraq the second time as a first step in a grander design to further incorporate the oil-rich Middle East within the American orbit. The fact that it may not work out that way does not take anything away from the original motives. Intervention in Iraq also fits a century-long pattern of hard military imperialism: the pattern began with the United States' smashing Filipino nationalists at the turn of the twentieth century to control the Philippines as a stepping-stone to the giant China market; it continued in Vietnam as a way to stop the spread of communism and to maintain open economies in the region; and is now playing itself out in the oil-rich Middle East that the United States hopes to dominate.

Judged from the standpoint of whether America's imperial interventions bring it benefits, the evidence from the most recent period again suggests that the United States does economic imperialism better than military imperialism. The US efforts to deal with the Latin American debt crisis of the 1980s supports the first part of this conclusion. As we have seen, the United States used economic coercion to ensure cooperation by Latin American elites, who were willing to pass on the costs of policy reform to both the lower strata and the future generations of Latin America. The costs of American intervention to Americans were minimal, except for the loss of some international goodwill. In turn, the US government and US-dominated multilateral institutions helped to maintain the profits and solvency of major American banks. Latin American markets were opened up further to American goods and capital. By contrast, US-military intervention in Iraq has cost the Americans dearly and the rewards remain uncertain. Since the goals of US intervention were murky to begin with, it is difficult to assess whether any of them have been met or are likely to be met. If the goals had been minimal—namely, to get rid of a thuggish, possibly anti-American dictator with access to oil wealth—that much the Iraq War certainly achieved. However, much of this goal was already accomplished after the first Gulf War, after which Saddam was still in power but well contained, and even willing to allow foreign oil companies to invest in Iraqi oil. The grander goal of remaking Iraq in America's image, and then going beyond to impose an American peace on the entire region, remains, at best, illusive, and more likely, with growing anti-Americanism and the spread of militancy, even more distant than before the second war.

The impact of American interventions on developing countries—both economic and military—has been negative. As to economic imperialism, I document below that American efforts to ensure that banks were repaid their debts contributed to a lost decade of growth in Latin America. Beyond the lost decade, moreover, forced economic openness reinforced economic dependency of Latin American countries on their northern giant. The consequences are evident if one juxtaposes the experience of Asian countries during the same period (say, from 1980 to 2005), with that of Latin America. Asian countries pursued a more autonomous development path in which national states directed their respective economies. This pattern of development—the Asian financial crisis notwithstanding—produced high growth rates, modest inequalities, industrial development, and high value-added exports. By contrast, economic growth in Latin American countries remained sluggish, with sharp income inequalities. Most Latin American countries also continued to export commodities in exchange for manufactured goods.

The negative impact of America's war in Iraq is there for anyone to see. What makes a moral judgment a little complicated is the fact that Saddam Hussein was a despotic, ruthless dictator who killed many of his own citizens, probably close to a quarter million over a period of twenty-five years.[2] By contrast, as noted, nearly a half million Iraqis died under American occupation between 2003 and 2011, the year most American troops left Iraq. Since then, US troops have had to return to deal with militancy. The Iraqi state remains weak and corruption and poverty remain endemic, even as oil extraction continues to grow.

What follows is a brief overview of the political and economic context within which America's most recent interventions have unfolded, and my discussion of the cases of the Latin American debt crisis and the war in Iraq.

Background

A number of developments during the 1970s challenged America's confidence in itself as a global hegemon. As we have seen, the Vietnam War had put enormous pressure on the American economy. By the end of the war (say, 1974–75), the US economy had gone into a sharp recession, probably the worst since the 1930s. The Vietnam Syndrome—a sense that wars against forces of national liberation were hard to win—was reinforced by the domestic costs associated with such interventions. At the same time, the Japanese and German economies had also recovered so successfully that they—and others—started exporting more to the United States than they were importing from it. During the Vietnam era, for the first time in the twentieth century, the United States became a net debtor nation. While Richard Nixon is often remembered for matters other than his policy acumen, well before William J. Clinton and the talk of "globalization," he recognized in 1971 that in "the last third of the century . . . economic power will be the key to other kinds of power."[3] Nixon proceeded unilaterally to reverse America's declining economic situation—and thus to also recover America's global political position—by pressuring Japan and other economies to revalue their currencies. He also took the United States off the gold standard.[4] The Bretton Woods system then began to collapse. A sharp increase in oil prices orchestrated by OPEC finally sounded the death knell of the old system of fixed exchange rates. To deal with its domestic economic problems, the United States killed the system that had provided some "international financial discipline;" as a result, "the door" was now open "for the vast expansion of private, national, and international debt that occurred in the late 1970s and early 1980s," and that, in turn, contributed mightily to the debt crises that followed.[5]

During the late 1970s, global political developments added to American anxieties. Important among these was the Islamic Revolution in 1979 that led to the overthrow of the Shah.[6] This was of both political and economic significance for the United States. According to the Nixon Doctrine, Iran under the Shah was to play the role of a pro-US regional supervisor of sorts in the oil-rich Persian Gulf. And the heavy purchases of American arms the Shah was making with his oil money both helped the US arms industry and enhanced Iran's regional power status. The revolution put an end to this cozy alliance. The Islamic

Revolution in Iran also contributed to the Soviet intervention in Afghanistan, in late 1979, although that was also triggered by internal political developments in Afghanistan that were threatening the hold of pro-Soviet rulers in that country. Both of these developments—the revolution in Iran and Soviet imperialism in Afghanistan—threatened US influence over the critical Gulf region. President Carter reacted with the Carter Doctrine, a declaration that the Gulf and its oil were vital to America's interests. Carter also increased defense spending in general, paving the way for the sharp increases to come under Reagan, and, more specifically, built military bases and authorized the Rapid Deployment Joint Force in the Middle East.[7] This was the beginning of a steady growth of the US military role in the Persian Gulf.

The revolution in Iran also disrupted the production and export of Iranian oil. OPEC used the occasion to impose a second round of sharp increase in oil prices in 1979, which had widespread global ramifications. Following the first round of increase in oil prices, in 1973, the United States and Saudi Arabia had already reached a tacit agreement to continue the denomination of oil in dollars. This arrangement was kept in place after the second increase, and was helpful for the United States because American hegemony rested in part on the central "role of the dollar in the international monetary system."[8] America's global role was also helped by the fact that allies like Saudi Arabia bought US Treasury securities (or, "Treasuries") with their large oil earnings, easing the strain on the US balance of payments.[9] Elsewhere, the impact of the sharp increase in oil prices was far from benign. I will return below to a fuller discussion of related issues. For now, what is important to note is the impact on American policies, also with global ramifications. The second round of oil-price increases contributed to more inflation in the United States. This in turn led to the Volcker Shock, named after the head of US Federal Reserve Bank at the time, Paul Volcker, who increased interest rates sharply. Although inflation was tamed as a result, these policies also induced a recession in the United States and elsewhere. Many developing countries that had borrowed with a plan to export to advanced industrial countries were now hit hard because of the shrinking demand for their exports. The costs of debt servicing for indebted developing countries—especially those in Latin America, which had borrowed from American banks, often at variable interest rates—also skyrocketed due to high interest rates. When international liquidity dried up in 1982, the debt crisis was upon the world. Once again, then, the United States had pursued policies that would help its own economy, but have a deleterious impact elsewhere.

These developments—the loss in Vietnam, domestic economic problems, the assertiveness of the OPEC, revolution in Iran, and Soviet intervention in Afghanistan—had created a sense in the United States that its global power might be in decline. Writing in 1977, Henry Kissinger reflected that the decline had probably begun in the late 1960s, when the "Soviet nuclear stockpile" approached parity. In addition, he suggested, "[T]he economic strength of Europe and Japan was bound to lead them to seek larger political influence," and "developing countries" would continue to demand "greater power and participation." As a result, though it was still the strongest nation in the world, by the 1970s, the United States, according to Kissinger, was "no longer preeminent."[10] On objective grounds, each of Kissinger's anxieties was debatable: Soviet nuclear parity rested on a rotten economic base; Japan and Germany could not readily translate their economic strength into military power; and the developing world was hardly unified. But never mind. American decline was as much a state of mind as it was an objective reality. President Carter underscored the national "malaise" in his famous speech of 1979, in which he suggested that the United States was facing "a crisis of confidence . . . that strikes at the very heart and soul and spirit of our national will."[11] Prominent scholars such as Robert Gilpin and Paul Kennedy contributed to this "declinist" mindset by focusing on either the growing economic prowess of Japan, or on issues of "imperial overreach."[12] *Business Week* captured the national mood when it suggested that "the country is entering the decade of the 1980s as a wounded, demoralized colossus."[13]

Instead of turning inward, however, Americans elected Ronald Reagan as its president, who became the instrument for the global reassertion of American power. Reagan was a strong anticommunist. His foreign affairs focus was mainly on the Soviet Union. Yet, circumstances soon demanded that he focus on other parts of the world, especially the debt crisis in Latin America. (I will return to a fuller discussion of U.S. economic interventions in Latin America during the last decades of the century. For now, some background on the Reagan era that sheds light on the nature of U.S. interventions may be useful.) Reagan's genius was an effort to beat the usual trade-off between guns and butter. Early in his presidency, he gave tax breaks to the rich and sharply increased defense spending. As the budget deficit grew, so did the pressure to cut social spending. Reagan packaged such cuts in a broader program of releasing market forces by shrinking the state. The outlines of a neoliberal revolution were now in place. The lower strata and the future generations in the United States would pay for the rapid increase in military spending. Foreigners would also help finance America's military buildup. The high interest rates triggered by Volcker's policies attracted large capital inflows that, in turn, helped both the budgetary and balance-of-payment deficits.[14] Further global implications of America's neoliberal turn included the fact that, supported by a more robust military, the United States was again ready to pressure other states—especially the Soviet Union, but also others—to fall in line with American goals and interests. Even allies would have to bend to the new

American assertiveness: for example, the Plaza Accord of 1984 pressured Japan and Germany to revalue their currencies to make American exports more competitive; and, of course, as we will see, the state had to be rolled back in much of the developing world to serve the American interest in a more open global economy.

During this period, a major economic shift that is relevant for understanding patterns of American interventions in the developing world was the ascendance of finance, both within the American political economy and globally. Trends within the United States and in the international economy fed each other. The shift toward the dominance of finance began even before the Reagan era, was encouraged by Reagan's deregulation policies, and matured during the Clinton years. As noted, the economic recovery of Japan and Europe threatened the competitiveness of the American economy, especially in manufacturing. Between 1979 and 1995, for example, some 43 million jobs were lost in the United States. If manufacturing contributed 28 percent, and finance 18 percent of the American GDP in 1975, by 1995 the share of manufacturing had declined to 22 percent and that of finance had increased to 27 percent.[15] Measured somewhat differently, the value of assets created by financial institutions within the United States grew from some 55 percent to 95 percent of the GDP between 1980 and 2000.[16] Not surprisingly, this shift was also reflected in who within the US economy was making the most profits: between 1980 and 2005, the profits of the financial sector grew by 800 percent, whereas that of nonfinancial sectors grew "only" by 250 percent.[17] The importance of Wall Street—that is, of finance—in American politics then grew, in part because American politicians were forced to recognize the structural shifts in the American economy, and also because the financial and personnel links adjoining Wall Street and American politics increasingly became denser.

These developments within the United States were influenced by changes abroad and in turn, pushed the world further toward financial globalization. The issue of the destruction of the Bretton Woods system is discussed above. And again, the OPEC price increases, along with the agreement of America's client states in the Middle East to denominate oil sales in dollars, further contributed to a sharp increase in Eurodollars. So, just as American industry was facing stiff competition from Japan and others, US-based banks found new economic opportunities overseas. Overseas branches of American commercial banks, which were not regulated by American banking laws, became a major depository of OPEC dollars. Awash in oil money and believing that "countries do not go bankrupt," American banks then pushed loans to middle-income, developing countries—especially in Latin America—at relatively low, but variable, interest rates. More than exports and direct investments, financial flows across national boundaries now emerged as the key dimension of globalization: if, in 1979, global financial transactions amounted to a sum twelve times greater than total exports, by 1984, this sum had jumped to nearly twenty times.[18] For American banks, domestic business had languished during the 1970s. In search of new sources of profit, the "international activities" of American banks "exploded" instead, "accounting for 95 percent of the earnings growth of the nation's ten largest banks" during the 1970s and "probably more than half their total earnings."[19] As we will see, the approach of the US government to Latin America's debt crisis in the 1980s was deeply influenced by the need to ensure that major American banks—now heavily exposed beyond the national borders—remained profitable.

Reagan, in sum, increased defense spending sharply, deregulated the domestic economy, and preached the ideology of free-market capitalism. This militaristic neoliberalism at home had its global counterparts, too: structural adjustment programs in debt-ridden developing countries and military interventions in such small places as Grenada. Reagan's overseas interventions were relatively limited, though, certainly compared to what followed. Reagan's morning-in-America notwithstanding, the Vietnam Syndrome had still not been fully defeated within the United States and the Soviet Union was still intact. It would take the end of the Cold War—and, eventually, 9/11—to overcome these hesitations. The Cold War started to decline in the mid-1980s with Gorbachev's rise to power in the Soviet Union. Gorbachev then took unprecedented steps aimed at modernizing the Soviet Union. These actions unleashed forces—probably unanticipated—that led to the reunification of Germany, the toppling of dominoes within the Soviet empire, and the end of the Soviet Union. The Cold War was over. While Americans were more surprised than anything by these developments, they were quick to claim "victory."[20] What followed was first a sense of triumphalism—the "end of history" variety[21]—and then the hubris to finally remake the world in the American image.

America's post–Cold War global assertiveness in the developing world has proceeded along both economic and military lines; both soft and hard interventions have been aimed at taming states in the developing world. Clinton focused on opening the world economy. In turn, the two Bushes, George H. W. Bush and George W. Bush, especially Bush II, sought to vanquish recalcitrant states via military interventions. This difference across administrations was more of means than of goals; the shared goal since the end of the Cold War has been to reassert America's global dominance.[22] Fighting communism was the main rationale for a variety of foreign policies during the Cold War, including high military expenditures, overseas bases, military alliances, and strengthening capitalist economies. None of these policies let up after the Soviet Union's implosion. The Cold War was over but American global assertiveness was not. New measures included maintaining high military expenditures; the forced opening of state-led

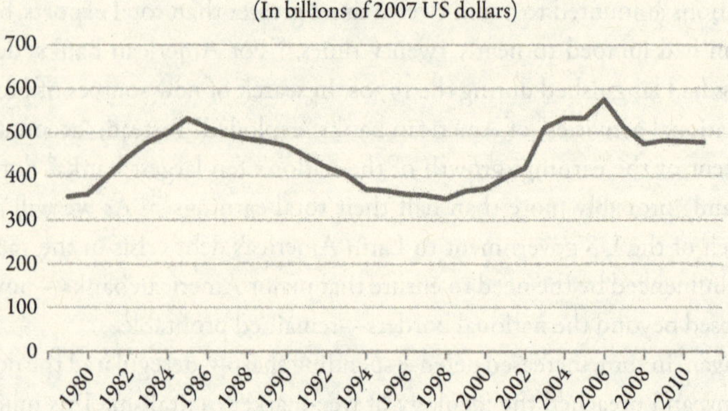

FIGURE 6.1 US defense spending, 1979–2011.

Source: Based on data in Calleo, *Follies of Power*, p. 89. Data beyond 2011 are not provided here because that was the year US troops pulled out of Iraq, which is more or less the end point of this study.

economies; the expansion of NATO; pressure on nonconformist states; the expansion of military bases worldwide; and military interventions, especially in the Middle East. Whether the US achieves its global goals or not, the post–Cold War policy pattern reflects a sustained ambition to maintain global hegemony that limits the autonomy of other nations.

The pattern of US military expenditures underscores these global ambitions (see Figure 6.1). Following the Vietnam War, defense spending in the United States declined but was maintained at a fairly high level during the 1970s, in the name of continuing the Cold War. This Cold War high, say around 1979, provides a base line for assessing future patterns. As is evident in Figure 6.1, this spending started its upward trend in the late Carter years and then shot up sharply during the Reagan years; the underlying reasons have been discussed. Reagan's high levels were unsustainable without increasing taxes. Well before the end of the Cold War, then, military spending had started declining, but never below the Cold War high. What is even more telling is that, even after the collapse of the Soviet Union, US defense spending never went below the levels of the Cold War high. If communism was the real enemy in the past, what was the United States preparing to fight now? America's gigantic military expenditures in the post–Cold War era have continued to be larger than the combined defense expenditures of the next seven to eight largest military spenders in the world, including China, Russia, Britain, France, and India. Why?

Official rationales for high military spending in the post–Cold War period provided a shifting kaleidoscope but are nevertheless telling. Arguing against any "peace dividend," the *Defense Planning Guide* stated, in 1992, that even though the Cold War had ended, the US military should remain so strong and overwhelming that "no country would be tempted to compete."[23] Colin Powell added that the new global enemy instead was "instability," which could, of course, emerge anywhere. The Pentagon declared in early 1993 that it was now fighting for a worldwide "open economic system."[24] This fit well with the emerging priorities of the new Clinton Administration, with its renewed focus on the American economy. Clinton indeed prioritized the economy, but the underlying rationale was that "American economic power was essential to the preservation of the nation's survival as the sole superpower."[25] When Clinton sought simultaneously to maintain the military budget at a high level, he was pushing at open doors; the US Congress added even more to the military budget than was requested, arguing that "a flourishing arms industry was necessary to keep thousands of Americans employed";[26] the profits from the arms industry were not, of course, underscored in the official document. Last, a government document drawn up under Paul Wolfowitz's supervision argued that America's "first objective," following the end of the Cold War, "is to prevent the re-emergence of a new rival." This goal required that the United States "prevent any hostile power from dominating a region whose resources would, under consolidated control, be sufficient to generate global power."[27] This last suggestion pointed to a "preventive" military strategy that was used as a rationale for the Iraq War, a subject to which I return in due course.

Some coherence can be imposed on these seemingly disparate rationales for high military spending following the end of the Cold War. First, the United States was keen to maintain its overwhelming superiority in a unipolar world. There is no indication in the official record that the United States could live with, and even less that it would encourage, a more multipolar world; instead, no country should even be "tempted to compete." Second, how would the United States ensure such overwhelming power superiority? The aim would be to "prevent" the emergence of any "hostile" rival. Any regional power seeking to dominate its own region should be nipped in the bud, well before it used the regional base to emerge as a global challenger. And third, what did the United States hope to achieve with such overwhelming power? Chances are that most American policymakers were persuaded that American power is a force for good in the world; most rulers in the world convince themselves of their own goodness. In fact, American power was to serve American interests in maintaining an orderly world with open economies. Over the twentieth century, American elites had come to associate the well-being of the country with an international order populated by open-market democracies. Even the fight against communism was a subset of this broader goal because in practice, communist countries were extreme forms of state-controlled economies that threatened to close off global economic spaces. When the Cold War ended, one major challenger to American designs was eliminated. The United States was then in a position—or hoped that it was in a position—to finally impose an American order of pliable states with open economies across the world. Whether the economic challenge posed by China in the twenty-first century will prove to be a turning point in America's open economy global project is an issue that will only become clear in the near future.

Within this broader post–Cold War ambition of global dominance, Clinton pursued economic and Bush II military imperialism. The broader context in which these American approaches to the developing world unfolded is now discussed in brief before proceeding to the two specific cases of such interventions: imposing the Washington Consensus on Latin America and the Iraq War. Clinton was a "centrist," or a "new" democrat, who shifted the Democratic Party toward the right of center, helped put together a winning electoral coalition, revived economic growth, but also brought the party closer to banking and corporate interests.[28] While his secretary of state, Madeline Albright, was not shy about the unilateral use of military force abroad,[29] the focus of the Clinton era was on matters economic. Clinton and his team believed that the American capacity to prevail as the sole superpower would remain a function of America's economic health. Their approach to the economy was also more conservative than those of earlier Democratic presidents. Clinton focused on balancing the budget, to gain credibility with Wall Street. The embrace of Wall Street was also evident in Clinton's appointing Wall Street bankers, for example, Robert Rubin of Goldman Sachs, and in his continuing the financial deregulation begun under Reagan. Whether the Clinton era can be understood as the era during which the Wall Street "captured" Washington or not,[30] there is no doubt that in addition to traditional business interests, industry and foreign investors, financial interests now also came to be heavily represented within the US government.

The global counterpart of this shift in the domestic political economy was a focus on the opening of markets everywhere. The locus of foreign policy shifted from the State to the Treasury, Commerce, and other economic departments. Clinton's top economic policy advisers—Ronald Brown, Mickey Kantor, and Samuel Berger—were intensely focused on "opening foreign markets to American exports and gaining American corporations greater access to the cheap labor and natural resources of less-developed countries."[31] A senior government official explained that Clinton's economic team pursued "commercial diplomacy" with a sense of "mission": "We used Washington's official muscle to help firms reach overseas markets. The culture was electric: we set up an economic 'war room' and built a 'trading floor' that tracked the world's largest commercial projects."[32] With the Cold War over, even allies were now fair game when it came to forced economic opening. For example, the Clinton team put enormous pressure on

Japan to "liberalize"; the Japanese economy went into "free fall" during 1994 and 1995.[33] I return to a discussion of the pressure on countries such as South Korea to also open their economies to American financial interests, which, in turn, contributed to the Asian financial crisis in 1997. Meanwhile, the American economy grew handsomely under Clinton.

It was in this context that the United States began taking an approach to the developing countries that came to be known as the Washington Consensus on development. A move in this direction had already begun during the Reagan years under the rubric of structural-adjustment programs. During the 1980s, these programs were put together—rather haphazardly—to ensure that indebted countries continued to make payments on their debts in exchange for policy changes. During the Clinton era, the policies demanded of developing countries became a full-fledged ideology of development. Key elements of this policy package are well known and basically added up to getting prices right: developing countries were supposed to free their economies from state guidance and open them to the forces of private enterprise, including foreign capital and goods. These policy-reform packages were promoted to the leaders of developing countries as the best route to their own economic development. As we will see, the impact of such policies was a lot more ambiguous. These policy reforms are thus better viewed as one more element in the post–Cold War American effort to open the global economy by "rolling back the state" in the developing world.[34] The countries most vulnerable to pressures from the United States—or from multilateral organizations, in which the United States wielded considerable influence—were Latin American countries. This was not only because they were highly indebted, but also because their loans were commercial (rather than official, as in much of sub-Saharan Africa), and they have traditionally depended on foreign investment to sustain growth. By contrast, many Asian countries with high domestic-savings rates were able to withstand the pressures to embrace the Washington Consensus on development. I document below that during the 1980s and the 1990s, growth and equity performance of many Asian countries was superior (at least prior to the Asian financial crisis) to those of Latin American countries that embraced the Washington Consensus.

The second case I discuss is the US military intervention in Iraq under Bush II. This case tempts one to attribute imperial hubris to a specific president or to a handful of decision-makers. However, it is important to keep the longer-term pattern of US interest in the oil-rich Middle East in mind. As noted, President Carter had declared it a region of vital interest following the revolution in Iran and the Soviet intervention in Afghanistan. Reagan (and the Soviet Union) then sided with Iraq in the Iran-Iraq War, with the hope of thwarting Iran's regional ambitions. Saddam's post–Cold War regional imperial effort to gobble up Kuwait cost him dearly and led to the First Iraq War, in which the United States easily prevailed. As to why the United States did not "finish the job" after its decisive victory—meaning, depose Saddam—the reasons offered at the time included that the effort would have been costly in terms of lives and treasure; Saddam could easily hide; the United States would be forced to undertake a costly occupation of Iraq; the United States did not want to strengthen the regional hands of Iran; and the US military was not well-equipped for "nation-building."[35] In retrospect, these earlier cautions appear a lot more prescient than was the hubris of Bush II in the new millennium.

As noted, Clinton is best known, and rightly so, for his economic focus, but it is worth underscoring how eager some of his senior staff members were to go to war in Iraq. Saddam's refusal to capitulate to each and every American demand, such as to open his military sights for "inspection" in 1997, provided opportunities for US decision-makers to ratchet up their demands and plan for a war. Even though Iraq had been crushed militarily and by now posed minimal military threat, "regime change" in Iraq was the standing policy of the Clinton Administration.[36] Both Secretary Albright and Samuel Berger, who was Clinton's national security adviser, argued that "time had come to get rid of Saddam."[37] The Joint Chief of Staff's *Strategic Assessment 1999* then considered an oil war in the Persian Gulf as a serious contingency. It was reasoned that "a new war would eliminate once and for all the influence of Saddam Hussein, gain control of his oil, and extend our influence into the vacuum created in the oil-rich lands of southern Eurasia by the demise of the Soviet Union."[38] Those outside the government at that time, such as Wolfowitz, also argued that "the only way to protect America's vital interests in the Persian Gulf region" was to overthrow Saddam.[39] The political support for such a war in Iraq, however, was absent during the Clinton years. It would take the tragedy of 9/11 to provide the opportune political moment for the second war in Iraq.

Bush II was elected by a slim margin. As a matter of fact, his victory was a result of a controversial decision by the US Supreme Court, which many interpreted as partisan. And yet, Bush II decided to take the United States into two major wars, in Afghanistan and Iraq, respectively. While the wars followed 9/11—a set of grievous events that understandably created a mood in the United States for some sort of revenge, especially in Afghanistan—it is important to underscore that the hostility toward Iraq was already palpable. As noted, the need for regime change in Iraq had been spelled out in Clinton's second term. During the presidential election in 2000, then, such key advisers to Bush II as Wolfowitz and Condoleezza Rice argued for removing Saddam. Bush's other advisers included Dick Cheney, Donald Rumsfeld, and eventually, in the second tier, I. Lewis Libby Jr. and Douglas Feith. They and other neoconservatives, as they came to be dubbed, wanted to invade Iraq again. "[T]en days" into the new administration, it was all about "Iraq," recalled Paul O'Neil, the Treasury Secretary to Bush II.[40] Well before 9/11, then, key US decision-makers were bent on regime change in Iraq. The underlying reasons are not always easy to discern: some wanted the war because they were concerned about Israel's long-term security; others were well connected to the oil industry and thought that Middle East oil ought to be controlled by pro-US governments; some were simply riding the post–Cold War euphoria, bent on establishing a *Pax Americana* in the Middle East; and yet others had even more expansive goals in mind, namely, to pursue a preemptive war to warn all comers in a unipolar world that they should not even be tempted to challenge America's global designs. All these rationales for attacking Iraq shared one common belief, namely, that deposing Saddam was an essential first step toward something grand, whatever that might be, including promoting democracy in the Middle East.

If Clinton in the post–Cold War period prioritized globalization as a strategy of opening up developing country economies, Bush II focused on military interventions. During the Bush II era, US military spending shot up sharply. While some of this spending financed the wars in Afghanistan and Iraq, new American military bases were also opened up in such faraway places as Kenya, Ethiopia, Turkmenistan, Kyrgyzstan, Tajikistan, Bahrain, Qatar, and Djibouti. Some of these bases were a response to the perceived threat of terrorism, others less so. By the end of the Bush II era, the United States had some seven hundred military, naval, and air bases in nearly a hundred countries.[41] In light of such evidence, it is astonishing that some observers maintain that the United States does not run, or seek to run, a global empire. With the demise of the Soviet Union, opening economies and taming insubordinate states across the world continued as key American imperial goals.

From the Debt Crisis to the Washington Consensus in Latin America

To preview what follows, I argue that the debt crisis that began in 1982 provided the occasion for the United States to demand policy reforms in Latin American countries. The United States successfully used the IMF to ensure that Latin American countries first tightened their belts, so the debt owed to American banks continued to be serviced regularly. As we have seen, although the bank profits were sustained, substantial capital was transferred out of Latin America, leading to a lost decade of development. From the standpoint of American banks, the debt crisis was more or less over by the late 1980s, when their debt exposure to Latin American countries became more manageable. However, many Latin American countries still owed large sums to American banks, and these economies remained deeply troubled. The United States then took further advantage of these vulnerabilities. The piecemeal policy reforms demanded by the United States at the outset of the debt crisis had also (say, by 1990), morphed into a full-scale development ideology of the Washington Consensus on development.[42]

Between 1982 and 1998—the year Hugo Chavez was elected the president of Venezuela, after which a series of left-leaning leaders denounced the Washington Consensus and won elections across Latin America—the United States pressured Latin American countries to embrace the Washington Consensus on development. A segment of Latin American elites was eager to cooperate. Although the prospects of renewing economic growth via these free-market policies were uncertain, two other likely outcomes drove the move toward a new economic model: the new policies promised to shift the costs of adjustment away from the Latin American elites and toward the lower strata and to future generations; and the forced opening of Latin American economies created opportunities for American economic interests. This is what followed: some economic growth returned to Latin American countries during the 1990s, but overall economic performance in Latin America in the post-1980 period (say, 1980–2005) remained anemic when compared to the region's pre-1980 performance and that of many Asian countries during the same time period.

To understand the era of debt and Washington Consensus, it may be useful to begin with some very brief background on the political economy of Latin America. After World War II, many Latin American countries experimented with democracy and import-substitution industrialization.[43] A shift toward import substitution had already begun before the war, especially during the 1930s, when an economic depression in the West limited the foreign exchange earnings of Latin American countries, thus discouraging imports of manufactured goods and encouraging national manufacturing. Following the War, Latin American middle classes forged uneasy alliances with working classes so as to diversify their respective economies, away from dependence on commodity exports.[44] Getulio Vargas and Juan Peron—in Brazil and Argentina, respectively—typified this nationalist and populist project. But these were uneasy alliances because landowning oligarchies, which depended on commodity exports for their wealth, were powerful in most of the Latin American countries, and by the same token, indigenous capitalism was relatively weak.[45] The interests of urban middle classes and those of workers also pulled in different directions. Unlike in other parts of the developing world (say, in India or China during the same period), Latin American leaders pursued easy import substitution. That is to say, rulers in Latin America were not in a position to impose overt costs on any social group to build a national industrial economy. They chose to attract foreign investors (instead of national investment, private or public) to produce consumer goods (instead of heavy industry) behind tariff walls. This model of development facilitated growth and industrialization for a few decades, along with sharp inequalities and other economic problems, which were barely held together by populist leaders.

The deepening of democracy in Latin American countries during the 1950s put pressure on the narrow ruling elite to incorporate the excluded masses. The Cuban Revolution of 1959 encouraged anti-imperial leftists in Latin America, on the one hand, and scared well-entrenched interests, on the other hand. Given the Cold War context, President Kennedy intervened in the region with the Alliance for Progress in 1961, with the hope of forestalling further revolutions and encouraging reforms. How this process of growing political polarization played out in Chile is discussed in chapter 5. It is worth recalling that the United States helped train the military forces of many Latin American countries during the 1950s. These militaries then became powerful pro-US power blocs in the region. Very simply put, when entrenched economic interests in Latin America were threatened by the mobilization of popular forces, militaries intervened in country after country during the 1960s, overthrowing civilian rulers and establishing military governments across the region.[46]

This historical background is important for the current analysis because it was these military rulers, many rather pro-US, who oversaw the growing debt of Latin American countries during the 1970s. What happened? Why did these repressive rulers, who were committed to restoring growth, bungle their respective economies so heroically? Or, maybe they did not bungle them after all, but were up against external forces that they could not control. The specific case of Brazil, arguably the most important Latin American country and also the largest debtor, may help us understand the underlying dynamics better and to take sides in rival interpretations.[47] Following the military coup in 1964, Brazilian generals were committed to the ruthless use of state power to both cower the political society and to promote economic growth. The model of development they adopted sought to continue import substitution and to diversify toward export promotion. The agents of development were mainly the state sector and foreign investors, although indigenous investors also played a role.[48] The Brazilian economy boomed under the military, so much so that the experience came to be dubbed the "Brazilian miracle." The leading sector of this miracle was foreign-investor-led growth in the production of automobiles. Concomitant with this focus was the growth in petroleum imports. Brazilian growth was thus highly import-intensive: for every 1 percent growth in the GDP, imports grew by 2 percent. As long as exports were growing, this may have been fine, but then came the OPEC-directed increases in the price of oil in 1973 and 1979.

Brazil's military rulers considered lowering their growth ambitions in the face of the adverse terms of trade caused by the increase in oil prices. However, the limited legitimacy the generals enjoyed was performance-based legitimacy, as distinct from procedural legitimacy, and it rested on their capacity to promote economic growth. Political compulsions thus pushed them to pursue rapid economic growth, which was increasingly financed by external borrowing. Interest rates on accumulating Eurodollars were relatively low and countries like Brazil, ruled by generals and with booming economies, were favored not only by the US government, but also by American bankers. Debt-led growth under such circumstances appeared to be rational. The Brazilian economy also adjusted well to the first increase in the price of oil. High levels of debt notwithstanding, the Brazilian economy sustained high levels of growth in the post-1974 period. It was the second oil-price increase that hit Brazil and many other Latin American countries hard; oil prices doubled and Brazil's share of oil imports rose from some 30 percent to 50 percent of total imports. But Brazilian leaders still did not lower their growth commitment. They continued to borrow. The generals hoped to grow their way out of the accumulating debt. This, too, might have worked. Certainly, there was much admiration for the continuing Brazilian miracle among the global investor community. Then came the Volcker Shock. The interest rates on Brazilian debt rose dramatically in 1981, to 17 percent to 18 percent per annum. Even this might have been manageable, but then access to finance dried up when Mexico's inability to service its debt in 1982 created a herd-like panic among American bankers.

The roots of debt crisis in all Latin American countries had some unique features, including in Brazil. Nevertheless, the Brazilian path to the crisis highlights a feature that many Latin American countries shared, namely, that borrowing for growth made some sense during the 1970s. This was especially the case for Latin American countries with low domestic-savings rates, which have often depended on foreign savings to sustain economic growth. It was also not the case that leaders of Latin America used foreign borrowing irresponsibly, only to pursue import substitution, or worse, channeled the loans toward consumption. This may have been true for a case here or there, but as the Brazilian case underscores, leaders on balance sought to invest in productive activities, with the hope of promoting domestic production and exports. Both American bankers and the American government supported these efforts; they were keen that Eurodollars circulate, because this process helped the profits of banks, on the one hand, and, on the other hand, it helped to sustain growth in the American economy, which was increasingly less competitive in manufacturing goods and looked to finance as the more dynamic sector. The tragedy was that when the project of debt-led growth went awry in Latin America, the costs were not shared among the principal instigators of the drama. Instead, the US government used its hegemonic position to ensure that American banks did not fail. Sections of Latin American

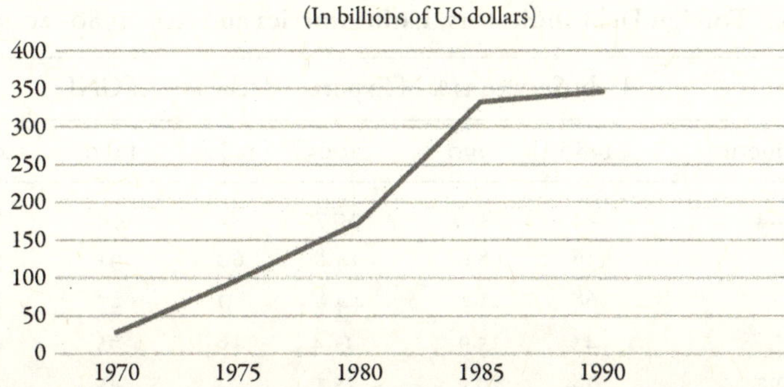

FIGURE 6.2 Total Latin American debt outstanding, 1970–1990.
Source: World Bank, *World Debt Tables, 1991–92*, vol. 1, *External Debt of Developing Countries*, p. 136. (Washington, DC: World Bank, 1991).

elites cooperated in implementing US-sponsored adjustment strategies, as long as the costs of debt-repayments were shifted to the less well-off citizens of Latin America.

With the ready availability of petrodollars in the post-1974 period, American banks lent and Latin American countries borrowed heavily. As is clear in Figure 6.2, the debt rose rapidly from the mid-1970s on, at a rate of some 24 percent per annum.[49] Latin American debt in 1982—around the time Mexico nearly defaulted—approached $200 billion (or more than a half-trillion in 2018 dollars). Four Latin American countries incurred nearly half of this debt: Brazil, Mexico, Argentina, and Venezuela. Moreover, nine banks lent 65 percent of the money lent by American banks.[50] The debt was thus highly concentrated: nine American banks and four Latin American countries constituted the core of the crisis. Two other characteristics of this debt should be underlined. First, 75 percent of this debt had floating interest rates, tied to Libor. The implication is obvious: once interest rates rose, so would the costs of servicing the debt. It is thus clear in Figure 6.2 that post-1982, when Latin American countries took out very few new commercial loans, the overall debt level kept rising (also see Table 6.1), both because of the enhanced cost of the debt and the new loans (mostly official, such as from the IMF) needed to keep servicing the old debt. Second, nearly 80 percent of the debt was sovereign debt; that is, it was either incurred by Latin American governments or was private debt but guaranteed by these governments.[51] The significance of this is that the problem of debt for Latin American countries was not only a foreign exchange problem but also one of mobilizing national resources to pay off the foreign debt. Balance-of-payment deficits and budgetary deficits were thus closely linked.

Table 6.1 Foreign Debt Indicators, Latin America and Asia, 1980–2005

	Debt Service as % of Exports			Debt as % of GNI		
Latin America	**1980**	**1990**	**2005**	**1980**	**1990**	**2005**
Argentina	42	37	20.7	36	46	75
Bolivia	36	38.6	14.8	60	92	77
Brazil	68	22.2	44.8	31	27	22
Chile	45	25.9	15.4	46	65	42
Columbia	18	40.9	35.3	21	45	29
Ecuador	35	32.5	30.6	52	132	49
Mexico	51	20.7	17.2	31	41	22
Peru	46	10.8	26.0	48	79	39
Venezuela	30	23.3	9.1	44	72	32
Average	**41.2**	**28.0**	**24.0**	**41**	**66**	**71**
Asia	**1980**	**1990**	**2005**	**1980**	**1990**	**2005**
Bangladesh	26	25.8	5.3	22	40	30
China	4	11.7	3.1	—	16	12
India	10	31.9	19.1	11	27	15
Indonesia	14	33.0	22.0	28	64	48
Malaysia	7	12.6	5.6	27	36	40
Pakistan	18	21.3	10.2	39	50	30
Philippines	29	27.0	16.7	54	69	58
South Korea	20	11.3	—	55	13	24
Taiwan	—	0.5	4.9	14	11	26
Thailand	20	16.9	14.6	26	33	30
Vietnam	—	—	2.6	—	—	37
Average	**16.4**	**19.2**	**10.4**	**31**	**36**	**32**

Sources: Most data for debt service as a percentage of exports is from United Nations, *Human Development Report*, various years. Data for Taiwan and for South Korea (1990) is from the Asian Development Bank. Most data for debt as percentage of gross national income (GNI) is from online development indicators of the World Bank. The data for South Korea and Taiwan (1990, 2005) is from the Asian Development Bank. The South Korean and Taiwanese data for 1980 is actually from 1983 and is taken from Albert Fishlow, "Some Reflections on Comparative Latin American Economic Performance and Policy" (Wider Working Papers, 22, August 1987, Table 1).

As noted earlier, in 1981 the US Federal Reserve Bank started pursuing a tight monetary policy. This led to high interest rates. The debt service costs of Latin American countries then skyrocketed. Mexico was the first one to plead an inability to pay in 1982. While the IMF and the US Federal reserve took early initiatives to ensure that a default did not trigger a broader financial crisis, the US government—in cooperation with the exposed banks—quickly took the lead in both diagnosing and prescribing solutions to the crisis.[52] The "primary concern" of the United States was the "risk" that a series of defaults might cause to "the major U.S. commercial banks;" by contrast, the "economic and political disarray within the debtor countries" that might result from proposed solutions was, for the most part, "ignored."[53] The die for the proposed set of solutions was cast rather early, as the United States dealt with a potential Mexican default.[54] The rescheduling of debt from then on would ensure that the indebted countries had enough financial resources to continue to service their debts. Since commercial loans had mostly vanished, new loans would come either from such official institutions as the IMF or from some remaining commercial sources, but only after a sort of good housekeeping seal of approval from the IMF. In return, indebted countries would have to tighten their belts, or implement demand-compression policies, starting with trimming budget deficits and then moving to deeper reforms. Demand compression would reduce imports and thus save foreign exchange for debt payments. If these policies hurt economic growth in indebted countries, so be it.

After 1982, the United States sought to ensure—rather vigorously—that the debts owed to American banks by Latin Americans were serviced regularly. The US government helped pull together a coalition of all those who were owed money, especially major American banks, but also European and Japanese banks. The United States used the IMF as the main organization to implement debt rescheduling and the related austerity programs on indebted countries. In the words of Gilpin, a keen observer of power relations, "the creditors successfully imposed their will on the debtors."[55] While the creditors formed a cartel, of sorts, similar efforts by debtors failed to cohere. I return below to a discussion of the efforts of Latin American countries—mostly in vain—to come together to forge a Cartagena Consensus in lieu of the Washington Consensus on how to deal with debt. The creditor's coalition chose instead to negotiate with the indebted countries one by one, offering promises here and threats there. The main mechanism to deal with the debt crisis was thus the classic imperial strategy of "divide and conquer,"[56] even though now the foot soldiers of conquest were IMF economists, armed with equations and PowerPoint presentations, aimed at developing-country finance ministers. While PowerPoint presentations maybe new, pressure to ensure debt repayment is not; we thus noticed in chapter 2 how Britain enforced debt collection in countries as diverse as Argentina, Egypt and

China. Of course, much had changed in the intervening years, but coercive pressure on finance ministers at the periphery to ensure that the debt of metropolitan bankers is paid off has a long history.

The United States in the mid-1980s transformed the IMF from a Keynesian agency, designed originally to deal with global market imperfections, into a debt-collecting organization that now purveyed free-market ideologies.[57] This transformation was deliberate. Reagan appointed James Baker—first, his chief of staff, and then his secretary of the treasury—to deal with the debt crisis. Baker and others in turn saw in the "IMF and other financial institutions an opportunity to advance important US objectives, such as keeping indebted Third World governments from defaulting on their obligations to US banks, and persuading them to open their economies to trade, investment, and private enterprise."[58] Baker then targeted the IMF to pursue US objectives: "[U]nder our proposals, debtor nations such as Mexico, Argentina, Brazil, and Venezuela will receive new IMF or World Bank loans only if they adopt and begin implementation of 'supply-side' policies to reattract flight capital and foreign investment, reduce the relative share of public investment, and provide market incentives for long-term growth . . . We do envision a central role for the IMF."[59] The management of the IMF embraced these pressures from its major shareholder and turned them into a new economic ideology: in addition to stabilizing the macro economy, countries restructuring their loans would now have to undertake such deep microeconomic changes as deregulation, liberalization, and privatization. Instead of pausing to ask if such deep interventions in the political economy of other countries violated global norms of sovereignty, the IMF asked instead, "[H]ow ambitious should we be in seeking to overhaul the institutional elements of a country's economy?"[60]

The United States and the IMF evolved their approach to the debt crisis without paying too much attention to the needs of the indebted countries. Latin American countries quickly sensed that the Washington-based "solutions" to the debt crisis would put the onus mainly on them, sparing the banks, and would also hurt the growth of their respective economies. Meeting in Cartagena in June 1984, the major indebted countries came up with an alternate proposal that assured the creditors that their debts would be paid, but also argued that the costs of the debt ought to be shared and that the policy reform should be pro-growth. The analysis at the heart of this "Cartagena Consensus" was that the debt problem was really a growth problem caused by restrictive economic policies of the United States. Any solution to the debt problem should thus avoid severe austerity programs that would further sacrifice economic growth in Latin American countries.[61] Whatever the truth value of this alternate analysis, the political position of Latin American countries was relatively weak. As is often the case, the views that prevailed were those of the powerful.

There is some evidence to suggest that the United States and the IMF pressured Latin American countries to undertake structural adjustments, knowing that the policies would ensure debt repayment but not economic growth in these countries. Even if this claim is a tad too strong, doubts about the growth-promoting impact of structural adjustment policies were certainly entertained at the highest levels. For example, Ernest Stern, then a vice president at the World Bank, noted the Bank's pessimism in 1984 about "the adjustment process and the resumption of growth."[62] Joseph Stiglitz argued much more strongly, in retrospect of course, that IMF's policy prescriptions for the developing world were never meant to be growth promoting; their primary goal, instead, was to ensure debt repayment to major banks.[63] Recent research has also documented that the representatives of the US government were aware in the post-1982 period that "belt tightening" and "getting prices right" would not promote economic growth and yet chose to "package" neoliberal policies in the rhetoric of growth promotion. Such "rhetorical strategy," according to recent evidence, "had been purposefully devised at the top of the U.S. treasury."[64] And, of course, if anyone in Washington listened to developing countries, the message was loud and clear: demand compression would create recessions rather than growth.

The main concern of the US government and of the IMF in the post-1982 period was that American banks did not suffer. This they achieved heroically, and then some. The incomes (from1980 to1986) of the top ten US banks exposed in the Latin American debt crisis are recorded in Figure 6.3. It is clear that not only

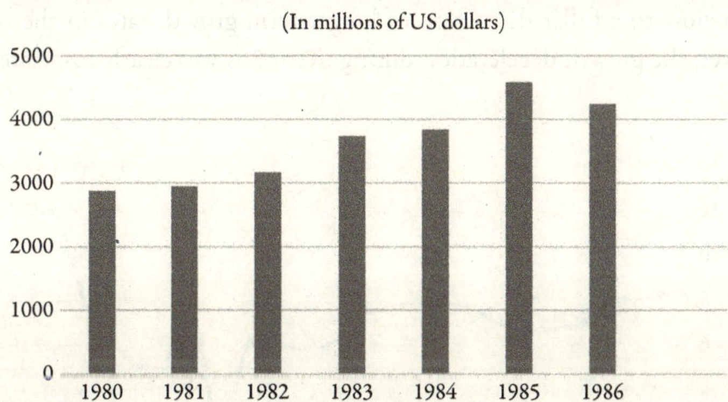

FIGURE 6.3 Incomes of top ten US banks, 1980–1986.

Source: Calculated from data in Sachs and Huizinga, "U.S. Commercial Banks and the Developing Country Debt Crisis," table 7 (p.56). The banks included are Citicorp, Bank America, Chase Manhattan, Manufacturers Hanover, J. P. Morgan, Chemical, Security Pacific, First Interstate, Bankers Trust, and First Chicago. These ten banks lent nearly 70 percent of the total money lent by US banks to Latin America.

did the banks not suffer, but their incomes also continued to rise in the post-1982 period. Moreover, bank stocks during these years paralleled the index of stock prices during these years.[65] As far as the banks were concerned, the crisis had been averted. This does not mean that Latin American countries quickly paid off their debts. Instead, it only suggests that the debts continued to be serviced. Over these years it also became clear that the principal on the loans was never likely to be paid back; for example, the value of the Latin American debt on secondary markets declined sharply, to less than half the original value, by 1987.[66] US banks then took a hit in 1987, when many of them wrote off part of these loans. The related decline in the return on bank assets in 1987 is evident in Figure 6.4. What is also noteworthy in Figure 6.4, however, is the quick recovery of bank incomes. The return on banking assets has grown steadily from 1990 onward. This trend is consistent with the earlier observation about the growing importance of finance in American economy from the 1970s onward.

Latin American countries paid dearly to ensure that the incomes of American banks did not suffer. Between 1982 and 1987, for example, the conditions imposed by the United States and the IMF on Latin American countries led to a net transfer of some 4 percent to 5 percent of the region's GDP per year to service the debt of American banks.[67] This was international usury on a grand scale. According to one set of scholars, the net transfer of resources from Latin America during this period exceeded even that "recorded by Germany after the First World War, when it had to pay war reparations to the allies."[68] If economic growth in the region prior to the debt crisis (say, 1975–1982) was over 4 percent per annum, this growth rate decelerated to 2 percent per annum during 1983–1989.[69] (I return below to a fuller discussion of longer-term growth rates in the region.) Moreover, the growth deceleration during the 1980s was clearly associated with

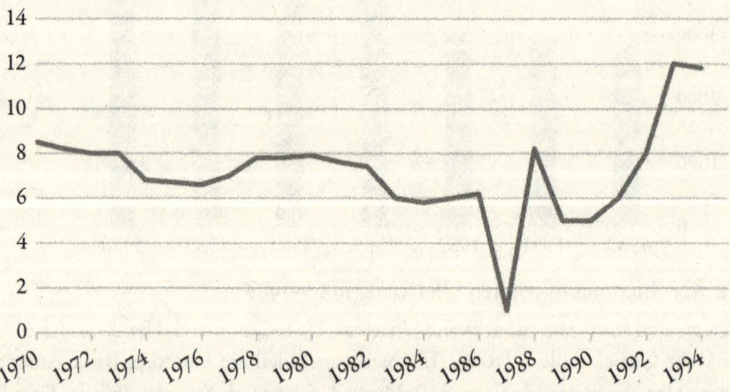

FIGURE 6.4 Return on assets, US banking industry, 1970–1994 (in %).
Source: World Bank, *An Examination of the Banking Crisis*, p. 209.

a decline in capital formation, which resulted from "external shocks," rather than from any decline in national savings.[70] Between 1982 and 1985 alone, per capita incomes in the region—already mired in poverty, inequality, and teetering military governments—declined by some 10 percent. In light of such evidence, it is incredible that the World Bank concluded in 1994 that the "strategy" pursued by the United States and the international financial institutions (IFIs) vis-à-vis the Latin American debt crisis was "successful;"[71] clearly, the World Bank's idea of success was that a meltdown of US banks was avoided. A scholarly conclusion about the role of IMF and the World Bank is more appropriate instead: the approach of the IFIs mainly served "the political interests of the major shareholders, especially the United States, and by extension, of the commercial banks."[72]

The United States and the American banks considered the debt crisis to be more or less over by the end of the 1980s. The US Federal Reserve started lowering interest rates in 1990 and maintained that trend for several years.[73] The cost of servicing debts for Latin American countries thus declined (see Table 6.1). The inflow of dollars into Latin America also resumed. The IMF-imposed policy changes in Latin American countries may have increased the confidence of the Wall Street in these countries. More likely, however, the dollar inflow into Latin America in the 1990s was driven by a recession and low interest rates in the United States.[74] The sharp differential in interest rates made Latin American countries more attractive for Americans seeking higher rates of return. It is telling that the resumption of US financial flows into Latin America in the early 1990s were not loans from US commercial banks or direct foreign investment, but a variety of pension and hedge funds chasing higher interest rates. These inflows did ease the liquidity concerns, but, as we will see, their impact on economic growth in Latin America was mixed at best.

As the debt crisis was easing in Latin America, the world changed. With the end of the Cold War, neoliberal ideas became triumphant during the 1990s. As noted, President Clinton and his advisers prioritized economic issues and then put enormous pressure on countries—where they had some leverage, of course—to open up their economies to American goods and capital. The pressure on Latin American countries to embrace free-market models of development was then enormous. What had begun as policy reform aimed at easing the debt crisis now became the full-blown ideology of development of the Washington Consensus, which has also been described as neoliberalism. A section of the Latin American elite even cooperated—more willingly in some countries, merely acquiescing in others—with the United States and the IFIs to move Latin America in these new directions. To understand this willy-nilly cooperation, it may be worth recalling that debates over appropriate development strategies were hardly new in Latin America. With the rise of dependency theory in the 1950s, for example, the debates between structuralists and monetarists were a perennial feature of the Latin American economic thinking. Since these debates had distributional consequences, they readily overlapped with political debates between the left and the right. What the debt crisis did was to discredit the prevailing model of development, with its focus on state intervention and import substitution. Pressure from the United States and the IFIs then strengthened the hands of pro-market elites at the expense of nationalist and leftist forces in Latin America. The new development agenda was now to roll back the state.

The core policy prescriptions associated with the Washington Consensus on development are well known and not worth repeating in any detail here.[75] The argument was that growth and distribution in Latin America would both be better served by shrinking the state, including privatization, getting various prices right (especially exchange and interest rates), and opening economies to foreign goods, investment and finance—especially finance. Moves toward such neoliberal policies had already begun in one country or another in Latin America, say, for example, in Chile following the coup in 1973. The debt crisis provided an opportunity for the IFIs to press these policies more broadly, in exchange for new loans and restructuring debt. As discussed, there were doubts—even within the IFIs—about whether such policies would help resume growth in Latin America. Such doubts did not gain much traction, however, because of the more pressing need to rescue American banks. What is worth underscoring is that even after the debt crisis eased for the banks, such doubts were again forgotten—or at least not raised openly—among the powerful policymakers in Washington. Globalization was the new, self-serving agenda of Washington in the post–Cold War world, and opening economies worldwide was the specific goal. The importance of finance in the American economy was growing during this period and the Clinton presidency manifested the new American urgency to liberalize finance. The debt crisis was over in Latin America, but opening Latin American economies for the long haul—for their own good, of course—was the new goal of US decisionmakers and the IFIs in the 1990s, and there was a growing concern with financial liberalization.

While the globalization agenda was indeed global, Latin American countries were especially vulnerable to American pressures. The underlying reasons were both political and economic. A contrast with some of the more important countries of Asia will help underscore the more dependent nature of Latin American political economies.[76] Debt indicators of select Latin American and Asian countries are presented in Table 6.1. A number of observations are in order. First, the debt service to export ratio in Latin America in the post-1980 period did decline, but it was still more than double that of Asian countries by 2005. More telling is the second observation: the debt in relation to national income continued to rise in Latin America throughout this period and was again more than double that of the Asian average by 2005. These high levels of debt meant that Latin American countries still had to periodically enter into debt-related negotiations with the IFIs throughout the 1990s. What made Latin American countries more desperate to reach agreements with the IFIs was another background condition: relatively low rates of domestic savings. For example, the savings rate of Latin American countries in 2000 averaged some 20 percent (or 18.4 percent without the oil-rich Venezuela), whereas the average in Asia was 29 percent (or 28 percent without China).[77] Latin American countries thus had much greater need for foreign savings to sustain high rates of growth. Foreign investors, in turn, often wanted assurances from the IMF or the Word Bank or both that specific countries were "reformed" enough to offer safe and attractive investment opportunities. The options for Latin American countries were, then, limited: either agree to policy reforms prescribed by the IFIs or risk alienating foreign investors. Most Latin American countries then embraced—again, some more ardently than others, of course—the Washington Consensus on development during the 1990s.[78]

What were the costs and benefits of the spread of the Washington Consensus for both the United States and for Latin America? The impact of how the debt crisis of the 1980s was settled is discussed above. Since the debt was relatively concentrated—with some nine-ten American banks and a handful of Latin American countries as the main actors—it is easier to trace the winners and the losers, with the evidence suggesting that the US government rescued American banks at the expense of Latin American countries. By contrast, the spread of the Washington Consensus was a more diffuse phenomenon. Who benefited and who lost is thus more difficult to establish. With this caveat, the impact on Latin America is easier to trace than the impact on the United States; this is because the United States plays a much more significant role in Latin America than Latin America does in the United States. Still, it is valid to ask if the United States achieved what it hoped to achieve by pressuring Latin American countries to roll back state intervention in their economies. When we look at the changing patterns of US trade and capital flows with Latin America, the evidence suggests that the changes indeed moved in the direction of benefiting American economic interests.

Figure 6.5 depicts the aggregate pattern of US exports to Latin America during 1985 and 2005. US exports to Latin America jumped sharply around 1990 and remained at a fairly high level during the 1990s. Clearly, the heyday of Washington Consensus in Latin America was good for US exporters. Toward the end of the period under consideration, Chinese goods started entering Latin America and put pressure on US exports to the region; the resulting downward trend is also evident in Figure 6.5. In and of itself, growth in US exports to Latin

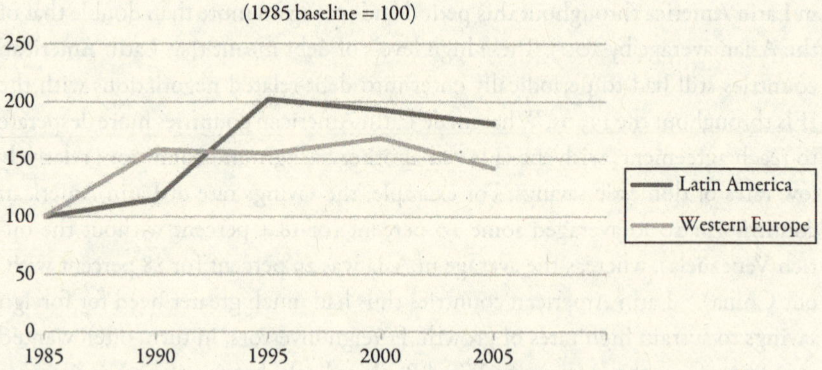

FIGURE 6.5 US exports to Latin America and Western Europe, 1985–2005.
Source: My calculations, based on data from the United States Census Bureau. The original data was in nominal prices. I used the consumer price index to change the data into 1985 prices (in millions of dollars) and then used 1985 as the base of 100 to create a growth index.

America does not tell us very much about costs and benefits of this trade; this could merely be a good, liberal story of all boats rising with growing trade. But it is important to note that US exports to Latin America grew in the context of serious balance-of-payment pressures and sluggish economic growth in Latin America.[79] Latin American commodity exports also grew but barely managed to pay for imports while the levels of foreign debt (as a share of the national income) in Latin America continued to rise (see Table 6.1). Clearly, US exports to Latin America grew despite continuing economic problems in the latter.

As important is that US exports to Western Europe, its main traditional market, remained relatively sluggish during this period (see Figure 6.5). In a way, then, the United States was compensating for a declining share in its traditional markets with the forced opening of Latin America. The United States exported high-tech equipment and industrial goods to Latin America: For example, automobiles and related parts went mainly to Colombia, Chile, Mexico, and Venezuela; telecommunication equipment went to Argentina, Mexico, Paraguay, and Venezuela; computers went to Argentina, Brazil, Colombia, Chile, and Paraguay; and aircraft and related equipment went to Argentina, Brazil, and Colombia.[80] It is worth recalling that these were the types of high value-added products for which the United States faced increasing competition, not only in Western Europe, but also from Japan, South Korea, and Taiwan. US capital flows into Latin America during this period are recorded in Figures 6.6 and 6.7.[81] Both the graphs underscore the well-known fact that capital flows into Latin America, both direct investments and portfolio investments, dried up in the aftermath of the debt crisis. As we have seen, these capital flows resumed again in the late 1980s when the debt

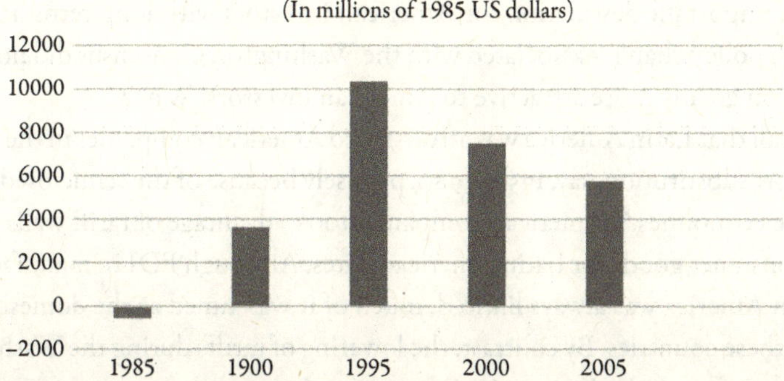

FIGURE 6.6 US direct investment in Latin America, 1985–2005.
Source: My calculations, based on data from the United States Department of Commerce, Bureau of Economic Analysis. The original data was in nominal prices. I used the consumer price index to change the data into 1985 prices.

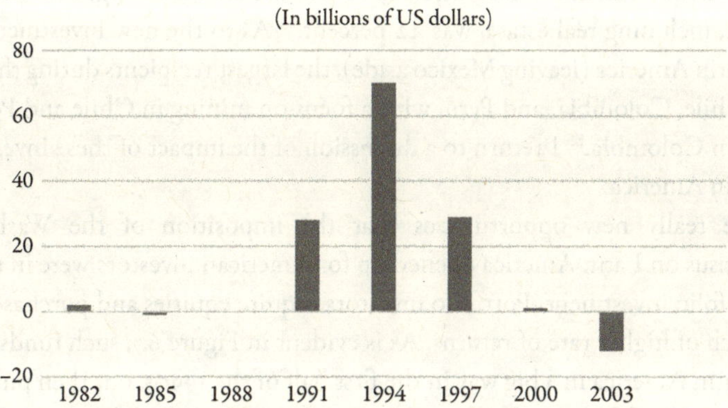

FIGURE 6.7 Portfolio investment in Latin America, 1982–2003.
Source: Based on data from Graciela L. Kaminsky, "International Capital Flows, Financial Stability and Growth," *United Nations, Department of Economic and Social Affairs*, Working Paper No. 10, ST/ESA/2005/DWP/10, 2005. The data should be treated as broadly indicative of trends rather than precise.

crisis eased; the Latin American economies were forced to reform—especially enabling free movement of capital from abroad; and interest rates in the United States declined in relation to those in Latin America. American foreign direct investment (FDI) in Latin America increased after 1990, and then went down again after 2000, but none of this was dramatic. The real dramatic shifts were in portfolio investment, and I will return to that issue. Meanwhile, the stock of US FDI in Latin America as a share of its global stock remained more or less stable, in the 10 percent to 12 percent range, during the 1990s.[82] While Latin America was thus an important destination for American investors with long-term horizons, even the policy changes associated with the Washington Consensus did not make the region greatly more attractive to American investors. Why?

Recall that Latin America was attractive to American companies in the heyday of import substitution, say, 1950–1980, precisely because of the semiclosed nature of those economies.[83] American companies took advantage of tariff walls to produce consumer goods for Latin American elites. Although FDI in manufacturing in Latin America was always limited, much of it was aimed at the domestic markets of these countries. By contrast, the lowering of tariffs during the Washington Consensus years in Latin America is better for American exporters of goods than it is for direct investors. In addition, given the higher wages, Latin America does not provide as attractive a base for exports as many of the lower-wage countries of Asia. The result is that US investments in manufacturing in Latin America continue to be limited.[84] For example, only 30 percent of the stock of US foreign investment in Latin America in 2000 was in manufacturing, whereas that in finance, including real estate, was 42 percent.[85] As to the new investment flows into Latin America (leaving Mexico aside), the largest recipients during the 1990s were Chile, Colombia, and Peru, with a focus on mining in Chile and Peru and on oil in Colombia.[86] I return to a discussion of the impact of these investments on Latin America.

The really new opportunities that the imposition of the Washington Consensus on Latin America opened up for American investors were in the area of portfolio investment. Portfolio investors acquire equities and purchase bonds in search of higher rate of returns. As is evident in Figure 6.7, such funds moved into Latin America in a big way in the first half of the 1990s, but then pulled out just as rapidly following the second financial crisis in Mexico in 1996, and even more sharply, following the Asian financial crisis in 1997. A notable characteristic of these investments is their volatility. They come and they go as they please. That is the whole point of the Washington-based demand that developing countries should remove all capital controls if they want access to savings from advanced industrial countries. Clinton and Rubin worked with the IMF to push the liberalization of capital markets in the developing world throughout the 1990s. The realization that such speculative investment can play havoc on developing-country economies is growing across the developing world.[87] Meanwhile, from the US perspective, the more open the world is for portfolio investors, the better it is for the American financial sector, as well as for the finance-dependent American economy.

Last, how do we assess the impact of Washington Consensus policies on Latin American patterns of development? We need to proceed cautiously here because policies demanded by Washington—the US government, the World Bank, and the IMF—were accepted unevenly across a vast region. Causal connections are difficult to trace because patterns of both economic growth and inequality are produced by a variety of complex underlying factors. Bounded by these caveats, a few claims can be made.[88] The economic performance of Latin America between 1980 and 2005 was pretty dismal (see Table 6.2): during these 25 years—arguably the heyday of Washington Consensus—the economies of the region grew at an average low rate of 2.5 percent per annum. The population of the region during these years grew at an average rate of 1.8 percent per annum. Per capita income of the population grew at less than 1 percent per annum for the duration. Even if we set aside the lost decade of the 1980s—though we should not, since the IMF and US policymakers promised that the debt-reduction strategy it was offering would be growth enhancing—per capita incomes in the region grew at only a little more than 1 percent per annum during 1990–2005. Income inequality in the region toward the end of the period was also extremely high, and urban unemployment in the major countries of the region had grown from some 7 percent in 1980 to 13 percent in 2002.[89]

How dismal was this performance? Since all assessments of economic performance are relative, it may be helpful to compare Latin America's record during the Washington Consensus years to not only its own earlier record, but also to Asian countries during the same period that pursued a more nationalist model of development, premised on significant state intervention. It is clear in Table 6.2 that the average economic growth rate of Latin American countries during 1965–1980 was some 5 percent per annum, or double the growth rate during 1980–2005. The ISI period in retrospect, then, does not look as bad as the neoliberal supporters of the Washington Consensus made it out to be. The comparison of Latin American with Asian countries during the post-1980 period is even more revealing. As documented in Table 6.2, the economies of the important Asian countries grew at an average rate of 5.9 percent per annum (or 5.5 percent, without the Chinese outlier), more than double than the rate of Latin American countries during 1980–2005. And they did so with much more modest levels of inequalities: At the end of the period under consideration, the ratio of earnings of the top and bottom 20 percent in Latin America was nearly 20 (or 18, without the Bolivian outlier) to 7 in Asia.

In light of these facts, it would be very difficult for supporters of Washington Consensus to claim that policies prescribed by the United States, the IMF, and the World Bank helped facilitate either growth or equality in Latin America.[90] The question that does remain is whether the Washington Consensus was indeed responsible for Latin America's poor economic performance during the quarter century following the debt crisis of 1982. To restate the caveat offered earlier, the causal connections are not straightforward. Latin America has a long history of

Table 6.2 Growth and Inequality in Latin America and Asia, 1965–2005

Annual GDP Growth (%)				Income Inequality
Latin America	1965–1980	1980–2005	1990–2005	(ratio, top 20% to bottom 20%)
Argentina	3.4	1.8	3.6	17.8
Bolivia	4.4	2.1	3.7	42.3
Brazil	9.0	2.7	2.7	21.8
Chile	1.9	4.4	5.8	15.7
Colombia	5.7	3.2	3.0	25.3
Ecuador	6.3	2.6	3.0	17.3
Mexico	6.5	2.1	2.7	12.4
Peru	3.9	2.6	4.6	15.2
Venezuela	3.7	1.3	1.5	16.0
Average	5.0	2.5	3.4	20.4
Asia	1965–1980	1980–2005	1990–2005	(ratio, top 20% to bottom 20%)
Bangladesh	—	4.4	5	4.9
China	7.3	10.2	10.3	12.2
India	3.0	6.1	6.3	5.6
Indonesia	7.0	5.1	4.4	5.2
Malaysia	7.4	5.9	6.3	12.4
Pakistan	6.1	5.4	4.1	4.3
Philippines	5.7	2.7	3.8	9.3
South Korea	10.0	7.0	5.4	4.7
Taiwan	10.0	5.5	5.0	6.1
Thailand	7.3	5.8	4.6	7.7
Vietnam	—	6.8	7.8	4.9
Average	7.1	5.9	5.7	7.0

Sources: The GDP growth data (1980–2005) is calculated from the World Bank, *World Development Indicators*. The earlier growth data (1965–80) is taken from Carlos Aquino Rodriguez, "Differences in the Economic Development of Latin America and East Asian Countries," paper presented at a conference of the Latin America–Caribbean and Asia-Pacific Economic and Business Association (LAEBA), Tokyo (Sept. 29–30, 2003). The growth data for Taiwan is from the Asian Development Bank and is approximate. The growth data for Vietnam is from 1985–2005. The income inequality data is taken from the United Nations, *Human Development Report*, 2007/8. The income inequality data for Taiwan is from the Asian Development Bank. The averages are simple and not weighted averages; GDP weighted averages would be swamped by China and India, and in most cases, would support my argument even more strongly.

economic booms, busts, and sharp inequalities; path dependence would suggest that these trends are likely to be sticky. Nevertheless, the pressures from Washington led the Latin American countries to open their economies, shrink their states, and embrace a more laissez faire model of development. Latin American countries also continued to depend heavily on foreign resources to finance their growth. This dependent model contrasts with the more nationalist models pursued in most Asian countries during this period. States in most Asian countries remained important economic actors. National economic resources in Asian countries primarily drove economic growth. The global integration that Asian countries sought was also strategic, aimed more at capturing export markets and less at opening their capital markets to the advantage of foreigners. On balance, the more nationalist models pursued in Asia produced impressive economic growth with modest inequalities. To the extent that Washington pressured Latin American countries to embrace a more dependent, laissez faire approach to development, Washington Consensus was partially responsible for the region's poor economic performance during the period under consideration.

It is clear in Figure 6.8 that countries with high foreign debt in 1980—mostly in Latin America—grew at lower rates than most Asian countries with less debt. One underlying mechanism linking debt to growth—in the 1980s at least—has already been suggested, namely, that debt repayments led directly to lower rates of capital formation and thus to lower economic growth in Latin American countries. For the period as a whole, an additional and more indirect point should also be underscored. High levels of debt made Latin American countries more vulnerable to policy pressures from Washington than were countries in Asia; debt restructuring by the IMF and the World Bank was always conditioned on policy reform. This vulnerability was enhanced by the fact that most Latin American countries saved less than the Asian countries. These lower savings are evident in Figure 6.9, as is the association between higher rates of domestic savings and higher economic growth in much of Asia. In sum, high foreign debt and low domestic savings made Latin American countries dependent on foreign resources, both over the short run to maintain debt servicing and over the longer term to resume and sustain economic growth. This dependence limited the policy autonomy of the Latin American countries. The policies prescribed by Washington served Washington's interests first, and hurt the prospects of sustained growth with equity in Latin America.

Having greater policy autonomy, what did Asian countries do differently during this period from countries in Latin America? The issue is clearly complex, not only because Asia and Latin America are both diverse regions, but also because economic policies in the two regions differed on numerous dimensions, and some of the key differences predated the period under consideration. This is

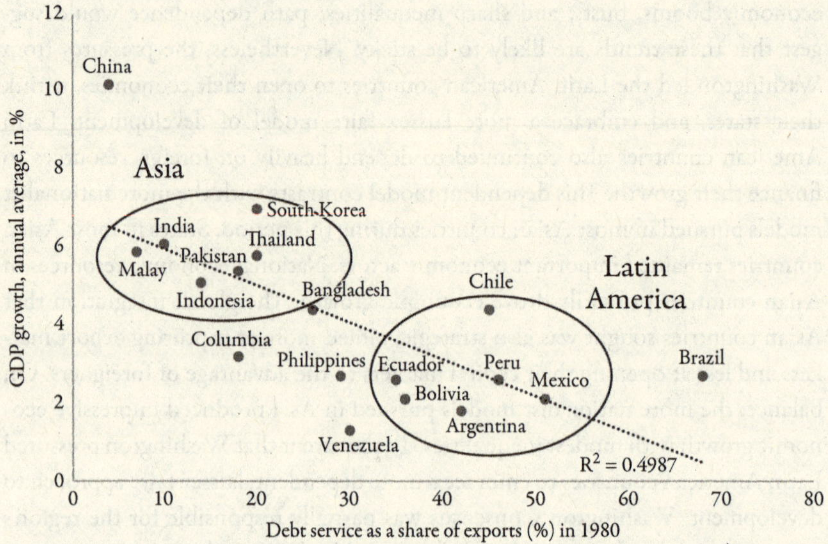

FIGURE 6.8 Foreign debt and GDP growth, Latin America and Asia, 1980–2005.
Source: Data from Kohli, "Nationalist versus Dependent Capitalist Development," tables 1 and 3. The 'R-squared' without China is 0.4417.

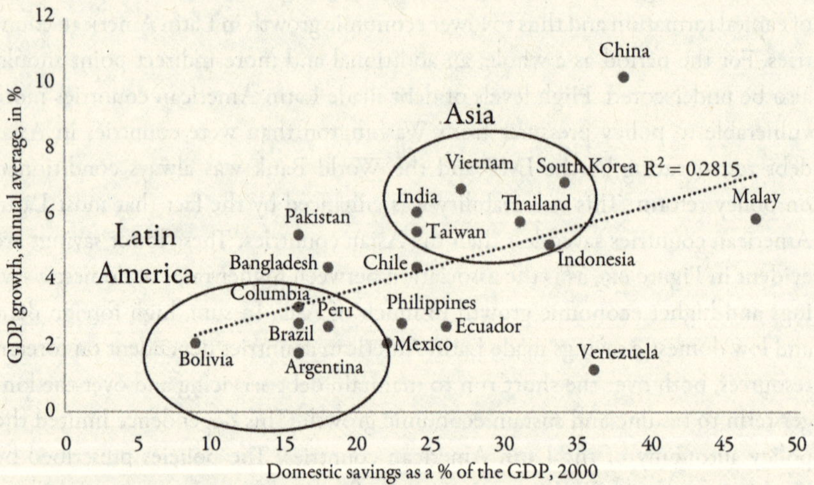

FIGURE 6.9 Domestic savings and GDP growth, Latin America and Asia, 1980–2005.
Source: Data from Kohli, "Nationalist versus Dependent Capitalist Development," tables 1 and 2. The 'R-squared' without the two outliers China and Venezuela is 0.3952.

also no place for a detailed comparison of Asian and Latin American development strategies.[91] The main point to note is that the development models of Asia and Latin America during this period differed significantly. On balance, and to repeat, Asian countries pursued a nationalist capitalist model of development, while Latin American countries were pressured to continue along a dependent capitalist path.[92] Asian countries created economies with high domestic-savings rates, the careful channeling of foreign investment into priority areas, significant capacity to export manufactured goods, and limited foreign debt. These economic trends emerged from the planned activities of effective national states and helped to stimulate economic growth with equity. By contrast, many countries in Latin America that were pressured into embracing the Washington Consensus remained more dependent on the global economy, with lower domestic savings rates, smaller roles for national capital, higher dependence on foreign capital to supplement limited mobilization of domestic resources, exports focused on lower value-added commodities, and relatively high levels of foreign debt. These trends, too, resulted from the policy choices of different types of states at the helm in Latin America, ones that were less effective, had sharp elite-mass gaps, and were more globally complicit. We have seen the poor economic results of this model.

One key difference across Asia and Latin America that is worth emphasizing is the focus in Asia on manufacturing. Active states in most of the Asian countries deliberately encouraged a shift to higher value-added goods during this period, especially for exports. The results are evident in Figure 6.10. The exports of Asian countries—of low-wage countries like Bangladesh, as well as of higher-wage countries like South Korea—were mostly manufactured goods. By contrast, the exports of Latin America, which grew considerably during this period, remained largely commodities. Mexico was the one significant exception to this trend in Latin America; the maquiladora type of investments facilitated by NAFTA help explain much of Mexico's manufactured exports back to the United States. For the rest, forced trade openness during this period created serious disincentives for manufacturing within Latin America. We have seen the commensurate increase in the exports of manufactured goods from the United States to Latin America in the post-1990 period. Desperately in need of foreign capital flows, Latin American countries were also in no position to demand that foreign investors promote manufactured exports. That new foreign investment during this period moved into commodities is also documented here. But the impact of the portfolio investments on actual production is hard to trace. What we do know is that the volatile nature of such investments has been a source of periodic financial and related economic difficulties in the region.

Last, to return to a central theme of this study: if Latin Americans have indeed pursued a more dependent model of development in comparison to

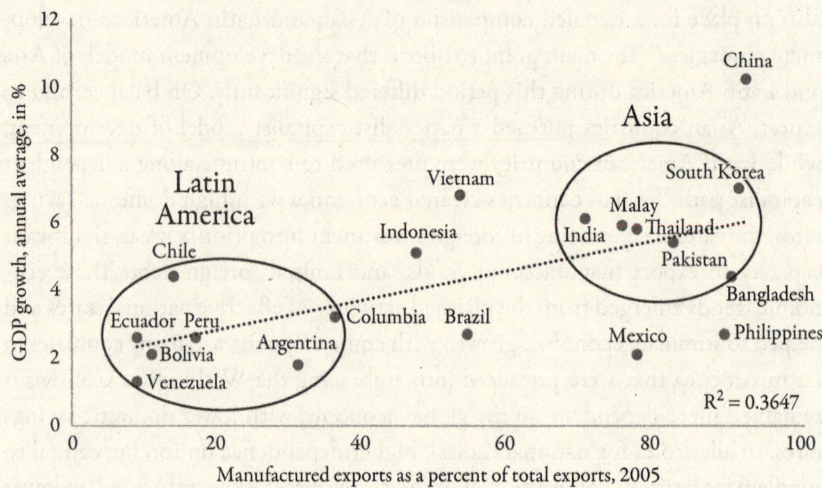

FIGURE 6.10 Manufactured exports and GDP growth, Latin America and Asia, 1980–2005.

Source: Data from Kohli, "Nationalist versus Dependent Capitalist Development," tables 1 and 5. The 'R-squared' without China is 0.3152.

countries in Asia, what are the deeper determinants of these alternate paths? My main proposition is that the origins of the differing pathways traversed by Asia and Latin America are political, rooted in differing patterns of state intervention that reflect the different processes of state formation in the two regions around the period of World War II. Decolonization in Asia created significant political discontinuities, which led to modified class relations, altered external relations, and more nationalist development choices. By contrast, there was no such discontinuity in Latin America in the post–World War II period; state and class formations modified, of course, but only incrementally and continuing along the grooves of dependent development of a much earlier historical origin. If political autonomy is an economic asset for a developing country, Asian countries, on balance, carved out more such autonomy via a variety of struggles than did the states of Latin America. A brief look back at the divergent historical trajectories of Asia and Latin America may be useful before concluding this discussion.

Following World War II, for example, China had a major communist revolution, and in India, the world's most significant noncommunist nationalist movement came to power. The Asian giants began their sovereign development experiments by focusing first and foremost on state consolidation. Once in power, the nationalistically inclined Chinese communists minimized Western economic and political influence on China, eliminated China's comprador classes, and created a well-organized state that penetrated the Chinese society deeply. Although

India's democratic state was less efficacious than the Chinese communist state, India's nationalist leaders also prioritized sovereignty and state consolidation. They, too, minimized the role of the old landed classes that had collaborated with the British and kept new political and economic dependencies at bay. In the early decades (say, from 1950 to 1980), then, the Asian giants used the power of newly consolidated states to create nearly autarkic economies. These experiments were hardly without costs. There were in fact serious costs in areas of state repression and state-led upheavals (China), slow and lingering poverty (India), and sluggish economic growth (both China and India). That said, there is no denying that state consolidation laid the foundation for a nationalist model of development in both China and India on which the post-1980 economic success was built.

Decolonization created a variety of political outcomes in the rest of Asia, with one shared commonality, namely, the creation of sovereign, new, and, for the most part, effective states. For example, the Japanese lost World War II and, along with that, their power and investments in their colonies of Korea and Formosa. This led to new political beginnings in the partial countries of South Korea and Taiwan. The Dutch were forced out of Indonesia, as were the British from Malaysia. The French and the Americans were both eventually defeated militarily in Vietnam. Although there were exceptions (e.g., the Philippines), well-organized mass nationalist or revolutionary forces (or both) consolidated power in most of the Asian countries after the war. It might be objected that countries like South Korea or Pakistan very quickly developed new dependencies, this time on the United States. This is true but with one important qualification: these new dependencies were mainly a product of the Cold War and thus were security-oriented. For the most part, countries like South Korea were left alone to pursue their own economic development, even gaining preferential resources and treatment from the United States as a quid pro quo for security arrangements.

In contrast to Asia, decolonization in Latin America was a thing of the distant past. State consolidation had occurred mainly in the interwar period. Unlike the Asian pattern of anticolonial mass mobilization, the underlying processes leading to state consolidation in Latin America often involved struggles between rival elites, especially struggles between centralizing and regional elites. Following World War II, newer political formations emerged in many Latin American countries, too, but there was more continuity than discontinuity in the social base of state power, in patterns of economic dependency, and in developmental choices. Most of these regimes readily embraced the emerging Western alliance, led by the United States. Consider again, for example, the case of the most important Latin American country, Brazil. Although a new democratic regime of sorts replaced an authoritarian regime after the war, significant elements of continuity characterized the pre– and post–World War II political economy of Brazil. Getulio Vargas, the authoritarian leader of the prewar period, even came back to power, this time as a democratically elected president.

The Cuban Revolution marked a moment of potential change in Latin American politics, in the direction of activist states supported by mass politics. From João Goulart to Allende, a variety of nationalists, populists, and social democrats emerged to give voice to new political forces of the region. The United States—the regional hegemon, committed to open economies, especially in its backyard—sought to co-opt the emerging political restlessness in a liberal direction via the Alliance for Progress. When these efforts did not succeed, the United States just as readily threw its weight behind more reactionary political forces that would provide favorable economic policies and a bulwark against any possible rise of the left. This tilted the balance of power within Latin American societies, retarding the trend toward nationalist and plebiscitary politics. Landed oligarchs; foreign investors; and militaries, which were often trained in the United States, felt threatened by the new direction. A variety of military coups that occurred in Latin American countries during the 1960s and the 1970s brought to power elites who were inclined, on the one hand, to cooperate politically and economically with the United States and, on the other hand, to pursue a highly elitist and a dependent model of development at home.

While anticolonial mass movements consolidated power in many Asian countries during the 1950s and the 1960s, similar political forces were thwarted in Latin America. What emerged instead in the latter was a variety of narrower elitist arrangements under American tutelage. These contrasting political developments cast the die for a longer-term divergence in political and economic evolution of the two regions. Among the developmental changes in the two regions that can be traced back to these earlier contrasts in state construction are: Land reforms and related patterns of inequalities; strategies for dependence on foreign capital; and the role of national capital and indigenous technology, including trained manpower, in industrialization strategies. These contrasting policy choices often reinforced the character of developmental states of the two regions, more nationalist in Asia and more dependent in Latin America.

In sum, although there were many false starts, and a fair amount of learning via trial and error, on balance, nationalist states consolidated power in most Asian countries between 1950 and 1980, eliminating or mitigating the power of traditional intermediaries, minimizing the role of foreign capital, and laying the foundations for the development of indigenous technology and heavy industry. As noted, the ruling elites in Latin America, by contrast, continued to rely heavily on foreign capital, failed to mitigate internal economic inequalities and the related elite-mass political gap, and constructed political economies that remained dependent on the outside world. These political differences are at the root of the fact that nationalist states of Asia have coped with post-1980 globalization from a position of relative strength, making concessions when necessary, but also taking advantages of available opportunities. By contrast, the indebted and dependent countries of Latin America have just as often confronted globalization on bended knee. When pressured by the United States, the IMF, and the World Bank, Latin elites during the 1980s and the 1990s readily embraced policies based on the Washington Consensus on development. The results, as we have seen, included higher rates of economic growth and lower inequalities in much of Asia during 1980 to 2005 relative to Latin America.

Middle East, Mainly Iraq

The United States invaded Iraq for a second time in 2003. The results of this intervention continue to unfold. Although US troops formally withdrew from the country in 2011, they returned in 2014. US-military involvement in Iraq at the time of writing has again diminished, although the United States could choose to return at any time.[93] The United States continues to train Iraqi military and police forces.[94] The internal political situation in Iraq, though seemingly calmer, is far from settled; and the United States is likely to remain a major political factor in the future evolution of Iraq. Much has also been written on US interventions in Iraq, some of it of rather good quality.[95] But questions remain, particularly those concerning US motives, mechanisms, and the impact of its imperialism: Why did the United States invade and occupy Iraq? How did the United States seek to turn Iraq into a client state? And what was the impact of the US invasion, especially on Iraq? To repeat my core argument briefly, I suggest that the United States invaded Iraq as a first step in some vague but grand post–Cold War design to establish pro-American democracies and thus to finally incorporate the oil-rich Middle East within the American orbit.[96] The war has not yielded the results leaders in the United States expected. American imperial ambitions have again confronted nationalist resistance.

It may be useful to begin the discussion with some background on Iraq.[97] Although the region in which Iraq now exists is very much part of the ancient cradle of civilization, the modern state of Iraq has relatively recent colonial origins. Iraq is unlike modern Iran or Turkey, the two Middle Eastern states that can trace their political lineage back to the grand empires of the Safavids or the Ottomans. Iraq is also unlike Egypt, which can trace a long history as a political unit. Iraq was, instead, cobbled together by the British after World War I from three outlying Arab provinces of the Ottoman Empire: Basra, Baghdad, and Mosul. As already noted (chapter 2), the weakening of Ottoman Empire throughout the nineteenth century was attended by growing British economic penetration of that empire following the imposition of the Treaty of Balta Liman in 1838. Following the opening of the Suez Canal in 1869, which brought steamship navigation to the Tigris, British economic interest in modern-day southern Iraq grew. For example, British goods, mainly textiles, sold briskly in the regions of Baghdad and Basra during the second half of the nineteenth century; if British exports to the region in 1868–70 were £51,000, by 1907–9 they had grown sharply, to over £3 million.[98] Prior to World War I, Britain had also secured the rights, via the so-called railway partitions, to build railways in modern-day southern Iraq. Oil exports were still to come, but toward the end of the nineteenth century, there was already growing awareness that southern Iraq was rich in oil deposits, and the same was likely to be the case in the northern province of Mosul.

At the onset of war, the British—with the help of troops from British India—sought to protect its economic and strategic interests (routes to India, and all that) and captured the provinces of Basra, Baghdad, and Mosul from the Ottomans during 1914–17.[99] British interest in Basra and Baghdad was, of course, formally recognized by the secret Sykes-Picot Agreement (formally known as the Asia Minor Agreement), which the Allied powers signed in 1916, but which the Bolsheviks then made public following the Russian Revolution. After the war, France gave up its control over Mosul to the British, in exchange for a right to the oil of the region.[100] The British then created the state of Iraq out of the three former regions of the Ottoman Empire. But no sooner had the British created Iraq (and sought to impose British rule), than they were faced with a major revolt by the Iraqis, in 1920. The British eventually put down this revolt, but only by using brutal military force, which included the bombing of civilians. Such were the beginnings of modern-day Iraq.

As the troubled Ottoman Empire sought to reorganize itself in the early twentieth century, it became clear to many Arab intellectuals and activists that their desire to achieve greater autonomy for the Arab provinces within the empire was not likely to be met. Some of them then organized politically, entertaining the idea of separate political units headed by Arab kings. These political beginnings had their counterparts in Basra and Baghdad, where secret societies favoring greater self-determination for Arabs had come into being before World War I.[101] Knowing that this would weaken the Ottomans even further, the British encouraged political activism among the Arabs, including by sponsoring local militias and armed groups to act against the Ottomans. In exchange for Arab support against the Ottomans, the British even promised Arabs greater self-determination after the war. Many British men on the spot, of whom T. E. Lawrence, "Lawrence of Arabia," is the most well-known, offered these assurances to the Arabs if they agreed to side only with the Allies during the war. When the

British captured Baghdad in 1917, the commanding officer announced: "[O]ur armies do not come into your cities and lands as conquerors or enemies, but as liberators . . . . The Arab race may rise once again to greatness!"[102] Shortly thereafter, Churchill suggested that the idea that the British sought Iraqi oil was "too absurd for acceptance."[103] For neither the first time nor the last, imperial lies were propagated for convenience and then discarded as needs changed.

The British quickly changed their tune and sought to organize Iraq as a colony, along the lines of India. It is not surprising that local opinion did not take kindly to the broken promises. The authorities in cities like Basra and Baghdad opposed the British designs. The British arrested and exiled these leaders. Local opposition to British colonial ambitions then spread to the entire political class, the clerics, and to educated Iraqis. While it is fair to assume that Iraqi identity at this time was not all that well developed, the British were, nevertheless, clear outsiders. They were now trying to impose their rule on Arab Muslims, a people with a strong sense of themselves. What gave the Iraqi opposition teeth was that the Arab soldiers who had fought against the Ottomans—with Britain's blessing—now turned against the British. The thin British forces on the ground were in danger of losing. London ordered the aerial bombing of opposition forces in 1920, killing southern Iraqis by the thousands, and bludgeoned them into submission. What this early encounter also clarified for the British, however, was that Iraq was probably not ready to be turned into a full-fledged colony. At the same time, Britain's relative global power was also declining, and Woodrow Wilson was promising self-determination to the peoples of the old empires. Old-fashioned colonialism may well not have been suitable for the newly acquired territories of the Middle East. Indirect rule was likely to be more suitable. The British proceeded to install the Hashemite Prince Faisal as the titular king of Iraq, who—and whose successors—remained deeply dependent on Britain until the end of monarchy in 1958.

Following the occupation, the British dominated Iraq, first as a mandate and then as an independent monarchy, for nearly four decades. A few developments during this semicolonial phase are worth underscoring, to give a sense of the country the United States invaded in 2003. First, the British rule in Iraq rested on a compliant monarchy and, below that, on a class of landowners that the British virtually created from the ranks of tribal leaders and city merchants.[104] The landowners came to control giant territories, and they often turned into absentee landlords. Not only were these estates not very productive, but this pattern of land ownership also contributed to a highly unequal society. When Iraqi nationalism grew, say, from the 1930s onward, the demands against imperialism went hand in hand with a reform of the social structure that underpinned British rule, namely, the system of large landowners. Nationalism and "socialism"—a word that often concealed many different political preferences—came to be inextricably linked in Iraq.

Second, from early on, the apex of the indigenous power structure in Iraq came to be controlled by Sunnis. For example, the senior officers of the armed force that was built in the nominally independent post-1932 Iraq were "Sunnis almost to a man."[105] Over time, the armed force came to exercise enormous influence over the state. Although Iraq was a majority Shia country (more than 50 percent at the time), with a significant Kurdish population (around 20 percent) concentrated in Mosul, a power concentration in the hands of Sunnis was not a good beginning for a future nation-state. What made these religious and ethnic distinctions especially potent was the fact that most of the Shia were relatively poor. An overlap between class and ethnic divisions is a powerful political force in any polity.

Third, the nationalist currents that emerged in Iraq were real, but they failed to cohere. The potency of underlying nationalism was evident not only in 1920 but also in 1941. With the British preoccupied with the World War II, elements among the Iraqi elites sought to forge an alliance with the Axis powers as a means to drive the British out of Iraq. Britain was then forced to militarily reconquer Iraq to ensure influence over the strategic Persian Gulf. Unlike Indian nationalism, however, Iraqi nationalism never became a coherent political force. Divisions among more conservative or more left-leaning currents are common to most anticolonial nationalist movements. They existed in Iraq, too, but the most powerful political force in British-dominated Iraq was a communist political party. Iraqi communists were relatively well organized, supported by Moscow, and combined Iraq's social and national issues rather successfully.[106] As the Cold War emerged, they were also brutally repressed during the last decade of the monarchy while the British watched, with their military bases intact in Iraq. The communists remained a political force in Iraq—at least until Saddam concentrated brutal power during the 1970s—but they were excluded from power at critical moments. The civilian base of the Iraqi nationalist movement was thus left without a cohesive core. This vacuum was eventually filled by the armed forces, the Ba'ath political party, and by strongmen.

Last, there is the issue of oil, always oil. The dependent King Faisal signed contracts with British companies in 1925 that gave them exclusive rights to extract oil from Iraqi oil fields well into the future.[107] In exchange, the Iraqi government was promised small royalty payments. French companies also joined the oil consortium; recall that Clemenceau expected access to oil when he surrendered Mosul to the British. Americans, the champions of self-determination, also insisted on a share of the Iraqi oil. Standard Oil then joined the group of Western companies that came to be called the Iraq Petroleum Company (IPC). British companies dominated this consortium. After signing few more contracts, the IPC, from 1930 onward, controlled all the oil extraction of Iraq. Once oil was discovered in a big way, the British high commissioner for Iraq sent a memo back to London: "[T]he discoveries of immense quantities of oil . . . make it now impossible to abandon control of Iraq without damaging important British and foreign interests."[108] The IPC controlled how much oil was to be extracted and the price at which it was to be sold. The Iraqi government did not even control the value of the local currency, which remained linked to sterling. As one might expect, the Iraqi economy and government resources came to increasingly depend on oil revenues. Oil production and exports grew rapidly, especially after World War II; by 1953, nearly half of Iraq's national income originated from oil exports.[109] The stakes for who would control the production and sale of Iraqi oil were thus increasingly high: the British wanted to somehow hold on to the Iraqi black gold. But Iraqi nationalists had different ideas.

The revolution of 1958 initiated a prolonged period of political fragmentation in Iraq that arguably came to an end only when Saddam Hussein consolidated power during the late 1970s.[110] Major developments during this phase included the overthrow of the monarchy; the slow but steady abolition of large landed estates; the growing role of the state in the economy, including the nationalization of IPC in 1972; the emergence of urban middle classes at the political forefront; and considerable political instability, evident in frequent, and irregular, government changes, as well as in state-sponsored violence against all opposition. Among these developments, two sets in particular help us understand the political instability and the role of oil as both developed in Iraq.

The overthrow of the monarchy was fed by a widely shared nationalist antipathy toward the ancien régime, which was viewed both as serving narrow Iraqi interests and dependent on the British. Except for the communists, however, the middle-class nationalists neither were well organized nor enjoyed systematic mass support. The political class was thus highly factionalized, often along personalistic lines. The result was that rulers came and went in the post-1958 period with great frequency. One set of rulers would capture power, say, with the help of the armed force, and would proceed to eliminate supporters of the past rulers and to seek new support, say, from the communists, or by promulgating some popular policies. Since Iraqi rulers lacked a firm power base and procedural legitimacy, another set of challengers would wait for an opportunity to capture power and once they did, the pattern would repeat itself. Social divisions fed the political instability: many Shias were poor and supported the communist party; better-off Sunnis dominated the state sector, including the military; and the Kurdish population in the north was never readily assimilated into a coherent nation-state.

It was in this political milieu that the Ba'ath political party and Saddam Hussein emerged as a major political force in Iraq. The Ba'ath were inspired by themes of Arab nationalism. While they generally proclaimed adherence to some sort of socialism, many members of the Ba'ath were also strongly anticommunist. Their anticommunist credentials even attracted the CIA, which supported the coups in 1961 and 1968 that helped the anticommunist Ba'ath consolidate power.[111] These fissures were reinforced by ethnic divisions because Arab nationalism, both inside and outside Iraq, was associated with the Sunni leaders. Most Iraqi Shias stayed away from the Ba'ath party, at least until it consolidated power. The Ba'ath came to offer an anti-imperialist alternative to the well-organized communists in Iraq that both appealed to the Sunni elites, including those in the armed forces, and to a broader cross-section of the population that was readily susceptible to nationalist mobilization. Saddam Hussein had risen to power while managing the security apparatus of the Iraqi state, an Iraqi Beria of sorts, and he used this base to place those loyal to him in positions of power, in both the Ba'ath and the state structure. During the 1980s, Saddam then used this combination of bureaucratic and personal power to unleash state terror on a variety of opposition groups.

The political fragmentation notwithstanding, there was consensus across the Iraqi political class as to what the role of the government ought to be. Public policies during this period thus led to the breaking down of large estates, the increasing role of the government in facilitating economic development, and, of course, to taking control of Iraqi oil away from foreign companies. It was the latter that was crucial for Iraq. As noted, Iraq depended on oil for much of its exports and income. A belief was widely shared across the political class that national control over oil was essential for the betterment of Iraqis. But wresting control back from the British-owned companies was not going to be easy. The specter of Mossadegh haunted the rulers of all the oil-producing countries. Before nationalizing the IPC, the Ba'ath rulers of Iraq made concessions (temporary ones, as it turned out) to their political enemies at home—both Kurds and the communists—to create some sense of domestic cohesion. They also entered a "friendship treaty" with the Soviet Union in the event of sanctions—or worse—from the West. This, however, was in 1972, when Britain had already withdrawn from much of the Middle East and the United States was distracted by Vietnam. Countries like Libya had also won some significant victories against the oil companies in 1970. The power balance between Middle Eastern countries and Western oil companies was thus shifting.[112]

After Iraq nationalized the IPC in 1972, oil nationalization in Syria followed. Within a year, OPEC raised the price of oil. In short order, the Iraqi political economy was transformed. The decision to nationalize oil was highly popular in Iraq; it will be important to keep this in mind considering the opposition to the United States within Iraq, because the US-dominated Iraqi governments have reversed this nationalization and brought back foreign corporations. During the 1970s, oil nationalization boosted the popularity of the Ba'ath government, of whom Saddam was very much a part. According to two historians, "[N]o action by any Iraqi government since the 1958 revolution was greeted with such universal enthusiasm, and the Ba'ath was able to live off the moral capital generated by this act for many years."[113] The new oil income in due course allowed the Iraqi state and rulers to consolidate their hold over the Iraqi society.

Oil majors propagated the view that countries like Iraq were incapable of managing oil production and sales. But as Greg Muttitt has documented with great care, this was definitely not true for Iraq.[114] Iraq had plenty of well-educated engineers and managers who could run the Iraqi oil industry competently. Iraq's share of world-oil production rose steadily after nationalization and peaked toward the end of the decade, when Saddam led Iraq into a war with Iran.[115] Meanwhile, enormous oil resources enabled the power of the Iraqi state to grow, both vis-à-vis its own citizens and in relation to its neighbors. For example, the Ba'ath-dominated state canceled taxes and used oil resources to fund welfare programs. A new social contract, common to many oil exporters, emerged: citizens would benefit from the largesse of the state, but they had better not question the state's authority. Those who did not fall in line suffered; both communists and Kurds were repressed harshly. An underground Shia opposition led by clerics also started to emerge. The Ba'ath also used the oil resources to buy armaments, more and more from Western countries. Many multinational corporations (MNCs) also won contracts for new projects in Iraq. What the oil majors had lost, defense manufacturers and other private companies had gained. Iraq also started moving away from its close relations with the Soviet Union and integrating more with the West, especially in terms of forging economic and military links.

Saddam Hussein became president of Iraq in 1979, around the same time the Islamic Revolution was unfolding in neighboring Iran. As I have noted, the Iranian revolution triggered Soviet intervention in Afghanistan and a second round of hikes in oil prices. The Carter Doctrine that followed underscored that American eyes were now sharply on the Middle East. No sooner did Saddam accede to power than he led Iraq into a ruinous war with Iran. Nearly a half million people, mostly Iranians, died during the decade-long war. At the end of the war there was no clear-cut victor; neither was it clear that anyone had gained anything from the war. Why did Saddam initiate it? Iran and Iraq were two major regional powers and some conflict was inevitable. The revolution in Iran must have been terrifying to Saddam, both because it might encourage Iraqi Shias to follow suit and because Iran had supported the Iraqi Kurds against the Ba'ath regime in the past. Saddam may have calculated that the troubled political situation in Iran gave him a temporary military advantage. However, he miscalculated seriously—and not for the last time—that he could easily defeat a much bigger power like Iran. The decade-long, stalemated conflict left Iraq with a weaker economy but a substantial, mobilized military. These conditions encouraged the Iraqi annexation of Kuwait and the US reaction that was the first Gulf War, in 1990.

Before focusing directly on US interventions in Iraq, it is important to note the support that the United States and other Western powers had extended to Iraq during the 1980s. The Shah of Iran had been a major American proxy in the Gulf. With that proxy lost, the United States prepared to police the Gulf directly. The Carter Doctrine "implied" nothing less than "the conversion of the Persian Gulf into an informal American protectorate"; there was no other short route to "safeguard the uninterrupted flow of oil."[116] The Americans then created a new military command—the United States Central Command (CENTCOM)—to exert ongoing influence over the Gulf; the commanding officer frankly suggested that his task was "to ensure the unimpeded flow of oil from the Arabian Gulf."[117] The United States also started searching for new military bases in or near the Gulf. In this context, Saddam's foolish forays into Iran drew American attention. Revolutionary Iran—fully armed because of the earlier American military support of the Shah—quickly recovered its stride and pushed Iraq back hard. The United States decided that it could not sit by and let the Iranian mullahs defeat Iraq and become the lords of the Gulf. The notorious record of the Ba'ath as rulers notwithstanding, the United States started supporting Iraq in the Iran-Iraq war, at first indirectly and, eventually, directly. As is well known, Reagan sent Rumsfeld to meet with Saddam. The photograph of the two of them shaking hands in 1983, even as Saddam was using chemical weapons against both Iran and the Kurds, stands as a prize image in any effort to catalog imperial hypocrisies. Conservative, moneyed US allies in the Gulf, such as the Saudis and the Kuwaitis, fearing a revolutionary Iran, also supported Saddam with funds. The United States "covertly" supplied "Iraq with sophisticated weapons through third countries," which included giving the Iraqis the means to manufacture chemical and biological weapons.[118] And last, toward the end of the war, the United States signed a five-year cooperation agreement with Iraq in 1987 that included $1 billion in food aid.

Saddam was a brutal, megalomaniacal leader, but at the end of the 1980s, he had reasons to believe that he and the United States were on the same side.

A wiser leader in Iraq would have demobilized the bloated armed force in the aftermath of the Iran-Iraq War and would have used the oil resources to create a prosperous country. Instead, Saddam chose to continue on the path of war and regional imperialism. In the past, even before the astronomical rise in oil prices during the 1970s, Iraqi leaders had toyed with the idea of annexing Kuwait. Since the British had made such a mess of creating arbitrary mandates out of former Ottoman territories, it was not difficult for the leaders in the region to disagree with one set of boundaries or another. Little Kuwait had thus been in Iraq's cross-hairs for a while. Saddam, pressed financially at home after the Iran-Iraq War, argued that oil-rich Kuwait should help out, say, by excusing the war-related loans, especially because the war had been fought in part to protect the oil-rich feudal states in the region from revolutionary Iran. As tensions escalated, the United States failed to discourage Saddam from annexing Kuwait. Following the war with Iran, for example, Saddam had informed April Glaspie, the US ambassador to Iraq at the time, that he was deeply irritated with Kuwait, implying that, if Kuwait refused to help, he might be compelled to take action against it. Instead of discouraging such a move, Glaspie responded, "[W]e have no opinion on the Arab-Arab conflicts, like your border disagreement with Kuwait." According to one scholarly observer, since the United States had also previously told Saddam that Washington had "no special defense or security commitments to Kuwait," it is likely that the United States "effectively" gave Saddam a "green light" on Kuwait.[119]

Be that as it may, Saddam annexed Kuwait and the United States responded sharply, achieving a quick military victory and forcing Saddam out of Kuwait. All that is well known.[120] Some of the reasons the United States left Saddam in power in Iraq were suggested earlier in the chapter, as was the fact that Saddam continued to irritate the United States during the 1990s. As I have noted, senior members of the Clinton Administration were keen to remove Saddam from power. However, the opportune moment for a second war with Iraq arose only after 9/11. Even though Iraq or the Iraqis had nothing to do with 9/11, the provocative tragedy created an open season for US ambitions in the Middle East and beyond. For example, on the theory that every crisis is also an opportunity, Condoleezza Rice called a meeting of the National Security Council within days of the attacks and asked members "to think about 'how do you capitalize on these opportunities' to fundamentally change American doctrine, and the shape of the world, in the wake of September 11."[121] With the demise of the Soviet Union, and 9/11, the United States might have calculated that it was now in a position to push back postcolonial nationalism in the Middle East, eliminate any potential security threats, create pliable democracies, and open the oil-rich economies of the region. The worldwide project to roll back the state had already begun with

Reagan. One early manifestation of that, as we have seen, was the imposition of the Washington Consensus in Latin America. Militaristic interventions in more contested regions of the developing world had to wait until the threat of a Soviet involvement had truly vanished. The start of the new millennium provided new opportunities. Could this be the beginning of yet another American century?

The second American war in Iraq was moved both by American concerns that were specific to Iraq and by the post–Cold War euphoria to remake the world in America's image. As Bush II came to power, to repeat, his foreign policy advisers included the likes of Rice, Rumsfeld, and Cheney in the first rank, Wolfowitz, Feith, and Libby in the second rank, and at a little further distance, defense policy advisers such as Richard Perle.[122] Many observers called this group, along with their other compatriots in Washington, the "neocons," short for neoconservatives; Colin Powell supposedly referred to them as the "fucking crazies."[123] Several members of this group argued—well before 9/11—that Saddam should be removed from power, offering their own reasons as to why. For example, one year before becoming the US vice president, Cheney—then the CEO of Halliburton, an oil company—expressed his concern to other oil executives in London about the growing scarcity of future global oil supplies and suggested that the solution would have to come from the Middle East, "where the prize ultimately lies."[124] Cheney was thus one of the strong supporters of the second Iraq war. Wolfowitz, whom Bob Woodward described as the "intellectual godfather and the fiercest advocate for toppling Saddam,"[125] had openly argued for getting rid of Saddam during the 1990s, including penning an article with former US diplomat Zalmay Khalilzad, in 1997, entitled, "Overthrow Him."[126] When Wolfowitz was subsequently questioned about why the United States chose to invade Iraq and not another axis-of-evil state, say, North Korea, his response was telling: "Let's look at it simply. The most important difference between North Korea and Iraq is that economically, we had no choice in Iraq. The country swims on a sea of oil."[127] Perle, who was close to both Wolfowitz and Feith, counseled Benjamin Netanyahu in 1996 that "removing Saddam Hussein from power" had to be an Israeli "strategic" priority, and that the American and Israeli interests in the region were identical.[128] And Rumsfeld argued at an NSC meeting in early 2001 in the following terms: "Imagine what the region (the Middle East) would look like without Saddam and with a regime that is aligned with US interests. . . . It would change everything in the region and beyond it. It would demonstrate what US policy is all about."[129]

It is already clear in this last quote that for some US policymakers, Iraq was only part of a broader design. Iraq was to be a first step in the post–Cold War world toward remaking the Middle East in the American image. Rice thus argued for bringing democracy and free enterprise to Iraq and beyond, because such cherished American goals ought not to "stop at the edge of Islam."[130] Rumsfeld added urgency to the task: "Need to move swiftly. . . . Go massive, sweep it all up, things related or not."[131] The war also followed from the new US national security doctrine, formulated in 2002, which argued that "the best defense is a good offense" and asserted: "We will not hesitate to act alone, if necessary, to exercise our right of self-defense by acting pre-emptively."[132] One analyst underlined the doctrine's implied commitment to remaining the "unchallengeable superpower," and to use "unilateral" and "pre-emptive" wars to ensure this outcome, calling it "revolution" in US foreign policy.[133] Senator Edward Kennedy criticized the preemptive doctrine as "a call for twenty-first century American imperialism that no other nation can or should accept."[134] Be that as it may, it is the case that the war in Iraq was to be a "war of choice," waged with some grand goals in mind. In the words of Bush II—who was ultimately responsible for the war—the war was aimed at ensuring that American values prevailed because these values were "right and true for every person, in every society."[135]

Why did the United States go to war in Iraq for a second time in 2003? A full understanding of this important question will surely evolve over time as more evidence becomes available. For now, it is evident that members of Bush's war council espoused a range of reasons. I have not emphasized here some of the other reasons that were also offered at the time, such as the need to destroy Saddam's weapons of mass destruction. While some in the war council may have believed that Iraq was a genuine security threat, America's own intelligence on whether Saddam possessed nuclear weapons, or could do so readily, was far from definite.[136] In retrospect, the focus on weapons of mass destruction turned out to be so empty of substance that Rumsfeld later admitted that arguing this line to justify the war was "a public relations error."[137] It is also the case that there was little evidence to suggest that Saddam supported anti-American terrorism. And Iraq, by 2002, was hardly a military threat. What, then, does one make of the more credible reasons offered by Bush II and his advisers to invade Iraq a second time? There is no reason to doubt that oil and the security of Israel were uppermost in the minds of some of the policymakers who wanted to get rid of Saddam and establish a pro-American regime, instead.[138] But it was hardly the case that Iraq's oil was not readily available in the world market. Saddam was even willing to invite some foreign investors into Iraq for further explorations. With his pathetic army, moreover, Saddam hardly threatened the security of nuclear-armed Israel in 2002. Both goals could have been enhanced via policies that were a lot less expensive and destructive than a trillion-dollar war that killed a half million Iraqis. So while oil and Israel were part of the motives, they do not quite provide a satisfactory answer to the question: Why the second Iraq war?

United States invaded Iraq in 2003 because American policymakers saw the war as a first step toward the domination of the Middle East. Following the end of the Cold War, the United States chose to reassert its global ambitions, both to further open semi-open economies and to tame militaristic states that might pose regional challenges. To recapitulate the discussion on motives leading to US intervention in Iraq, the United States had long considered the Middle East of great strategic value, especially because more than half the world's oil is located in the region. Once Britain decided to withdraw from regions east of the Suez, the United States hoped that such pro-US regimes as the monarchies in Iran and Saudi Arabia—with Israel in the background—would be sufficient to police the region. When these plans went awry in 1979, the United States started building its own military presence in the region. This was because no regional power could be allowed to dominate the Middle East. In American perceptions, only the United States has such imperial prerogatives around the globe. The United States even chose to support the odious regime of Saddam Hussein during the Iraq-Iran war to limit Iran's regional power. When Saddam misunderstood his American supporters and overplayed his hand, the United States hit back hard. Although Saddam was weakened, he remained a potential threat to America's regional design. He was an ambitious leader who could use Iraq's oil resources to rebuild military power in the future. As previously noted, the United States had already decided that such regional ambitions in the post–Cold War world had to be nipped in the bud. The United States could only dominate the Middle East if pro-US regimes were in power across the region. This was the key. Only friendly regimes would allow the United States to maintain military bases and facilitate ready access to oil. Unfriendly regimes had to go. Iraq was thus in the American crosshairs, waiting to happen. How dare a tin-pot dictator challenge the ambitions of the mighty United States, especially in a region of such great importance? American decision-makers then turned the tragedy of 9/11 into an opportunity to take out Saddam and to turn Iraq into a client state. It was hoped that this would be a first step in establishing the United States as a regional overlord of the Middle East.

What Bush and his war council truly expected when they waged a second war in Iraq may only become clear when secret documents are declassified, and maybe not even then. For now, what seems evident is that the United States expected a short war, whereby Saddam would be removed from power, and a pro-American regime would be installed instead.[139] With its overwhelming power superiority, why did the United States fail to carry out this plan in Iraq? Scores of books have documented American mistakes in Iraq: too few forces on the ground; poor planning for a post-Saddam Iraq, including the failure to provide basic security; the decision to destroy the existing state structure; imagining Iraq mainly in sectarian terms and thus reinforcing religious/ethnic divisions; depending too heavily on self-serving Iraqi exiles; brutal disrespect for local mores, evident especially in Abu Ghraib; and then losing the will to "stay the course," withdrawing US troops and leaving Iraq in near civil-war conditions, with a poorly functioning state, only to return when ISIS threatened. These insights are valuable, and I incorporate some of them in my analysis.

Most such analyses, however, start from the faulty assumption that American intentions in Iraq "were basically good,"[140] but that somehow "mistakes" were made, and then the United States "lost Iraq." This is a deeply biased perspective. It ignores the "original sin" of an imperial intent. Iraq was not America's to lose. Iraq was a sovereign country when the United States invaded it. Yes, it was poorly governed. But it was sovereign. The United States wanted to undermine that sovereignty and mold Iraq for its own self-serving purposes. It is not surprising that what the United States confronted in Iraq was a fairly classic struggle between imperialism and nationalism: most Iraqis did not want the United States to rule them, either directly or via puppets. The United States could bludgeon such opposition, which they tried to do, or leave, which they also tried, though half-heartedly. The in-between "solution" of creating a pro-American regime in Iraq is still a work in progress. Over time, the conflict in Iraq became a lot messier, of course, once sectarians, thugs, criminals, and terrorists entered the fray. It is important to recall, however, that such patterns often unfold when basic state structures do not function; life without a Leviathan can be "nasty, brutish and short."

American leaders hoped to accomplish their goals in Iraq on the cheap. They did not want to mobilize additional military manpower at home for the war or to tax the American people. As one cynical observer of Bush's approach to the second Iraq war quipped, "[W]e are at war, let us party." This approach was reinforced by two other factors. First, changing US military doctrines emphasized technology, rather than manpower, to win wars.[141] America's overwhelming technological superiority was indeed more than sufficient to quickly defeat and depose Saddam, but it was far from sufficient to "win the peace." Second, American leaders had expected the Iraqis to treat them as "liberators." Because they were based on this assumption of civilian support, the American preparations for establishing order in postwar Iraq turned out to be deeply flawed. Faced instead with growing opposition, the American leaders had to improvise postwar governance. As Jay Garner, the first head of US administration in Iraq, testified to Congress some three weeks after the invasion, "[T]his is an ad hoc operation, glued together over about four or five weeks' time . . . [We] didn't really have enough time to plan."[142] Imagine the irresponsibility of invading and occupying a foreign country the size of California—both in terms of population and area—without adequate preparation!

There is nothing new about wanting to pursue imperialism on the cheap. As we have seen, "imperialism on the cheap" could have been the British motto in the nineteenth century. However, imperialism on the cheap works best when two conditions are present: local collaborators are readily available and these collaborators can as readily control and pacify the local population. The British found these conditions in many of the countries they colonized in the nineteenth century, formally or informally. However, the rise of nationalism and mass politics in twentieth century altered the social structures of countries on the periphery. This means that though local collaborators are still available for those seeking to build empires, their ranks are thinner because of nationalist competitors. More important, the spread of plebiscitarian politics across the world has dissolved key building blocks of old-fashioned imperialism. These were the feudal-like social arrangements whereby the maharajas, sultans, tribal chiefs, and latifundistas or the pashas of the past could deliver the compliance of local populations. These vertical authority structures are vanishing fast, if they are not already gone, and are being replaced by the emergence of mass politics. Imposing imperial order from the outside is much more complicated in the modern era, when the would-be subjects can be readily mobilized along nationalist lines.

As a result of these slow but steady changes, the British had considerable difficulty imposing an imperial order on Iraq in the first half of the twentieth century. This is clear even in the highly synoptic discussion here. Any book on the history of Iraq is likely to discuss at least four such notable encounters: the British had to put down a full-scale nationalist revolt in Iraq in 1920; they had to reconquer Iraq in 1941 to ensure that Iraqi nationalists did not take advantage of World War II conditions to enhance their political autonomy; the revolution against the British-supported monarchy in 1958 was very nearly the beginning of the modern republic of Iraq; and the nationalization of British-owned oil companies in 1972 was deeply popular in Iraq. Had the Americans paid attention to this past, they would not have assumed—or, at least, should not have assumed—that the Iraqis would welcome them as liberators. After all, this was not World War II, when the United States helped defeat the Germans and Americans were indeed welcomed in Europe as liberators. This was Iraq circa 2003, a country with a well-developed sense of both Arab and Iraqi nationalism, and with a strong tradition of anti-imperialism.

No sooner had American forces entered Baghdad in April 2003 (and Saddam was removed from power) than lawlessness began spreading rapidly in the capital city and beyond. As is well known, state authority in Iraq collapsed and American forces failed to fill the vacuum. Iraqi government buildings, hospitals, and university libraries were looted, as were museums filled with precious artifacts dating to ancient Mesopotamia. Losses from the looting ran into billions of dollars. The only building the American military protected was the one that houses the oil ministry. As former US Ambassador Peter Galbraith explained to congressional committee, "[I]n the three weeks following the US takeover (in Iraq), unchecked looting effectively gutted every important public institution in the city—with the notable exception of the oil ministry."[143] When Rumsfeld was subsequently criticized for the American failure to provide basic security, his response was nonchalant: "Stuff happens." He went on to equate criminal looting as a type of "freedom."[144]

Was this early failure to provide basic security deliberate or just incompetent? With the limited evidence available, it is difficult to tell. The failure was probably in part a result of the limited number of US troops on the ground. If so, it has to be understood as a result of the US policy to do Iraq on the cheap, at least at the outset. But the failure to secure order also had a deliberate quality.[145] Allowing the relics of the Iraqi past and the Ba'athist state to be destroyed fit the American design to start with a tabula rasa in Iraq. (I return to this issue.) The protection of oil fields and of the oil ministry was certainly deliberate. This is prime evidence against the American claim that they were not invading Iraq for its oil. Again, it is difficult to attribute the second Iraq war *entirely* to oil; that would be too simplistic. However, it is also the case that oil was very much on the mind of American leaders as war plans were being made. Before the war, for example, "working groups" met in Washington and London to consider the fate of Iraqi oil after the war. The two most pressing issues on the table were the extent to which foreign oil companies could get back into the country, and whether Iraqi oil revenues could be used to pay the costs of the war—a war indemnity, of sorts.[146] It is not unreasonable, then, to suggest that the orders to protect Iraqi oil came with the orders to invade Iraq. How else can one explain the fact that US soldiers protected only the oil ministry, while every other part of the Iraqi public sector was looted and gutted?

The Americans were initially welcomed in Baghdad but that welcome did not last long. Graffiti soon appeared on walls throughout the city, complete with spelling mistakes that underscored their authenticity, "all donne, go home."[147] More seriously, organized opposition to the US occupation had started to emerge nearly right away. Saddam had seriously eviscerated political life in Iraq, but even he was not capable of eliminating mosques and preachers. It is not surprising that the earliest opposition to US occupation was expressed within the frame of religion. For example, Muqtada al-Sadr was the scion of the Sadr family, who had impressive credentials as Shia clerics and martyrs.[148] With Saddam gone, young Muqtada emerged from hiding and started preaching right away. He also revived the religious and political network developed by his late father. Though he was very much a leader of one Shia faction, his message was anti-US and nationalist: Iraq was for Iraqis, and the United States should get out of Iraq. He and his Sadrist movement also stepped into the authority vacuum created by the state's collapse. They started policing the areas where they held sway; imposing their Islamic mores on followers; running Sharia courts; and providing social services, including running hospitals. The influence of the movement spread quickly and widely, especially among poor Shias, some of whom had supported the communists in the past. The Sunnis were in disarray but their clerics and scholars also got together, with the same message: Iraq is for Iraqis.

American military and civilian leaders in Iraq were dismayed. They refused to acknowledge—at least openly—that the perception of Americans as liberators was short-lived. They claimed that the opposition to the American presence had been instigated by supporters of Saddam and other Ba'athists who had lost power. That a nationalist opposition had emerged nearly instantaneously was a proposition the Americans did not want to entertain.[149] Nevertheless, the opposition was there for anyone to see. What the re-emergence of politics—and related violence—quickly clarified for the American leadership was that Iraq was not going to be easy to govern, and certainly not if the aim was to ensure that the new regime pursued American goals. The initial plan to topple Saddam and hand power over to a pro-US Iraqi figure, such as Ahmad Chalabi, now had to be shelved. A longer-term occupation would be needed to achieve American goals. This was an important moment in US intervention in Iraq. By the time Rumsfeld sent Paul Bremer to replace Ryan Crocker as the head of US administration in Iraq, a plan that resembled the establishment of an informal empire had been abandoned. A longer-term, formal occupation was about to begin. Observers could be excused for believing that the Americans were the new British, yet another imperial power in Iraq. And what did Iraq have that the United States want? As one skeptic commented, "[I]t wasn't the sand."[150]

Bremer was a self-confident member of Washington's neoconservative crowd and wanted to bring capitalism and free markets to Iraq. He lasted in Iraq for about only a year but during that short period, he initiated actions that deeply hurt the future development of Iraq. Several of these deserve comment, but within the frame of a caveat: many critics have heaped scorn on Bremer, but it is well to recall that he was implementing policies that were made in Washington. Bremer reported to Rumsfeld, who reported to Bush. Yes, Bremer acted like a viceroy, but viceroys are appointed by imperial states. Bremer's follies were really the follies of the US government. Soon after his arrival, Bremer let it be known that unlike his predecessor, he had not come to hand state power back to the Iraqis. A longer-term US occupation was to be the new policy. This immediately confirmed the worst fears of the Iraqi nationalists, even the moderate ones. Resistance to the US occupation rose steadily thereafter, and included armed attacks on the American military. I will return to further discussion of the growing nationalist opposition to US occupation.

Bremer proceeded to dissolve the Iraqi state, both the civil bureaucracy and the armed force. Why the US government chose to do this remains baffling, especially because the consequences for governance were downright deleterious. This was not even effective imperialism. The overt rationale was to get rid of all the members of the Ba'ath party in the state apparatus. However, many Iraqis had joined the Ba'ath party, not because they were die-hard believers in the ideology, which was mainly nationalist in any case, but because that was how you got a government job in Saddam's Iraq. Since nearly all the senior positions were held by party members, all Iraqis in the top tiers of management at "every government ministry and government-affiliated institution," including "teachers and doctors" were fired. This amounted to the dismissal of some 120,000 public servants.[151] The disbanding of the army also led to the dismissal of some 400,000 soldiers (with one month's salary as severance). The old state was suddenly gone. A new one could only emerge slowly. Meanwhile, the occupying Americans simply did not have the wherewithal to either ensure order or provide social services. Worse, the dispossessed army officers and soldiers joined the ranks of the angry men opposed to US occupation. Many of these men were battle-hardened and armed. In one fell swoop, US policies had released an enormous amount of free-floating and dangerous anger in Iraq.

Why did the United States disband the Iraqi state? The odious Saddam had already been deposed. Why destroy the core of the state structure, as well? A full answer may only emerge when classified documents are released. Limited evidence suggests that the decision was part of the American design to eviscerate the institutions that represented the Iraqi nation. The Ba'ath had been champions of anti-British Iraqi nationalism. Over time, "Ba'athism and Iraq's national identity became synonymous."[152] What the United States wanted was to destroy this past and to start fresh instead, with new institutions that would reflect American priorities: a democratic state; a commitment to an open economy, especially to foreign investment in oil; and foreign policies aligned with America's regional goals. Members of a Ba'athist state were likely to oppose such goals. As Rumsfeld explained, "[T]he coalition will work with forward-looking Iraqis and actively oppose the old regime's enforcers."[153] It was easy for Americans to persuade themselves that "forward-looking"—read, pro-American—rulers in Iraq would be good not only for America, but also for Iraqis. With the arrogance that comes with power and a sense of virtue, Bremer and his associates set out to destroy the Iraqi state, with fatal consequences not only for Iraq, but also for America's imperial ambitions.

All imperialists need an advisory council of natives to give some legitimacy to their rule. True to form, Bremer created such a council. This action was par for the course—even the British created had such institutions in India, nearly a century before. What is notable is how Americans chose to imagine the Iraq that needed to be represented in such a council. This was mainly in terms of ethnic groups: A handful of Shias and another handful of Kurds will join the council and be close to power, and if possible, a few pro-American Sunnis can also join.[154] Dismantling the state was already being viewed as an action against Iraqi Sunnis. American efforts to divide the political pie along ethnic lines hardened the ethnic divisions in Iraq. Scholars of ethnic politics well understand that the design of political institutions can either exacerbate or mitigate ethnic tensions.[155] Whether the United States chose ethnic representation as a divide-and-rule strategy, it came to be viewed as such within Iraq. Muqtada thus denounced "the illegitimate council created by the United States and its servants." A Sunni scholar who went on to head a key Sunni organization, the Association of Muslim Scholars, went further: "This council has divided Iraq along communal and ethnic lines for the first time in its history. It is the creation of the occupation forces . . . . It sows the seeds of hostility among the people of this society."[156] Prescient indeed!

Last, Bremer sought to dismantle the state's controls on the Iraqi economy, again, part and parcel of the imperial project to transform Iraq in America's image. To again quote Condoleezza Rice, neoliberalism did not have to stop at the "edge of Islam." The new policies announced by Bremer's provisional authority were nothing if not ambitious.[157] The changes proposed included 100 percent ownership of Iraqi assets by foreign investors (except for oil; more on that to come); full repatriation of profits by foreign investors; the slashing of tariffs and corporate taxes; a fully convertible new currency; and opening of the financial sector to foreign banks. According to the *Economist,* the changes represented "the kind of wish-list that foreign investors and donor agencies dream of for developing markets . . . [A]nd, if implemented, they could] create a poster-child for the recalcitrant region." Courtesy of American occupation, Iraq—an economy with some 30 million consumers, fed by oil wealth—was to be turned into a "capitalist's dream." Given the violence and political turmoil that followed in Iraq, only a few of these changes came to pass or were consequential, at least over the next decade. Their significance lay, instead, in exposing American intentions and hopes in Iraq: destroy the old nationalist state; replace it with a weak client regime in which the United States would play the referee to bickering ethnic groups; and turn the whole country into a bazaar for Western business interests.

Why Bremer did not privatize Iraq's oil industry with the stroke of a pen and open it up to foreign investors right away also remains something of a mystery. It is less mysterious, however, if one situates the issue in the broader context.

Muttitt has argued persuasively that the American interest in Iraqi oil was not so much that American corporations controlled it but that adequate oil supplies were readily available on the world market at low prices.[158] As noted earlier, the United States also had a strong interest in ensuring that profits from the Iraqi oil industry did not feed the regional ambitions of another Saddam. It would be an added gain if OPEC could be weakened in the process. So the denationalization of Iraqi oil was very much in American interest and part of the American plan. However, denationalization of oil had to be done a little more systematically than Bremer's destruction of the Iraqi state or his proposed opening of the non-oil economy to all comers. Even if the United States did not care much about Iraq or Iraqis, they did value its oil. The Russian model of rapid privatization that fed crony capitalism was to be avoided to ensure that oil supplies did not dwindle. Enabling a rapid takeover of state-owned Iraqi oil by American corporations would have also cost the Americans hugely in terms of global legitimacy; self-serving greed would have neutralized all claims that there was a higher purpose behind the war. And the firms of America's coalition partners wanted a piece of Iraqi oil too. For all these reasons, the American approach to the Iraqi oil sector was more gradual. Although the Iraqi oil industry has now indeed been largely denationalized, only some of it passed into the hands of American corporations.

Bremer's brief tenure as the de facto viceroy in Iraq fed virulent opposition to American control of Iraq. Remnants of the old regime dispersed and put up fierce resistance against the US military. Religious leaders also started mobilizing, both against American military targets and American civilians, ensconced within the green zone. The United States versus Iraqi nationalism thus emerged as one serious line of conflict within Iraq. Hoping to diffuse some of this conflict, Bush ordered Bremer back to the United States. Iraq was now to be ruled by pro-US Iraqis instead. With 160,000 US troops still in Iraq, the idea that Iraq was again a sovereign country in 2004 was not a serious proposition. Nevertheless, the political shift was real enough to encourage another line of growing conflict: Who among the Iraqis would exercise the limited power Iraq might be able to wrest from the Americans? Internal political cleavages were already numerous. Saddam had slapped a brutal lid on these conflicts. Again, American occupation had not only failed to provide adequate authority to secure order after Saddam but had also further fueled ethnic imaginations. New lines of conflict now also emerged. Between 2004 and 2011, when US troops finally left Iraq, internecine conflict within Iraq escalated, first along some identifiable cleavages, but then became more and more confusing as thugs, other criminal elements, and supporters from neighboring countries entered the fray. The US had sought to liberate Iraqis in 2003 but left behind a nearly failed state in 2011, with nearly a half million Iraqis dead.[159]

The details of the variety of conflicts that emerged during the American occupation of Iraq do not concern us here. The main point to understand instead is how and why these conflicts frustrated the goal of creating a stable-but-subservient state in Iraq. In short, Iraqi nationalism foiled American hopes for a subservient Iraq and numerous internecine conflicts made stability illusive. Bremer's viceroyship fueled a full-fledged nationalist revolt in Iraq. A poll conducted during that period showed that two-thirds of Iraqis viewed the "coalition authority" as "occupying powers," and only 15 percent viewed them as "liberators."[160] Another poll conducted a few months later found that 81 percent of Iraqis wanted the US-led forces to leave, and only 7 percent wanted them to stay.[161] Most Iraqis also believed that the United States was in Iraq mainly for their oil. According to one observer, it was "difficult for Americans to understand" that they were deeply "hated by ordinary Iraqis."[162] These sentiments then gave rise to a range of nationalist responses, more or less organized, more or less militant. For example, the Shia cleric Ayatollah Sistani demanded that the United States allow elections in Iraq and then leave; he also issued a fatwa to that effect. Muqtada al-Sadr and some of the more militant clerics preached fire-and-brimstone at mosques, sermonizing that the United States should leave Iraq, while demonstrators proclaimed "death to the U.S." and "death to Israel."[163] Armed attacks on coalition forces grew from an "average of six per day in June 2003 to fifteen per day in August and fifty in September."[164] In short order, the United States had a nationalist insurgency on its hands, with US military commanders freely admitting that what they faced was "a classical guerilla type of campaign against us."[165] The parallels with Vietnam were hard to ignore.

The major difference from Vietnam was, of course, that a well-organized communist party had not spearheaded the opposition to the American occupation in Iraq. The political society of Iraq was, in contrast, highly fragmented, and became more so under American occupation. Saddam had incorporated many Shias into the upper reaches of his regime, but his rule had been viewed widely as one of minority Sunnis over Iraq's Shia majority, as well as over Iraq's other main minority, the Kurds. With Saddam gone, Shias rightly felt that it was now their turn at power. American occupation encouraged ethnic schisms.[166] Early American efforts to give Iraqis representation along ethnic lines created a sense at the outset that the majority Shia would be the new ruling class of Iraq. The Kurds cooperated with the Americans but pushed to enhance regional autonomy more than a new, united Iraq. The United States thus worked with Shias, especially the more moderate factions, and the Kurds, and treated Sunnis as the enemy. Sunnis were viewed by American military commanders as mainly Ba'athists and former allies of Saddam. Most of the Iraqis imprisoned by Americans were Sunnis, and they were often treated harshly, without much regard for the norms of warfare. The exposure of the treatment of Iraqi prisoners at Abu Ghraib may well have turned all regional and even global opinion against the Americans.[167] Abu Ghraib was to Iraq what the My Lai massacre was to Vietnam; both undermined any limited legitimacy the United States might have enjoyed in select quarters.

The treatment of Sunnis fueled anger against both the Americans and their moderate Shia cooperators. The fact that members of the new police force—created during American occupation—were mostly Shias, did not help the cause of achieving a unified secular state. Resistance to American occupation now took the form of attacks by militant Sunni groups against the Shias. Car bombs and suicide bombers targeted Shias, including in their holy city Najaf, with devastating results. The militant groups responsible for these attacks, for example, those led by Zarqawi, morphed into the Iraqi al-Qaeda. The Shias, in turn, increasingly had access to state agencies, especially after the nominal elections of 2005, which gave them control over many of the ministries. In power the Shias used special police commandos to attack Sunnis. Instead of providing security and order, the new Iraqi state—very much a product of American endeavors—now became party to the growing ethnic fratricide.

The bombing of the al-Askari mosque in Samarra in 2006 turned into a free-for-all ethnic bloodletting. The mosque was deeply revered by the Shias, who understandably reacted with fury. Numerous Sunni mosques were destroyed in turn. Over the next several months, violence escalated throughout Iraq, but especially in Baghdad. State security forces joined the fray. Rival militias killed for revenge or for gain. Sadr probably lost control over his own Mahdi army, which then joined in the acts of terror and revenge. The Iranians supported some groups within Iraq, and Osama bin Laden's forces supported others. One wonders why the 150,000 US troops still present in the country at the time failed to calm the situation. Once again, was this deliberate or just incompetent? Or, to be fair, maybe no one could control such ethnic hatreds until they declined on their own due to the parties' sheer exhaustion. In any case, the death and destruction was enormous. In the words of one close observer: "Across Baghdad drifted the stench of death . . . . Corpses were dumped in ditches or backstreets. At 120 degrees Fahrenheit, they rotted quickly . . . . In July 2006 more than 3,400 civilians were killed, straining the ability of morgues to keep up. In Baghdad alone more than sixty people were killed every day."[168]

The American project to turn Iraq into a pro-American poster child for democracy and neoliberalism was now in tatters. Whenever America's imperial interventions get bogged down—*quagmire* is a favored American description of these events—domestic politics intervenes. And so it was with Iraq. Opposition to the war grew, and Bush lost both houses of Congress in 2006. The pressure to salvage whatever was possible and get out of Iraq became the new theme. Bush fired Rumsfeld. The surge led by General David Petraeus in 2007 may have brought some of the worst violence under control. However, it is as likely that rival participants in ethnic warfare were exhausted; instead of further engagement, they chose to withdraw into segregated lives. Moderate Sunni leaders also cut their ties with al-Qaeda and forged some ties with the US military.[169] The violence subsided, but we know, in retrospect, that it was only a lull.

The lull allowed the United States to pressure the puppet Iraqi government to pass laws that would enable foreign investors to take over Iraq's oil industry.[170] All the conflict and death notwithstanding, Iraqi oil was denationalized. It is operated now by MNCs from a variety of countries. The lull enabled President Obama to follow through on his election promise to withdraw US troops from Iraq. The American hope was that some US troops would stay on in Iraq; that is the preferred American way to end conflicts. The dependent rulers of Iraq, too, would have preferred that outcome, but they also needed some semblance of sovereignty to maintain legitimacy. The delicate negotiations failed and US troops withdrew from Iraq, bringing the second Gulf War to an end. Or so it seemed. American troops returned to Iraq in 2014 to deal with the challenge of ISIS in Iraq and beyond.[171] Some 5,000 troops remain in Iraq; apparently, they are training Iraqi security forces, but the details of their activities are not fully public. An analysis of post-2011 developments, however, is not part of the current study. Our discussion ends here, with the withdrawal of American forces in 2011.

To recapitulate, US intervention in Iraq, and in the broader Middle East, is still unfolding. As this book goes to press Iran is again in American crosshairs. The last word on the subject of US role in the Middle East is not likely to be written for a while. The factors that led the United States to invade Iraq a second time were not always clear. We know that such avowed goals as destroying Saddam's weapons of mass destruction turned out to be false. Based on fragmentary evidence, I have suggested instead that Americans hoped for a quick military victory in Iraq. American decision-makers thought a quick victory would enable them to engineer a pro-US ruling government in Iraq, along with an open economy, in which oil production was controlled by foreign investors. Understood as such, intervention in Iraq was part of the US global project to roll back the state. Iraq was an attractive candidate for this broader project because it was ruled by a third-rate dictator; it was a major source of oil; and a successful intervention in Iraq might have become a template for establishing *Pax Americana* throughout the strategically vital Middle East. As the analysis above has highlighted, however, US intervention in Iraq has not followed any script that American decision-makers might have hoped for or imagined. The US intervention in Iraq is not quite a failed intervention on the scale of Vietnam, but it also does not provide a ready model for America's future imperial efforts.

The US underestimated the power of Iraqi nationalism. After the United States had deposed Saddam, most Iraqis wanted it to leave. The depth of anti-US sentiment made it difficult for the United States to establish a client regime and get out. Iraqi nationalists organized quickly and expressed their opposition to the United States along both more and less militant pathways. The United States then intervened more deeply. Bremer dismantled the Ba'athist state and the entire Iraqi armed force, probably hoping that a pro-US regime would thus be easier to construct. Without a functioning state, however, militancy only grew. Since US occupation forces cooperated more with some indigenous groups than others, anti-US opposition soon took the form of nationalist Iraqis attacking collaborating Iraqis, and vice-versa. As often happens when there is no functioning Leviathan, soon there was no pattern to the violence, just more and more of it. Between 2003 and 2011, when 150,000 American troops occupied the country, nearly a half million Iraqis died. Should someone be held responsible for crimes against humanity?

Since US goals in Iraq were murky, it is difficult to assess the relative success or failure of the US intervention. The United States clearly achieved some of its minimal goals: Saddam Hussein was deposed; Iraq is not likely to re-emerge as a regional power; and Iraqi oil has been denationalized. The Iraqi state has indeed been rolled back. The question that ought to haunt American decision-makers is whether the enormous human and financial costs of the war were worth these gains. The question is especially poignant because Iraq's power was eviscerated during the First Gulf War, and Saddam was willing to let MNCs come and explore new oil fields in Iraq. The toll of the American intervention on the Iraqi state and society was, however, phenomenal. It is a deeply legitimate ambition of a proud people to desire a wealthy and a powerful nation-state in the contemporary world. Iraq was an artificial creation of the British, and Saddam was an odious dictator. However, many postcolonial states share such characteristics with Iraq. Over time, the Iraqis may well have deposed Saddam on their own and may well have used their oil resources to build a state and society to their own liking. But that was not to be. Had Iraq not had oil, it is hard to imagine that the United States would have expended so many resources to shape and control it. In the words of Cheney, Saddam was a potential regional threat, not because he was an odious dictator, but because he had regional ambitions and because he "has lots of money coming in from oil reserves."[172] During the process of deposing Saddam, however, the United States has also ensured that a strong and a unified Iraqi state will not emerge, certainly not over the short- to medium term.

Conclusion

Following the end of the Cold War, American interventions in the developing world have not ceased. During the Cold War, it was possible for US policymakers and observers to argue that US interventions, such as in Iran, Guatemala, Vietnam, or Chile, were defensive actions against aggressive communists. However, a longer-term perspective that takes into account US interventions both before and after the Cold War casts doubt on the merit of such interpretations. The evidence is consistent with an alternate interpretation developed in this study: US interventions over the twentieth century have sought to tame developing-country nationalists who stand in the way of the American search for economic opportunities overseas. The forced opening of peripheral economies is the one consistent theme that runs through a variety of US—or, for that matter, British—interventions across different eras. Although not all the evidence neatly fits this argument—evidence never does achieve a perfect fit—much of it does. For the most part, the American interventions following the Spanish-American War and during the Cold War, too, fit the pattern that began before the Cold War and now continues beyond it.

I have not analyzed all US interventions in the developing world in the post–Cold War period in this chapter. Those I have focused on capture significant trends. The Cold War faded, but US ambition to remain the unchallenged global hegemon did not diminish. If anything, American leaders interpreted the decline of the Soviet Union as a victory for democracy and free-market capitalism. Unchallenged power and ideological self-assurance proved to be a heady brew. Since then, the United States has pursued its interests in the developing world with renewed moral certainty. As we have seen, it was reasoned that forcibly opening semiclosed economies and taming insubordinate states on the periphery would not only enhance American interests but would benefit—and be welcomed by—the citizens of the developing world. Armed with real power and hubris then, American decision-makers sought to impose the Washington Consensus on development on a range of countries, on the one hand, and intervened militarily in the oil-rich Middle East, on the other hand. An analysis of US economic actions in Latin America and of military occupation of Iraq help us understand the causes and consequences of this most recent phase of American imperialism.

The United States pressured Latin American countries to pursue open-market economies, first to ensure that the debts of American banks were paid, and then, when the debt-crisis was more or less under control, to enhance the access of American producers and investors to markets south of the border. Of course, the IMF and the World Bank, the two multilateral institutions in which the United States wields significant influence, did the actual work of pressuring Latin American governments to open their economies. It is noteworthy that for the most part, governments in Latin America decided to accept these pressures. Such "cooperation" is essential for the functioning of an informal empire. Thus, Latin American governments really did not entertain default on debts as a serious option. One wonders what the US reaction to such a move might have been. The option of pursuing a more autonomous development path was also not realistic for Latin American governments. This is because regional economies have long been dependent economies that exchange commodities for manufactured goods, and rely on foreign rather than domestic savings for economic growth. The embrace of Washington Consensus policies hurt rather than improved the economic performance of Latin American countries: economic growth during the free market era, say, 1980 to 2005, remained sluggish, with sharp inequalities, and a continued dependence on commodity exports and foreign investors. That citizens of the region reacted angrily and elected left-of-center governments, who opposed the Washington Consensus, is then not all that surprising.

Unlike in Latin America, American domination of the Middle East is more recent and a work in progress. Once British forces pulled out of the oil-rich region in 1971, the United States stepped in. When American proxies could not carry on the task of policing the region, direct US-military presence increased during the 1980s. American military interventions have increased sharply in the post–Cold War period, including in Libya, Syria, Afghanistan, and Iraq. The second war in Iraq was planned as a decisive step in a vague but grand scheme to incorporate the oil-rich Middle East into the American orbit. The hope was to roll back the state in much of the Middle East, so that foreign investors would have access to the oil of the region, and client regimes—pliable democracies—would ensure that key allies like Israel and Saudi Arabia are not threatened in the future. The American war in Iraq has not followed any anticipated script. Unlike Latin America, the building blocks to create stable but subservient regimes are not readily available, certainly not in Iraq. The United States seriously underestimated Iraqi nationalism. The strength of anti-US reaction forced the United States to occupy Iraq. Whether deliberately or not, US policies unleashed ethnic fratricide in Iraq. While 150,000 US troops occupied Iraq, nearly half a million Iraqis died. The United States did succeed in ensuring that Iraq's oil was denationalized. Slowly but surely, Iraqi oil has again passed into the hands of foreign investors. Whether or not the United States construes its intervention as a victory, for now the Iraqi state has been eviscerated, and Iraqi citizens have paid a heavy cost for America's regional ambitions.

Conclusion

Western imperialism has fundamentally shaped the developing world. The focus of the present study has been on the role of Great Britain and the United States in this historical process. Britain and the United States were the dominant capitalist powers of the nineteenth and the twentieth centuries respectively. Why they expanded into the global periphery and how they molded parts of it that came under their sway have been my principal concerns in the book. The subject is vast, and I am painfully aware of all that has not been covered. Yet based on the historical materials analyzed, it is time to pull together the main themes. The central argument can be restated briefly: time and again, the pursuit of national economic prosperity led hegemonic powers to expand into peripheral areas of the world. Limiting the sovereignty of states on the periphery was the main method of ensuring that peripheral economies stay open and accessible to Anglo-American economic interests. Loss of sovereignty, however, greatly hurt the life chances of people living in Asia, the Middle East, Africa, and Latin America. Sovereign states may not be sufficient to facilitate economic progress, but sovereignty is a precondition for the emergence of effective states. Effective states, in turn, are surely necessary to propel countries toward prosperous, industrial societies. Some exceptions notwithstanding, imperialism—both formal and informal—has thus repeatedly undermined the prospects of steady economic progress in the global periphery.

This argument has been developed with reference to a range of empirical materials, starting with the British role in India in the eighteenth century and ending with the recent American intervention in Iraq. To conclude the study, I go over some of the same ground that was covered in the introductory chapter, while trying to minimize repetition; the logic of the bare argument will now be fleshed out instead with historical examples. I first set aside some preparatory issues again, such as the use of the term "imperialism," and why compare Britain and the

How Britain and the United States Shaped the Global Periphery. Atul Kohli, Oxford University Press (2020).

DOI: 10.1093/oso/9780190069629.001.0001

United States. The core of the conclusion then revisits the central themes of the study: why imperialists imperialize, how to make sense of the varieties of imperialism, and what the impact of imperialism is on countries in the global periphery. The book ends with some musings on the future of imperialism, including the emerging role of China.

Some Preparatory Issues, Revisited

Cases of both formal and informal empire are analyzed in this book. The more specific focus is British and US interventions in the global periphery during the nineteenth and the twentieth centuries. Before summarizing the key conclusions, it may be useful to clarify again the use of key concepts, and to justify again why I have chosen to examine some cases and not others.

Imperialism is a controversial term. It is used in this study to characterize situations in which powerful states seek to control the political and economic life of weaker states or people. Most observers are not likely to take exception to the use of the term *imperialism* when control of one state over another includes direct territorial control, as in formal colonies. Few will thus object—on definitional grounds, at least—that the British colonization of India and Nigeria or the American control of the Philippines and Cuba in the first half of the twentieth century were instances of imperialism. Controversy arises instead when such control is exercised indirectly. Informal empire is a more debatable concept because nominally sovereign states are free to exercise sovereign authority, at least in principle. Was British influence, say, over Argentina in the nineteenth century or American influence over Iran during the Shah's reign really instances of informal empire? While my answer is yes, serious scholars can propose different answers to such questions.

My understanding of informal empire has both conceptual and empirical elements. It helps to conceptualize the autonomy of states in the world arena as varying along a continuum, with colonies and fully sovereign states occupying the two ends of the continuum, and client states, which are part of informal empires, falling somewhere in between. Client states—or semi-sovereign states, or semicolonies—thus exercise more autonomy than colonies but less than fully sovereign states. The limits on their autonomy are best understood in real historical situations. Recall the definition of informal empire that was proposed in the introduction, with three key elements: imperial powers exercise veto power over key policies in client states; under normal circumstances the ruling elite in the metropole and the periphery collaborate; and when such relations of domination and subordination are challenged, imperial powers use (or are in a position to use) coercion to seek compliance. The exercise of veto power, elite collaboration, and the use of coercion are all observable and can be verified empirically before characterizing a relationship as informal imperialism.

The use of coercion is especially significant for assessing a relationship as imperial. That is why I avoid characterizing mere exercise of influence or economic expansion from the metropole into the periphery as imperialism. Economic expansion becomes imperialistic when it is forced. British intervention in Egypt and China involved overt use of military force to either initiate or sustain economic access. Covert and forceful interventions helped the United States overthrow regimes in Iran and Chile when it deemed their governments to be inimical to American economic interests; following the CIA-supported coups, pro-American dictators replaced the elected nationalist rulers of Iran and Chile. The US military interventions in Vietnam and Iraq were so obviously imperialistic that they hardly require any definitional justification. By contrast, overt military intervention by the British was rare in Argentina and in the American imposition of the Washington Consensus on Latin America. These cases may thus be more debatable as instances of informal empire. Nevertheless, in my analysis of British influence on Argentina, I document numerous instances of forceful British interventions that either helped to install pro-British rulers in power in Argentina, or ensured that economic policies pursued in Argentina remained favorable to British economic interests. In the economic opening of Latin America, the American-led economic coercion was both deliberate and powerful enough to seriously constrain the policy choices of Latin American governments.

Once informal empire is understood as a variant of imperialism, the logic of a comparative focus on British and American imperialism is easier to explicate. A suggestion in the introduction was that British and American empires are empires of growth, analytically distinguishable from traditional land empires. It is not necessary to repeat those observations. What is important is to justify the claim that the British and American empires are indeed similar enough to warrant serious comparative analysis. A scholarly reluctance to comparing the British and American empires may rest in an understanding of Britain in the nineteenth century as mainly a colonial power, but the United States in the twentieth century as an anticolonial one. This contrast has merit only if the focus is on formal empire, that is, on colonialism. Britain and the United States were the dominant capitalist powers of the nineteenth and the twentieth centuries, respectively. They both sought to lead and shape the world in their respective centuries. Recall Lord Palmerston's suggestion that Britain stood "at the head of moral, social and political civilisation," and that it was Britain's task to "lead the way and direct the march of other nations." And then recall Woodrow Wilson's similar claim in the twentieth century that the United States was destined to be "the justest, the most progressive, the most honorable, the most enlightened nation in the world" and his urging Americans to "accept what is offered to us, the leadership of the world."[1]

Clothed in these moral justifications, both Britain and the United States pursued their respective economic interests in the global periphery. Britain complemented its formal empire with an informal one in the nineteenth century; the balance for the United States in the twentieth tilted toward the latter. The British first discovered the value of informal empire via trial and error. As the British economy became more competitive, in the late-eighteenth century members of the British political class came to understand that economic expansion might require only open economies on the periphery, rather than conquest. We thus note, in chapter 2, a British commander, Sir Ralph Abercrombie, arguing for the need to open Latin American economies because mere openness would ensure that Great Britain "would in reality possess nine parts in ten" of the great economic prize of southern America. And then we see again, around the same time period, the British ambassador to China, Lord Macartney, suggesting that the idea of conquering China was too "wild," especially because "all can be quietly got without it that was expected to be got with it." This idea that *all can be quietly got without conquest* then came to be the core insight behind the pursuit of informal empire. Castlereagh put this idea into practice in South America in the first half of the nineteenth century, and other British imperialists subsequently adapted it to meet local circumstances in Egypt and China.

The Americans learned from the British. As the American economy became more and more competitive in the new century, American leaders also sensed that economic openness around the world would create favorable opportunities for American industries. The British even helped Americans draft the Open Door notes, with reference to China. Opening doors of others then became the American ideology of informal empire for much of the twentieth century, especially in the post–World War II period. Those who stood in the way of open economies, both communists and nationalists, had to be tamed. Although conquest was not needed for economic expansion, the taming of recalcitrant governments to open economies often required force. Sustaining openness further required installing and maintaining stable-but-subservient regimes in power in client states. Many of the cases of American intervention I have discussed in the book followed this logic. If we broaden the focus to include both formal and informal empire, the shared features of the British and American empires become clearer. The British and American empires no longer look like apples and oranges. Instead, they look like apples of different varieties. The two empires then invite systematic comparative analysis, with a focus on both similarities and differences.

Since both Britain and the United States have run vast global empires, a final justification is needed for why I focus on some cases of British and American imperialism, and not others. The first justification is simply an admission of limitation: a discussion of more cases would have been desirable but there is only so much a team of one can accomplish. Within those limits, the choice of cases analyzed here was guided by a need to capture regional variation, and by the importance of the cases. No effort to generalize about causes and consequences of imperialism, for example, would be complete without taking the British experience in India into account. Theories of imperialism that base their conclusions mainly on the late nineteenth-century Scramble for Africa are especially limited when they neglect India. However, the scramble remains of great importance for a full understanding of British colonialism. Nigeria came to be one of the most important British colonies in sub-Saharan Africa; focusing on that case helps to further our understanding of what Eric Hobsbawm famously called the "Age of Empires."[2] In addition to formal colonies, Britain exercised enormous influence over Latin America, the Ottoman Empire, and Ch'ing China in the nineteenth century. My focus on Britain's vast informal empire in Argentina, Egypt, and China, then, complements the study of British colonialism.

By the time the United States emerged on the global scene following the Spanish-American War, the British century was nearly over and the American century was about to begin. In the words of Walter LaFeber, the Americans then started "searching for opportunity" overseas.[3] The American colonization of Cuba and the Philippines, as well as the efforts to seek influence in China, are the obvious cases with which to begin exploring early American imperialism. America's efforts to expand into the global periphery after World War II belied the popular views that United States was a friend of nationalism in the developing world. In the Cold War context, the United States used its enormous power superiority to thrash communists and, at times, even nationalists, who got in the way of the American design for a free world of open economies. The cases of Iran, Vietnam, and Chile reveal the underlying dynamics. Last, in the soft and hard US interventions in the developing world that have continued even after the end of the Cold War, Americans have used economic and military power to pursue their global ambitions. US efforts to reopen Latin American economies late in the twentieth century, and the most recent military intervention and occupation of Iraq in the twenty-first century, help us understand the continuing nature of

American imperialism, especially in light of British efforts to achieve similar goals nearly a century ago.

Why Imperialists Imperialize

The search for economic prosperity drove both Britain and the United States to establish influence over peripheral countries of the world. How strong is the support for this proposition? Strong, I suggest. I will recapitulate the logic of this argument, and then juxtapose it to alternate arguments and revisit historical developments—now in a schematic form, of course—to assess the validity of my explanation of the motives that drive modern imperialism.

It is important to set aside some misleading views about imperialism. First is the tendency among some observers to deny that imperialism continues in the modern world. Leaving aside apologists and court scholars, serious proponents of this view hold it because they tend to equate modern imperialism with colonialism.[4] Although I do not share this view, it is a respectable one. I have in this study instead treated the formal control and the informal control of one state over another as variants of imperialism. Understood this way, imperialism is well and alive in the twenty-first century. Second, a variety of observers still propose modern-day versions of the white man's burden to explain what drives contemporary imperialism. One serious version of this standpoint treats American efforts to promote democracy overseas as a driving force behind American expansionism.[5] This may be true here and there, but it will certainly not do as a general explanation of American interventions in the poor parts of the world. Missionaries notwithstanding, there is very little in the historical record to support a suggestion that the United States, or Britain, expanded overseas primarily to promote the well-being of peripheral countries.

A somewhat more serious suggestion that also needs to be set aside is that imperialism in the modern world does not pay, that it is often a mistake. This was the logic behind Joseph Schumpeter's argument against Lenin, in which he proposed that imperialism was moved, not so much by the profit motive of capitalists, as by the atavistic elements in society who still care about status and militarism.[6] Over the subsequent decades, numerous versions of the idea that imperialism is irrational or a mistake have been put forward. For example, a strong criticism of the American war in Vietnam was that it was a giant mistake: it was a product of mistaking nationalists for communists or of the mistaken concerns of ideologues worried about falling dominoes; or it was perpetuated by status-obsessed leaders who could not face defeat at the hands of a "fourth rate power." [7] This view allows well-meaning observers to criticize imperialist actions here and there, but it avoids a central question, why are such "mistakes" repeated over and over again, across space and time? The answer is, imperialism is not a mistake. There are instances in which imperialists fail to achieve their objectives, such as in Vietnam. However, a theory of motives ought not to be deduced from the outcomes. Imperialists imperialize because they hope to gain from such actions. Whether metropolitan states interpret the national economic interest narrowly, equating it with the interests of select capitalists, or more broadly has varied over time and place; what has not varied is that metropolitan states take the lead in imperialism, hoping for gain. Starting with the East India Company and culminating in the most recent American invasion of Iraq, one aim of the historical analysis in this book has been to identify what imperialists hoped to gain from imperialism. Serious analyses of what drives imperialism need to focus on the self-interested behavior of imperialists.

I have suggested that both Britain and the United States expanded into the global periphery to enhance national economic prosperity. This proposition competes with two other venerable, interest-oriented hypotheses: realist and Marxist. Realists often suggest that political interests of national security move imperialism; Marxists, by contrast, argue that imperial expansion really happens at the behest of the capitalists of the hegemonic powers.[8] Before revisiting the historical evidence in support of either proposition, it may be useful to focus for a moment on the underlying logic of these competing arguments. My argument that the pursuit of national economic prosperity is the taproot of imperialism begins with the claim that modern states pursue prosperity, both as an end in itself and because state leaders believe that national power is a function of economic buoyancy. For hegemonic capitalist states, the world is their oyster. Leaders of these states seek opportunities for national capitalists abroad as a means to enhance both prosperity and power. Hegemonic capitalist states typically seek to open peripheral economies, hoping that such openness will facilitate trade, investment, and financial opportunities for their national firms. When stable openness is not readily achievable in peripheral countries, imperialism becomes likely. Limiting the sovereignty of peripheral countries is the means by which hegemonic capitalist states ensure economic access in the world. Both formal and informal empire originates from this national logic of dominant capitalist states.

It will be evident to careful readers that the logic of my argument overlaps with that of both realism and Marxism, especially at the theoretical edges of these venerable paradigms. This is not surprising, since I draw on both scholarly traditions. But I am also seeking to move beyond. If the realist argument is that states pursue national security and admits that national security depends largely on a growing national economy, then my argument is nearly indistinguishable from some versions of realism. However, a focus on national-level factors as determinants of foreign behavior of dominant states is only a minority strain among realists.

Following Kenneth Waltz, the majority view is instead attracted to "system level explanations" in which national behavior is understood mainly as a product of balance-of-power politics in an "anarchic" world.[9] Benjamin Cohen thus argues that imperialism results from the urge of nations to maximize their power positions in an insecure world.[10] This is the core realist explanation of imperialism. I return below to the discussion of the empirical validity of such arguments and suggest that the real empirical challenge to a number of balance-of-power arguments arises when dominant capitalist states continue imperial expansion even when the global balance of power is not tight.[11]

Similarly, if the Marxist argument is that capitalist states have enough autonomy from the interests of specific capitalists to pursue the interests of capitalism as a national economic system, then my argument is, again, nearly indistinguishable from some versions of Marxism. However, once Marxist scholars admit that states can pursue what is good for the national economy irrespective of the demands of specific capitalists, then they have very nearly thrown the baby out with the bathwater; the argument is not really a Marxist one anymore.[12] The core Marxist argument of imperialism, which is deeply persuasive in some historical instances, instead, is when capitalists actually influence state elites to undertake aggressive actions aimed at opening markets or protecting investments or ensuring that loans are paid off. We have encountered many such cases in this volume. However, we have also encountered numerous other cases of imperial expansion in which the direct pressure of capitalists was missing, in which the state elite took the lead in both diagnosing what ailed the national economy and in suggesting cures, which included aggressive imperialism. The Weberian theoretical assumption that I embrace instead of strained Marxism is that state and class—or authority and association—are autonomous realms of human activity that influence each other.[13] This theoretical standpoint enables one to accommodate class analysis of state and imperialism—when needed—but without embracing a Marxist framework. Such a theoretical position is also consistent with a normative preference for social democracy and state sovereignty in the modern world.

If realists underemphasize the importance of economic elites as a force behind imperial expansion, Marxists underestimate the power of nationalism that also drives imperial interventions. To overcome these limitations, I have focused on the pursuit of national economic interest overseas as the key motive that propels imperialism. The core intuition is that imperialism is moved by a convenient marriage of the power interests of the state and the profit interests of the economic elite. How well does this proposition hold up against the empirical evidence analyzed in this book? On balance, the proposition holds up well against much of it, but not all. In what follows I provide a quick summary of this historical evidence.

Imperialism of the type represented by the East India Company began at the initiative of private interests, and received only limited support from the British state. There can be no doubt that this early example of imperialism was driven by economic motives, though there is room to disagree about the balance between private and public economic interests. Corporate initiative notwithstanding, over time the East India Company came to depend more and more on the British state. A company on its own simply could not rule a country of the size and complexity of India. The narrow goal of company profits then broadened to include finding ways to enrich the mother country. Beyond company profits, the East India Company became rulers of India and, in the process, devised, with the help of the British state, a variety of methods to use Indian resources to support British interests. These included financing a large armed force in India for British use, transferring Indian revenues to Britain to help the British state and economy, and opening the Indian economy under duress as a taker of British manufactured goods. The East India Company's role in India is a classic case of the marriage of force and profits as drivers of early British imperialism.

Throughout the nineteenth century, Britain complemented its formal empire with an informal one. As British hegemony consolidated, British influence over Latin America, the Ottoman Empire, and Ch'ing China also grew. It is difficult to sustain an analytical case that this expansion was driven by balance-of-power considerations, because by mid-century, Britain had few rivals. The evidence that Britain's primary concern was economic gain, ideally without coercion but with coercion if necessary, is overwhelming. To recall the underlying forces: Britain had a head start in the development of industry by the late eighteenth century, and industrialists needed markets for their goods. Britain also established naval superiority following the end of the Napoleonic Wars. British economic and political elites came to share the view that sustaining Britain's global dominance would require a buoyant capitalist economy. Economic buoyancy, in turn, demanded expansion into peripheral regions of the world. By mid-century, Lord Palmerston unequivocally espoused this position and went on to argue that it should be a key function of the British government to open overseas markets for merchants and the producers. Such dynamic capitalism would thus serve the interests of both the capitalists and the state. A marriage of force and profits is what drove Britain to seek gains across the world. When indigenous rulers did not readily succumb to British ambitions, Britain subjugated them using force until open economies could be established. This is the main pattern leading to the creation of Britain's informal empire in Argentina, Egypt, and China.

In Argentina and Brazil, the British in the first half of the nineteenth century first sought outlets for their growing textile industry, and then sought to build railways, and finally, lent these countries large sums of money as a profitable business venture. It used force periodically to establish and maintain these economic interactions. Still, within a comparative context, Britain's use of overt force in Argentina, for example, was less pronounced than it was in Egypt and China. Instead, a ruling class of European origin came to fore in Argentina, whose members made fortunes in a dependent economy, and were often happy to facilitate stable subservience. By contrast, the ancient civilizations of Egypt and China did not as readily capitulate to Britain. Muhammad Ali sought to emulate European industrial gains in Egypt via an early Egyptian version of the Meiji Restoration. His efforts were brutally undercut by the British, who turned Egypt into a supplier of high-quality cotton for the British textile industry. Egypt, along with Turkey, did absorb its share of British manufactured goods and substantial foreign loans, including for the Suez Canal. Given Egypt's location, strategic concerns were also more important in British imperialism there than in Argentina or China. But it was domestic opposition to imperialism that eventually precipitated a colonial-type of takeover of Egypt. Last, economic motives were paramount in China, first, to push the opium trade to facilitate revenue transfers to Britain from India, and then to sell manufactured goods, and, finally, to absorb foreign investments and loans. Force was used overtly to open the Chinese economy, and the British used their military superiority to construct a variety of mechanisms to ensure subservience, including control over public finances.

I used the examples of post-1857 India and Nigeria to analyze patterns of British colonialism. The argument that national economic interest was the motive force behind imperialism holds up for both cases, but more strongly for India than for Nigeria. Britain's establishment of a formal colony in India in 1857 poses a real challenge to balance-of power-arguments for imperialism. British power at the time was mostly unchallenged, and no system-level threat was pushing Britain to hold on to India. And yet the British crushed a major anti-British military revolt by Indians to turn India into a Crown colony. It is notable that at mid-century hardly anyone in Britain questioned the need to hold on to India. A central motive was that the economic importance of India for both state and private capital in Britain was already well established, and sustained benefits were expected. There was also the concern that any indecisiveness about India would have broader ramifications because it could indicate to others that the British capacity—or willingness—to run a global empire might be in decline. India was thus already central to British prosperity and power in the middle of the nineteenth century. It is therefore no surprise that Britain used ruthless force to hold on to India for another century.

And India met the British expectations of economic rewards. The major vehicle via which Britain continued to derive economic benefits from India during Crown rule was still trade. Britain was under pressure from other late industrializers, and the captive Indian market helped the British textile industry to sustain growth in the second half of the nineteenth century, and beyond. Over time, other products entered the picture, especially during the second industrial revolution. The importance of India for managing Britain's balance of payments also continued during the post-1858 phase. In addition, British investments in India became sizable, often supported by rates of return that were guaranteed by the colonial state, for example, in the railways. India provided jobs for the British in substantial numbers, and indentured Indians replaced African slaves as a source of labor on British plantations in the West Indies. The British Indian Army also continued to support Britain's global rule, at no cost whatsoever to the British taxpayer. Some of India's economic importance to Britain declined after the First World War (see chapter 3). The shift eased the pain of decolonization for Britain in the middle of the twentieth century.

Nigeria was of considerably less economic importance for Britain. Except for Egypt and South Africa, this was probably also true for most of Britain's other colonies in tropical Africa. Nevertheless, the economic benefits Nigeria eventually yielded do not tell us much about the original motives to colonize Nigeria; it is clear instead that economic motives were at the forefront when Britain began its imperial journey into Nigeria. George Goldie and his company, the Royal Niger Company—reminiscent of the East India Company—initially spearheaded the colonial efforts. It is the case that by the time Europeans entered the frenzy to divide up Africa late in the nineteenth century, political and economic conflict among European powers was indeed growing. That is why balance-of-power theories of imperialism find support for their views in the Scramble for Africa. But since this point of view does not help to explain other instances of imperialism analyzed in this book, I have doubts that it applies all that well to this historical episode either. I argue instead that of the various theories developed to explain the Scramble for Africa, economic theories remain the most relevant, though not of the Hobson-Lenin variety.

Arguments that prioritize strategic considerations especially make no sense for West African countries like Nigeria. The whole region was of limited strategic significance. Unlike Egypt, Nigeria was not a route to anywhere. And if, instead, the argument is that the need to save the old empire in India is what drove the urge to acquire a new empire,[14] then given the economic importance of India to Britain, this argument is quite consistent with economic arguments. I thus argue that what moved the British to colonize Nigeria was the urge to seek access to possible markets in the African interior. Competition with other European powers was real, but in West Africa this competition was mainly about trade. The British were irked by the French use of protectionism, and they hoped that open access would provide important raw materials in exchange for their manufactured goods, which, toward the end of the century, faced increasing competition elsewhere in the world. Some of this hope was borne out, even in Nigeria, though not as much as in, say, Egypt or South Africa, not to mention India.

When we move to cases of American expansion into the poor regions of the world, national economic interests still help to explain the underlying motives, though there are some qualifications, even important ones. Following the Spanish-American War, the United States established colonies, or near colonies, in both the Caribbean and the Pacific. What drove this early imperial expansion? The pressures to expand overseas had been building in the decades following the Civil War, when the United States developed a powerful industrial economy. With the example of Britain very much on the minds of influential Americans, arguments emerged that great powers must seek commercial opportunities beyond their borders and that they need to build military power to support such ambitions. So, along with an industrial economy, the United States developed a powerful navy. The boom-and-bust character of a buoyant capitalist economy added to the argument that ready access to overseas markets could smooth such fluctuations, facilitating steady economic growth and national power. Much of the global periphery was already colonized, however, and so the United States sought access to the few remaining open economic spaces. The largest among these was China. The temptations of the China market loomed large in America's early overseas imagination. The Philippines was initially deemed a desirable acquisition because it would provide ready access to China. Closer to home, Britain was still a major presence in such large economies as Argentina, Brazil, and even Mexico. Still, with the American economy becoming more competitive, and American naval power growing, new opportunities were opening up in the Caribbean and Central America. This was because weaker European powers like Spain were ready to be expelled from their few remaining colonial outposts.

Nationalist revolts against Spanish colonialism in Cuba and the Philippines provided opportunities for the United States to intervene, avowedly in support of indigenous nationalists. However, America's quick naval victories over Spain did not lead to independence for Cuba or the Philippines, but to the suppression of indigenous nationalists and, some opposition to imperialism within the United States notwithstanding, to the creation of new American colonies. By establishing naval bases in the Philippines, the United States became a Pacific power. This enabled it to claim a right, in a condominium with other major imperial powers, to full and open access to the Chinese market, which had been the big prize all along. A stronger presence in the Caribbean led the United States to appropriate Panama from Colombia and to build the Panama Canal. The canal was of great value, not only to the United States Navy, but also to manufacturing interests on the American East Coast. It made access to the Pacific much easier and trade routes more profitable. The rulers of some weaker southern neighbors were also tamed to either favor American investors or to ensure payment of debt owed to Americans, or even to Europeans. The American leaders McKinley, Theodore Roosevelt, and Taft encouraged these developments both because of their close ties to America's economic elite and because they viewed overseas expansion as essential for America's prosperity and global might.

During the Cold War, American leaders often justified their interventions in developing countries in terms of a fight against communism. If one takes such justifications at face value, American expansionism during this period could be interpreted either as propelled by balance-of-power politics or as an ideological struggle. But a closer analysis of the US interventions in Iran, Vietnam, and Chile reveals that economic motives were never too far from what shaped the American approach to the developing world. This is not to deny that Cold War tensions shaped American reactions, especially in a case like Vietnam. Yet, as I argue in chapter 5, these specific cases of American intervention need to be understood in an even broader context. More than Britain, the United States came to understand its hegemonic role as a global system of power. After it emerged as the world's most powerful state following the Second World War, it then used its power superiority to mold a world order that fit its values and interests, the centerpiece of which was to be an open global economy. While capitalist Europe and Japan joined this global order, many others did not. In addition to the Soviet Union and its neighboring empire, a variety of communist and nationalist leaders in the developing world chose to pursue state-led development and closed or semiclosed their economies. The United States tolerated some of these pursuits but confronted those communists and nationalists that stood (or were perceived to be standing) in the way of its desire to establish an open global economic order.

What really moved the Americans to intervene in the developing world was the threat posed by assertive nationalists in the developing world—some more radical than others—to America's hegemonic ambitions. Iran's Mossadegh thus not only threatened key economic interests of Britain, an already weakened ally, but also threatened to create an unacceptable norm for who controls the production, supply, and profits of an important commodity—oil. The United States orchestrated Mossadegh's overthrow and replaced him with a pliable client who was willing to fit into America's broader design. The revolutionary nationalism of Ho Chi Minh similarly threatened important interests of France, another weakened ally. The more the United States got involved in Vietnam, the more America's global credibility became an issue. American efforts to preserve its reputation as a global power that would contain communism prolonged a costly and tragic war, which the United States eventually lost. And Chile's Allende posed a direct threat to American corporations, but he also created a broader danger by encouraging a nationalist and a democratic socialist pathway to development in America's backyard. He, too, was overthrown with the help of the CIA and replaced by a pro-American dictator. American interventions during the Cold War followed a pattern similar to earlier American interventions at the turn of the twentieth century: they were aimed at taming the nationalists of poor countries to create open economic spaces.

After the decline of the Soviet Union, the United States chose to expand *Pax Americana* with the hope of further opening semiclosed economies, on the one hand, and taming anti-American despots, on the other hand. The American efforts in the post–Cold War period to impose the Washington Consensus on Latin American countries and the invasion and the occupation of Iraq both have to be understood in this broader context. The early priority of the United States government during the Latin American debt crisis was to ensure the solvency of major American banks, and so it worked through the IMF, the World Bank, and other multilateral institutions to deal with Latin American governments. These institutions offered loans to Latin American countries so that they could continue to repay their loans to commercial banks. In exchange, Latin American countries were asked to undertake policy changes, or "structural reforms," to ensure that they would have enough resources to continue to service their debts. Over time these policy packages were dubbed the "Washington Consensus" on development. Responding to pressure from the United States and the US-controlled multilateral institutions, countries in Latin America (and elsewhere) embraced these policies during the 1990s. The United States and these multilateral institutions maintained a discourse that policy reform was pro-growth, even though it was understood that the economic opening associated with the Washington Consensus could jeopardize economic growth in Latin America. The poor countries of Latin America were thus pressured to embrace these policies to benefit American economic interests.

American domination of the oil-rich Middle East is more recent and remains a work in progress. When British forces pulled out of the region, in 1971, the United States stepped in. When American proxies, such as the Shah of Iran, could not carry on the task of policing the region, direct US-military presence increased during the 1980s. American military interventions have increased sharply in the post–Cold War period in Libya, Syria, Afghanistan, and Iraq. As this book goes to press, in 2019, Iran is again a target of American wrath. The tragedy of 9/11 gave the US an opportunity to pursue regime change in Iraq. This was to be a first step towards a more ambitious hope of establishing pro-American regimes in the oil-rich Middle East. The hope was to roll back the state in much of the Middle East so that foreign investors would have access to the region's oil and client regimes would ensure that key allies like Israel and Saudi Arabia are not threatened in the future. The American war in Iraq did not turn out as anticipated. The outcome is still unfolding. The uncertainty of the outcome does not take anything away from the original motive to invade Iraq: get rid of a brutal dictator and establish a pro-American regime as a first-step toward remaking the oil-rich Middle East in the American image.

To sum up the discussion on motives that drive imperialism, both Britain and the United States used their power superiority to expand into poor countries of the world. The two hegemonic powers of the nineteenth and the twentieth centuries established colonial control over some parts of the world, and installed pliable regimes in power in other parts of the world. I return to the issue of why they chose formal empire in some places and during some periods, versus informal empire elsewhere and during other periods. The main motive that drove the expansion of both Britain and the United States was search for economic opportunity. The suggestion of some scholars that imperial expansion is best understood as an effort to enhance national security simply does not stand up to evidence examined in this book, except in a few cases. For example, the late nineteenth-century burst of imperial European powers is one important instance that makes some sense when interpreted as a result of balance-of-power politics. The American war in Vietnam can also be credibly analyzed as an American effort to stop the spread of communism and thus the power of the Soviet Union. However, as I have documented, a strictly political analysis in both cases is rather incomplete. More importantly, a balance-of-power interpretation does not explain the numerous other cases of imperialism analyzed in the book. This is because all realist explanations of imperialism face an important, logical problem: Why do hegemonic powers that do not face any real challenge to their power, still choose to imperialize little powers?[15]

The answer I develop focuses on the need of hegemonic powers to enhance national prosperity. This is because there is no end to human want: the more prosperous the better. Moreover, sustained prosperity also ensures a relative power edge, prolonging hegemony. Both Britain and the United States thus used their power superiority to open up markets of lesser powers. Open economies elsewhere created opportunities for British and American business to trade, invest, and lend money. There is some evidence in the cases analyzed above to support a Marxist interpretation of imperialism; imperialism often benefited metropolitan capitalists. But the reason I have not embraced a Marxist interpretation is because, time and again, imperial actions were spearheaded by metropolitan states. And it is not easy to establish that these states responded only to the interests of their capitalists; at times they did, and in other instances they did not. It is thus better to begin with the assumption that state elites have broader horizons. They pursue a national agenda, even though in some instances the view of the "nation" entertained by the rulers is narrow and nearly indistinguishable from those of the economic elite. Metropolitan rulers choose to open economies on the global periphery to enhance economic growth at home. This helps metropolitan capitalists but the fruits of sustained growth are also national. The root cause of imperialism is thus the pursuit of national economic prosperity.

Varieties of Imperialism

The means imperialists use to seek economic access in peripheral countries is political leverage, if not control. Imperialism takes different forms because the strategies for establishing and maintaining political influence vary depending on the circumstances. One major variation that we encounter throughout this study is that between formal and informal empire. What factors lead imperialists to colonize some countries and to pursue informal imperialism in others? Why do strategies for establishing informal empire vary? As we revisit the historical evidence that helps us answer these questions, keep in mind that the various British imperial efforts best help us understand the logic of formal versus informal empire. The American approaches to informal empire, in turn, help us home in on the political constraints that incline hegemonic powers to pursue different paths to creating client states.

The choice between formal and informal empire was a serious one for the British in the nineteenth century, more so than for Americans in the twentieth. We have seen that territorial control over India was already well advanced in the eighteenth century. But the industrializing, capitalist Britain of the nineteenth century seemed to prefer informal control in places as diverse as Latin America and the Ottoman and Ch'ing empires. If one juxtaposes these nineteenth-century cases to that of India, one could conclude that true colonialism was a product of a mercantilist age that came to an end with the emergence of thriving capitalism. Historical developments, however, complicate the argument, because at the end of the nineteenth century, Britain colonized large parts of Africa. So what led the British to seek territorial control in some places but not others?

In a well-known formulation, Gallagher and Robinson argued that Britain preferred an informal empire in the nineteenth century but resorted to territorial control only when informal collaboration failed to secure ready access to the peripheral economies.[16] Based on the evidence discussed in this volume, this argument is not fully persuasive. The major exception to Gallagher and Robinson's argument is India. Britain sought territory in India from the outset. Land revenue from India made the Raj profitable. Even when it was faced with a major revolt in the mid-nineteenth century, there was never a question of running India informally. If capitalist Britain really preferred informal rule, why did it establish

Crown rule over India at the height of the Victorian era? A second problem with the Gallagher and Robinson argument is that Britain's informal empire often bred the conditions for formal empire. The cases of Egypt and Nigeria both exhibit the evolution along such a continuum. In parts of the British Empire, then, informal versus formal rule were really not alternate choices as much as they were stages.

Recall that the British wanted peripheral countries to be "well kept" and "always accessible." The British choice of formal versus informal empire in the nineteenth century then often depended on whether they could secure stable subservience in one part of the global periphery or another; since conditions varied, so did strategy. Moderately well- governed countries with rulers who could be made to collaborate were the best candidates for informal empire, and, as we saw in chapter 2, this is what the British found in Argentina, especially after the violence that followed independence from Spain had settled down. The fact that the British and Argentine economies proved to be highly complementary helped because the Argentinian upper classes also benefited from the arrangement; on balance, then, the Argentinian rulers were ready collaborators. Another condition that helped the emergence of an informal empire in Latin America was the power and the interest of the United States in the region. The Monroe Doctrine, though ultimately not sufficient to dissuade the British from recolonization—the British navy was far superior to the American navy at the time—was a factor. Britain's informal empire in Argentina ensured that the lion's share of the benefits would accrue to British business interests, but left open the prospect of gain for the Argentinian elite and, over time, allowed the Americans to make inroads.

At the other end of the continuum of informal to formal rule, the main condition that seems to be associated with formal colonial rule is the absence of centralized rule in the periphery. In the words of George Goldie, quoted in chapter 3, "[T]here can be no permanence of commerce without political power" in countries without a stable central government. Although India and Nigeria were colonized under very different circumstances, they did share a critical condition: absence of central authority. Without such authority, the question of whom to collaborate with was moot. Establishing territorial control and central authority had to precede a search for collaborators at lower levels. Formal colonialism, in other words, was a prerequisite for taking sustained economic advantage of peripheral countries in which central authority was either weak or missing.

Recall the case of the East India Company in India under Aurangzeb (see chapter 1). When the company lost a military engagement to the Mughal ruler in 1690, trade with India had to be sustained on commercial terms for nearly half a century. The disintegration of the Mughal Empire in the eighteenth century created opportunities for the company to both initiate the long-term process of territorial control and alter the terms of economic interactions in favor of Britain. More than a century later, the colonial advance in Nigeria followed similar patterns. After Britain established a colony on Lagos, in 1861, it carried on trade with West Africa for a few decades, without the need to colonize the area. The need to expand trade, however, required access to the interior. This was difficult. Indigenous strongmen were an impediment. More importantly, there was no central authority that could be pressured into facilitating the building of railways, searching and establishing rights over mines, expanding the production of exportable crops, and opening interior markets for British manufactured goods. The fact that the French and the Germans wanted similar access only strengthened the need to establish territorial control, which the British eventually did.

In-between the cases of easy informal empire and hard colonialism are the cases of British imperialism in Egypt and China. Both were moderately well governed in the early nineteenth century. The rulers of these ancient civilizations were not willing to give Britain the ready economic access it had gained in Argentina. Muhammad Ali and the Ch'ing emperors resisted British encroachments, but were ultimately not strong enough to prevail. Britain used military power to destroy Muhammad Ali's nascent efforts to modernize Egypt and to pry open China for the opium trade. Subsequent rulers in the two countries were then forced to collaborate willy-nilly. The comparison of British attitudes toward China and India at mid-century is instructive and worth reiterating: while there was general consensus in Britain that the next step for India was to become a Crown colony, there was a strong common view that to turn China into a Crown colony would be foolishness. The key distinction underlying the different attitudes was that the Ch'ing Empire was still very much intact and the conquest of China would have been very expensive. Moreover, "all could be quietly got" without conquest in China. To repeat, this was indeed the spirit that moved the British to seek informal empire: If you can get economic advantage without a formal empire, then why not? This attitude kept the British from colonizing Egypt for a while, but then circumstances changed. A patriotic revolt—the Urabi Revolt—threatened the smooth operation of the informal empire in Egypt. The British therefore crushed the revolt and moved toward full colonialism to recreate stable subservience in Egypt, and in so doing, they also initiated the Scramble for Africa. In sum, the main proposition that historical materials analyzed in this book support is that imperialists colonize when they can, but settle for an informal empire when they face resistance.

The Americans, after a brief flirtation with formal colonialism, came to prefer informal imperialism. As in the case of Britain, the logic that drove this preference was again that of political constraints, especially the growing significance of mass nationalism in the twentieth century. To revisit some of the historical evidence analyzed in this book: as the United States sought economic opportunities abroad after the Spanish-American War, they faced a variety of constraints. Some were internal, for example, given its anticolonial heritage, many in the United States were reluctant to establish European-style colonies in the poor countries of the world. Others were external: American power relative to other global powers was far from overwhelming in the early twentieth century, and much of the global periphery was already colonized. The United States also faced strong nationalist resistance in the former Spanish colonies on which it sought to impose an American order. To create economic opportunities overseas, therefore, the United States experimented before settling on informal empire as the preferred path. It pursued the path of hard militarism to establish a real colony in the Philippines and a near colony in Cuba. It enforced a variety of regime changes in Central America and the Caribbean to ensure that pro-American governments ruled the countries in its backyard. And it joined a coalition of imperialists to keep China stable and open. These early pathways—hard militarism, regime change, and multilateral domination—pointed toward the American way to empire in the twentieth century and beyond.

Hard militarism has been a recurring American strategy for taming recalcitrant governments on the global periphery, evident in the cases of the Philippines, Vietnam, and Iraq. When faced with strong nationalist resistance in the Philippines, the United States deployed thousands of American soldiers in a three-year war that led to the death of some 200,000 Filipino civilians. American aims in the Philippines were vague but resistance to American domination was strong. The combination of vague goals on the way to something grand and a strong nationalist resistance seems to attract hard militarism as an imperial strategy. Both Vietnam and Iraq also followed this pattern. The United States intervened in Vietnam, first to help the French, and then to stop the spread of communism in Southeast Asia. Over time, even when it became clear that South Vietnam was not likely to survive as an autonomous state, US military intervention continued with the goal of preserving America's credibility. American goals in the most recent intervention in Iraq were again rather vague, but remaking Iraq was seen as a first step toward establishing *Pax Americana* in the oil-rich Middle East. When faced with strong resistance, a prolonged military confrontation again followed.

Establishing and maintaining pro-American governments in power has been the main American route to an informal empire. This path was first evident in the early twentieth century in the south-of-the-border countries Nicaragua, Cuba, and Honduras. The curtailing of the powers of the Cuban government via the Platt Amendment was an early indicator of how the Americans would approach informal empire, with an emphasis on creating the trappings of democracy and manipulating constitutions. After granting the Philippines formal sovereignty, the US again fine-tuned this model of nominal independence but substantial control over policy via encouraging—or imposing—pro-American governments in power. The United States even offered its Philippine model to the French in Vietnam as a route to preserving their own substantial interests while granting formal sovereignty. With the rise of mass nationalism in the post–World War II period, however, open efforts to control policy in peripheral countries faced more and more obstacles. The spread of anticolonial norms also made overt interventions costly in terms of loss of legitimacy. The United States then pursued the use of covert methods to install friendly governments in power. Both the cases of Mossadegh in Iran and Allende in Chile (chapter 4) underscore this pattern. In contrast to the hard militarist approach, American intervention in these countries also points to the alternate set of conditions that give rise to a covert approach: when America's goals were specific—say, creating economic opportunities for corporations—and its relative power advantage considerable, then covert regime change emerged as the appropriate strategy to implant pliable rulers in a world in which national self-determination had become a valued norm.

Covert support for coups against Mossadegh and Allende led to the installation of the Shah and of Pinochet to do America's bidding. Similar cases that are not discussed in this this book might include the US-supported overthrow of Arbenz in Guatemala and the assassination of Lumumba in Congo. The case of Vietnam was, of course, a lot more overt, but the American hope there, too, was to create a stable-but-subservient regime in South Vietnam. The covert overthrow and the death of Diem followed a pattern similar to that in Iran and Chile. Once it had installed client regimes, the United States used a variety of carrots and sticks to promote the stability and subservience of the pro-American governments, most commonly foreign aid, especially military aid, but also military bases, which limited national autonomy. The United States hoped that given its enormous power and economic resources, most client states would simply take America's preferences seriously; after all, it is an old axiom of politics that the truly powerful need not use their power to secure preferred outcomes. More so than in the case of Britain, the credibility of American commitments has thus become a key resource for the functioning of America's informal empire.

Another American approach to establishing influence over peripheral countries is to collaborate with other industrialized countries with shared interests. The case of American expansion into China (chapter 4) suggests that multilateral collaboration was needed to establish dominance when the power resources of the United States were not sufficient to accomplish the task at hand. It established a system of multilateral institutions with the hope of promoting both global prosperity and its own interests. The IMF and the World Bank, in particular, have provided the United States some cover while it pursues naked self-interest in the developing world. We saw this in the American efforts to ensure that Latin American countries paid off their debts to American banks during the 1980s, and then again when the United States sought to impose Washington-approved economic policies on the developing world, especially on indebted Latin America (chapter 6).

Besides formal and informal empire, this study sheds light on varieties of imperialism along a few other dimensions. One comparison that runs throughout the study is obviously of British and American forms of imperialism. A few concluding observations are again in order. As noted in the introduction and again in chapter 4 (and elsewhere), some of the major differences in the British and American approaches to global empire stem from the fact that America's continental economy in the twentieth century was relatively self-sufficient, certainly in comparison to that of the British Isles in the nineteenth century. As a result, the United States, like the British, sought overseas markets, but without desperately needing them. Imperialism for Americans has thus always been a matter of choice. Time and again, this has added an element of tentativeness to America's imperial quest. America's giant economy also enabled it to create military might that was far superior to that of its nearest competitors. This, in turn, enabled the Americans to pursue imperial interventions, which, unlike Britain's, were not always cost-effective. As in the case of Vietnam, the United States, after a period of remorse, readily absorbs the costs of its hubris and moves on to the next one, as in Iraq. It is too early to tell whether or not President Trump's moves to withdraw some American forces from abroad are the beginning of a new period of post-Iraq remorse.

Other important differences between British and American imperialism stem from the obvious fact that they unfold a century apart. The emergence of democracy in the metropolitan centers and of mass politics in the periphery has altered the nature of imperialism. To reiterate, Britain's pursuit of imperialism was made easier because it found ready collaborators in peripheral countries who could control and pacify the local population. Nationalism and mass politics in twentieth century altered the social structures of countries on the periphery. The spread of plebiscitarian politics across the world has dissolved some of the key building blocks of old-fashioned imperialism. The maharajas, the sultans, tribal chiefs, latifundistas, and the pashas of the past who collaborated with the British are now being replaced by the emergence of mass politics. Imposing imperial order from the outside is a much more complicated task when one must confront mobilized nationalists. More recent American interventions in Vietnam and Iraq underscore this changing nature of imperialism.

A last observation on varieties of imperialism is a negative one. The historical evidence examined in this study could be construed to suggest that the nature of imperialism has changed over time, from a focus on free trade in the nineteenth century, to protection of overseas corporate investments in the mid-twentieth century, and then to a preoccupation with finance in the late twentieth century and beyond. Based on such a classification, Marxist scholars may even theorize that the changing nature of imperialism reflects the changing needs of capitalism.[17] Such an argument would not be wrong, but would be based on oversimplification. Some simplification is essential for theory building, but oversimplification leads to misleading theories. No taxonomy that makes a case that the nature of imperialism has changed neatly from a focus on trade, to investment, and then to finance survives empirical scrutiny. For example, the British expansion into India well preceded Britain's commitment to free trade. British interests in Argentina, Egypt, and China then combined interests in trade, investment, and finance. According to Lenin, finance-led imperialism—the highest stage of capitalism—had already arrived at the turn of the twentieth century. American expansion following the Spanish-American War sought both trading and investment opportunities. Some of the post–World War II American interventions (Iran, Chile) indeed focused on protecting the interests of multinational corporations, but were also punctuated by Vietnam. And yes, financial interests indeed played a dominant role in Washington's efforts to ensure that Latin American countries paid back their debts to American banks during the 1980s. However, the demands of the Washington Consensus also included demands for opening of trade and investment opportunities. And then there is the case of American intervention in Iraq; in the era of high finance, it is a case of really old-fashioned imperialism in which natural resources again played an important role.

Impact of Imperialism

I have argued in this book that imperialists gain from imperialism at the expense of the imperialized. This is hardly a novel argument. Time and again, developing-country nationalists and critical scholars of imperialism and dependency have made the same point. There are several reasons, however, why it is worth traveling this well-trodden path again. First, the claims of dependency scholarship have faded so much that some now claim with impunity that, on balance, the impact of colonialism was positive, such as that of Britain on India.[18] On the American side, too, many deny that America seeks to undermine the sovereignty of other nations, or if it does, American empire is essentially benign.[19] I have sought to counter those arguments. Second, between the covers of this book I have also accumulated the most recent data available to support the argument of costs and benefits of imperialism. Where such data does not support the main argument, I have just as readily qualified the claims.

The causal mechanisms that drive my analysis are also distinguishable, especially from the more Marxist critics of imperialism. Nowhere in this study, for example, have I claimed that capitalism, as a global economic system, is in and of itself a source of exploitation and imperialism. I have also not criticized free trade or foreign investment or financial flows across national boundaries as necessarily a source of unequal exchange. Much depends on the terms on which such economic interactions take place. Such terms are often set by sovereign states out of self-interest. That is why I emphasize the central role of sovereignty and coercion in understanding imperialism. Imperialists undermine the sovereignty of peripheral states. Economic exchange between metropolitan and peripheral countries is, then, structured by superior political power. Imperialists benefit at the expense of the imperialized because of a relationship of domination and subservience. Kwame Nkrumah understood this when he argued, "[S]eek ye first the political kingdom." Others of his generation, such as Nehru, Nasser, Mao, and Ho Chi Minh, shared this political intuition, even though they pursued different pathways to national liberation and to effective developmental states. I have sought in this study to systemize the logic and data that supports the inclination of developing-country nationalists, past and present. The positive historical models of what might have been that inform my analysis include the Meiji Restoration in Japan as a path to modernity in the nineteenth century, and both China and India in the more recent period that underscore the progress that can be made when sovereign and capable states direct socioeconomic development.

I now revisit the argument developed in this study about the costs and benefits of imperialism for both metropolitan and peripheral countries. The case of India looms large in any full understanding of British colonialism. As I documented in chapters 1 and 3, ample evidence supports the claim that Britain benefited at the expense of India. We saw in those chapters that during the first century of British rule, the East India Company squeezed India's rural economy hard. The methods the company then devised to use India's resources to support British interests included financing a large armed force in India for British use, transferring Indian revenues to Britain to help the British state and economy, and opening the Indian economy under duress as a taker of British manufactured goods. Both the British state and private interests thus benefited. By contrast, India's nascent industries were destroyed. More important, India lost significant portions of its savings to the East India Company—every year, every decade, for a century—which the company used for a variety of purposes other than the economic betterment of India. This pattern of costs and benefits continued over the next century of formal British colonial rule over India, though with some modifications. British capital continued to benefit via trade, investments, and financial flows. Other private benefits included creating jobs for British citizens in India and the use of Indian labor in other British colonies in the West Indies. The British state benefited most directly from the use of a vast Indian army for which it did not pay anything. Other indirect national benefits included help with balance of payments, transfer of revenues from India via home charges, and an overall contribution of the Indian colony to Britain's economic buoyancy and thus, to power.

As to impact on India, one should acknowledge that two centuries of British rule in India left behind such positive legacies as the creation of a modern state and railways. The balance between costs and benefits, however, tilted sharply in the negative direction. It is a remarkable fact that the per capita earnings of Indians barely budged over the entire colonial century, and certainly stagnated during the first half of the twentieth century. Among the British acts of commission and omission that contributed to this outcome was a policy pattern that I characterize as one of "squeeze and neglect." The British continued in the post-1857 period to squeeze substantial amount of savings out of the Indian economy on a regular basis, and spent nearly two-thirds of these monies on nothing more than on running the Raj. Land policies facilitated revenue extraction but created disincentives for private investment in agriculture. Public investments in support of the rural economy, especially in irrigation, were minimal. Since nearly 90 percent of Indians at that time lived in the countryside, the stagnant incomes in India can to a significant degree be explained by the limited gains in agricultural productivity. Industrial growth was minimal, and forced economic openness made it difficult for Indians to initiate new industries. When the British left India after nearly two centuries of rule, they left behind a country with a poor, illiterate population with an average life expectancy of thirty-two years.

British colonialism in sub-Saharan Africa was of a much shorter duration. Though British gains in Africa were modest, the impact of British rule was deep and often deleterious. Setting aside the cases of settler colonies, the tragedy of British colonialism in Africa was that Britain dragged rudimentary societies into the modern world but did not leave them with the tools to cope with that modernity. The case of Nigeria (chapter 3) helps document some of the underlying dynamics. The focus of British rule in Nigeria was the promotion of trade but also the taxing of that trade to finance colonial rule. A colonial pattern of exchange of commodities for manufactured goods evolved. Production growth in cash crops was mainly extensive. The British did not invest in technologies to improve agricultural productivity. Except for some export crops, subsistence agriculture dominated the economy and underwent hardly any significant improvement. The industrial impulse was weak and what impulse there was the British actively discouraged. The legacy of poorly constructed state structures looms especially large as a blot on the British record. The contributing factors in Nigeria included the failure to create a central government that was run by a professional civil service with a capacity to tax incomes; and the accentuation of local identities and identity struggles around regions. The state failure came to be mirrored in a fractured nationalist movement. After gaining independence, the Nigerian state was relatively dysfunctional. This was a tragedy of first order because a well-functioning state, which gives meaning to national sovereignty, remains a key institution in the modern world to facilitate development and upward mobility.

To recapitulate the importance of the informal empire for Britain, it is helpful to recall a fairly simple point: for much of the nineteenth century, foreign trade played a central role in sustaining the buoyancy of Britain's export-led economy. Even though a fair amount of this trade depended on the competitiveness of British products, those with the political power to protect their economies (Germany, the United States, France, and even some of the white Dominions) used tariffs and other measures to regulate their trade. These policy options were closed to countries in the orbit of Britain's formal and informal empire. The result was that these countries evolved into providers of raw materials for the expansion of British manufacturing and, in turn, absorbed British manufactured products. As the century wore on, those with excess capital in Britain also sought opportunities for direct investment and loans abroad. In the uncertain conditions of peripheral economies, the British state often intervened to ensure satisfactory rates of return on such investments. Along with Britain's economic interactions with formal colonies like India, then, and with the white Dominions of Canada and Australia, informal colonies in Latin America, the Middle East, and in East Asia helped sustain Britain's economic dynamism and global leadership position during the nineteenth century.

Britain's handsome gains from its economic interactions with Latin America, and with the Ottoman and Ch'ing Empires, had to be shared with the elites in client states. This was the cost of running the informal empire. The consequences for peripheral countries included rising incomes for the indigenous elite, but lopsided development characterized by sharp inequalities and commodity-dependent economies. The impact of informal imperialism was thus both positive and negative, and quite complex, but on balance it tended to be less pernicious than that of formal colonial control. Unlike India, Egypt and Argentina experienced steady economic growth during the nineteenth century. Not all of the countries in the orbit of informal empire experienced such steady growth (for example, China), but many did. This growth can, of course, be partly explained by the nature of complementarities between the metropolitan and peripheral economies. But sustained growth within the scope of informal empire also had political roots: since these peripheral countries were not quite colonies, they enjoyed some political autonomy. As long as they were prepared to export commodities in exchange for manufactured goods, the terms of trade were mostly commercial, facilitating the growth of the incomes of both the commodity producers and the economy as a whole. Commodity-exporting economies gave rise to agrarian oligarchies, which became politically influential and supported limited sovereignty in exchange for economic benefits as a class.

Over time, the limits on sovereignty also took an economic toll. Countries in the orbit of Britain's informal empire may have experienced economic growth, but they failed to evolve into complex economies with an industrial base. Even in Argentina, where the economy indeed grew, and grew well during some periods, growth was lopsided insofar as it rested mainly on the development of a ranching economy. Britain discouraged the emergence of nationalist rulers and made it difficult to use tariff and other policy instruments to create a more complex economy with an industrial base. In the case of Egypt, even the growth was not continuous. It is telling that the Egyptian economy grew in periods when local khedives maintained some degree of sovereign control over their economies. As British control became decisive later in the century, economic growth vanished. Meanwhile, Egypt became one large cotton farm, feeding the British textile industry, incapable of diversifying beyond simple commodity production. While China's economic penetration remained limited to treaty ports, the Chinese state was repeatedly drained of resources and delegitimized by imperial incursions, which contributed to its demise. A common theme, then, runs through the cases of informal empire: irrespective of economic growth here and there, Britain undermined the possibility of a more nationalist building of more complex economies on the global periphery. To repeat: there were to be no Meiji restorations within the scope of Britain's informal empire. Many countries continued to struggle with this nineteenth-century legacy during the twentieth century, and beyond.

Finally, we can summarize the impact of US interventions in the twentieth century. An important caveat ought to precede this concluding discussion. The harm that the United States inflicted on specific developing countries is easier to document than are the American gains. The latter is difficult because the United States is a giant economy. Unlike Britain, American economic dynamism does not depend heavily on overseas interactions. Nevertheless, two observations are pertinent. First, the economic benefits of imperialism for the United States have to be assessed in relation to the cost of acquiring and maintaining them. Given America's giant economy and power resources, the cost of most imperial forays into peripheral states for the United States is marginal. When the costs are significant, as, for example, in the Philippines or Iraq, they are borne by taxpayers and soldiers, while the eventual gains are mainly private. Second, the United States has often intervened with broader considerations in mind, especially in the post–World War II period. The coup in Iran was aimed as much at deposing Mossadegh as it was to setting acceptable global norms for the control of natural resources. The aims of deposing Allende included forestalling the spread of a democratic socialist model of development to the rest of Latin America. And the 2003 invasion of Iraq was aimed as much at getting rid of Saddam Hussein as it was a first step toward establishing *Pax Americana* in the oil-rich Middle East. When assessing American gains, then, it is important to bear in mind that American goals often went beyond specific interventions, although the diffuse nature of these goals also makes it difficult to assess whether the Americans achieved them.

With this caveat, we can now revisit the historical evidence on the impact of American interventions in the global periphery. Following the Spanish-American War, the United States established sway over the Philippines, Cuba, and other countries in Central America and the Caribbean, and sought the opening of China. Early in the twentieth century, the United States exported less than 10 percent of its products, and America's overseas investments were also trivial. Many in the United States believed that economic expansion abroad was the next frontier, because it would both help smooth out the boom-and-bust quality of rapid capitalist expansion and provide long-term outlets to the problem of glut in the American economy. The results of American efforts suggest that this thinking was not wrong. As I documented in chapter 4, US trade expanded rapidly in its newly acquired colonies of Cuba and the Philippines. Trade also jumped sharply in China following the Open Door policy, although the progress there was not steady. American direct investments overseas also grew sharply after the Spanish-American War, especially in Cuba. The evidence, then, supports the contention that perceived economic needs within the United States led to imperial expansion, and both trade and investment followed the flag.

America's impact on its protectorates was malign. Both Cuba and the Philippines experienced some commodity-led economic growth, but mainly over the short term. Over the longer term, American protectorates became classic colonies that produced commodities and took manufactured goods. Commodity producers became wealthy and powerful. While these groups, and their political representatives, were happy to cooperate with the United States, they seldom commanded enough legitimacy to establish orderly polities. Economic inequalities and illegitimate rulers gave rise to poorly governed societies. The American impact on China was more limited, but again, it did not make a positive contribution. For example, a variety of modernizing forces were beginning to emerge in China during this period, some aimed at expelling foreigners and others at reforming or abolishing the monarchy. More often than not, the United States opposed these forces; instead, the United States joined other imperial powers in failed efforts to create a stable-but-subservient China, which paved the way to a half century of political instability. American influence thus encouraged commodity-producing economies and undermined nationalist leaders who may have commanded the majority support needed to create effective, developmental states.

The United States intervened in numerous developing countries during the Cold War. The cases of Iran, Vietnam, and Chile (chapter 5) help us reach some conclusions about the impact of these interventions. What did the United States gain by supporting a coup against Mossadegh, entering into a prolonged conflict in Vietnam, and orchestrating another coup against an elected leader in Chile? In Iran and Chile, the United States certainly succeeded in overthrowing elected nationalist leaders and in replacing them with authoritarian, pro-American rulers, who facilitated benefits for American corporations. These interventions also served broader American goals, although the causal links are more diffuse. The coup in Iran, for example, probably forestalled efforts to nationalize oil by other countries for a couple of decades. Western control over oil helped steady supply of cheap oil in the 1950s and the 1960s, which fed the economic recovery of Western Europe and Japan. The coup that overthrew Allende put other Latin American countries on notice that the United States would be setting the limits on what development models can be pursued south of the American border. Democratic socialism and leftward drift was certainly to be discouraged. The preferred direction of change, instead, was a movement toward open economies, which Pinochet initiated in Chile, and which then gained sharp momentum during the era of the Washington Consensus.

Judged from the standpoint of imperial gains, America's prolonged intervention in Vietnam provided a sharp contrast to its more limited interventions in Iran and Chile. The American war in Vietnam was about as clear a case of failed imperialism as is found in this book. Not only was the effort to stop Ho Chi Minh extremely expensive for Americans in human and material terms, but also, when the war ended and the Americans withdrew, Vietnam was unified under the leadership of communists. Hegemony rests not only on domination but also on some legitimacy; the United States lost a lot of high moral ground as a result of the Vietnam War. Ironically, the United States also lost credibility in the aftermath, something that American leaders thought was worth fighting for. Unlike the covert interventions in Iran and Chile, then, what distinguished the failed American intervention in Vietnam was the overt confrontation with well-organized nationalists. America's military might notwithstanding, these overt confrontations against mobilized nationalism are difficult to win. The more recent American invasion of Iraq further underscores this point. If this book were meant to be a guide to how to do imperialism in the modern era (it is not), one might conclude that instead of confronting developing-country nationalism, the

United States is more likely to achieve its goals when it works quietly with pro-American elites in the poor countries of the world.

The negative impact of American interventions on Iran, Vietnam, and Chile can also be reiterated briefly. Democracy in both Iran and Chile—more nascent in Iran than in Chile—was deeply damaged by American interventions. As important, American interventions empowered ruling coalitions that favored open and dependent economies in these countries. Chilean economy under Pinochet did grow but the growth remained commodity dependent. Nationalist coalitions that might diversify economies via deliberate industrialization thus failed to emerge in both Iran and Chile, at least over the short to medium term. By contrast, America's loss in Vietnam paved the road in that country toward a nationalist consolidation of power. The war, of course, devastated Vietnam; the communist government that emerged victorious has been highly repressive. Nevertheless, Vietnam is now charting its own development journey, with positive results that include near eradication of poverty and high rates of economic growth.

I analyzed American interventions in the post–Cold War period in chapter 6, focusing on economic imperialism in Latin America and military imperialism in Iraq. American gains in Latin America were clearer than in Iraq. During the 1980s, the US government and US-dominated multilateral institutions used economic coercion to ensure cooperation by Latin American elites. Policies dictated from Washington helped maintain the profits and solvency of major American banks. Latin American markets were opened up further to American goods and capital during the 1990s. By contrast, the US-military intervention in Iraq cost America dearly, and the rewards remain uncertain. If the main goal of the Second Iraq War was to remove Saddam from power, that much the United States did achieve. But Saddam was contained after the first Iraq war. Was a trillion-dollar war really needed to achieve this modest goal? If the quiet goal was, instead, access to Iraqi oil, what else was Saddam going to do with Iraqi oil but sell it in the global market place? Saddam was willing to invite foreign investors to explore new oil reserves. If the goal was to create a stable and democratic Iraq as a showcase for *Pax Americana* in the Middle East, that goal remains well beyond the American reach. Iraqis on their own may create a stable Iraq in due course, but it will not be thanks to American efforts.

The impact of post–Cold War American interventions on Latin America and the Middle East continues to be negative. American efforts to ensure that US banks were paid back contributed strongly to a lost decade of growth in Latin America. Beyond the lost decade, forced economic openness reinforced economic dependency of Latin American countries on their northern giant. The consequences are clearly evident if one juxtaposes the experience of Asian countries during the same period, say, 1980 to 2005, with that of Latin America. Asian countries pursued a more autonomous development path that led to relatively rapid economic growth, modest inequalities, industrial development, and higher value-added exports. The negative impact of the American invasion and occupation of Iraq is even clearer. I have documented that a half million Iraqis died during this period. That happens to be twice as many Iraqis as butchered by Saddam! American efforts to ensure that Iraq is governed by pro-American rulers who are not only elected but are also effective remains a work in progress. Meanwhile, a weak and corrupt state governs Iraq, and its only real accomplishment, so far, has been to ensure that foreign-owned companies continue to extract and export Iraqi oil.

To sum up, the evidence supports the claim that Britain and the United States benefited from their respective global empires in the nineteenth and the twentieth centuries. Moreover, these benefits came at the expense of the imperialized. Seeking economic benefits, both Britain and the United States used their superior power to pry open poor parts of the world. Their key aims were to limit the exercise of sovereign state power and to open the economies of peripheral countries. Both formal and informal empire facilitated this goal, although to different degrees, and this economic expansion helped both hegemonic states sustain economic growth and prosperity at home. From the standpoint of the developing world, however, loss of sovereignty had a pernicious impact. In a world of states, sovereign and effective states are essential instruments for the well-being of a people. The evidence in this study helps underscore an inverse relationship between imperialism and development: the less control a state has over its own affairs, the less likely it is that the people of that state will experience steady and inclusive economic progress. We thus notice that fully colonized countries experienced the least economic progress. The economic prospects of semi-sovereign states were a little better, though again, limited. Only fully sovereign and effective states have succeeded in leading poor countries toward prosperity in the modern world.

The Future of Imperialism

Imperialism is an age-old phenomenon. In one form or another, it is likely to continue. There is insight in Thucydides's suggestion that the "weak" will always be "subject to the strong," and that the powerful seldom turn down "the opportunities of aggrandizement offered by superior strength."[20] But one problem with such venerable claims is that they tend to absolve the strong for exploiting the weak. Another problem is the danger of near banality passing for ancient wisdom: if there will always be rich and poor, then should we not worry about inequality? If some citizens will always commit crimes, then should we not try to find ways to mitigate the harm of such behavior? A commitment to a better world suggests that we seek to right the wrongs of the past. In a world of states, then, it is important to strengthen arrangements that discourage powerful states from imposing their will on weaker ones. It may well be the case that institutions cannot readily restrain the powerful in an "anarchic world."[21] If so, it is at least important to dissect the self-serving claims of the powerful; at minimum, the mighty should not to be allowed to define what is right. Throughout this volume I have interrogated several interrelated claims made by hegemonic states of the modern era: we really do not run an empire; if we do, it is only because it was offered to us; even when it was not offered to us, we had to take it, not for greed, but for the sake of our own security; and, in any case, the impact of our empire was, on balance, benign. My analysis has underscored the ways in which each of these claims is deeply misleading.

With this core analysis in mind, I have a few final, speculative thoughts on the future of imperialism. Extrapolating from the recent past, two sets of comments are especially pertinent. First, what is the likely trajectory of American interventions in the developing world in the near future? Second, will emerging powers like China follow the expansionist patterns analyzed in this book? Is China also moving toward building an informal empire? As I turn to discuss these questions, an obvious but important caveat ought to be borne in mind: peering into the future is hazardous. Nevertheless, if the analysis of the past is correct, it ought to have some bearing on future projections.

The United States has never really needed an empire. The analysis in this volume has suggested instead that unlike Britain, which really needed an empire to sustain prosperity in the nineteenth century, the United States in the twentieth century had merely wanted one. The tentativeness in the American imperial project is a function of this difference between need and want. American gains from imperial interventions in the global periphery have also been uneven. A case can be made that during the post–World War II period, the United States has been more successful in achieving its goals—at least short- to medium-term goals—via covert (or indirect) rather than overt, military interventions. For example, the former suggestion is supported by American interventions in Iran and Chile and by the most recent imposition of the Washington Consensus on Latin American countries. By contrast, US intervention in Vietnam was a heroic failure. The most recent military intervention in Iraq is still unfolding. But it is unlikely that the partial success in Iraq in deposing a despot and opening the oil wells of that country to foreign capital will ever be judged worth the cost in treasure, loss of life, and the unstable polity that the United States has left behind.

The relative failures of US military interventions in the developing world are also comprehensible. Of course, the United States is a military giant and, if it so chose, it could readily defeat and occupy any (or most) developing countries. But that is not the American goal. The United States does not want colonies. What it wants instead are stable-but-subservient regimes in the global periphery. And these are increasingly hard to construct via military interventions. As I argue throughout this book, the building blocks of old-fashioned nineteenth century imperialism—ready collaborators in the periphery who benefited from maintaining commodity-exporting economies and clientelistic polities—have dissolved in the global periphery. Mass politics has replaced clientelism nearly everywhere. Plebiscitarian politics, in turn, encourages a variety of nationalists to the fore. Imperial efforts to overtly shape and control the politics of a developing country then readily run up against developing-country nationalism. Diem and others in South Vietnam, for example, could thus never be considered legitimate rulers of a sovereign South Vietnam; they were in fact puppets and were seen as such by the Vietnamese, no match for a Ho Chi Minh. The same is true elsewhere, such as in contemporary Iraq.

This does not mean that modern-day imperialists cannot find ready collaborators in the developing world, or that commodity-producing elites and their political representatives do not have much to gain from quiet collaboration with industrialized countries, especially the United States. But as democracy spreads in peripheral countries, subservient rulers face power challenges from a variety of nationalists. The American preference for democracy, on the one hand, but for promotion of stable-but-subservient regimes in the developing world, on the other, are thus inherently in tension. When economic stakes are high, as in the case of oil-rich Saudi Arabia, the United States quietly sets aside the goal of democracy in favor of supporting the power of a stable-but-subservient regime.

What is the likely shape of US interventions in the developing world in the near future? Enormous power disparities and the prospect of economic gain will tempt the United States to intervene in one developing country or another. Global norms of noninterference in the affairs of sovereign nations may put some brakes on imperial ambitions. American citizens' awareness that US interventions in the developing world often bring misery to the lives of those who are already destitute may also retard the imperial urge. However, neither global norms nor public opinion is likely to make imperialism a relic of the past. The post–World War II record examined here sharply supports this projection. The more pertinent issue is what form American imperialism will take in the near future. Again, the record examined here suggests that the United States does economic imperialism better than military imperialism. To the extent that imperialism is rational, one should expect the United States to eschew military interventions but continue to seek economic advantage in the global periphery via the use of covert and indirect interventions. As this book goes to press, Iran and Venezuela, which both possess enormous oil resources, are the focus of American angst. Will the United States intervene militarily in these countries? A cost-benefit analysis of the past suggests that the United States ought not to pursue a military option in these countries. But what complicates this rational suggestion is the enormous power surplus that the United States enjoys in the world. This power surplus, in turn, enables American leaders to periodically ignore the costs of interventions, which, in any case, are borne largely by American taxpayers and soldiers, and to indulge their whims and hubris.

China is now an emerging global power with a buoyant economy. How well do China's expansionist tendencies fit my arguments about the nature of great-power imperialism? The short answer is, it's too early to tell. China's expansionism has developed only over the past two decades. The trends I have analyzed in this study unfolded over a much longer time period. Nevertheless, some patterns are already discernable. China's economic expansion overseas reflects its internal economic needs. This much we should expect based on the British and American experiences. China, too, is pursuing its national economic interest overseas, such as seeking access to raw materials, outlets for capital surplus, and opportunities to export higher value added products. So far, it has resisted the use of military power to take economic advantage abroad. This may well change in the near future, especially in the countries in China's own backyard, but so far, the global military presence of the United States continues to be a major deterrent. This trend has historical parallels in the nineteenth century, when the United States, wary of British power, shied away from the use of military force in Latin America, proclaimed the Monroe Doctrine, and focused instead on economic expansion. In the language of this study, then, China's economic expansion in the early twenty-first century is exacerbating the economic dependency of numerous developing countries on the emerging manufacturing giant, but there is little evidence—at least so far—that China is building an informal empire.

China's economic interactions with the developing world are increasingly a focus of scholarly inquiries.[22] For my purpose, the details can be set aside. To conclude the book, I draw on this literature only to comment, very briefly, on the motives, mechanisms, and impact of China's expansionism. After four decades of rapid economic growth, China now produces nearly 25 percent of the world's manufactured output and holds the world's largest foreign exchange reserves. Moreover, it is committed to maintaining a high rate of economic growth in the near future. As with Britain and the United States in the past, China's commitment to national prosperity has led it to seek markets and profitable outlets for its financial reserves in other developing countries. Considering China's rapid economic growth, the trends are dramatic.

On the trade front, for example, rapid economic growth in manufacturing has led China to ensure a steady supply of raw material imports. By 2015, China was importing more than half of the world's total imports of iron ore, aluminum, and soya beans.[23] China's exports, by contrast, are mainly manufactured goods. These trends are especially notable in China's trade with other developing countries. They are also reminiscent of colonial and neocolonial patterns of exchange of raw materials for manufactured goods. China's foreign direct investment in other developing countries has also grown rapidly. Much of this growth is spearheaded by Chinese state-owned firms, especially oil and mining companies searching for natural resources abroad. The driving motive includes the need to promote "China's national economic development."[24] Last, China's giant foreign exchange reserves allow it to lend money to developing countries, again mainly to promote its own exports. Chinese sovereign funds and portfolio investments have mostly moved to advanced economies; however, its bank loans and trade credits to the developing world are tied to securing market access. The construction of infrastructure abroad is a focus of Chinese efforts, too, especially via the creation of such policy banks as the Asian Infrastructure Investment Bank and the New Development Bank (better known as the BRICS bank). China's most recent initiative, One Belt, One Road, is also focused on loans to promote construction projects in neighboring Asia and Europe.[25] In addition to projecting economic power, the hope is, again, to promote the exports of heavy industries that are likely to be underutilized as China shifts to a focus on domestic consumption and as domestic infrastructure needs are saturated.

Much of Chinese global economic expansion is steered by the Chinese state. In this important sense, the driving force behind China's economic expansion is clearly the country's national economic needs, as interpreted by its state elite. Although the state may have competing interests within (as it surely does), there is no denying that state-owned entities are dominant in the buying and selling of goods overseas, managing projects, and in providing loans for specific purposes in the developing world. Political and economic motives are thus closely intertwined in China's overseas expansion. The Chinese pattern of overseas expansion by state-owned firms is in contrast to the private actors that drove economic expansion in Britain and the United States. This fact created a problem for interpreting the overseas actions of the British and American states, because it gives rise to the question, were forceful interventions moved by the narrow interests of the economic elite or by some broader understanding of the national economic interest entertained by the political elite? Although historical evidence can be marshaled to support either proposition, I argue that on balance, one need not treat these as rival propositions. The pursuit of national economic prosperity by hegemonic powers is the taproot of imperialism. This focus on national economic prosperity as the driver of overseas economic expansion then finds strong support in the case of China. Private firms still play a secondary role in the Chinese economy. Much of the expansion by state-owned firms reflects the Chinese need to support its own economic growth. More sharply than in the cases of Britain and the United States, the Chinese case underscores the value of the proposition that the search for national economic prosperity generates a tendency toward overseas economic expansion.

If the motives driving China's overseas economic expansion are similar to that of Britain and the United States in the past, the mechanisms are not. China has rarely needed to use force to access the economies of other developing countries. The open world economy created by the United States has served China's economic interests well. Moreover, the timing of China's economic expansion has been propitious. Just as the Washington Consensus on development was losing steam in the new millennium, China's rapid economic growth provided seemingly attractive economic opportunities for the developing world. Commodity producers in Africa and Latin America eagerly sought Chinese markets to boost economic growth at home, and they imported cheap Chinese manufactured goods. Chinese finance and expertise helped infrastructure projects in a variety of developing countries, especially in Africa. When Chinese efforts to seek access to commodities have run into nationalist opposition, bribes, rather than military interventions, have so far sufficed to nip the resistance in bud.[26]

The closest China has come thus far to using force to seek economic advantage overseas is the acquisition of a port from an indebted Sri Lanka.[27] Such use of economic coercion by China to acquire economic assets abroad resembles past patterns of informal empire analyzed in this study. If China continues to use economic or military coercion along these lines to seek economic advantage in, say, other highly indebted countries, such as Pakistan, then China, too, will join the ranks of modern imperial nations. But until now, China's use of force for profits in the world is a phenomenon of marginal significance. (More significant is China's use of force to seek strategic goals, especially in its own neighborhood; that, however, is not the focus of the present study.) To the extent that I have emphasized that the use of coercion is central to any understanding of informal imperialism, China does not fit the pattern, at least not yet.

How is this exception to be explained? China's reluctance to use force to pursue economic advantage in the developing world is not likely the result of a commitment to noninterference in the affairs of other nations. Such ideological vows melt away when stakes are high or when opportunities arise. More likely, China has either not needed to use force or has been deterred from doing so. Among the prime candidates for such deterrence is, of course, the power of the United States—especially in Latin America. Other candidates are moderately well-functioning states in other parts of the developing world, such as in the rest of Asia. For example, Mahathir Mohammed, the recently reelected president of Malaysia, successfully renegotiated the inflated costs of a China-sponsored railroad project in 2019.[28] If my analysis is correct, the most likely region(s) where China is likely to use force for profits is Africa, where in the future, China's economic stakes may become high enough to justify such actions, but where such countervailing factors as US power or strong national states are likely to be missing.

Last, what do emerging trends tell us about the likely impact of China's economic expansion on the developing world? The issue is already being debated vigorously in Africa, Latin America, and elsewhere.[29] As one might expect, proponents of the idea can point to the economic benefits to be had by integrating with the Chinese economy: higher economic growth; ready availability of capital, without pressure to undertake policy reform; and access to China's skill at building infrastructure. Conversely, those who are wary can point to other trends: the perpetuation of dependent development as commodities continue to be exchanged for manufactured goods, the possibility of falling into debt traps, and the real danger of deindustrialization in countries that have some industrial base. Both sides of the argument can be supported with evidence.

What is important to note from the standpoint of the historical materials analyzed in this study is that none of these contradictory trends ought to be surprising. As we have seen, Argentina grew in the nineteenth and early twentieth centuries while exporting agricultural products to Britain and the United States, but this pattern of development was lopsided without a diversified economy; nor could commodity-led growth be sustained when external conditions turned unfavorable. Chinese demand for raw materials has similarly helped economic growth in a number of African and Latin American countries (though it is notable that these trends are already decelerating along with China's economic growth). Chinese loans and infrastructure projects may well benefit some select countries that carefully assess the costs and benefits of such investments; nevertheless, the danger of falling into a debt trap is ever present. Since China has eschewed the use of force so far, its economic interactions with other developing countries mostly follow commercial principles.[30] This allows for developing countries that integrate with China to gain some economic benefits. On balance, however, integration with China is now accentuating a pattern of dependent development in countries of Africa, Latin America, and even in a few Asian countries. Leaders in some of these countries may be in a position to break these patterns and promote diversified and inclusive economies, but the historical record of dependent economies is not too encouraging.

To conclude: imperialism in the modern world is an economic phenomenon. It is pushed by powerful states that seek economic advantage for their dynamic economies. Both the colonialism and informal empire of the past few centuries have resulted from such use of force for profits. On the whole, the impact on peripheral countries has been negative. However, these trends of the past are not about to vanish. The powerful will always be tempted to take advantage when they can. It is for the leaders of peripheral countries to be wary of this omnipresent danger. And when such leaders themselves become part of the problem—and quietly collaborate with external powers for narrow advantages—it is then up to the citizens of these countries to expose them and to demand new rulers who will put the interests of their respective nations first. Sovereign, effective states remain indispensable for improving the life chances of the poor in the modern world.

Notes

INTRODUCTION

1. For Obama's foreign policy address, delivered on Thursday, May 23, 2013, in which he said this, see the *New York Times,* May 24, 2013. Trump's boast was made in the context of a threat to North Korea and Iran and was reported in the *New York Times*, September 19, 2017.
2. Whether one notices that all empires have something in common or that some empires are more similar than other empires depends partly on the purpose of study. One important recent book that treats most empires as worthy of comparative historical analysis within a single frame is Jane Burbank and Fredrick Cooper, *Empires in World History* (Princeton, NJ: Princeton University Press, 2010). Another study that came to my attention only as my own book goes to press is, Krishan Kumar, *Visions of Empire: How Five Imperial Regimes Shaped the World* (Princeton: Princeton University Press, 2017).
3. For an overview of how thinking about the economic origins of national power shifted from mercantilists to free traders, including Adam Smith, see Albert Hirschman, *National Power and the Structure of Foreign Trade* (Berkeley: University of California Press, 1980).
4. One could object that this is really not the case because those who were on the periphery of traditional land empires, that is, those who mainly paid tribute but were not fully incorporated into empires, also constituted an informal empire of sorts. While this may be the case, it is also true that land empires were seldom divided along the lines of an industrial core and an agrarian periphery.
5. See Atul Kohli, *State-Directed Development: Political Power and Industrialization in the Global Periphery* (New York: Cambridge University Press, 2004), esp. chap. 1.
6. As examples of the first set of views, see D. K. Fieldhouse, *Economics and Empire, 1830–1914* (Ithaca, NY: Cornell University Press, 1973); and David B. Abernathy, *The Dynamics of Global Dominance: European Overseas Empires, 1415–1980* (New Haven, CT: Yale University Press, 2000). For the second set of views, see Vladimir I. Lenin, *Imperialism, The Highest Stage of Capitalism: A Popular Outline* (English reprint, London: Lawrence and Wishart, 1944). Original Russian edition

published in 1916. It may interest the reader that the definition proposed here is also the commonsensical understanding of imperialism. Webster's dictionary, for example, defines imperialism as *the policy, practice, or advocacy of extending the power and dominion of a nation especially by direct territorial acquisition or by gaining indirect control over the political or economic life of other areas.*

7. See Joseph A. Schumpeter, *Imperialism and Social Classes* (New York: A. M. Kelly, 1951). Original edition published in 1919.
8. See John Gallagher and Ronald Robinson, "The Imperialism of Free Trade," *Economic History Review*, 2nd ser., 6, no. 1 (1953): 1–15.
9. For a review of theories of imperialism, see Wolfgang J. Mommsen, *Theories of Imperialism* (Chicago: University of Chicago Press, 1980). A survey of Marxist theories of imperialism is available in Anthony Brewer, *Marxist Theories of Imperialism* (London: Routledge and Kegan Paul, 1980); and a more recent effort to extend Marxist insights is David Harvey, *The New Imperialism* (New York: Oxford University Press, 2003). A realist account of imperialism is Benjamin Cohen, *The Question of Imperialism* (New York: Basic Books, 1973). The classic liberal account of imperialism is, of course, Schumpeter, *Imperialism and Social Classes.* Also see Michael W. Doyle, *Empires* (Ithaca, NY: Cornell University Press, 1986).
10. Two useful historical studies that cover somewhat similar ground as this study are Tony Smith, *The Pattern of Imperialism* (New York: Cambridge University Press, 1981); and Julian Go, *Patterns of Empire: The British and American Empires, 1688 to the Present* (New York: Cambridge University Press, 2011).
11. See Kenneth Waltz, *Theory of International Politics* (Reading, MA: Addison-Wesley, 1979).
12. The theme that specific imperial actions need to be understood as part of maintaining imperial systems is emphasized by Charles S. Maier, *Among Empires: American Ascendancy and its Predecessors* (Cambridge, MA: Harvard University Press, 2006).
13. This argument can be juxtaposed to the suggestion of Gallagher and Robinson that Britain preferred informal empire in the nineteenth century because it facilitated free trade. According to them, Britain was only moved to acquire African colonies at the end of the century when faced by political compunctions. See Gallagher and Robinson, "Imperialism of Free Trade." This argument comes across even more strongly in their subsequent work: Ronald Robinson and John Gallagher, *Africa and the Victorians: The Official Mind of the Imperialism*, with Alice Denny (1961; new paperback edition, London: I.B. Tauris, 2015). I return to this issue in more detail in the conclusion of chapter 3 and in the Conclusion to the volume.
14. The scholarship on this theme is extensive. As one good example, see Gabriel Kolko, *Confronting the Third World: United States Foreign Policy, 1945–1980* (New York: Pantheon Books, 1988). As an excellent and a more recent example of the impact of United States foreign policy in a non-communist setting, see

Gary J. Bass, *The Blood Telegram: Nixon, Kissinger, and a Forgotten Genocide* (New York: Alfred A. Knopf, 2013).

15. A ready review of the dependency literature is Gabriel Palma, "Dependency: A Formal Theory of underdevelopment or a Methodology for the Analysis of Concrete Situations of Underdevelopment?," *World Development* 6, no. 7–8 (1978): 881–924. For more recent thinking on related themes, see Patrick Heller, Dietrich Rueschemeyer, and Richard Snyder, eds., "Dependency and Development in a Globalized World," special issue of *Studies in Comparative International Development*, December 2009. Prominent recent works that have also addressed the issue of the impact of colonialism from different perspectives include James Mahoney, *Colonialism and Post-Colonial Development: Spanish America in a Comparative Perspective* (New York, Cambridge University Press, 2010); and Daron Acemoglu, Simon Johnson, and James A. Robinson, "The Colonial Origins of Comparative Development: An Empirical Investigation," *American Economic Review* 91, no. 5 (Dec. 2001): 1369–1401.
16. Dani Rodrik, in an important recent book, calls the more extreme versions of these demands *hyper-globalization*. See Rodrik's *The Globalization Paradox* (New York: W. W. Norton, 2011).
17. Many scholars in the dependency tradition understood this point well. I only extend their insights in a more political direction.
18. For a suggestion along these lines for the British Empire, see Niall Ferguson, *Empire: The Rise and Demise of British World Order and the Lessons for Global Power* (New York: Basic Books, 2003). On the American side, the view that United States' influence on the world is essentially benign is much more common, even among some scholars who do not deny that the United States runs an empire. See, for example, John Lewis Gaddis, *We Now Know: Rethinking Cold War History* (Oxford: Clarendon Press, 1997).
19. Gallagher and Robinson, "Imperialism of Free Trade."
20. See, for example, Paul Baran, *The Political Economy of Growth* (New York: Monthly Review Press, 1957).
21. For a good discussion of the importance of sovereignty, see Georg Sorensen, *Changes in Statehood: The Transformation of International Relations* (New York: Palgrave, 2001), esp. chap. 10.
22. Since I discussed the conditions that give rise to effective developmental states in earlier studies, that subject is not covered in any detail in this book. See, for example, Kohli, *State-Directed Development*.

CHAPTER 1

1. The phrase is generally attributed to Sir George Macartney, a former British governor of Madras, who claimed, during the signing of Treaty of Paris in 1773 following

the end of the Seven Years' War with France, that Britain now controlled "a vast empire, on which the sun never sets."

2. The word *factories* here does not refer to what we understand today by the word. In the historical context, *factors* were representatives—intermediaries—who carried out trade and other activities on behalf of the East India Company in India. *Factories,* then, refers to a group of *factors* who established communities, often coastal and often armed and fortified.
3. For example, a good overview account of the East India Company in this genre is Philip Lawson, *The East India Company: A History* (London: Longman, 1993). An earlier study was P. J. Marshall, *Problems of Empire: Britain and India, 1757–1813* (London: Allen and Unwin, 1968). Two useful recent volumes that focus on the internal workings of the East India Company are H. V. Bowen, *The Business of Empire: The East India Company and Imperial Britain, 1756–1833* (Cambridge: Cambridge University Press, 2006); and Emily Erikson, *Between Monopoly and Free Trade: The English East India Company, 1600–1757* (Princeton, NJ: Princeton University Press, 2014).
4. See, for example, a number of important contributions in Dharma Kumar, ed., *The Cambridge Economic History of India* [hereafter cited as *CEHI*], vol. 2: *c.1757–c.1970* (Cambridge: Cambridge University Press, 1983). Also see Ratnalekha Ray, *Change in Bengal Agrarian Society, c. 1760–1850* (Delhi: Manohar, 1979); and Sushil Chaudhury, *From Prosperity to Decline: 18th Century Bengal* (Delhi: Manohar, 1999). A more recent volume that came to my attention after this chapter was drafted is Tirthankar Roy, *The East India Company: The World's Most Powerful Corporation* (New Delhi: Penguin Books, 2012).
5. One study that moves in that direction is K. N. Chaudhuri, *The Trading World of Asia and the East India Company, 1660–1760* (Cambridge: Cambridge University Press, 1978). Also see by the same author *The Economic Development of India under the East India Company* (Cambridge: Cambridge University Press, 1971).
6. The phrase *development of underdevelopment* draws attention to the argument proposed by some dependency scholars that European economic expansion into the global periphery helped European economic development while simultaneously sowing the seeds of underdevelopment in Asia, Africa, and Latin America. See, for example, Andre Gunder Frank, *Dependent Accumulation and Underdevelopment* (London: MacMillan, 1978); and Immanuel Wallerstein, *Modern World System*, 3 vols. (San Diego, CA: Academic Press, 1974, 1980, 1989). While I am respectful of this literature, especially of Wallerstein's monumental contributions, I depart from it analytically in my emphasis on both national and political factors as part of the causal dynamics.
7. See Lawson, *East India Company*, chap. 2. Also see K. N. Chaudhuri, *The East India Company: The Study of an Early Joint-Stock Company, 1600–1640* (London: F. Cass, 1965).

8. For a variety of different perspectives, see Christopher Hill, *Reformation to Industrial Revolution: A Social and Economic History of Britain, 1530–1780* (London: Weidenfeld and Nicolson, 1968); Lawrence Stone, *The Causes of the English Revolution, 1529–1642* (London: Routledge, 1972); Conrad Russell, *Causes of the English Civil War* (Oxford: Clarendon Press, 1990); and Austin Woolrych, *Britain in Revolution, 1625–1640* (New York: Oxford University Press, 2002).
9. Hill, *Reformation to Industrial Revolution*, p. 13.
10. "The greatest triumph of the Tudors was the ultimately successful assertion of royal monopoly of violence." See Lawrence Stone, *The Crisis of Aristocracy, 1558–1641* (Oxford: Clarendon Press, 1965).
11. Quoted in Lawson, *East India Company*, p. 3.
12. On the importance of limited royal support for England's early colonial expansion, see John C. Appleby, "War, Politics and Colonization, 1558–1625," in Nicholas Canny, ed., *The Origins of Empire*, vol. 1 of *The Oxford History of the British Empire* (New York: Oxford University Press, 2001), pp. 55–78. Hereafter cited as "*OHBE*, vol. 1."
13. Historians debate the issue of how centralized and effective Mughal rule was. On one side of the debate are scholars of the "Aligarh School," who emphasize relative centralization and effectiveness. See, for example, Irfan Habib, *The Agrarian System of Moghul India, 1556–1707*, rev. ed. (Delhi: Oxford University Press, 1999); and S. Moosvi, *People, Taxation and Trade in Mughal India* (Oxford: Oxford University Press, 2008). More recent scholarship on the Mughals has focused on nonstate actors, creating a more fluid picture of Moghul rule. See, for example, Farhat Hasan, *State and Locality in Mughal India: Power Relations in Western India, c. 1572–1730* (Cambridge: Cambridge University Press, 2004); and Munis D. Faruqui, *The Princes of the Mughal Empire, 1504–1719* (Cambridge: Cambridge University Press, 2012). A good review of the literature is in Muzaffar Alam and Sanjay Subrahmanyam, *Writing the Mughal World: Studies on Culture and Politics* (New York: Columbia University Press, 2011), pp. 1–32.
14. See Tapan Ray Chaudhri, "The Mid-Eighteenth-Century Background," in Kumar, *CEHI*, vol. 2, pp. 3–35.
15. Recent research supports this view of relative prosperity of Mughal India. See Stephen Broadberry, Johann Custodis, and Bishnupriya Gupta, "India and the Great Divergence: An Anglo-Indian Comparison of Per Capita GDP, 1600–1871," *Explorations in Economic History* 58 (2015): 58–75. Broadberry and his colleagues estimate that per capita GDP of Mughal India around the year 1600 was some 60 percent of British per capita GDP (table 13, p. 70).
16. One prominent American historian of India described Akbar's empire as "probably the most powerful in the world at the time." See Stanley Wolpert, *A New History of India* (New York: Oxford University Press, 1982), p. 134.

17. For the account in this paragraph I am drawing on P. J. Marshall, "The English in Asia to 1700," in *OHBE*, vol. 1, pp. 264–85.
18. The correspondence of the ambassador Thomas Roe back to the court of James I provides important insights into the early British understanding of India: "It cannot be denyed that this King is one of the mightiest Princes in Asia, as well in extent of territory as in revenew; equall to the Turke, far exceeding the Persian. But the Gouerment so vncertayne, without written law, without Policye, the customes mingled with barbarism, religions infinite." Thomas Roe to the Kings Majestie, January 29, 1615. See William Foster, ed., *The Embassy of Thomas Roe to India* (Nendeln, Lichtenstein: Kraus Reprint, 1967), p. 120. What is noteworthy, on the one hand, is the admiration of power and wealth; but, on the other hand, a sense of cultural superiority manifest in the suggestion that customs of Mughal India were *barbaric*. This sense of barbarism—of the other—will be important throughout the study of imperialism because over time this attitude often justified metropolitan imposition of political control over the *barbaric other*, including in the writings of a variety of liberal thinkers.
19. See Chaudhuri, *English East India Company*, p. 91.
20. Ibid., table II, p. 22.
21. Ibid., chap. 5.
22. See Lawson, *East India Company*, chap. 2.
23. Chaudhuri, *East India Company*, p. 30. To put the sum of £20,000 in perspective, the annual average tax receipt of the English exchequer during the period 1663 to 1667—when the earliest reliable data are available—was £1.65 million. See Patrick K. O'Brien, "The Political Economy of British Taxation, 1660–1815," *Economic History Review*, n.s., 41, no. 1 (Feb., 1988): 1–32, table 2.
24. Immanuel Wallerstein characterizes the period 1625–75 as the period of Dutch hegemony in the global capitalist economy. See Wallerstein, *Modern World System II*, chap. 2.
25. For contending interpretations, see the sources in note 8 above.
26. Hill, *Reformation to Industrial Revolution*, p. 51.
27. An important recent study argues that 1688 was the real dividing line, after which "gentlemanly capitalism"—an alliance of the commercialized landed classes and London merchants—became hegemonic within the English state and spearheaded imperial expansion. See P. J. Cain and Anthony Hopkins, *British Imperialism, 1688–2000*, 2nd ed. (New York: Longman, 2002). Based on my reading of the historical literature, I find Hill's emphasis on 1640 as the real dividing line more persuasive. See his *Reformation to Industrial Revolution.* Still, for the purposes of this study, the demarcation of exact historical breaks is not that important. I am comfortable with a rough view that during the second half of the seventeenth century, power in England shifted away from the monarchy and the old nobility. Power increasingly came to reside in the Parliament. Moreover, the prominence of new

moneyed interests in Parliament, both in the countryside and in London, grew. Both 1640 and 1688 confirmed these trends.

28. Ibid., p. 73.
29. Ibid., p. 70.
30. Nicholas Canny, "Origins of Empire: An Introduction," in *OHBE*, vol. 1, p. 21.
31. My own rough estimates suggest that exports were worth less than 0.3 percent of the economy of Mughal India at the time. This estimate is based on the following calculations: exports from India to England in 1700 in current prices were worth some £500,000. See Chaudhuri, *Trading World of Asia,* table C.2, p. 509. The GDP of Mughal India in 1700, also in nominal prices, was some £191 million. This estimate in turn is derived from Broadberry, Custodis, and Gupta, "India and the Great Divergence." I used the Mughal GDP in 1600 as a benchmark that Broadberry and his coauthors provide in table 15, p. 70, to calculate this estimate. I used their index numbers for growth of Indian GDP (1600–1871), and their price deflators (tables 11 and 9, respectively) to calculate India's nominal GDP for various years. I also followed their suggested exchange rates of Rs. 8 to £1 for pre-1750 figures and Rs.10 to £1 for post-1750 figures. I am indebted to both Professors Bishnupriya Gupta and Stephen Broadberry for suggesting how to derive these estimates from their data. They are not at all responsible if I have misused their data in any way.
32. Hill, *Reformation to Industrial Revolution*, pp. 125, 128.
33. Canny, "Origins of Empire," in *OHBE*, vol. 1, pp. 22.
34. Ibid., p. 22.
35. One respected historian of the East India Company thus notes that the East India Company officials bribed English politicians to seek favorable legislation. See P. J. Marshall, "English in Asia to 1700," in *OHBE*, vol. 1, p. 282. Conversely, it may also be suggested—without stretching the evidence—that the legislative support provided to the East India Company from English MPs (especially those who held stock in the company) did not always follow the logic of enhancing the public good.
36. Ibid., p. 279. Also see Chaudhuri, *Trading World of Asia*, p. 547.
37. Lawson, *East India Company,* p. 57.
38. This theme is central to Chaudhuri, *Trading World of Asia*, which is probably the most significant existing economic history of the East India Company. Chaudhuri's conclusion on why trade was armed is important: "The ultimate answer must be that profits from armed trading were higher than in the case of peaceful commerce," p. 114.
39. Cited in Hill, *Reformation to Industrial Revolution*, p. 193.
40. Cited in Chaudhuri, *Trading World of Asia*, p. 454.
41. Quoted in Chaudhury, *From Prosperity to Decline*, p. 312.
42. See P. J. Marshall, "The British in Asia: Trade to Dominion, 1700–1765," in P. J. Marshall, ed., *The Eighteenth Century*, vol. 2 of *The Oxford History of the British*

Empire, vol. 2 (Oxford: Oxford University Press, 1998), p. 498. Hereafter cited as "*OHBE*, vol. 2."

43. Cited in Chaudhuri, *Trading World of Asia*, p. 117.
44. See Irfan Habib, "The Eighteenth Century in Indian History," in P. J. Marshall, ed., *The Eighteenth Century in Indian History: Evolution or Revolution?* (New Delhi: Oxford University Press, 2003).
45. See W. H. Moreland, *The Agrarian System of Moslem India* (Allahabad: Central Book Depot, 1929); and Habib, *Agrarian System of Mughal India*. Also see Faruqui, *Princes of the Mughal Empire*, where on page 9 he catalogues the variety of reasons historians suggest for the disintegration of the Mughals, including the one emphasized here. Also see C. A. Bayly, *Imperial Meridian: The British Empire and the World, 1780–1830* (London: Longman, 1989). Bayly puts more emphasis on the "growth of regions" as a cause of disintegration, not only of the Moghuls, but also of the Safavids and the Ottomans (see chaps. 1 and 2). I do not find this analysis too persuasive for Moghul India. There is some evidence that trade and commerce grew under the Moghuls, but the mainstay of the economy was agriculture. There is no evidence to indicate improvements in agricultural productivity or of per capita agricultural growth. The data in Broadberry, Custodis, and Gupta, "India and the Great Divergence," tables 12 and 13, indicates a steady decline in Indian per capita incomes during the eighteenth century. The struggle between the Mughal rulers and their regional intermediaries was in all probability a classic political struggle that had a zero-sum quality because it rested on a relatively stagnant economic base. Moreover, Bayly seems to suggest that the disintegration of the Mughals was in some senses a cause of British imperialism in India. The logic of this well-known peripheral thesis is also not all that persuasive; disintegration may create an opportunity for imperialism, but an opportunity is neither a cause nor a motive. Interested readers may note that much of the more recent scholarship on the Mughal Empire (see note 13 above) has not so much revised the Habib type of interpretation of the Mughal state as stepped away from political-economy issues, while following the "cultural turn" in historical studies.
46. Bayly is, of course, quite right when he suggests that "it was not quite clear in the conditions of the early eighteenth century what was the metropolis and what the periphery." Bayly, *Imperial Meridian*, p. 3. However, the diverging roots of what would become the metropole and what the periphery were already evident in the seventeenth century. For recent data on the declining per capita GDP in India in the seventeenth and eighteenth centuries—while the same in Britain was growing—see Broadberry, Custodis, and Gupta, "India and the Great Divergence," table 12, p. 69. Another related study that only came to my attention as this book was going to press, is Prasannan Parthasarthi, *Why Europe Grew Rich and Asia Did Not: Global Divergence, 1600–1850* (New York: Cambridge University Press, 2011).

47. See E. J. Hobsbawm, *Industry and Empire: From 1750 to the Present Day* (New York: New Press, 1999), chap. 1.
48. See Marshall, "English in Asia to 1700," p. 279.
49. Chaudhuri, *Trading World of Asia*, p. 238.
50. Marshall, *Problems of Empire*, p. 82.
51. Lawson, *East India Company*, p. 80.
52. Ibid., chap. 4.
53. Chaudhuri, *Trading World of Asia*, p. 119.
54. Chaudhury, *From Prosperity to Decline*, p. 310. The figure Chaudhury cites is in Indian rupees. I converted rupees into British pounds at the rate of 8:1, which is the best estimate available of exchange rate during that period (see note 31).
55. See Chaudhuri, *Trading World of Asia*, p. 111.
56. These numbers are based on Dutch sources. See Irfan Habib, "The Eighteenth Century in Indian History," in P. J. Marshall, ed., *The Eighteenth Century in Indian History: Evolution or Revolution?* (New Delhi: Oxford University Press, 2003), p. 104.
57. See Angus Maddison, *Contours of the World Economy, 1–2030 A.D.* (Oxford: Oxford University Press, 2007), table A.4, p. 379. The English economy in 1700 was already larger than the Dutch economy, but only by a factor of 2 or 3. The sharp divergence over the eighteenth century resulted in part from the divergent growth rates but also from the joining of England and Scotland in 1707 to become Great Britain.
58. See Hobsbawm, *Industry and Empire*.
59. See P. J. Marshall, "Introduction," to the *OHBE*, vol. 2, p. 1.
60. Hobsbawm, *Industry and Empire*, p. 10.
61. Cain and Hopkins, *British Imperialism*, p. 92.
62. I have relied heavily on Hobsbawm, *Industry and Empire*. In addition, a short, clear study that remains relevant is T. S. Ashton, *The Industrial Revolution* (Oxford: Oxford University Press, 1948); for a cultural argument of sorts, see David Landes, *The Unbound Prometheus: Technological Change and Industrial Development in Western Europe, 1750 to Present* (Cambridge: Cambridge University Press, 2003); and Wallerstein, *Modern World System III*, offers a distinctive global interpretation but also provides a useful review of relevant literature. Based on studies of national accounts, some scholars have sought to challenge the idea of "revolution" altogether, arguing instead that it was a gradual change; see N. F. R. Crafts, *British Economic Growth during the Industrial Revolution* (Oxford: Oxford University Press, 1985). This view in turn has been challenged; see Maxine Berg and Pat Hudson, "Rehabilitating the Industrial Revolution," *Economic History Review*, n.s., 45, no. 1 (Feb. 1992): 24–50. A useful survey of relevant debates is D. Cannandine, "The Past and Present in the English Industrial Revolution," *Past and Present* 103 (May 1984): 149–58. A recent study that focuses mainly on proximate and economic determinants of the Industrial Revolution is Robert C. Allen,

The British Industrial Revolution in Global Perspective (Cambridge: Cambridge University Press, 2009). Two much broader studies that shed light on social and institutional origins of modernization are Barrington Moore Jr., *Social Origins of Dictatorship and Democracy: Lord and Peasant in the Making of the Modern World* (Boston: Beacon Press, 1993); and Douglas North, *Institutions, Institutional Change and Economic Performance* (Cambridge: Cambridge University Press, 1990).

63. The discussion in this paragraph follows Hobsbawm, *Industry and Empire*, esp. chaps. 2 and 3.
64. Ibid., p. 32.
65. See Marshall, "British in Asia," in *OHBE*, vol. 2, p. 491.
66. See, for example, Chaudhury, *From Prosperity to Decline*, chap. 11.
67. See Bayly, *Imperial Meridian*, chap. 4. To be fair, Bayly's focus is broader than why Clive conquered Bengal. He is trying to explain the motives that drove the British Empire during the late eighteenth century. His suggestion is that a political and ideological interpretation of the empire is superior to an economic one, especially an economic interpretation that might emphasize the need to export manufactured goods. I agree with Bailey that the second half of the eighteenth century is still too early for manufacturing interests to drive foreign policy in Britain. However, I disagree with his claim that the motives were not economic. Britain's ruling classes were thoroughly commercialized, and Bailey's suggestion (in chapter 5) that the power of the gentry represents some sort of atavism, reminiscent of Schumpeter's argument about the taproot of imperialism, is simply not tenable. (One should recall that Schumpeter's argument was inspired more by the German Junkers and less by the profit-seeking British gentry). Bayly recognizes some of these tensions when he deviates from his central argument to also suggest that British imperialism was moved by a remarkable consensus across ruling classes, including "a revived and prosperous landed class with an emboldened professional and business class" (p. 12), and the underlying motive was "of course—a ruthless search for profit" (p. 16).
68. Cain and Hopkins, *British Imperialism*, chap. 2.
69. Clive of India continues to fascinate historians. A recent study is Brad C. Faught, *Clive: Founder of British India* (Washington DC: Potomac Books, 2013). Numerous earlier studies of Clive also exist and can be readily found by following the references in this book. One useful earlier study that situates Clive within the broader context of eighteenth century British politics is Lucy S. Sutherland, *The East India Company in Eighteenth-Century Politics* (Oxford: Oxford University Press, 1952).
70. See Hill, *Reformation to Industrial Revolution*, pp. 188–190.
71. Ibid., p. 188.
72. Ibid., p. 189.
73. Sutherland notes that corruption in British political life during this period, not to mention within the East India Company, was widespread; she also suggests why

this was so in a manner that is still highly relevant for understanding corruption anywhere: "The private and public interests of those taking part in political life were insufficiently distinguished either by the sanctions of political organization or by the influence of an informed public opinion." See Sutherland, *East India Company*, p. 51.

74. See O'Brien, "Political Economy of British Taxation," tables 2 and 3, for figures on income of the British government.
75. Hill, *Reformation to Industrial Revolution*, p. 193.
76. Ibid., p. 193.
77. Lawson, *East India Company*, p. 96.
78. Marshall, "British in Asia," *OHBE*, vol. 2, p. 506.
79. Bowen, *Business of Empire*, p. 83. For those interested in British political thinking about the East India Company during this period, Edmund Burke's speech on Fox's India Bill in 1783 (a bill leading up to the Pitt's India Act in 1784) makes for fine reading. It is readily available online at: http://ota.ox.ac.uk/id/4069.
80. Bowen, *Business of Empire*, p. 8.
81. Cited in Lawson, *East India Company*, p. 128.
82. Marshall, *Problems of Empire*, p. 15.
83. Ibid, p. 83.
84. Bowen, *Business of Empire*, p. 200.
85. Marshall, *Problems of Empire*, p. 83.
86. See John F. Richards, "The Finances of the East India Company in India, c. 1766–1859" (Working Paper no. 153/11, Department of Economic History, London School of Economics, 2011), table 3.
87. See Bowen, *Business of Empire*, p. 40.
88. An overview of the early origins of the British Indian army is available in Stephen Cohen, *The Indian Army: It's Contribution to the Development of a Nation* (Berkeley: University of California Press, 1971), chap. 1.
89. Lawson, *East India Company*, p. 133.
90. One scholar argues that this was a central factor pushing Britain toward greater military and political control over India. See Bayly, *Imperial Meridian*, p. 59.
91. William Playfair, a British mathematician, cited in Bowen, *Business of Empire*, p. 11.
92. See Esteban, "India's Contribution to the British Balance of Payments", p. 175.
93. Ibid., p. 156.
94. Bowen, *Business of Empire*, table 9.2, p. 272.
95. See Maddison, *Contours of the World Economy*, table B.1, p. 384.
96. Bowen, *Business of Empire*, p. 277.
97. While it is hard to attach a number to these activities, they are summarized ibid., pp. 288–94.
98. Ibid., p. 295.

99. Cited in H. V. Bowen, "British India, 1765–1813: The Metropolitan Context," in *OHBE*, vol. 2, p. 533.
100. This claim was made in 1968 by Marshall, *Problems of Empire*, p. 92.
101. Cited in Bowen, *Business of Empire*, p. 41.
102. For such an argument, see Linda Colley, *Britons: Forging the Nation, 1707–1837*, 2nd ed. (New Haven, CT: Yale University Press, 2005).
103. Maddison, *Contours of the World Economy*, p. 128.
104. From Richards, "Finances of the East India Company," table 3.
105. John F. Richards, "Imperial Finance under the East India Company, 1762–1859," in Durba Ghosh and Dane Keith Kennedy, eds., *Decentering Empire: Britain, India and the Postcolonial World* (New Delhi: Oriental Longman, 2006), p. 50.
106. See Richards, "Finances of the East India Company," table 3. Richards reports in this table that military expenditures averaged 66 percent during this period; what he is reporting, however, is the share of "Indian charges" of the East India Company. I have reported instead the military expenditures, as well as the revenues used to buy exportable goods (listed in Richards's table under the headings of "Cargoes" and "Net Remittances"), as shares of the total revenues.
107. S. Bhattacharya, "Eastern India," in Kumar, *CEHI*, vol. 2, p. 289.
108. B. Chaudhuri, "Eastern India," Kumar, *CEHI*, vol. 2, p. 299.
109. A. K. Sen, *Poverty and Famines: An Essay on Entitlement and Deprivation* (Oxford: Clarendon Press, 1981).
110. Chaudhuri, "Eastern India," Kumar, *CEHI*, vol. 2, p. 299.
111. Ibid., p. 299.
112. Cited ibid., p. 301.
113. One good study of the impact of the settlement on Bengali Zamindari class is Ray, *Change in Bengal Agrarian Society*. A more recent study that focuses on the impact on the regional rural economy is Rajat Datta, *Society, Economy and Market: Commercialization in Rural Bengal, c. 1760–1800* (New Delhi: Manohar, 2000).
114. Chaudhuri, "Eastern India" in Kumar, *CEHI*, vol. 2, p. 157.
115. See Richards, "Finances of the East India Company," table 7. Some of the data discussed in this and the next paragraph also appear in table 9.
116. I estimate that India's nominal GDP in 1801 was £219 million (see note 31 above for details of how I calculated India's historical GDP in nominal terms). Table 9, p. 68, in Broadberry, Custodis, and Gupta, "India and the Great Divergence" suggests that the East India Company in 1801 controlled about one quarter of India's overall territory. The annual product of the territory controlled by the East India Company was then one quarter of the overall GDP, or roughly in the range of £55 million. Also see Table 1.3 for related data.
117. Such examples—and others—were of course at the heart of the influential argument on Britain's informal empire proposed by Gallagher and Robinson. See

John Gallagher and Ronald Robinson, "The Imperialism of Free Trade," *Economic History Review*, 2nd ser., 6, no. 1 (1953): 1–15.

118. Yes, Clive and Hastings were criticized in Parliament and a brief reformist period followed under Cornwallis. However, as Washbrook emphasizes, the militarism re-emerged fairly soon thereafter. See David Washbrook, "India, 1818–1860: The Two Faces of Colonialism," in *OHBE*, vol. 1, pp. 395–421.
119. See Cain and Hopkins, *British Imperialism.* While I have taken these quotes from here and there between pages 82 and 100, I do not think that I have taken any quote out of context. My main disagreement with the argument put forward by Cain and Hopkins in their important book is that they underestimate the importance of manufactured exports in the spread of British imperialism. For such an argument that directly disagrees with Cain and Hopkins with reference to the East India Company and India, see J. R. Ward, "The Industrial Revolution and British Imperialism, 1750–1850," *Economic History Review*, n.s., 47, no. 1 (Feb. 1994): 44–65.
120. See note 31 above for how I calculated India's nominal GDP. In a recent work Tirthankar Roy, working backward from estimates of 1913 Indian GDP—assuming a 1 percent growth rate between 1860 and 1913—estimates India's real GDP in 1860 at £507.8 million. See his *An Economic History of Early Modern India* (Abingdon, UK: Routledge, 2013), table 5.1, p. 76. The substantial discrepancy in my estimates based on data from Broadberry, Custodis, and Gupta, "Great Divergence," and those of Roy probably result from the fact that my estimates extrapolate from Mughal data, and the Mughals controlled only a little more than half of what was then India. However, since the East India Company during this period also did not control all of India, I think that estimates based on forward extrapolation of Broadberry and colleagues data are likely to me more accurate than Roy's backward extrapolation, which also rests on assumed growth rates. Roy's estimates are also in real prices, not nominal prices.
121. See Richards, "Finances of the East India Company," table 6. Britain's nominal GDP in 1850 was some £468 million; see Stephen Broadberry, Bruce M. S. Campbell, Mark Overton, Bas van Leeuwen, and Alexander Apotolides, "Historical National Accounts for Britain, 1300–1850," unpublished manuscript available at: https://www.academia.edu/385400/historical_national_accounts_for_britain_1300-1850_some_preliminary_estimates. The data on nominal GDP is in the linked excel file. The East India Company's Indian revenues in that year were some £20 million or about 4 percent of Britain's nominal GDP.
122. See Washbrook, "India, 1818–60".
123. Ibid.
124. Richards, "Finances of the East India Company," table 8.
125. Ibid., table 12.
126. Bowen, *Business of Empire*, p. 259.

127. See East India Company, *Home Accounts of the East India Company: 1 May 1835* (House of Commons, London, July 23, 1835), List no. 1, 2. The East India Company's monopoly on tea trade was abolished in 1833. This led to a decline in the East India Company's earnings from tea, but it did not diminish opium trade. On the contrary, opium trade flourished in subsequent years, especially after China was forcibly opened up. The East India Company's revenues from the opium monopoly in India also grew substantially.
128. Washbrook, "India, 1818–60," p. 404. One is forced to wonder how such important British thinkers as Jeremy Bentham, John Stuart Mill, and Thomas Malthus—all employees of the East India Company—coped morally with the brutal immorality of such actions of the East India Company.
129. Bowen, *Business of Empire*, pp. 257–58.
130. Chaudhuri, *Economic Development of India, 1814–58*, p. 2. Some specific information in this paragraph is also taken from this source, table 2, pp. 26 and 34; the direct quote appears on p. 26.
131. From East India Company's petition to Parliament in 1840, cited ibid, p. 17.
132. Ibid., p. 36.
133. Cited in Mamta Aggarwal, "Short Essay on Economic Drain during British India," *History Discussion* website, downloaded November 2, 2013, accessed July 3, 2018, http://www.historydiscussion.net/history-of-india/short-essay-on-economic-drain-during-british-india/728.
134. Bhattacharya, "Eastern India," in Kumar, *CEHI*, vol. 2, p. 290 (Bhattacharya is in turn citing the well-known work of A. K. Bagchi).
135. See Divekar, "Western India," in Kumar, *CEHI*, vol. 2, pp. 348–349. It is worth noting that in 1851, toward the end of the time period under consideration, Parsis took the lead in establishing India's first cotton mill, the Bombay Spinning and Weaving Company, which catered to low-end cloth that the British were not exporting to India. One can only wonder how much faster India's textile industry would have grown if a sovereign Indian government—like its counterparts in the United States and Germany around that time—could have used protectionism to support a range of such industries.
136. Kumar, "South India," in Kumar, *CEHI*, vol. 2, p. 359.
137. A comment from East India Company directors, cited in Bowen, *Business of Empire*, p. 255.
138. See Broadberry, Custodis, and Gupta, "India and the Great Divergence" , pp. 26–27.
139. Ibid.," table 12, p. 69.
140. See, for example, D. K. Fieldhouse, *Economics and Empire, 1830–1914* (Ithaca, NY: Cornell University Press, 1973).
141. See Gallagher and Robinson, "Imperialism of Free Trade," for a further discussion of those who put forward such free-trade views and for what is wrong with such views.

CHAPTER 2

1. A full definition of an informal empire is provided in chapter 1.
2. Palmerston made this statement in 1848 and has been quoted widely. I took the quote from Ronald Hyam, *Britain's Imperial Century, 1815–1914: A Study of Empire and Expansion* (London: B. T. Batsford, 1976), p. 49.
3. See Martin Lynn, "British Policy, Trade, and Informal Empire in the Mid-Nineteenth Century," in Andrew Porter, ed., *The Nineteenth Century*, vol. 3 of *The Oxford History of the British Empire* (Oxford: Oxford University Press, 1999), p. 106.
4. A useful overview volume is Rory Miller, *Britain and Latin America in the Nineteenth and Twentieth Century* (London: Longman, 1993). An earlier study that remains relevant is Stanley J. Stein and Barbara H. Stein, *The Colonial Heritage of Latin America: Essays on Economic Dependence in Perspective* (New York: Oxford University Press, 1970). A collection with diverse perspectives is V. Bulmer-Thomas, ed., *Britain and Latin America: A Changing Relationship* (New York: Cambridge University Press, 1989).
5. See Atul Kohli, *State-Directed Development: Political Power and Industrialization in the Global Periphery* (New York: Cambridge University Press, 2004), chap. 4.
6. See, for example, Şevket Pamuk, "Anatolia and Egypt during the Nineteenth Century: A Comparison of Foreign Trade and Foreign Investment," in Şevket Pamuk, *The Ottoman Economy and Its Institutions* (Farnham, UK: Ashgate, 2009), chap. 11.
7. See John Gallagher and Ronald Robinson, "The Imperialism of Free Trade," *Economic History Review*, 2nd ser., 6, no. 1 (1953): 1–15.
8. See D. C. M. Platt, "Further Objections to an 'Imperialism of Free Trade,' 1830–60," *Economic History Review*, 2nd ser., 26, no. 1 (1973): 77–91. A useful volume that brings together debates around the concept of informal empire is Wm. Roger Louis, ed., *The Robinson and Gallagher Controversy* (New York: Franklin Watts, 1976).
9. See P. J. Cain and Anthony Hopkins, *British Imperialism, 1688–2000*, 2nd ed. (New York: Longman, 2002).
10. See, for example, Platt's own arguments in D. C. M. Platt, ed., *Business Imperialism: An Inquiry Based on British Experience in Latin America* (Oxford: Clarendon Press, 1977), pp. 10–11.
11. See, for example, François Crouzet, "Toward an Export Economy: British Exports during the Industrial Revolution," *Exploration in Economic History* 17 (January 1, 1980): 48–93.
12. See Charles Issawi, "Egypt since 1800: A Study in Lop-sided Development," *Journal of Economic History* 21, no. 1 (March 1961): 1–25. The classic dependency analysis of Latin America along these lines is, of course, Fernando Henrique Cardoso and Enzo Faletto, *Dependency and Development in Latin America* (Berkeley: University of California Press, 1979). For a lively debate on whether internal or external factors were more important in China's failure to modernize in the nineteenth century,

see Philip C. C. Huang, ed., *The Development of Underdevelopment in China: A Symposium* (New York: M. E. Sharpe, 1980).

13. See, for example, H. S. Ferns, *Britain and Argentina in the Nineteenth Century* (Oxford: Oxford University Press, 1960), chap. 1.
14. Quoted in David Rock, "The British in Argentina: From Informal Empire to Post Colonialism," in Matthew Brown, ed., *Informal Empire in Latin America: Culture, Commerce and Capital* (Oxford: Blackwell, 2008), p. 57.
15. This quote is from Castlereagh's "Memorandum for the Cabinet, Relative to South America," May 1, 1807, cited in Miller, *Britain and Latin America*, p. 35.
16. Ibid.
17. See Hyam, *Britain's Imperial Century*, p. 168.
18. See Alan K. Manchester, *British Preeminence in Brazil, Its Rise and Decline: A Study in European Expansion* (Chapel Hill: University of North Carolina Press, 1933), chap. 4.
19. Miller, *Britain and Latin America*, p. 43.
20. Ibid., p. 44.
21. See Richard Graham, "Sepoys and Imperialists: Techniques of British Power in Nineteenth-Century Brazil," *Inter-American Economic Affairs* 23 (1969): 23–37.
22. See Ferns, *Britain and Argentina*, chaps. 1–4. Those unfamiliar with this historical period may wish to know that Home Popham was a British naval officer, who aspired to be another Lord Clive, and who took it upon himself to invade Buenos Aires in 1806 in the hope of claiming it from the Spanish and to open it for British merchants for commerce. The invasion failed and Popham was court-martialed. Nevertheless, Popham was feted by London merchants, and British government sent in reinforcements to support Popham's invading force; this second attack was also repulsed by a patriotic coalition of local merchants and ranchers; while the Spanish crown did not support this anti-British resistance, the role of local Spanish authorities is debated by historians. A similar coalition then came to the fore during 1808–10 in Argentina, when the authority of the Spanish crown disintegrated under the weight of Napoleon's armies.
23. Two good historical overviews of Argentine political economy are David Rock, *Argentina, 1516–1982: From Spanish Colonization to the Falklands War* (Berkeley: University of California Press, 1985); and H. S. Ferns, *The Argentine Republic, 1516–1971* (New York: Barnes and Noble Books, 1973).
24. Juan Eugenio Corradi, "Argentina," in Ronald Chilcote and Joel C. Edelstein, eds., *Latin America: The Struggle with Dependency and Beyond* (New York: John Wiley and Sons, 1983), p. 320.
25. Quoted in Ferns, *Britain and Argentina*, p. 51.
26. Rock, *Argentina, 1516–1982*, p. 116.
27. See Corradi, "Argentina," pp. 321–3.
28. A useful study of political change in nineteenth century Buenos Aires is Jeremy Adelman, *Republic of Capital: Buenos Aires and the Legal Transformation of the Atlantic World* (Stanford, CA: Stanford University Press, 1999).

29. All direct quotes from Castlereagh are taken from Ferns, *Britain and Argentina*, pp. 47–48.
30. See Manuel Llorca-Jaña, *The British Textile Trade in South America in the Nineteenth Century* (Cambridge: Cambridge University Press, 2012), p. 19.
31. Ferns, *Britain and Argentina*, p. 76.
32. See Rock, *Argentina, 1516–1982*, p. 100.
33. To be precise, Canning made this statement in 1824, one year after Britain recognized South American states and one year before he negotiated the Friendship Treaty. This statement is cited widely. I took it from Lynn, "British Policy, Trade, and Informal Empire," p. 102.
34. Miller, *Britain and Latin America*, pp. 40–41.
35. Ibid., p. 40.
36. Also see Llorca-Jaña, *British Textile Trade*, tables 2.2 and 2.4, the sources from which Table 2.1 is derived.
37. See Rock, *Argentina, 1516–1982*, p. 100.
38. See Llorca-Jaña, *British Textile Trade*, pp. 284 and 183. Fern in his later work also estimated that in 1829 gold and silver bullion exports from Argentina constituted 16 percent of its total exports. See Fern, *Argentine Republic*, p. 29.
39. See Rock, *Argentina, 1516–1982*, pp. 100–103.
40. D. C. M. Platt, "Dependency in Latin America: A Historian Objects," *Latin American Research Review* 15, no. 1 (1980): 115. Platt in this essay also develops his argument to include finance and to subsequent periods. I will return to those other issues below.
41. See Platt, "Further Objections to an 'Imperialism of Free Trade,' 1830–60," (abridged version) in Wm. Roger Louis, ed., *Robinson and Gallagher Controversy*, p. 155.
42. Llorca-Jaña, *British Textile Trade*, esp. chap. 2.
43. See Rock, *Argentina, 1516–1982*, pp. 102–3.
44. See Ferns, *Britain and Argentina*, chap. 6.
45. The felicitous phrase is used by Miller, *Britain and Latin America*, p. 7.
46. Rosas was also a controversial figure who has excited a lot of conflicting interpretations, especially among Argentine historians. Given the focus of this study most of these debates are not all that germane. For a quick overview of the historiography of Rosas, see Jeffrey Shunway, "Juan Manuel de Rosas," *Oxford Bibliographies Online*, https://www.oxfordbibliographies.com.
47. See Corradi, "Argentina," p. 325.
48. See his *Argentine Republic*, p. 50.
49. Gore (a British diplomat in Argentina) to Palmerston, January 4, 1852, cited in Knight, "Britain and Latin America," p. 135.
50. Palmerston quoted in Miller, *Britain and Latin America*, p. 51
51. Ibid., p. 56.
52. Quoted in Ferns, *Britain and Argentina*, p. 259.
53. Cited in Knight, "Britain and Latin America," p. 144.

54. See Ferns, *Britain and Argentina*, pp. 252–54.
55. See Miller, *Britain and Latin America*, p. 83.
56. See Ferns, *Britain and Argentina*, p. 288.
57. See Rock, *Argentina, 1516–1982*, chap. 4.
58. See Corradi, "Argentina," pp. 327–30.
59. Ferns, *Britain and Argentina*, p. 301.
60. Ibid, p. 314.
61. Ibid, p. 320.
62. Miller thus notes with reference to this period that "diplomats, consuls and naval officers became deeply involved in internal politics," in both Argentina and Brazil. See Miller, *Britain and Latin America*, p. 54.
63. Those with a more than passing interest in these matters may wish to know a little more about the relevant literature. The view that British-Latin American trade during the first half of the nineteenth century was not all that significant is of course associated with D. C. M. Platt, *Latin America and British Trade, 1806–1914* (London: A. and C. Black, 1972). While for Argentina Platt depended on Ferns, *Britain and Argentina*, which was published in 1960, Ferns himself revised his own views significantly by 1973 when he published *Argentine Republic*. This shift was based on the availability of new data that suggested that volume of trade was a lot greater than revealed by the earlier data on value; the latter was misleading because of decline in textile prices during this period. In spite of the shift by Ferns, a variety of scholars continued to adhere to Platt's view that this early phase was one of economic disappointment for Britain. For those paying closer attention, it was already clear by 1980 from the data provided in Crouzet, "Toward an Export Economy," that British-Latin American trade had grown handsomely during this first phase. It is surprising that more scholars did not pay attention to this emerging data, including Cane and Hopkins, *British Imperialism*. Among the first to fully challenge Platt's views—gently but decisively—was Miller, *Britain and Latin America*, whose study remains one of the best treatments of the subject. A recent volume published in 2012 (Llorca-Jaña, *British Textile Trade in South America*) totally discredits the view that trade during this period was insignificant.
64. See Crouzet, "Toward an Export Economy," table 10, p. 73.
65. Miller, *Britain and Latin America*, p. 75.
66. Ferns, *Argentine Republic*, pp. 32–35.
67. See Luis Bertola and Jose Antonio Ocampo, eds., *Economic Development of Latin America since Independence* (Oxford: Oxford University Press, 2012), table 24.
68. See Ricardo D. Salvatore and Carlos Newland, "Between Independence and the Golden Age: The Early Argentine Economy," in Gerrardo Della Paolera and Alan P. Taylor, *A New Economic History of Argentina* (Cambridge: Cambridge University Press, 2003), p. 21.

69. See Llorca-Jaña *British Textile Trade in South America*, p. 284.
70. Ibid., p 183; also see Miller, *Britain and Latin America*, p. 78.
71. These historical growth rates are taken from Leandro Prados de la Escosura, "Lost Decades? Economic Performance in Post-Independence Latin America," *Journal of Latin American Studies*, 41 (2009) : table 6, p. 301.
72. Prados notes, ibid., table 6, p. 301, that Brazil's per capita economic growth between 1820 and 1870 was 0.1 percent per annum. Also see Nathaniel H. Leff, *Underdevelopment and Development in Brazil*, vol. 1 (London: George Allen and Unwin, 1982), p. 38.
73. See Celso Furtado, *The Economic Growth of Brazil: A Survey from Colonial to Modern Times* (Berkeley: University of California Press, 1963), Parts 2, 3, and 4.
74. Kohli, *State-Directed Development*, chap. 4.
75. It should be qualified that the decline in indigenous manufacturing was slow and only hastened after 1840. See Llorca-Jaña, *British Textile Trade*, pp. 257–70.
76. See Stanley and Stein, *Colonial Heritage of Latin America*, p. 146.
77. See Rock, *Argentina, 1516–1982*, p. 119.
78. The estimate is from Lyman Johnson and cited in Salvatore and Newland, "Between Independence and the Golden Age," p. 32.
79. Rock, *Argentina, 1516–1982*, p. 119.
80. Ibid., p. 132.
81. See Miller, *Britain and Latin America*, p. 142.
82. In the words of one scholar, Argentine elites chose "dependent development through foreign investment over autonomous development." See Corradi, "Argentina," p. 330.
83. Miller, *Britain and Latin America*, chap. 3; and Knight, "Britain and Latin America," p. 134. A "revisionist" account of sorts is Fernando Rocchi, *Chimneys in the Desert: Argentina during the Export Boom Years, 1870–1930* (Stanford, CA: Stanford University Press, 2006), esp. chap. 7.
84. The direct quote as well as the account of the incident is drawn from Rock, *Argentina, 1516–1982*, pp. 148–49.
85. Ibid., p. 150.
86. Miller, *Britain and Latin America*, p. 138.
87. See Ferns, *Britain and Argentina*, p. 437.
88. Corradi, "Argentina," p. 331.
89. Knight, "Rethinking British Informal Empire", p. 45.
90. Cited ibid., p. 45.
91. See Rock, *Argentina, 1516–1982*, pp. 159–60.
92. See Ferns, *Britain and Argentina*, p. 372.
93. Knight, "Rethinking British Informal Empire," p. 45.
94. Ferns, *Britain and Argentina*, p. 429.
95. Miller, *Britain and Latin America*, p. 5.

96. Ibid., p. 5.
97. Knight, "Britain and Latin America," 135.
98. Miller, *Britain and Latin America*, tables 5.5, p. 111, and 6.2, p. 122, respectively.
99. Knight, "Britain and Latin America," 135.
100. Miller, *Britain and Latin America*, tables 5.4, p. 109, and 5.2, p. 106.
101. Ibid, table 6.2, p. 122.
102. Ibid., table 5.6, p. 112.
103. Ibid., p. 113.
104. Ibid., table 6.2, p. 122.
105. The focus on the importance of finance in late nineteenth-century British imperialism is of course an old one, dating to Hobson and Lenin. More recently, a version of this argument has been developed by Cain and Hopkins, *British Imperialism*. They, in their brief discussion of the Argentine case (pp. 252–67), focus mainly on the Barings crisis of 1890.
106. Ferns, *Britain and Argentina*, p. 337.
107. It may be worth noting in passing that there were such beginnings. In 1853, indigenous businessmen established the first Argentine railway, the *Ferrocarril al Oeste*, with support from the government of Buenos Aires. That the railway was fairly successful further complicates the issue of why more such efforts were not undertaken. This rail line was eventually sold to a British company in the fire sale that followed the settlement of the Barings financial crisis in 1891, and it provoked nationalist reaction. If all that sounds familiar to observers of subsequent financial crises, it should. That history repeats itself—Marx notwithstanding—is not so much farce as tragedy, insofar as elites fail to learn lessons from the past. For details of this Argentine railway experiment, see ibid., esp. pp. 313, 452.
108. Ibid., pp. 325–27.
109. I analyzed the political and economic changes in Brazil during this phase in Kohli, *State-Directed Development*, pp. 137–52. For my analysis, in turn, I drew quite heavily on Steven Topik, *The Political Economy of the Brazilian State, 1889–1930* (Austin: University of Texas Press, 1987).
110. See, for example, Rocchi, *Chimneys in the Desert*, table 1.4, p. 22.
111. See Madison, *Contours of the World Economy*, table 6.6, p. 309, where he notes that the per capita GDP of Egypt had not changed between 1500 and 1820; the population of Egypt is noted in his table 4.7, p. 229. A quick overview of Egyptian history during this period is readily available in Afaf Lutfi Al-Sayyid Marsot, *A History of Egypt: From the Arab Conquest to the Present*, 2nd ed. (Cambridge: Cambridge University Press, 2007), chaps. 3 and 4.
112. Cited in John Marlowe, *A History of Modern Egypt and Anglo-Egyptian Relations* (Hamden, CT: Archon Books, 1965), p. 15.
113. The best study of Egypt under Muhammad Ali remains Afaf Lutfi Al-Sayyid Marsot, *Egypt in the Reign of Muhammad Ali* (Cambridge University Press,

1984). Also useful is Helen Anne B. Rivlin, *The Agricultural Policy of Muhammad Ali in Egypt* (Cambridge, MA: Harvard University Press, 1961).

114. See Marlowe, *History of Modern Egypt,* p. 27. Carl Brown also tersely noted that, claims of propping up the "sick-man of Europe" aside, "no one in Europe," including the English, had any interest in "reconstituting the Ottoman Empire." See L. Carl Brown, *International Politics and the Middle East: Old Rules, Dangerous Games* (Princeton, NJ: Princeton University Press, 1984), p. 34.
115. The two important studies by Marsot and Rivlin were cited in note 113. In addition, see Khaled Fahmy, "The Era of Muhammad 'Ali Pasha, 1805–45," in M. W. Daly, ed., *The Cambridge History of Egypt* [hereafter cited as *CHE*], vol. 2 (Cambridge: Cambridge University Press, 1998), pp. 139–79. Useful analyses of Muhammad Ali's policies are also available in the following broader studies: Charles Issawi, *An Economic History of the Middle East and North Africa* (New York: Columbia University Press, 1982); Roger Owen, *The Middle East and the World Economy, 1800–1914* (London: Methuen, 1981); and Alan Richards, *Egypt's Agricultural Development, 1800–1980: Technical and Social Change* (Boulder, CO: Westview Press), 1982).
116. See Marsot, *Egypt in the Reign of Muhammad Ali,* p. 97.
117. The themes of personal rule and inefficiency are emphasized in Fahmy, "Era of Muhammad 'Ali Pasha."
118. For factual information that follows I am drawing on the sources listed in note 115, this chapter. Specific citations are provided only when the information needs some authoritative support.
119. For a discussion of Egypt's own imperial activities in the region, see Hassan Ahmed Ibrahim, "Egyptian Empire, 1805–85," in Daly, *CHE,* vol. 2, pp. 198–216.
120. See Marlowe, *History of Modern Egypt,* p. 35.
121. Marsot, *Egypt in the Reign of Muhammad Ali,* p. 137.
122. See Patrick O'Brien, "The Long-Term Growth of Agricultural Production in Egypt: 1821–1962," in P. M. Holt, ed., *Political and Social Change in Modern Egypt* (London: Oxford University Press, 1968), tables 5 and 6, p. 179.
123. See Owen, *Middle East in the World Economy,* table 4, p. 67.
124. Cited in Marsot, *Egypt in the Reign of Muhammad Ali,* p. 167.
125. See Issawi, *An Economic History of the Middle East,* p. 188.
126. See Issawi, "Egypt Since 1800," p. 5.
127. Marsot, *Egypt in the Reign of Muhammad Ali,* p. 181.
128. Issawi, "Egypt since 1800," p. 6.
129. See Hyam, *Britain's Imperial Century,* p. 244.
130. Cited in Marsot, *Egypt in the Reign of Muhammad Ali,* p. 230.
131. See Hyam, *Britain's Imperial Century,* p. 244.
132. Marsot, *Egypt in the Reign of Muhammad Ali,* p. 171.
133. Ibid., p. 174.

134. See, for example, Rivlin, *Agricultural Policy of Muhammad 'Alī*, p. 199, where she makes this suggestion, without providing much support for the argument except to repeat the observations of self-interested British consuls of the period, who argued that Egypt should pursue its comparative advantage in growing cotton. Also see Owen, *Middle East in the World Economy*, pp. 75–76, where he seems to rest his case on the untenable claim that all import-substituting industrialization is doomed to failure because these experiments end up being import intensive. I have argued against this position elsewhere; see Kohli, *State-Led Industrialization*.
135. Cited in Marsot, *Egypt in the Reign of Muhammad Ali*, pp. 174–75.
136. Issawi, "Egypt since 1800," p. 7. A similar conclusion is reached by Marsot, *Egypt in the Reign of Muhammad Ali*, esp. on p. 177.
137. "Klondike on the Nile" is a chapter heading in David S. Landes, *Bankers and Pashas: International Finance and Economic Imperialism in Egypt* (Cambridge, MA: Harvard University Press, 1958).
138. Cited in Hyam, *Britain's Imperial Century*, p. 250.
139. See F. Robert Hunter, "Egypt under the Successors of Muhammad Ali," in Daly, *CHE*, vol. 2, p. 185.
140. Ibid., p. 185.
141. I am drawing the factual information in this paragraph from Issawi, "Egypt since 1800," pp. 8–10.
142. Cited in Issawi, *Economic History of the Middle East*, p. 51.
143. For details see John Marlowe, *World Ditch: The Making of the Suez Canal* (London: Macmillan, 1964); and for a quick overview, Marlowe, *History of Modern Egypt*, chap. 3.
144. See Marsot, *History of Egypt*, p. 79.
145. See Issawi, *Economic History of the Middle East*, p. 68.
146. Marsot, *History of Egypt*, p. 79.
147. Marlowe, *History of Modern Egypt*, p. 71.
148. Ibid., p. 74.
149. Ibid., p. 75.
150. Hunter, "Egypt under the Successors of Muhammad Ali," p. 188.
151. See Issawi, "Egypt since 1800," p. 10. Also excellent for financial developments during this phase, with a special emphasis on the role of the French, is Landes, *Bankers and Pashas*.
152. See Marlowe, *History of Modern Egypt*, p. 91.
153. For accounts of Cromer, see Robert Tignor, "Lord Cromer: Practitioner and Philosopher of Imperialism," *Journal of British Studies* 2, no. 2 (May 1963): 142–59; and John Marlowe, *Cromer in Egypt* (London: Elek, 1970).
154. See Marsot, *History of Egypt*, p. 84.
155. See Donald M. Reid, "The 'Urabi Revolution and the British Conquest, 1879–1882," in Daly, *CHE*, vol. 2, pp. 219–20.
156. See ibid., for a persuasive analysis along these lines.

157. One relatively recent study on which I have drawn is Robert T. Harrison, *Gladstone's Imperialism in Egypt: Techniques of Domination* (Westport, CT: Greenwood Press, 1995).
158. See, for example, Ronald Robinson and John Gallagher, *Africa and the Victorians: The Official Mind of Imperialism*, with Alice Denny (1961; repr. London: I. B. Tauris, 2015).
159. This line of thinking is associated with Robinson, among others, ibid.
160. Cited in ibid., p. 4.
161. Cited in Hyam, *Britain's Imperial Century*, p. 252.
162. See their *British Imperialism*.
163. A brief but excellent overview of this period is readily available in Afaf Lutfi al-Sayyid-Marsot, "The British Occupation of Egypt from 1882," in Louis, ed., *OHBE*, vol. 3, pp. 651–65.
164. These eloquent words are from Hyam, *Britain's Imperial Century*, p. 255.
165. Ibid., p. 256.
166. Owen, *Middle East in the World Economy*, p. 224.
167. Pamuk, "Anatolia and Egypt," p. 44.
168. For a favorable account of Cromer's rule, see Marlowe, *History of Modern Egypt*, esp. chap. 7.
169. Owen, *Middle East in the World Economy*, pp. 218–19.
170. See O'Brien, "Agricultural Production in Egypt", table 6, p. 179, and table 8, p. 180.
171. O'Brien notes that "investment in irrigation system during this period did not occur on a scale sufficient to add" new lands for cultivation at the same rate as in the earlier period. See ibid., p. 186.
172. See Owen, *Middle East in the World Economy*, p. 225.
173. Hyam, *Britain's Imperial Century*, p. 258.
174. See B. Hansen, *The Political Economy of Poverty, Equity and Growth: Egypt and Turkey* (Oxford: Oxford University Press, 1991), table 1.
175. Pamuk, "Anatolia and Egypt," pp. 40–41.
176. Owen, *Middle East in the World Economy*, p. 241.
177. Ibid., p. 242. It should be added that in spite of the Cromer's much-touted "administrative efficiency," the absolute amount of Egyptian public debt hardly declined between 1878 and 1914, remaining at nearly £100 million. See Pamuk, "Anatolia and Egypt," table 2b, p. 43.
178. Pamuk, "Anatolia and Egypt", table 3b, p. 46.
179. Ibid., table 4b, p. 47.
180. Ibid., p. 48.
181. Issawi, "Egypt since 1800."
182. Cited in V. J. Puryear, *International Economics and Diplomacy in the Near East, 1834–4* (1935; Hamden, CT: Archon Books, 1969), p. 213.
183. Cited in Peter Ward Fay, *The Opium War, 1840–42* (Chapel Hill: University of North Carolina Press, 1975), p. 12.

184. Hyam, *Britain's Imperial Century*, p. 352.
185. Ibid., p. 352.
186. Michael Greenberg, *British Trade and the Opening of China, 1800–1842* (Cambridge: Cambridge University Press, 1951), pp. 43–44.
187. Ibid., p. 1.
188. Good accounts of how the old Canton trade operated are available in Frederic Wakeman, "The Canton Trade and the Opium War," in *The Cambridge History of China (CHC)*, vol. 10, ed. John K. Fairbank (Cambridge: Cambridge University Press, 2008), 163–212; Greenberg, *British Trade and Opening of China*; and Fay, *Opium War*. A recent useful volume is Julia Lovell, *The Opium Wars: Drugs, Dreams and the Making of China* (London: Picador, 2011).
189. Greenberg, *British Trade and Opening of China*, p. 8.
190. Cited in Fay, *Opium War*, p. 46.
191. This is based on a quick and rough calculation: Crouzet suggests that Britain's exports in 1831 were 11 percent of its national product. See Crouzet, "Toward Export Economy," table 14, p. 79. Broadberry estimates that Britain's nominal GNI in 1831 was £382 million, giving us a rough estimate of exports in that year of £42 million. See Broadberry, et al, "Historical National Accounts for Britain." (The raw data is in the Excel attachment to the paper.)
192. Dean, "British Informal Empire" makes such a case but as far as I can make out does not take into account the opium exports to China from British India. If so, this crucial omission makes his argument untenable.
193. See D. A. Farnie, *The English Cotton Industry and the World Market, 1815–1896* (Oxford: Clarendon Press, 1979), table 5, p. 91.
194. Greenberg, *British Trade and the Opening of China*, p. 16.
195. See Wakeman, "Canton Trade," p. 173.
196. Fay, *Opium War*, p. 18.
197. Ibid., p. 55.
198. Ibid., p. 55.
199. Jonathan Spence, "Opium Smoking in Ch'ing China," in Fredric Wakeman and Carolyn Grant, eds., *Conflict and Control in Late Imperial China* (Berkeley: University of California Press, 1975), p. 148.
200. Fay, *Opium War*, p. 59.
201. Spence, "Opium Smoking in Ch'ing China," p. 151.
202. See Alejandra Irigoin, "A Trojan Horse in Daoguang China? Explaining the Flows of Silver in and out of China" (working paper 173/13; Department of Economic History, London School of Economics, 2013).
203. Wakeman, "Canton Trade," p. 172.
204. Spence, "Opium Smoking in Ch'ing China", p. 150.
205. Ibid., p. 150.
206. Cited in Fay, *Opium War*, p. 49.

207. Ibid, p. 89.
208. See Peter Lowe, *Britain and the Far East: A Survey from 1819 to the Present* (London: Longman, 1981), p. 11.
209. Cited in J. Y. Wong, "The Building of an Informal British Empire in China in the Middle of the Nineteenth Century," *Bulletin of the John Ryland University Library of Manchester* 59, no. 2 (Spring 1977): 477.
210. John K. Fairbank, "Creation of the Treaty System," in Fairbank, ed., *CHC*, V. 10, p. 216.
211. Greenberg, *British Trade and the Opening of China*, pp. 194–195.
212. Wakeman, "Canton Trade," p. 178.
213. Cited in Wong, "Building of an Informal British Empire," p. 474.
214. Greenberg, *British Trade and the Opening of China*, xi.
215. Fay, *Opium War*, p. 190.
216. Lowe, *Britain and the Far East*, p. 14.
217. Fay, *Opium War*, p. 193–94.
218. Frances V. Moulder, *Japan, China and the World Economy* (Cambridge and New York: Cambridge University Press, 1977), p. 106.
219. Fairbank, "Creation of the Treaty System," p. 213.
220. Greenberg, *British Trade and the Opening of China*, p. 215.
221. Fay, *Opium War*, p. 195.
222. Greenberg, *British Trade and the Opening of China*, p. 215.
223. Lowe, *Britain in the Far East*, p. 15.
224. Gull, *British Economic Interests in the Far East*, p. 50.
225. Cited in Dean, "British Informal Empire," p. 70.
226. Two important studies of the period are John King Fairbank, *Trade and Diplomacy on the China Coast: The Opening of Treaty Ports, 1842–1854* (Stanford, CA: Stanford University Press, 1969); and Fredric Wakeman Jr., *Strangers at the Gate: Social Disorder in South China, 1839–1861* (Berkeley: University of California Press: 1966).
227. These specific figures are from W. C. Costin, *Great Britain and China, 1833–1860* (Oxford: Clarendon Press, 1937), p. 118. The upward trend during this period is also clear in Figure 2.1.
228. Lowe, *Britain in the Far East*, p. 34.
229. Cited ibid., p. 35.
230. Cited ibid., p. 34.
231. In addition to Wakeman, *Strangers at the Gate*, see Philip A. Kuhn, *Rebellion and Its Enemies in Late Imperial China: Militarization and Social Structure, 1796–1864* (Cambridge, MA: Harvard University Press, 1970). A recent study is Stephen R. Platt, *Autumn in the Heavenly Kingdom: China, the West and the Epic Story of the Taiping Civil War* (New York: Alfred A. Knopf, 2012).

232. I am drawing on Philip A. Kuhn, "The Taiping Rebellion," in John Fairbank, ed., *CHC*, V. 10, pp. 264–317.
233. A pro-British accounting of the war is available; see Douglas Hurd, *The Arrow War: An Anglo-Chinese Confusion, 1856–1860* (London: Collins, 1967).
234. Jürgen Osterhammel, "Britain and China, 1842–1914," *OHBE*, vol. 3, p. 146.
235. Cited in Hyam, *Britain's Imperial Century*, p. 360.
236. Sir William Harcourt apparently argued in this context that "we have already as much empire as the nation can carry." Cited ibid., p. 362.
237. See Albert Feuerwerker, *The Chinese Economy, ca. 1870–1911*, Michigan Papers in Chinese Studies 5 (Ann Arbor: University of Michigan, Center for Chinese Studies, 1969), table 21, p. 66.
238. See Lowe, *Britain in the Far East*, p. 54.
239. Osterhammel, "Britain and China," p. 149.
240. Fairbank, "Creation of the Treaty System," in Fairbank, *CHC*, V. 10, p. 215.
241. Gull, *British Economic Interests in the Far East*, p. 52.
242. Farnie, *English Cotton Industry*, table 5, p. 91.
243. Ibid., table 5, p. 91.
244. Spence, "Opium Smoking in Ch'ing China," p. 151.
245. See his "The Creation of the Treaty System," in Fairbank, *CHC*, V. 10, p. 213.
246. Dean, "British Informal Empire," 73. It should be added that Dean uses the same figures to build a broader argument that Britain's economic gains from China were minimal. As noted, I do not find this broader argument persuasive because Dean ignores the crucial role of the opium trade in Anglo-Chinese relations. In addition, he ignores the fact that British indemnities on China made the Chinese bear the costs of British imperial expansionism. Thereafter, economic gains to the British were free of any real cost, icing on the imperial cake. Also, 10 percent of governmental revenues is nothing to scoff at; to put that share in perspective, 9 percent of federal revenues in the United States in 2010 originated from corporate income tax.
247. One good study that does so is Moulder, *Japan, China and the World Economy*.
248. One set of debates is brought together in Huang, *Development of Underdevelopment in China*. Most textbooks on China's development review related debates, focusing on cultural, imperial, economic, and/or state-society relations as factors that could be considered the most salient for understanding China's failure to take off in the nineteenth century, especially when compared to Japan. See, for example, Kenneth Lieberthal, *Governing China: From Revolution through Reform* (New York: W. W. Norton, 1995).
249. See, for example, Barrington Moore Jr., *Social Origins of Dictatorship and Democracy: Lord and the Peasant in the Making of the Modern World* (Boston: Beacon Press, 1966).

250. Cain and Hopkins suggest, in *British Imperialism* (pp. 365–66), that British trade in China went into serious disrepair toward the end of the century, and so British firms turned to finance and services to substitute for old trade. The trade data do not support this view. While there was indeed a decline in China's imports to Britain, British exports grew, as did the overall trade in the new century. The new financial interest in China was thus an addition to the older interest in trade.
251. Gull, *British Economic Interests in the Far East*, p. 52.
252. For this discussion I am drawing on Remer, *Foreign Investments in China*; and Chi-Ming Hou, *Foreign Investment and Economic Development in China* (Cambridge, MA: Harvard University Press, 1965).
253. Ibid., table 22, p. 100.
254. Remer, *Foreign Investments in China*, table 1, p. 347.
255. Cain and Hopkins, *British Imperialism*, p. 372. A detailed history of the HSBC is available in Frank H. H. King, *The History of the Hong Kong and Shanghai Banking Corporation*, vols. 1 and 2 (Cambridge: Cambridge University Press, 1987 and 1988).
256. Gull, *British Economic Interests in the Far East*, p. 70.
257. For details, see Immanuel C. Y. Hsu, "Late Ch'ing Foreign Relations, 1866–1905," in Fairbank and Liu, *CHC*, pp. 70–141; and Joseph Esherick, *The Origins of the Boxer Uprising* (Berkeley: University of California Press, 1987).
258. Cain and Hopkins, *British Imperialism*, pp. 360–80.
259. Lord Clarendon, a disciple of Palmerston and Britain's foreign secretary during the period, quoted in Hyam, *Britain's Imperial Century*, p. 361.
260. Jürgen Osterhammel, "British Business in China, 1860s–1950s," in P. T. Davenport-Hines and Geoffrey Jones, eds., *British Business in Asia since 1860* (Cambridge: Cambridge University Press, 1989), p. 195.
261. Gull, *British Economic Interests in the Far East*, p. 102.
262. One example of the former is Robert F. Dernberger, "The Role of the Foreigner in China's Economic Development," in Dwight H. Perkins, *China's Modern Economy in Historical Perspective* (Stanford, CA: Stanford University Press, 1983); and one of the latter is Moulder, *Japan, China and the World Economy*. A good discussion of related debates is Huang, *Development of Underdevelopment in China*.
263. Lippit, "Development of Underdevelopment in China," in Huang, *Development of Underdevelopment in China*, p. 26.
264. Feuerwerker, *Chinese Economy*, pp. 17–31.
265. See Hou, *Foreign Investment and Economic Development in China*.
266. Feuerwerker, *Chinese Economy*, provides an estimate of Chinese GDP in the 1880s of some 3.3 million Chinese taels. I converted the figure in taels to sterling at a rough exchange rate of three taels to one sterling pound.
267. Cited in Cain and Hopkins, *British Imperialism*, p. 399.

CHAPTER 3

1. See Atul Kohli, *State-Directed Development: Political Power and Industrialization in the Global Periphery* (New York: Cambridge University Press, 2004), chaps. 6 and 8.
2. As specialists will readily recognize, this argument comes from Ronald Robinson and John Gallagher, *Africa and the Victorians: The Official Mind of the Imperialism*, with Alice Denny (1961; repr., London: I.B. Tauris, 2015).
3. In making this argument I am following Eric Hobsbawm, *The Age of Empire, 1875–1914* (New York: Vintage Books, 1989), chap. 3.
4. Cited in Ronald Hyam, *Britain's Imperial Century, 1815–1914: A Study of Empire and Expansion* (London: B. T. Batsford, 1976), p. 72.
5. A recent account by a journalist cites a number as high as ten million. See Amresh Misra, *War of Civilizations: India, 1857 AD*, 2 vols. (Allahabad, India: Rupa, 2008). These high numbers, however, remain to be vetted by professional historians.
6. Hyam, *Britain's Imperial Century*, p. 224.
7. Robinson and Gallagher, *Africa and the Victorians*, p. 13.
8. See D. A. Farnie, *The English Cotton Industry and the World Market, 1815–1896* (Oxford: Clarendon Press, 1979), table 5, p. 91.
9. The statement was made by Sir George Gray with reference to the mutiny in India at the Cape on August 7, 1857, quoted in Hyam, *Britain's Imperial Century*, p. 71.
10. Thomas R. Metcalf, *The Aftermath of Revolt: India, 1857–1870* (Princeton, NJ: Princeton University Press, 1964), p. ix.
11. Studies of the subject include Philip Mason, *A Matter of Honor: An Account of the Indian Army, Its Officers and Men* (New York: Holt, Rinehart and Winston, 1974); and David E. Omissi, *The Sepoy and the Raj: The Indian Army, 1860–1940* (Basingstoke, UK: Macmillan, 1994). Also relevant are Stephen P. Cohen, *The Indian Army: Its Contribution to the Development of a Nation* (Berkeley: University of California Press, 1971); and Stephen P. Rosen, *Societies and Military Power: India and Its Armies* (Ithaca, NY: Cornell University Press, 1996).
12. See Hyam, *Britain's Imperial Century*, p. 207.
13. Two good studies of the ICS are David C. Potter, *India's Political Administrators: From ICS to IAS* (Delhi: Oxford University Press, 1996); and B. B. Misra, *The Bureaucracy in India: A Historical Analysis of Development up to 1947* (Delhi: Oxford University Press, 1977).
14. See, for example, Dharma Kumar, "The Fiscal System," in Dharma Kumar, ed., *The Cambridge Economic History of India, V. II* (Cambridge: Cambridge University Press, 1983), pp. 928–29. [hereafter cited as *CEHI*, vol. 2]
15. Ibid., table 12.8, p. 931. Also see Table 3.4 in this chapter.
16. This is bit of an exaggeration. Late in the century, for example, Lord Curzon, Viceroy of India (1898–1905), had some deliberate plans to improve and modernize the Indian economy, though he made little headway with them. They were shelved by subsequent viceroys in the name of laissez faire.

17. See K. N. Chaudhuri, "Foreign Trade and Balance of Payments," in Kumar, *CEHI*, vol. 2. tables 10.7A and 10.7C, pp. 833 and 837. By some other estimates, the trade jumped seven, not ten, times. See Hyam, *Britain's Imperial Century*, p. 206.
18. Hyam, *Britain's Imperial Century*, p. 207.
19. See Chaudhuri, "Foreign Trade and Balance of Payments", table 21.A, p. 864.
20. Ibid., table 10.7A, p. 833.
21. See Robin J. Moore, "Imperial India, 1858–1914," in Andrew Porter, ed., *The Nineteenth Century*, vol. 3 of *The Oxford History of the British Empire* (Oxford: Oxford University Press, 2001), p. 441.
22. See Chaudhuri, "Foreign Trade and Balance of Payments," table 10.18, p. 858.
23. See P. J. Cain and Anthony Hopkins, *British Imperialism, 1688–2000*, 2nd ed. (New York: Longman, 2002), p. 289.
24. I am drawing here on Chaudhuri, "Foreign Trade and Balance of Payments," pp. 865–69. Also see Peter Harnetty, "The Imperialism of Free Trade: Lancashire and the Indian Cotton During 1859–1862," *Economic History Review*, 2nd ser., 18, 2 (1965): 333–49.
25. See Hyam, *Britain's Imperial Century*, p. 231.
26. Moore, "Imperial India," p. 442.
27. Details of British capital movements within the empire are available in Lance E. Davis and Robert A. Huttenback, *Mammon and the Pursuit of Empire: The Economics of British Empire* (Cambridge: Cambridge University Press, 1988).
28. See Tara Sethia, "Railways, Raj and the Indian States," in Clarence B. Davis, Kenneth E. Wilburn Jr., and Ronald E. Robinson, eds., *Railway Imperialism* (New York: Greenwood Press, 1991): 103–20.
29. Ibid., p. 106.
30. See, for example, Marcelo de Paiva Abreu, "British Business in Brazil: Maturity and Demise (1850–1950)," *Revista Brazileira de Economia* 52, no. 4 (Oct. /Dec. 2000): 394.
31. See, for example, Dadabhai Naoroji, *Poverty and Un-British Rule in India* (London: Swan Sonnenschein and Company, 1901); and Romesh Chunder Dutt, *Economic History of India in the Victorian Age* (London: K. Paul, Trench and Trubner, 1906).
32. The troop figures are from Moore, "Imperial India," p. 422; the cost figure is from Judith Brown, "India," in Judith Brown and Wm. Roger Louis, eds., *The Twentieth Century*, vol. 4 of *The Oxford History of the British Empire* (Oxford: Oxford University Press, 1999), p. 429.
33. Brown, "India," in Brown and Louis, *Twentieth Century*, p. 430.
34. Ibid., p. 425.
35. See Sumit Sarkar, *Modern India, 1885–1947* (London: Macmillan, 1989), p. 4.
36. Two good studies that are consistent with my own understanding are Sarkar, *Modern India*; and Bipin Chandra, et al., *India's Struggle for Independence, 1857–1947* (New Delhi: Penguin, 1998).

37. I developed this argument in a little more detail in Kohli, *State-Directed Development*, pp. 240–47.
38. See Anil Seal, "Imperialism and Nationalism in India," in John Gallagher et al., eds., *Locality, Province and Nation: Essays on Indian Politics, 1870–1940* (Cambridge: Cambridge University Press, 1973).
39. Cited in Chandra, *India's Struggle for Independence*, p. 166.
40. See Barrington Moore Jr., *Social Origins of Dictatorship and Democracy* (Boston: Beacon Press, 1966).
41. See Kohli, *State-Directed Development*, chaps. 6 and 7.
42. The term was popularized by Gunnar Myrdal, *Asian Drama: An Inquiry into the Poverty of Nations* (New York: Pantheon, 1968).
43. See Cain and Hopkins, *British Imperialism*, p. 544.
44. Chaudhuri, "Foreign Trade and Balance of Payments," p. 838.
45. See D. K. Fieldhouse, "Metropolitan Economics of Empire," in Brown and Louis, eds., *Twentieth Century*, table 4.4, p. 102, and table 4.2, p. 100. There is no discrepancy between these figures and the seemingly higher figure for capital inflows prior to WW I cited above in chapter 3; the earlier figures were capital flow for the period while these figures are for accumulated capital or capital stock.
46. Ibid., p. 102.
47. The quote is from ibid., p. 102.
48. A useful discussion on related issues is available in Cain and Hopkins, *British Imperialism*, chap. 23.
49. Tomlinson, *Economy of Modern India*, p. 6.
50. Ibid., p. 25.
51. For one good discussion of such issues see Myrdal, *Asian Drama*, chap. 22.
52. See Daniel Thorner, *Agrarian Prospects for India: Five Lectures on Land Reforms Delivered in 1955 at the Delhi School of Economics* (Delhi: Delhi University Press, 1956).
53. It ought to be a matter of considerable shame for Indian nationalists that they, too, failed to reverse these trends in the post-independence period. For a good study of related issues that is especially focused on regional variations in attainments in education and health in post-independence India, see Prerna Singh, *How Solidarity Works for Welfare: Subnationalism and Social Development in India* (New York: Cambridge University Press, 2015).
54. This discussion on limited industrialization in colonial India draws on my own earlier work. See Kohli, *State-Directed Development*, esp. pp. 247–55. A useful study is Rajat K. Ray, *Industrialization in India: Growth and Conflict in the Private Corporate Sector, 1914–47* (Delhi: Oxford University Press, 1979).
55. This is an important theme in Amiya Bagchi, *Private Investment in India, 1900–1939* (Cambridge: Cambridge University Press, 1972). For an alternative account that stresses low rates of return in jute processing as an explanation, see Morris D.

Morris, "The Growth of Large-Scale Industry to 1947," in Kumar, *CEHI*, vol. 2, pp. 553–76.

56. See B. R. Tomlinson, *The Political Economy of the Raj, 1914–1947: The Economics of Decolonization in India* (London: Macmillan, 1979), p. 34.
57. A good study is A. G. Hopkins, *An Economic History of West Africa* (London: Longman, 1973).
58. See Hyam, *Britain's Imperial Century*, p. 265.
59. Lord Palmerston, quoted in Cain and Hopkins, *British Imperialism*, p. 306.
60. See H. L. Wesseling, *Divide and Rule: The Partition of Africa, 1880–1914* (Westport, CT.: Praeger, 1996), p. 187.
61. Ibid., pp. 186–94.
62. See, for example, John E. Flint, *Sir George Goldie and the Making of Nigeria* (London: Oxford University Press, 1960).
63. Wesseling, *Divide and Rule*, p. 190.
64. I am drawing here on my own earlier and more detailed discussion in Kohli, *State-Directed Development*, pp. 293–301. A good overview of Nigerian history is Michael Crowder, *The Story of Nigeria*, 4th ed. (London: Faber and Faber, 1978), esp. chaps. 2–11.
65. The story of Jaja goes that he was a shrewd businessman who understood Western ways. He lived in a Western-style palace and sent his sons for schooling in Glasgow. When British traders found his demands meddlesome, the British consul invited him aboard his ship for discussions, and with British gunships pointing at his island, essentially kidnapped him and sent him away, first to the Gold Coast and then to the West Indies. See Wesseling, *Divide and Rule*, pp. 193–94.
66. Useful studies are Robert S. Smith, *Kingdom of the Yoruba*, 2nd ed. (London: Methuen, 1976); and Peter C. Lloyd, *The Political Development of Yoruba Kingdoms in the Eighteenth and Nineteenth Centuries* (Occasional paper no. 31, London: Royal Anthropological Institute, 1971).
67. This does not mean that the colonization of these areas was either smooth or rapid. For details see I. F. Nicolson, *The Administration of Nigeria, 1900–1960*, (Oxford: Clarendon Press, 1969), p. 85.
68. A brilliant and pioneering study along these lines was Onwuka K. Dike, *Trade and Politics in the Niger Delta, 1830–1885: An Introduction to the Economic and Political History of Nigeria* (London: Oxford University Press, 1956). The logic of Dike's argument was subsequently generalized in Hopkins, *Economic History of West Africa*.
69. For a more balance-of-power type of argument, with a focus on the role of the dominant kingdom, Oyo, see J. F. A. Ajayi, "The Aftermath of the Fall of Old Oyo," in J. F. A. Ajayi and Michael Crowder, eds., *History of West Africa* (New York: Columbia University Press, 1973). The historiography of the commercial transition is reviewed in Robin Law, introduction to Robin Law, ed., *From*

Slave Trade to "Legitimate" Commerce: The Commercial Transition in Nineteenth-Century West Africa (Cambridge: Cambridge University Press, 1995).

70. The quotes, respectively, are from Crowder, *Story of Nigeria*, p. 68; James S. Coleman, *Nigeria: Background to Nationalism* (Berkeley: University of California Press, 1958), pp. 40–41; and R. Olufemi Ekundare, *An Economic History of Nigeria, 1880–1960* (New York: Homes and Meir, 1973), p. 35.
71. Ekundare, *An Economic History of Nigeria*, pp. 40–41.
72. See Gerald K. Helleiner, *Peasant Agriculture, Government, and Economic Growth in Nigeria* (Homewood, IL: Richard D. Irwin, 1966), p. 2.
73. Good studies include R. A. Adeleye and C. C. Stewart, "The Sokoto Caliphate in the Nineteenth Century," in J. F. A. Ajayi and Michael Crowder, eds., *History of West Africa*, 2nd ed. (London: Longman, 1987), vol. 2: pp. 86–131; and Murray Last, "The Sokoto Caliphate and Borno," in J. F. A. Ajayi, ed., *UNESCO General History of Africa*, vol. 1: *Africa in the Nineteenth Century until the 1880s* (Berkeley: University of California Press, 1989), pp. 555–99.
74. A telling anecdote is that when Goldie prepared to send an expedition up the Niger to explore the northern interior, the chief rabbi of London sent a letter along with him in case the explorers encountered any Jews.
75. One scholar thus describes Sokoto as the "most complexly organized" in West Africa. See Michael Watts, *Silent Violence: Food, Famine and Peasantry in Northern Nigeria* (Berkeley: University of California Press, 1983), p. 49.
76. Kohli, *State-Directed Development*, p. 297.
77. See Paul E. Lovejoy, "Plantations in the Economy of the Sokoto Caliphate," *Journal of African History* 19, no. 3 (1978): 341–68. For a fine-grained analysis of one specific emirate, see Polly Hill, *Population, Prosperity and Poverty: Rural Kano, 1900 and 1970* (Cambridge: Cambridge University Press, 1970).
78. Wesseling thus concludes that it is "rather sad to recall" that the European colonization of Africa—so important for Africa—was "of such small importance to Europe itself." See his *Divide and Rule*, p. 373.
79. The reference is to his well-known book, Hobsbawm, *Age of Empire, 1875–1914*.
80. Hobson and Lenin are often referred to together because Lenin popularized key elements of Hobson's arguments. Hobson's book still makes for a fine reading, because of the clarity of his prose and the forcefulness of his argument. See J. A. Hobson, *Imperialism: A Study* (New York: James Pott and Company, 1902); and V. I. Lenin, *Imperialism: The Highest Stage of Capitalism* (Sydney, Australia: Resistance Books, 1999). Originally published as a pamphlet in Russian in 1916.
81. Cain and Hopkins have gone the furthest in recent scholarship to argue for the importance of the finance and service sectors in Britain's overseas expansion. Even they suggest that the "City was not prepared to pour money into Tropical Africa." See Cain and Hopkins, *British Imperialism*, p. 566.

82. This argument was, of course, forcefully put forward by Robinson and Gallagher, *Africa and the Victorians.* A more general argument about political factors, especially balance-of-power politics, being the driving force behind imperialism is Benjamin J. Cohen, *The Question of Imperialism: The Political Economy of Dominance and Dependence* (New York: Basic Books, 1973).
83. See Hopkins, *Economic History of West Africa.*
84. See Cain and Hopkins, *British Imperialism*, p. 304.
85. Max Weber, quoted in Hobsbawm, *Age of Empire*, p. 56.
86. Ibid., p. 62. In this paragraph I am drawing on Hobsbawm, pp. 62–64.
87. The omission of France here is deliberate. Following the defeat in Franco-Prussian War, the French economy remained sluggish at the end of the century. The French colonial impulse during this period was moved less by the search for markets and more by a desire to export its internal class conflict, as was evident in the Paris Commune of 1871. See, for example, Wesseling, *Divide and Rule*, pp. 11–18.
88. Cited in Hobsbawm, *Age of Empire*, p. 67.
89. Cited in Hyam, *Britain's Imperial Century*, p. 273.
90. Ibid., pp. 278–79.
91. Ibid., p. 281.
92. For two very different interpretations of Lugard's role in Nigeria, see Margery Perham, *Lugard: The Years of Authority, 1898–1945* (London: Oxford University Press, 1960); and Nicolson, *Administration of Nigeria*, chap. 6. I also spent time reading the "Lugard papers" at the Bodleian Library, Oxford University, in the summer of 2017. While specific information drawn from these sources is cited here, two general observations maybe pertinent for other researchers. First, one gets a sense of the need Lugard feels to impress his superiors in London as to how well he is performing in the wilderness. This, in turn, suggests that the men on the spot were not as free to do what they wanted, as some accounts have suggested. Second, Lugard is deeply pleased when he reports back to London about the peaceful turnout of all the emirs, in their colorful traditional regalia, to pay homage to the representative of the British Crown in Kano, who was, of course, Lugard himself. This correspondence underscores what we already know—namely, the pomposity, superiority, and paternalism with which the British colonial authorities treated the "natives." From here on I will cite material drawn from these papers as "Lugard papers." At the Bodleian Library, they are available under Papers of Frederick D. Lugard, Papers Relating to Nigeria (1892–1944), Commonwealth and African Studies, especially boxes 56–59.
93. Over time, given the need for taxation, security, and helping traders and missionaries, the mission of the colonial state in Nigeria, as well as in other parts of tropical Africa, expanded. See, for example, D. K. Fieldhouse, *Colonialism, 1870–1945: An Introduction* (London: Weidenfeld and Nicolson, 1981), pp. 16–20. I will return to this issue.

94. On related debates within Britain, see Andrew Roberts, "The Imperial Mind," in A. D. Roberts, ed., *The Cambridge History of Africa*, vol. 7: *From 1905 to 1940* (Cambridge: Cambridge University Press, 1986), pp. 24–76.
95. In a key speech in 1914, Lugard—then recently appointed the governor-general of Nigeria—declared that the amalgamation of Nigeria will maintain laws and other regional systems distinct under one governor-general. See "Speech by the governor-general (Sir F. Lugard)," January 1, 1914, Lugard papers, file 2, box 58. Subsequently, Lugard wrote about his experiences in glowing terms, of course. See Frederick Lugard, *The Dual Mandate in British Tropical Africa* (London: W. Blackwood and Sons, 1922). For the importance of the Indian experience in molding the preference for indirect rule in Africa, see Mahmood Mamdani, *Citizen and Subject: Contemporary Africa and the Legacy of Late Colonialism* (Princeton, NJ: Princeton University Press, 1996).
96. For details, see Jeremy White, *Central Administration in Nigeria, 1914–1948* (Dublin: Irish Academic Press, 1981).
97. For a discussion of how the Lagos consulate was administered, see Nicolson, *Administration of Nigeria*, pp. 51–79.
98. See D. C. Dorward, "British West Africa and Liberia," in Roberts, *Cambridge History of Africa*, vol. 7, esp. p. 403.
99. See White, *Central Administration in Nigeria*, p. 41.
100. See, for example, James S. Coleman, *Nigeria: Background to Nationalism* (Berkeley: University of California Press, 1958), chap. 12.
101. See Nicolson, *Administration of Nigeria*, pp. 228–30. I am also drawing here on my own earlier work in *State-Directed Development*, p. 306.
102. Kohli, *State-Directed Development*, p. 49.
103. See Philip Terdoo Ahire, *Imperial Policing: The Emergence and Role of Police in Colonial Nigeria, 1860–1960* (Philadelphia: Open University Press, Milton Keynes, 1991), chaps. 1 and 2. The factual information on the police that follows is drawn from this source.
104. See Helleiner, *Peasant Agriculture*, pp. 296–97. This low rate is more apparent than real, however, because it does not take into account the "taxes" that indigenous authorities collected and were allowed to keep as the "cost" of providing indirect rule. Figures for such taxation are not readily available.
105. See Watts, *Silent Violence*, pp. 160–66.
106. See Ekundare, *Economic History of Nigeria*, p. 116; and A. W. Pim, "Public Finance," in Margery Perham, ed., *Mining, Commerce and Finance in Nigeria* (London: Faber and Faber, 1948), pp. 225–79.
107. See Fieldhouse, *Colonialism*, 27–28.
108. See J. F. A. Ajayi and Michael Crowder, "West Africa, 1919–1939: The Colonial Situation," in Ajayi and Crowder, *History of West Africa*, 2nd ed. (Harlow, England: Longman, 1987), vol. 2, pp. 593–4.

109. See Helleiner, *Peasant Agriculture*, pp. 232–34.
110. Ibid., chap. 1.
111. The figures are from a report from J. E. W. Hood to Sir Lugard, in the Lugard Papers, file 7, box 59. The dependence of revenues on growth of trade is evident in the same set of figures, where it is reported that revenues during the same period jumped from £0.6 million in 1901 to £7.7 million in 1927.
112. For a discussion along these lines, see Sara Berry, "Cocoa and Economic Development in Western Nigeria," in Carl K. Liedholm and Carl Eicher, eds., *Growth and Development in Nigerian Economy* (East Lansing: Michigan State University Press, 1970), pp. 16–27.
113. See, for example, Lugard Papers, file 3, box 59.
114. See Helleiner, *Peasant Agriculture*, pp. 6–7.
115. See Ekundare, *Economic History of Nigeria*, pp. 156 and 200.
116. Ibid., 157.
117. See Helleiner, *Peasant Agriculture*, p. 16.
118. See Carl Liedholm, "The Influence of Colonial Policy on the Growth and Development of Nigeria's Industrial Sector," in Liedholm and Eicher, *Growth and Development*, p. 57.
119. Ibid., p. 57. Also see D. C. Dorward, "British West Africa and Liberia," in Roberts, *Cambridge History of Africa*, vol. 7, p. 410.
120. See Ajayi and Crowder, "West Africa, 1919–1939," pp. 594–97.
121. See Coleman, *Nigeria*, p. 83.
122. By the early 1940s literacy in the Roman script was about 18 percent in the west, 16 percent in the east, and 2 percent in the north. See White, *Central Administration in Nigeria*, p. 118.
123. See his *Nigeria*, 202. Also see J. B. Webster, "African Political Activity in British West Africa, 1900–1940," in Ajayi and Crowder, *History of West Africa*, v. 2, chap. 17.
124. A good essay that provides an overview of British thinking during the post-WW II period of decolonization is Wm. Roger Louis, "The Dissolution of the British Empire," in Brown and Louis, eds., *The Twentieth Century*, pp. 329–56.
125. Cited ibid., p. 329.
126. Ibid., where this point is brilliantly made, p. 329.
127. See his *Nigeria*, p. 50.
128. Cited in Crowder, *Story of Nigeria*, p. 236.
129. See Coleman, *Nigeria*. Also of use is Richard Sklar, *Nigerian Political Parties: Power in an Emergent African Nation* (Princeton, NJ: Princeton University Press, 1963).
130. My interpretation of these post-independence developments, which are not discussed in this study, are in Kohli, *State-Directed Development*, chap. 9. A fine study of the forces that contributed to the demise of Nigeria's first republic is Larry Diamond, *Class, Ethnicity and Democracy in Nigeria: The Failure of the First Republic* (Syracuse, NY: Syracuse University Press, 1988).

131. See Nicolson, *Administration of Nigeria*, pp. 256–300.
132. A caveat should be added: Nigerian data are not always reliable. Here I am drawing on Helleiner, *Peasant Agriculture*; Ekundare, *Economic History*; and Sayre P. Schatz, *Nigerian Capitalism* (Berkeley: University of California Press, 1977).
133. See Ekundare, *Economic History*, p. 295.
134. In the words of Ekundare, "Most Nigerians lacked any knowledge of managerial and technical skills required for industrial development." Ibid., p. 295.
135. See Michael Crowder, "The 1939–45 War and West Africa," in Ajayi and Crowder, *History of West Africa*, vol. 2, p. 679.
136. For such an argument applied to sub-Saharan Africa as a whole, see Robert Bates, *Markets and States in Tropical Africa* (Berkeley: University of California Press, 1981).
137. See Helleiner, *Peasant Agriculture*, p. 307.
138. As an example, see Niall Ferguson, *Empire: The Rise and Demise of the British World Order and the Lessons for Global Power* (New York: Basic Books, 2003).
139. The reference is to Immanuel Wallerstein, *The Modern World System*, vols. 1–3 (New York: Academic Press, 1974, 1980, 1989) The fourth volume was published by the University of California Press in 2011.
140. This point is forcefully made by Cain and Hopkins, *British Imperialism*, chap. 24.
141. Wesseling, *Divide and Rule*, p. 370.
142. See, for example, A. K. Sen, *Poverty and Famines: An Essay on Entitlement and Deprivation* (Oxford: Clarendon Press, 1981). Also see Madhushree Mukherjee, *Churchill's Secret War: The British Empire and the Ravaging of India during World War II* (New York: Basic Books, 2010).
143. This is certainly the suggestion in Joseph A. Schumpeter, *Imperialism and Social Classes*, translated by Heinz Norden, edited by Paul M. Sweezy (New York: A. M. Kelly, 1951). Original German edition was published in 1919.
144. This argument comes across more strongly in Robinson and Gallagher, *Africa and the Victorians*, though it was already evident—and to my mind, better stated—in their earlier seminal article, John Gallagher and Ronald Robinson, "The Imperialism of Free Trade," *Economic History Review*, 2nd ser., 6, no. 1 (1953): 1–15.

CHAPTER 4

1. Some of the earlier literature is reviewed in Ernst May, *American Imperialism: A Speculative Essay* (New York: Athenaeum, 1968), 3–17. A good effort to combine economic arguments with ideological and *realpolitik* considerations is John M. Dobson, *America's Ascent: The United States Becomes a Great Power, 1880–1914* (DeKalb: Northern Illinois University Press, 1978), pp. 1–24. For a more recent study that builds on the foundational economic views of Charles Beard and William Appleman Williams, see Andrew J. Bacevich, *American Empire: The Realities and Consequences of U.S. Diplomacy* (Cambridge, MA: Harvard

University Press, 2002). The best book on the subject remains Walter LaFeber, *The American Search for Opportunity, 1865–1913*, vol. 2 of *The Cambridge History of American Foreign Relations* (Cambridge: Cambridge University Press, 1993).

2. Examples of regionally specific but high-quality scholarship include Thomas J. McCormick, *China Market: America's Quest for Informal Empire, 1893–1901* (Chicago: Quadrangle Books, 1967); H. W. Brands, *Bound to Empire: The United States and the Philippines* (New York: Oxford University Press, 1992); David Healy, *Drive to Hegemony: The United States in the Caribbean, 1898–1917* (Madison: University of Wisconsin Press, 1988); and Walter LaFeber, *Inevitable Revolutions: The United States in Central America* (New York: W. W. Norton, 1983).
3. The relevant literature is very large indeed, offering a variety of interpretations. While I consulted this literature widely, some of which is cited below, I found the writings of Walter LaFeber especially persuasive. In addition to LaFeber, *American Search for Opportunity*; and LaFeber, *Inevitable Revolutions*, see Walter LaFeber, *The New Empire: An Interpretation of American Imperialism, 1860–1898* (Ithaca, NY: Cornell University Press, 1963); and Walter LaFeber, Richard Polenberg, and Nancy Woloch, *The American Century: A History of the United States since the 1890s*, 7th ed. (Armonk, NY: M. E. Sharpe, 2013). I gratefully acknowledge the influence of LaFeber's insights on my understanding of this period.
4. See, for example, Lance E. Davis et al., *American Economic Growth: An Economist's History of the United States* (New York: Harper and Row, 1972), chap. 2.
5. The protectionist history of the United States is often forgotten now amid the din of free trade. It is worth recalling that US protectionism was quite deliberate in the nineteenth century and was a major source of political controversy across the industrializing North and the agrarian South. As early as 1791, Alexander Hamilton, in his *Report on Manufacturers, 1791*, proposed to the US Congress—and the Congress accepted—high tariffs to protect and encourage the nascent American industry in terms that would be quite understandable to any developing-country nationalist of the twentieth century: "The United States cannot exchange with Europe on equal terms; and the want of reciprocity would render them the victim of a system which would induce them to confine their views to Agriculture, and refrain from Manufactures." And then again, in the mid-nineteenth century, President Ulysses S. Grant argued: "For centuries England has relied on protection . . . there is no doubt that it is to this system that it owes its present strength. After two centuries England has found it convenient to adopt free trade because it thinks that protection can no longer offer it anything. Very well then, Gentlemen, my knowledge of our country leads me to believe that within 200 years, when America has gotten out of protection all that it can offer, it too will adopt free trade." Quoted in Ha-Joon Chang, *Kicking Away the Ladder: Development Strategy in Historical Perspective* (London: Anthem Press, 2002), p. 63.
6. See LaFeber et al., *American Century*, p. 4.

7. See LaFeber, *New Empire*, pp. 6–7.
8. The concept of a "promotional state" is developed in Emily Rosenberg, *Spreading the American Dream: American Economic and Cultural Expansion* (New York: Hill and Wang, 1981).
9. The comparative growth figures and the size of national product are taken from Angus Maddison, *Contours of the World Economy, 1–2030 AD* (Oxford: Oxford University Press, 2007), tables A.2 (p. 377), A.4 (p. 379), and A.5 (p. 380).
10. See Davis et al., *American Economic Growth*, table 14.1 (p. 554). For the British data, as well as for an elaboration of the concept of an "export economy," see François Crouzet, "Toward an Export Economy: British Exports during the Industrial Revolution," *Exploration in Economic History* 17, no. 1 (January 1980): 81.
11. LaFeber et al., *American Century*, p. 19.
12. Much of the information in this paragraph is drawn from LaFeber, *American Search for Opportunity*, chap. 2.
13. See Brands, *Bound to Empire*, p. 3.
14. See Thomas Piketty, *Capital in the Twenty-First Century* (Cambridge, MA: Belknap Press of Harvard University Press, 2014), fig. 4.6.
15. McCormick, *China Market*, pp. 24–25.
16. The reference is to the well-known thesis of Fredrick Jackson Turner, first presented in 1893 and subsequently published as chapter 1 of his book *The Frontier in American History* (New York: Henry Holt and Company, 1921).
17. See Stephen Skowronek, *Building a New American State: The Expansion of National Administrative Capacities, 1877–1920* (New York: Cambridge University Press, 1982).
18. Earlier instances of imperial forays might include Liberia in the 1830s; Commodore Perry in Japan in the 1850s; the reassertion of the Monroe Doctrine in Santo Domingo in the 1870s; and the emergence of banana companies (led by Minor Keith) as significant powers in Costa Rica, Honduras, and Guatemala from 1880s onward.
19. Cited in LaFeber, *New Empire*, pp. 26, 30.
20. Cited in LaFeber, *American Search for Opportunity*, pp. 8, 10.
21. See Dobson, *America's Ascent*, pp. 6–7.
22. Ibid, p. 29.
23. Cited in A. T. Volwiler, "Harrison, Blaine and American Foreign Policy, 1889–1893," in William Appleman Williams, ed., *The Shaping of American Diplomacy: 1750–1914*, vol. 1, 2nd ed. (Chicago: Rand McNally, 1970), p. 298.
24. Mahan's writings and influence have been discussed by a number of scholars. Here I am drawing on Kenneth Wimmel, *Theodore Roosevelt and the Great White Fleet: American Sea Power Comes of Age* (Washington, DC: Brassey's, 1998), esp. chap. 3.
25. Direct quotes are from ibid. p. 61.
26. Cited in McCormick, *China Market*, p. 21.
27. Wimmel, *Theodore Roosevelt*, pp. 89–92.

28. See Brands, *Bound to Empire*, pp. 3–8.
29. Ibid., p. 8.
30. Cited in LaFeber, *New Empire*, p. 183.
31. As late as 1889 the US state department "remained a bastion of the spoils system" and foreign policy was often directed by a handful of individuals. Moreover, what there was of formal US foreign policy was "not of earthshaking importance." See Dobson, *America's Ascent*, p. 28.
32. Ibid., p. 181.
33. Cited in Brands, *Bound to Empire*, p. 9.
34. See Dobson, *America's Ascent*, p. 6.
35. Cited in LaFeber, *New Empire*, p. 193.
36. See McCormick, *China Market*; and Brands, *Bound to Empire*.
37. Brands, *Bound to Empire*, p. 9.
38. Ibid., p. 10.
39. Cited in Dobson, *America's Ascent*, p. 80.
40. Ibid., p. 85.
41. A couple of years later, the American minister to China, Charles Denby, wrote back that a "partition" of China "would destroy our markets." This would be a major setback because "the Pacific Ocean is destined to bear on its bosom a larger commerce than the Atlantic." Quoted in Thomas Schoonover, *Uncle Sam's War of 1898 and the Origins of Globalization* (Lexington: University Press of Kentucky, 2003), p. 69.
42. A detailed history of that war that remains relevant is David F. Trask, *The War with Spain in 1898* (New York: Macmillan, 1981).
43. A fine study of the regional base of disagreements in American foreign policy is Peter Trubowitz, *Defining the National Interest: Conflict and Change in American Foreign Policy* (Chicago: University of Chicago Press, 1998), esp. chap. 2, which discusses "the great debates of the 1890s."
44. Cited in LaFeber, *American Search for Opportunity*, p. 133.
45. Williams, *Shaping of American Diplomacy*, p. 336.
46. Ibid., p. 337.
47. Brands, *Bound to Empire*, p. 16.
48. Ibid., p. 15.
49. This view is associated with Ernest R. May. See Dobson, *America's Ascent*, p. 88.
50. See Wimmel, *Theodore Roosevelt*, pp. 96–97.
51. Dobson, *America's Ascent*, p. 87.
52. I use the term *Caribbean* loosely to include the island nations in the Caribbean and the Central American nations that border the Caribbean Sea.
53. See David Healy, *Drive to Hegemony: The United States in the Caribbean, 1898–1917* (Madison: University of Wisconsin Press, 1988), p. 15. Healy's estimate of US investments in Cuba at this time is $30 million, but many others suggest a figure closer to $50 million. For example, see LaFeber, *American Search for Opportunity*, p. 149.

54. Basic information about Cuban history is readily available. See, for example, Louis A. Pérez, *Cuba: Between Reform and Revolution*, 5th ed. (New York: Oxford University Press, 2015); Clifford L. Staten, *The History of Cuba*, 2nd ed. (Santa Barbara, CA: Greenwood, 2015).
55. Cited in Healy, *Drive to Hegemony*, p. 36.
56. Cited in Philip S. Foner, *The Spanish-Cuban-American War and the Birth of American Imperialism, 1895–1902*, vol. 1 (New York: Monthly Review Press, 1972), p. 209.
57. William McKinley, "Message to the Congress Requesting a Declaration of War with Spain," April 11, 1898, American Presidency Project (website), https://www.presidency.ucsb.edu/documents/message-congress-requesting-declaration-war-with-spain .
58. See Louis A. Perez, *Cuba between Empires, 1878–1902* (Pittsburgh, PA: University of Pittsburgh Press, 1983).
59. The US companies that signed this memorandum are listed in Foner, *Spanish-Cuban-American War*, p. 231. It should be added that US business was not united in its demand for a war with Spain, although most businesses ended up supporting the war effort, especially following a short and speedy victory.
60. See Stephen Kinzer, *Overthrow: America's Century of Regime Change from Hawaii to Iraq* (New York: Times Books), p. 36.
61. Ibid., p. 39.
62. Cited in LaFeber, *American Search for Opportunity*, p. 155.
63. Ibid., p. 154.
64. Cited in Dobson, *America's Ascent*, p. 142.
65. For details see ibid., pp. 144–46.
66. See, for example, "Platt Amendment, 1903," Documents related to American Foreign Policy, 1898–1914. https://www.mtholyoke.edu/acad/intrel/platt.htm.
67. Cited in LaFeber, *American Search for Opportunity*, p. 152.
68. It may be worth pointing out that Great Britain, the most sophisticated imperial nation of the world at that time, did not share America's self-perception that it was "exceptional." For example, once the United States had acquired Cuba, Lord Salisbury, the British colonial secretary at that time, suggested that the US situation in Cuba was quite similar to that of Britain in Egypt during that period. In both cases, Salisbury predicted—quite accurately—that the United States and Britain would prevail against local nationalists and would continue to rule well into the future. See Foner, *Spanish-Cuban-American War*, vol. 2, p. 395.
69. See Richard Gott, *Cuba: A New History* (New Haven, CT: Yale University Press, 2004), p. 129.
70. See, for example, Jules R. Benjamin, *The United States and Cuba: Hegemony and Dependent Development, 1880–1934* (Pittsburgh, PA: University of Pittsburgh Press, 1978); and a more recent essay, Rémy Herrera, "When the Names of

Emperors Were Morgan and Rockefeller . . . : Prerevolutionary Cuba's Dependency with Regard to U.S. High Finance," *International Journal of Political Economy* 34, no. 4 (Winter 2004/5): 24–48.

71. Ibid., fig. 2, p. 35.
72. See Healy, *Drive to Hegemony*, p. 204.
73. Ibid., p. 205.
74. Herrera, "When the Names of Emperors Were Morgan and Rockefeller," p. 42.
75. A good discussion can be found in Louis Pérez, *Cuba under the Platt Amendment, 1902–1934* (Pittsburgh, PA: University of Pittsburgh Press, 1986).
76. Jules R. Benjamin, *The United States and the Origins of the Cuban Revolution* (Princeton, NJ: Princeton University Press, 1990).
77. Herrera, "When the Names of Emperors Were Morgan and Rockefeller," p. 32.
78. See Diaz et al., *Study on Cuba*, chap. 21, for further evidence.
79. See Maddison, *Contours of the World Economy,* table 4a, p. 124.
80. More specifically, measured in 1990 international Geary-Khamis dollars, Cuba's per capita income in 1929 was 1639, whereas that of Nicaragua was 1750 and of Guatemala 1720. Ibid., table 4b, pp. 145–46.
81. Herrera, "When the Names of Emperors were Morgan and Rockefeller," p. 40.
82. See Maddison, *Contours of the World Economy,* table 4b, p. 135.
83. This argument was originally proposed by Celso Furtado, *Economic Growth of Brazil* (Berkeley: University of California Press, 1961), chap. 31. For my review of debates surrounding this important argument, see Atul Kohli, *State-Directed Development: Political Power and Industrialization in the Global Periphery* (New York: Cambridge University Press, 2004), pp. 161–65.
84. A detailed study is Jorge I. Dominguez, *Cuba: Order and Revolution* (Cambridge, MA: Belknap Press of Harvard University Press, 1978).
85. See Benjamin, *United States and the Origins of the Cuban Revolution*, p. 69.
86. Estimates of direct US foreign investment in 1914 are put at $2.7 billion; and in 1930, at $8 billion. See US Bureau of the Census, *Historical Statistics of the United States, Colonial Times to 1970*, Bicentennial ed., Part 2 (Washington, DC: Bureau of the Census, 1975).
87. Jean Daniel's interview with President John F. Kennedy, cited in Jean Daniel, "Unofficial Envoy: An Historic Report from Two Capitals," *New Republic*, Dec. 14, 1963, pp. 15–20.
88. Theodore Roosevelt to Bishop Joseph Bucklin, February 23, 1904. Theodore Roosevelt Digital Library, Dickinson State University, http://www.theodoreroo-seveltcenter.org/Research/Digital-Library/Record?libID=o281261.
89. See "Roosevelt Corollary to the Monroe Doctrine, 1904," ourdocuments.gov, https://www.ourdocuments.gov/doc.php?flash=false&doc=56&page=transcript.
90. One study of this period is Bruce J. Calder, *The Impact of Intervention: The Dominican Republic during the U.S. Occupation of 1916–1924* (Austin: University of Texas Press, 1984).

91. A useful history of the building of the Panama Canal is David McCullough, *The Path between the Seas: The Creation of the Panama Canal, 1870–1914* (New York: Simon and Schuster, 1977).
92. See "Rutherford B. Hayes: Foreign Affairs," Miller Center website, University of Virginia, http://millercenter.org/president/biography/hayes-foreign-affairs.
93. Cited in Howard C. Hill, "The Taking of Panama," in Williams, *Shaping of American Diplomacy*, p. 441.
94. See LaFeber, *American Century*, p. 51.
95. Kinzer, *Overthrow*, p. 61.
96. Healy, *Drive to Hegemony*, p. 93.
97. Dobson, *America's Ascent*, p. 159.
98. LaFeber, *Inevitable Revolutions*, p. 45.
99. LaFeber, *American Search for Opportunity*, p. 220.
100. Kinzer, *Overthrow*, pp. 64–68.
101. See LaFeber, *Inevitable Revolutions*, pp. 46–49.
102. See LaFeber, *American Search for Opportunity*, p. 195.
103. See Warren Cohen, *America's Response to China: A History of Sino-American Relations*, 5th ed. (New York: Columbia University Press, 2010), p. 14.
104. See, for example, Charles S. Campbell, "American Business Interests and the Open Door in China," *Far Eastern Quarterly* 1, no. 1 (November 1941): 43–58.
105. McCormick, *China Market*, p. 14.
106. Among others, this argument was made by Charles Denby, the US ambassador to China at that time. See note 41, this chapter.
107. McCormick, *China Market*, p. 107.
108. Ibid., p. 107.
109. For sources, see notes 50 and 51, this chapter.
110. McCormick, *China Market*, p. 107.
111. See Tony Smith, *America's Mission: The United States and the Worldwide Struggle for Democracy*, expanded ed. (Princeton, NJ: Princeton University Press, 2012), p. 39.
112. More specifically, Chamberlain (then the colonial secretary), conveyed this policy suggestion to John Hay (then US ambassador to Great Britain) via Arthur Balfour at the Foreign Office. See Dobson, *America's Ascent*, p. 178. The importance of this specific information is that it underscores the British origins of what eventually became America's Open Door policy. I will return to that discussion below.
113. General accounts of American colonial experience in the Philippines include Stanley Karnow, *In Our Image: America's Empire in the Philippines* (New York: Random House, 1989); Brands, *Bound to Empire*; William J. Pomeroy, *The Philippines: Colonialism, Collaboration and Resistance* (New York: International Publishers, 1992); and Frank H. Golay, *Face of Empire: United States–Philippine Relations, 1899–1946* (monograph no. 14; Madison: Center for South East Asian Studies, University of Wisconsin, 1998).

114. See Karnow, *In Our Image*, p. 15.
115. See Brands, *Bound to Empire*, p. 45.
116. Karnow, *In Our Image*, p. 12.
117. See Pomeroy, *Philippines*, p. 2; and Brands, *Bound to Empire*, chap. 3.
118. One detailed study of internal political debates in the United States over Philippines is Richard E. Welch Jr., *Response to Imperialism: The United States and the Philippine-American War, 1899–1902* (Chapel Hill: University of North Carolina Press, 1979).
119. Cited in Brands, *Bound to Empire*, p. 32.
120. See Smith, *America's Mission*, pp. 50–59.
121. I have developed this argument elsewhere. See Kohli, *State-Directed Development*, chaps. 1–3.
122. Paul Hutchcroft, *Booty Capitalism: The Politics of Banking in the Philippines* (Ithaca, NY: Cornell University Press, 1998).
123. See Brands, *Bound to Empire*, p. 75.
124. See Richard Hooley, "American Economic Policy in the Philippines, 1902–1940," *Journal of Asian Economics* 16 (2005): 2.
125. Ibid, pp. 472–73.
126. Ibid., p. 478.
127. See Pomeroy, *Philippines*, pp. 8–9. For a more detailed analysis of American educational (and other) policies in the Philippines (in comparison to Puerto Rico), see Julian Go, *American Empire and the Politics of Meaning: Elite Political Cultures in the Philippines and Puerto Rico during U.S. Colonialism* (Durham, NC: Duke University Press, 2008).
128. Hooley, "American Economic Policy," p. 471.
129. See Glen Anthony May, *Social Engineering in the Philippines: The Aims, Execution, and Impact of American Colonial Policy, 1900–1913* (Westport, CT: Greenwood Press, 1980), p. xvii.
130. Growth data for the Philippines during the colonial period are not reliable. Hooley's recent estimates are much higher than those provided by Maddison, though Maddison's estimates are based on Hooley's earlier estimates. To make the matter more confusing, Hooley presents Maddison's estimates, along with his own data, but without any explanation for the discrepancy. See Hooley, "American Economic Policy," table 1, p. 466, for his estimates, and table 5, p. 477, for Maddison's estimates; and Angus Maddison, *Monitoring the World Economy, 1820–1992* (Paris: Organisation for Economic Co-operation and Development, 1995), table B-10E, p. 158. It is reassuring that the growth trends in both Hooley and Maddison follow a similar pattern. For magnitude-of-growth data I have chosen to rely on Maddison's data, mainly because it is standardized for cross-country comparisons.
131. See Brands, *Bound to Empire*, chaps. 4 and 5.
132. It should be added that enough loopholes were left in such legislation to enable, say, the US Sugar Trust to acquire 80,000 acres of land in 1910. Taft himself invested in a promising holding.

133. See Pomeroy, *Philippines*, p. 5.
134. See Hooley, "American Economic Policy", p. 475.
135. Ibid, table 1. Given the doubts about the reliability of data, I am only reporting trends rather than exact magnitude of the changes.
136. See, for example, Thomas Pepinsky, "Trade Competition and American Decolonization," *World Politics* 67, no. 3 (July 2015): 387–422.
137. Brands, *Bound to Empire*, p. 121.
138. See William Appleman Williams, *The Tragedy of American Diplomacy* (New York: Dell, 1962), esp. chap. 1.
139. For a review of this tradition in US foreign policy, see Dobson, *America's Ascent*, esp. p. 10.
140. See Campbell, "American Business Interests and the Open Door in China."
141. See Cohen, *America's Response to China*, pp. 43–44.
142. The comment was made by Major L. L. Seaman, an American who witnessed the rebellion first-hand and who was also the president of China Society of America. It is cited in Marilyn Young, "The Quest for Empire," in Ernst R. May and James C. Thomson Jr., *American-East Asian Relation: A Survey* (Cambridge, MA: Harvard University Press, 1972), p. 139.
143. For this discussion I am drawing on McCormick, *China Market*, pp. 183–86. All the direct quotes in this paragraph are on these pages.
144. Roosevelt to Brooke Adams cited in LaFeber, *American Search for Opportunity*, p. 188.
145. For a balance-of-power type of interpretation of US Far East policy during this period, see James C. Thomson Jr., Peter W. Stanley, and John Curtin Perry, *Sentimental Imperialists: The American Experience in East Asia* (New York: Harper and Row, 1981).
146. See Wimmel, *Theodore Roosevelt and the Great White Fleet*.
147. See Peter Schran, "Commercial Relations between U.S. and China," in Ernst R. May and John K. Fairbank, eds., *America's China Trade in Historical Perspective*, Harvard Studies in American-East Asian Relations 11 (Cambridge, MA: Harvard University), esp. tables 46, 47, and 37.
148. See Tony Smith, *The Pattern of Imperialism: The United States, Great Britain and the Late-Industrializing World since 1815* (New York: Cambridge University Press, 1981), esp. chap. 4.
149. The data on foreign investment are from the US Bureau of Census, *Historical Statistics*, pp. 869–70.

CHAPTER 5

1. I use the term "Third World" only in the context of the Cold War, when use of the term was both common and had a clear referent. My preferred term during other time periods is the more generic "developing world."

2. The literature on these themes is substantial. I list only some of the literature I consulted. On the economic dimensions of reconstruction in Europe, see Michael J. Hogan, *The Marshall Plan: America, Britain, and the Reconstruction of Western Europe, 1947–52* (New York: Cambridge University Press, 1987); Alan S. Milward, *The Reconstruction of Western Europe, 1945–1951* (Berkeley: University of California Press, 1984); Fred L. Block, *The Origins of International Economic Disorder: A Study of the United States International Monetary Policy from World War II to the Present* (Berkeley: University of California Press, 1977); Richard N. Gardner, *Sterling-Dollar Diplomacy in Current Perspective: The Origins and Prospects of Our International Economic Order* (New York: Columbia University Press, 1980); and Charles P. Kindleberger, *The Marshall Plan Days* (Boston: Allen and Unwin, 1987). For broader perspectives, see Lawrence Kaplan, *The United States and NATO: The Formative Years* (Lexington: University of Kentucky Press, 1984); and G. John Ikenberry, *After Victory: Institutions, Strategic Restraint and the Rebuilding of Order after Major Wars* (Princeton, NJ: Princeton University Press, 2001). On the Asian side, see Akira Iriye, *The Cold War in Asia: A Historical Introduction* (Englewood Cliffs, NJ: Prentice Hall, 1974); and William S. Borden, *The Pacific Alliance: United States Foreign Economic Policy and Japanese Trade Recovery, 1947–1955* (Madison: University of Wisconsin Press, 1984). The theme that colonial links would need to be maintained to facilitate economic recovery in Western Europe is stressed in Melvyn P. Leffler, *A Preponderance of Power: National Security, the Truman Administration, and the Cold War* (Stanford, CA: Stanford University Press, 1992). Essays that update the themes in this earlier literature are readily available in Melvyn P. Leffler and Odd Arne Westad, eds., *Cambridge History of the Cold War*, vol. 1: *Origins* (New York: Cambridge University Press, 2010).
3. Interpretations of the Cold War vary enormously. For a range of perspectives, see John Lewis Gaddis, *We Now Know: Rethinking Cold War History* (Oxford: Clarendon Press, 1997); Walter LaFeber, *America, Russia, and the Cold War, 1945–1996*, 8th ed. (New York: McGraw-Hill, 1997); Thomas J. McCormick, *America's Half-Century: United States Foreign Policy in the Cold War and After*, 2nd ed. (Baltimore: Johns Hopkins University Press, 1995); Warren Cohen, *America in the Age of Soviet Power, 1945–1991*, vol. 4 of *The Cambridge History of American Foreign Relations* (New York: Cambridge University Press: 1993); and Leffler, *Preponderance of Power.* In addition, see the more recent introductory essays on a variety of specialized subjects in Leffler and Westad, *Cambridge History of the Cold War*, vol. 1: *Origins.*
4. The best literature on US interventions in the developing world tends to be region specific. I will refer to case-specific literature in due course. Some general treatments of the subject might include the following: Robert A. Packenham, *Liberal America and the Third World: Political Development Idea in Foreign Aid and Social Science* (Princeton, NJ: Princeton University Press: 1976); H. W. Brands, *The Specter of Neutralism: The United States and the Emergence of the Third World, 1947–60* (New York: Columbia University Press, 1989); T. E. Vadney, *The World*

since 1945 (New York: Penguin Books, 1987); Scott L. Bills, *Empire and Cold War: The Roots of US–Third World Antagonism, 1945–47* (New York, St. Martin's Press, 1990); Odd Arne Westad, *The Global Cold War: Third World Interventions and the Making of Our Times* (New York: Cambridge University Press, 2005); and Stephen Kinzer, *Overthrow: America's Century of Regime Change from Hawaii to Iraq* (New York: Times Books, Henry Holt, 2006).

5. Readers might object that all the cases I have chosen serve to highlight the negative impact of American interventions. A focus on South Korea or Taiwan, for example, might lead to different conclusions. In the defense of my choice of cases for this study, I have analyzed the impact of US intervention in South Korea elsewhere. See Atul Kohli, *State-Directed Development: Political Power and Industrialization in the Global Periphery* (New York: Cambridge University Press, 2004), chaps. 1–3. The analysis below will be informed by this earlier study.
6. The literature and sources of information on specific interventions are cited in the body of this chapter.
7. Cited in William Appleman Williams, *The Tragedy of American Diplomacy* (New York: Dell, 1962), p. 57.
8. Compare this to Palmerston's well-known quote some half-century earlier (quoted in chapter 2), when he suggested that in the mid-nineteenth century, Britain stood "at the head of moral, social and political civilisation," and that it was Britain's task to "lead the way and direct the march of other nations." Liberal arrogance, not to mention hypocrisy, seems not only recurring, but also boundless. The Wilson quote here is taken from his address to the National Press Club in 1916, extracts of which are reproduced in Edgar Eugene Robinson and Victor J. West, *The Foreign Policy of Woodrow Wilson, 1913–1917* (New York: MacMillan, 1917).
9. Cited in Ray S. Baker, *Woodrow Wilson and World Settlement* (Garden City, NY: Doubleday, Page and Company, 1922), p. 326
10. The statements of Wilson and Bryan are taken from Williams, *Tragedy*, pp. 66 and 62, respectively.
11. For a detailed study that takes the American commitment to spread democracy more seriously than is implied here, see Tony Smith, *America's Mission: The United States and the Worldwide Struggle for Democracy*, expanded ed. (Princeton, NJ: Princeton University Press, 2012).
12. For details see Walter LaFeber, Richard Polenberg, and Nancy Woloch, *The American Century: A History of the United States since the 1890s*, 7th ed. (Armonk, NY: M. E. Sharpe, 2013), chap. 5.
13. Ibid., p. 98.
14. I have drawn heavily in this and the previous paragraph from LaFeber, ibid., chap. 5.
15. See McCormick, *America's Half-Century*, p. 25.
16. For an overview of some of these complex debates, as well as for a guide to further readings, see LaFeber, *America, Russia, and the Cold War*, chap. 1.

17. Cited in Williams, *Tragedy*, p. 233.
18. Ibid., p. 235.
19. The shared consensus is well revealed in the discussions during the full testimony. See *Post-War Economic Policy and Planning: Hearings Before the Special Committee on Post-War Economic Policy and Planning*, House of Representatives, 78th Congress, second session, 1944 The digitized full text is readily available online from the Hathi Trust Digital Library.
20. The importance of economic themes during this period is also emphasized in Leffler, *Preponderance of Power*; and Ikenberry, *After Victory*.
21. Cited in McCormick, *America's Half-Century*, p. 33.
22. Ibid., p. 33.
23. See Leffler, *Preponderance of Power*, pp. 2 and 5.
24. See LaFeber, *America, Russia*, p. 26.
25. This is a central theme of McCormick, *America's Half-Century*, esp. p. xviii.
26. For some of the relevant literature, see notes 2 and 3, this chapter.
27. Such a "revisionist" assessment of postwar Soviet capabilities is provided in Matthew A. Evangelista, "Stalin's Postwar Army Reappraised," *International Security* 7, no. 3 (Winter 1982–3): 110–38; the findings of the intelligence report are summarized on pp. 133–34.
28. The argument that Americans feared the emergence of "national capitalist" pathways that might not follow American rules for a system of global capitalism is well developed in Block, *Origins*, pp. 1–10.
29. The useful phrase is from Cohen, *America in the Age of Soviet Power*, p. 35.
30. See, for example, Ikenberry, *After Victory*.
31. For a good discussion, see Block, *Origins*.
32. As Truman stated: "[I]f we were to turn our back on the world, areas such as Greece, weakened and divided as a result of the war, would fall into the Soviet orbit without much effort on the part of Russians." See Leffler, *Preponderance of Power*, p. 143.
33. Cited in Andrew J. Bacevich, *American Empire: The Realities and Consequences of U.S. Diplomacy* (Cambridge, MA: Harvard University Press, 2003), p. 5.
34. A number of analysts have made this general point. See, for example, Leffler, *Origins*, chap. 4; LaFeber, *America, Russia*, pp. 50–57; McCormick, *America's Half-Century*, chap. 4; and Cohen, *America in the Age of Soviet Power*, pp. 35–40. As to the specific case of Greece, given its proximity to the Middle East, it was also of strategic and economic significance. For example, *Time* magazine during the period noted that "the loud talk was all of Greece and Turkey but the whispers behind the talk were of the ocean of oil to the south." Quoted in McCormick, *America's Half-Century*, p. 76.
35. See note 2, this chapter, for some of the more important literature on the Marshall Plan.

36. I am especially drawing here on Block, *Origins*; and McCormick, *America's Half-Century*.
37. McCormick, *America's Half-Century* p. 78. Block's conclusion is also worth restating: "The Marshall Plan . . . provided a means of financing a large export surplus and influencing Western Europe's economic course." See Block, *Origins*, p. 87.
38. For the examples that follow, see LaFeber, *America, Russia*, pp. 2–3.
39. See Cohen, *America in the Age of Soviet Power*, p. 10.
40. See Leffler, *Preponderance of Power*, p. 15. Leffler's measured conclusion as to "who started the Cold War" is also worth citing in full: "[I]n view of the overwhelming power of the United States and in view of the relative restraint exhibited by Kremlin *outside its immediate periphery*, US officials might have displayed more tolerance for risk. The terms laid out by the Truman administration for a cooperative relationship were clearly skewed to sustain America's preponderant position in the international system" (p. 99, original italics).
41. See Cohen, *America in the Age of Soviet Power*, p. 57.
42. See Leffler, *Preponderance of Power*, p. 7.
43. Cited ibid., p. 17.
44. While this statement is attributed to Senator Thomas Connally of Texas, for a further discussion that his was not a lone, idiosyncratic voice, see LaFeber, *America, Russia*, p. 83.
45. For details see ibid., chap. 4.
46. For example, this is a central theme in Tony Smith, *The Pattern of Imperialism* (New York: Cambridge University Press, 1981).
47. Cited in LaFeber, et al., *American Century*, p. 227.
48. For such an interpretation, see Leffler, *Preponderance of Power.* His own observations are worth quoting: "Because they defined power in terms of control over or access to resources, US officials could usually pursue economic and strategic objectives in tandem" (p. 14).
49. It may be noted here that though Americans took for granted their own need to control the "new world," this did not lead them to have much sympathy for the Russian need to control its backyard in Eastern Europe.
50. Leffler, *Preponderance of Power,* p. 80.
51. See, for example, Robert Vitalis, *America's Kingdom: Mythmaking on the Saudi Oil Frontier* (Stanford, CA: Stanford University Press, 2005).
52. In Leffler's words: "In order to align Western Europe, West Germany, and Japan permanently with the United States, American officials were convinced that they had to narrow the dollar gap and help their industrial allies sell their goods, earn dollars, and purchase foodstuffs and raw materials in the underdeveloped periphery." *Preponderance of Power*, p. 17.
53. See McCormick, *America's Half-Century*, p. 113.
54. See "An Estimate of Conditions in Asia and Pacific at the Close of the War in the Far East and the Objectives and Policies of the United States," Policy Paper

prepared in the Department of State, Washington, DC, June 22, 1945, in *Foreign Relations of the United States*, 1945, vol. 6. All the direct quotes in this paragraph are from this document, pp. 557–58.

55. See Dean Rusk to H. Freeman Matthews, January 31, 1951, in *Foreign Relations of the United States*, 1951, vol. 6, p. 24.
56. National Security Council Study on United States Objectives, Policies and Courses of Action in Asia, in *Foreign Relations of the United States, 1951*, vol. 6, p. 57. When referring to "the present world situation" the officials are probably referring to the growing US anxieties in Asia at the time caused by the Chinese revolution and the war in Korea. The importance of this passage, however, is less the specific context of 1951 than the type of governance strategy the United States had put in place in the Philippines since granting it full independence in 1946, well before the Chinese revolution and the Korean War.
57. See Leffler, *Preponderance of Power*, p. 314.
58. See Borden, *Pacific Alliance*.
59. Cited ibid., p. 339.
60. Many scholars have made this observation. See, for example, McCormick, *America's Half-Century*, p. 100. Among the original documents, where this American perception is laid out, see Dean Rusk to H. Freeman Matthews, January 31, 1951, in *Foreign Relations of the United States, 1951*, vol. 6, pp. 16–26. This document is revealing since it underlines Rusk's near obsession with the economic resources and markets of the region and how the US and other industrial allies must have access to them.
61. For such an argument, see Andrew J. Rotter, *The Path to Vietnam: Origins of the American Commitment to Southeast Asia* (Ithaca, NY: Cornell University Press, 1987).
62. Cited in LaFeber, *America, Russia*, p. 98.
63. See Policy Planning Staff, "Basic Issues Raised by Draft NSC, 'Reappraisal of U.S. Objectives and Strategy for National Security,'" *Foreign Relations of the United States, 1952–54*, vol. 2, p. 65. I first saw this document cited in Leffler, *Preponderance of Power*, and then followed it up. The early official use in the United States of the concepts of "center" and "periphery"—well before dependency theory popularized them—raises intriguing questions about sociology of knowledge that I will not pursue here.
64. A similar observation is made by Niall Ferguson, in *Colossus: The Price of America's Empire* (New York: Penguin Press, 2004), p. 12. He uses the term "full spectrum dominance" to characterize how the United States created and operated its post-WWII system of global power, a type of domination more akin to an empire than hegemony.
65. See Cohen, *America in the Age of Soviet Power*, pp. 89–90.
66. Cited in LaFeber et al., *American Century*, p. 278.
67. The documents are available online; see Malcolm Byrne, ed., "CIA Confirms Role in 1953 Iran Coup," *National Security Archive Electronic Briefing Book no. 435*, posted August 19, 2013. It should be noted that CIA's admission was hardly news

for many in the know. Most Iranians took it for granted that the United States was behind the coup. Among American observers a fine account was provided by Stephen Kinzer, *All the Shah's Men: An American Coup and the Roots of Middle Eastern Terror* (Hoboken, NJ: John Wiley and Sons, 2003). Scholars specializing in the subject had also reached such judgments earlier: in the words of Gasiorowski, for example, "[T]he CIA planned, financed, and led the coup, with limited help from Britain." See Mark J. Gasiorowski, "Conclusion: Why Did Mossadegh Fall?," in Mark J. Gasiorowski and Malcolm Byrne, eds., *Mohammad Mossadegh and the 1953 Coup in Iran* (Syracuse, NY: Syracuse University Press, 2004), p. 263.

68. While good scholars often recognize that multiple factors move real world events, relative emphasis on one set of factors over others is also evident in respective studies. For example, Gasiorowski concludes that what really moved the United States to intervene in Iran was the fear that Iran would fall to the Soviet Union. Ibid., p 273. By contrast, control over oil is stressed in an outstanding recent volume to which I am greatly indebted in the writing of this section on Iran. See Ervand Abrahamian, *The Coup: 1953, the CIA, and the Roots of Modern U.S.-Iranian Relations* (New York: New Press, 2013).

69. I discuss very briefly some of the constraints faced by the Ottomans in chapter 2, and by the Mughals in chapter 1. One study that compares and contrasts these three Muslim empires in the context of growing British power overseas is, C. A. Bayly, *Imperial Meridian: The British Empire and the World, 1780–1830* (London: Longman, 1989). An overview of Iran under the Safavids is available in Peter Jackson and Laurence Lockhart, eds., *Cambridge History of Iran*, vol. 6: *The Timurid and Safavid Periods* (Cambridge: Cambridge University Press, 1986).

70. Essays covering a variety of specialized subjects on the nineteenth- and twentieth-century history of Iran are available in P. Avery, G. R. G. Hambly and C. Melville, eds., *Cambridge History of Iran*, vol. 7: *From Nadir Shah to the Islamic Republic* (Cambridge: Cambridge University Press, 1991). It is notable that this volume does not contain a separate chapter on Mossadegh and the coup that overthrew him, arguably the most important turning point in modern Iranian history.

71. I am drawing here on Abrahamian, *The Coup*, esp. p. 10.

72. A fine new biography of Mossadegh is Christopher de Bellaigue, *Patriot of Persia: Muhhammad Mossadegh and a Tragic Anglo-American Coup* (New York: HarperCollins, 2012). A useful earlier volume that covers similar ground but with a different emphasis and interpretations—especially, Mossadegh as a democrat—is Homa Katouzian, *Musaddiq and the Struggle of Power in Iran*, rev. ed. (London: I.B. Tauris, 1999). For general background on Iran during this time period, see M. Reza Ghods, *Iran in the Twentieth Century: A Political History* (Boulder, CO.: Lynne Rienner, 1989).

73. See Abrahamian, *The Coup*, p. 40.

74. See James A. Bill, *The Eagle and the Lion: The Tragedy of American-Iranian Relations* (New Haven, CT: Yale University Press, 1988), p. 63. This theme of the importance of sovereignty and "control" is also emphasized in Abrahamian, *The Coup*, pp. 82–93.
75. See Abrahamian, *The Coup*, p. 52.
76. Bellaigue, *Patriot of Persia*, p. 2, 3.
77. This characterization of Mossadegh's close supporters actually came from reports of the British embassy. See Abrahamian, *The Coup*, p. 52. In this paragraph I am drawing on Abrahamian for much of the information.
78. For those not familiar with communist categories, in a hierarchy of enemies, "comprador bourgeoisie" were worse than "national bourgeoisie." Ever since Lenin there had been a sense that Soviet leaders might be able to work with national but not comprador elements in the developing world because the latter were not even patriotic; they were in cahoots with foreign powers.
79. Abrahamian, *The Coup*, p. 79.
80. An eminently readable account of the global role of big oil companies during the Cold War years is Anthony Sampson, *The Seven Sisters: The Great Oil Companies and the World They Shaped* (New York: Bantam Books, 1976).
81. Cited in Kinzer, *Overthrow*, p. 119.
82. See Mary Ann Heiss, "The International Boycott of Iranian Oil and the Anti-Mossadegh Coup of 1953," in Gasiorowski and Byrne, *Mohammad Mossadegh*, p. 180.
83. Ibid., p. 178.
84. Ibid., p. 185.
85. Bill, *Eagle and the Lion*, p. 60.
86. For early American involvement in Iran, I am drawing—for factual information, though not always for interpretation—on ibid., chap. 1.
87. Ibid., p. 19.
88. Ibid., pp. 52–53.
89. See Memorandum by the Deputy Assistant Secretary of State for Near Eastern, South Asian, and African Affairs (Berry), March 14, 1951, in *Foreign Relations of the United States, 1952–54*, vol. 10: *Iran: 1951–1954*.
90. See, for example, *Foreign Relations of the United States, 1952–54*, vol. 10: *Iran: 1951–1954*. Even a cursory review of these declassified documents reveals the continuous back and forth between the United States and Britain over Iran.
91. To be fair, McGhee subsequently sought to distance himself from the coup. See the introduction to James A. Bill and Wm. Roger Louis, eds., *Musaddiq, Iranian Nationalism, and Oil* (Austin: University of Texas Press, 1988), esp. p. 17.
92. See Maziar Behrooz, "The 1953 Coup in Iran and the Legacy of the Tudeh," in Gasiorowski and Byrne, eds., *Mohammad Mossadegh*, pp. 102–25.
93. Cited in Abrahamian, *The Coup*, p. 165.
94. Bellaigue, *Patriot of Persia*, pp. 184–85.

95. Ibid., p. 221.
96. Abrahamian, *The Coup*, p. 173.
97. Bellaigue, *Patriot of Persia*, p. 160.
98. See "Study Prepared by the Staff of the National Security Council," in *Foreign Relations of the United States, 1952–54*, vol. 10.
99. Abrahamian, *The Coup*, p. 147.
100. Cited in Bill, *Eagle and the Lion*, p. 86.
101. Ibid., p. 172.
102. See Kinzer, *Overthrow*, p. 124.
103. Bellaigue, *Patriot of Persia*, p. 228.
104. Two Americans who directly participated in fomenting the coup have penned informative—if embellished and self-serving—accounts of it. See Kermit Roosevelt, *Countercoup: The Struggle for the Control of Iran* (New York: McGraw Hill, 1979); and Donald Wilber, *Regime Change in Iran: Overthrow of Premier Mossadeq in Iran, November 1952–August 1953* (London: Russell Press, 2006). Abrahamian, *The Coup*, especially chap. 3, offers scholarly and much needed corrections to these accounts. An earlier good account is Kinzer, *All the Shah's Men.* Though it is primarily a political biography, Bellaigue, *Patriot of Persia*, is also very well researched and useful.
105. See Bellaigue, *Patriot of Persia*, p. 254.
106. See Hadi Salehi Esfahani and M. Hashem Pesaran, "Iranian Economy in the Twentieth Century: A Global Perspective," *Iranian Studies* 42, no. 2 (April 2009): fig. 19.
107. See Kinzer, *Overthrow*, p. 136.
108. See, for example, Richard H. Immerman, *The CIA in Guatemala: The Foreign Policy of Intervention* (Austin: University of Texas Press, 1982); Piero Gleijeses, *Shattered Hope: The Guatemala Revolution and the United States, 1944–1954* (Princeton, NJ: Princeton University Press, 1991); and Greg Grandin, *The Blood of Guatemala: A History of Race and Nation* (Durham, NC: Duke University Press, 2000).
109. During the summer of 2016, I taught a course, "America's War in Vietnam," at the Vietnam National University, Hanoi. The students in the class were from Princeton University and the Vietnam National University (Social Science and Humanities Campus, Hanoi). During the class, I invited a number of speakers with a deep knowledge of the Vietnam War and its legacy. These included: Chuck Searcy, Quang Minh Pham, Ton-Nu-Thi Ninh, Le Ma Luong, Pham Hong Tung, Nguyen Khac Huynh, Nguyen Manh Ha, Bao Ninh, Vu Thanh Tu Anh, and Ted Osias. I learned from all these knowledgeable individuals.
110. Among the best overviews that have survived the test of time is, Marilyn B. Young, *The Vietnam Wars, 1945–1990* (New York: Harper Collins, 1991). Another good overview that incorporates new scholarship based on Vietnamese sources is, George C. Herring, *America's Longest War: The United States and Vietnam, 1950–1975*, 5th ed. (Boston: McGraw Hill, 2014). A useful guide to further readings on

a variety of more specialized themes is available in David L. Anderson, ed., *The Columbia History of the Vietnam War* (New York: Columbia University Press, 2011). For legal dimensions of the war, see Richard A. Falk, *The Vietnam War and International Law* (Princeton, NJ: Princeton University Press (4 volumes), 1968–1976.

A recent volume that focuses on developments in Vietnam and is based on Vietnamese documents is, Lien-Hang T. Nguyen, *Hanoi's War: An International History of the War for Peace in Vietnam* (Chapel Hill: University of North Carolina Press, 2012). Of course, some observers continue to defend the American intervention in Vietnam; for a review of this and other bodies of literature on the Vietnam War, see Gary R. Hess, *Vietnam: Explaining America's Lost War* (West Sussex, U.K.: Wiley Blackwell, 2015).

111. A good realist account that makes such a case is Cohen, *America in the Age of Soviet Power;* in his words, "No vital American interest was threatened by events in Indochina," p.179. While much of the critical literature on Vietnam war emphasizes the point that Ho Chi Minh was as much a nationalist as a communist, an eloquent, liberal case against the war in Vietnam was made by US Senator George S. McGovern, "America in Vietnam," in Patrick J. Hearden, *Vietnam: Four American Perspectives* (West Lafayette, Indiana: Purdue University Press, 1990), pp. 11–36.
112. In making this argument I am especially influenced by McCormick, *America's Half-Century.* Also see Thomas J. McCormick, "American Hegemony and the Roots of Vietnam War," in Hearden, *Vietnam*, pp. 81–108.
113. For a quick overview of early Vietnamese history, see William J. Duiker, *Vietnam: Revolution in Transition*, Boulder, CO: Westview Press, 1995), chap. 2.
114. English language literature on French colonialism in Vietnam is meager. A good early account that remains relevant is, Ngo Vinh Long, *Before the Revolution: The Vietnamese Peasants under the French*. Cambridge: MIT Press, 1973). Useful insights can also be gained from such general histories of Vietnam as, Joseph Buttinger, *Vietnam: A Dragon Embattled* (New York: Praeger, 1967); Ellen Hammer, *Vietnam: Yesterday and Today* (New York: Holt, Rinehart and Winston, 1966); and a fine recent volume, Christopher Goscha, *Vietnam: A New History* (New York: Basic Books, 2016).
115. Duiker, *Vietnam*, p. 30.
116. Ibid., p. 36.
117. This transformation was very well captured in a local study in central Vietnam that was based on oral interviews with peasants with memories of colonial rule. See James Walker Trullinger, Jr., *Village at War: An Account of Revolution in Vietnam* (New York: Longman, 1980), chap. 2.
118. Select writing of such early nationalists as Nguyen Dinh Chieu (1861), Phan Boi Chau (1907), and Phan Chu Trinh (1907) are readily available in Michael H. Hunt, *A Vietnam War Reader: A Documentary History from American*

and Vietnamese Perspectives (Chapel Hill: University of North Carolina Press, 2010), pp. 4–7. A good account of early Vietnamese nationalism is also available in, John T. McAlister, Jr., *Vietnam: The Origins of Revolution (*New York: Doubleday, 1971).

119. See William J. Duiker, *Ho Chi Minh* (New York: Hyperion, 2000), p. 571.
120. Ibid., p. 570.
121. See Ho Chi Minh, "Statement on behalf of the new Indochinese Communist Party, 18 February 1930," in Hunt, *A Vietnam War Reader*, p. 11.
122. Ho Chi Minh, "Proclamation of the Viet Minh-led Independence struggle, 6 June 1941," ibid, p.12.
123. See Trullinger, *Village at War*, p. 42.
124. See "President Franklin D. Roosevelt and Premier Joseph Stalin, discussion at the Teheran conference, 28 November 1943," in Hunt, *A Vietnam War Reader*, pp. 22–23.
125. Cited in Young, *Vietnam Wars*, p. 12.
126. See Rotter, *Path to Vietnam*, chap. 4. I am drawing on Rotter in this and the following paragraph.
127. Ibid., p. 88. This information is for the early 1950s, which is not likely to be all that different from the situation at the end of the war.
128. "Secretary of State to the Embassy of France," May 13, 1947, in *Foreign Relations of the United States*, 1947, V. VI, pp. 95–96.
129. For the lack of evidence on Soviet support for the Vietminh in the late 1940s, see Rotter, *Path to Vietnam*, p. 101.
130. Dean Rusk to H. Freeman Matthews, Jan. 31, 1951, *Foreign Relations of the United States,* 1951, V. VI, p. 25.
131. See Nguyen, *Hanoi's War*, chap. 1.
132. This point came across clearly in my discussions (during July and December of 2016, in Hanoi and Ho Chi Minh City, respectively) with Madame Ton Nu Thi Ninh, former Vietnamese ambassador, member of the National Assembly, and the former translator for Pham Van Dong.
133. Cited in Young, *Vietnam Wars*, p. 31.
134. See Herring, *America's Longest War*, pp. 38–45.
135. Kahin—the foremost historian of the Vietnam War—suggests that the American decision to create and maintain a noncommunist South Vietnam in 1954 was "the most fundamental decision of its thirty-year involvement" in Vietnam. See George McT. Kahin, *Vietnam: How America Became Involved in Vietnam* (New York: Alfred A. Knopf, 1986), p. 66.
136. To be fair, the United States was not a signatory to the Geneva Accords.
137. See, for example, Qiang Zhai, *China and the Vietnam Wars, 1950–1975* (Chapel Hill: University of North Carolina Press, 2000).
138. See Nguyen, *Hanoi's War*, chap. 1. For an analysis of Le Duan's strong communist commitments, see Tuong Vu, *Vietnam's Communist Revolution: The Power and Limits of Ideology (*New York: Cambridge University Press, 2016).

139. I learned much about Vietnamese land reforms of 1953–56 from Professor Quang Minh Pham of the Vietnam National University, Social Science Campus, Hanoi. He presented his research to my class in Hanoi, on June 30, 2016 (also see footnote 109).
140. Lien-Hang portrays this struggle over Proposition 15—a key party document that helped eventually shift the party's priority to South-first—as a struggle in which Le Duan essentially pressured Ho Chi Minh to sideline Giap. The evidence she provides, however, is thin. See Nguyen, *Hanoi's War*, p. 39. It is just as likely that once Diem and the United States had decided, in 1956, that there were to be no national elections, Ho recognized that the only road to national unification was a more militant struggle in the South. Who else was better suited to lead this effort than Le Duan, with his deep experience and sympathy for the revolutionaries in the south?
141. For details see Kahin, *Intervention*, chaps. 3–7; Herring, *America's Longest War*, chaps. 2–3; and Young, *Vietnam Wars*, chaps. 4–5.
142. For my analysis of the legacy of Japanese colonialism in Korea, see Kohli, *State-Directed Development*, chaps. 1–3.
143. A good cloak-and-dagger account of who-did-what-to-whom-at-what-time is available in Kinzer, *Overthrow*, chap. 7.
144. See Cohen, *America in the Age of Soviet Power*, p. 155.
145. See Anderson, *Columbia History of the Vietnam War*, p. 35.
146. Cited in Young, *Vietnam Wars*, p. 79 and p. 80 respectively.
147. For a scathing, well-deserved critique of the role played by these and other technocratic advisers, see Young, *Vietnam Wars*, chaps. 4–8.
148. The strategic-hamlet program, for example, that aimed to clear procommunist peasants from selected hamlets in South Vietnam, was based on the recommendation of one Robert Thompson, a British Royal Air Force officer with experience in killing communists in Malaya. His visit to the White House is recorded in the Kennedy Papers at the John F. Kennedy Presidential Library and Museum, Boston, Box 197, 3/20/63—3/29/63, document #146.
149. Ibid., Box, 197, 10/1/62—10/6/62, document # 4.
150. In addition to the sources cited above in footnote 105, see Kahin, *Intervention*; Patrick J. Hearden, *The Tragedy of Vietnam* (New York: Harper Collins, 1991); and William S. Turley, *The Second Indochina War: A Concise Political and Military History*, 2nd ed., (Lanham, Maryland: Rowman and Littlefield, 2009). Useful local studies of the conflict include, Trullinger, *Village at War;* and Eric M. Bergerud, *The Dynamics of Defeat: The Vietnam War in Hau Nghia Province* (Boulder, CE: Westview Press, 1991). From the Vietnamese side, see "The Military History Institute of Vietnam," *Victory in Vietnam: The Official History of the People's Army of Vietnam, 1954–1975* (trans. Merle L. Pribbenow,) (Lawrence, Kansas: University of Kansas Press, 2002).
151. See "Johnson, speech at Johns Hopkins University, Baltimore, 7 April, 1965," in Hunt, *Vietnam War Reader*, p. 70.
152. See "Johnson, White House meeting, 21 July 1965," Ibid., p. 81.

153. See "Johnson, Meeting at the White House, 22 July 1965," p. 82.
154. Cited in Young, *Vietnam Wars*, p. 141.
155. See Anderson, *Columbia History of the Vietnam War*, p. 48.
156. For a good overview, with a guide to further readings, see Melvin Small, "Hey, Hey, LBJ! American Domestic Politics and Vietnam War," in Anderson, ed., *Colombia History of the Vietnam War*, pp. 333–56.
157. For details, see Herring, *America's Longest War*, pp. 179–85.
158. For details, see Nguyen, *Hanoi's War*, chap. 3.
159. See, for example, Turley, *Second Indochina War*, p. 141.
160. See, for example, Martin Gilens and Benjamin Page, "Testing Theories of American Politics: Elites, Interest Groups and Average Citizens," *Perspectives on Politics*, September 2014, v.12, no.3, pp. 563–81.
161. I am drawing here on Herring, *America's Longest War*, pp. 252–59.
162. Cited in ibid., p. 257.
163. For the argument that the economic crisis of 1968 contributed to Johnson's decision to deescalate the Vietnam War in 1968, see Gabriel Kolko, *Anatomy of a War: Vietnam, the United States, and the Modern Historical Experience* (New York: Pantheon Books, 1985), chap. 25. Another fine study that both explains the nature of the 1968 economic crisis and provides detailed evidence of how the crisis influenced Johnson's Vietnam policies is, Robert M. Collins, "Economic Crisis of 1968 and the Waning of the 'American Century,'" *American Historical Review*, April 1996 101, no. 2, pp. 396–422.
164. Collins, "Economic Crisis of 1968," p. 412.
165. All of these direct quotes are cited in ibid. p. 415 and 416.
166. For fine analyses of this phase of the Vietnam War, along with strong moral condemnation, see Herring, *America's Longest War*, chap. 7; and Young, *Vietnam Wars*, chaps. 12–13. For a guide to further reading, see Jeffrey P. Kimball, "Richard M. Nixon and the Vietnam War," in Anderson, *Columbia History of Vietnam War*, pp. 217–246.
167. See Henry Kissinger, "The Vietnam Negotiations," *Foreign Affairs*, January 1969, 47. no. 2, pp. 211–34.
168. All the direct quotes are in Ibid., p 218 and 219.
169. A frustrated Kissinger remarked to the National Security Council in July 1969, "I refuse to believe that a little fourth-rate power like Vietnam does not have a breaking point."
170. See, for example, Nguyen, *Hanoi's War*, part 4.
171. For a balanced discussion, see Kenton Clymer, "Cambodia and Laos in the Vietnam War," in Anderson, ed., *Columbia History of the Vietnam War*, pp. 357–84.
172. See, for example, Herring, *America's Longest War*, pp. 291–96.
173. The literature on the US intervention in Chile is sizable and often of good quality. I cite the most relevant sources in due course. What needs to be acknowledged at the outset are the heroic efforts of Peter Kornbluh to pull together the

important secret documents released by the US government. See Peter Kornbluh, *The Pinochet File: A Declassified Dossier of Atrocity and Accountability* (A National Security Archive Book) (New York: New Press, 2004). The first two chapters of this volume, along with the declassified documents appended to each chapter, are indispensable for understanding how and why the United States promoted a coup against Allende.

174. Two recent studies that move in this direction are: Jonathan Haslam, *The Nixon Administration and the Death of Allende's Chile* (New York: Verso, 2005); and Kristian Gustafson, *Hostile Intent: U.S. Covert Operations in Chile, 1964–1974* (Washington D.C.: Potomac Books, 2007). For a good critique of such arguments, see Lubna Z. Qureshi, *Nixon, Kissinger, and Allende: U.S. Involvement in the 1973 Coup in Chile*, (Lanham, MD: Lexington Books, 2009).
175. Specialists on Latin America will readily recognize that this well-known argument comes from Guillermo O'Donnell, *Modernization and Bureaucratic Authoritarianism*, (Berkeley: Institute of International Studies, University of California, 1973). It is important to note the O'Donnell wrote his study before the coup in Chile. Subsequently, others sought to extend his argument to the Chilean case. For a critical discussion of O'Donnell's important hypothesis, see David Collier, ed. *The New Authoritarianism in Latin America* (Princeton, NJ: Princeton University Press, 1979).
176. In a much earlier study—with a different set of analytical concerns and without the benefit of the data that has become available since—I, too, had suggested in passing that the absence of a well-organized social democratic party had contributed to Allende's failure. See Atul Kohli, *The State and Poverty in India: The Politics of Reform* (New York: Cambridge University Press, 1987), p. 232.
177. American officials often stressed the importance of the "communist threat" as the rationale for anti-Allende policies. For a scholarly account that situates such American fears within the broader context of US foreign policy during the Cold War, see John Lewis Gaddis, *Strategies of Containment: A Critical Reappraisal of American National Security Policy during the Cold War* (New York, Oxford University Press, 2005). Recent studies that take into account new evidence but also stress the importance of economic factors behind US intervention instead include: Kornbluh, *Pinochet File;* Qureshi, *Nixon, Kissinger, and Allende;* and Kinzer, *Overthrow*, chap. 8.
178. Cited in Kornbluh, *Pinochet File*, p. xiii.
179. Details about Chile during the nineteenth century are readily available in any standard historical account, the best of which in the English language is probably, Brian Loveman, *Chile: The Legacy of Hispanic Capitalism*, 3rd ed. (New York: Oxford University Press, 2001). Also see Simon Collier and William Sater, *A History of Chile, 1808–1994* (New York: Cambridge University Press, 1999).
180. For supporting data and details see Manuel Llorca-Jaña, *The British Textile Trade in South America in the Nineteenth Century* (New York: Cambridge University

Press, 2012). Some of the controversies related to this claim were discussed in chapter 2.

181. A good political-economy account of early Chilean history is available in Marcelo J. Cavarozzi and James F. Petras, "Chile," in Ronald H. Chilcote and Joel C. Edelstein, eds., *Latin America: The Struggle with Dependency and Beyond* (New York: John Wiley and Sons, 1983), pp. 491–578.
182. Ibid., p. 504.
183. See, for example, Gabriel Palma, "External Disequilibrium and Internal Industrialization: Chile, 1914–1935," in Christopher Abel and Colin M. Lewis, *Latin America, Economic Imperialism and the State: The Political Economy of the External Connection from Independence to the Present* (London: Athlone Press, 1985), pp. 318–38.
184. A fine study of the economic programs of these respective leaders is Barbara Stallings, *Class Conflict and Economic Development in Chile, 1958–1973* (Stanford, CA: Stanford University Press, 1978).
185. See Paul E. Sigmund, *The Overthrow of Allende and the Politics of Chile, 1964–1976* (Pittsburgh: University of Pittsburgh Press, 1977), p. 24.
186. Ibid., p. 31.
187. Quoted in Qureshi, *Nixon, Kissinger, and Allende*, p. 24.
188. Ibid., p. 23.
189. See, for example, Lars Schoultz, *Beneath the United States: A History of U.S. Relations towards Latin America* (Cambridge, MA: Harvard University Press, 1998).
190. The trade and investment data in this paragraph are available on line, drawn from United States Census Bureau, *Bicentennial Edition: Historical Statistics of the United States, Colonial Times to 1970*, September 1975, Part 2, chapter U, p. 903 for trade data and p. 870 for investment data.
191. By early 1970s these programs were widely considered a failure. A good account is Jerome Levinson and Juan de Onís, *The Alliance that Lost its Way: A Critical Account of the Alliance for Progress* (Chicago: Quadrangle Books, 1972).
192. See, for example, Paul Sigmund, *The United States and Democracy in Chile*, A Twentieth Century Fund Book (Baltimore: Johns Hopkins University Press, 1993), chap. 2.
193. Kinzer, *Overthrow*, pp. 174–75.
194. See Kornbluh, *Pinochet File*, p. 5.
195. Ibid., p. 5.
196. The figure for Chilean officers trained by the United States is from Kinzer, *Overthrow*, p. 176.
197. Sigmund, *Overthrow of Allende*, p. 31.
198. Kornbluh, *Pinochet File*, p. 4.
199. Kinzer, *Overthrow*, p. 175.
200. Cited in Qureshi, *Nixon, Kissinger, and Allende*, p. 33.
201. See Stallings, *Class Conflict and Economic Development in Chile*, chap. 9.

202. Cited in Sigmund, *Overthrow of Allende*, p. 103. Kissinger's lose use of the term "Communist" in this context must be underscored. With his German background, Kissinger must have known the difference between social democracy and communism. As suggested above, Allende was a social democrat and not a communist. In Chile at that time Socialist and Communist parties were distinct political parties—though in coalition—and Allende was a leader of the Socialists. That Kissinger chose to ignore such subtle, but important, distinctions must be understood as part of his deliberate effort to join Washington's discourse in which anyone on the left risked being labeled a communist.
203. These conclusions are cited in Kornbluh, *Pinochet File*, p. 8. All the materials quoted in this paragraph are taken from these conclusions. I should add that my interpretation of these materials is not the same as that of Kornbluh.
204. Ibid., p. 9.
205. See CIA, Richard Helms Handwritten Notes, "Meeting with the President on Chile at 1525," September 15, 1970. A copy of this memo is appended in ibid., p. 36.
206. See CIA, Memorandum, "Genesis of Project FUBELT," September 16, 1970, ibid., p. 37.
207. See Kinzer, *Overthrow*, p. 172.
208. See, for example, Kornbluh, *Pinochet File*, chaps. 1 and 2.
209. Kinzer, *Overthrow*, p. 171.
210. Ibid., p. 186.
211. Cited in Qureshi, *Nixon, Kissinger, and Allende*, p. 12.
212. Cited in Kornbluh, *Pinochet File*, p. 10.
213. Cited in Qureshi, *Nixon, Kissinger, and Allende*, p. 54.
214. Cited in Kornbluh, *Pinochet File*, p. 11.
215. Qureshi, *Nixon, Kissinger, and Allende*, p. 55.
216. Cited in Kinzer, *Overthrow*, p. 213.
217. See "The White House **Secret** Memorandum for the President, "NSC Meeting, November 6—Chile," November 5, 1970, reproduced in Kornbluh, *Pinochet File*, pp. 121–28.
218. Cited in Kinzer, *Overthrow*, p. 177.
219. All the material in quotations in this paragraph is from the Kissinger memo. I use italics only when the text is underlined in the original.
220. It may well be—as a matter of fact, it is rather likely—that Kissinger penned what he already knew to be Nixon's thinking, just giving it more analytical flair. Be that as it may, for the record of the NSC meeting that—in addition to Nixon and Kissinger—included Secretary of State William Rogers, Secretary of Defense Melvin Laird, Director of CIA Richard Helms and Generals William Westmoreland and Alexander Haig, see "The White House, **SECRET** Memorandum of Conversation, "NSC Meeting—Chile (NSSM 97)," November 6, 1970," appended in Kornbluh, *Pinochet File*, p. 116.

221. Cited in Qureshi, *Nixon, Kissinger, and Allende*, p. 55. According to Qureshi, this conversation took place on June 11, 1971, and is recorded on Tape 517-4, Nixon Presidential Materials Project.
222. In addition to the various sources cited so far (especially Kornbluh, Qureshi, Kinzer, and Sigmund), see John Dinges, *The Condor Years* (New York: New Press, 2004).
223. See, for example, Kornbluh, *Pinochet File*.
224. Ibid., p. 162.
225. Kinzer, *Overthrow*, p. 211.
226. See Kohli, *State-Directed Development*, Chs. 1–3.

CHAPTER 6

1. See Amy Hagopian, et al., "Mortality in Iraq, Associated with the 2003–2011 War and Occupation: Findings from a National Cluster Sample Survey by the University Collaborative Iraq Mortality Study," *PLOS Medicine*, Oct. 15, 2013, pp. 1–15.
2. Human Rights Watch, "War in Iraq," January 25, 2004.
3. Cited in Walter LaFeber, *America, Russia and the Cold War, 1945–1996*, 8th ed. (New York: McGraw-Hill, 1997), p. 264.
4. A good study is Joanne Gowa, *Closing the Gold Window: Domestic Politics and the End of Bretton Woods* (Ithaca, NY: Cornell University Press, 1983).
5. See Robert Gilpin, *The Political Economy of International Relations* (Princeton, NJ: Princeton University Press, 1987), pp. 140–42.
6. A useful study is Amin Saikal, *The Rise and Fall of the Shah: Iran from Autocracy to Religious Rule* (Princeton, NJ: Princeton University Press, 2009).
7. For a good discussion, see Andrew J. Bacevich, *America's War for the Greater Middle East: A Military History* (New York: Random House, 2017), chap. 1.
8. See Gilpin, *Political Economy of International Relations*, p. 134.
9. See David Spiro, *The Hidden Hand of American Hegemony: Petrodollar Recycling and International Markets* (Ithaca, NY: Cornell University Press, 1999).
10. Cited in Walden Bello, *Dilemmas of Domination: The Unmaking of the American Empire* (New York: Henry Holt, 2005), p. 220, note 16.
11. This speech is known as the Malaise Speech, even though Carter never used the word *malaise*. For a full text of the speech, see Jimmy Carter, "Address to the Nation on Energy and National Goals," July 15, 1979, available at: https://millercenter.org/the-presidency/presidential-speeches/november-8-1977-address-nation-energy.
12. See Gilpin, *Political Economy of International Relations*; and Paul Kennedy, *The Rise and Fall of the Great Powers: Economic Change and Military Conflict from 1500 to 1989* (New York: Vintage, 1989).
13. Cited in Walter LaFeber, Richard Polenberg, and Nancy Woloch, eds., *The American Century: A History of the United States since the 1890s* (Armonk, NY: M. E. Sharpe, 2013), p. 367.

14. For such an argument, see Leo Panitch and Sam Gindin, "Finance and American Empire," in Leo Panitch and Martijn Konings, eds., *American Empire and the Political Economy of Global Finance* (New York: Palgrave Macmillan, 2008), p. 34.
15. See LaFeber, et al., *American Century*, p. 461.
16. See Simon Johnson and James Kwak, *13 Bankers: The Wall Street Takeover and the Next Financial Meltdown* (New York: Vintage Books, 2011), p. 85.
17. Ibid., p. 60.
18. See Gilpin, *Political Economy of International Relations*, p. 144.
19. See Karin Lissakers, *Banks, Borrowers and the Establishment: A Revisionist Account of the International Debt Crisis* (New York: Basic Books, 1991), p. 45.
20. For good discussions of the end of the Cold War along these lines, see Warren I. Cohen, *America in the Age of Soviet Power, 1945–1991*, vol. 4 of *The Cambridge History of American Foreign Relations* (New York: Cambridge University Press, 1993), chap. 8; and Walter LaFeber, *America, Russia and the Cold War, 1945–1996*, 8th ed. (New York: McGraw-Hill, 1997), chap. 12.
21. The reference is to a book with this title that suggests that with the end of the Cold War, democracy and capitalism had won and that ideological struggles over how best to organize national political economies was over. See Francis Fukuyama, *The End of History and the Last Man* (London: Hamish Hamilton, 1992).
22. Some recent studies that make such an argument include (listed in no particular order): David Calleo, *Follies of Power: America's Unipolar Fantasy* (New York: Cambridge University Press, 2009); Walden Bello, *Dilemmas of Domination: The Unmaking of the American Empire* (New York: Henry Holt, 2005); Warren Cohen, *America's Failing Empire: U.S. Foreign Relations since the Cold War* (Malden, MA: Blackwell, 2005); Andrew J. Bacevich, *American Empire: The Realities and Consequences of U.S. Diplomacy* (Cambridge, MA: Harvard University Press, 2002); and Chalmers Johnson, *The Sorrows of Empire* (New York: Metropolitan Books, 2004).
23. Cited in Cohen, *America's Failing Empire*, p. 39.
24. Cited in Mark Lofgren, *The Deep State: The Fall of the Constitution and the Rise of a Shadow Government* (New York: Penguin Books, 2016), p. 108–9.
25. Cohen, *America's Failing Empire*, p. 55.
26. Cited in LaFeber, et al, *American Century*, p. 436.
27. Cited in Bello, *Dilemmas of Domination*, p. 41. It should be added that the first Bush Administration did not accept this 1992 document. However, Wolfowitz was back with a vengeance during Bush II, and was a key architect of the second intervention in Iraq. I return to a fuller discussion of that intervention below.
28. A good recent overview of the Clinton years is Nelson Lichtenstein, "A Fabulous Failure: Clinton's 1990s and the Origins of Our Times," *American Prospect*, January 29, 2018.
29. According to one observer, she was "itchy" to use military force, arguing with Colin Powell, then the chairman of the Joint Chiefs of Staff, "What is the point of

having this superb military that you are always talking about if we cannot use it?" See Lofgren, *Deep State*, p. 60.

30. For such an argument, see Johnson and Kwak, *13 Bankers*, chap. 4.
31. Cohen, *America's Failing Empire*, p. 58.
32. The official in question was Jeffrey Garten, undersecretary of commerce in the Clinton Administration. Cited in Johnson, *Sorrows of Empire*, p. 268. As a qualification it should be added that such comments could also just be self-serving.
33. Cohen, *America's Failing Empire*, p. 91.
34. The felicitous phrase "rolling back the state" is from Bello, *Dilemmas of Domination*.
35. See Cohen, *America's Failing Empire*, p. 26.
36. See Bob Woodward, *Plan of Attack* (New York: Simon and Schuster, 2004), p. 10.
37. Cited ibid., p. 96.
38. Johnson, *Sorrows of Empire*, p. 226.
39. Cited in Cohen, *America's Failing Empire*, p. 96.
40. Cited in Bello, *Dilemmas of Domination*, p. 39.
41. See, for example, Arno Mayer, "Two Parties, One Imperial Mission: The US Empire Will Survive Bush," *Le Monde Diplomatique*, October 29, 2008.
42. See, for example, John Williamson, "What Washington Means by Policy Reform," in John Williamson, ed., *Latin American Adjustment: How Much Has Happened?* (Washington DC: Institute for International Economics, 1990), 7–40.
43. Many overviews of Latin American political economy are readily available. Two useful accounts, which provide further references to other sources, are Francisco Panizza, *Contemporary Latin America: Development and Democracy beyond the Washington Consensus* (London: Zed Books, 2009); and Peter Kingstone, *The Political Economy of Latin America: Reflections on Neoliberalism and Development* (New York: Routledge, 2011).
44. On different pathways toward the incorporation of the working classes, see David and Ruth Collier, *Shaping the Political Arena* (Princeton, NJ: Princeton University Press, 1991).
45. The classic account of the historical development of class forces in Latin America is Fernando Henrique Cardoso and Enzo Faletto, *Dependency and Development in Latin America* (Berkeley: University of California Press, 1979).
46. For one good overview, see Karen L. Remmer, *Military Rule in Latin America* (Boston: Unwin Hyman, 1989).
47. For the following couple of paragraphs, I am drawing on my own earlier work. See Atul Kohli, *State-Directed Development: Political Power and Industrialization in the Global Periphery* (New York: Cambridge University Press, 2004), chap. 5. I will not cite again the numerous sources on which I depended in this earlier work.
48. See, for example, Peter Evans, *Dependent Development: The Alliance of Multinational, State, and Local Capital in Brazil* (Princeton, NJ: Princeton University Press, 1995).

49. See World Bank, *An Examination of the Banking Crisis of the 1980s and the Early 1990s*, vol. 1 (Washington, DC: World Bank, 1994), p. 194.
50. See Jeffrey Sachs and Harry Huizinga, "U.S. Commercial Banks and the Developing Country Debt Crisis," *Brookings Papers on Economic Activity* 2 (1987): 555.
51. See World Bank, *Examination of the Banking Crisis*, p. 193.
52. Numerous studies document the role of the United States in the debt crisis. Among those that I consulted are Lissakers, *Banks, Borrowers and the Establishment*; Gilpin, *Political Economy of International Relations*, chap. 8; Jeffrey Sachs and Harry Huizinga, "U.S. Commercial Banks and the Developing Country Debt Crisis;" Devesh Kapur, John P. Lewis, and Richard Webb, *The World Bank: Its First Half Century*, vol. 1 (Washington DC: Brookings Institution, 1997), chap. 11; and Alexander Kentikelenis and Sarah Babb, "Norm Substitution and the Rise of Structural Adjustment in the IMF," mimeo, University of Oxford, 2018.
53. Sachs and Huizinga, "U.S. Commercial Banks and the Developing Country Debt Crisis," pp. 555 and 560.
54. A good discussion of how the US approach to the Latin American debt crises originated with the "restructuring" of the Mexican debt in 1982 is Kapur et al., *World Bank*, p. 608.
55. Gilpin, *Political Economy of International Relations*, p. 319.
56. Ibid., p. 320.
57. I am drawing here on Kentikelenis and Babb, "Norm Substitution". This fine recent work in turn is based on newly released papers of James A. Baker and records of the IMF.
58. Ibid., p. 10.
59. Baker to Patrick Buchanan, a senior adviser to Reagan at that time, cited ibid., p. 10.
60. Cited ibid., p. 14.
61. See Gilpin, *Political Economy of International Relations*, p. 320.
62. Cited in Kapur et al. *World Bank,* p. 615.
63. See Joseph Stiglitz, *Globalization and Its Discontents* (New York: W. W. Norton, 2003).
64. Based on an interview with Charles Dallara, an assistant to James Baker, who worked simultaneously at the IMF and the US Treasury during this time period. The interview is cited in Kentikelenis and Babb, "Norm Substitution," p. 17.
65. World Bank, *Examination of the Banking Crisis*, p. 201.
66. See Sachs and Huizinga, "U.S. Commercial Banks and the Developing Country Debt Crisis", table 4, p. 564.
67. The estimate of 5 percent per annum as net transfers is suggested ibid. p. 560. The lower estimate of 4 percent is suggested in Robert Devlin and Ricardo French-Davis, "The Great Latin American Debt Crisis: A Decade of Asymmetric Adjustment," *Revista de Economia Politica* 15, no. 3 (59) (July–September 1995): 135.
68. Ibid., p. 135.

69. See Kapur et al., *World Bank*, table 11–6, p. 658.
70. See Devlin and French-Davis, "Great Latin American Debt Crisis," p.138.
71. See World Bank, *An Examination of the Banking Crisis*, p. 208.
72. Kapur et al., *World Bank*, p. 626.
73. It may interest the reader that higher interest rates in the United States in the mid-1990s again triggered a financial crisis in Mexico during 1994–96, the so-called peso crisis.
74. Devlin and French-Davis, "Great Latin American Debt Crisis," p. 119.
75. See, for example, Williamson, "What Washington Means by Policy Reform." For a critique, see Narcís Serra and Joseph Stiglitz, eds., *The Washington Consensus Reconsidered: Towards a New Global Governance* (New York: Oxford University Press, 2008).
76. I am drawing here on my two earlier essays. See Atul Kohli, "Coping with Globalization: Asian versus Latin American Strategies of Development, 1980–2010," *Brazilian Journal of Political Economy* 32, no. 4 (Oct.–Dec. 2012): 531-556; and Kohli, "Nationalist versus Dependent Capitalist Development: Alternate Pathways of Asia and Latin America in a Globalized World," *Studies in Comparative International Development* 44, no. 4 (December 2009): 386–410.
77. Ibid., table 2. Why the rates of savings were higher in Asia than Latin America is an important issue but this is not the place to discuss it. For my discussion of the subject, with specific reference to South Korea versus Brazil, see Kohli, *State-Directed Development*.
78. One good study of the underlying politics in select countries is, Judith Teichman, *The Politics of Freeing Markets in Latin America: Chile, Argentina and Mexico* (Chapel Hill: University of North Carolina Press, 2001).
79. It may interest the readers to note that US exports to East Asia also grew rapidly during this period, but the pattern was distinct in so far as the East Asian context was one of rapid economic growth.
80. See Cintia Quiliconi, "U.S.-Latin American Trade Relations," (Anti-Americanism Working Papers, 2005, Center for Policy Studies, Central European University, Budapest, Hungary, 2005), p. 13.
81. The data in Figure 6.8 are actually not only American but also all portfolio investment going into Latin America. Since the United States was the major source of portfolio investments in Latin America, the data captures broad trends of US investments in the region. The data for US portfolio investments in Latin America during the 1990s are not readily available. The main source of such data is an annual survey conducted by the US Treasury. These surveys began around 2000. Prior to that, the Treasury conducted two pilot surveys in 1994 and 1996, but the results are not readily available and may not be comparable. Even the US Bureau of Economic Analysis—now the easiest source of data on US portfolio investments—draws its data from the surveys conducted by the Treasury. I would like to acknowledge the help of the bureau's staff in sorting out these issues of data availability.

82. This claim is based on my own calculations from the Bureau of Economic Analysis data on "U.S. Investment Position Abroad on a Historical-Cost Basis."
83. For my discussion of this issue with reference to Brazil, see Kohli, *State-Directed Development*, chap. 5.
84. The one significant exception to this trend is of course the *maquiladoras* in Mexico. Given the large domestic market, Brazil also attracts US manufacturing investment.
85. See Barbara Stallings, "U.S. Financial Flows to Latin America," *Partnership for the Americas Commission, Background Document, BD-02* (Washington DC: Brookings, 2008).
86. See Sebastian Edwards, "Capital Flows to Latin America," in Martin Feldstein, ed., *International Capital Flows* (Chicago: University of Chicago Press, 1999), p. 15.
87. For a critique along these lines, with specific reference to Latin America, see Luiz Carlos Bresser-Pereira and Carmen Augusta Varela, "The Second Washington Consensus and Latin America's Quasi-Stagnation," *Journal of Post Keynesian Economics* 27, no. 2 (Winter 2004/5): 231–50. For more general critiques of financial openness, see Jagdish Bhagwati, "The Capital Myth: The Difference between Trade in Widgets and in Dollars," *Foreign Affairs* 77, May/June 1998; and Dani Rodrik, *The Globalization Paradox* (New York: W. W. Norton, 2011).
88. I am drawing here on my earlier work. See Kohli, "Nationalist versus Dependent Capitalist Development."
89. The urban unemployment data is calculated from Bresser-Pereira and Varela, "Second Washington Consensus," table 2, p. 234.
90. The World Bank quietly made such an admission in one of its postmortems, concluding that instead of the certainties of the Washington Consensus, the record suggests that "there is no unique set of rules" that will help facilitate economic growth in developing countries. See the World Bank, *Economic Growth in the 1990s: Learning from a Decade of Reform* (Washington DC: World Bank, 2005), xiii. I am not aware of any such mea culpa from the IMF or the US government.
91. For my own effort to explain some of these differences, see my two earlier essays: Kohli, "Coping with Globalization"; and Kohli, "Nationalist versus Dependent Capitalist Development." For more detailed comparison of South Korea, India, and Brazil, see Kohli, *State-Directed Development*.
92. This is not to deny or ignore the pressure on some Asian countries to pursue the Washington Consensus, especially on countries that were in clientelistic relationship to the United States. Important countries of the region, however, like China and India, resisted such pressures. When forced opening of capital markets contributed to the Asian financial crisis in the late 1990s, the harmful effects were also relatively short-lived, especially in the healthy economies like South Korea. For a set of essays that analyze the Asian financial crisis, see Andrew MacIntyre, T. J. Pempel and John Ravenhill, eds., *Crisis as Catalyst: Asia's Dynamic Political Economy* (Ithaca, NY: Cornell University Press, 2008). Also see Robert Wade, "Asian Debt-and-Development Crisis, 1997–?: Causes and Consequences," *World Development*, August 1998.

93. The United States still has some 5,000 troops in Iraq. The US Embassy in Iraq is among its largest in the world. The embassy occupies nearly a hundred acres of prime real estate along the Tigris in Baghdad—bigger than the Vatican—and employs a staff of some 6,000.
94. During 2017, for example, the US Congress appropriated $3.6 billion for such tasks. See *New York Times*, May 12, 2018.
95. Useful accounts that cover different facets include (an incomplete list, with the most recent publication listed first): Andrew J. Bacevich, *America's War for the Greater Middle East: A Military History* (New York: Random House, 2016); Greg Muttitt, *Fuel on the Fire: Oil and Politics in Occupied Iraq* (New York: New Press, 2012); Larry Diamond, *Squandered Victory: The American Occupation and the Bungled Effort to Bring Democracy to Iraq* (New York: Henry Holt, 2006); Rajiv Chandrasekaran, *Emerald City: Inside Baghdad's Green Zone* (New York: Alfred A. Knopf, 2006); David L. Phillips, *Losing Iraq: Inside the Postwar Reconstruction Fiasco* (New York: Basic Books, 2005); and Rashid Khalidi, *Resurrecting Empire: Western Footprints and America's Perilous Path in the Middle East* (Boston: Beacon Press, 2004).
96. After having lunch with President Bush, for example, his vice president Dick Cheney noted, "Democracy in the Middle East is just a big deal for him. It's what's driving him." Cited in Woodward, *Plan of Attack*, p. 412.
97. A good historical overview is Marion Farouk-Sluglett and Peter Sluglett, *Iraq since 1958: From Revolution to Dictatorship* (New York: I.B. Tauris, 1990). For those wanting to dig deeper, especially on the social origins of communism and of the Ba'ath in Iraq, see Hanna Batatu, *The Old Social Classes and the Revolutionary Movements of Iraq* (Princeton, NJ: Princeton University Press, 1978). Also see Geoff Simons, *Iraq: From Sumer to Saddam*, 2nd ed. (New York: St. Martin's Press, 1994).
98. See Batatu, *Old Social Classes*, pp. 239–40. In exchange, the main exports of Iraq were grains and dates. The British came to control much of the trade of the region. For further details of this trade, see Roger Owen, *The Middle East in the World Economy, 1800–1914* (London: Methuen, 1981), chaps. 7 and 11.
99. See Farouk-Sluglett and Sluglett, *Iraq since 1958*, p. 9.
100. According to Khalidi, France gave up Mosul to the British because Georges Clemenceau was in an "expansive mood after receiving a rapturous reception from the normally phlegmatic British public." See Khalidi, *Resurrecting Empire*, p. 94.
101. See Farouk-Sluglett and Sluglett, *Iraq since 1958*, pp. 6–7.
102. Cited in Larry Everest, *Oil, Power and Empire: Iraq and the U.S. Global Agenda* (Monroe, ME: Common Courage Press, 2004).
103. Cited in Muttitt, *Fuel on the Fire*, p. 8.
104. For details, see Batatu, *Old Social Classes*, Book one, Part two.
105. See Farouk-Sluglett and Sluglett, *Iraq since 1958*, p. 20. Of course, this Sunni domination predated the British colonial phase since the Ottoman rule was very much a Sunni affair.

106. For details, see Batatu, *Old Social Classes*, Book 2.
107. See Muttitt, *Fuel on the Fire*, p. 8.
108. Cited ibid, p. 8.
109. See Farouk-Sluglett and Sluglett, *Iraq since 1958*, pp. 35 and 42.
110. See any of the sources listed in note 93, this chapter, both for details and further references.
111. An official of the US National Security Council subsequently noted that the 1968 coup in Iraq created a "regime that was unquestionably midwifed by the United States and the CIA's involvement there was really primary." Cited in Johnson, *Sorrows of Empire*, p. 223.
112. See Daniel Yergin, *The Prize: The Epic Quest for Oil, Money and Power* (New York: Free Press, 2009), Part 5.
113. Farouk-Sluglett and Sluglett, *Iraq since 1958*, p. 147.
114. See Muttitt, *Fuel on the Fire*, chap. 2.
115. Ibid., vii.
116. Bacevich, *America's War for the Greater Middle East*, p. 29.
117. Ibid., 35.
118. See Farouk-Sluglett and Sluglett, *Iraq since 1958*, p. 267. Germany was one of the countries that supplied Saddam with the means to manufacture chemical weapons. For documentation, see David McDowall, *A Modern History of the Kurds* (London: I. B. Tauris, 2004), chap. 17.
119. See Steven M. Walt, "WikiLeaks, April Glaspie and Saddam Hussein," *Foreign Policy*, January 9, 2011, http://foreignpolicy.com/2011/01/09/wikileaks-april-glaspie-and-saddam-hussein/.
120. A fine account is Bacevich, *America's War for the Greater Middle East*, chap. 7.
121. Cited in Johnson, *Sorrows of Empire*, p. 229.
122. For details of how Bush interacted with his various advisers during the run up to the war, see Woodward, *Plan of Attack*.
123. Cited in Muttitt, *Fuel on the Fire*, p. 35
124. Cited in ibid., p. 4.
125. See Woodward, *Plan of Attack*, p. 21.
126. Zalmay Khalilzad and Paul Wolfowitz, "Overthrow Him," *Weekly Standard*, December 1, 1997.
127. Cited in Bello, *Dilemmas of Domination*, p. 54.
128. See Khalidi, *Resurrecting Empire*, p. 53.
129. Cited in Muttitt, *Fuel on the Fire*, p. 30.
130. See her interview in *Financial Times*, September 22, 2002. Rice subsequently sought the help of her former Stanford colleague Larry Diamond to lead such a democracy-building effort in Iraq. The tortured journey is well documented in Larry Diamond, *Squandered Victory: The American Occupation and the Bungled Effort to Bring Democracy to Iraq* (New York: Henry Holt, 2006).

131. Cited in Bacevich, *America's War for the Greater Middle East*, p. 222.
132. These quotes from the *National Security Strategy, 2002*, are taken from Khalidi, *Resurrecting Empire*, p. 3.
133. See Cohen, *America's Failing Empire*, p. 136.
134. Cited in Woodward, *Plan of Attack*, p. 203.
135. Cited in Khalidi, *Resurrecting Empire*, p. 3.
136. Cited in Woodward, *Plan of Attack*, p. 354.
137. Cited in Bacevich, *America's War for the Greater Middle East*, p. 239.
138. Gilpin thus argued, "The 2003 American attack against Iraq was engineered by two powerful groups within the Bush Administration, the ultra-nationalists and the neo-conservatives. The ultra-nationalists' motive was to gain control of the oil resources in the Middle East and elsewhere in the region in order to gain and sustain American global primacy. While the neo-conservatives shared this objective, they also wanted a radical restructuring of geopolitical relations in the area in order to promote the long-term security of Israel." See Robert Gilpin, "War Is Too Important to Be Left to Ideological Amateurs," *International Relations* 19, no. 1 (2005): 5–18, abstract, p. 5.
139. In the discussion that follows I draw on the accounts listed in note 92, this chapter. Also see Anthony Shadid, *Night Draws Near: Iraq's People in the Shadow of War* (New York: Henry Holt, 2005); Nir Rosen, *In the Belly of the Green Bird: The Triumph of the Martyrs in Iraq* (New York: Free Press, 2006); and Emma Sky, *The Unraveling: High Hopes and Missed Opportunities in Iraq* (New York: Public Affairs, 2016).
140. See Diamond, *Squandered Victory*, 297. Two good books on Iraq that do not share this benign view are Bacevich, *America's War for the Greater Middle East*, and Muttitt, *Fuel on the Fire*.
141. Bacevich, *America's War for the Greater Middle East*, esp. chap. 12.
142. Cited in Diamond, *Squandered Victory*, p. 31.
143. Cited ibid., p. 282.
144. Ibid., p. 282.
145. US ambassador Barbara Bodine subsequently told a documentary filmmaker in an interview that "there were instructions from Washington *not* to intervene to stop the looting." Muttitt, *Fuel on the Fire*, p. 44.
146. Ibid., chap. 3.
147. Ibid., p. 74.
148. For a close up study of the Muqtada-led movement, as well as other opposition movements, see Rosen, *In the Belly of the Green Bird*.
149. This theme that a nationalist opposition emerged early and that the United States refused to acknowledge it appears in many accounts of the US war in Iraq. See, for example, Bacevich, *America's War for the Greater Middle East*, chap. 13; Muttitt, *Fuel on the Fire*, chap. 9; and Diamond, *Squandered Victory*, chap. 2.

150. Muttitt, *Fuel on the Fire*, p. 39.
151. Phillips, *Losing Iraq*, p. 145.
152. Ibid., p. 148.
153. Cited in ibid., p. 146.
154. See Muttitt, *Fuel on the Fire*, chap. 7.
155. See, for example, Donald L. Horowitz, *Ethnic Groups in Conflict* (Berkeley: University of California Press, 1985).
156. Both the quotes are from Muttitt, *Fuel on the Fire*, p. 75–76.
157. These policies were announced at a World Bank/IMF jamboree in Dubai. See "Let's All Go to the Yard Sale," *Economist*, September 27, 2003. The information and quotes in this paragraph are from this article.
158. See Muttitt, *Fuel on the Fire*.
159. See note 1, this chapter, for the source from which this figure is taken.
160. Cited in Diamond, *Squandered Victory*, p. 51.
161. Cited in Muttitt, *Fuel on the Fire*, 95.
162. Rosen, *In the Belly of the Green Bird*, p. 3.
163. Ibid., p. 15.
164. Muttitt, *Fuel on the Fire*, p. 80.
165. Bacevich, *America's War for the Greater Middle East*, p. 258.
166. This theme is developed in Muttitt, *Fuel on the Fire*, chaps. 11 and 12. I am drawing here on Muttitt's work, esp. pp. 135–40.
167. See Bacevich, *America's War for the Greater Middle East*, pp. 264–66.
168. Muttitt, *Fuel on the Fire*, p. 140.
169. See Bacevich, *America's War for the Greater Middle East*, pp. 286–87.
170. Muttitt, *Fuel on the Fire*, Part 4.
171. For an overview of this phase, see Bacevich, *America's War for the Greater Middle East*, chap. 17.
172. Cited in Woodward, *Plan of Attack*, p. 190.

CONCLUSION

1. These quotes from Palmerston and Wilson were cited in chapter 2, note 2; and chapter 5, note 7, respectively.
2. The reference is to Eric Hobsbawm, *The Age of Empire, 1875–1914* (New York: Vintage Books, 1989).
3. The reference is to Walter LaFeber, *The American Search for Opportunity, 1865–1913*, vol. 2 of *The Cambridge History of American Foreign Relations* (Cambridge: Cambridge University Press, 1993).
4. See, for example, David B. Abernethy, *The Dynamics of Global Dominance: European Overseas Empires, 1415–1980* (New Haven, CT: Yale University Press, 2000), esp. p. 20.

5. See, for example, Tony Smith, *America's Mission: The United States and the Worldwide Struggle for Democracy* (Princeton, NJ: Princeton University Press, 2012).
6. See his *Imperialism and Social Classes*, 1919, reprinted in English: (New York: A. M. Kelly, 1951).
7. See Marilyn B. Young, *The Vietnam Wars, 1945–1990* (New York: Harper Collins, 1991). The mistake thesis notwithstanding, this remains one of the best books on the US intervention in Vietnam.
8. Both realism and Marxism provide well-established interpretations of imperialism. For one realist analysis, see Benjamin Cohen, *The Question of Imperialism* (New York: Basic Books, 1973). The variety of Marxist approaches to the study of imperialism are reviewed in Anthony Brewer, *Marxist Theories of Imperialism* (London: Routledge and Kegan Paul, 1980).
9. See Kenneth Waltz, *Theory of International Politics* (Reading, MA: Addison-Wesley, 1979). For a fuller discussion of varieties of realist thought, see John J. Mearsheimer, *The Tragedy of Great Power Politics* (New York: W. W. Norton, 2001).
10. Cohen, *Question of Imperialism*, p. 245.
11. An exception that argues for "offensive realism" is Mearsheimer, *Tragedy of Great Power Politics*.
12. For the "foundational" Marxist argument about the "relative autonomy of the state," see Nicos Poulantzas, *State, Power and Socialism*, Verso edition, trans. by Patrick Camiller (New York: Schocken Books, 1980); for a recent application of this type of Marxism to the study of imperialism, see Sam Gindin and Leo Panitch, *The Making of Global Capitalism: The Political Economy of American Empire* (London: Verso, 2012).
13. For a fuller discussion of the related ideas of Max Weber, see Reinhard Bendix, *Max Weber: An Intellectual Portrait* (Berkeley: University of California Press, 1978).
14. See Ronald Robinson and John Gallagher, *Africa and the Victorians: The Official Mind of Imperialism*, with Alice Denny (London: I.B. Tauris, 2015). First published in 1961.
15. For one realist answer to this question, see Mearsheimer, *Tragedy of Great Power Politics*.
16. This argument comes across more strongly in Robinson and Gallagher, *Africa and the Victorians*, though it was already evident—and to my mind, better stated—in their earlier, seminal article. See John Gallagher and Ronald Robinson, "The Imperialism of Free Trade," *Economic History Review*, 2nd ser., 6, no. 1 (1953): 1–15.
17. For a learned discussion of variety of such Marxist arguments, with a special focus on the relationship of capital accumulation to state formation, see Giovanni Arrighi, *The Long Twentieth Century: Money, Power, and the Origins of our Times* (London: Verso Books, 1994).
18. See Niall Ferguson, *Empire: The Rise and Demise of British World Order and the Lessons for Global Power* (New York: Basic Books, 2003). For broader-but-hurried claims along

these lines see Bruce Gilley, "The Case for Colonialism," *Third World Quarterly*, 2017. This controversial essay was subsequently withdrawn by the journal but is available at https://www.nas.org/academic-questions/31/2/the_case_for_colonialism.

19. See, for example, John Lewis Gaddis, *We Now Know: Rethinking Cold War History* (Oxford: Clarendon Press, 1997).
20. See Thucydides, *The Peloponnesian War* (Baltimore, MD: Penguin Books), p. 55.
21. For a good discussion of the role of institutions in the context of global power inequalities, see Robert O. Keohane, *After Hegemony: Cooperation and Discord in the World Political Economy*, rev. ed. (Princeton, NJ: Princeton University Press, 2005).
22. Three works are notable among the studies that I consulted, both for their insights and as sources for further bibliographical references: Rhys Jenkins, *How China Is Reshaping the Global Economy: Development Impact in Africa and Latin America* (New York: Oxford University Press, 2018);; Barbara Stallings, *Dependency in the 21st Century? The Political Economy of China-Latin American Relations* (New York: Cambridge University Press), forthcoming; and Deborah Brautigam, *The Dragon's Gift: The Real Story of China in Africa* (New York: Oxford University Press, 2009).
23. See Jenkins, *How China Is Reshaping the Global Economy*, table 3.1.
24. Ibid. chap. 4, p. 8 (online version).
25. See, for example, Elizabeth Economy, *The Third Revolution: Xi Jinping and the Chinese State* (New York: Oxford University Press, 2018); and Min Ye, "Fragmentation and Mobilization: Domestic Politics of the Belt and Road in China," *Journal of Contemporary China*, published online, January 26, 2019, available at: https://doi.org/10.1080/10670564.2019.1580428.
26. It is possible that China has used covert means to influence decisions in one developing country or another, but these have not come to light.
27. See, for example, Maria Abi-Habib, "How China Got Sri Lanka to Cough Up a Port," *New York Times*, June 25, 2018.
28. See Alexandra Stevenson, "China Yields on Malaysia Rail Project as Global Infrastructure Project Is Reexamined," *New York Times*, April 12, 2019.
29. To get a flavor of these debates, see Jenkins, *How China Is Reshaping the Global Economy*; Stallings, *Dependency in the 21st Century*; and Brautigam, *Dragon's Gift*.
30. I say mostly because the Chinese economy is heavily state-led, with a variety of subsidies and political considerations built into both production and exchange. All economic interactions with China are thus necessarily in part political.

Select Bibliography

Abernathy, David B. *The Dynamics of Global Dominance: European Overseas Empires, 1415–1980.* New Haven, CT: Yale University Press, 2000.

Abrahamian, Ervand. *The Coup: 1953, the CIA, and the Roots of Modern U.S.-Iranian Relations.* New York: New Press, 2013.

Acemoglu, Daron, Simon Johnson, and James A. Robinson. "The Colonial Origins of Comparative Development: An Empirical Investigation." *American Economic Review* 91, no. 5 (December 2001): 1369–1401.

Adeleye, R. A., and C. C. Stewart. "The Sokoto Caliphate in the Nineteenth Century." In J. F. A. Ajayi and Michael Crowder, eds., *History of West Africa*, vol. 2, 2nd ed., pp. 86–131. London: Longman, 1987.

Adelman, Jeremy. *Republic of Capital: Buenos Aires and the Legal Transformation of the Atlantic World.* Stanford, CA: Stanford University Press, 1999.

Aggarwal, Mamta. "Short Essay on Economic Drain during British India." History Discussion (website). Posted November 2, 2013. Accessed July 3, 2018. http://www.historydiscussion.net/history-of-india/short-essay-on-economic-drain-during-british-india/728.

Ahire, Philip Terdoo. *Imperial Policing: The Emergence and Role of Police in Colonial Nigeria, 1860–1960*. Philadelphia: Open University Press, 1991.

Ajayi, J. F. A. "The Aftermath of the Fall of Old Oyo." In J. F. A. Ajayi and Michael Crowder, eds., *History of West Africa*. vol. 2, pp. 129–66 New York: Columbia University Press, 1974.

Ajayi, J. F. A., and Michael Crowder, "West Africa, 1919–1939: The Colonial Situation." In J. F. A. Ajayi and Michael Crowder, eds., *History of West Africa*, vol. 2, 2nd ed., pp. 593–94. Harlow, UK: Longman, 1987.

Alam, Muzaffar, and Sanjay Subrahmanyam. *Writing the Mughal World: Studies on Culture and Politics*. New York: Columbia University Press, 2011.

Allen, Robert C. *The British Industrial Revolution in Global Perspective*. Cambridge: Cambridge University Press, 2009.

Al-Sayyid Marsot, Afaf Lutfi. "The British Occupation of Egypt from 1882." In Andrew Porter, ed., *The Nineteenth Century*, vol. 3 of *The Oxford History of the British Empire*, pp. 651–65. Oxford: Oxford University Press, 1999.

Al-Sayyid Marsot, Afaf Lutfi. *A History of Egypt: From the Arab Conquest to the Present.* 2nd ed. Cambridge: Cambridge University Press, 2007.

Al-Sayyid Marsot, Afaf Lutfi. *Egypt in the Reign of Muhammad Ali.* Cambridge: Cambridge University Press, 1984.

Anderson, David L., ed. *The Columbia History of the Vietnam War*. New York: Columbia University Press, 2011.

Appleby, John C. "War, Politics and Colonization, 1558–1625." In Nicholas Canny, ed., *The Origins of Empire*, vol. 1 of *The Oxford History of the British Empire*, pp. 55–78. Oxford: Oxford University Press, 2001.

Arrighi, Giovanni. *The Long Twentieth Century: Money, Power, and the Origins of Our Times*. London: Verso Books, 1994.

Ashton, T. S. *The Industrial Revolution.* Oxford: Oxford University Press, 1948.

Avery, P. G., R. G. Hambly, and C. Melville, eds. *Cambridge History of Iran*. Vol. 7: *From Nadir Shah to the Islamic Republic.* Cambridge: Cambridge University Press, 1991.

Bacevich, Andrew J. *American Empire: The Realities and Consequences of U.S. Diplomacy.* Cambridge, MA: Harvard University Press, 2002.

Bacevich, Andrew J. *America's War for the Greater Middle East: A Military History.* New York: Random House, 2016.

Bagchi, Amiya. *Private Investment in India, 1900–1939*. Cambridge: Cambridge University Press, 1972.

Baker, Ray S. *Woodrow Wilson and World Settlement.* Garden City, NY: Doubleday, Page and Company, 1922.

Ballantyne, Tony, and Antoinette Burton. "Empires and the Reach of the Global." In Emily S. Rosenberg, ed., *A World Connecting, 1870–1945*, pp. 285–434. Cambridge, MA: Belknap Press of Harvard University Press, 2012.

Baran, Paul. *The Political Economy of Growth*. New York: Monthly Review Press, 1957.

Bass, Gary J. *The Blood Telegram: Nixon, Kissinger, and a Forgotten Genocide.* New York: Alfred A. Knopf, 2013.

Batatu, Hanna. *The Old Social Classes and the Revolutionary Movements of Iraq.* Princeton, NJ: Princeton University Press, 1978.

Bates, Robert. *Markets and States in Tropical Africa*. Berkeley: University of California Press, 1981.

Bayly, C. A. *Imperial Meridian: The British Empire and the World, 1780–1830.* London: Longman, 1989.

Behrooz, Maziar. "The 1953 Coup in Iran and the Legacy of the Tudeh." In Mark J. Gasiorowski and Malcolm Byrne, eds., *Mohammad Mosaddeq and the 1953 Coup in Iran*, pp. 102–25. Syracuse, NY: Syracuse University Press, 2004.

Bello, Walden. *Dilemmas of Domination: The Unmaking of the American Empire*. New York: Henry Holt, 2005.

Bendix, Reinhard. *Max Weber: An Intellectual Portrait*. Berkeley: University of California Press, 1978.

Benjamin, Jules R. *The United States and Cuba: Hegemony and Dependent Development, 1880–1934*. Pittsburgh, PA: University of Pittsburgh Press, 1978.

Benjamin, Jules R. *The United States and the Origins of the Cuban Revolution*. Princeton, NJ: Princeton University Press, 1990.

Berg, Maxine, and Pat Hudson. "Rehabilitating the Industrial Revolution." *Economic History Review*, n.s., 45, no. 1 (February 1992): 24–50.

Bergerud, Eric M. *The Dynamics of Defeat: The Vietnam War in Hau Nghia Province*. Boulder, CO: Westview Press, 1991.

Berry, Sara. "Cocoa and Economic Development in Western Nigeria." In Carl K. Liedholm and Carl Eicher, eds., *Growth and Development in Nigerian Economy*, pp. 16–27. East Lansing: Michigan State University Press, 1970.

Bertola, Luis, and Jose Antonio Ocampo, eds. *Economic Development of Latin America since Independence*. Oxford: Oxford University Press, 2012.

Bhagwati, Jagdish. "The Capital Myth: The Difference between Trade in Widgets and in Dollars." *Foreign Affairs* 77, May/June 1998, pp. 7–12.

Bhattacharya, S. "Eastern India." In Dharma Kumar, ed., *The Cambridge Economic History of India*, vol. 2, pp. 270–95. Cambridge: Cambridge University Press, 1983.

Bill, James A. *The Eagle and the Lion: The Tragedy of American-Iranian Relations*. New Haven, CT: Yale University Press, 1988.

Bill, James A., and Wm. Roger Louis, eds. *Musaddiq, Iranian Nationalism, and Oil*. Austin: University of Texas Press, 1988.

Bills, Scott L. *Empire and Cold War: The Roots of US–Third World Antagonism, 1945–47*. New York: St. Martin's Press, 1990.

Block, Fred L. *The Origins of International Economic Disorder: A Study of the United States International Monetary Policy from World War II to the Present*. Berkeley: University of California Press, 1977.

Borden, William S. *The Pacific Alliance: United States Foreign Economic Policy and Japanese Trade Recovery, 1947–1955*. Madison: University of Wisconsin Press, 1984.

Bowen, H. V. *The Business of Empire: The East India Company and Imperial Britain, 1756–1833*. Cambridge: Cambridge University Press, 2006.

Bowen, H. V. "British India, 1765–1813: The Metropolitan Context." In P. J. Marshall, ed., *Oxford History of the British Empire: The Eighteenth Century*, vol. 2, pp. 530–51. Oxford: Oxford University Press, 1998.

Brands, H. W. *Bound to Empire: The United States and the Philippines*. New York: Oxford University Press, 1992.

Brands, H. W. *The Specter of Neutralism: The United States and the Emergence of the Third World, 1947–60*. New York: Columbia University Press, 1989.

Brautigam, Deborah. *The Dragon's Gift: The Real Story of China in Africa*. New York: Oxford University Press, 2009.

Bresser-Pereira, Luiz Carlos, and Carmen Augusta Varela. "The Second Washington Consensus and Latin America's Quasi-Stagnation." *Journal of Post Keynesian Economics* 27, no. 2 (Winter 2004/5): 231–50.

Brewer, Anthony. *Marxist Theories of Imperialism*. London: Routledge and Kegan Paul, 1980.

Broadberry, Stephen, Bruce M. S. Campbell, Mark Overton, Bas van Leeuwen, and Alexander Apotolides, "Historical National Accounts for Britain, 1300–1850," unpublished manuscript. https://www.academia.edu/385400/historical_national_accounts_for_britain_1300-1850_some_preliminary_estimates.

Broadberry, Stephen, Johann Custodis, and Bishnupriya Gupta. "India and the Great Divergence: An Anglo-Indian Comparison of Per Capita GDP, 1600–1871." *Explorations in Economic History* 58 (2015): 58–75.

Brown, Judith. "India." In *The Oxford History of the British Empire*, vol. 4: *The Twentieth Century*, edited by Judith Brown and Wm. Roger Louis, pp. 421–46. Oxford: Oxford University Press, 1999.

Brown, L. Carl. *International Politics and the Middle East: Old Rules, Dangerous Games*. Princeton, NJ: Princeton University Press, 1984.

Bulmer-Thomas, V., ed., *Britain and Latin America: A Changing Relationship*. New York: Cambridge University Press, 1989.

Burbank, Jane, and Fredrick Cooper. *Empires in World History*. Princeton, NJ: Princeton University Press, 2010.

Buttinger, Joseph. *Vietnam: A Dragon Embattled*. New York: Praeger, 1967.

Byrne, Malcolm, ed. "CIA Confirms Role in 1953 Iran Coup." *National Security Archive Electronic Briefing Book No. 435*. Posted August 19, 2013. https://nsarchive2.gwu.edu/NSAEBB/NSAEBB435/.

Cain, P. J., and Anthony Hopkins. *British Imperialism, 1688–2000*. 2nd ed. New York: Longman, 2002.

Calder, Bruce J. *The Impact of Intervention: The Dominican Republic during the U.S. Occupation of 1916–1924*. Austin: University of Texas Press, 1984.

Calleo, David. *Follies of Power: America's Unipolar Fantasy*. New York: Cambridge University Press, 2009.

Campbell, Charles S. "American Business Interests and the Open Door in China." *Far Eastern Quarterly* 1, no. 1 (November 1941): 43–58.

Cannandine, D. "The Past and Present in the English Industrial Revolution." *Past and Present* 103, no. 1 (May 1984):149–58.

Canny, Nicholas. "The Origins of Empire: An Introduction." In Nicholas Canny, ed., *Oxford History of the British Empire: The Origins of the Empire*, vol. 1, pp. 1–33. Oxford: Oxford University Press, 1998.

Cardoso, Fernando Henrique, and Enzo Faletto, *Dependency and Development in Latin America*. Berkeley: University of California Press, 1979.

Carter, Jimmy. "Address to the Nation on Energy and National Goals." July 15, 1979. https://millercenter.org/the-presidency/presidential-speeches/november-8-1977-address-nation-energy.

Cavarozzi, Marcelo J., and James F. Petras. "Chile." In Ronald H. Chilcote and Joel C. Edelstein, eds., *Latin America: The Struggle with Dependency and Beyond*, pp. 491–578. New York: John Wiley and Sons, 1983.

Chandra, Bipin, et al. *India's Struggle for Independence, 1857–1947*. New Delhi: Penguin, 1998.

Chandrasekaran, Rajiv. *Emerald City: Inside Baghdad's Green Zone*. New York: Alfred A. Knopf, 2006.

Chang, Ha-Joon. *Kicking Away the Ladder: Development Strategy in Historical Perspective*. London: Anthem Press, 2002.

Chaudhri, Tapan Ray. "The Mid-Eighteenth-Century Background." In Dharma Kumar, ed., *The Cambridge Economic History of India*, vol. 2, pp. 3–35. Cambridge: Cambridge University Press, 1983.

Chaudhuri, B. "Eastern India." In Dharma Kumar, ed., *The Cambridge Economic History of India*, vol. 2, pp. 295–331. Cambridge: Cambridge University Press, 1983.

Chaudhuri, K. N. *The East India Company: The Study of an Early Joint-Stock Company, 1600–1640*. London: F. Cass, 1965.

Chaudhuri, K. N. *The Economic Development of India under the East India Company*, Cambridge: Cambridge University Press, 1971.

Chaudhuri, K. N. "Foreign Trade and Balance of Payments." In Dharma Kumar, ed., *The Cambridge Economic History of India*, vol. 2, pp. 804–77. Cambridge: Cambridge University Press, 1983.

Chaudhuri, K. N. *The Trading World of Asia and the East India Company. 1660–1760*, Cambridge: Cambridge University Press, 1978.

Chaudhury, Sushil. *From Prosperity to Decline: 18th Century Bengal*. Delhi: Manohar, 1999.

Chomsky, Noam. *Hegemony or Survival: America's Quest for Global Dominance*. New York: Henry Holt and Company, 2003.

Clymer, Kenton. "Cambodia and Laos in the Vietnam War." In David L. Anderson, ed., *The Columbia History of the Vietnam War*, pp. 357–84. New York: Columbia University Press, 2011.

Cohen, Benjamin J. *The Question of Imperialism: The Political Economy of Dominance and Dependence*. New York: Basic Books, 1973.

Cohen, Stephen P. *The Indian Army: Its Contribution to the Development of a Nation*. Berkeley: University of California Press. 1971.

Cohen, Warren I. *America in the Age of Soviet Power, 1945–1991*. Cambridge History of American Foreign Relations 4. New York: Cambridge University Press, 1993.

Cohen, Warren I. *America's Failing Empire: U.S. Foreign Relations since the Cold War*. Malden, MA: Blackwell, 2005.

Cohen, Warren. *America's Response to China: A History of Sino-American Relations*. 5th ed. New York: Columbia University Press, 2010.

Coleman, James S. *Nigeria: Background to Nationalism.* Berkeley: University of California Press, 1958.

Colley, Linda. *Britons: Forging the Nation, 1707–1837*. 2nd ed. New Haven, CT: Yale University Press, 2005.

Collier, David, ed. *The New Authoritarianism in Latin America*. Princeton, NJ: Princeton University Press, 1979.

Collier, David, and Ruth Collier. *Shaping the Political Arena*. Princeton, NJ: Princeton University Press, 1991.

Collier, Simon, and William Sater. *A History of Chile, 1808–1994*. New York: Cambridge University Press, 1999.

Collins, Robert M. "Economic Crisis of 1968 and the Waning of the 'American Century.'" *American Historical Review* 101, no. 2 (April 1996): 396–422.

Corradi, Juan Eugenio. "Argentina." In Ronald Chilcote and Joel C. Edelstein, eds., *Latin America: The Struggle with Dependency and Beyond*, pp. 305–408. New York: John Wiley and Sons, 1983.

Costin, W. C. *Great Britain and China, 1833–1860*. Oxford: Clarendon Press, 1937.

Crafts, N. F. R. *British Economic Growth during the Industrial Revolution*. Oxford: Oxford University Press, 1985.

Crouzet, François. "Toward an Export Economy: British Exports during the Industrial Revolution." *Exploration in Economic History* 17 (January 1980): 48–93.

Crowder, Michael. "The 1939–45 War and West Africa." In J. F. A. Ajayi and Michael Crowder, eds., *History of West Africa*, vol. 2, pp. 665–92, 2nd ed. London: Longman, 1987.

Crowder, Michael. *The Story of Nigeria*. 4th ed. London: Faber and Faber, 1978.

Daniel, Jean. "Unofficial Envoy: An Historic Report from Two Capitals." *New Republic*, December 14, 1963, pp. 15–20.

Datta, Rajat. *Society, Economy and Market: Commercialization in Rural Bengal, c. 1760–1800*. New Delhi: Manohar, 2000.

Davis, Lance E., and Robert A. Huttenback. *Mammon and the Pursuit of Empire: The Economics of British Empire*. Cambridge: Cambridge University Press, 1988.

Davis, Lance E., Richard A. Easterlin, William N. Parker, et al. *American Economic Growth: An Economist's History of the United States*. New York: Harper and Row, 1972.

De Bellaigue, Christopher. *Patriot of Persia: Muhhammad Mossadegh and a Tragic Anglo-American Coup*. New York: Harper Collins, 2012.

De Paiva Abreu, Marcelo. "British Business in Brazil: Maturity and Demise (1850–1950)." *Revista Brazileira de Economia* 52, no. 4 (Oct.–Dec. 2000): 383–413.

Dernberger, Robert F. "The Role of the Foreigner in China's Economic Development." In Dwight H. Perkins, ed., *China's Modern Economy in Historical Perspective*, pp. 19–48. Stanford, CA: Stanford University Press, 1983.

Devlin, Robert, and Ricardo Ffrench-Davis. "The Great Latin American Debt Crisis: A Decade of Asymmetric Adjustment." *Revista de Economia Politica* 15, no. 3 (59), (July–September 1995).

Diamond, Larry. *Class, Ethnicity and Democracy in Nigeria: The Failure of the First Republic*. Syracuse, NY: Syracuse University Press, 1988.

Diamond, Larry. *Squandered Victory: The American Occupation and the Bungled Effort to Bring Democracy to Iraq*. New York: Henry Holt, 2006.

Dike, Onwuka K. *Trade and Politics in the Niger Delta, 1830–1885: An Introduction to the Economic and Political History of Nigeria*. London: Oxford University Press, 1956.

Dinges, John. *The Condor Years*. New York: New Press, 2004.

Divekar, V. D. "Western India." In Dharma Kumar, ed., *The Cambridge Economic History of India*, vol. 2, pp. 332–51. Cambridge: Cambridge University Press, 1983.

Dobson, John M. *America's Ascent: The United States Becomes a Great Power, 1880–1914*. DeKalb: Northern Illinois University Press, 1978.

Dominguez, Jorge I. *Cuba: Order and Revolution*. Cambridge, MA: Belknap Press of Harvard University Press, 1978.

Dorward, D. C. "British West Africa and Liberia." In A. D. Roberts, ed., *The Cambridge History of Africa, 1905–1940*, vol. 7, pp. 399–459. Cambridge: Cambridge University Press, 1986.

Doyle, Michael W. *Empires*. Ithaca, NY: Cornell University Press, 1986.

Duiker, William J. *Ho Chi Minh*. New York: Hyperion, 2000.

Duiker, William J. *Vietnam: Revolution in Transition*. Boulder, CO: Westview Press, 1995.

Dutt, Romesh Chunder. *Economic History of India in the Victorian Age*. London: K. Paul, Trench and Trubner, 1906.

Economy, Elizabeth. *The Third Revolution: Xi Jinping and the Chinese State*. New York: Oxford University Press, 2018.

Edwards, Sebastian. "Capital Flows to Latin America." In Martin Feldstein, ed., *International Capital Flows*, pp. 5–56. Chicago: University of Chicago Press, 1999.

Ekundare, R. Olufemi. *An Economic History of Nigeria, 1880–1960*. New York: Homes and Meir, 1973.

Erikson, Emily. *Between Monopoly and Free Trade: The English East India Company, 1600–1757*. Princeton, NJ: Princeton University Press, 2014.

Esfahani, Hadi Salehi, and M. Hashem Pesaran. "Iranian Economy in the Twentieth Century: A Global Perspective." *Iranian Studies* 42, no. 2 (April 2009): 177–211.

Esherick, Joseph. *The Origins of the Boxer Uprising*. Berkeley: University of California Press, 1987.

Evangelista, Matthew. "Stalin's Postwar Army Reappraised." *International Security* 11, no. 3 (Winter 1982–83): 110–38.

Evans, Peter. *Dependent Development: The Alliance of Multinational, State, and Local Capital in Brazil*. Princeton, NJ: Princeton University Press, 1995.

Everest, Larry. *Oil, Power and Empire: Iraq and the U.S. Global Agenda*. Monroe, ME: Common Courage Press, 2004.

Fahmy, Khaled. "The Era of Muhammad 'Ali Pasha, 1805–45." In M. W. Daly, ed., *The Cambridge History of Egypt*, vol. 2, pp. 139–79. Cambridge: Cambridge University Press, 1998.

Fairbank, John K. "The Creation of the Treaty System." In John K. Fairbank, ed., *The Cambridge History of China*, vol. 10, pp. 213–63. Cambridge: Cambridge University Press, 2008.

Fairbank, John King. *Trade and Diplomacy on the China Coast: The Opening of Treaty Ports, 1842–1854*. Stanford, CA: Stanford University Press, 1969.

Falk, Richard, A. *The Vietnam War and International Law*. 4 vols. Princeton, NJ: Princeton University Press, 1968–1976.

Farnie, D. A. *The English Cotton Industry and the World Market, 1815–1896*. Oxford: Clarendon Press, 1979.

Farouk-Sluglett, Marion, and Peter Sluglett. *Iraq since 1958: From Revolution to Dictatorship*. New York: I.B. Tauris, 1990.

Faruqui, Munis D. *The Princes of the Mughal Empire, 1504–1719*. Cambridge: Cambridge University Press, 2012.

Faught, Brad C. *Clive: Founder of British India*. Washington, DC: Potomac Books, 2013.

Fay, Peter Ward. *The Opium War, 1840–42*. Chapel Hill: University of North Carolina Press, 1975.

Ferguson, Niall. *Colossus: The Price of America's Empire*. New York: Penguin Press, 2004.

Ferguson, Niall. *Empire: The Rise and Demise of the British World Order and the Lessons for Global Power*. New York: Basic Books. 2003.

Ferns, H. S. *The Argentine Republic, 1516–1971*. New York: Barnes and Noble Books, 1973.

Ferns, H. S. *Britain and Argentina in the Nineteenth Century*. Oxford: Oxford University Press, 1960.

Feuerwerker, Albert. *The Chinese Economy, ca. 1870–191*. Michigan Papers in Chinese Studies 5. Ann Arbor: University of Michigan, Center for Chinese Studies, 1969.

Fieldhouse, D. K. *Colonialism, 1870–1945: An Introduction*. London: Weidenfeld and Nicolson, 1981.

Fieldhouse, D. K. *Economics and Empire, 1830–1914*. Ithaca, NY: Cornell University Press, 1973.

Fieldhouse, D. K. "The Metropolitan Economics of Empire." In Judith Brown and Wm. Roger Louis, eds., *The Oxford History of the British Empire: The Twentieth Century*, vol. 4, pp. 88–113. Oxford: Oxford University Press, 1999.

Flint, John E. *Sir George Goldie and the Making of Nigeria*. London: Oxford University Press, 1960.

Foner, Philip S. *The Spanish-Cuban-American War and the Birth of American Imperialism, 1895–1902*. Vol. 1. New York: Monthly Review Press, 1972.

Frank, Andre Gunder. *Dependent Accumulation and Underdevelopment*. London: MacMillan, 1978.

Fukuyama, Francis. *The End of History and the Last Man*. London: Hamish Hamilton, 1992.

Furtado, Celso. *The Economic Growth of Brazil: A Survey from Colonial to Modern Times*. Berkeley: University of California Press, 1963.

Gaddis, John Lewis. *Strategies of Containment: A Critical Reappraisal of American National Security Policy during the Cold War*. New York: Oxford University Press, 2005.

Gaddis, John Lewis. *We Now Know: Rethinking Cold War History*. Oxford: Clarendon Press, 1997.

Gallagher, John, and Ronald Robinson. "The Imperialism of Free Trade." *Economic History Review*, 2nd ser., 6, no. 1 (1953): 1–15.

Gardner, Richard N. *Sterling-Dollar Diplomacy in Current Perspective: The Origins and Prospects of Our International Economic Order*. New York: Columbia University Press, 1980.

Gasiorowski, Mark J. "Conclusion: Why Did Mosaddeq Fall?" In Mark J. Gasiorowski and Malcolm Byrne, eds. *Mohammad Mosaddeq and the 1953 Coup in Iran*, pp. 261–80. Syracuse, NY: Syracuse University Press, 2004.

Ghods, M. Reza. *Iran in the Twentieth Century: A Political History*. Boulder, CO: Lynne Rienner, 1989.

Gilens, Martin, and Benjamin Page. "Testing Theories of American Politics: Elites, Interest Groups and Average Citizens." *Perspectives on Politics* 12, no. 3 (September 2014): 563–81.

Gilley, Bruce. "The Case for Colonialism." *Third World Quarterly*, 2017. This controversial essay was subsequently withdrawn by the journal but was available in September 2019 at: https://www.nas.org/academic-questions/31/2/the_case_for_colonialism.

Gilpin, Robert. *The Political Economy of International Relations*. Princeton, NJ: Princeton University Press.

Gilpin, Robert. "War Is Too Important to Be Left to Ideological Amateurs." *International Relations* 19, no. 1 (2005): 5–18.

Gindin, Sam, and Leo Panitch. *The Making of Global Capitalism: The Political Economy of American Empire*. London: Verso, 2012.

Gleijeses, Piero. *Shattered Hope: The Guatemala Revolution and the United States, 1944–1954*. Princeton, NJ: Princeton University Press, 1991.

Go, Julian. *American Empire and the Politics of Meaning: Elite Political Cultures in the Philippines and Puerto Rico during U.S. Colonialism*. Durham, NC: Duke University Press, 2008.

Go, Julian. *Patterns of Empire: The British and American Empires, 1688 to the Present*. New York: Cambridge University Press, 2011.

Golay, Frank H. *Face of Empire: United States-Philippine Relations, 1899–1946*. Madison: Center for South East Asian Studies, University of Wisconsin, Monograph Number 14, 1998.

Goscha, Christopher. *Vietnam: A New History*. New York: Basic Books, 2016.

Gott, Richard. *Cuba: A New History*. New Haven, CT: Yale University Press, 2004.

Gowa, Joanne. *Closing the Gold Window: Domestic Politics and the End of Bretton Woods*. Ithaca, NY: Cornell University Press, 1983.

Graham, Richard. "Sepoys and Imperialists: Techniques of British Power in Nineteenth-Century Brazil." *Inter-American Economic Affairs* 23 (1969): 23–37.

Grandin, Greg. *The Blood of Guatemala: A History of Race and Nation*. Durham, NC: Duke University Press, 2000.

Greenberg, Michael. *British Trade and the Opening of China, 1800–1842*. Cambridge: Cambridge University Press, 1951.

Gustafson, Kristian. *Hostile Intent: U.S. Covert Operations in Chile, 1964–1974*. Washington DC: Potomac Books, 2007.

Habib, Irfan. "The Eighteenth Century in Indian History." In P. J. Marshall, ed., *The Eighteenth Century in Indian History: Evolution or Revolution?*, pp. 100–22, New Delhi: Oxford University Press, 2003.

Habib, Irfan. *The Agrarian System of Moghul India, 1556–1707*. Rev. ed. Delhi: Oxford University Press, 1999.

Hagopian, Amy, Abraham D. Flaxman, Tim K. Takoro, et al. "Mortality in Iraq, Associated with the 2003–2011 War and Occupation: Findings from a National Cluster Sample Survey by the University Collaborative Iraq Mortality Study." *PLOS Medicine*, Oct. 15, 2013, pp. 1–15.

Hammer, Ellen. *Vietnam: Yesterday and Today*. New York: Holt, Rinehart and Winston, 1966.

Hansen, B. *The Political Economy of Poverty, Equity and Growth: Egypt and Turkey*. Oxford: Oxford University Press, 1991.

Harnetty, Peter. "The Imperialism of Free Trade: Lancashire and the Indian Cotton during 1859–1862." *Economic History Review*, 2nd ser., 18 (1965): 333–45.

Harrison, Robert T. *Gladstone's Imperialism in Egypt: Techniques of Domination*. Westport, CT: Greenwood Press, 1995.

Harvey, David. *The New Imperialism*. New York: Oxford University Press, 2003.

Hasan, Farhat. *State and Locality in Mughal India: Power relations in Western India, c. 1572–1730*. Cambridge: Cambridge University Press, 2004.

Haslam, Jonathan. *The Nixon Administration and the Death of Allende's Chile*. New York: Verso, 2005.

Healy, David. *Drive to Hegemony: The United States in the Caribbean, 1898–1917*. Madison: University of Wisconsin Press, 1988.

Hearden, Patrick J. *The Tragedy of Vietnam*. New York: Harper Collins, 1991.

Heiss, Mary Ann. "The International Boycott of Iranian Oil and the Anti-Mosaddeq Coup of 1953." In Mark J. Gasiorowski and Malcolm Byrne, eds., *Mohammad Mosaddeq and the 1953 Coup in Iran*, pp. 178–200. Syracuse, NY: Syracuse University Press, 2004.

Helleiner, Gerald K. *Peasant Agriculture, Government, and Economic Growth in Nigeria*. Homewood, IL: Richard D. Irwin, 1966.

Heller, Patrick, Dietrich Rueschemeyer, and Richard Snyder, eds. *Dependency and Development in a Globalized World*. Special issue of *Studies in Comparative International Development* 44, no. 4 (December 2009).

Herrera, Rémy. "When the Names of Emperors Were Morgan and Rockefeller ... Prerevolutionary Cuba's Dependency with Regard to U.S. High Finance." *International Journal of Political Economy* 34, no. 4 (Winter 2004/5): 24–48.

Herring, George C. *America's Longest War: The United States and Vietnam, 1950–1975*. 5th ed. Boston: McGraw Hill, 2014.

Hess, Gary R. *Vietnam: Explaining America's Lost War*. Chichester, UK: Wiley Blackwell, 2015.

Hill, Christopher. *Reformation to Industrial Revolution: A Social and Economic History of Britain, 1530–1780*. London: Weidenfeld and Nicolson, 1968.

Hill, Howard C. "The Taking of Panama." In William Appleman Williams, ed., *The Shaping of American Diplomacy, , 1750–1914*, pp. 506–10, Chicago: Rand McNally, 1956.

Hill, Polly. *Population, Prosperity and Poverty: Rural Kano, 1900 and 1970*. Cambridge: Cambridge University Press, 1970.

Hirschman, Albert. *National Power and the Structure of Foreign Trade*. Berkeley: University of California Press, 1980.

Ho Chi Minh. "Proclamation of the Viet Minh-led Independence struggle, 6 June 1941." In Michael H. Hunt, ed., *A Vietnam War Reader: A Documentary History from American and Vietnamese Perspectives*, p. 12. Chapel Hill: University of North Carolina Press, 2010.

Ho Chi Minh. "Statement on behalf of the new Indochinese Communist Party, 18 February 1930." In Michael H. Hunt, ed., *A Vietnam War Reader: A Documentary History from American and Vietnamese Perspectives*, pp. 10–12. Chapel Hill: University of North Carolina Press, 2010.

Hobsbawm, Eric. *The Age of Empire, 1875–1914*. New York: Vintage Books, 1989.

Hobsbawm, Eric J. *Industry and Empire: From 1750 to the Present Day*. New York: New Press, 1999.

Hobson, J. A. *Imperialism: A Study*. New York: James Pott and Company, 1902.

Hogan, Michael J. *The Marshall Plan: America, Britain, and the Reconstruction of Western Europe, 1947–52*. New York: Cambridge University Press, 1987.

Hooley, Richard. "American Economic Policy in the Philippines, 1902–1940." *Journal of Asian Economics* 16, no. 3 (2005): 464–88.

Hopkins, A. G. *American Empire: A Global History*. Princeton, NJ: Princeton University Press, 2018.

Hopkins, A. G. *An Economic History of West Africa*. London: Longman, 1973.

Horowitz, Donald L. *Ethnic Groups in Conflict*. Berkeley: University of California Press, 1985.

Hou, Chi-Ming, *Foreign Investment and Economic Development in China*. Cambridge MA: Harvard University Press, 1965.

Hsu, Immanuel C. Y. "Late Ch'ing Foreign Relations, 1866–1905." In John K. Fairbank and Kwang-Ching Liu, eds. *Cambridge History of China*, vol. 11, *Late Ching 1800–1911*, part 2, pp. 70–141. Cambridge: Cambridge University Press, 1980.

Huang, Philip C. C., ed. *The Development of Underdevelopment in China: A Symposium*. New York: M. E. Sharpe, 1980.

Human Rights Watch. *War in Iraq: Not a Humanitarian Intervention*, January 25, 2004. https://www.hrw.org/news/2004/01/25/war-iraq-not-humanitarian-intervention.

Hunt, Michael H. *A Vietnam War Reader: A Documentary History from American and Vietnamese Perspectives*. Chapel Hill: University of North Carolina Press, 2010.

Hunter, F. Robert. "Egypt under the Successors of Muhammad Ali." In M. W. Daly, ed., *The Cambridge History of Egypt*, vol. 2, 180–97. Cambridge: Cambridge University Press, 1998.

Hurd, Douglas. *The Arrow War: An Anglo-Chinese Confusion, 1856–1860*. London: Collins, 1967.

Hutchcroft, Paul. *Booty Capitalism: The Politics of Banking in the Philippines*. Ithaca, NY: Cornell University Press, 1998.

Hyam, Ronald. *Britain's Imperial Century, 1815–1914: A Study of Empire and Expansion*. London: B. T. Batsford, 1976.

Ibrahim, Hassan Ahmed. "The Egyptian Empire, 1805–85." In M. W. Daly, ed., *The Cambridge History of Egypt*, vol. 2, 198–216. Cambridge: Cambridge University Press, 1998.

Ikenberry, G. John. *After Victory: Institutions, Strategic Restraint and the Rebuilding of Order after Major Wars*. Princeton, NJ: Princeton University Press, 2001.

Immerman, Richard H. *The CIA in Guatemala: The Foreign Policy of Intervention*. Austin: University of Texas Press, 1982.

Irigoin, Alejandra. "A Trojan Horse in Daoguang China? Explaining the Flows of Silver in and out of China." Working paper 173/13. Department of Economic History, London School of Economics, 2013.

Iriye, Akira. *The Cold War in Asia: A Historical Introduction*. Englewood Cliffs, NJ: Prentice Hall, 1974.

Issawi, Charles. "Egypt since 1800: A Study in Lop-sided Development." *Journal of Economic History* 21, no. 1 (March 1961): 1–25.

Issawi, Charles. *An Economic History of the Middle East and North Africa*. New York: Columbia University Press, 1982.

Jackson, Peter, and Laurence Lockhart, eds. *Cambridge History of Iran*. Vol. 6: *The Timurid and Safavid Periods*. Cambridge: Cambridge University Press, 1986.

Jenkins, Rhys. *How China Is Reshaping the Global Economy: Development Impact in Africa and Latin America*. New York: Oxford University Press, 2018.

Johnson, Chalmers. *The Sorrows of Empire*. New York: Metropolitan Books, 2004.

Johnson, Simon, and James Kwak. *13 Bankers: The Wall Street Takeover and the Next Financial Meltdown*. New York: Vintage Books, 2011.

Kahin, George McT. *Vietnam: How America Became Involved in Vietnam*. New York: Alfred A. Knopf, 1986.

Kaplan, Lawrence. *The United States and NATO: The Formative Years*. Lexington: University of Kentucky Press, 1984.

Kapur, Devesh, John P. Lewis, and Richard Webb. *The World Bank: Its First Half Century*. Vol. 1. Washington, DC: Brookings Institution, 1997.

Karnow, Stanley. *In Our Image: America's Empire in the Philippines*. New York: Random House, 1989.

Katouzian, Homa. *Musaddiq and the Struggle of Power in Iran*. Rev. ed. London: I.B. Tauris, 1999.

Kennedy, Paul. *The Rise and Fall of the Great Powers: Economic Change and Military Conflict from 1500 to 1989*. New York: Vintage, 1989.

Kentikelenis, Alexander, and Sarah Babb. "Norm Substitution and the Rise of Structural Adjustment in the IMF." Mimeo, University of Oxford, 2018.

Keohane, Robert O. *After Hegemony: Cooperation and Discord in the World Political Economy*. Rev. ed. Princeton, NJ: Princeton University Press, 2005.

Khalidi, Rashid. *Resurrecting Empire: Western Footprints and America's Perilous Path in the Middle East*. Boston: Beacon Press, 2004.

Khalilzad, Zalmay, and Paul Wolfowitz. "Overthrow Him." *Weekly Standard*, December 1, 1997.

Kimball, Jeffrey P. "Richard M. Nixon and the Vietnam War." In David L. Anderson, ed., *The Columbia History of the Vietnam War*, pp. 217–246. New York: Columbia University Press, 2011.

Kindleberger, Charles P. *The Marshall Plan Days*. Boston: Allen and Unwin, 1987.

King, Frank H. H. *The History of the Hong Kong and Shanghai Banking Corporation*. 2 vols. Cambridge and New York: Cambridge University Press, 1987.

Kingstone, Peter. *The Political Economy of Latin America: Reflections on Neoliberalism and Development*. New York: Routledge, 2011.

Kinzer, Stephen. *All the Shah's Men: An American Coup and the Roots of Middle Eastern Terro*r. Hoboken, NJ: John Wiley and Sons, 2003.

Kinzer, Stephen. *Overthrow: America's Century of Regime Change from Hawaii to Iraq*. New York: Times Books, Henry Holt, 2006.

Kissinger, Henry. "The Vietnam Negotiations." *Foreign Affairs*, January 1969 47. no. 2, pp. 211–34.

Knight. Alan. "Britain and Latin America." In Andrew Porter, ed., *The Oxford History of the British Empire. the Nineteenth Century*, vol. 3, pp. 122–45. Oxford: Oxford University Press, 1999.

Kohli. Atul, "Coping with Globalization: Asian versus Latin American Strategies of Development, 1980–2010." *Brazilian Journal of Political Economy* 32, no. 4, (Oct.–Dec. 2012): 531–56.

Kohli, Atul. "Nationalist versus Dependent Capitalist Development: Alternate Pathways of Asia and Latin America in a Globalized World." *Studies in Comparative International Development* 44, no. 4 (December 2009): 386–410.

Kohli, Atul. *The State and Poverty in India: The Politics of Reform*. New York: Cambridge University Press, 1987.

Kohli, Atul. *State-Directed Development: Political Power and Industrialization in the Global Periphery*. New York: Cambridge University Press, 2004.

Kolko, Gabriel. *Anatomy of a War: Vietnam, the United States, and the Modern Historical Experience*. New York: Pantheon Books, 1985.

Kolko, Gabriel. *Confronting the Third World: United States Foreign Policy, 1945–1980*. New York: Pantheon Books, 1988.

Kornbluh, Peter. *The Pinochet File: A Declassified Dossier of Atrocity and Accountability*. National Security Archive Book. New York: New Press, 2004.

Kuhn, Philip A. "The Taiping Rebellion." In John K. Fairbank, ed., *The Cambridge History of China*, vol. 10, pp. 264–317. Cambridge: Cambridge University Press, 2008.

Kuhn, Philip A. *Rebellion and Its Enemies in Late Imperial China: Militarization and Social Structure, 1796–1864*. Cambridge, MA: Harvard University Press, 1970.

Kumar, Dharma, ed. *The Cambridge Economic History of India*, vol. 2: *c.1757–c.1970*. Cambridge: Cambridge University Press, 1983.

Kumar, Dharma. "The Fiscal System." In Dharma Kumar, ed., *The Cambridge Economic History of India*, pp. 905–46. Cambridge: Cambridge University Press, 1983.

Kumar, Dharma. "South India." In Dharma Kumar, ed., *The Cambridge Economic History of India*, pp. 352–75. Cambridge: Cambridge University Press, 1983.

Kumar, Krishan. *Visions of Empire: How Five Imperial Regimes Shaped the World*. Princeton, NJ: Princeton University Press, 2017.

LaFeber, Walter. *The American Search for Opportunity, 1865–1913*. Cambridge History of American Foreign Relations 2. Cambridge: Cambridge University Press, 1993.

LaFeber, Walter. *America, Russia and the Cold War, 1945–1996*. 8th ed. New York: McGraw-Hill, 1997.

LaFeber, Walter. *Inevitable Revolutions: The United States in Central America*. New York: W. W. Norton, 1983.

LaFeber, Walter. *The New Empire: An Interpretation of American Imperialism, 1860–1898*. Ithaca, NY: Cornell University Press, 1963.

LaFeber, Walter, Richard Polenberg. and Nancy Woloch. *The American Century: A History of the United States since the 1890s*. 7th ed. Armonk, NY: M. E. Sharpe, 2013.

Landes, David S. *Bankers and Pashas: International Finance and Economic Imperialism in Egypt*. Cambridge, MA: Harvard University Press, 1958.

Landes, David. *The Unbound Prometheus: Technological Change and Industrial Development in Western Europe, 1750 to Present*. Cambridge: Cambridge University Press, 2003.

Last, Murray. "The Sokoto Caliphate and Borno." In J. F.A. Ajayi, ed., *UNESCO General History of Africa*, vol. 1: *Africa in the Nineteenth Century until the 1880s*, pp. 555–99. Berkeley, University of California Press, 1989.

Law, Robin. "Introduction" In Robin Law, ed., *From Slave Trade to "Legitimate" Commerce: The Commercial Transition in Nineteenth-Century West Africa*, pp. 1–32. Cambridge: Cambridge University Press, 1995.

Lawson, Philip. *The East India Company: A History*. London: Longman, 1993.

Leff, Nathaniel H. *Underdevelopment and Development in Brazil.* Vol. 1. London: George Allen and Unwin, 1982.

Leffler, Melvyn P. *A Preponderance of Power: National Security, the Truman Administration, and the Cold War.* Stanford, CA: Stanford University Press, 1992.

Leffler, Melvyn P., and Odd Arne Westad, eds. *Cambridge History of the Cold War.* Vol. 1: *Origins.* New York: Cambridge University Press, 2010.

Lenin, Vladimir I. *Imperialism, the Highest Stage of Capitalism: A Popular Outline.* London: Lawrence and Wishart, 1944. Original edition published in Russian in 1916.

Levinson, Jerome, and Juan de Onís. *The Alliance That Lost Its Way: A Critical Account of the Alliance for Progress.* Chicago: Quadrangle Books, 1972.

Lichtenstein, Nelson. "A Fabulous Failure: Clinton's 1990s and the Origins of Our Times." *American Prospect*, January 29, 2018.

Lieberthal, Kenneth. *Governing China: From Revolution through Reform.* New York: W. W. Norton, 1995.

Liedholm, Carl. "The Influence of Colonial Policy on the Growth and Development of Nigeria's Industrial Sector." In Carl K. Liedholm and Carl Eicher, eds., *Growth and Development in Nigerian Economy*, pp. 52–61. East Lansing: Michigan State University Press, 1970.

Lissakers. Karin, *Banks, Borrowers and the Establishment: A Revisionist Account of the International Debt Crisis.* New York: Basic Books, 1991.

Llorca-Jaña, Manuel. *The British Textile Trade in South America in the Nineteenth Century.* New York: Cambridge University Press, 2012.

Lloyd, Peter C. *The Political Development of Yoruba Kingdoms in the Eighteenth and Nineteenth Centuries.* Occasional Paper No. 31. London: Royal Anthropological Institute, 1971.

Lofgren, Mark. *The Deep State: The Fall of the Constitution and the Rise of a Shadow Government.* New York: Penguin Books, 2016.

Long, Ngo Vinh. *Before the Revolution: The Vietnamese Peasants under the French.* Cambridge, MA: MIT Press, 1973.

Louis, Wm. Roger. "The Dissolution of the British Empire." In Judith Brown and Wm. Roger Louis, eds., *The Oxford History of the British Empire: The Twentieth Century*, vol. 4, pp. 329–56. Oxford: Oxford University Press, 1999.

Louis, Wm. Roger, ed. *The Robinson and Gallagher Controversy.* New York: Franklin Watts, 1976.

Lovejoy, Paul E. "Plantations in the Economy of the Sokoto Caliphate." *Journal of African History* 19, no. 3 (1978): 341–68.

Lovell, Julia. *The Opium Wars: Drugs, Dreams and the Making of China.* London: Picador, 2011.

Loveman, Brian. *Chile: The Legacy of Hispanic Capitalism.* 3rd ed. New York: Oxford University Press, 2001.

Lowe, Peter. *Britain and the Far East: A Survey from 1819 to the Present*. London: Longman, 1981.

Lugard, Frederick. *The Dual Mandate in British Tropical Africa*. London: W. Blackwood and Sons, 1922.

Lynn, Martin. "British Policy, Trade, and Informal Empire in the Mid-Nineteenth Century." In Andrew Porter, ed., *The Oxford History of the British Empire, the Nineteenth Century*, vol. 3, pp. 101–21. Oxford: Oxford University Press, 1999.

MacIntyre, Andrew, T. J. Pempel, and John Ravenhill, eds. *Crisis as Catalyst: Asia's Dynamic Political Economy*. Ithaca, NY: Cornell University Press, 2008.

Maddison, Angus. *Contours of the World Economy, 1–2030 A.D.* Oxford: Oxford University Press, 2007.

Maddison, Angus. *Monitoring the World Economy, 1820–1992*. Paris: Organisation for Economic Cooperation and Development, 1995.

Mahoney, James. *Colonialism and Post-Colonial Development: Spanish America in a Comparative Perspective*. New York: Cambridge University Press, 2010.

Maier, Charles S. *Among Empires: American Ascendancy and Its Predecessors*. Cambridge, MA: Harvard University Press, 2006.

Mamdani, Mahmood. *Citizen and Subject: Contemporary Africa and the Legacy of Late Colonialism*. Princeton, NJ: Princeton University Press, 1996.

Manchester, Alan K. *British Preeminence in Brazil, Its Rise and Decline: A Study in European Expansion*. Chapel Hill: University of North Carolina Press, 1933.

Marlowe, John. *Cromer in Egypt*. London: Elek, 1970.

Marlowe, John. *A History of Modern Egypt and Anglo-Egyptian Relations*. Hamden, CT: Archon Books, 1965.

Marlowe, John. *World Ditch: The Making of the Suez Canal*. London: Macmillan, 1964.

Marshall, P. J. "The British in Asia: Trade to Dominion, 1700–1765." In P. J. Marshall, ed., *Oxford History of the British Empire: The Eighteenth Century*, vol. 2, pp. 487–507. Oxford: Oxford University Press, 1998.

Marshall, P. J. "The English in Asia to 1700." In Nicholas Canny, ed., *The Oxford History of the British Empire, The Origins of Empire*, vol. 1, pp. 264–85. Oxford: Oxford University Press, 2001.

Marshall, P. J. *Problems of Empire: Britain and India, 1757–1813*. London: Allen and Unwin, 1968.

Mason, Philip. *A Matter of Honor: An Account of the Indian Army, Its Officers and Men*. New York: Holt, Rinehart and Winston, 1974.

May, Ernst. *American Imperialism: A Speculative Essay*. New York: Athenaeum, 1968.

May, Glen Anthony. *Social Engineering in the Philippines: The Aims, Execution, and Impact of American Colonial Policy, 1900–1913*. Westport, CT.: Greenwood Press, 1980.

Mayer, Arno. "Two Parties, One Imperial Mission: the US Empire Will Survive Bush." *Le Monde Diplomatique*, October 29, 2008.

McAlister, John T., Jr. *Vietnam: The Origins of Revolution*. New York: Doubleday, 1971.

McCormick, Thomas J. "American Hegemony and the Roots of Vietnam War." In Patrick J. Hearden, *Vietnam: Four American Perspectives*, pp. 81–108. West Lafayette, IN: Purdue University Press, 1990.

McCormick, Thomas J. *America's Half-Century: United States Foreign Policy in the Cold War and After*. 2nd ed. Baltimore: Johns Hopkins University Press, 1995.

McCormick, Thomas J. *China Market: America's Quest for Informal Empire, 1893–1901*. Chicago: Quadrangle Books, 1967.

McCullough, David. *The Path between the Seas: The Creation of the Panama Canal, 1870–1914*. New York: Simon and Schuster, 1977.

McDowall, David. *A Modern History of the Kurds*. London: I.B. Tauris, 2004.

McGovern, George S. "America in Vietnam." In Patrick J. Hearden, *Vietnam: Four American Perspectives*, pp. 11–36. West Lafayette, IN: Purdue University Press, 1990.

McKinley, William. "Message to the Congress Requesting a Declaration of War with Spain." American Presidency Project (website), April 11, 1898. https://www.presidency.ucsb.edu/documents/message-congress-requesting-declaration-war-with-spain.

Mearsheimer, John J. *The Tragedy of Great Power Politics*. New York: W. W. Norton, 2001.

Metcalf, Thomas R. *The Aftermath of Revolt: India, 1857–1870*. Princeton, NJ: Princeton University Press, 1964.

Military History Institute of Vietnam. *Victory in Vietnam: The Official History of the People's Army of Vietnam, 1954–1975*. Translated by Merle L. Pribbenow. Lawrence: University of Kansas Press, 2002.

Mill, John Stuart. *Essays on Equality, Law, and Education*. Vol. 21 of *Collected Works of John Stuart Mill*. Toronto: University of Toronto Press, 1984.

Miller, Rory. *Britain and Latin America in the Nineteenth and Twentieth Century*. London: Longman, 1993.

Milward, Alan S. *The Reconstruction of Western Europe, 1945–1951*. Berkeley: University of California Press, 1984.

Misra, Amresh. *War of Civilizations: India, 1857 AD*. 2 vols. Allahabad, India: Rupa Publishers, 2008.

Misra, B. B. *The Bureaucracy in India: A Historical Analysis of Development up to 1947*. Delhi: Oxford University Press, 1977.

Mommsen, Wolfgang J. *Theories of Imperialism*. Chicago: University of Chicago Press, 1980.

Moore, Barrington, Jr. *Social Origins of Dictatorship and Democracy: Lord and Peasant in the Making of the Modern World*. Boston: Beacon Press, 1966.

Moore, Robin J. "Imperial India, 1858–1914." In Andrew Porter, ed., *The Oxford History of the British Empire: The Nineteenth Century*, vol. 3, pp. 422–46. Oxford: Oxford University Press, 2001.

Moosvi, S. *People, Taxation and Trade in Mughal India*. Oxford: Oxford University Press, 2008.

Morefield, Jeanne. *Empires without Imperialism: Anglo-American Decline and the Politics of Deflection*. New York: Oxford University Press, 2014.

Moreland, W. H. *The Agrarian System of Moslem India*. Allahabad: Central Book Depot, 1929.

Morris, Morris D. "The Growth of Large-Scale Industry to 1947." In Dharma Kumar, ed., *The Cambridge Economic History of India*, vol. 2, pp. 553–576. Cambridge: Cambridge University Press, 1983.

Moulder, Frances V. *Japan, China and the World Economy*. Cambridge: Cambridge University Press, 1977.

Mukherjee, Madhushree. *Churchill's Secret War: The British Empire and the Ravaging of India during World War II*. New York: Basic Books, 2010.

Muttitt, Greg. *Fuel on the Fire: Oil and Politics in Occupied Iraq*. New York: New Press, 2012.

Myrdal, Gunnar. *Asian Drama: An Inquiry into the Poverty of Nations*. New York: Pantheon, 1968.

Naoroji, Dadabhai. *Poverty and Un-British Rule in India*. London: Swan Sonnenschein and Company, 1901.

Nguyen, Lien-Hang T. *Hanoi's War: An International History of the War for Peace in Vietnam*. Chapel Hill: University of North Carolina Press, 2012.

Nicolson, I. F. *The Administration of Nigeria, 1900–1960*. Oxford: Clarendon Press, 1969.

North, Douglas. *Institutions, Institutional Change and Economic Performance*. Cambridge: Cambridge University Press, 1990.

O'Brien, Patrick. "The Long-Term Growth of Agricultural Production in Egypt: 1821–1962." In P. M. Holt, ed., *Political and Social Change in Modern Egypt*, pp. 162–95. London: Oxford University Press, 1968.

O'Brien, Patrick K. "The Political Economy of British Taxation, 1660–1815." *Economic History Review*, n.s., 41, no. 1 (February 1988): 1–32.

O'Donnell, Guillermo. *Modernization and Bureaucratic Authoritarianism*. Berkeley: Institute of International Studies, University of California, 1973.

Omissi, David E. *The Sepoy and the Raj: The Indian Army, 1860–1940*. Basingstoke, UK: Macmillan, 1994.

Osterhammel, Jürgen. "Britain and China, 1842–1914." In Andrew Porter, ed., *Oxford History of the British Empire: The Nineteenth Century*, vol. 3, pp. 146–69. Oxford: Oxford University Press, 1999.

Osterhammel, Jürgen. "British Business in China, 1860s–1950s." In P. T. Davenport-Hines and Geoffrey Jones, eds., *British Business in Asia since 1860*, pp. 189–216. Cambridge: Cambridge University Press, 1989.

Owen, Roger. *The Middle East and the World Economy, 1800–1914*. London: Methuen, 1981.

Packenham, Robert A. *Liberal America and the Third World: Political Development Idea in Foreign Aid and Social Science*. Princeton, NJ: Princeton University Press, 1976.

Palma, Gabriel. "Dependency: A Formal Theory of Underdevelopment or a Methodology for the Analysis of Concrete Situations of Underdevelopment?" *World Development* 6, no. 7–8 (1978): 881–924.

Palma, Gabriel. "External Disequilibrium and Internal Industrialization: Chile, 1914–1935." In Christopher Abel and Colin M. Lewis, eds., *Latin America, Economic Imperialism and the State: The Political Economy of the External Connection from Independence to the Present*, pp. 318–38. London: Athlone Press, 1985.

Pamuk, Şevket. "Anatolia and Egypt during the Nineteenth Century: A Comparison of Foreign Trade and Foreign Investment." In Şevket Pamuk, *The Ottoman Economy and Its Institutions*, pp. 37–55. Farnham, UK: Ashgate, 2009.

Panitch, Leo, and Sam Gindin. "Finance and American Empire." In Leo Panitch and Martijn Konings, eds., *American Empire and the Political Economy of Global Finance*, pp. 17–47. New York: Palgrave Macmillan, 2008.

Panizza, Francisco. *Contemporary Latin America: Development and Democracy beyond the Washington Consensus*. London: Zed Books, 2009.

Parker, Jason. *Hearts, Minds, Voices: US Cold War Public Diplomacy and the Formation of the Third World*. New York; Oxford University Press, 2016.

Parthasarthi, Prasannan. *Why Europe Grew Rich and Asia Did Not: Global Divergence, 1600–1850*. New York: Cambridge University Press, 2011.

Pepinsky, Thomas. "Trade Competition and American Decolonization." *World Politics* 67, no. 3 (July 2015): 387–422.

Pérez, Louis A. *Cuba between Empires, 1878–1902*. Pittsburgh, PA: University of Pittsburgh Press, 1983.

Pérez, Louis A. *Cuba: Between Reform and Revolution*. 5th ed. New York: Oxford University Press, 2015.

Pérez, Louis. *Cuba under the Platt Amendment, 1902–1934*. Pittsburgh, PA: University of Pittsburgh Press, 1986.

Perham, Margery. *Lugard: The Years of Authority, 1898–1945*. London: Oxford University Press, 1960.

Phillips, David L. *Losing Iraq: Inside the Postwar Reconstruction Fiasco*. New York: Basic Books, 2005.

Piketty, Thomas. *Capital in the Twenty-First Century*. Cambridge MA: Belknap Press of Harvard University Press, 2014.

Pim, A. W. "Public Finance." In Margery Perham, ed., *Mining Commerce and Finance in Nigeria*, pp. 225–79. London: Faber and Faber, 1948.

Platt, D. C. M. "Dependency in Latin America: A Historian Objects." *Latin American Research Review* 15, no. 1 (1980): 113–30.

Platt, D. C. M. "Further Objections to an 'Imperialism of Free Trade,' 1830–60." *Economic History Review*, 2nd ser., 26, no. 1 (1973): 77–91.

Platt, D. C. M., ed. *Business Imperialism: An Inquiry Based on British Experience in Latin America*. Oxford: Clarendon Press, 1977.

Platt, D. C. M. *Latin America and British Trade, 1806–1914*. London: A. and C. Black, 1972.

Platt, Stephen R. *Autumn in the Heavenly Kingdom: China, the West and the Epic Story of the Taiping Civil War*. New York: Alfred A. Knopf, 2012.

Pomeroy, William J. *The Philippines: Colonialism, Collaboration and Resistance*. New York: International Publishers, 1992.

Potter, David C. *India's Political Administrators: From ICS to IAS*. Delhi: Oxford University Press, 1996.

Poulantzas, Nicos. *State, Power and Socialism*. Verso ed. Translated by Patrick Camiller. New York: Schocken Books, 1980.

Prados de la Escosura, Leandro. "Lost Decades? Economic Performance in Post-Independence Latin America." *Journal of Latin American Studies* 41, no. 2 (May 2009): 279–307.

Puryear, V. J. *International Economics and Diplomacy in the Near East, 1834–4*. Hamden, CT: Archon Books, 1969. First published in 1935.

Quiliconi, Cintia. "U.S.-Latin American Trade Relations." *Anti-Americanism Working Papers*. 2005. Center for Policy Studies, Central European University: Budapest, Hungary, 2005.

Qureshi, Lubna Z. *Nixon, Kissinger, and Allende: U.S. Involvement in the 1973 Coup in Chile*. Lanham, MD: Lexington Books, 2009.

Ray, Rajat K. *Industrialization in India: Growth and Conflict in the Private Corporate Sector, 1914–47*. Delhi: Oxford University Press, 1979.

Ray, Ratnalekha. *Change in Bengal Agrarian Society, c. 1760–1850*. Delhi: Manohar, 1979.

Reid, Donald M. "The 'Urabi Revolution and the British Conquest, 1879–1882." In M. W. Daly, ed., *The Cambridge History of Egypt*, vol. 2, pp. 217–38. Cambridge: Cambridge University Press, 1998.

Remmer, Karen L. *Military Rule in Latin America*. Boston: Unwin Hyman, 1989.

Richards, Alan. *Egypt's Agricultural Development, 1800–1980: Technical and Social Change*. Boulder, CO: Westview Press, 1982.

Richards, John F. "The Finances of the East India Company in India, c. 1766–1859." Working Paper No. 153/11. London: Department of Economic History, London School of Economics, 2011.

Richards, John F. "Imperial Finance under the East India Company, 1762–1859." In Durba Ghosh and Dane Keith Kennedy, eds., *Decentering Empire: Britain, India and the Postcolonial World*, pp. 16–50. New Delhi: Oriental Longman, 2006.

Rivlin, Helen Anne B. *The Agricultural Policy of Muhammad Ali in Egypt*. Cambridge, MA: Harvard University Press, 1961.

Roberts, Andrew. "The Imperial Mind." In A. D. Roberts, ed., *The Cambridge History of Africa*, vol. 7: *From 1905 to 1940*, pp. 24–76. Cambridge: Cambridge University Press.

Robinson, Edgar Eugene, and Victor J. West. *The Foreign Policy of Woodrow Wilson, 1913–1917*. New York: MacMillan, 1917.

Robinson, Ronald, and John Gallagher. *Africa and the Victorians: The Official Mind of the Imperialism*. With Alice Denny. London: I.B. Tauris, 2015. Original edition published in 1961.

Rocchi, Fernando. *Chimneys in the Desert: Argentina during the Export Boom Years, 1870–1930*. Stanford, CA: Stanford University Press, 2006.

Rock, David. "The British in Argentina: From Informal Empire to Post Colonialism." In Matthew Brown, ed., *Informal Empire in Latin America: Culture, Commerce and Capital*, pp. 49–77 . Oxford: Blackwell, 2008.

Rock, David, *Argentina, 1516–1982: From Spanish Colonization to the Falklands War*. Berkeley: University of California Press, 1985.

Rodrik, Dani. *The Globalization Paradox*. New York: W. W. Norton, 2011.

Roosevelt, Kermit. *Countercoup: The Struggle for the Control of Iran*. New York: McGraw Hill, 1979.

Rosen, Nir. *In the Belly of the Green Bird: The Triumph of the Martyrs in Iraq*. New York: Free Press, 2006.

Rosen, Stephen P. *Societies and Military Power: India and Its Armies*. Ithaca, NY: Cornell University Press, 1996.

Rosenberg, Emily. *Spreading the American Dream: American Economic and Cultural Expansion*. New York: Hill and Wang, 1981.

Rotter, Andrew J. *The Path to Vietnam: Origins of the American Commitment to Southeast Asia*. Ithaca, NY: Cornell University Press, 1987.

Roy, Tirthankar. *An Economic History of Early Modern India*. Abingdon, UK: Routledge, 2013.

Roy, Tirthankar. *The East India Company: The World's Most Powerful Corporation*. New Delhi: Penguin Books, 2012.

Russell, Conrad. *Causes of the English Civil War*. Oxford: Clarendon Press, 1990.

Sachs, Jeffrey, and Harry Huizinga. "U.S. Commercial Banks and the Developing Country Debt Crisis." *Brookings Papers on Economic Activity*, 2, 1987.

Saikal, Amin. *The Rise and Fall of the Shah: Iran from Autocracy to Religious Rule*. Princeton, NJ: Princeton University Press, 2009.

Salvatore, Ricardo D., and Carlos Newland. "Between Independence and the Golden Age: The Early Argentine Economy." In Gerrardo Della Paolera and Alan P. Taylor, eds., *A New Economic History of Argentina*, pp. 19–45. Cambridge: Cambridge University Press, 2003.

Sampson, Anthony. *The Seven Sisters: The Great Oil Companies and the World They Shaped*. New York: Bantam Books, 1976.

Sarkar, Sumit. *Modern India, 1885–1947*. London: Macmillan, 1989.

Schatz, Sayre P. *Nigerian Capitalism*. Berkeley: University of California Press, 1977.

Schoonover, Thomas. *Uncle Sam's War of 1898 and the Origins of Globalization*. Lexington: University Press of Kentucky, 2003.

Schoultz, Lars. *Beneath the United States: A History of U.S. Relations towards Latin America*. Cambridge, MA: Harvard University Press, 1998.

Schran, Peter. "Commercial Relations between U.S. and China." In Ernst R. May and John K. Fairbank, eds., *America's China Trade in Historical Perspective*, pp. 151–204. Harvard Studies in American-East Asian Relations 11. Cambridge, MA: Harvard University Press, 1986.

Schumpeter, Joseph A. *Imperialism and Social Classes*. Translated by Heinz Norden. New York: A. M. Kelly, 1951. Original German edition published in 1919.

Seal, Anil. "Imperialism and Nationalism in India." In John Gallagher, Gordon Johnson, and Anil Seal, eds. *Locality, Province and Nation: Essays on Indian Politics, 1870–1940*, pp. 1–28. Cambridge: Cambridge University Press, 1973.

Sen, A. K. *Poverty and Famines: An Essay on Entitlement and Deprivation*. Oxford: Clarendon Press, 1981.

Serra, Narcís, and Joseph Stiglitz, eds. *The Washington Consensus Reconsidered: Towards a New Global Governance*. New York: Oxford University Press, 2008.

Sethia, Tara. "Railways, Raj and the Indian States." In Clarence B. Davis, Kenneth E. Wilburn Jr., and Ronald E. Robinson, eds., *Railway Imperialism*, pp. 103–20. New York: Greenwood Press,1991.

Shadid, Anthony. *Night Draws Near: Iraq's People in the Shadow of War*. New York: Henry Holt, 2005.

Shunway, Jeffrey. "Juan Manuel de Rosas." *Oxford Bibliographies Online*. https://www.oxfordbibliographies.com.

Sigmund, Paul E. *The Overthrow of Allende and the Politics of Chile, 1964–1976*. Pittsburgh, PA: University of Pittsburgh Press, 1977.

Sigmund, Paul. *The United States and Democracy in Chile*. Twentieth Century Fund Book. Baltimore: Johns Hopkins University Press, 1993.

Simons, Geoff. *Iraq: From Sumer to Saddam*. 2nd ed. New York: St. Martin's Press, 1994.

Singh, Prerna. *How Solidarity Works for Welfare: Subnationalism and Social Development in India*. New York: Cambridge University Press, 2015.

Sklar, Richard. *Nigerian Political Parties: Power in an Emergent African Nation*. Princeton, NJ: Princeton University Press, 1963.

Skowronek, Stephen. *Building a New American State: The Expansion of National Administrative Capacities, 1877–1920*. New York: Cambridge University Press, 1982.

Sky, Emma. *The Unraveling: High Hopes and Missed Opportunities in Iraq*. New York: Public Affairs, 2016.

Small, Melvin. "Hey, Hey, LBJ! American Domestic Politics and Vietnam War." In Anderson, David L. Anderson, ed., *The Columbia History of the Vietnam War*, pp. 333–56. New York: Columbia University Press.

Smith, Robert S. *Kingdom of the Yoruba*. 2nd ed. London: Methuen, 1976.

Smith, Tony. *America's Mission: The United States and the Worldwide Struggle for Democracy*. Expanded ed. Princeton, NJ: Princeton University Press, 2012.

Smith, Tony. *The Pattern of Imperialism: The United States, Great Britain and the Late-Industrializing World since 1815*. New York: Cambridge University Press, 1981.

Sorensen, George. *Changes in Statehood: The Transformation of International Relations*. New York: Palgrave, 2001.

Spence, Jonathan. "Opium Smoking in Ch'ing China." In Fredric Wakeman and Carolyn Grant, eds., *Conflict and Control in Late Imperial China*, pp. 143–73. Berkeley: University of California Press, 1975.

Spiro, David. *The Hidden Hand of American Hegemony: Petrodollar Recycling and International Markets*. Ithaca, NY: Cornell University Press, 1999.

Stallings, Barbara. *Dependency in the 21st Century? The Political Economy of China-Latin American Relations*. New York: Cambridge University Press, forthcoming.

Stallings, Barbara. "U.S. Financial Flows to Latin America." *Partnership for the Americas Commission, Background Document, BD-02*. Washington, DC: Brookings, 2008.

Stallings, Barbara. *Class Conflict and Economic Development in Chile, 1958–1973*. Stanford, CA: Stanford University Press, 1978.

Staten, Clifford L. *The History of Cuba*. 2nd ed. Santa Barbara, CA: Greenwood, 2015.

Stein, Stanley J., and Barbara H. Stein, *The Colonial Heritage of Latin America: Essays on Economic Dependence in Perspective*. New York: Oxford University Press, 1970.

Stiglitz, Joseph. *Globalization and Its Discontents*. New York: W. W. Norton, 2003.

Stone, Lawrence. *The Causes of the English Revolution, 1529–1642*. London: Routledge, 1972.

Stone, Lawrence. *The Crisis of Aristocracy, 1558–1641*. Oxford: Clarendon Press, 1965.

Sutherland, Lucy S. *The East India Company in Eighteenth-Century Politics*. Oxford: Oxford University Press, 1952.

Teichman, Judith. *The Politics of Freeing Markets in Latin America: Chile, Argentina and Mexico*. Chapel Hill: University of North Carolina Press, 2001.

Thomson, James C., Jr., Peter W. Stanley, and John Curtin Perry. *Sentimental Imperialists: The American Experience in East Asia*. New York: Harper and Row, 1981.

Thorner, Daniel. *Agrarian Prospects for India: Five Lectures in Land Reforms Delivered in 1955 at the Delhi School of Economics*. Delhi: Delhi University Press, 1956.

Thucydides. *History of the Peloponnesian War*. Baltimore, MD: Penguin Books, 1954.

Tignor, Robert. "Lord Cromer: Practitioner and Philosopher of Imperialism." *Journal of British Studies* 2, no. 2 (May 1963): 142–59.

Tomlinson, B. R. *The Political Economy of the Raj, 1914–1947: The Economics of Decolonization in India*. London, Macmillan, 1979.

Topik, Steven. *The Political Economy of the Brazilian State, 1889–1930*. Austin: University of Texas Press, 1987.

Trask, David F. *The War with Spain in 1898*. New York: Macmillan, 1981.

Trubowitz, Peter. *Defining the National Interest: Conflict and Change in American Foreign Policy*. Chicago: University of Chicago Press, 1998.

Trullinger, James Walker, Jr. *Village at War: An Account of Revolution in Vietnam*. New York: Longman, 1980.

Turley, William S. *The Second Indochina War: A Concise Political and Military History*. 2nd ed. Lanham, MD: Rowman and Littlefield, 2009.

Turner, Fredrick Jackson. *The Frontier in American History*. New York: Henry Holt, 1921.

U.S. Bureau of the Census. *Historical Statistics of the United States, Colonial Times to 1970*. Bicentennial ed. Part 2. Washington, DC: U.S. Bureau of the Census, 1975.

Vadney, T. E. *The World since 1945*. New York: Penguin Books, 1987.

Vitalis, Robert. *America's Kingdom: Mythmaking on the Saudi Oil Frontier*. Stanford, CA: Stanford University Press, 2005.

Volwiler, A. T. "Harrison, Blaine and American Foreign Policy, 1889–1893." In William Appleman Williams, ed., *The Shaping of American Diplomacy*, 2nd ed., vol. 1, *1750–1914*. 295–301, Chicago: Rand McNally, 1970.

Vu, Tuong. *Vietnam's Communist Revolution: The Power and Limits of Ideology*. New York: Cambridge University Press, 2016.

Wade, Robert. "Asian Debt-and-Development Crisis, 1997–? Causes and Consequences." *World Development* 26, no. 8 (August 1998): 1535–53.

Wakeman, Frederic. "The Canton Trade and the Opium War." In John K. Fairbank, ed., *The Cambridge History of China*, vol. 10, pp. 163–212. Cambridge: Cambridge University Press, 2008.

Wakeman, Frederic, Jr. *Strangers at the Gate: Social Disorder in South China, 1839–1861*. Berkeley: University of California Press, 1966.

Wallerstein, Immanuel. *The Modern World System*. 3 vols. New York: Academic Press, 1974, 1980, 1989. The fourth volume was published by the University of California Press (Berkeley), in 2011.

Walt, Steven M. "WikiLeaks, April Glaspie and Saddam Hussein." *Foreign Policy*, January 9, 2011. http://foreignpolicy.com/2011/01/09/wikileaks-april-glaspie-and-saddam-hussein/.

Waltz, Kenneth. *Theory of International Politics*. Reading, MA: Addison-Wesley, 1979.

Ward, J. R. "The Industrial Revolution and British Imperialism, 1750–1850." *Economic History Review*, n.s., 47, no. 1 (February 1994): 44–65.

Washbrook, David. "India, 1818–1860: The Two Faces of Colonialism." In Andrew Porter, ed., *Oxford History of the British Empire: The Nineteenth Century*, vol. 3, pp. 395–421. Oxford: Oxford University Press, 1999.

Watts, Michael. *Silent Violence: Food, Famine and Peasantry in Northern Nigeria*. Berkeley: University of California Press, 1983.

Webster, J. B. "African Political Activity in British West Africa, 1900–1940." In J. F. A. Ajayi and Michael Crowder, eds., *History of West Africa*, vol. 2, 2nd ed., chap. 17. London: Longman, 1987.

Welch, Richard E., Jr. *Response to Imperialism: The United States and the Philippine-American War, 1899–1902*. Chapel Hill: University of North Carolina Press, 1979.

Wesseling, H. L. *Divide and Rule: The Partition of Africa, 1880–1914*. Westport, CT: Praeger, 1996.

Westad, Odd Arne. *The Global Cold War: Third World Interventions and the Making of Our Times*. New York: Cambridge University Press, 2005.

Westad, Odd Arne. *The Global Cold War: Third World Interventions and the Making of Our Times*. New York: Cambridge University Press, 2011.

White, Jeremy. *Central Administration in Nigeria, 1914–1948,* Dublin: Irish Academic Press, 1981.

Wilber, Donald. *Regime Change in Iran: Overthrow of Premier Mossadeq in Iran, November 1952–August 1953*. London: Russell Press, 2006.

Williams, William Appleman. *The Tragedy of American Diplomacy*. New York: Dell, 1962.

Williamson, John. "What Washington Means by Policy Reform." In John Williamson, ed., *Latin American Adjustment: How Much Has Happened?*, pp. 7–40. Washington, DC: Institute for International Economics, 1990.

Wimmel, Kenneth. *Theodore Roosevelt and the Great White Fleet: American Sea Power Comes of Age*. Washington, DC: Brassey's, 1998.

Wolpert, Stanley. *A New History of India*. New York: Oxford University press, 1982.

Wong, J. Y. "The Building of an Informal British Empire in China in the Middle of the Nineteenth Century." *Bulletin of the John Ryland University Library of Manchester* 59, no. 2 (Spring 1977): 472–85.

Woodward, Bob. *Plan of Attack*. New York: Simon and Schuster, 2004.

Woolrych, Austin. *Britain in Revolution, 1625–1640*. New York: Oxford University Press, 2002.

World Bank. *Economic Growth in the 1990s: Learning from a Decade of Reform.* Washington, DC: World Bank, 2005.

World Bank. *An Examination of the Banking Crisis of the 1980s and the Early 1990s*. Vol. 1. Washington, DC: World Bank, 1994.

Ye, Min. "Fragmentation and Mobilization: Domestic Politics of the Belt and Road in China." *Journal of Contemporary China,* online, January 26, 2019. https://doi.org/10.1080/10670564.2019.1580428.

Yergin, Daniel. *The Prize: The Epic Quest for Oil, Money and Power*. New York: Free Press, 2009.

Young, Marilyn B. *The Vietnam Wars, 1945–1990*. New York: Harper Collins, 1991.

Young, Marilyn. "The Quest for Empire." In Ernst R May and James C. Thomson Jr., eds., *American-East Asian Relation: A Survey*, pp. 131–42. Cambridge, MA: Harvard University Press, 1972.

Zhai, Qiang. *China and the Vietnam Wars, 1950–1975*. Chapel Hill: University of North Carolina Press, 2000.

ARCHIVAL SOURCES

Baker Papers. Papers of James A. Baker III, Seeley G. Mudd Library, Princeton University.

Foreign Relations of the United Sates, various volumes. https://www.archives.gov/research/foreign-policy/other-resources.

Foster, William, ed. *The Embassy of Thomas Roe to India*. Nendeln and Lichtenstein: Kraus Reprint, 1967.

Kennedy Papers. Papers of John F. Kennedy at the John F. Kennedy Presidential Library and Museum, Boston.

Lugard papers. Papers of Frederick D. Lugard, Papers Relating to Nigeria (1892–1944), Commonwealth and African Studies, Bodleian Library, Oxford University.

Index

Notes: Bibliography and passing references to places and concepts are not indexed. *For the most part the endnotes are also not indexed. For the benefit of digital users, indexed terms that span two pages (e.g., 52–53) may, on occasion, appear on only one of those pages.*